# Economic Thinkers

# Economic Thinkers

## A Biographical Encyclopedia

DAVID A. DIETERLE, EDITOR

AN IMPRINT OF ABC-CLIO, LLC
Santa Barbara, California • Denver, Colorado • Oxford, England

Copyright 2013 by ABC-CLIO, LLC

All rights reserved. No part of this publication may be reproduced, stored in a retrieval system, or transmitted, in any form or by any means, electronic, mechanical, photocopying, recording, or otherwise, except for the inclusion of brief quotations in a review, without prior permission in writing from the publisher.

**Library of Congress Cataloging-in-Publication Data**

Economic thinkers : a biographical encyclopedia / David A. Dieterle, editor.
    pages cm
  Includes bibliographical references and index.
  ISBN 978–0–313–39746–2 (hardcopy : alk. paper) — ISBN 978–0–313–39747–9 (ebook) 1. Economists—Biography—Encyclopedias. I. Dieterle, David Anthony, editor of compilation.
  HB76.E26   2013
  330.092′2—dc23              2013002956

ISBN: 978–0–313–39746–2
EISBN: 978–0–313–39747–9

17 16 15 14 13    1 2 3 4 5

This book is also available on the World Wide Web as an eBook.
Visit www.abc-clio.com for details.

Greenwood
An Imprint of ABC-CLIO, LLC

ABC-CLIO, LLC
130 Cremona Drive, P.O. Box 1911
Santa Barbara, California 93116-1911

This book is printed on acid-free paper ∞

Manufactured in the United States of America

# Contents

| | |
|---|---|
| Alphabetical List of Entries | vii |
| Guide to Related Topics: Chronology | xi |
| Guide to Related Topics: Geography | xv |
| Guide to Related Topics: Economic Concepts and Philosophies | xix |
| Preface | xxxiii |
| Introduction: The Family Tree of Economics | xxxv |
| **Encyclopedia Entries** | 1 |
| Appendix: Nobel Laureates | 501 |
| Glossary | 503 |
| Selected Bibliography | 523 |
| About the Editor and Contributors | 529 |
| Index | 531 |

# Alphabetical List of Entries

Akerlof, George
Alchian, Armen
Allais, Maurice
Arrow, Kenneth
Aumann, Robert
Bastiat, Frédéric
Bauer, Otto
Becker, Gary
Bentham, Jeremy
Bernanke, Ben
Beveridge, William
Bhagwati, Jagdish
Böhm-Bawerk, Eugen von
Boserup, Ester
Buchanan, James
Burns, Arthur
Cantillon, Richard
Carlyle, Thomas
Cassel, Gustav
Child, Josiah
Clark, John Bates
Coase, Ronald
Colbert, Jean-Baptiste
Collier, Paul
Debreu, Gérard
de Soto, Hernando
Diamond, Peter
Draghi, Mario
Duflo, Esther
Dupuit, Jules
Easterly, William
Edgeworth, Francis
Ekelund, Robert
Ely, Richard
Engels, Friedrich
Engle, Robert
Fischer, Stanley
Fisher, Irving
Fogel, Robert

Friedman, Milton
Frisch, Ragnar
Gaidar, Yegor
Galbraith, John Kenneth
George, Henry
Granger, Sir Clive
Greenspan, Alan
Haavelmo, Trygve
Haberler, Gottfried von
Harrod, Sir Roy
Harsanyi, John
Hayek, Friedrich von
Hazlitt, Henry
Heckman, James
Heilbroner, Robert
Heller, Walter
Hicks, Sir John
Hilferding, Rudolf
Hobbes, Thomas
Hobson, John
Hollander, Samuel
Hoppe, Hans-Hermann
Hornick, Philipp Wilhelm von
Huang, Qin Shi
Hume, David
Hurwicz, Leonid
Irwin, Douglas
Jevons, William Stanley
Johnson, Harry
Kahn, Alfred
Kahneman, Daniel
Kaldor, Nicholas
Kalecki, Michal
Kantorovich, Leonid
Keynes, John Maynard
Khaldun, Ibn
Klein, Lawrence
Knight, Frank
Koopmans, Tjalling

## ALPHABETICAL LIST OF ENTRIES

Kregel, Jan
Krueger, Anne
Krugman, Paul
Kuznets, Simon
Kydland, Finn
Laffer, Arthur
Lagarde, Christine
Lange, Oskar
Leontief, Wassily
Lewis, Sir Arthur
List, Friedrich
Locke, John
Lucas, Robert, Jr.
Machlup, Fritz
Malthus, Thomas
Mankiw, Gregory
Markowitz, Harry
Marshall, Alfred
Marx, Karl
Maskin, Eric
McFadden, Daniel
Meade, James
Meltzer, Allan
Menger, Carl
Merton, Robert
Mill, John Stuart
Miller, Merton
Mirrlees, James
Mises, Ludwig von
Modigliani, Franco
Morgenstern, Oskar
Mortensen, Dale
Mun, Thomas
Mundell, Robert
Murphy, Kevin
Myerson, Roger
Myrdal, Gunnar
Nash, John
North, Douglass
North, Sir Dudley
Ohlin, Bertil
Okun, Arthur
Olson, Mancur
Oster, Emily
Ostrom, Elinor
Pareto, Vilfredo
Pasinetti, Luigi
Petty, Sir William

Phelps, Edmund
Phillips, A. W. H.
Pigou, A. C.
Pissarides, Christopher
Prescott, Edward
Quesnay, François
Reich, Robert
Reisman, George
Ricardo, David
Rivlin, Alice
Roach, Stephen
Robbins, Lionel
Robertson, Sir Dennis
Robinson, Joan
Romer, Christina
Romer, Paul
Rosen, Sherwin
Roth, Alvin
Rothbard, Murray
Roubini, Nouriel
Sachs, Jeffrey
Samuelson, Paul
Sargent, Thomas
Say, Jean-Baptiste
Schelling, Thomas
Scholes, Myron
Schultz, Theodore
Schumacher, Ernst
Schumpeter, Joseph
Schwartz, Anna
Selten, Reinhard
Sen, Amartya
Senior, Nassau
Sennholz, Hans
Shapley, Lloyd
Sharpe, William
Shiller, Robert
Shultz, George
Simon, Herbert
Simon, Julian
Simons, Henry
Sims, Christopher
Singh, Manmohan
Smith, Adam
Smith, Vernon
Solow, Robert
Sowell, Thomas
Spence, Michael

Sraffa, Piero
Stern, Nicholas
Steuart, James
Stigler, George
Stiglitz, Joseph
Stone, Sir Richard
Summers, Lawrence
Sunstein, Cass
Sweezy, Paul
Taussig, Frank
Thaler, Richard
Thunen, Johann
Thurow, Lester
Tinbergen, Jan
Tobin, James
Trichet, Jean-Claude
Tullock, Gordon
Turgot, Jacques

Tyson, Laura
Veblen, Thorstein
Vickrey, William
Viner, Jacob
Volcker, Paul
Walpole, Sir Robert
Walras, Leon
Webb, Beatrice
Weber, Max
Wicksell, Knut
Wicksteed, Philip
Wieser, Friedrich von
Williams, Walter
Williamson, Oliver
Wolf, Martin
Xiaochuan, Zhou
Yellen, Janet
Zoellick, Robert

# Guide to Related Topics: Chronology

## TWENTY-FIRST CENTURY (2000–PRESENT)

Akerlof, George (1940– )
Bernanke, Ben (1953– )
Collier, Paul (1949– )
de Soto, Hernando (1941– )
Diamond, Peter (1940– )
Draghi, Mario (1947– )
Duflo, Esther (1972– )
Easterly, William (1957– )
Fischer, Stanley (1943– )
Greenspan, Alan (1926– )
Heckman, James (1944– )
Hoppe, Hans-Hermann (1949– )
Irwin, Douglas (1962– )
Klein, Lawrence (1920– )
Kregel, Jan (1944– )
Krueger, Anne (1934– )
Krugman, Paul (1953– )
Kydland, Finn (1943– )
Laffer, Arthur (1940– )
Lagarde, Christine (1956– )
Mankiw, Gregory (1958– )
Maskin, Eric (1950– )
McFadden, Daniel (1937– )
Meltzer, Allan (1928– )
Merton, Robert (1944– )
Mirrlees, James (1936– )
Mortensen, Dale (1939– )
Murphy, Kevin (1950– )
Myerson, Roger (1951– )
Oster, Emily (1980– )
Ostrom, Elinor (1933– )
Reich, Robert (1946– )
Rivlin, Alice (1931– )
Roach, Stephen (1945– )
Romer, Christina (1958– )
Roth, Alvin (1947– )
Roubini, Nouriel (1959– )
Sachs, Jeffrey (1951– )
Sargent, Thomas (1943– )
Sen, Amartya (1933– )
Shiller, Robert (1946– )
Sims, Christopher (1942– )
Sowell, Thomas (1930– )
Spence, Michael (1943– )
Stern, Nicholas (1946– )
Stiglitz, Joseph (1943– )
Summers, Lawrence (1954– )
Sunstein, Cass (1954– )
Thaler, Richard (1945– )
Trichet, Jean-Claude (1942– )
Williams, Walter (1936– )
Wolf, Martin (1946– )
Xiaochuan, Zhou (1948– )
Yellen, Janet (1946– )
Zoellick, Robert (1953– )

## TWENTIETH CENTURY (POST–WORLD WAR II, 1945–99)

Alchian, Armen (1914–2013)
Arrow, Kenneth (1921– )
Aumann, Robert (1930– )
Becker, Gary (1930– )
Bhagwati, Jagdish (1934– )
Boserup, Ester (1910–99)
Buchanan, James (1919–2013)
Burns, Arthur (1904–87)
Debreu, Gérard (1921–2004)
Ekelund, Robert (1940– )
Engle, Robert (1942– )
Fogel, Robert (1926–2013)
Friedman, Milton (1912–2006)
Gaidar, Yegor (1956–2009)

Galbraith, John Kenneth (1908–2006)
Granger, Sir Clive (1934–2009)
Haavelmo, Trygve (1911–99)
Haberler, Gottfried von (1900–95)
Harsanyi, John (1920–2000)
Hayek, Friedrich von (1899–1992)
Hazlitt, Henry (1894–1993)
Heilbroner, Robert (1919–2005)
Heller, Walter (1915–87)
Hicks, Sir John (1904–89)
Hollander, Samuel (1937– )
Hurwicz, Leonid (1917–2008)
Johnson, Harry (1923–77)
Kahn, Alfred (1917–2010)
Kahneman, Daniel (1934– )
Kaldor, Nicholas (1908–86)
Kalecki, Michal (1899–1970)
Kantorovich, Leonid (1912–86)
Knight, Frank (1885–1972)
Koopmans, Tjalling (1910–85)
Kuznets, Simon (1901–85)
Lange, Oskar (1904–65)
Leontief, Wassily (1905–99)
Lewis, Sir Arthur (1915–91)
Lucas, Robert, Jr. (1937– )
Machlup, Fritz (1902–83)
Markowitz, Harry (1927– )
Meade, James (1907–95)
Miller, Merton (1923–2000)
Modigliani, Franco (1918–2003)
Morgenstern, Oskar (1902–77)
Mundell, Robert (1932– )
Nash, John (1928– )
North, Douglass (1920– )
Okun, Arthur (1928–80)
Olson, Mancur (1932–98)
Pasinetti, Luigi (1930– )
Phelps, Edmund (1933– )
Phillips, A. W. H. (1914–75)
Pissarides, Christopher (1948– )
Prescott, Edward (1940– )
Reisman, George (1937– )
Romer, Paul (1955– )
Rosen, Sherwin (1938–2001)
Rothbard, Murray (1926–95)
Samuelson, Paul (1915–2009)
Schelling, Thomas (1921– )
Scholes, Myron (1941– )
Schultz, Theodore (1902–98)
Schumacher, Ernst (1911–77)
Schwartz, Anna (1915–2012)
Selten, Reinhard (1930– )
Sennholz, Hans (1922–2007)
Shapley, Lloyd (1923– )
Sharpe, William (1934– )
Shultz, George (1920– )
Simon, Herbert (1916–2001)
Simon, Julian (1932–98)
Singh, Manmohan (1932– )
Smith, Vernon (1927– )
Solow, Robert (1924– )
Stigler, George (1911–91)
Stone, Sir Richard (1913–91)
Sweezy, Paul (1910–2004)
Thurow, Lester (1938– )
Tinbergen, Jan (1903–94)
Tobin, James (1918–2002)
Tullock, Gordon (1922– )
Tyson, Laura (1947– )
Vickrey, William (1914–96)
Volcker, Paul (1927– )
Williamson, Oliver (1932– )

# EARLY TWENTIETH CENTURY (PRE–WORLD WAR II, 1900–45)

Allais, Maurice (1911–2010)
Bauer, Otto (1881–1938)
Beveridge, William (1879–1963)
Cassel, Gustav (1866–1945)
Coase, Ronald (1910– )
Ely, Richard (1854–1943)
Fisher, Irving (1867–1947)
Frisch, Ragnar (1895–1973)
Hilferding, Rudolf (1877–1941)
Hobson, John (1858–1940)
Keynes, John Maynard (1883–1946)
Mises, Ludwig von (1881–1973)
Myrdal, Gunnar (1898–1987)
Ohlin, Bertil (1899–1979)
Pareto, Vilfredo (1848–1923)
Pigou, A. C. (1877–1959)

Robertson, Sir Dennis (1890–1963)
Robbins, Lionel (1898–1984)
Robinson, Joan (1903–83)
Schumpeter, Joseph (1883–1950)
Simons, Henry (1899–1946)
Sraffa, Piero (1898–1983)
Viner, Jacob (1892–1970)
Weber, Max (1864–1920)
Wicksteed, Philip (1844–1927)
Wieser, Friedrich von (1851–1926)

## NINETEENTH CENTURY (1800–1899)

Bastiat, Frédéric (1801–50)
Böhm-Bawerk, Eugen von (1851–1914)
Carlyle, Thomas (1795–1881)
Clark, John Bates (1847–1938)
Dupuit, Jules (1804–66)
Edgeworth, Francis (1845–1926)
Engels, Friedrich (1820–95)
George, Henry (1839–97)
Jevons, William Stanley (1835–82)
List, Friedrich (1789–1846)
Marshall, Alfred (1842–1924)
Marx, Karl (1818–83)
Menger, Carl (1840–1921)
Mill, John Stuart (1806–73)
Ricardo, David (1772–1823)
Say, Jean-Baptiste (1767–1832)
Senior, Nassau (1790–1864)
Taussig, Frank (1859–1940)
Thunen, Johann (1783–1850)
Veblen, Thorstein (1857–1929)
Walras, Leon (1834–1910)
Webb, Beatrice (1858–1943)
Wicksell, Knut (1851–1926)

## EIGHTEENTH CENTURY (1700–1799)

Bentham, Jeremy (1748–1832)
Cantillon, Richard (1680–1734)
Hume, David (1711–76)
Malthus, Thomas (1766–1834)
Quesnay, François (1694–1774)
Smith, Adam (1723–90)
Steuart, James (1712–80)
Turgot, Jacques (1727–81)

## SEVENTEENTH CENTURY (1600–1699)

Child, Josiah (1630–99)
Colbert, Jean-Baptiste (1619–83)
Hobbes, Thomas (1588–1679)
Hornick, Philipp Wilhelm von (1638–1712)
Locke, John (1632–1704)
North, Sir Dudley (1641–91)
Petty, Sir William (1623–87)
Walpole, Sir Robert (1676–1745)

## FIFTEENTH–SIXTEENTH CENTURY

Mun, Thomas (1571–1641)

## FOURTEENTH CENTURY

Khaldun, Ibn (1332–1406)

## PREHISTORIC: ANCIENT GREECE AND ROME

Huang, Qin Shi (259–210 BCE)

# Guide to Related Topics: Geography

## NORTH AMERICA

**United States**

Akerlof, George
Alchian, Armen
Arrow, Kenneth
Becker, Gary
Bernanke, Ben
Buchanan, James
Burns, Arthur
Clark, John Bates
Debreu, Gérard (naturalized)
Diamond, Peter
Easterly, William
Ekelund, Robert
Ely, Richard
Engle, Robert
Fisher, Irving
Fogel, Robert
Friedman, Milton
Galbraith, John Kenneth
George, Henry
Greenspan, Alan
Harsanyi, John
Hazlitt, Henry
Heckman, James
Heilbroner, Robert
Heller, Walter
Hurwicz, Leonid
Irwin, Douglas
Kahn, Alfred
Klein, Lawrence
Knight, Frank
Kregel, Jan
Krueger, Anne
Krugman, Paul
Kuznets, Simon (naturalized)
Laffer, Arthur
Leontief, Wassily
Lucas, Robert, Jr.
Machlup, Fritz
Mankiw, Gregory
Markowitz, Harry
Maskin, Eric
McFadden, Daniel
Meltzer, Allan
Merton, Robert
Miller, Merton
Morgenstern, Oskar
Mortensen, Dale
Murphy, Kevin
Myerson, Roger
Nash, John
North, Douglass
Okun, Arthur
Olson, Mancur
Oster, Emily
Ostrom, Elinor
Phelps, Edmund
Prescott, Edward
Reich, Robert
Reisman, George
Rivlin, Alice
Roach, Stephen
Romer, Christina
Romer, Paul
Rosen, Sherwin
Roth, Alvin
Rothbard, Murray
Roubini, Nouriel
Sachs, Jeffrey
Samuelson, Paul
Sargent, Thomas
Schelling, Thomas
Schultz, Theodore
Schwartz, Anna
Sennholz, Hans
Shapley, Lloyd

GUIDE TO RELATED TOPICS: GEOGRAPHY

Sharpe, William
Shiller, Robert
Shultz, George
Simon, Herbert
Simon, Julian
Simons, Henry
Sims, Christopher
Smith, Vernon
Solow, Robert
Sowell, Thomas
Spence, Michael
Stigler, George
Stiglitz, Joseph
Summers, Lawrence
Sunstein, Cass

Sweezy, Paul
Taussig, Frank
Thaler, Richard
Thurow, Lester
Tobin, James
Tullock, Gordon
Tyson, Laura
Veblen, Thorstein
Vickrey, William
Viner, Jacob
Volcker, Paul
Williams, Walter
Williamson, Oliver
Yellen, Janet
Zoellick, Robert

*Canada*
Hollander, Samuel (naturalized)
Hurwicz, Leonid

Mundell, Robert
Scholes, Myron

*West Indies (Barbados)*
Lewis, Sir Arthur

## Europe

*Austria*
Bauer, Otto
Böhm-Bawerk, Eugen von
Haberler, Gottfried von
Hayek, Friedrich von
Hilferding, Rudolf
Hornick, Philipp Wilhelm von

Machlup, Fritz
Menger, Carl
Mises, Ludwig von
Schumpeter, Joseph
Wieser, Friedrich von

*Denmark*
Boserup, Ester

*England*
Bentham, Jeremy
Beveridge, William
Child, Josiah
Coase, Ronald
Collier, Paul
Harrod, Sir Roy
Hayek, Friedrich von
Hobbes, Thomas
Hobson, John

Hollander, Samuel (born)
Jevons, William Stanley
Keynes, John Maynard
Locke, John
Malthus, Thomas
Marshall, Alfred
Meade, James
Mill, John Stuart
Mun, Thomas

North, Sir Dudley
Petty, Sir William
Pigou, A. C.
Pissarides, Christopher
Ricardo, David
Robertson, Sir Dennis
Robbins, Lionel
Robinson, Joan

Schumacher, Ernst
Senior, Nassau
Stern, Nicholas
Stone, Sir Richard
Walpole, Sir Robert
Webb, Beatrice
Wicksteed, Philip
Wolf, Martin

*France*
Allais, Maurice
Bastiat, Frédéric
Cantillon, Richard
Colbert, Jean-Baptiste
Debreu, Gérard (born)
Duflo, Esther
Dupuit, Jules

Lagarde, Christine
Quesnay, François
Say, Jean-Baptiste
Trichet, Jean-Claude
Turgot, Jacques
Walras, Leon

*Germany*
Aumann, Robert
Engels, Friedrich
Hilferding, Rudolf
Hoppe, Hans-Hermann
List, Friedrich

Marx, Karl
Selten, Reinhard
Thunen, Johann
Weber, Max

*Ireland*
Cantillon, Richard

Edgeworth, Francis

*Italy*
Draghi, Mario
Modigliani, Franco
Pareto, Vilfredo

Pasinetti, Luigi
Sraffa, Piero

*Netherlands*
Koopmans, Tjalling

Tinbergen, Jan

*Norway*
Frisch, Ragnar
Haavelmo, Trygve

Kydland, Finn

*Poland*
Hurwicz, Leonid (born)
Kalecki, Michal

Lange, Oskar

## GUIDE TO RELATED TOPICS: GEOGRAPHY

*Russia*
Gaidar, Yegor
Kantorovich, Leonid
Kuznets, Simon (born)
Leontief, Wassily (born)

*Scotland*
Carlyle, Thomas
Hume, David
Mirrlees, James
Smith, Adam
Steuart, James

*Sweden*
Cassel, Gustav
Myrdal, Gunnar
Ohlin, Bertil
Wicksell, Knut

*Wales*
Granger, Sir Clive

## Asia

*China*
Huang, Qin Shi
Xiaochuan, Zhou

*India*
Beveridge, William (born)
Bhagwati, Jagdish
Sen, Amartya
Singh, Manmohan

*Israel*
Fischer, Stanley (naturalized)
Hollander, Samuel (naturalized)
Kahneman, Daniel

## South America

*Peru*
de Soto, Hernando

## Africa

*Zambia*
Fischer, Stanley (born)

*Tunisia*
Khaldun, Ibn

## Oceania

*New Zealand*
Phillips, A. W. H.

# Guide to Related Topics: Economic Concepts and Philosophies

### AGRICULTURAL ECONOMICS
Schultz, Theodore

### Antitrust
Williamson, Oliver

### Austrian School of Economic Thought
Böhm-Bawerk, Eugen von
Haberler, Gottfried
Hayek, Friedrich von
Hazlitt, Henry
Hoppe, Hans-Hermann
Machlup, Fritz
Menger, Carl
Mises, Ludwig von
Riesman, George
Robbins, Lionel
Sennholz
Wicksteed, Philip
Wieser, Friedrich von

### Behavioral Economics
Becker, Gary
Kahneman, Daniel
Shiller, Robert
Sunstein, Cass
Thaler, Richard

### Business Cycles
Burns, Arthur
Kalecki, Michal
Kydland, Finn
Marx, Karl
Schumpeter, Joseph
Tinbergen, Jan

### Capitalism
de Soto, Hernando
Gaidar, Yegor
Greenspan, Alan
Turgot, Jacques

### Chicago School
Friedman, Milton
Rosen, Sherwin
Simons, Henry
Stigler, George

## Circular Flow of Economic Activity

Quesnay, François
Smith, Vernon

## Classical

Cantillon, Richard
Dupuit, Jules
Ekelund, Robert
Friedman, Milton
Galbraith, John Kenneth
George, Henry
Hume, David
Keynes, John Maynard
Knight, Frank
List, Friedrich
Locke, John
Malthus, Thomas
Marshall, Alfred
Mill, John Stuart
Petty, Sir William
Pigou, A. C.
Say, Jean-Baptiste
Schumpeter, Joseph
Smith, Adam

## Comparative Advantage

Ricardo, David

## Conspicuous Consumption

Veblen, Thorstein

## Consumer Surplus

Marshall, Alfred

## Costs and Outputs

Alchian, Armen
Wieser, Friedrich von

## Creative Destruction

Greenspan, Alan
Schumpeter, Joseph

## Development Economics

Collier, Paul
Duflo, Esther
Easterly, William
Fischer, Stanley
Kaldor, Nicholas
Kregel, Jan
Krueger, Anne
Lewis, Sir Arthur
Murphy, Kevin
Oster, Emily
Romer, Paul
Roubini, Nouriel
Sachs, Jeffrey
Sargent, Thomas
Sen, Amartya
Singh, Manmohan
Stern, Nicholas

# GUIDE TO RELATED TOPICS: ECONOMIC CONCEPTS AND PHILOSOPHIES

## Diminishing Marginal Returns

Thunen, Johann

## Econometrics

Debreu, Gérard
Edgeworth, Francis
Engle, Robert
Fisher, Irving
Frisch, Ragnar
Haavelmo, Trygve
Heckman, James
Hurwicz, Leonid
Kantorovich, Leonid
Klein, Lawrence
Koopmans, Tjalling
McFadden, Daniel
Myerson, Roger
Nash, John
Okun, Arthur
Oster, Emily
Prescott, Edward
Pissarides, Christopher
Sargent, Thomas
Schelling, Thomas
Schumacher, Ernst
Selten, Reinhard
Shapley, Lloyd
Sims, Christopher
Thunen, Johann
Tinbergen, Jan
Tyson, Laura
Walras, Leon

## Economic Development of Developing Countries

Boserup, Ester
Collier, Paul
Duflo, Esther
Easterly, William
Fischer, Stanley
Kaldor, Nicholas
Kregel, Jan
Krueger, Anne
Lewis, Sir Arthur
Murphy, Kevin
Oster, Emily
Sachs, Jeffrey
Schultz, Theodore
Schumpeter, Joseph
Sen, Amartya
Stern, Nicholas

## Economic Growth

Allais, Maurice
Arrow, Kenneth
Becker, Gary
Burns, Arthur
Keynes, John Maynard
Khaldun, Ibn
Lewis, Sir Arthur
Lucas, Robert, Jr.
Murphy, Kevin
Pasinetti, Luigi
Phillips, A. W. H.
Schumacher, Ernst
Solow, Robert
Stone, Sir Richard

## Economic History

Bernanke, Ben
Carlyle, Thomas
Ekelund, Robert
Fogel, Robert
Heilbroner, Robert
Hollander, Samuel
North, Douglass
Reisman, George

Robbins, Lionel
Romer, Christina
Rothbard, Murray
Schwartz, Anna
Sraffa, Piero
Viner, Jacob

## Economic Institutions

Simon, Herbert

## Economic Rent

George, Henry
Hobson, John
Senior, Nassau
Thunen, Johann
Tullock, Gordon

## Economic Systems

Gaidar, Yegor
Haberler, Gottfried
Heilbroner, Robert
Lange, Oskar
Marx, Karl
Murphy, Kevin
North, Sir Dudley
Simon, Julian
Webb, Beatrice
Weber, Max

## Economics of Crime

Becker, Gary

## Economics of Environment

Collier, Paul
Sachs, Jeffrey
Simon, Julian
Stern, Nicholas

## Economics of Family

Becker, Gary

## Economics of Health

Duflo, Esther
Oster, Emily

## Economics of Information

Stigler, George

## Economics of Population

Boserup, Ester

## Economics of War and Peace
Robbins, Lionel

## Economies of Scale
Krugman, Paul

## Elasticity
Marshall, Alfred

## Equilibrium Price
Allais, Maurice
Lange, Oskar

## Experimental Economics
Roth, Alvin
Selten, Reinhard
Smith, Vernon

## Finance Economics
Granger, Sir Clive
Johnson, Harry
Markowitz, Harry
Merton, Robert
Miller, Merton
Modigliani, Franco
Mundell, Robert
Scholes, Myron
Sharpe, William
Summers, Lawrence
Tobin, James
Volcker, Paul

## Fiscal Policy
Kydland, Finn
Laffer, Arthur
Mises, Ludwig von
Stiglitz, Joseph
Yellen, Janet

## Game Theory
Aumann, Robert
Harsanyi, John
Hurwicz, Leonid
Maskin, Eric
Morgenstern, Oskar
Myerson, Roger
Nash, John
Roth, Alvin
Schelling, Thomas
Selten, Reinhard
Shapley, Lloyd

## General Equilibrium Theory
Arrow, Kenneth
Edgeworth, Francis
Galbraith, John Kenneth
Hicks, Sir John

Keynes, John Maynard
Mankiw, Gregory
Marshall, Alfred
Pareto, Vilfredo

Quesnay, François
Say, Jean-Baptiste
Smith, Vernon

### Global Economics

Roach, Stephen
Roubini, Nouriel
Sachs, Jeffrey
Sargent, Thomas

Singh, Manmohan
Thurow, Lester
Wolf, Martin

### Growth Theory

Romer, Paul

### Human Capital

Becker, Gary

Schultz, Theodore

### Immigration

Bhagwati, Jagdish

### Imperfect Competition

Robinson, Joan

### Imperialism

Hobson, John

### Incentives

Myerson, Roger

### Income Distribution

Thurow, Lester

### Indifference Curves

Edgeworth, Francis

### Inflation

Allais, Maurice
Alchian, Armen

Burns, Arthur
Fisher, Irving

Greenspan, Alan
Locke, John

Wicksell, Knut
Volcker, Paul

## Institutions

Ely, Richard
North, Douglass
Tyson, Laura

Veblen, Thorstein
Williamson, Oliver

## International Policy Reform

Bhagwati, Jagdish
Collier, Paul
Lagarde, Christine
Machlup, Fritz
Meade, James

Roach, Stephen
Schelling, Thomas
Singh, Manmohan
Stiglitz, Joseph
Zoellick, Robert

## International Trade

Bhagwati, Jagdish
Haberler, Gottfried
Hicks, Sir John
Johnson, Harry
Lucas, Robert, Jr.

Meade, James
Ohlin, Bertil
Zoellick, Robert
Taussig, Frank
Viner, Jacob

## Keynesianism

Arrow, Kenneth
Diamond, Peter
Galbraith, John Kenneth
Harrod, Sir Roy
Kalecki, Michal
Keynes, John Maynard
Krugman, Paul
Mankiw, Gregory

Ohlin, Bertil
Okun, Arthur
Pareto, Vilfredo
Robinson, Joan
Solow, Robert
Sraffa, Piero
Summers, Lawrence
Thurow, Lester

## Labor Economics

Heckman, James
Kydland, Finn
Mortensen, Dale
Olson, Mancur
Pissarides, Christopher

Rosen, Sherwin
Spence, Michael
Senior, Nassau
Summers, Lawrence

## Labor Theory of Value

Hicks, Sir John
Marx, Karl

Weber, Max

## Libertarianism

Rothbard, Murray
Riesman, George
Sennholz, Hans
Sowell, Thomas
Williams, Walter

## Linear Programming

Kantorovich, Leonid

## Macroeconomics

Alchian, Armen
Greenspan, Alan
Haberler, Gottfried
Harrod, Sir Roy
Kalecki, Michal
Kuznets, Simon
Leontief, Wassily
Menger, Carl
North, Sir Dudley
Phelps, Edmund
Prescott, Edward
Roubini, Nouriel
Samuelson, Paul
Simon, Julian
Sims, Christopher
Solow, Robert
Stone, Sir Richard
Wicksell, Knut
Yellen, Janet

## Marginal Rate of Substitution

Edgeworth, Francis

## Marginal Utility Theory/Marginal Productivity

Clark, John Bates
Dupuit, Jules
Jevons, William Stanley
Marshall, Alfred
Menger, Carl
Wicksteed, Philip

## Market Design

Roth, Alvin

## Marxism

Bauer, Otto
Engels, Friedrich
Hilferding, Rudolf
Marx, Karl
Sweezy, Paul

## Mercantilism

Cantillon, Richard
Child, Josiah
Colbert, Jean-Baptiste
Hornick, Philip Wilhelm von

# GUIDE TO RELATED TOPICS: ECONOMIC CONCEPTS AND PHILOSOPHIES

Mun, Thomas
Steuart, James

Walpole, Sir Robert

## Microeconomics

Kantorovich, Leonid
Menger, Carl
Smith, Vernon
Sraffa, Piero
Stigler, George

Stiglitz, Joseph
Vickrey, William
Wicksteed, Philip
Wieser, Friedrich von

## Monetarism

Bernanke, Ben
Burns, Arthur
Draghi, Mario
Fisher, Irving
Friedman, Milton

Greenspan, Alan
Schwartz, Anna
Volcker, Paul
Yellen, Janet

## Money, Banking, and Monetary Policy

Bernanke, Ben
Burns, Arthur
Draghi, Mario
Fisher, Irving
Friedman, Milton
Greenspan, Alan
Hayek, Friedrich von
Huang, Qin Shi
Johnson, Harry
Kydland, Finn
Machlup, Fritz
Meltzer, Allan
Menger, Carl
Mises, Ludwig von

Myrdal, Gunnar
Ohlin, Bertil
Reisman, George
Ricardo, David
Rivlin, Alice
Robertson, Sir Dennis
Sargent, Thomas
Schwartz, Anna
Sraffa, Piero
Tobin, James
Volcker, Paul
Wicksell, Knut
Yellen, Janet
Xiaochuan, Zhou

## Monopoly

Allais, Maurice
Child, Josiah

Sweezy, Paul

## Monetary Theory

Lucas, Robert, Jr.
Simons, Henry

Stiglitz, Joseph

### Moral Philosophy
Hume, David  
Smith, Adam

### National Income Accounting
Stone, Sir Richard

### Neoclassical
Cassel, Gustav  
Irwin, Douglas  
Pigou, A.C.  
Tullock, Gordon

### Neo-Keynesian
Duflo, Esther  
Okun, Arthur  
Romer, Christina  
Stiglitz, Joseph  
Tobin, James

### Neo-Ricardian
Pasinetti, Luigi

### Physiocrats
Quesnay, François  
Turgot, Jacques

### Political Economy
Cantillon, Richard  
Dupuit, Jules  
Edgeworth, Francis  
Ekelund, Robert  
Friedman, Milton  
Gaidar, Yegor  
Galbraith, John Kenneth  
George, Henry  
Hobbes, Thomas  
Keynes, John Maynard  
Knight, Frank  
Kydland, Finn  
Laffer, Arthur  
List, Friedrich  
Locke, John  
Malthus, Thomas  
Maskin, Eric  
Menger, Carl  
Mirrlees, James  
Petty, Sir William  
Reich, Robert  
Reisman, George  
Say, Jean-Baptiste  
Senior, Nassau  
Simon, Herbert  
Smith, Adam  
Sowell, Thomas  
Stern, Nicholas  
Steuart, James  
Turgot, Jacques  
Walpole, Sir Robert  
Weber, Max

## Price Theory

Friedman, Milton
Gaidar, Yegor
Marshall, Alfred
Menger, Carl
Stigler, George
Vickrey, William

## Private Property/Property Rights

Alchian, Armen
Coase, Ronald
de Soto, Hernando
Engels, Friedrich
Locke, John
Maskin, Eric
Williams, Walter

## Production Theory

Khaldun, Ibn

## Profit Maximization

Thunen, Johann

## Public Choice Theory

Arrow, Kenneth
Buchanan, James
McFadden, Daniel
Olson, Mancur
Ostrom, Elinor
Tullock, Gordon

## Public Finance/Taxation

Gaidor, Yegor
Simons, Henry
Singh, Manmohan
Stern, Nicholas
Stone, Sir Richard
Summers, Lawrence
Trichet, Jean-Claude
Vickrey, William
Walpole, Sir Robert
Wieser, Friedrich von
Williamson, Oliver

## Public Policy/Administration

Colbert, Jean-Baptiste
Diamond, Peter
Hayek, Friedrich von
Heller, Walter
Kahn, Alfred
Keynes, John Maynard
North, Sir Dudley
Ohlin, Bertil
Schelling, Thomas
Senior, Nassau
Shultz, George
Singh, Manmohan
Sowell, Thomas
Stern, Nicholas
Steuart, James
Tinbergen, Jan
Trichet, Jean-Claude
Tyson, Laura

## Quantity Theory of Money

Friedman, Milton
Locke, John

Wieser, Friedrich von

## Rational Expectations

Lucas, Robert, Jr.

Sims, Christopher

## Savings and Investment

Cassel, Gustav

## Social Choice Theory

Sen, Amartya

## Social Economics

Akerlof, George
George, Henry

Kalecki, Michal
Wieser, Friedrich von

## Socialism

Bauer, Otto
Ely, Richard
Engels, Friedrich
Heilbroner, Robert
Hilferding, Rudolf

Lange, Oskar
Marx, Karl
Robinson, Joan
Sweezy, Paul
Webb, Beatrice

## Stockholm School of Economics

Cassel, Gustav
Myrdal, Gunnar

Ohlin, Bertil
Wicksell, Knut

## Supply Side

Laffer, Arthur

Okun, Arthur

## Tariffs

Taussig, Frank

Irwin, Douglas

## Theory of the Firm

Allais, Maurice
Child, Josiah

Sraffa, Piero

## Theory of Value

Khaldun, Ibn

## Trade

Bastiat, Frederic
Cantillon, Richard
Child, Josiah
Krugman, Paul
Hayek, Friedrich von
Irwin, Douglas
Johnson, Harry
Mises, Ludwig von
North, Sir Dudley
Ohlin, Bertil
Quesnay, François
Senior, Nassau
Steuart, James
Taussig, Frank
Tyson, Laura
Walpole, Sir Robert

## Unemployment

Beveridge, William
Burns, Arthur
Murphy, Kevin
Pissarides, Christopher
Solow, Robert
Yellen, Janet

## Utility Theory

Bentham, Jeremy
Harsanyi, John
Mill, John Stuart
Williamson, Oliver

## Welfare Theory

Arrow, Kenneth
Diamond, Peter
Hicks, Sir John
Lange, Oskar
Pigou, A. C.

# Preface

From before the Chinese dynasties into the new global economy, economic thinkers and leaders have shaped the ideas, concepts, and philosophies that have given us our capacity to study the economic behavior of individuals, individually and collectively. *Economic Thinkers: A Biographical Encyclopedia* explores over 200 of the major economic thinkers and thought leaders in the world of economics.

One of the attractions of studying economics is the complexity of the discipline. Our aim was to explore this complexity through some of those economists who have been the influencers of today's economic world. This encyclopedia is about economic history. This encyclopedia is about economic philosophy. This encyclopedia is about economics as a scientific discipline. Economics has been the topic of philosophers, politicians, citizens, writers, speakers, and barroom patrons since virtually the beginning of time. Economics is a discipline that began as a religious doctrine, transcended into a philosophy, and morphed into a social science and ultimately an exercise in mathematics.

The journey of economics is a continuum of people and events. Our encyclopedic journey begins before the time of Christ with the biography of Qin Shi Huang as his biography tells how the Chinese established standard measurements and money, and continues progressing through history to our latest Nobel laureates. We also view the development of economics as a science continually being expanded even as *Economic Thinkers* is published.

Economics is woven into the timeline of many historical events. A very long time ago my favorite subject in elementary school was social studies. I loved history and studying about the people, places, and events that made us who we are today. I especially remember my fifth-grade social studies when I learned about the explorers and their discoveries of new routes and new worlds. Little was I aware of the economic significance of all these people and events. To me (and to my teacher) it was a history lesson with some geography thrown in for good measure. As I look back, I think of the opportunity lost to also explore our economic history with those same people and events who have defined our "economic self." *Economic Thinkers* is a response to that hole in the lesson.

All too often economics has been elevated to some esoteric subject to be understood and appreciated by the elite of those who have had a graduate education in the subject. *Economic Thinkers* works to explode that notion and bring 210 of economics' great thinkers to the general reader, student, and beginning researcher. Both the general and experienced student of economics will gain a better understanding of the economic world around them and how it came to be, and provide a glimpse into the future of where it might be heading.

The encyclopedia contains the biographies of more than 200 great economic thinkers throughout history. One of the major challenges as the project unfolded was selecting the 200 economists. The experienced economics reader might wonder why a certain economist is included while another is not. However, there was a method to our madness. Even the nonexperienced user will most likely be familiar with the likes of Adam Smith, John Maynard Keynes, or Karl Marx. Our intent was to include a broad base of economic philosophies, economic disciplines such as history, development economics, and econometrics, along with thought leaders and policy implementers from the influential economic institutions. I am the first to acknowledge that economics has been developed through the efforts of many more than the 200 economic thinkers selected here. The general reader and the student who uses *Economic Thinkers* is going to be introduced to the world of economics through the economists chosen and the many subdisciplines, topics, eras, and philosophers.

The Introduction to *Economic Thinkers* passes briefly through time and the economists who define the eras. The A–Z entries provide brief biographies on over 200 of the great economic thinkers from yesterday and today. Topic finders help organize the entries by time period, geographical location, and major conceptual contributions. An Appendix includes a list of Nobel laureates. Thank you for your interest in coming on the journey.

A big thank-you goes out to all of the contributors without whose efforts this project would not have succeeded. The contributors to *Economic Thinkers* are some of the nation's finest college professors and high school AP economics teachers. Their passion for economics and their devotion to the discipline was evident throughout the development of the project. I owe them a major debt of gratitude.

I would like to thank Brian Romer, and Alison Bjerke from ABC-CLIO for their support and expertise throughout the project. Brian gave me the opportunity and Alison made us look good. I also want to thank Laura Bullard for her editorial and research assistance. Of course a project like this can be undertaken only with the support of family and friends. I owe a big thanks to each and every one of them for their patience and understanding. Thank you, Babe, for always being my inspiration. You are Beautiful.

*David A. Dieterle*

# Introduction:
# The Family Tree of Economics

## Introduction

A family tree is a chart or table showing the lines of descent specific to a family. Like a family, economic thought has its own family tree of individuals whose ideas and thinking have given us today's science of economics. Economics has been the topic of philosophers, politicians, citizens, writers, speakers, and barroom patrons since virtually the beginning of time. It is a discipline with roots in religious doctrine that transcended into a philosophy, morphed into a social science, and ultimately was taken over by mathematics.

If we journey back in time and view economic history through the prism of the great economic thinkers, we find ourselves on different early paths. One path is that of the early philosophers from Aristotle, the Bible, and earlier. Or, we can venture back in time on the path of the practitioners, the doers. They are represented by the businesspeople who practiced economics in their daily lives as early merchants, traders, and businessmen of their day.

## The Early Philosophers

The early philosophers of what was to become economics included the early Greeks, Aristotle, and the Romans. Later, in the thirteenth century, St. Thomas Aquinas and the scholastics of the church academies added to economic thinking. In the eighteenth century, an important line of economic philosophers came from France in the Physiocrats. François Quesnay and the Physiocrats have been labeled the first economic philosophers.

## The Early Practitioners

While there were early businessmen who promoted the virtues of an economy, the economic lineage of the early practitioners began to take shape in the seventeenth and eighteenth centuries with the mercantilists. The mercantilists were the merchants whose main practice was to export goods and import gold or other valuable monetary commodities. They viewed an economy as a zero-sum game: for every winner there is a loser. Their aim was to be the winner as the accumulator of gold, achieving that end by exporting goods to the rest of the known world. Mercantilism led to the age of exploration in a search for new lands and commodities such as gold and spices. New routes to India by land and sea with discoveries of the New World were products of the age. New lands meant more goods to export to accumulate more gold for the nation's treasury. And then—

### Along Comes Smith

In the midst of the eighteenth century, mercantilism was the key economic philosophy, but the philosophical thinking of the Physiocrats was gaining an audience in France. Then a diminutive Scottish political economy and morals professor brought the world of economics to a convergent trunk in the family tree. With the publication of *An Inquiry into the Nature and Causes of the Wealth of Nations* in 1776, Adam Smith moved the subject of economics from the zero-sum game of the mercantilists and the purely philosophical and theoretical world of the Physiocrats to the win-win economic system of trade, specialization, and self-interest. Through Adam Smith and *The Wealth of Nations*, a classical approach to economics was spawned on the family tree. Classical economics was more than just one more branch on the tree but rather a trunk where philosophers and practitioners converged.

### The Classical Economists: The Common Trunk

Adam Smith provided a new line of economic thinking and sparked the advent of the classical era. The writings of both the supporters and the critics of Adam Smith became the prevalent economic writings of the nineteenth century. What Adam Smith started, others continued. With the writings of David Ricardo, John Stuart Mill, Alfred Marshall, Leon Walras, and a host of other economists, political economists, and moral philosophers, the nineteenth century became a beehive of activity of economic writings, ideas, and theories that gave the science of economics its own distinctive scientific personality.

Not all nineteenth-century economists, philosophers, and writers were content to build on what Adam Smith began. Soon enough another line of economic thought appeared, discounting Smith's emphasis on growth, trade, and self-interest. It was argued that Smith's ideas would lead to an abuse of the masses and to a class warfare, which would bring down an economy. Karl Marx, a classical economist by education, led a group of economic thinkers into a new direction of economic thought. This line of thinking was to spawn yet another branch on the economics family tree, the branch of a command economy and socialism.

### The New Political Economy: Keynes

Between the writings of the classical writers and the writings of Karl Marx, the economics family tree seemed to be separating just as it had in the beginning. The separation was magnified in the twentieth century as the world of economics became more intertwined with the world of politics and government. The comingling of economic theory and thought with government expanded in the middle of the century with the advent of John Maynard Keynes and his *General Theory of Employment, Interest and Money*.

The classical economic writers along with a new school of economic thought emanating from Austria continued to write and promote economics from a philosophical, theoretical, and historical context. Yet the economic landscape was changing, and the prevalent economic practitioners were not just the participants from the business world but also those from the political world. Keynes, and the new group of economists known as Keynesians, had infused their economic thinking into government policies. Keynes had invented macroeconomics. Meanwhile, the economic ideas of Karl Marx were also gaining momentum around the globe. Going forward in the twentieth century, economics and government were now forever intricately linked as never before, even for the economic philosophers.

As Keynes and his new ideas were changing the economic way of thinking, two other groups of economists were having their own say. The Austrian School of economic thought led by Ludwig von Mises and Friedrich von Hayek were promoting just the opposite of Keynes. They were promoting a view of not more government but less government and more individual participation. Another group of economists were promoting the importance of focusing on the money supply and its critical function in an economy. The monetarists led by Milton Friedman concerned themselves with the role of central banks and central banking as the key to a vibrant, growing economy.

### The Quantitative Revolution

As the middle of the twentieth century became the end of the century, another branch of the economics family tree began to sprout. As Keynes launched new practices for measuring the macroeconomy, the advent of quantitative mathematics and statistics gained a foothold and became the major influence on economic thought. Econometrics took hold of economic thinking so that it became more important for economists to understand calculus than to know the writings of Adam Smith. The likes of Gérard Debreu, James Heckman, and Irving Fisher changed the course of economics from a historical and philosophical practice to a mathematical one. As a review of the Nobel laureates aptly reveals, the economic thinking in the latter years of the twentieth century was confined to expanding the world of economic thought and theory through mathematical derivation or statistical analysis. Even economic history through the work of Nobel laureate Douglass North was converted to a set of mathematical equations and formula-creating cliometrics.

### The New Branches on the Tree

The human element of the economics tree has not disappeared completely. Behavioral economics has sprouted new branches with the works of Daniel Kahneman and others. Kahneman's work exemplifies the interdisciplinary nature of economics as he is educated and trained as a psychologist, yet was awarded the Nobel Prize in Economics for his pioneering work in this new discipline of behavioral economics. Developing countries are also being studied in new ways as Esther Duflo implements experimental trials into her research. These are two examples of how the family tree of economics continues to sprout new branches and will do so in the future. With each new branch the tree grows bigger, stronger, and more interesting. With each new branch, the great economic thinkers make economics come alive for all of us.

# A

## AKERLOF, GEORGE

Born: June 17, 1940, in New Haven, Connecticut; American; social economics, Nobel Prize (2001); Major Work: "The Market for 'Lemons': Quality Uncertainty and the Market Mechanism" (1970).

George Akerlof is known for his work in growth theory and how markets worked. As a Keynesian economist, he had a unique perspective emphasizing the social aspect of economics. His economics is interdisciplinary in scope incorporating sociology, psychology, and social psychology into his economic thought and writings. An example of the topics he popularized in his work and writings are looting and bankruptcy. He won the Nobel Prize in Economics with Michael Spence and Joseph Stiglitz in 2001 for their work on asymmetric information in markets.

George Arthur Akerlof was born on June 17, 1940, to a Swedish father and German-Jewish mother in New Haven, Connecticut. His father, while a well-accomplished chemist, relocated on several occasions, finally settling in Princeton, New Jersey, where young Akerlof spent his formative school years. While in elementary school, he remembers his first insights into the world of economics. During a period when his father was unemployed, he realized there was a spin-off effect by which others would also lose their jobs, resulting in less money being spent in the economy. Even at an early age, he realized that this domino effect would create an ever-shrinking economy. Young Akerlof had his first encounter with Keynesian economics.

Growing up during two great American events, the Great Depression and World War II, Akerlof had a very inquiring social perspective as a young man. His interests ranged widely in the social sciences from history to economics. His brother, who frequented the lab with their father, followed in their father's footsteps to become a scientist. Such was not the path for young George Akerlof.

His interests and academic intrigue led his studies in the direction of economics and the social sciences. Contrary to his family's advice to pursue a career in law, Akerlof went to Yale and excelled in his studies as a young economist. He received his bachelor's degree from Yale in 1962. He continued his graduate studies in economics, earning his PhD at the Massachusetts Institute of Technology (MIT) in 1966. He accepted a position at the University of California, Berkeley, receiving tenure in 1969. It was during this time at Berkeley that he wrote "The Market for 'Lemons,'" which would later be the work on which his Nobel Prize was based.

In 1973 and 1974, he served on the Council of Economic Advisers as a senior economist during President Nixon's presidency. Due to his lack of a research background, lack of ability to write like a bureaucrat, and lack of loyalty when it came to

George Akerlof speaks with reporters at his Berkeley, California, home shortly after discovering he won the 2001 Nobel Prize. (AP/Wide World Photos)

party politics, he considered himself ill-suited for the position. However, professionally he considered the experience quite rewarding, broadening his skills in the areas of both labor economics and empirical economics.

Having failed to receive a promotion to full professor at Berkeley, he served on the Federal Reserve Board in Washington, DC, for a year. He then accepted a position at the prestigious London School of Economics. During his appointment at the London School, he was the Cassel Professor of Economics with Respect to Money and Banking.

Upon his return to Berkeley where he still had a faculty appointment, his research focus was changing. He had previously focused on the macroeconomic impact of microeconomic structures including asymmetric information and jobs. His research was now addressing issues such as fairness and the social traditions regarding unemployment. The paper he wrote and presented on involuntary unemployment led to his interest in sociology. This newfound interest in sociology led to additional writings on economic theory with a sociology base.

Several theories and ideals were made popular by Akerlof through his writings. One was "identity economics" as discussed in the *Quarterly Journal of Economics* (2000). The topic of looting was addressed in "The Economic Underworld of Bankruptcy for Profit" (1993), which he coauthored with Paul Romer. His paper "Efficiency Wage Models of the Labor Market" was coauthored with his wife, Janet Yellen. Continuing his integration of the social sciences with his economics, Akerlof and coauthor Robert Shiller proposed a macroeconomic framework that incorporates human behavior in their book, *Animal Spirits*. Incorporating all the idiosyncrasies of human behavior, they explore economic policy issues joining economics and psychology.

During his career as an economist, George Akerlof was honored with many prizes, awards, prestigious fellowships, and positions. His accomplishments include the Lawrenceville Medal, serving as the nonresident senior fellow at the Brookings Institution, the Guggenheim Fellowship, the Richard and Rhoda Goldman Distinguished Professor in the College of Letters and Science, studying as a Fulbright fellowship scholar, a fellow of the Econometric Society, and a fellow of the American Academy of Arts and Sciences.

The Nobel Prize in Economics, the most prestigious honor in economics, was bestowed on George Akerlof in 2001. The prize was awarded jointly to George Akerlof, Michael Spence, and Joseph Stiglitz for their analyses of the asymmetric information nature of markets. The study for which Akerlof is most noted is his previously mentioned study on asymmetric information in reference to the used-car market. "The Market for 'Lemons': Quality Uncertainty and the Market Mechanism" is the study on how imperfect or asymmetric information in the market for used cars creates market failures and alters behavior in consumers. This Nobel-honoring article was first published in the 1970 *Quarterly Journal of Economics*.

Akerlof has served as the Koshland Professor of Economics at the University of California, Berkeley. He is married to a fellow economist, Janet Yellen, who serves as current vice chairman of the Federal Reserve Bank's Board of Governors and is a professor of economics at the University of California, Berkeley. His son, Robert, currently serves as postdoctoral associate in applied economics at his father's graduate alma mater, MIT.

*See also:* Shiller, Robert; Spence, Michael; Stiglitz, Joseph; Yellen, Janet

## Selected Works by George Akerlof

Akerlof, George. "The Market for 'Lemons': Quality Uncertainty and the Market Mechanism." *The Quarterly Journal of Economics* 84, no. 3 (1970): 488–500.

Akerlof, George, and Rachel E. Kranton. "Identity Economics." *The Quarterly Journal of Economics* 115, no. 3 (2000): 715–53.

Akerlof, George, and Paul Romer. "Looting: The Economic Underworld of Bankruptcy for Profit." In *Explorations in Pragmatic Economics: Selected Papers of George A. Akerlof*, 232–74. New York: Oxford University Press, 2005.

Akerlof, George, and Robert Shiller. *Animal Spirits: How Human Psychology Drives the Economy, and Why It Matters for Global Capitalism*. Princeton, NJ: Princeton University Press, 2009.

Akerlof, George, and Janet Yellen. *Efficiency Wage Models of the Labor Market*. Cambridge: Cambridge University Press, 1986.

## Selected Works about George Akerlof

Akerlof, George. "Autobiography." 2011. Nobelprize.org. http://nobelprize.org/nobel_prizes/economics/laureates/2001/akerlof.html (accessed March 2011).

Akerlof, George. "Prize Lecture." Nobelprize.org. http://nobelprize.org/nobel_prizes/economics/laureates/2001/akerlof-lecture.html (accessed March 2011).

"George Akerlof Wins Nobel Prize in Economics." University of California, Berkeley. http://berkeley.edu/news/features/2001/nobel/index.html (accessed March 10, 2011).

Scheib, Arielt. "George Akerlof." Jewish Virtual Library. http://www.jewishvirtuallibrary.org/jsource/biography/akerlof.html (accessed March 18, 2011).

*Victoria Green*

## ALCHIAN, ARMEN

Born: April 12, 1914 in Fresno, California; Died: February 19, 2013, in Los Angeles; American; macroeconomic theory, inflation, costs and output, property rights; Major Work: "Information Costs, Pricing and Resource Unemployment" (1969).

Armen Alchian provided scholars with significant insights into several fields of economics. In macroeconomics, Alchian was instrumental in identifying the relationship between inflation and wages and clarifying why money is necessary for an efficiently functioning economy. In microeconomics, he clarified the relationship between costs and production. He also countered the argument for property rights. While his body of work was not weighty in size, it was impressive in breadth and depth and it broadened the understanding of economics.

Armen Albert Alchian was born in Fresno, California, in April 12, 1914. He attended Fresno State College for two years before transferring to Stanford University. He earned a BA from Stanford in 1936. He continued his graduate studies at Stanford, earning his PhD in economics in 1943. Upon graduation, he had a brief tenure at the University of Oregon as an instructor. During World War II, he served as a statistician for the Air Force. Following World War II, he joined the faculty at the University of California, Los Angeles.

Alchian, while often cited for his work in microeconomics, was also responsible for important contributions in macroeconomic theory. Within the study of macroeconomic theory, he stands out as a contrarian voice to what were some of the prevailing ideas of his day, particularly on the effects of inflation. Alchian emphasized the importance of detailed historical data when testing economic theories with empirical evidence. The hallmark of an engaged thinker, he would not accept claims without evidence to back them up.

This is most clearly illustrated in the work he did concerning "wage lag" inflation. Wage lag inflation favorably affects firms at the expense of laborers. Many economists believed that labor markets operated differently than other markets. Most of his contemporary economists believed inflation did not have an effect on wages. Wages would not follow as the general price level of goods and services in an economy began to rise. Although these claims were made by economists, it was Alchian who applied empirical historical data and discovered that in reality there was barely any evidence to support the wage lag theory. He was able to establish that labor markets functioned much in the same way as all other markets.

His work on inflation went beyond his study of the wage lag theory. He also developed detailed ideas about the impact of anticipated inflation versus unanticipated inflation. Alchian conducted much of his work on this area of inflation during the late 1950s and early 1960s when price indices were showing little inflation. But in subsequent decades when the U.S. inflation rate began to rise, Alchian's ideas became reality as economists witnessed a transition from a world where people expected and experienced price stability to a world with persistently higher than expected inflation. His work and experiences showed the need to include inflationary expectations when modeling its effects. He did this by showing that if inflation is unanticipated, holders of cash will behave in a certain way and generate a certain set of implications. If on the other hand holders of cash do expect inflation, they will behave differently, generating an entirely different set of expectations.

A second area Alchian was known for exploring is the role of money in an economy, specifically addressing the questions of what is money and why is it used. In a short essay titled "Why Money?," Alchian explored what money is and why it exists. In this essay, Alchian also demonstrated his ability to use plain language to clarify complicated issues and make them accessible to everyone. For Alchian, a thorough understanding of money serves as an important basis for the understanding of monetary policy. In "Why Money?," he identified three conditions that give rise to the use of a commodity as money. When there is a commodity about which everyone is informed, then everyone will be a specialist in that good and it will be used as money. Alchian also illustrated how what a society considers "money" has a low "recognition cost." As such, its quality and characteristics are readily identifiable by everyone. It can be used to facilitate almost every trade and therefore satisfies the characteristics as to what can serve as money.

Even with his important contributions to macroeconomics, his work in microeconomics represents even greater contributions to the field. Two notable areas of his work are developments in understanding the relationship between costs and output in the productions process and the implications of private property.

Prior to his work on costs and output in the production process, it was commonly held that a firm's costs depend only on the output. In his work entitled "Costs and Outputs" (1959), Alchian held that costs are actually determined by several dimensions within a well-defined production process. In his work, he outlined what these dimensions are and describes how costs respond to those variables when they are allowed to change separately. His work in this field constituted a departure from classical theory of production.

In his work on private property, Alchian attempted to clarify important issues surrounding property rights by explaining the structure of property rights, the social consequences that result from a particular structure of property rights, and the way in which a particular structure of property rights comes into being. Alchian submitted that what is owned is not the property itself but the right to use it in a particular socially accepted way. Alchian rejected the critics who say property rights take away from human rights by asserting that property rights are human rights and that a well-defined enforceable system will lead to better outcomes for society.

Armen Alchian's long career and groundbreaking work qualify him as one of the most important economic thinkers of modern times. His insights into both macro- and microeconomic theory have shed light on the subject in way no one previously had. His unique ability to make difficulty concepts accessible to any interested party also set him apart as skilled educator. In 1996, he was named a distinguished fellow of the American Economic Association.

Amen Alchian died on February 19, 2013, at his home in Los Angeles, He was 98.

*See also:* Coase, Ronald; de Soto, Hernando

### Selected Works by Armen Alchian

Alchian, Armen. *Economic Forces at Work*. Springville, UT: Liberty Press, 1977.
Alchian, Armen. "Information Costs, Pricing, and Resource Unemployment." *Economic Inquiry* 7 (1969): 109–28.
Alchian, Armen. "Why Money?" *Journal of Money, Credit and Banking* 9 (1977): 133–40.
Alchian, Armen, and Daniel K. Benjamin. *Choice and Cost under Uncertainty*. Indianapolis, IN: Liberty Fund, 2006.

### Selected Works about Armen Alchian

Baird, Charles W. "Alchian and Menger on Money." *Review of Austrian Economics* 13 (2000): 115–20.
Gavin, William T., and Jerry L. Jordan. "Armen Alchian's Contribution to Macroeconomics." *Economic Inquiry* 34 (1996): 496–505.
Lott, John R., ed. *Uncertainty and Economic Evolution: Essays in Honor of Armen A. Alchian*. New York: Routledge, 1997.
Orr, Daniel. "Costs and Outputs: An Appraisal of Dynamic Aspects." *The Journal of Business* 37 (1964): 51–56.

*John E. Trupiano*

## ALLAIS, MAURICE

Born: May 31, 1911, in Paris, France; Died: October 9, 2010, in Paris, France; French; market behavior, microeconomics, Nobel Prize (1988); Major Works: *In Quest of Economic Discipline* (1943), *Economy and Interest* (1947).

Maurice Allais was the first French citizen to receive the Nobel Prize in Economics. In 1988, Allais won the Nobel for his role in the understanding of market behavior and the efficient use of resources. Allais's work also centered on setting efficient prices for state-owned monopolies, as in his native France. Allais's ideas did not receive timely worldwide recognition as he published his works in French. Other English-speaking economists who published similar ideas around the same time, like Sir John Hicks and Paul Samuelson, took the spotlight instead. Samuelson even commented that had Allais's early writings been published in English, economic theory might have taken a different direction. Allais also made important discoveries related to growth theory in 1947 that were later credited to Edmund Phelps (in 1961). Allais died in 2010.

Maurice Felix Charles Allais was born in Paris on May 31, 1911, to a working-class family. His father died in a German prison camp during World War I and his mother raised him under difficult financial circumstances. A mathematics teacher persuaded Allais to study science rather than history. An exceptionally bright student at the Lycée Louis-le-Grand, Allais later trained as an engineer at the École Polytechnique, graduating first in his class. He then worked for several years as a mining engineer. During this time period, Allais also served in the French Alpine Army.

In the 1930s, Allais traveled to the United States where he witnessed the devastation of the Great Depression. He would later write that his travels to the United States were initiated by his desire to understand why the Depression happened and figure out how he could help find solutions to the world's problems. This desire led him to study economics. He saw economics as a way of helping people solve their problems.

After the armistice, Allais returned to work at the Corps National des Mines and began a self-study of economics. In *In Quest of an Economic Discipline* (1943), Allais mathematically proved, in an abstract model of a market in which goods are traded between households and firms, that equilibrium prices are efficient. His results show that the law of supply and demand works in theory as well as in practice.

Allais was also interested in the efficient use of public monopolies. He opposed the French postwar nationalization of several industries, but developed principles used to determine effective pricing and resource allocation in state-owned utilities and other monopolistic enterprises. He showed that even in state-run monopolies, resource allocation is most efficient when using some type of pricing system rather than direct regulation. This work was significant for younger economists working for state-owned monopolies in guiding their investment and pricing decisions. It also proved useful for regulating private sector monopolies in an age of denationalization.

Allais also discovered what came to be called the "golden rule of accumulation" in his book *Economy and Interest* (1947). The rule states that to maximize real income, the optimum rate of interest should equal the growth rate of the economy. This concept was the foundation for work by Edmund Phelps and Robert Solow, both of whom became Nobel laureates, and it was also important for the monetary theories of Milton Friedman.

In 1944, Allais became an economics professor at the École Nationale Supérieure des Mines in Paris where he would spend his career. He also became the director of a research unit at the Centre de la Recherche Scientifique from 1946 on and earned his doctorate from the University of Paris in 1949.

Allais is credited with introducing a mathematical rigor into the French discipline of economics, which at that time was mostly nonquantitative. His work also provided the foundation that allowed his student Gérard Debreu (1983 Nobel laureate) to prove that perfect markets can reach a stable equilibrium.

The overlapping generations model also debuted in Allais's work. Allais suggested that in stimulating an economy, it is helpful to use a model consisting of two generations, young and old. At each step, the old generation dies, the young generation grows old, and a new young generation appears. The model received little notice at the time, but more than a decade later Paul Samuelson introduced the same idea independently.

In 1953, Allais discovered and resolved a paradox about how people behave when choosing between various risks. The Allais paradox is an equation that predicts responses to risk. He collected convincing mathematical proof that people act in ways that are inconsistent with the standard theory of utility, which forecasts that people will behave as rational economic beings. Allais's work illustrates that people often put emotional considerations first, and overturns classical economic thought.

In the mid-1950s, Allais introduced the concept of psychological time when explaining inflation as a response to the growth in the money supply. In stable economies, people may take as much as two years to respond to an increase in the money supply by inflating prices, but in rapidly changing situations, such as in the case of hyperinflation, the time response may be as short as a few days. Allais proposed that economic models should use psychological time as a more accurate representation to changing circumstances than chronological time.

In the course of his career, Allais was not only a Nobel laureate but also received 14 scientific prizes from 1933 until 1987. One of the most notable was the Gold Medal of the National Center for Scientific Research, the most distinguished honor in French science, for Allais's lifetime work. Allais was a copious writer, both in the length of his pieces (his books typically ran 800–900 pages) and in the variety of subjects he addressed. As well as works on economic theory and physics, he also wrote books on history. He was appointed an officer of the Legion of Honor in 1977 and grand officer in 2005. He was promoted to Grand Cross of the Legion of Honor in 2010.

Maurice Allais died on October 9, 2010, at his home near Paris. He was 99.

*See also:* Debreu, Gérard; Hicks, Sir John; Samuelson, Paul

### Selected Works by Maurice Allais

Allais, Maurice. *A la Recherche d'une discipline économique, première partie: l'Économie pure.* Paris: Ateliers Industria, 1943.

Allais, Maurice. *Économie et Intérêt.* 2 vols. Paris: Imprimerie Nationale, 1947.

Allais, Maurice. *The General Theory of Surpluses.* 2 vols. Paris: Institut de Sciences Mathématiques et Économiques, 1981.

Allais, Maurice. "Le Comportement de l'homme rationnel devant le risqué: critique des postulates et axioms de l'école américaine." *Econometrica* 21 (October 1953): 503–46.

### Selected Works about Maurice Allais

Allais, Maurice. "Autobiography." Nobelprize.org. http://nobelprize.org/nobel_prizes/economics/laureates/1988/allais-autobio.html (accessed January 2011).

Allais, Maurice, and Bertrand R. Munier. *Markets, Risk and Money: Essays in Honor of Maurice Allais.* Theory and Decision Library B. New York: Springer: 1995.

"Chevalier Maurice." *The Economist* 75 (October 22, 1988): 75.

Douglas, Martin. "Maurice Allais, Nobel Winner, Dies at 99." *New York Times.* http://www.nytimes.com/2010/10/12/business/economy/12allais.html (accessed January 2011).

Maler, Karl-Goran. *Economic Sciences, 1981–1990: The Sveriges Riksbank (Bank of Sweden) Prize in Economic Sciences in Memory of Alfred Nobel.* Hackensack, NJ: World Scientific, 1992.

"Maurice Allais." *The Telegraph.* http://www.telegraph.co.uk/news/obituaries/finance-obituaries/8056996/Maurice-Allais.html (accessed January 2011).

Pool, Robert. "Market Theorist Gets Nobel Nod." *Science* 242, no. 4878 (1988): 511–12.

Vane, Howard R., and Chris Mulhearn. *The Nobel Memorial Laureates in Economics: An Introduction to Their Careers and Main Published Works.* Northampton, MA: Edward Elgar, 2007.

*Kathryn Lloyd Gustafson*

# ARROW, KENNETH

Born: August 23, 1921, in New York City; general equilibrium theory, welfare theory, economic growth, Nobel Prize (1972); Major Work: *Social Choice and Individual Values* (1951).

Kenneth J. Arrow is an American economist. In 1972 he, along with Sir John Hicks, won the Nobel Prize in Economics for work on general equilibrium and welfare economics. Arrow is also known for his work in the area of public choice, for he introduced and defended the impossibility theorem in his dissertation.

Kenneth Joseph Arrow was born on August 23, 1921, in New York City. He did his undergraduate work at the City College of New York, where he received a bachelor of science in social science with a major in mathematics in 1940. He then received an MA in mathematics from Columbia University in 1941. At that point, he switched to the Economics Department at Columbia for further graduate work, having completed his PhD course work in 1942, although he was still in search of a dissertation. His dissertation research was interrupted by military service during World War II in the U.S. Army Air Corps, where he served as weather officer, rising to the rank of captain. It was here that he had his first published paper, "On the Optimal Use of Winds for Flight Planning."

Upon his return from the military, Arrow was at Columbia for a brief period before joining the Cowles Commission at the University of Chicago in 1947. Time spent with other young econometricians and mathematically oriented economists proved to be a significant influence.

Arrow became affiliated with the RAND Corporation in 1948 and continued that relationship into the 1970s. It was early in his time at RAND that he arrived at an idea for his dissertation. He sought to apply the newly emerging field of game theory to large groups, such as countries. His research was published in 1951 under the title *Social Choice and Individual Values*. The work introduced the "impossibility theorem," which stated that, given certain assumptions, it was impossible to find a voting construct that would provide an outcome that most voters preferred. This provided and continues to provide great insights into social welfare theory as well as voter behavior in the public arena.

In 1949, Arrow joined the Economics Department at Stanford University where he would stay until leaving to join the faculty at Harvard in 1968. While at Stanford, some of his most significant early works were published: the aforementioned *Social Choice and Individual Values*, several articles on competitive equilibrium with Leonid Hurwicz from 1958 to 1960, and his contribution to "Toward a Theory of Price Adjustment" in *Allocation of Economic Resources* edited by Moses Abramovitz in 1959. Also while at Stanford, Arrow won the John Bates Clark Medal in 1957. It was while at Stanford that he also began his research into economic growth. His article "The Economic Implications of Learning by Doing" is a precursor to modern growth theory and the role of human capital.

In 1968, Arrow accepted a position at Harvard University. He would remain on the faculty at Harvard until returning to Stanford in 1979. While at Harvard, Arrow would continue his work in the areas of information, market efficiency, and public choice, producing several articles and books of note. These include *Public Investment, the Rate of Return, and Optimal Fiscal Policy* (with Mordecai Kurz) in 1970; *Essays on the Theory of Risk-Bearing* in 1970; *General Competitive Analysis* (with Frank Hahn) in 1971; and *The Limits of Organization* in 1974. Each of these provided insights into the role of information in markets or decision making. Arrow also produced significant research in the economics of discrimination and of health care.

Upon his return to Stanford in 1979, he became the Joan Kenney Professor of Economics and professor of economic research. During this second period at Stanford, Arrow continued his work on the impact of information in the market and decision making, as well as providing important insights into topics as widely divergent as income distribution and globalization.

Arrow retired in 1991 but remains professor emeritus at Stanford. He continues his research into areas of information economics, growth, and the environment.

*See also:* Hicks, Sir John

### Selected Works by Kenneth Arrow

Arrow, Kenneth J. *Behavior under Uncertainty and Its Implications for Policy*. No. TR-399. Standord, CA: Center for Research on Organizational Efficiency, Stanford University, 1983.

Arrow, Kenneth J. *Essays on the Theory of Risk-Bearing*. Chicago: Markham, 1971.

Arrow, Kenneth J. *Handbook of Mathematical Economics*. Vol. 1. Handbooks in Economics. Amsterdam: North Holland, 1987.

Arrow, Kenneth J. *The Limits of Organization*. New York: Norton, 1974.

Arrow, Kenneth J. *Social Choice and Individual Values*. Hoboken, NJ: Wiley, 1951.

Arrow, Kenneth J. *Theoretical Issues in Health Insurance*. Essex, UK: University of Essex, 1973.

Arrow, Kenneth J. "Toward a Theory of Price Adjustment." In *Studies in Resource Allocation Processes*. Edited by Kenneth Joseph Arrow and Leonid Hurwicz, 380–90. Cambridge: Cambridge University Press, 1959.

Arrow, Kenneth J., and Frank H. Hahn. *General Competitive Analysis*. Amsterdam: North Holland, 1971.

Arrow, Kenneth, and Mordecai Kurz. *Public Investment, the Rate of Return, and Optimal Fiscal Policy*. Washington, DC: RFF Press, 1970.

### Selected Works about Kenneth Arrow

Arrow, Kenneth J. "Autobiography." Nobelprize.org. http://www.nobelprize.org/nobel_prizes/economics/laureates/1972/arrow-autobio.html.

Chichilnisky, Graciela, ed. *Markets, Information and Uncertainty: Essays in Economic Theory in Honor of Kenneth J. Arrow*. Cambridge: Cambridge University, 1999.

Hammer, Peter J., Deborah Haas-Wilson, Mark A. Peterson, and William M. Sage., eds. *Uncertain Times: Kenneth Arrow and the Changing Economics of Health Care*. Durham, NC: Duke University Press, 2003.

"Kenneth Arrow." In *The Concise Encyclopedia of Economics*, ed. David R. Henderson. The Library of Economics and Liberty. http://www.econlib.org/library/Enc/bios/Arrow.html.

"Kenneth Arrow." The RAND Corporation. http://www.rand.org/pubs/authors/a/arrow_kenneth.html (accessed February 2011).
"Kenneth Arrow." Stanford University. http://economics.stanford.edu/faculty/arrow (accessed March 2011).
Scheib, Ariel. "Kenneth Arrow." Jewish Virtual Library. http://www.jewishvirtuallibrary.org/jsource/biography/arrow.html (accessed October 2012).

*Timothy P. Schilling*

## AUMANN, ROBERT

Born: June 8, 1930, in Frankfurt, Germany; Israeli; mathematician, game theory, Nobel Prize (2005); Major Work: *Lectures on Game Theory* (1989).

Robert Aumann was the first to introduce the formal analysis of infinitely repeated games, focusing on noncooperative encounters, a subject of game theory. Game theory is a branch of both economics and applied mathematics. Economics is like a game, in which action is or is not taken, based on the anticipated action of other players in the game. Outcomes result from the encounters between players who have mixed, similar, or opposing interests from each other. Based on these interests, players may or may not cooperate for any set of outcomes. Aumann's research showed that noncooperative relations or encounters, over the long run, hold up—this is known as the "folk theorem." In 2005, Aumann was awarded the Nobel Prize in economics.

Robert John Aumann was born on June 8, 1930, in the city of Frankfurt (on the Main), Germany, into an orthodox Jewish family. His mother was college educated in London and his father made a comfortable living as a wholesale textile merchant. In 1938, the family lost all their assets as the Nazis were coming to power. They then emigrated to New York. While in high school, he found a passion for mathematics, especially "the axioms, theorems, proofs, and constructions of Euclid's geometry." In college, Aumann's mathematics passion continued as he found analytic and algebraic number theory fascinating.

Robert J. Aumann completed his PhD at the Massachusetts Institute of Technology (MIT). In his undergraduate years, he preferred to study classical mathematics; however, at MIT his interests moved toward modern branches of mathematics, such as algebraic topology. His focus was in knot theory, a branch of algebraic topology. Aumann's thesis was published in the *Annals of Mathematics* in 1956.

According to Aumann, his knowledge of game theory was limited to early conversations he had with MIT instructor John Nash (also a Nobel economics laureate). After earning his PhD, Aumann began his research in game theory as a solution to solving a problem given him as a consultant for the Analytical Research Group (ARG): how do you defend a city from an attack by an air squadron, knowing that most are decoys, yet a few of the aircraft have nuclear weapons?

Aumann is most recently known for sharing the 2005 Nobel Prize in Economics with Thomas C. Schelling. The cowinners described their contribution to economics and game theory as the ability to use game-theory analysis to broaden the understanding of conflict and cooperation.

Aumann's research and publications include extensive collaborations with over 30 award-winning scientists. His notable collaborators include Thomas C. Schelling, Lloyd Shapley (coauthored the book *Values of Non-Atomic Games*), and Michael Maschler. He also collaborated with John Harsanyi, Reinhard Selten, Gérard Debreu, Dick Stearns, Herb Scarf, Harold Kuhn, Jim Mayberry, Jacques Drèze, Mordecai Kurz, Sergiu Hart, Bezalel Peleg, Adam Brandenburger, Frank Anscombe, Abraham Neyman, Benjy Weiss, Micha Perles, Joe Kruskal, Roger Myerson, Roberto Serrano, and Motty Perry.

*See also:* Debreu, Gérard; Harsanyi, John; Nash, John; Schelling, Thomas

## Selected Works by Robert Aumann

Aumann, Robert J. *Lectures on Game Theory*. Boulder, CO: Westview Press, 1989.

Aumann, Robert J., and Michael B. Maschler with collaboration of Richard E. Stearns. *Repeated Games with Incomplete Information*. Cambridge, MA: MIT Press, 1995.

Aumann, Robert J., and Lloyd S. Shapley. *Values of Non-Atomic Games*. Santa Monica, CA: RAND, 1968.

## Selected Works about Robert Aumann

Aumann, Robert J. "Autobiography." Nobelprize.org. http://nobelprize.org/nobel_prizes/economics/laureates/2005/aumann.html (accessed March, 2011).

"Robert J. Aumann." Hebrew University of Jerusalem. http://www.ma.huji.ac.il/~raumann/ (accessed October 2012).

*Steven Downing*

## BASTIAT, FRÉDÉRIC

Born: June 30, 1801, in Bayonne, Aquitaine, France; Died: December 24, 1850, in Rome; French; proponent of free trade; Major Work: *The Law* (1850).

Frédéric Bastiat was a French economist and journalist who championed free trade and laissez-faire government. His career as an economist began in 1844 during a time when France was undergoing a trend toward socialism. Most of his works were published around the time of the French Revolution of 1848. Bastiat's arguments against socialism are characterized by their clear organization, use of parables, and understandable writing style. In his most famous work, *The Law*, Bastiat argues that government should exist only to protect our God-given rights, which are life, liberty, and property. This work was published in June, just a few months prior to his death. Bastiat died in 1850.

Claude Frédéric Bastiat was born on June 30, 1801, in Bayonne, Aquitaine, France. Bayonne, Aquitaine, is located in the south of France on the Bay of Biscay. Bastiat was orphaned at the age of nine and was raised by his paternal grandparents. His youth was spent on his grandfather's farm in Mugron in the south of France. Not fond of working on the farm, he spent most of his time reading. At the age of 17, he left school to work at his uncle's trading company. While working at his uncle's firm, he perceived that its inability to flourish was due in part to the government's restrictive economic controls. It was at this time that young Bastiat declared that his ambition was "nothing less than to become acquainted with politics, history, geography, mathematics, mechanics, natural history, botany, and four or five languages."

Bastiat was particularly inspired by the works of Jean-Baptiste Say and Adam Smith. Their ideas convinced Bastiat that social and economic progress could not exist outside of a free-market economy. At the age of 24, Bastiat's grandfather died, leaving him the countryside family estate in Mugron. Bastiat spent the next 20 years running the farm and quietly debating politics with his friends. During the Revolution of 1830, Bastiat became inspired to join the cause in the name of driving out oppressive government rule in France. His analytical thinking and dedication to the cause of the Revolution did not go unnoticed. Soon after the Revolution of 1830, Bastiat was named justice of the peace in Mugron, and two years later he was elected to membership in the General Council of Landes.

Even under a new ruler, Louis Phillipe, France soon fell into the same oppressive patterns. Soon poor citizens were not allowed to vote, the publication of negative articles about Louis Phillipe were stopped, and he used the power of government to benefit some citizens at the expense of others. Bastiat witnessed the once

Frédéric Bastiat, a French economist and journalist, championed free trade and laissez-faire government. (Bettmann/Corbis)

promising ruler fall into the Socialist patterns of his predecessors and became even more convinced that increasing government regulation was not beneficial to the citizens of society.

Bastiat was particularly sensitive to the issue of tariffs. After traveling to Spain and Portugal, and having seen them mirror some of the same mistakes France had made, he became more passionate about free trade and fighting government protectionism. To defend himself against criticism from fellow Frenchmen, he began reading English works. It was while reading *The Globe and Traveler* that he discovered the ideas of Englishman Richard Cobden, and the Anti-Corn-Law League. Inspired by his findings, Bastiat submitted a treatise on tariffs to the *Journal des Economistes*. The article was printed in October 1844 and Bastiat's career as a journalist began.

Bastiat's articles were popular with the readers and he became a regular contributor to the *Journal des Economistes*. Bastiat's writings were characterized by their satirical wit and use of parables. The early articles that he wrote were collectively published as *Economic Sophisms* in 1845. One of the articles contained in *Economics Sophisms* uses the analogy of a broken railroad to explain how tariffs are counterproductive. The illustration tells a fictitious story of a railroad built between Spain and France to facilitate trade. Soon, the producers in each country complain that the importing country is now able to provide certain goods at lower prices, which threaten the profitability and security of their businesses. The producers demand that tariffs be enacted to artificially raise the price of the competing goods. Bastiat suggests that the tariffs negate the benefit of the cost of building the railroad in the first place and the consumer suffers by not enjoying the most competitive price. He sarcastically suggests that instead of tariffs, the government should simply destroy the railroad anywhere that competition threatens to lower the price to consumers.

One of his most famous parables attacking protectionism is "The Petition of the Candlemakers." In this satirical essay, he requests a law be passed to require the closing of doors, curtains, and all openings in order to block out the sun, which is unfairly competing with the candle makers' products. In it, on behalf of the candle makers, Bastiat declares that the candle makers' occupation is under attack by the sun, which certainly has an unfair competitive advantage. The sun can provide an abundance of light at a very low price. Bastiat goes on to claim this law against the sun is absolutely necessary to prevent this French industry, candle making, from totally disappearing.

In 1846, Bastiat established the Association of Free Trade and began his own newspaper devoted to free trade, *Le libre-echange*. He began a journey through France to establish affiliate free-trade associations. The free-trade movement in France failed to gain popularity and Bastiat's association ceased to exist in 1848. Bastiat was elected to the French National Assembly in 1848. He continued to write, lecture, and serve in the Assembly until his death in 1850.

In June of 1850, Bastiat returned to Mugron for a few days and penned his most famous work, *The Law*. In his last work, Bastiat warned against socialism and again praised limited government and individual freedom. In *The Law*, he asserts his belief that the responsibility of the law is to preserve life, liberty, and property. He argued that instead, the law was being used to benefit one group of citizens to the detriment of another group.

Frédéric Bastiat died on December 24, 1850, in Rome at the age of 49 after contracting tuberculosis. Bastiat's works are still considered relevant arguments against the effects of socialism. His works are better known in the United States than in France. Since Bastiat offered no unique economic theories, some current economists do not consider him an economist in his own right but instead a talented journalist and communicator.

*See also:* Say, Jean-Baptiste; Smith, Adam

### Selected Works by Frédéric Bastiat

Bastiat, Claude Frédéric. *Economic Harmonies*. 1850. Edited by George B. De Huszar. Translated by W. H. Boyers. Irvington-on-Hudson, NY: Foundation for Economic Education, 1997.

Bastiat, Claude Frédéric. *Economic Sophisms*. 1845. Translated by A. Goddard, 1964. Irvington-on-Hudson, NY: Foundation for Economic Education, 1996.

Bastiat, Claude Frédéric. *The Law*. 1850. Translated by Dean Russell. Irvington-on-Hudson, NY: Foundation for Economic Education, 1995.

Bastiat, Claude Frédéric. *Selected Essays on Political Economy*. 1848. Translated by S. Cain, 1964. Irvington-on-Hudson, NY: Foundation for Economic Education, 1995.

### Selected Works about Frédéric Bastiat

Böhm-Bawerk, Eugen. *Capital and Interest: A Critical History of Economical Theory*. Translated with a preface and analysis by William Smart. New York: Kelley, 1970.

Kirzner, Israel M. *The Economic Point of View: An Essay in the History of Economic Thought*. 2nd ed. Kansas City, MO: Sheed and Ward, ca. 1976.

Roche, G. C. *Frederic Bastiat: A Man Alone*. New Rochelle, NY: Arlington House, 1971.

*Aimee Register Gray*

## BAUER, OTTO

Born: September 5, 1881, in Vienna, Austria-Hungary; Died: July 4, 1938, in Paris, France; Austrian; Austro-Marxist; Major Work: *Die Nationalitätenfrage und die Sozialdemokratie* (1907).

Otto Bauer was a leading thinker in the Austro-Marxist movement of the early twentieth century. Bauer promoted a form of socialism that would gradually overcome capitalism through state expropriation of property while also attempting to avoid civil war between the bourgeois and proletariat. He served as secretary of state for foreign affairs under Chancellor Karl Renner in the post–World War I Austrian Social Democratic Party, and advocated (unsuccessfully) for the Austrian *Anschluss* with Germany immediately after the war. He spent the remainder of his life in exile following a failed revolution attempt. Bauer died in 1938.

Otto Bauer was born on September 5, 1881, in Vienna, Austria-Hungary, to Jewish parents. He became involved in Austria's Parliament in 1904 and would stay active through 1934, as well as being active in an underground movement while in exile. He earned a PhD in law from the University of Austria in 1906. He was editor of *Der Kampf*, which was the journal of the Austrian Social Democratic Party. During World War I, he served in the Austrian army and was a prisoner of war in Russia. Upon his return in 1917, he became a leader of the nation's left wing in politics.

In his major work, *The Nationalities Question and Social Democracy* (1907), Bauer addressed the theory of national character, or what constitutes a nation. He would define national character as "the sum total of characteristics which distinguish the people of one nationality from the people of another nationality—the complex of physical and spiritual characteristics which distinguish one nation from another," and nation as "an aggregate of people bound into a community of character by a common destiny."

In a 1914 pamphlet, *The High Cost of Living*, Bauer attacked capitalism. His arguments included that fact that the increase in the cost of living was international. He also made links to the rise of populations in countries where technology and industry had increased. He claimed that the real task of socialism was to solve the difficulties of providing for the needs of the people in the face of scarcity in proportion to their production.

In the pamphlet *The Road to Socialism* (1919), Bauer explained his ideas about the expropriation of capitalist property. He believed that the industrialist leaders should be compensated for their losses, but he proposed that capital taxes should be levied to help cover the costs. He would state in a 1924 pamphlet, *The Struggle for Power*, that the voting of the people is preferable to resorting to violence, but that the threat or possibility of using armed force would help to make voting possible.

Bauer viewed Marxism as the inevitable outcome in countries throughout Europe, especially in Russia. He believed that as the Russian workers led the revolt, the end result would not be a leadership from the proletariat but that the dictatorship would come from the "bourgeois democracy," which was more of a "state capitalism." He believed that ending the dictatorship should be peaceful and nonviolent. He would go on to say in *Between Two Wars* (1937) that the Soviet Union had achieved socialism, in part, because the state was large enough to maintain itself with its own raw materials and not have to rely on the international community. Austro-Marxism, as viewed by Bauer, rejected the Communist method of consolidating power by violent revolution, but sought to use parliamentary decisions to achieve a similar goal.

In the late 1920s, a dichotomy was growing in Austria between the Socialists, influenced by Bauer, and the *Heimwehr*, influenced by Fascist Italy, resulting in a new Austrian constitution in 1929. As depression hit Austria and political conflict continued, the Austro-Marxists lost influence with the Social Democratic Party. Fighting broke out between the *Heimwehr* and Social Democrats in 1934, and Bauer would be exiled to Brno, Czechoslovakia.

In *Between Two Wars*, Bauer would state his idea of "integral socialism." This idea aimed to unite the Social Democratic and the Communist movements not on common methods but with consistent political goals. In a sense, he was admitting the inability of Austro-Marxists and Social Democrats to succeed in bringing about the socialism he desired, while also seeking a way to influence Communists. He did not want a union of the two at the expense of one, but rather a change and strengthening of both.

Toward the end of his life, while in exile Bauer met with Ernst Fischer. Fischer described Bauer's belief in the necessity of a strong state for socialism to work and his admiration for the successes of the Soviet Union. He believed in the ideal of the "self-management of a classless society" and the looming World War II would be the impetus required to start the Socialist revolution in Europe. He refused a request to return to Moscow with Fischer to help the Communists reach their goals.

He fled Austria in 1934, initially to Czechoslovakia, and later to Paris, France. By the time of his death, he had lost influence in the theoretical debate between Socialists and Communists. He has been recognized for his influence in promoting a democratic socialism.

Otto Bauer died in exile July 4, 1938, in Paris, France.

*See also:* Marx, Karl

## Selected Works by Otto Bauer

Bauer, Otto. *Die Nationalitätenfrage und die Sozialdemokratie* (1907). Minneapolis: University of Minnesota Press, 2000.

Bauer, Otto. *Die österreichische Revolution* [The Austrian Revolution] (1923). London: Parsons, 1925.

## Selected Works about Otto Bauer

Bourdet, Yvon. *Otto Bauer et la Revolution*. Paris: EDI, 1968.

Braunthal, Julius. *Otto Bauer*. Vienna, Austria: Volksbuchhandlung, 1961.

Fischer, Ernst. "Ernst Fischer Solicits Otto Bauer for the Popular Front in 1936." *International Socialist Review* 30, no. 3 (May–June 1969): 44–48. Translated by Einde O'Callaghan. Originally published in *Weg und Ziel*, July–August 1968. http://www.marxists.org/history/etol/newspape/isr/vol30/no03/fischer.html (accessed March 18, 2011).

Frank, Pierre. "Otto Bauer: A Representative Theoretician of Austro-Marxism." *International Socialist Review* 30, no. 3 (May–June 1969): 36–41. Translated by Einde O'Callaghan. Originally published in French in *Quatrième Internationale*, 1969. http://www.marxists.org/history/etol/writers/frank/1969/01/bauer.htm (accessed December 2010).

Reichetseder, Manuel. "The February 1934 Austrian Uprising and the Weaknesses of 'Austro-Marxism.'" http://www.marxist.com/february-1934-austrian-uprising.htm (accessed December 2010).

*Joseph Lee Hauser*

# BECKER, GARY

Born: December 2, 1930, in Pottsville, Pennsylvania; American; behavioral economics, economic growth, Nobel Prize (1992); Major Work: *The Economic Approach to Human Behavior* (1977).

Gary Becker is an American economist who applied the idea that individuals are rational, optimizing creatures seeking to maximize wealth or other utility. In doing so, he has been able to offer explanations for many behaviors outside the traditional sphere of economic activity. In 1992, he won the Nobel Prize in Economics for his application of economic analysis to human behavior and interaction, including nonmarket activities.

Gary Stanley Becker was born on December 2, 1930, in the small coal-mining town of Pottsville, Pennsylvania. His family moved to Brooklyn, New York, when he was quite young. Upon graduating from high school, Becker attended Princeton University, graduating summa cum laude with an AB in 1951. He then went to the University of Chicago for graduate work, receiving an AM in 1953 and his PhD in 1955.

Becker held the post of assistant professor at the University of Chicago from 1954 to 1957. It was during this time that he developed several influential relationships including Milton Friedman (Nobel Prize 1976) and Theodore W. Schultz (Nobel Prize 1979). It was here that he worked on *The Economics of Discrimination*, which grew out of his PhD dissertation. In it, Becker used economic analysis to examine the effects of prejudice on the economic life of minorities, including earnings, employment, and occupations. Becker showed that, contrary to the Marxian view, discrimination hurt the person who discriminated, especially in competitive situations. The work received good reviews in major journals. However, Becker felt his research and work were not having an impact. Despite encouragement from Friedman, Schultz, and others, in 1957 Becker left the University of Chicago, accepting a joint appointment at Columbia University and the National Bureau of Economic Research (NBER).

While at Columbia, Becker began focusing on the role of human capital in the economy. He published *Human Capital*, which was a result of one of his first research projects for NBER in 1964. In 1967, he authored *Human Capital and the Personal Distribution of Income*. This same year he won the John Bates Clark Medal. Becker recognized education as an investment in human capital and an important component for economic growth. While at Columbia, he began to produce articles on what had previously been viewed as "noneconomic," the economics of the family and the economics of crime. He also instituted a workshop, modeled after the workshops at the University of Chicago. The workshops were about labor and "related" subjects. But as he and his later codirector, Jacob Mincer, felt that most subjects were "related," the workshops were wide-ranging and drew significant student interest.

While he remained affiliated with NBER, Becker left Columbia and returned to the University of Chicago in 1970. It was at this time that he became friends with George Stigler and they coauthored a number of articles. He continued to expand his own research in the studies of "noneconomic" activity.

*The Economic Approach to Human Behavior* was published in 1976. Becker saw family formation, family size, and family dissolution as choices subject to rational, utility-maximizing objectives. His *Treatise on the Family* was a major work on the subject and was followed by numerous articles using economics to shed light on family activity. In 1983, Becker was offered a joint appointment by the Sociology Department at the University of Chicago, which he accepted. This was verification that his method of analysis had gained validity outside of the economics profession.

In 1985, Becker was approached by *Business Week* to write a monthly column on economic issues. He accepted on an experimental basis because he had previously written only for academic audiences. However, he believes his writing style improved as he learned to make his case without using professional jargon and in a shorter format. He has produced a number of books for general audiences including *The Economics of Life* (with Guity Nashat-Becker) in 1996 and *Uncommon Sense* (with Richard Posner) in 2009.

In addition to being a member of the NBER, he remains affiliated with the Hoover Institution and the American Enterprise Institute for Public Policy Research. He has been active in the American Economic Association (serving both as president and vice president), the Econometric Society, and the Economic History Association. Becker has been elected to the Mount Pelerin Society, the American Academy of Arts and Sciences, the National Academy of Sciences, and the Pontifical Academy of Sciences.

He has received honorary degrees from a number of institutions including Hebrew University in Jerusalem, Princeton University, Columbia University, the Warsaw School of Economics, University of Economics in Prague, and Harvard University. In addition to winning the Nobel Prize for Economic Sciences in 1992, he has received the National Medal of Science in 2000, the Heartland Prize in 2002, the Hayek Award in 2003, the Presidential Medal of Freedom in 2007, and the Bradley Prize in 2008.

*See also:* Friedman, Milton; Schultz, Theodore; Stigler, George

## Selected Works by Gary Becker

Becker, Gary S. *Accounting for Tastes*. Cambridge, MA: Harvard University Press, 1996.

Becker, Gary S. *The Economic Approach to Human Behavior*. Chicago: University of Chicago Press, 1977.

Becker, Gary S. *The Economics of Discrimination*. 2nd ed. Chicago: University of Chicago Press, 1971.
Becker, Gary S. *Human Capital and the Personal Distribution of Income: An Analytical Approach*. 3rd ed. Chicago: University of Chicago Press, 1994.
Becker, Gary S. "Investment in Human Capital: A Theoretical Analysis." *Journal of Political Economy* 70 (1962): 9–49.
Becker, Gary S. *A Treatise on the Family*. Cambridge, MA: Harvard University Press, 1981.
Becker Gary S., and Gilbert Ghez. *The Allocation of Time and Goods over the Life Cycle*. Cambridge, MA: National Bureau of Economic Research, 1975.
Becker, Gary S., and Kevin Murphy. *Social Economics*. Cambridge, MA: Belknap Press/ Harvard University Press, 2003.
Becker, Gary S., and Guity Nashat. *The Economics of Life*. New York: McGraw-Hill, 1996.
Becker, Gary S., and Richard Posner. *Uncommon Sense*. Chicago: University of Chicago Press, 2009.

**Selected Works about Gary Becker**

"An Interview with Gary Becker." http://www.minneapolisfed.org/publications_papers/pub_display.cfm?id=3407 (accessed March 2011).
Becker, Gary. "Autobiography." Nobelprize.org. http://nobelprize.org/nobel_prizes/economics/laureates/1992/becker-autobio.html (accessed October 2010).
Hoover Institution. "Gary Becker." http://www.hoover.org/fellows/9904 (accessed December 10, 2010).
*Prize Lectures in Economic Sciences 1991–1995*. The Sveriges Riksbank Prize in Economic Sciences in Memory of Alfred Nobel. Edited by Torsten Persson. Singapore: World Scientific Publishing, 1997.

*Timothy P. Schilling*

# BENTHAM, JEREMY

Born: February 15, 1748, in London, England; Died: June 6, 1832, in London, England; utility theory; Major Works: *Defense of Usury* (1787), *An Introduction to the Principles of Morals and Legislation* (1789).

Jeremy Bentham was an English philosopher, jurist, and legal and social reformer. His concept of the utility of consumer satisfaction, and its impact on markets, is still a major influence on economic and political thought today. Bentham quantified the utility of individual actions on the basis of the utility (satisfaction) gained by the action. Bentham's approach to studying decision making is known as utilitarianism. His utilitarian critiques of law helped to promote liberal social and legal reform. Bentham died in 1832.

Jeremy Bentham was born in Spitalfields, London, England, on February 15, 1748, to a wealthy Tory family. He was discovered reading a multivolume history of England as a toddler and went on to study Latin at age three. His grandfather and father were both lawyers and expected Bentham to follow in their footsteps. At the age of 12, he was sent to Queen's College, Oxford, where he earned his bachelor's degree. He continued at Lincoln's Inn to study law with a student seat in the King's Bench division of the High Court. Bentham earned his master's degree in 1766, trained as a lawyer, and was called to the bar in 1769.

Bentham disappointed his father by spending most of his time focused on the theoretical aspects of legal abuses within the English system rather than practicing law. Bentham was dissatisfied with the complexity of British law. He spent the remainder of his life criticizing the existing law and suggesting ways to improve it.

Bentham was influenced by philosophers of the Enlightenment and by thinkers such as John Locke, David Hume, Baron de Montesquieu, and Claude Adrien Helvétius. He felt that many of the problems of his day resulted from the accumulation of inherited power in the hands of a few wealthy landowners.

Bentham emphasized reason over tradition and clarity in the use of terms. He sought to eliminate the use of any legal words that led to "fictitious" ownership. He did not believe in "natural rights," "natural law," or "social contracts." Bentham felt that any people within a society always had some kind of restriction imposed upon them. Laws were necessary for social order and well-being and must have government to enforce them. Without law, anarchy would result. Bentham believed that the individual's economic and personal best interest is reflected in the use of a government elected by the people.

Bentham wrote *Defense of Usury* in 1785 while visiting his brother, an engineer in the Russian armed forces. Bentham shows himself as a follower of Adam Smith, but critiques him for not following the logic of his own principles.

One of Bentham's most significant contributions was his moral principle of utilitarianism, outlined in his book *An Introduction to the Principles of Morals and Legislation* (1789). A basic tenet of utilitarianism is that pleasure and pain motivates all human action. This thesis is also known as psychological hedonism. The right action or choice is that which causes "the greatest happiness for the greatest number." All individuals refer to utility or satisfaction in their choices either explicitly or implicitly, and it is morally appropriate to pursue the action that maximizes pleasure.

Bentham devised a method to assess the moral status of any action called the hedonic calculus or felicific calculus. The ancient Greek philosophy of hedonism promotes the idea that pleasure seeking is one's moral duty. Bentham's method of calculating the pleasures and pains of a course of action, however, allows for an objective public discussion. He advocated that it was the role of the legislature to identify different interests and make decisions to promote the most satisfaction for the most people.

This became known as utility theory, a way of measuring consumer behavior. The principle of utility theory emphasizes human equality, as each person's happiness counts the same as every other person's. Bentham's ideas proved influential to his peers. They helped to shape his student John Stuart Mill's viewpoints and became a significant part of liberal political objectives. Bentham was also declared an honorary citizen of France due to his correspondence with leaders of the French Revolution. Bentham also convinced Adam Smith to change his views on interest rates.

Bentham believed monetary expansion was the key to achieving full employment. He advocated the use of minimum wage and guaranteed employment to make this happen. His work laid the foundation for the maximization principle in the economics of the consumer, the firm, and the optimum in welfare economics.

Bentham is also credited with helping to shape contemporary philosophical and economic vocabulary with terms such as "international," "maximize," "minimize," and "codification."

His work greatly influenced political reform in England and neighboring countries. Upon his death, Bentham left his large estate to finance the University College of London—one of the first English universities to admit all regardless of family background or political belief. His cadaver, as his will instructed, was dissected, embalmed, dressed, and placed in a chair in a cabinet in the hallway of the main building of the University College of London. Although Bentham published few books during his lifetime, he was a prolific writer, producing 10 to 20 manuscripts daily until his death. The University College of London's Bentham Project is working to publish a complete edition of Bentham's works and correspondence.

Jeremy Bentham died on June 6, 1832, in London, England.

*See also:* Hume, David; Mill, John Stuart; Smith, Adam

### Selected Works by Jeremy Bentham

Bentham, Jeremy. *Defence of usury: shewing the impolicy of the present legal restraints on the terms of pecuniary bargains: in a series of letters to a friend: to which is added, a Letter to Adam Smith ... on the discouragements opposed by the above restraints to the progress of inventive industry.* London: Messrs. D. Williams, Colles, White, Byrne, Lewis, Jones, and Moore, 1788.

Bentham, Jeremy. *An Introduction to the Principles of Morals and Legislation.* Oxford: Clarendon Press, 1789.

### Selected Works about Jeremy Bentham

Atkinson, Charles Milner. *Jeremy Bentham: His Life and Work.* New York: Kelly, 1969.
Everett, Charles Warren. *Jeremy Bentham.* London: Weidenfeld and Nicolson, 1969.
Mack, Mary Peter. *Jeremy Bentham: An Odyssey of Ideas, 1748–1792.* London: Heinemann, 1962.

*Kathryn Lloyd Gustafson*

## BERNANKE, BEN

Born: December 13, 1953, in Augusta, Georgia; American; monetary policy, chairman of the Federal Reserve System 2006–current; Major Works: "Nonmonetary Effects of the Financial Crisis in the Propagation of the Great Depression" (1983), *Essays on the Great Depression* (2004).

Ben Bernanke is an American economist who has served as chairman of the Federal Reserve System Board of Governors from 2006. Bernanke directed the Federal Reserve's response to the financial crisis of 2008–9. He served on the Fed Board of Governors from 2002 to 2005. He was first appointed chairman by President George W. Bush and was reappointed by President Obama in 2010. Prior to being named chairman of the Federal Reserve Board of Governors, he was a board governor since 2002. Prior to joining the Board of Governors, Bernanke was a tenured professor and chair of the Princeton University Department of Economics. Bernanke also served President George W. Bush as chairman of the Council of Economic Advisers.

Benjamin Shalom Bernanke was born on December 13, 1953, in Augusta, Georgia. Growing up in Dillon, South Carolina, as the grandson of Jewish immigrants, he graduated as high school class valedictorian. Bernanke earned his BA in economics from Harvard University with honors in 1975. He received his PhD in economics from Massachusetts Institute of Technology (MIT) in 1979. His dissertation adviser was future Bank of Israel central bank counterpart, Stanley Fischer.

Bernanke's dissertation, "Long-Term Commitments, Dynamic Optimization, and the Business Cycle," launched his career as a Depression-era economic historian. Upon graduation from MIT, Bernanke began his academic career in the Stanford University Graduate School of Business. Bernanke joined the faculty at Princeton University in 1985, becoming department chair in 1992—a position he would hold till 2002.

Bernanke's expertise and research on the economic causes and consequences of the Great Depression elevated his reputation as an equal to Milton Friedman and Anna Schwartz. In 1983, Bernanke published "Nonmonetary Effects of the Financial Crisis in the Propagation of the Great Depression." Bernanke made the case that the key causes and eventual collapse of the economy in 1929 and subsequent depression of the 1930s was a collapse of the banking system's failure to provide sufficient credit. This view goes beyond Friedman's response, which laid blame directly on the Federal Reserve and government. Later, in 2004, he would provide a summation of his views in *Essays on the Great Depression*.

Beyond his work on the Great Depression, he is the coauthor of two successful economics textbooks, both in their multiple editions. Bernanke has delivered lectures at the London School of Economics on monetary policy and theory. He directed the Monetary Economics Program of the National Bureau of Economic Research and edited the *American Economic Review*.

Ben Bernanke entered public service in 2002 when he accepted an offer from President George W. Bush to join the Federal Reserve Board of Governors. He remained on the Board of Governors till 2005 when he chaired President Bush's Council of Economic Advisers till 2006. In 2006, he was a top candidate to replace the retiring Alan Greenspan as chairman of the Federal Reserve Board of Governors. On February 1, 2006, Ben Bernanke succeeded Greenspan as chair, becoming the most important monetary economist in the nation. He also chairs the Federal Open Market Committee, the committee responsible for key monetary policy decisions.

Though he soundly defended the Federal Reserve's actions, Bernanke was not without his critics. He was criticized for the Federal Reserve's role in backing of JP Morgan Chase in order for Chase to buy Bear Stearns, the Troubled Asset Relief Program (TARP), and with the U.S. Treasury the bailout of AIG.

An avowed monetarist and student of the Great Depression, Bernanke feared deflation more than inflation. As a result, he publicly advocated supplying as much money as necessary to the monetary system to avoid a deflationary spiral. Using a helicopter analogy in a speech to describe his monetary views, Bernanke was labeled (mostly by his critics) "Helicopter Ben."

Known as "quantitative easing" on three different occasions (QE I, II, III), the Fed went into the business of buying and adding depreciated assets to the Federal Reserve's balance sheet. In return, the Federal Reserve supplies sufficient quantities of dollars into the monetary system, keeping interest rates at historical lows. In responding to these crises, under Ben Bernanke the Federal Reserve took on more direct actions then quite possibly at any time since its inception in 1913.

Bernanke's honors included being named Fellows of the American Academy of Arts, Guggenheim, and the Econometric Society. He also was a member of the National Bureau of Economic Research (NBER) and NBER's Business Cycle Dating Committee.

*See also:* Fischer, Stanley; Friedman, Milton; Greenspan, Alan; Schwartz, Anna; Volcker, Paul

### Selected Works by Ben Bernanke

Bernanke, Ben S. *Essays on the Great Depression*. Princeton, NJ: Princeton University Press, 2004.

Bernanke, Ben S. "Nonmonetary Effects of the Financial Crisis in the Propagation of the Great Depression." *American Economic Review* 73, no. 3 (June 1983): 257–76.

Bernanke, Ben S., Andrew B. Abel, and Dean Croushore. *Macroeconomics*. 6th ed. Boston: Addison-Wesley, 2007.

Bernanke, Ben S., and Alan S. Blinder. "The Federal Funds Rate and the Channels of Monetary Transmission." *American Economic Review* 82, no. 4 (September 1992): 901–21.

Bernanke, Ben S., and Robert H. Frank. *Principles of Macroeconomics*. New York: McGraw-Hill, 2007.

Bernanke, Ben S., Mark Gertler, and Mark Watson. "Systematic Monetary Policy and the Effects of Oil Price Shocks." C.V. Starr Center for Applied Economics, May 27, 1997.

Bernanke, Ben S., Thomas Laubach, Frederic S. Mishkin, and Adam S. Posen. *Inflation Targeting: Lessons from the International Experience*. Princeton, NJ: Princeton University Press, 2001.

### Selected Works about Ben Bernanke

"Ben Bernanke." *Forbes*. http://www.forbes.com/profile/ben-bernanke/ (accessed October 2012).

"Ben Bernanke; Chairman of the Federal Reserve (since January 2006)." *Washington Post*. http://www.washingtonpost.com/politics/ben-bernanke/gIQA3UaU9O_topic.html (accessed October 2012).

"Ben Bernanke's Greatest Challenge." *60 Minutes*. http://www.cbsnews.com/stories/2009/03/12/60minutes/main4862191.shtml (accessed October 2012).

"Ben S. Bernanke." Board of Governors of the Federal Reserve System. http://www.federalreserve.gov/aboutthefed/bios/board/bernanke.htm (accessed October 2012).

Harris, Ethan S. *Ben Bernanke's Fed: The Federal Reserve after Greenspan*. Cambridge, MA: Harvard Business Press, 2008.

Lowenstein, Roger. "The Education of Ben Bernanke." *New York Times*. http://www.nytimes.com/2008/01/20/magazine/20Ben-Bernanke-t.html (accessed October 2012).

Wessel, David. *In Fed We Trust: Ben Bernanke's War on the Great Panic*. New York: Crown Business, 2009.

David A. Dieterle

## BEVERIDGE, WILLIAM

Born: March 5, 1879, in Rangpur, India; Died: March 16, 1963, in Oxford, Oxfordshire, England; English; unemployment; Major Work: *Social Insurance and Allied Services* (1942).

Baron William Beveridge was the founder of the British welfare state. Beveridge was considered the leading authority on unemployment insurance due to his early work beginning in 1907. In fact, Beveridge took a lifelong interest in the problem of unemployment and it was his influence that helped shape Britain's social policies and institutions through the Beveridge Report (1942). It would become the desire of the British government to provide economical housing for the poor, great health care for all, and pensions that would allow for a comfortable retirement. Most of the recommendations from his report were implemented in 1948 when the British National Health Service was established. Beveridge died in 1963.

Baron William Henry Beveridge was born on March 5, 1879, in Rangpur, India. His father served as a judge in the Indian Civil Service. Beveridge attended Balliol College and Oxford University. Although trained as a lawyer, Beveridge became interested in social services and wrote articles about it for the *Morning Post*. He was highly influenced by the

William Beveridge is considered the founder of the British welfare state including the British National Health Service. (Library of Congress)

Fabian Society Socialists, who believed in the advancement of their ideals including clean simplified living for all. This society laid many of the foundations of the British Labour Party, which is still in existence today.

In 1908, Beveridge joined the Board of Trade and helped organize the national system of labor exchanges, becoming its director from 1909 to 1916. During the Victorian era in 1907, Beveridge traveled to Germany to learn more about its state welfare and Socialist reforms for the working class. More than 25 years earlier, Germany—the leading Socialist government of the time—began to provide accident, health, and pension insurance and thereby became the model of the United Kingdom's own reforms. He worked closely with David Lloyd George on old-age pensions and national insurance, and it was Beveridge's influence regarding these social reforms that led to the passing of the 1911 National Insurance Act.

From 1914 to 1918, during World War I, Beveridge was involved in mobilizing and controlling manpower. Following the war, Beveridge was knighted and made permanent secretary to the Ministry of Food.

Lord Beveridge left civil service in 1919 and became the director of the London School of Economics and Political Science where he stayed until 1937. From 1937 to 1945, he served as master of University College, Oxford.

After World War II, the British government commissioned a report to determine the ways it should rebuild. This report, titled *Social Insurance and Allied Services*, was written in 1942, and later became known as the Beveridge Report. It was Beveridge's most famous work, and became the blueprint for a complete national network of health and social services that would meet the needs of the British people for hospital-based and personal care, public health and preventative services, and social support of the elderly and the handicapped. It also included a children's allowance to ensure adequate food and clothing. This national system of comprehensive social insurance proposed that people of working age should pay a weekly contribution for national insurance. In return, it would provide paid benefits to people who were sick, unemployed, retired, or widowed. In other words, a minimum standard of living "below which no one should be allowed to fall" would be established. Beveridge recommended that the government should find ways of fighting the five "Giant Evils" of "Want, Disease, Ignorance, Squalor and Idleness."

Beveridge served in Parliament from 1944 to 1945 as a member of the Liberal Party. During this time he wrote two books regarding full employment, which, by his definition, was an unemployment rate of no more than 3 percent. He saw full employment as the key to accomplishing his social welfare program described in the Beveridge Report. It was this report that led to the setting up of the modern welfare state in 1945 by Britain's new prime minister, Clement Attlee. (The National Health Service was also established by Attlee in 1948 and allowed for free medical treatment for all. Built upon the 1911 National Insurance Act, the new national system or "social security" now provided much greater benefits.)

In 1946 he was honored by the Queen and bestowed the title of baron. He became a leader of the Liberals in the House of Lords. His final work, *Power and Influence* (1953), is an autobiography that contains documents, excerpts from his articles and speeches, and a selected bibliography of his published work.

Baron William Beveridge died on March 16, 1963, in Oxford, Oxfordshire, England.

*See also:* Keynes, John Maynard

**Selected Works by William Beveridge**

Beveridge, William. *Full Employment in a Free Society.* New York: Norton, 1944.
Beveridge, William. *Insurance for All and Everything.* London: Longmans, Green, 1924.
Beveridge, William. *Prices and Wages in England from the Twelfth to the Nineteenth Century.* London: Frank Cass, 1939.
Beveridge, William. *Social Insurance and Allied Services.* London: HMSO, 1942.
Beveridge, William. *Unemployment: A Problem of Industry.* London: Longmans, Green, 1910.

**Selected Works about William Beveridge**

BBC Historic Figures. "William Beveridge." http://www.bbc.co.uk/history/historic_figures/beveridge_william.shtml (accessed January, 2011).
Berry, Stephen. "The Rise and Fall of the British Welfare State." The Libertarian Alliance. http://www.la-articles.org.uk/ws.htm (accessed January 2011).
Beveridge, Janet. *Beveridge and His Plan.* London: Hodder and Stoughton, 1954.
Harris, Jose. *William Beveridge: A Biography.* Oxford: Clarendon Press, 1997.
NNDB Tracking the Entire World. "William Beveridge." http://www.nndb.com/people/080/000196489/ (accessed January 2011).

*Carol Lynn Nute*

# BHAGWATI, JAGDISH

Born: July 26, 1934, in Mumbai, India; Indian-American; international trade, economic policy reforms, immigration; Major Works: *India: Planning for Industrialization* (1970), *India* (1975), *In Defense of Globalization* (2004), *Termites in the Trading System: How Preferential Agreements Undermine Free Trade* (2008).

Jagdish Bhagwati joined the faculty at the Massachusetts Institute of Technology (MIT) where he was the Ford International Professor of Economics from 1968 to 1980. His early work at MIT is credited for laying the foundation for the current economic reforms in India. Bhagwati stresses that global trade is a two-way exchange benefiting both parties (countries). Of note is his argument against critics of offshoring. Bhagwati suggests that offshoring is only one facet of free trade and with time the United States will benefit from other countries offshoring labor back to the United States, particularly India. The end result will be higher standards of living for citizens in both India and the United States.

Jagdish Natwarlal Bhagwati was born in Mumbai, India, on July 26, 1934. He did his undergraduate work at Sydenham College in Mumbai. He then attended Cambridge and MIT where he received his doctorate in 1967. His early works included a number of publications, two of which were *India: Planning for Industrialization* (1970) and *India* (1975). It was during his tenure at MIT that he founded and edited the *Journal of International Economics*. Bhagwati left MIT to join the faculty at Columbia University.

Jagdish Bhagwati is credited for laying the foundation for the current economic reforms in India and supporting global trade. (Council on Foreign Relations)

During his time at Columbia, Bhagwati continued as a prolific writer and a vociferous defender of free trade. He wrote many of his most popular works during this period including *Protectionism*, *World Trading System at Risk*, *A Stream of Windows: Reflections on Trade, Immigration and Democracy*, *The Wind of the Hundred Days*, and in 2004 *In Defense of Globalization*, which he wrote to combat an antiglobalization sentiment gaining supporters and momentum. In his follow-up book, *Termites in the Trading System*, Bhagwati discusses the harmful consequences that can result from preferential trade agreements.

Bhagwati is also a regular contributor to the *New York Times*, the *Wall Street Journal*, and the *Financial Times*, writing on trade policy and trade issues. He also founded and edited another academic journal, *Economics and Politics*, while at Columbia. He also provides reviews for *New Republic* and the *Times Literary Supplement*. He also contributes to the blogs *Project Syndicate* and *The American Interest*.

As a professor, Bhagwati has worked with a great many students. Two of his former students include Dartmouth professor Douglas Irwin and Princeton professor, writer, and Nobel laureate Paul Krugman.

Bhagwati has been the economic policy adviser to the director-general for the General Agreement on Tariffs and Trade (GATT) from 1991 to 1993. He served as special policy adviser to the United Nations on globalization in 2000, and as external adviser to the director-general of the World Trade Organization in 2001. He serves as a member of UN Secretary-General Kofi Annan's advisory group of the New Partnership for Africa's Development (NEPAD) process in Africa. Additionally, Bhagwati serves as a senior fellow in international economics at the Council of Foreign Relations where he also publishes and as a director at the National Bureau of Economic Research where he has authored a large number of articles over the years.

In a professional capacity, Bhagwati is a fellow of the Econometric Society. He is a member of the American Philosophical Society and the American Academy of Arts and Sciences. He has been honored as a distinguished fellow of the American Economic Association. As a result of his research and advisory efforts, Bhagwati has been awarded honorary degrees at a number of schools including Erasmus University (Netherlands), Sussex University in the United Kingdom, and the London School of Economics.

He was chosen as one of the world's 100 Most Influential Policy Intellectuals by the respected periodicals *Prospect* (UK) and *Foreign Policy* (United States). Internationally, he has received the Padma Vibhushan award from the government of India, and the Order of the Rising Sun, Gold and Silver Star from the government of Japan.

*See also:* Collier, Paul; Duflo, Esther; Easterly, William; Krugman, Paul; Sachs, Jeffrey

## Selected Works by Jagdish Bhagwati

Bhagwati, Jagdish. *In Defense of Globalization*. Oxford: Oxford University Press, 2004.
Bhagwati, Jagdish. *Essays in Development Economics*. Vol. 1, *Wealth and Poverty*. Edited by Gene Grossman. Cambridge, MA: MIT Press, 1985.
Bhagwati, Jagdish. *Essays in Development Economics*. Vol. 2, *Dependence and Interdependence*. Edited by Gene Grossman. Cambridge, MA: MIT Press, 1985.
Bhagwati, Jagdish. *Free Trade Today*. Princeton, NJ: Princeton University Press, 2002.
Bhagwati, Jagdish. *India: Planning for Industrialization: Industrialization and Trade Policies since 1951*. Oxford: Oxford University Press, 1970.
Bhagwati, Jagdish. *India in Transition: Freeing the Economy*. New York: Oxford University Press, 1993.
Bhagwati, Jagdish. *Protectionism*. Cambridge, MA: MIT Press, 1988.
Bhagwati, Jagdish. *A Stream of Windows: Unsettling Reflections on Trade, Immigration, and Democracy*. Cambridge, MA: MIT Press, 1998.
Bhagwati, Jagdish. *Termites in the Trading System: How Preferential Agreements Undermine Free Trade*. Oxford: Oxford University Press, 2008.
Bhagwati, Jagdish. *The Wind of the Hundred Days*. Cambridge, MA: MIT Press, 2000.
Bhagwati, Jagdish. *The World Trading System at Risk*. Princeton, NJ: Princeton University Press, 1991.
Bhagwati, Jagdish, and Alan Blinder. *Offshoring of American Jobs: What Response from U.S. Economic Policy?* Edited by Benjamin M. Friedman. Cambridge, MA: MIT Press, 2009.

## Selected Works about Jagdish Bhagwati

Balasubramanyam, V. N., and David Greenaway, eds. *Trade and Development: Essays in Honor of Jagdish Bhagwati*. London: Palgrave Macmillan, 1996.
Feenstra, Robert C., Gene M. Grossman, and Douglas A. Irwin. *The Political Economy of Trade Policy: Papers in Honor of Jagdish Bhagwati*. Cambridge, MA: MIT Press, 1996.
Koekkoek, Ad. *International Trade and Global Development: Essays in Honor of Jagdish Bhagwati*. Abington, Oxford, UK: Taylor & Francis, 1991.

*Timothy P. Schilling*

# BÖHM-BAWERK, EUGEN VON

Born: February 12, 1851, in Vienna, Austria; Died: August 27, 1914, in Vienna, Austria; Austrian; Austrian School economist; Major Works: *Capital and Interest* (vols. 1, 2, and 3, 1884–90).

Eugen von Böhm-Bawerk's early contributions led to the further advancement of the Austrian School of economics. His contribution to the Austrian School was his theory of capital and interest. He published three volumes of his magnum opus, *Capital and Interest*. A focus of his writings were the basis of the Austrian School's theory of the business cycle, later communicated by von Mises and Hayek. Early in his career he wrote a damaging critique of Karl Marx's exploitation theory. As Austrian finance minister he advocated for tax reform, a fixed gold standard, and a balanced budget. Böhm-Bawerk died in 1914.

Böhm-Bawerk was born February 12, 1851 in Vienna, Austria. He was studying law at the University of Vienna when he read Carl Menger's *Principles of Economics*. He became a dedicated supporter of Menger's theories and those of the Austrian School of economics. Böhm-Bawerk's unique contribution to the Austrian School was his theory of capital and interest. Following his studies, Böhm-Bawerk taught at the University of Innsbruck. He was appointed minister of finance in 1895, serving till 1900. In 1904, he returned to teaching economics, at the University of Vienna.

Böhm-Bawerk's principal contributions to economics were his theories of interest and capital. During the 1880s, he first published two of the three volumes of his magnum opus, *Capital and Interest*. The first volume of *Capital and Interest*, titled *History and Critique of Interest Theories*, was published in 1884. This first volume is an exhaustive survey of the alternative treatments of interest including the use theories on productivity and abstinence as only two of many put forward by Böhm-Bawerk. Böhm-Bawerk stated that interest would be paid to the owners of capital, irrespective to who owned the capital. Economists today continue to accept this argument.

Böhm-Bawerk did not go beyond monetary theory in his thinking and writings. If he had, he would have conveyed the Austrian School's theory of the business cycle. His bull's-eye concentric circles could have reflected how lower interest rates create new money, eventually misallocating resources and creating unsustainable growth leading to economic crises. This was later communicated by Ludwig von Mises and Friedrich von Hayek.

Böhm-Bawerk's economics analysis was one of the first serious analyses of Karl Marx and his works. Early in his career he wrote a damaging critique of the exploitation theory. Böhm-Bawerk submitted that capitalists do not exploit their workers. Just the opposite: capitalists provide workers an income before they receive any revenue from their production. Böhm-Bawerk maintained that the exploitation of workers did not create interest. He also maintained that production was cyclical. Therefore some financing that Marx attributed to workers must go toward capital. Böhm-Bawerk's alternative views of the exploitation theory gained him recognition in the discipline of economic thought. This rebuttal to Marx and socialist doctrine brought a new spectrum in economic thought to capitalism.

Böhm-Bawerk's work in the area of capital change formulated the early Austrian thought in the relationship between saving and consumption. He asserted a trade-off between consumption and saving. Savings could increase only with a decrease of consumption, and vice versa. This zero sum was broadened to the relationship between saving and capital formation. Using his bull's-eye model, he asserted that capital increases in the inner rings could be accomplished only with increased savings in the outer rings. In a market economy, the relative value of the capital among the different rings would determine the economic activity of businesses.

Böhm-Bawerk was a classical liberal, yet he would not fit the Austrian economist label by today's standards. His writings exhibited a concern for completely unfettered free markets. Combining his theory of interest and theory of marginal value proposed by his early champion Menger, Böhm-Bawerk showed that given a market wage rate, capitalists engage in activities that employ a full labor force.

Böhm-Bawerk presented a bull's-eye type of figure to more fully illustrate his work on capital and interest. This bull's-eye pattern of concentric rings portrayed timing in the production of goods. The center circle (the bull's-eye) represented the factors of production (land and labor). Each succeeding concentric circle represented a new time frame in the production process till the final outside circle represented the final good. Böhm-Bawerk also used the bull's-eye illustration to represent an orderly economy. Even though the bull's-eye model was static by design, it was intended to reflect a dynamic analysis of change.

On his economic theories, Böhm-Bawerk also had his detractors, both within the Austrian School and outside it. From within the Austrian School, it was considered that his theory relied too much on psychology and subjective. From outside the Austrian School, many thought his work lacked mathematical strength and that his perspective was historical.

Later in his career, Böhm-Bawerk served as the Austrian minister of finance. He held this position at various times during the 1890s till 1904. As finance minister, he advocated for tax reform and a rigorous preservation of a fixed gold standard and a balanced budget. His tax reforms were considered very successful.

He also eliminated the long-standing sugar subsidy. He increased the financial demands to the support the army, creating serious budget imbalances. This led to his resignation in 1904. He was later honored by being the image on Austria's 100-schilling note.

After his service in the Austrian government, he returned to teaching. In 1904, he became chair at the University of Vienna. He joined Friedrich von Wieser on the faculty as well as succeeding the retired Menger. His legacy of work continued through the work of his students during Böhm-Bawerk's tenure including Ludwig von Mises and Joseph Schumpeter.

Eugen Böhm-Bawerk died in Vienna on August 27, 1914.

*See also:* Hayek, Friedrich von; Marx, Karl; Menger, Carl; Mises, Ludwig von; Schumpeter, Joseph

### Selected Works by Eugen von Böhm-Bawerk

Böhm-Bawerk, Eugen von. *Capital and Interest.* Vol. 1, *History and Critique of Interest Theories* (1884). South Holland, IL: Libertarian Press, 1959.
Böhm-Bawerk, Eugen von. *Capital and Interest.* Vol. 2, *Positive Theory of Capital* (1889). South Holland, IL: Libertarian Press, 1959.
Böhm-Bawerk, Eugen von. *Capital and Interest.* Vol. 3, *Value and Price* (1890). Translated by George Huncke and Hans F. Senholz. South Holland, IL: Libertarian Press, 1959.
Böhm-Bawerk, Eugen von. "The Positive Theory of Capital and Its Critics." *Quarterly Journal of Economics* 9 (1895): 113–31.

### Selected Works about Eugen von Böhm-Bawerk

Garrison, Roger W. "Austrian Capital Theory: The Early Controversies." *History of Political Economy* 22, Suppl. (1990): 133–54. Published as Bruce J. Caldwell, ed., *Carl Menger and His Legacy in Economics*. Durham, NC: Duke University Press, 1990.
Hennings, Klaus H. *The Austrian Theory of Value and Capital: Studies in the Life and Work of Eugen von Böhm-Bawerk*. Brookfield, VT: Edward Elgar, 1997.
Kirzner, Israel. *Essays on Capital and Interest: An Austrian Perspective*. Brookfield, VT: Edward Elgar, 1996.
Kuenne, Robert E. *Eugen von Böhm-Bawerk*. Columbia Essays on Great Economists, no. 2. New York: Columbia University Press, 1971.
Schumpeter, Joseph A. *Ten Great Economists*. New York: Oxford University Press, 1951.

*David A. Dieterle*

## BOSERUP, ESTER

Born: May 18, 1910, in Copenhagen, Denmark; Died: September 24, 1999, in Geneva, Switzerland; Dutch; economic development; Major Work: *The Conditions of Agricultural Growth: The Economics of Agrarian Change under Population Pressure* (1965).

Ester Boserup is renowned in the post–World War II era for positing and challenging the neo-Malthusian view that food supply can only grow slowly and is the main factor governing the rate of population growth. She proposed that the primary stimulus to agricultural productivity is population growth itself by developing a model of economic development that groups land use into five different types in order of increasing intensity. For her works on agricultural change, gender, and development, she received three honorary doctorate degrees in the agricultural (Wageningen University), economic (Copenhagen University), and human sciences (Brown University). Boserup was elected foreign associate of the National Academy of Sciences, United States, in 1989. Boserup died in 1999.

Ester Boserup was born Ester Børgesen on May 18, 1910, in Copenhagen, Denmark. She was the only daughter of an engineer who died when Boserup was two. After his death, financial hardship forced her mother to move the family to live with other family members and to take up menial work to support the family. With encouragement by her mother and the awareness of having a better prospect in life through education, Ester studied diligently and entered the university when she was 19. During university, against the background of the Great Depression, her search for alternatives to the prevailing theories of equilibrium and marginal utility led her to join a Socialist intellectual debating group and to her choice of two divergent topics (American Institutionalist School and the Marxian theory of crises) for a multidisciplinary degree in theoretical economics, sociology, and agricultural policy.

Following her graduation, she published her first article, which compared Keynes's theory of propensity to consume with the Marxist theory of underconsumption and began her research work at the United Nations and its agencies on agricultural trade policy in the late 1940s. In the early years of her career, her unconventional views were already attracting attention.

From 1957 to 1960, she and her economist husband, Mogens Boserup, worked on a joint project assessing the future of India using Western models of development. While traveling about the country, she observed women working in the fields, noted the agricultural impact of various forms of tenure, and learned about the flexibility of agricultural labor, which made her question many of the Western-based assumptions about agricultural production, particularly the theories relating to surplus labor, population density, and migration. This experience transformed her view of development and she became increasingly convinced that the prevailing theory of zero marginal productivity and agrarian surplus population in densely populated developing countries was an unrealistic theoretical construction.

Returning to Denmark, Boserup combined consultancies with her research and writing as she penned her most important work, *The Conditions of Agricultural Growth: The Economics of Agrarian Change under Population Pressure* (1965). Boserup offered a powerful set of ideas that had far-reaching impacts on interdisciplinary research and real-world practice and became the subjects of intensive academic scrutiny. Based mainly on the experience of Asian countries, the book challenged the dominant Malthusian paradigm (accepted by the majority of classical economists) that at any given time there is in any given community a warranted rate of population increase with which the actual growth of population tends to conform.

In this work, Boserup proposed using a new approach in which population growth rather than the impact of new technologies is the primary mechanism of agrarian development within traditional communities. She maintained that population pressure can lead to agricultural intensification as the principal means of increasing agricultural output and to the adoption of improved methods of production. Population growth, Boserup argued, is independent of food supply, and population increase is a cause of changes in agriculture. This theory of agricultural development is more subtle and complex than that of any of her predecessors.

More than a simple rejection of Malthus's economic development theory, Boserup aimed at explaining all the characteristics of agriculture in any specific area and time according to the resource endowment—the land-labor ratio. Boserup asserted that the more dense population is the more intensive cultivation becomes. Thus she grouped land use into five different types in order of increasing intensity: (1) forest-fallow or slash and burn (15–20 years of fallow),

(2) bush-fallow (6–10 years), (3) short-fallow (1–2 years), (4) annual cropping (a few months), and (5) multicropping (no fallow). For Boserup, this land use typology is not just a classification scheme but a characterization of the main stages of the evolution of agriculture from prehistoric times to the present.

Boserup asserted that methods of cultivation and fertilization to produce more crops per acre become more labor intensive with the shortening of fallow periods. This increase requires far more human labor to produce these higher yields. Although Boserup's central argument was not widely accepted, the ideas put forward in the book are an insightful interpretation of agrarian change.

In addition to this landmark book, Boserup also made other major contributions to the literature on development: *Woman's Role in Economic Development* (1970) and *Population and Technological Change: A Study of Long-Term Trends* (1981). Both books addressed the two major topics to which she had devoted most of her research and writings in the 1970s and 1980s.

In the *Woman's Role in Economic Development*, Boserup argued that although gender is one of the main criteria for the division of labor in all societies, there is a great diversity in this division of labor between the sexes across societies. She emphasized population density and the availability of land as the primary factors that are related to the work and subsequent status of women. This division of labor is not limited to farming systems; it carries over into nonfarm activities as well.

Boserup's main contribution to economics was a more complex picture of the relationships between population, agricultural production, and the environment than was initially put forward by the English economist Thomas Robert Malthus. Her model had great influence on the social evolutionary theory of Mark Cohen, Marvin Harris, and Gerhard Lenski.

Ester Boserup died on September 24, 1999, in Geneva, Switzerland, at the age of 89.

*See also:* Keynes, John Maynard; Malthus, Thomas; Marx, Karl

### Selected Works by Ester Boserup

Boserup, Ester. *The Conditions of Agricultural Growth: The Economics of Agrarian Change under Population Pressure*. Piscataway, NJ: Transactions, 1965.

Boserup, Ester. *Economic and Demographic Relationships in Development*. Baltimore: Johns Hopkins University Press, 1980.

Boserup, Ester. *My Professional Life and Publications, 1929–1998*. New York: Museum Tusculanum Press, 1999.

Boserup, Ester. *Woman's Role in Economic Development*. London: Earthscan, 1970.

### Selected Works about Ester Boserup

Jain, Devaki. *Women, Development and the UN*. Bloomington: Indiana University Press, 2005.

Tinker, Irene. *A Tribute to Ester Boserup: Utilizing Interdisciplinarity to Analyze Global Socio-Economic change*. Edited by Lourdes Beneria. London: Routledge Press, 2003.

Turner, B. L., II, and M. Fischer-Kowalski. "Ester Boserup: An Interdisciplinary Visionary Relevant for Sustainability." *Proceedings of the National Academy of Sciences of the United States of America* 107 (2010): 21963–65.

*Ninee Shoua Yang*

## BUCHANAN, JAMES

Born: October 2, 1919, in Murfreesboro, Tennessee; Died: January 9, 2013, in Blacksburg, Virginia; American; public choice theory, Nobel Prize (1986); Major Work: *The Calculus of Consent: Logical Foundations of Constitutional Democracy* (1962).

James Buchanan is an American economist who founded the subdiscipline of economics called public choice theory. Public choice theory analyzes the actions of individuals in a democracy, and seeks to explain what they do by examining their individual goals. By studying the incentives of politicians, voters, and other people in public functions, Buchanan believed that we could gain a more real and less ideal understanding of how our society works. Buchanan died in 2013.

James McGill Buchanan was born October 2, 1919 in Murfreesboro, Tennessee to a family that was both important and poor. His grandfather, John P. Buchanan, had been governor of Tennessee, which brought prestige to the family but not wealth. Buchanan's family expected him to continue the proud family tradition by becoming a lawyer-politician. However, the onset of the Great Depression meant that they would be unable to send him to Vanderbilt University, which was their first choice, opting instead for Middle Tennessee State Teacher's College in Murfreesboro. Buchanan milked cows throughout all four years of college to pay for school, which he did in 1940. Shortly thereafter, he was drafted into the navy with the U.S entry into World War II.

After the war, Buchanan attended graduate school at the University of Chicago. After earning a doctorate from Chicago and spending a research year in Italy, he launched into a career as a political economist, which has lasted his whole life and in which he has held professorships at the University of Virginia, UCLA, Florida State University, the University of Tennessee, Virginia Polytechnic Institute, and George Mason University. He was awarded the Nobel Prize for Economics in 1986.

Buchanan believed all economic analysis had to begin with the study of individual choices. He wrote that governments, nations, communities, ethnic groups, or any other type of groups cannot be said to make decisions or choices—all groups are made up of people who are trying to get the most benefit for the least cost. In short, he applied the economic concepts of cost-benefit analysis to politics. Therefore, in Buchanan's analysis, one would consider not what the government or a policy would do in a certain situation but what politicians seeking reelection, voters seeking public money, or bureaucrats seeking a larger budget would do.

A second piece of Buchanan's economic thought was the importance of free exchange in economics. He emphasized that the main way people get what they want is through trade. On the other hand, people can also get what they want through force. To analyze how people might choose whether to trade or whether to use force, he thought of an imaginary world that is in a state of nature in which no government exists—the same philosophical approach used by Thomas Hobbes and John Locke.

Buchanan reasoned that in a state of nature, people would divide their time between production, predation (taking things by force), and protection of their property. In such a situation, everyone could become wealthier if they did not have to worry about predation and protection and could simply focus on producing things. Therefore people would have an incentive to create a government that could protect people and their property. A good government with a good constitution would allow for the maximum amount of trade because people would not have to worry about defending themselves. Therefore, he claimed, the creation of the "rules" of politics, or the constitution, was the most important part of the political process.

However, he also saw problems on the horizon. Buchanan noted that in a democracy, each citizen has an incentive to try to vote money out of other citizens' pockets and into his or her own. This would not be a problem if a constitution prevented it, as he believed the American constitution did in fact do. However, in *Democracy in Deficit: The Political Legacy of Lord Keynes* (1977), he wrote that the Keynesian idea that a government could use public debt to produce goods and services for the common good ignored the principle that politicians and bureaucrats act just as everyone else does—in their own self-interest. Rather, public debt was more likely to be used to make projects that would get politicians reelected and bureaucrats better funding. When the government goes beyond its role of protecting its citizens, it takes society back to the state of nature. People will cease to pursue their self-interest through production and trade. They will begin to pursue self-interest by gathering political force and take the fruits of others' work.

To limit the government, Buchanan recommended nothing less than change on the constitutional level. He suggested a balanced-budget rule, larger-majority requirements for the spending of public money, and the creation of specific taxes for specific projects. He opposed the concept of broad-based taxes that are funneled into a pool of government revenue.

In Buchanan's works, the state is viewed as a combination of self-interested individuals, similar to a market, but with different incentives. Buchanan best summarized his work as the notion that people, given a set of constraints, will seek the best position for them personally regardless if they are a producer or consumer in the marketplace, a politician, or a government bureaucrat.

James Buchanan died on January 9, 2013, in Blacksburg, Virginia, at the age of 93.

*See also:* Hobbes, Thomas; Keynes, John Maynard; Locke, John

### Selected Works by James Buchanan

Buchanan, James. *The Calculus of Consent: Logical Foundations of Constitutional Democracy.* Ann Arbor: University of Michigan Press, 1962.

Buchanan, James. *Public Principles of Public Debt: A Defense and Restatement.* Homewood, IL: Irwin, 1958.

Buchanan, James. *What Should Economists Do?* Indianapolis, IN: Liberty Fund, 1979.
Buchanan, James, and Gordon Tulloch. *The Logical Foundations of Constitutional Liberty.* Vol. 1. Indianapolis, IN: Liberty Fund, 1999.
Buchanan, James, and Richard E. Wagner. *Democracy in Deficit: The Political Legacy of Lord Keynes.* Indianapolis, IN: Liberty Fund, 1977.

### Selected Works about James Buchanan

Brennan, G., H. Kliemt, and R. D. Tollison, eds. *Method and Morals in Constitutional Economics: Essays in Honor of James M. Buchanan.* Berlin: Springer, 2002.
Reisman, David. *The Political Economy of James Buchanan.* Basingstoke, UK: Macmillan, 1990.
Younkins, Edward W. *Champions of a Free Society.* Lanham, MD: Lexington Books, 2008.

*Stephen H. Day*

## BURNS, ARTHUR

Born: April 27, 1904, in Stanislawow, Galicia (now Ivano-Frankivsk, Ukraine); Died: June 6, 1987, in Baltimore, Maryland; American; monetary policy, economic growth; Major Works: *Economic Research and the Keynesian Thinking of Our Time* (1946), *Prosperity without Inflation* (1957), *Reflections on an Economic Policy Maker* (1978).

Arthur Burns was the chairman of the Board of Governors of the Federal Reserve System from 1970 until 1978. (UPI-Bettmann/Corbis)

Arthur Burns was the chairman of the Board of Governors of the Federal Reserve System from 1970 until 1978. Though his record of academic work and government service continued on far beyond his time as head of the central bank, he is most commonly remembered for his work at the Federal Reserve, particularly for his part in creating the policies that led to economic stagnation and inflation during the 1970s. Burns died in 1987.

Arthur Frank Burns was born in April 27, 1904 in Stanisławów, Galicia (now Ivano-Frankivsk, Ukraine). He emigrated with his parents to New Jersey when he was a little boy. Burns earned both his bachelor's and doctoral degrees from Columbia University. After earning his PhD, he was hired at the new National Bureau of Economic Research, which was located at Columbia. Here, he gathered copious amounts of data on various industries, which he used to predict economic business cycles.

Burns's research during this period focused on booms and busts in the American economy. He carefully measured aspects of the business cycle, looking into the behavior of many different industries to create a complex yet somewhat predictable view of the economy. Burns believed that recessions occurred not so much because of lack of aggregate demand, as the popular Keynesian theory posited, but because several industries happened to slump at the same time. Such theory promised to be valuable for macroeconomic forecasting, and it gave Burns the reputation as a respectable, impartial scientist.

Burns's nuanced and moderately conservative work got the attention of the Eisenhower administration, and he was recruited to serve on the Council of Economic Advisers in 1953, which he did until 1956. Burns is credited with convincing President Eisenhower not to attempt an aggressive fiscal policy when responding to a recession. When the economy improved in 1954 without significant fiscal stimulus, Burns's fame as an approachable, wise adviser grew. In 1968, this reputation served to elevate Burns as a counselor to the newly elected President Richard Nixon, and in 1970 Burns was appointed chairman of the Board of Governors of the Federal Reserve System.

Burns inherited an economy beset by both rising unemployment and rising inflation. He embarked upon a policy of fighting unemployment with "easy" monetary policy (i.e., keeping interest rates low in order to stimulate economic activity) while fighting inflation with a variety of schemes to discourage large companies from increasing wages and prices. He failed on both counts, as both unemployment and inflation continued to increase. Throughout his tenure as chairman of the Federal Reserve, Burns kept interest rates at a level that is now considered dangerously low. In 1978, Burns was replaced by G. William Miller before Paul Volcker fought skyrocketing inflation, not with wage and price controls (as Nixon and Burns had done), but with tighter monetary policy. This policy worked, and the Burns era of the Federal Reserve became known as a lost decade.

During the time of Arthur Burns's tenure as Federal Reserve chair, it was not clear that inflation was mostly about money. Many economists believed that inflation had to do with factors such as the power of unions and the price of oil. Attributing inflation to "real" factors such as these made monetary policy of secondary importance. More interesting, however, was the influence of President Nixon and Treasury Secretary John Connally. Nixon was convinced that he had lost the 1960 presidential election because tight monetary policy had raised unemployment, and he did not intend to lose the 1972 election for the same reason. He was recorded in the White House tapes in 1971 saying: "I've never seen anybody beaten on inflation in the United States. I've seen many people beaten on unemployment." Nixon and Connally cynically urged, threatened, and manipulated Burns to keep an expansive monetary policy. They leaked hints to the press that Burns would no longer be an adviser and that the Federal Reserve might lose its independence if interest rates were not kept low. These threats seem to have been effective in convincing Burns to agree to a looser monetary policy than he would have held without their persuasion.

Thus, throughout the 1970s, inflation surged despite wage freezes, price freezes, and federal anti-inflation councils, and without a significant drop in unemployment. Since that time, economists have refocused on the importance of controlling the money supply as a means to stop inflation. Burns was appointed ambassador to West Germany by President Ronald Reagan in 1981, where he served effectively until 1985.

Arthur Burns died in Baltimore, Maryland, on June 6, 1987.

*See also:* Greenspan, Alan; Volcker, Paul

## Selected Works by Arthur Burns

Burns, Arthur. *Economic Research and the Keynesian Thinking of Our Time.* Washington, DC: National Bureau of Economic Research, 1946.
Burns, Arthur. *The Management of Prosperity.* New York: Columbia Press, 1966.
Burns, Arthur. *Prosperity without Inflation.* New York: Fordham University Press, 1957.
Burns, Arthur. *Reflections of an Economic Policy Maker.* Washington, DC: American Enterprise Institute for Public Policy Research, 1978.
Burns, Arthur, and Jacob Koppel Javits. *The Defense Sector and the American Economy.* New York: New York University Press, 1968.
Burns, Arthur, and W. C. Mitchell. *Measuring Business Cycles.* Washington, DC: National Bureau of Economic Research, 1946.

## Selected Works about Arthur Burns

"Arthur Burns." Columbia 250. http://c250.columbia.edu/c250_celebrates/remarkable_columbians/arthur_burns.html (accessed April 2012).
"Arthur Burns, 1904–1987, Economist." HistoryCentral.com. http://www.historycentral.com/Bio/people/burns.html (accessed April 2012).
Wells, Wyatt C. *Economist in an Uncertain World: Arthur F. Burns and the Federal Reserve, 1970–78.* New York: Columbia University Press, 1994.

*Stephen H. Day*

# C

## CANTILLON, RICHARD

Born: ca. 1680 in County Kerry, Ireland; Died: May 1734 in London, England; Irish-French; political economy; Major Work: *Essai sur la Nature du Commerce in Général* [Essay on the Nature of Trade in General] (1755).

Richard Cantillon was best known for his treatise *Essai Sur la Nature du Commerce en Général*, which was written in French circa 1732 and published anonymously in England 20 years after his death. Cantillon was an Irishman who moved to France and made a personal fortune in banking and investing in British mercantilist John Law's Mississippi Company. Cantillon's *Essai* is considered the first dedicated treatise of economics as an analysis of the entire economic system. The broad scope of Cantillon's *Essai* implies that Richard Cantillon, not Adam Smith, is the rightful father of modern political economy and true founder of modern economics. The Physiocrats and French school knew Cantillon's work; however, he was not recognized with the fame of Smith until William Stanley Jevons, a cofounder of the marginalist revolution, rediscovered the *Essai* in the 1880s. Jevons writes that the Essai is "a systematic and connected treatise, going over in a concise manner nearly the whole field of economics ... It is thus, more than any other book I know, the first treatise on economics." Cantillon died in 1734.

Richard Cantillon was born in the 1680s in County Kerry, Ireland, to a family of Catholic landlords who had fought for the Stuart cause, and later lost their lands to Cromwell. Cantillon moved to France in 1708, took on French nationality, and then clerked as an assistant of the British paymaster general, James Brydges, in Spain where he organized payments to British prisoners of war during the War of Spanish Succession. In Paris, Cantillon's cousin—who also went by the name of Richard Cantillon—hired him to work in the family banking business. By 1716, Cantillon bought out his cousin and attained complete ownership of the Paris branch of the bank. He became very successful due to his contacts and connections throughout the major commercial centers of Western Europe.

Cantillon built a personal fortune investing in British mercantilist John Law's Mississippi Company and South Sea Bubble. Predicting an inevitable crash from Law's money-induced speculative bubble, Cantillon lent heavily to clients at high rates of interest that took into account future inflation. These clients then owed significant debt to Cantillon and brought with them much animosity and enmity. Cantillon did not agree with Law's inflationist theories, but understood their composition and eventual collapse. Until his death, debtors filed numerous lawsuits against Cantillon, which led to multiple murder plots and criminal accusations.

Cantillon's *Essai* is significant as it the first *general* inquiry into economic theory and quite different from the pamphleteers of this day. As such, the *Essai* influenced the early development of modern economic thought and thinkers such as Adam Smith, many of the Physiocrats, A. R. J. Turgot, and Jean-Baptiste Say. The treatise is one of the few referenced in Adam Smith's *Wealth of Nations*. The extensive range and influence led Jevons to call the *Essai* "the cradle of political economy."

Cantillon's *Essai* is distinctive for its organization using cause-and-effect methodology. Cantillon also wrote only of positive economics, excluding his own ethics or value judgments. Cantillon used the "ceteris paribus" assumption within his *Essai* as well as a small isolated state to eliminate extra complications within the model. This scientific approach and logical-deductive theorizing is impressive and unique when placed within historical context.

Cantillon significantly introduces and explains the concept of "entrepreneur" within the *Essai* as a risk taker who balances supply and demand in a market while bearing the risk of uncertainty. These entrepreneurs—farmers, independent craftsmen, merchants, and manufacturers—are different from "hired men" who earn a fixed income.

Cantillon also writes that demand and relative scarcity determine market price. Price as "intrinsic value" or price based on opportunity cost and the factors of production may differ from actual market price due to the forces of supply and demand. Intrinsic value was a measure of cost, yet it is important to note that Cantillon considered all resources as heterogeneous. It becomes quite difficult if not impossible to determine their respective intrinsic value because each piece of land or worker was of different quality. In addition, Cantillon explains the value of the alternative uses of land and labor, thus introducing the concept of opportunity cost to determine choice.

Cantillon wrote of monetary theory and the microeconomic aspect of monetary inflation. He explained how an increase in the volume of money in circulation will lead to an increase in the price level of goods and services where it enters the economy, as opposed to general inflation. He also explained that the forces of supply and demand of new money would influence the interest rate in the hands of money lenders. In addition, Cantillon disagreed with the mercantilist-monetarist goal of continual increases in the money supply. Other than extenuating circumstances, the money supply should remain stable.

Cantillon was also the first to clearly outline the creation of spatial theory of economics, population theory—which later influenced Malthus and Smith—and the business cycle.

Richard Cantillon played a significant role in the history of economic thought, although his *Essai* remained visible to few after its publication. Jevons served as a catalyst for renewed interest in the *Essai*, and Higgs's translation to English allowed significantly more readers to study the beginnings of modern economic thought.

Unfortunately, Cantillon's discharged cook ultimately murdered him and set Cantillon's house on fire to cover his crime.

Richard Cantillon died in his London home in May of 1734.

*See also:* Jevons, William Stanley; Malthus, Thomas; Say, Jean-Baptiste; Smith, Adam; Turgot, Jacques

### Selected Works by Richard Cantillon

Cantillon, Richard. *Essai sur la Nature du Commerce in Général* [Essay on the nature of trade in general] (1755). Edited and translated by Henry Higgs. London: Frank Cass and Co., 1959.

### Selected Works about Richard Cantillon

Brewer, Anthony. *Richard Cantillon: Pioneer of Economic Theory*. London: Routledge, 1992.

Hebert, Robert F. "Was Richard Cantillon an Austrian Economist?" *The Journal of Libertarian Studies* 7, no. 2 (Fall 1985): 269–79.

Murphy, Antoin E. *Richard Cantillon: Entrepreneur and Economist*. New York: Oxford University Press, 1987.

*Kathryn Lloyd Gustafson*

## CARLYLE, THOMAS

Born: December 4, 1795, in Ecclefechan, Dumfriesshire, Scotland; Died: February 5, 1881, in London, England; Scottish; British historian and essayist; Major Works: *Sartor Resartus* (1831), *The French Revolution* (1837), *History of Friedrich II of Prussia* (1858).

Thomas Carlyle was a Scottish-born historian and essayist. He was given credit for coining the term the "the dismal science," referring to economics or the political economy. The term had nothing to do with the topic of economics as a miserable or dull discipline. The phrase actually was a rebuttal to John Stewart Mill's *Principles of Political Economy* (1848). Carlyle held the view humans from all races were not the same. Three ideas were prominent in Carlyle's political beliefs. He protested against the doctrine of laissez-faire, he supported the organization of labor, and he advocated emigration. Carlyle died in 1881.

Thomas Carlyle was born in Ecclefechan, Dumfries, and Galloway, Scotland, on December 4, 1795, to James Carlyle and Margaret Aitken Carlyle. Born into a strict Calvinistic family of religion, discipline, and prudence, Carlyle seemed destined to join the ministry. He attended the village school at Ecclefechan and then attended Annan Academy. At the age of 14, Carlyle entered the University of Edinburgh to study mathematics and the classics. He graduated with a bachelor of arts degree. He prepared to enter the ministry at the Church of Scotland, yet to his family's dismay, he lost his faith in Christianity and decided against a career in theology. Instead, he became a schoolmaster for Annan and then Kirkcaldy Grammar School. With the help of his friend and mentor Edward Irving, in 1820 Carlyle landed a position as a tutor for Charles and Arthur Buller. Carlyle eventually

Thomas Carlyle was a Scottish-born historian and essayist credited for coining the term "the dismal science," though the term had nothing to do with describing the topic of economics. (AP/Wide World Photos)

moved to London, meeting some great literary figures including Samuel Taylor Coleridge and Matthew Arnold.

By 1824, Carlyle was a full-time writer and a prudent student of German. In 1826, Carlyle married the writer Jan Baillie Welsh and they moved to Craigenputtock where he wrote *Sartor Resartus* (1831). It was a general view about life, part autobiographical and part philosophy. *Sartor Resartus* was originally released as articles in *Fraser's Magazine* between November 1833 and August 1834. Even though *Sartor Resartus* was not well received by the press, it would eventually become one of Carlyle's most notable writings. Carlyle had a difficult time finding a publisher and it was not published as a book until 1838.

Carlyle's next challenge and first real, successful accomplishment would come in the form of his three-volume book, *The French Revolution* (1837). In *The French Revolution*, Carlyle focuses the reader's attention to the egotism of the nobility and of the monarchy. Carlyle lost the original manuscript when it was burned by a maid of J. S. Mill to whom Carlyle had loaned the original. When it was finally published in 1837, Carlyle's fame as a leading writer of the era was solidified.

In 1840 Carlyle published *Chartism*, taking a stance against the conventional economic theory of the day. Chartism was a working-class movement that was made up of groups such as miners, factory operatives, rail makers, carpenters, handloom weavers, and artisans. It was primarily an urban and industrial phenomenon, not very well known in agricultural areas. The theory of Chartism reflected the contradiction in society between the rich and poor. It gave a voice to many people who had a grievance about their own situation or a complaint about the current disorder. Carlyle's response to the question of the English condition was that an active government and a responsible social and political order could elevate Britain out of their slump.

Carlyle's pamphlet drew much attention. *Chartism* expressed his opinion that England lacked a mental or spiritual vigor and enthusiasm. Carlyle's beliefs brought about his next two works. His lecture *On Heroes, Hero-Worship, and the Heroic in History* showed his respect for strength, especially when combined with a God-given mission. *Past and Present* embodied his detailed vision of a hero.

By 1857, Carlyle compiled the history of Friedrich II of Prussia into *Frederick the Great*. This biography, consisting of six volumes, is considered Carlyle's greatest accomplishment in writing because it showcased his exemplary talent at recounting character and beautifully constructing language. Frederick the Great was one of Carlyle's heroes as he admired Frederick's everlasting strength, discipline, leadership, writing abilities, and his very hand in creating the Diplomatic Revolution. Carlyle called this masterpiece his own "thirteen years war." Consuming much of his time in writing *Frederick the Great*, the writing took a toll on his health.

Carlyle lived his last 15 years as a recluse. He was against the "analytic reasoning and quasi-scientific treatment of social questions by the rationalist political economists and advocated the more emotional and intuitive approach of the 18th and 19th century German thinkers" (*Petri Liukkonen* 2008). Two events did spark his interest in his final years. One was his defense of Governor Eyre of Jamaica who was dismissed for putting down a black rebellion. The other cause was the Franco-German War in which Carlyle claimed Germany should be the president of Europe.

Thomas Carlyle died on February 8, 1881, in London. Westminster Abbey was offered for his burial, but he requested to be placed beside his parents in Ecclefechan, Scotland.

*See also:* Mill, John Stuart

## Selected Works by Thomas Carlyle

Carlyle, Thomas. *Chartism*. New York: Wiley and Putnam, 1840.
Carlyle, Thomas. *The French Revolution*. Vol. 1, *The Bastille*. Boston: Charles C. Little and James Brown, 1837.
Carlyle, Thomas. *The French Revolution*. Vol. 2, *The Constitution*. London: J. M. Dent, 1897.
Carlyle, Thomas. *The French Revolution*. Vol. 3, *The Guillotine*. London: James Fraser, 1837.
Carlyle, Thomas. *On Heroes and Hero Worship and the Heroic in History*. London: Grant Richards, 1841.
Carlyle, Thomas. *History of Friedrich II of Prussia*. Leipzig: Bernard Tauchnitz, 1858.
Carlyle, Thomas. *Past and Present*. London: Chapman and Hall, 1843.
Carlyle, Thomas. *Sartor Resartus*. London: Chapman and Hall, 1831.

## Selected Works about Thomas Carlyle

Ashton, Rosemary. *Thomas and Jane Carlyle: Portrait of a Marriage*. London: Chatto and Windus, 2002.
Cumming, Mark. *The Carlyle Encyclopedia*. Madison, NJ: Farleigh Dickinson University Press, 2004.
Harold, Charles Frederick. *Carlyle and German Thought, 1819–34*. Hamden, CT: Archon Books, 1963.

Heffer, Simon. *Moral Desperado: A Life of Thomas Carlyle*. Gaithersburg, MD: Phoenix, 1996.
Jessop, Ralph. *Carlyle and Scottish Thought*. New York: St. Martin's Press, 1997.
Kaplan, Fred. *Thomas Carlyle: A Biography*. Berkeley: University of California Press, 1993.
Ralli, Augustus. *Guide to Carlyle*. Boston: Small Maynard, 1962.
Roe, Frederick William. *Thomas Carlyle as a Critic of Literature*. New York: Columbia University Press, 1910.
Rosenberg, John D. *Carlyle and the Burden of History*. Cambridge, MA: Harvard University Press, 1986.
Timko, Michael. *Carlyle and Tennyson*. New York: Macmillan, 1988.

*Samantha Lohr*

## CASSEL, GUSTAV

Born: October 20, 1866, in Stockholm, Sweden; Died: January 14, 1945, in Stockholm, Sweden; Swedish; role of interest rates, savings, investment; Major Work: *The Nature and Necessity of Interest* (1903).

Gustav Cassel was a prominent economist whose publications spanned nearly four decades. His work was rooted in the ideas of British Neoclassicism and marked by close attention to the role of interest. Cassel is also known for using mathematical models to describe the interdependence of markets, and he was an economist continually looking to push the boundaries through innovative thinking. Cassel was one of the original economists of the Stockholm School of economics. The Stockholm School included politically active Swedish economists active in their homeland politics. Cassel died in 1945.

Karl Gustav Cassel was born October 20, 1866 in Stockholm, Sweden. Cassel's pursuits were not always in economics. Prior to entering economics, he was an accomplished mathematician, earning a mathematics degree at the University of Uppsala. He took a teaching position at Stockholm University. Cassel belonged to a group of mathematical-based economists called Stockholm School of economics. Based at Stockholm University, they were influenced by the early works of French economist Leon Walras. It was after his teaching in Stockholm that he went to Germany and began publishing papers on economics.

Cassel was an innovative thinker who had great influence on economic thought in his time. Works such as *The Nature and Necessity of Interest* (1903) became the main thread of Swedish thought on the fundamental economic realities that underlie the relationship between savings and investment. This publication introduced Cassel's own standpoint on the concept of waiting and was also an attempt to resurrect Leon Walras's thoughts on the theory of capital. The core thought was that if the interest rate is equated to the price of borrowing, the factor market price is called "waiting," a term used earlier by Marshall. Waiting had two dimensions, value and time measured by dollar-years. For example, repaying a person $600 over three years at $200 per year constituted the equivalent of 600 dollar-years of waiting. Cassel submitted that positive interest rates would create incentives for people to postpone spending rather than spend now. Cassel's work was an extension of previous work by economists Alfred Marshal and William Stanley Jevons equating the theory of interest to standard price theory.

Cassel's earlier efforts viewed the price of money (interest rates) as determined by the supply and demand of money as the key element to an economy's equilibrium. Cassel's most inspiring publication, *The Theory of Social Economy* (1918), expanded that view as the basis for his general equilibrium theory. Originally published in Swedish, Cassel explained how price value, not utility value, created general equilibrium in an economy. His mathematical approach to general equilibrium theory was in the same manner as Walras.

Keynesians and Cassel had a bitter rivalry. Keynes also had the opposite view of interest rates. Keynes thought interest rates were a monetary phenomenon rather that a real device that could bring savings and investment into equality. The Austrians laid waste to any thoughts of Cassel from day one because he disagreed with Böhm-Bawerk's theory of capital and interest. Böhm-Bawerk's trade-off between consumption and savings formulated the early Austrian thought about the relationship between saving and consumption.

Cassel did father one of the greatest theories of his era in purchasing power parity (PPP) theory of exchange rates. This purchasing power parity theory is still widely applied today and receives international adulation. The implication of the concept is that the purchasing power of the two currencies should be equal within their own domestic economy. There should be parity between the purchasing power of one U.S. dollar in the United States and the purchasing power of its exchange value in Mexican pesos in Mexico. PPP worked on the basis that if exchange rates were not in parity, people would exploit the price differences by buying in U.S. dollars and selling in pesos until there was no price differential; i.e., the exchange rate or purchasing power of the currencies would change until equilibrium was achieved. There are similarities between PPP and the theory of supply and demand. When demand is high, it causes a shift from market equilibrium and more suppliers enter the market to take advantage of higher prices. This dynamic will continue until the market is brought back to equilibrium. The only problem with Cassel's theory is that it requires every country trading every good internationally, which does not happen. Most theories have some flaw. This problem does not tarnish the prominence of a great mind such as Cassel's. His reputation was established as an authority in monetary problems. His contributions were especially noteworthy at the Brussels Conference in 1920 and on the League of Nations Finance Committee in 1921. He also worked on Germany's reparation problems following World War I.

Gustav Cassel left a legacy of innovative thought. He was a forefather in the mathematical, quantitative approach to economics. Many famous economists and their papers were based on the work of Gustav Cassel.

Gustav Cassel died in Stockholm, Sweden, on January 14, 1945.

*See also:* Böhm-Bawerk, Eugen von; Jevons, William Stanley; Marshall, Alfred; Walras, Leon

## Selected Works by Gustav Cassel

Cassel, Gustav. *The Downfall of the Gold Standard*. Oxford: Clarendon Press, 1936.
Cassel, Gustav. *Fundamental Thoughts in Economics*. London: T. F. Unwin, 1925.

Cassel, Gustav. "Keynes' General Theory." *International Labor Review* 36 (1937): 437–45.
Cassel, Gustav. *The Nature and Necessity of Interest*. New York: Macmillan, 1903.
Cassel, Gustav. *The Theory of Social Economy*. London: Harcourt Brace, 1932.
Cassel, Gustav. *The World's Monetary Problems*. London: Constable and Co., 1921.

### Selected Works about Gustav Cassel

Brems, Hans. "Gustav Cassel Revisited." *History of Political Economy* 21, no. 2 (1989): 165–78.
"Cassel, Karl Gustav." In *An Encyclopedia of Keynesian Economics*. Edited by Thomas Cate, 90–93. Aldershot, UK: Edward Elgar, 1997.
Englund, Eric. "Gustav Cassel's Autobiography." *The Quarterly Journal of Economics* 57, no. 3 (1943): 466–93.
Humphrey, Thomas M. "Knut Wicksell and Gustav Cassel on the Cumulative Process and Price-Stabilizing Policy Rule." *Economic Quarterly* 88, no. 3 (2002): 59–83.

*John E. Trupiano*

# CHILD, JOSIAH

Born: 1630 in London, England; Died: June 22, 1699, in Wanstead, England; English; trade, mercantilism; Major Works: *Letter Observations Concerning Trade and the Interest of Money* (1668), *Observations upon the United Provinces of Netherlands* (1672), *A New Discourse of Trade* (1690).

Josiah Child was a mercantilist and a governor of the East India Company. His fame as an economist came mainly from his books: *Brief Observations Concerning Trades and the Interest of Money* (1668) and *A New Discourse of Trade* (1668 and 1690). In his writings, Child discussed a variety of topics such as interest rates, population, wage policy, and colonization. Despite Child's liberal views on many aspects of trade, he was a typical mercantilist. His writings lacked scientific originality and citation. Rather than explaining the reasons behind trading dilemmas or innovating new economic theories, Child was an advocate of certain policies that were mainly beneficial to his own trading business. He died in 1699.

Josiah Child was born in 1630 in London, England. He was the second son of Richard Child, a merchant of a well-known family. At the age of 25, Child started his own business of providing services to the navy under the Commonwealth. In 1659, he became the supplier of the East India Company. Child's relationship with the company grew closer, and in 1671 he became a stockholder. In 1673, he was elected to Parliament and continued to accumulate wealth. By 1674, he became the largest single stockholder of the company and was chosen as the director. In 1681, he became the elected governor of the East India Company. Until his death in 1699, Child served as the manager and the sole policy maker of the company.

Child is considered the father of mercantilism, which is the economic policy that was developed in Europe in the early modern period and dominated Western Europe from the early sixteenth to the late eighteenth century. Mercantilism considers wealth and money to be identical. Based on this theory, the main objective in international trade is to export the greatest amount of manufacturing products as possible and to import the least amount. The difference is the trade deficit, or trade surplus, in the form of valuable metals such as gold and silver. Accordingly, the prosperity of a nation depends on its supply of capital and the fact that the global volume of the international trade is fixed. Therefore the success of one nation depends on the failure of another. Mercantilism suggests that policy makers play a crucial role in advancing the economy through the use of restricting policies such as subsidies and tariffs.

During the second half of the seventeenth century, England was facing fierce commercial competition from the Netherlands. The Dutch were replacing the British dominance in foreign trade. Unlike the British, they were producing high-quality goods, using small but efficient ships, and their commercial law was simple and effective. Child, instead of exploring the reasons behind their wealth, concluded that Dutch superiority in commerce was because of their lower interest rates.

Although many eighteenth-century economic historians viewed Child as one of the pioneers of free trade and economic liberalism, Child was more like a self-interested advocate than a detached theorist, a follower rather than an innovator. In his pamphlet *Brief Observations Concerning Trade and the Interest of Money*, Child urged the Council of Trade and the Lords' Committee to reduce the rate of interest from 6 percent to 4 percent or less. He argued that a low rate of interest is the main cause of wealth in a nation and attributed the economic prosperity of the Dutch to their low interest rate of 3 percent.

Child considered himself as a supporter of competitive markets and free trade. He would, however, argue in favor of the monopolistic power of the East India Company in its trade with South Asia. He persuaded the policy makers toward a government-controlled interest rate and restricted trade among the British colonies. Child was a borrower, and it was beneficial for his trading business to keep the interest rate low. He had the mercantilist partiality in seeking certain policies. He advocated for the restricted trade right of the mother country with its colonies. Child supported the free market only for some people and only for certain restrictions on the market.

Economists of the eighteenth century had falsely considered Child an advocate of laissez-faire and one of the main precursors of Adam Smith. Child neither added anything new nor explained any of the economics theories of his time. He was a merchant who advocated for certain policies that appeared to benefit his own business. Regardless of his place in the history of economics, Child was an old-style economics writer. However, his writings did not serve to advance economic theories because they directed the reader to follow a certain policy or act in a specific way rather than teach a new truth or discuss the reasons behind specific facts. The old style of economics writing was not uncommon at the time. One could see that in other British economists of the seventeenth century such as William Petty, Dudley North, and John Locke. The old style of writing was being replaced by the first scientific economists during the late eighteenth century.

Josiah Child died in Wanstead, Essex, England, on June 22, 1699.

*See also:* Locke, John; North, Douglass; Petty, William; Smith, Adam

### Selected Works by Josiah Child

Child, Josiah. *Brief Observations Concerning Trade and the Interest of Money*. London: Calvert, 1668.

Child, Josiah. *A New Discourse of Trade*. London: Sowle, 1690.

### Selected Works about Josiah Child

Child, S. J., S. T. Culpeper, and Early English Books Online Ebook Collection. *A New Discourse of Trade: Wherein Is Recommended Several Weighty Points Relating to Companies of Merchants, the Act of Navigation, Naturalization of Strangers, and Our Woollen Manufactures, the Ballance of Trade . . . : And Some Proposals for Erecting a Court of Merchants for Determining Controversies*. Printed and sold by T. Sowle, 1751.

Johnson, E. A. J. *Predecessors of Adam Smith: The Growth of British Economic Thought*. New York: Kelley, 1960.

Letwin, W. *The Origins of Scientific Economics: English Economic Thought, 1660–1776*. London: Routledge, 2003.

*Elham Mahmoudi*

## CLARK, JOHN BATES

Born: January 26, 1847, in Providence, Rhode Island; Died: March 21, 1938, in New York City; American; marginal productivity theory; Major Works: *The Philosophy of Wealth: Economic Principles Newly Formulated* (1885), *The Distribution of Wealth: A Theory of Wages, Interest and Profits* (1899).

John Bates Clark was an early developer and leading proponent of using the value of marginal product theory to analyze an economy. Clark did not view the theory as a complete system but an initial start to further analysis. Motivated by the same puritan work ethic of his ancestors, Clark pursed economic theory in terms of its social-ethical impact. This led to his work with both static and dynamic economic models with an emphasis on the impact of social change on economic decision making. He was a religious churchgoing man and that is evident in the social-ethical predisposition of his work. John Bates Clark was a cofounder of the American Economic Association, which biennially awards the John Bates Clark Medal. Clark died in 1938.

John Bates Clark was born January 26, 1847 in New England. Clark graduated from Amherst College in 1872 and briefly considered entering the ministry but was persuaded by his mentors to continue along an academic path. He then pursued studies in Europe for three years, his main professor being Karl Knies. Upon returning to the United States, he began his first professorship at Carleton College. It was during this period that Clark suffered from an extended illness that severely limited his working capacity. Despite this illness, he was able to produce several essays that would become part of his book *The Philosophy of Wealth: Economic Principles Newly Formulated* (1885).

Following his tenure at Carleton College, Clark joined the faculty at Smith College and taught there until 1893. He also taught at his alma mater Amherst for three years starting in 1893 where he had many notable students including future president Calvin Coolidge. Clark would also go on to lecture at Johns Hopkins and Columbia University.

In his book *The Philosophy of Wealth*, Clark devotes much energy to a criticism of classical economic theory. One of its main concerns is the question of human motivation. Clark argues that although people make decisions by evaluating the costs and benefits of their next choice (at the margin), choices are also conditioned by the social setting in which they take place. This social setting is where economic processes and values develop. Instead of seeing individuals in an economy as only acting on self-centered concerns, as did the classical school, Clark views individual choices as a rational balance between self-centered concerns and social concerns.

Another important publication by Clark is *The Distribution of Wealth: A Theory of Wages, Interest and Profits* (1899). In this work Clark developed the theories on marginalism for which he would become widely known. It is interesting that although his theories were published later than his marginalist contemporaries', his work and conclusions appear to be arrived at independently. In this highly theoretical work, Clark defines components of an imaginary economy. He then applies his marginal theories in a theoretical environment in which he can hold constant the necessary factors. His work is a distinct variant of the marginal utility theory proposed by Jevons and Walras. Clark is noted for his work on the value of the marginal product theory. Clark submitted that the value of a real wage is only up to the level where it is equal to the value the labor adds to the product, thus promoting a relationship between the production of a good and its distribution in the marketplace.

One characteristic of Clark's was that he was not unyielding with his theories but adapted them over his life to fit changing situations as he saw them. In his 1907 book, *Essentials of Economic Theory*, he showed that the economic laws he analyzed applied only to economically developed nations in which resources were mobile and responded to market forces. The same theories, he claimed, were not applicable to developing nations. Therefore, Clark suggested, achieving equilibrium of a global economy in both developed and developing nations was not only something he viewed as too long term a matter for analysis but would also require unforeseeable technological advancements in order to secure a stable outcome.

Clark analyzed changes in an economy from two viewpoints. One view was a static view where economic equilibrium is achieved through competition. The second view was a dynamic view, which takes into account the effects of constant social change of a society. The dynamic changes he identified were growth of population, growth of capital, technical improvements, changes in market organization, and changes in consumer wants.

He was a cofounder of the American Economic Association and served as its third president. The American Economic Association awards the John Bates Clark Medal, one of the most prestigious awards in the field of economics, biennially to an American economist under the age of 40. Many recipients of this award have later received the Nobel Prize in Economics.

John Bates Clark died in New York City on March 21, 1938.

*See also:* Jevons, William Stanley; Walras, Leon

### Selected Works by John Bates Clark

Clark, John Bates. *The Philosophy of Wealth: Economic Principles Newly Formulated*. Boston: Ginn, 1885.
Clark, John Bates. *Capital and Its Earnings*. American Economic Association Monographs. Vol. 3, no. 2, 7–69. Baltimore: American Economic Association, 1888.
Clark, John Bates. *The Distribution of Wealth: A Theory of Wages, Interest and Profits*. New York: Macmillan, 1899.
Clark, John Bates. *The Problem of Monopoly: A Study of a Grave Danger and of the Natural Mode of Averting It*. London: Macmillan, Columbia University Press, 1904.
Clark, John Bates. *Social Justice without Socialism*. New York: Houghton Mifflin, 1914.

### Selected Works about John Bates Clark

Homan, Paul T. "John Bates Clark: Earlier and Later Phases of His Work." *Quarterly Journal of Economics* 42, no. 1 (November 1927): 39–69.
Prasch, Robert E. "John Bates Clark's Defense of Mandatory Arbitration and Minimum Wage Legislation." *Journal of the History of Economic Thought* 22, no. 2 (June 2000): 251–63.
Veblen, Thorstein. "Professor Clark's Economics." *Quarterly Journal of Economics* 22, no. 2 (February 1908): 147–95.

*John E. Trupiano*

# COASE, RONALD

Born: December 29, 1910, in Willesden, England; English; property rights, economics of law, Nobel Prize (1991); Major Works: "The Nature of the Firm" (1937), *British Broadcasting: A Study in Monopoly* (1950), "The Problem of Social Cost" (1960).

Ronald Coase wrote little compared to other famous economists, but what he did write made a tremendous impact on economic thought. Two of his journal articles have each started new subfields of economics: the economics of property rights and the economics of law.

Ronald Harry Coase was born on December 29, 1910, in Willesdale, England, just outside London. His parents were not well educated, both of them having dropped out of school by the age of 12. As a boy, his weak legs required him to wear metal braces; as a result he was sent to a school for physically handicapped children. When he was 12 years old he was admitted to a quality grammar school, and in 1929 he enrolled in the London School of Economics. In his last year at school, he took a study tour to the United States. During his visit he examined the structure of American industries. It was here, before he even graduated from college, that he gained his essential insight into the workings of companies for which he was to become famous and the concept of "transaction costs."

Upon graduation he taught at various British universities and, with the onset of World War II, entered government service, first for the Forestry Commission and then for the Offices of the War Cabinet. After the war he continued to teach college classes and also worked on a doctoral dissertation. Upon earning his PhD in 1951, he emigrated to the United States, where he taught at the University of Buffalo, the

University of Virginia, and finally the University of Chicago, from which he retired in 1979. After retirement, however, his work did not stop. He continued as a researcher at the University of Chicago in law and economics—a field that he himself created.

When Coase visited the United States in 1931–32, he collected data and made observations about how firms really work. In doing so, he stumbled across a question for which no one had produced an adequate answer: "Why do firms (companies) exist?" If people can specialize in whatever job gets them the most value, how could it possibly be efficient to hold workers captive in large companies? Should it not it be more efficient to make individual contracts with individual workers for each necessary task? Coase pointed out that all firms are like little Socialist economies: instead of individuals deciding what kind of economic activity to pursue, they have to follow orders from their managers.

In an article entitled "The Nature of the Firm," Coase solved this problem by discussing the idea of transaction costs. Each economic exchange has certain built-in costs, like bargaining costs, the costs to gather and interpret information, and the costs to protect trade secrets. These transaction costs interfere with market activity and provide an incentive for entrepreneurs to produce goods and services in-house by hiring workers and forming a company. Creating a hierarchy inside a firm can lower transaction costs, but only to a certain degree. Coase also noted that as a company gets larger, it becomes more difficult to manage, a problem called diseconomies of scale. Because of this, there is a limit to the size to which companies can grow (contrary to what Karl Marx believed). Rather, according to Coase firms will begin to make contracts with individuals and smaller companies to do the work that is inefficient for the firm to do itself.

Coase's second groundbreaking article came in 1960, "The Problem of Social Cost." It was published 23 years after "The Nature of the Firm." In the "The Problem of Social Cost," Coase attacked a generally held theory about how people interact in society, first posited by Arthur Pigou in 1920.

Externalities (spillover costs) are the costs and consequences of one decision imposed upon third parties external to the transaction. According to Pigou, the government can tax the entity creating the externality (such as pollution) to make them stop the behavior or at least to reduce it. The government could then use the tax money to deal with the effects of the behavior: in this case to clean up the pollution.

Coase's insight into externalities was that the situation could be solved by simply assigning clear property rights, or if that is not possible, by making one of the parties legally liable for the spillover costs incurred. The surprising conclusion is that the final amount of spillover will be the same regardless of who is liable for it. If the two parties involved are free to negotiate and trade with one another, they will make a deal to get the end result they both desire.

For example, if a factory is made liable for polluting the nearby neighborhood, then the factory will pay the neighbors for the right to pollute. Conversely, if the neighbors are held liable, then they will pay the factory to pollute less. If there are no transaction costs (and this is a big "if"), then the same amount of pollution will be produced either way, though the wealth of the parties involved may be different. This became known as the "Coase Theorem" and has had a definite real-world impact. Because of Coase's theorem, legislators and judges are now encouraged to define ownership (property rights) before issuing taxes or injunctions.

Primarily for his work on social costs and the Coase theorem, Ronald Coase was awarded the Nobel Prize in Economics in 1991. Coase spent much of the rest of his professional career editing the University of Chicago's *Journal of Law and Economics*.

At the age of 100, he was busy analyzing the growth of the Chinese economy and advising Chinese economists through the Coase China Society, while coauthoring a book entitled *How China Became Capitalist*.

*See also:* Pigou, A. C.; Stigler, George

**Selected Works by Ronald Coase**

Coase, Ronald. *British Broadcasting: A Study in Monopoly*. London: London School of Economics and Political Science, 1950.
Coase, Ronald. *Essays on Economics and Economists*. Chicago: University of Chicago Press, 1994.
Coase, Ronald. *The Firm, the Market, and the Law*. Chicago: University of Chicago Press, 1988.
Coase, Ronald. *How China Became Capitalist*. London: Palgrave Macmillan, 2011.
Coase, Ronald. "The Nature of the Firm." *Economica* 4, no. 16 (November 1937): 386–405.
Coase, Ronald. "The Problem of Social Cost." *Journal of Law and Economics* 3 (October 1960): 1–23.

**Selected Works about Ronald Coase**

Coase, Ronald. "Autobiography." Nobelprize.org. http://nobelprize.org/nobel_prizes/economics/laureates/1991/coase-autobio.html (accessed June 30, 2011).
Overtweldt, Johan van. *The Chicago School: How the University of Chicago Assembled the Thinkers Who Revolutionized Economics and Business*. Chicago: Agate B2, 2007.

*Stephen H. Day*

# COLBERT, JEAN-BAPTISTE

Born: August 29, 1619, in Reims, France; Died: September 6, 1683, in Paris, France; French; public administration and mercantilism; Major Works: *Lettres, instructions et memoires*, Vols. 1, 2.1, 2.2, 3.1, 3.2, 4, 5, 6, and 7 (1861–79).

Jean-Baptiste Colbert served as a prominent figure in the French political system as controller-general of finances for more than two decades of King Louis XIV's 72-year reign, one plagued by extravagant government spending and ostentatious use of government finances. Colbert, responsible for maintaining political and financial stability during this tumultuous period, successfully managed through tax reform and increased commerce for the state. Though he held other government positions during Louis's reign, it was as controller-general that Colbert left his mark on history. Colbert died in 1683.

Jean-Baptiste Colbert was born on August 29, 1619, in Reims, France, into a family of merchants who ascended through the bourgeoisie class as a result of a tenacious desire for upward mobility. They accomplished their goals through vast business dealings in international trade, the use of public office, and advantageous marriages. Colbert attended a Jesuit college, but not much is known about his early years.

Colbert's major contributions are related to his controller-general commission under the reign of the Sun King. He received his commission in 1665 as a result of his competitive fire and high political aspirations along with his role in revealing the highly publicized embezzlement scandal involving former controller-general Fouquet. Colbert's experience in government administration and his relationship with Jules Mazarin and Cardinal Richelieu, the boy king's counselors, played a pivotal role in his appointment as well.

As a result of a brutal recession, France faced problems with erratic taxation and an unorganized economic system. Louis charged Colbert with the task of stabilizing the French economy, coupled with ensuring Louis's continued personal prosperity. These tasks required Colbert to balance economic and social goals with financing Louis's extensive wars, implementing and executing public policy, and maintaining the Sun King's reputation for pretentious displays of wealth. He took on his new role knowing what he intended to do. He understood how he fit into Louis's administration and took pride in his position, his nation, and his king. Colbert attacked the French inefficiencies with a vast array of statistics, record keeping, and a tireless work ethic.

Colbert, using his mercantilist background, focused his administration's efforts on maintaining a favorable balance of trade. Aggressive trade policies helped strengthen the domestic economy and promoted new industries within the country. As the French empire grew, tariffs were imposed to keep newly acquired cities from trading with old partners abroad, encouraging domestic trade within the empire, and cultivating innovation and manufacturing. His reform efforts in industry created higher standards and expectations. Colbert's protectionist ideals focused his taxation efforts on customs duties, primarily on salt and land. Taxation allowed France to finance expenditures such as war, private and public works, and Louis's vast array of personal expenditures. Colbert is often quoted as saying "The art of taxation is to pluck the maximum amount of feathers for the minimum amount of hissing." He felt the purpose of his role was to reduce the environment of corruption in France's upper classes. To do so, he instituted a variety of indirect taxes to achieve this aim. Colbert's policies on taxation and mercantilism effectively bolstered the French economy. He used mercantilism as a tool by which to carve, chisel, and stabilize the domestic economy, and in doing so solidified France's standing as a world power.

As Colbert addressed the problems associated with the French economy, he called upon his experience and expertise of financial systems. Motivated by a desire to protect national interest, he assembled a massive database of national, legal, and financial documents that would be unmatched by any European power. These facts and figures would help him devise policies to strengthen the French cause, whether it was politically, militarily, or economically. His database consisted of more than 50,000 printed books and 15,000 manuscripts. His administrative system focused on facts and figures, calculations, and universal truths. Colbert founded the Academy of Sciences as well as many other academies across France. His desire to substantiate France's claim of superiority and excellence was of great concern, and his attention to that fact can be no better explained than by his acceptance of the palace of Versailles, Louis XIV's crowned jewel.

Part of Colbert's mission was to strengthen France's claim of supremacy. Versailles was the prime example of supremacy during the seventeenth century with all of its grandeur, extensive and exemplary architecture, and unmatched elegance. There was no greater example of excellence than that of Versailles. While not economically advantageous for France, Versailles helped create a greater demand for French goods; jobs were created, skills were developed and the overall standards were raised. Colbert came to appreciate Versailles for the greatness it represented.

Colbert was charged with the opportunity to reconcile Louis XIV's extravagant expenses in order to maintain political and financial stability on the European stage during the seventeenth century. His use of public office served France well during his tenure. His implementation of mercantilism and taxation created a more stable national economy. Colbert's carefully devised administrative system allowed France to continue to expand geographically and economically through the colonization and exploitation of their empire while trying to minimize some of the domestic inefficiencies. His system of administration perhaps brought more stability than his economic systems did. He served his king and his country for over two decades.

Jean-Baptiste Colbert died in Paris on September 6, 1683, at the age of 64.

*See also:* Quesnay, François

### Selected Works by Jean-Baptiste Colbert

Colbert, Jean-Baptiste. *Lettres, instructions et memoires de Colbert* (1861–79). Vols. 1, 2.1, 2.2, 3.1, 3.2, 4, 5, 6, and 7.
Colbert, Jean-Baptiste. *Speech to the Town and People of Marseilles* (1664).

### Selected Works about Jean-Baptiste Colbert

Cole, C. W. *Colbert and a Century of French Mercantilism.* 2 vols. New York: Columbia University Press, 1939.
Murat, Ines. *Colbert.* Charlottesville: University Press of Virginia, 1984.
Payne, George, and James Rainsford. *Lives of Cardinal de Retz, Jean Baptiste Colbert, John de Witt and Marquis de Luvois.* Vol. 2. Philadelphia: Carey, Lea, and Blanchard, 1837.
Soll, Jacob. *The Information Master: Jean-Baptiste Colbert's Secret State Intelligence System.* Ann Arbor: University of Michigan Press, 2009.
Trout, Andrew P. *Jean-Baptiste Colbert.* New York: Twayne, 1978.

*William S. Chappell*

## COLLIER, PAUL

Born: April 23, 1949, in Sheffield, England; English; economic development of developing countries, economics of Africa; Major Works: *The Bottom Billion: Why the Poorest Countries Are Failing and What Can Be Done about It* (2008), *The Plundered Planet* (2010).

Paul Collier is one of world's experts in the political and economic development of developing countries, especially of African nations. At St. Antony's College of Oxford University, he is the director of the Centre for the Study of African Economies. Collier's focus in Africa has been on the effects of civil wars and aid on a nation's economic and political environments. He has been credited as being one of the world's leading global thinkers. His book *The Bottom Billion: Why the Poorest Countries Are Failing and What Can Be Done about It* is considered one of the most influential books in the field of development economics.

Paul Collier was born April 23, 1949, in the Sheffield region of England. Following graduation from the prestigious King Edward VII School, he attended Oxford University, graduating with distinction. Receiving his PhD from Oxford University, he remained at his alma mater as a professor of economics. He interrupted his career at Oxford in 1998 to head the Development Research Group of the World Bank. Returning to Oxford in 2003, he became director of the Centre for the Study of African Economies (CSAE).

Collier's research and study on the governance of Africa's low-income countries, the impact of civil wars and aid on African countries' growth, and the economics of globalization and poverty on growth had public policy influence. He was a senior adviser to Prime Minister Tony Blair's Commission on Africa including a seminar for Mr. Blair at his 10 Downing Street address, along with the United Nations General Assembly.

Collier's writings began winning awards early in his career. In 1988, Collier's *Labour and Poverty in Rural Tanzania: Ujamaa and Rural Development in the United Republic of Tanzania* was awarded the Edgar Graham Book Prize.

Collier turned writing high-impact books into an annual event with three influential books in the years 2008, 2009, and 2010. In 2008, he wrote *The Bottom Billion: Why the Poorest Countries Are Failing and What Can Be Done about It*. Focusing largely on the 60 countries that contain the world's poorest people, he is critical of and exposes the ineffectiveness of foreign aid on these billion of the earth's inhabitants. In *The Bottom Billion*, Collier explains what he calls the four poverty traps for poor countries: the conflict trap, the natural resource trap, the landlocked with bad neighbors trap, and the bad governance trap. *The Bottom Billion* was awarded the Lionel Gelber, Arthur Ross, and Corine prizes in 2008 and the Estoril Global Issues Distinguished Book prize in 2009. Of the three books, *The Bottom Billion* was the most popular and widely read.

In 2009, Collier wrote *Wars, Guns, and Votes: Democracy in Dangerous Places* and in 2010 *The Plundered Planet: Why We Must and How We Can Manage Nature for Global Prosperity*. In *The Plundered Planet*, Collier constructs a set of illustrative formulas to convey the theme of sustainability of the earth's limited resources: Nature − Technology + Regulation = Starvation, Nature + Technology − Regulation = Plunder, and Nature + Technology + Regulation (good governance) = Prosperity. Using these formulas, Collier explores the extremes of the environmental mind-set against the context of solving our planet's poverty problems.

Paul Collier was honored as a Commander of the Order of the British Empire in 2008. The University of Sheffield bestowed an honorary doctor of letters on Dr. Collier for his work in global economic development and global poverty. In 2010 and 2011, Dr. Paul Collier was on *Foreign Policy* magazine's list of top global thinkers.

*See also:* Duflo, Esther; Easterly, William; Ostrom, Elinor; Sachs, Jeffrey

### Selected Works by Paul Collier

Collier, Paul. *The Bottom Billion: Why the Poorest Countries Are Failing and What Can Be Done about It.* Oxford: Oxford University Press, 2008.

Collier, Paul. *Labour and Poverty in Rural Tanzania: Ujamaa and Rural Development in the United Republic of Tanzania.* Oxford: Oxford University Press, 1991.

Collier, Paul. *The Plundered Planet: Why We Must, and How We Can, Manage Nature for Global Prosperity.* Oxford: Oxford University Press, 2010.

Collier, Paul. *Wars, Guns, and Votes: Democracy in Dangerous Places.* New York: HarperCollins, 2009.

### Selected Works about Paul Collier

Carnegie Council. "Paul Collier." http://www.carnegiecouncil.org/people/data/paul_collier.html (accessed April 2012).

"How to Help the Poorest, Springing the Traps." *The Economist*, August 2, 2007.

"Paul Collier." University of Oxford Department of Economics. http://www.economics.ox.ac.uk/index.php/staff/collier/ (accessed April 2012).

"Professor Paul Collier." Center for the Study of African Economies. http://www.csae.ox.ac.uk/members/biogs/collier.html (accessed October 2012).

*David A. Dieterle*

## DEBREU, GÉRARD

Born: July 4, 1921, in Calais, France; Died: December 31, 2004, in Paris, France; American; economic mathematician, Nobel Prize (1983); Major Work: "The Monograph"—*Theory of Value: An Axiomatic Analysis of Economic Equilibrium* (1959).

Gérard Debreu was a French-born economist and mathematician who became a naturalized citizen of the United States. Debreu was an officer of the French Legion of Honor and a commander of the French National Order of Merit. As a professor at the University of California, Berkeley, one colleague described Debreu as the most important contributor to the development of the mathematical models used in economics. Debreu is credited by many as the one who made economics into an authentic science. Debreu also had a major effect on the spirit of economics as he transformed economics from an art to a science. In 1975, Debreu became an American citizen. He was awarded the Nobel Prize in Economics in 1983 for his mathematical work on the basics ideas of supply and demand. Debreu died in 2004.

Gérard Debreu was born in Calais, a town in the far northern coast of France, on July 4, 1921. In the tradition of Calais industry, his father and maternal grandfather were in the lace-manufacturing business. Debreu's schooling began in 1939 at the College of the City of Calais. Before studying for his degree examination, he interrupted his studies of mathematics and enlisted in the French Army. He served in Germany as a member of the French occupational forces. Following D-Day, Debreu joined the French Resistance forces, serving till 1945. When he resumed his studies, his concept of mathematics was greatly influenced by Henri Cartan, alias Bourbaki. However, his focus had shifted from mathematics to economics while studying under economist Maurice Allais. His interest in economics heightened after reading Leon Walras's mathematical theory on general economic equilibrium.

As a Rockefeller Fellowship recipient, he came to the United States in 1948 to visit several U.S. universities including Harvard University, the University of California at Berkeley, the University of Chicago, and Columbia University. He also spent time at the University of Uppsala and University of Oslo as a Rockefeller fellow. As a result of the visits, in 1950 he began work for the Cowles Commission for Research in Economics as a research associate at the University of Chicago.

To a mathematical-oriented economics student, the Cowles Commission was the perfect place to study and hone his mathematical economics. During this time,

University of California professor Gérard Debreu poses at Berkeley in October 1983. He won the 1983 Nobel Prize in economics for refining the classic theory of supply and demand in economic systems. Gérard Debreu was born in 1921 in Calais, France. (AFP/Getty Images)

Debreu worked on the optimum theory of Vilfredo Pareto, his general equilibrium existence theory, and utility theory. In 1955, the Cowles Commission relocated to Yale University, and Debreu followed. He continued his work on market equilibrium and his monograph.

In 1959, Debreu published what became his seminal work, *Theory of Value: An Axiomatic Analysis of Economic Equilibrium* (Cowles Foundation Monographs Series). This classic became known simply as "the Monograph." This is one of the foundational works in mathematical economics. The Monograph establishes an axiomatic foundation for competitive markets. His main thesis was that price systems exist in which excess aggregate demand will vanish.

Debreu did not ignore disequilibrium. However, he addresses disequilibrium from a quantitative argument. According to Debreu, disequilibrium was not consistent economic theory. To Debreu, only equilibrium was the condition of economic models exist, i.e., a point where mathematics and economics align.

A major contribution of Debreu was viewing economics through the lens of mathematics. While discussion and questions surrounded the Monograph, Debreu was consistent in his defense of approaching economics as a quantitative science.

In 1960, Debreu left Yale and the Cowles Commission for Stanford's Center for Advanced Study in the Behavioral Sciences. In 1962, Debreu continued pursuit of his research and teaching activities when he joined the faculty at the University of California, Berkeley, teaching economics and mathematics. Debreu continued his research and teaching at UC Berkeley for the next 30 years till his retirement in 1991. During his tenure at UC Berkeley, he employed his expertise as economic adviser and lecturer on economic theory throughout Europe.

Debreu is also given credit for using mathematics to prove Adam Smith's "invisible hand" concept. His mathematical approach provided clarity and quantitative credibility to Smith's notion that the actions of individuals to benefit themselves also leads to benefits for all of society. Like Smith, Debreu's models make assumptions on the morality of individuals.

Debreu won the Nobel Prize in Economics in 1983 for his contributions to raising the reputation of economics to a science. Debreu was cited for integrating new mathematical analytical methods into economic theory, especially in his quantitative approach of the general equilibrium theory. In addition to the Nobel Prize, Debreu was also honored with the French Legion of Honor in 1976, as a member of the National Academy of Sciences, and as a commander in the French National Order of Merit.

He died at age 83 on December 31, 2004, in Paris. In Debreu's obituary, UC Berkeley professor Robert Anderson noted that "he really was the most important contributor to the development of formal math models within economics. He brought to economics a mathematical rigor that had not been seen before."

*See also:* Pareto, Vilfredo; Smith, Adam

## Selected Works by Gérard Debreu

Debreu, Gérard. *Mathematical Economics: Twenty Papers of Gérard Debreu*. Cambridge: Cambridge University Press, 1986.

Debreu, Gérard. *Theory of Value: An Axiomatic Analysis of Economic Equilibrium*. Cowles Foundation Monographs Series. New Haven, CT: Yale University Press, 1959.

Debreu, Gérard, and Kenneth Arrow. *Existence of Equilibrium for a Competitive Economy*. Cowles Foundation Monograph Series. New Haven, CT: Yale University Press, 1954.

## Selected Works about Gérard Debreu

Bourbaki, Nicholas. "The Architecture of Mathematics." *The American Mathematical Monthly* 57, no. 4 (1950): 221–32.

Bourbaki, Nicholas. *Elements of Mathematics: Theory of Sets*. Reading, MA: Addison-Wesley, 1968.

Bourbaki, Nicholas. "Foundations of Mathematics for the Working Mathematician." *The Journal of Symbolic Logic* 14, no. 1 (1949): 1–8.

Heilbroner, Robert L., and William S. Milberg. *The Crisis of Vision in Modern Economic Thought*. New York: Cambridge University Press, 1995.

Ingrao, Bruna, and Giorgio Israel. *The Invisible Hand: Economic Equilibrium in the History of Science*. Cambridge, MA: MIT Press, 1990.

Mandelbrot, Benoit B. "Chaos, Bourbaki, and Poincaré." *The Mathematical Intelligencer* 11, no. 3 (1989): 10–12.

Rubinstein, A. "Dilemmas of an Economic Theorist." *Econometrica* 74, no. 4 (2006): 865–83.

Weintraub, E. Roy. *How Economics Became a Mathematical Science*. Durham, NC: Duke University Press, 2002.

*David A. Dieterle*

## DE SOTO, HERNANDO

Born: 1941 in Arequipa, Peru; Peruvian; property rights; Major Works: *The Other Path* (1987), *The Mystery of Capital: Why Capitalism Triumphs in the West and Fails Everywhere Else* (2000).

Hernando de Soto is a Peruvian economist who believes that property rights are key to a working capitalist society. De Soto believes that the poor in Third World countries are unable to realize their economic potential because of their inability to obtain property rights. He founded the Institute for Liberty and Democracy in 1981 to act as a platform for research and to communicate his economic findings and beliefs. De Soto has won numerous awards for his work and has been an adviser to many world leaders.

Hernando de Soto Polar was born in Arequipa, Peru, in 1941 to a Peruvian diplomat father. His father was exiled in 1948 after a military coup, and moved the family to Europe. Raised in Europe with his younger brother, Álvaro, de Soto was educated in Switzerland, where he completed his postgraduate work at the Graduate Institute of International Studies. He became a successful economist, executive, and consultant in Europe before he earned enough money to retire at the age of 38. In 1979, de Soto returned to his native Peru to devote his life to solving the issue of global economic inequality.

De Soto had long wondered why, given intellectual and skill equality, Europe, North America, and Western nations thrived while Third World nations remained poor. When he moved back to Peru, he set out to research what made the difference. He found that in Third World countries, the legal system, in particular access to property rights, was not available to everyone. Third World citizens are subject to a legal system that will not allow them to accumulate and transfer capital. This, de Soto claims, is the key to making capitalism work as well in Third World countries as it does in other areas of the world.

In 1981, de Soto created the Institute for Liberty and Democracy (ILD) in Lima, Peru. The ILD's mission is to equip governments with knowledge, expertise, and resources to employ institutional reforms in property and business rights allowing citizens to be participants in using the market economy to elevate them out of poverty. He and his fellow ILD researchers initiated an investigation into the process of obtaining property rights in countries such as Peru, Egypt, and the Philippines. They discovered it to be extremely difficult. They found that in Lima, Peru, it would take over 200 bureaucratic steps and 21 years to obtain the title to a piece of land. In Egypt, it would take 17 years to get authorization to build on a sand dune, and in Manila, it might take 50 years to receive a land title.

In Peru in the 1980s, many of the poor were joining the murderous terrorist group the Shining Path to combat the government. De Soto published his book *The Other Path* in 1987 to reach out to potential Shining Path members and the Peruvian government. In it, he convinces Peru's farmers that they are future entrepreneurs and should join the legal economy instead of fight it. Because they did not have access to the capitalist system, the poor would operate extralegally in black or shadow markets. De Soto argued that if the black markets were legalized and provided the same protection that was given to legal markets, the free market could thrive. His efforts were unpopular with the terrorist group, and they made several attempts against his life before finally losing most of their power in 1992.

In his book *The Mystery of Capital*, de Soto explains the political responsibility of implementing a legal process for making property systems work for all citizens. He finds that because the poor do not own their land and cannot access capital, they are unable to expand their businesses. If the poor were given the land that they occupy, they would have the collateral needed for a loan and therefore could enjoy business growth. He also points out that the system that works so well in the United States has been established for only 100 years and contends that now that the formula is known, it can be copied expeditiously in other countries.

De Soto was chosen one of the five leading Latin American innovators of the century in 1999, and was named in the top 100 most influential people in the world in 2004 by *Time* magazine. He was named one of the 15 innovators in *Forbes'* 85th-anniversary edition. He has won numerous prizes for his work including the Freedom Prize (Switzerland), the Fisher Prize (United Kingdom), the Goldwater Award (United States), the Adam Smith Award (United States), the CARE Canada Award for Outstanding Development Thinking (Canada), the Americas Award (United States), the Academy of Achievement's Golden Plate Award in 2005, and the Most Outstanding of 2004 by the Peruvian National Assembly of Rectors.

De Soto gained early support from Margaret Thatcher, Richard Nixon, and Dan Quayle. He has also been an adviser to governments in Mexico, Egypt, Peru, El Salvador, Ghana, Russia, Afghanistan, and the Philippines. His foundation, the Institute for Liberty and Democracy, has been responsible for more than 400 laws and regulations in Peru that have opened up their economic system to the majority of citizens. De Soto's plans are being adopted by the unrecognized Eurasian country of Pridnestrovie and are gaining the attention of leaders worldwide.

*See also:* Collier, Paul; Duflo, Esther; Easterly, William; Ostrom, Elinor; Sachs, Jeffrey

## Selected Works by Hernando de Soto

de Soto, Hernando. *The Mystery of Capital: Why Capitalism Triumphs in the West and Fails Everywhere Else*. New York: Basic Books, 2000.
de Soto, Hernando. *The Other Path: The Economic Answer to Terrorism*. New York: Basic Books, 1987.

## Selected Works about Hernando de Soto

Berlau, John. "Providing Structure to Unstable Places; Hernando de Soto Puts Destabilized Countries on the Right Path by Securing Citizens' Confidence in Property Rights and Easing Legal Hurdles to Market Entrance." *Insight on the News*, July 8, 2003, 42.
Fernandez-Morera, Dario. "Outlaws and Addresses: Hernando de Soto's Path to Property Rights." *Reason Foundation* 25, no. 9 (February 1994): 28.
Wolverton, Marvin. "Review of *The Mystery Capital*." *Appraisal Journal*, July 1, 2003, 272.

*Aimee Register Gray*

## DIAMOND, PETER

Born: April 29, 1940, in New York City; American; public finance theory economics, public policy analysis, welfare economics, Nobel Prize (2010); Major Work: *Saving Social Security: A Balanced Approach* (with Peter R. Orzag) (2003).

Peter Diamond is an American economist known for his analysis of pensions and specifically the U.S. Social Security system. He was awarded the Nobel Prize in Economics in 2010 with Dale Mortensen and Christopher Pissarides. He served as an adviser on the Advisory Council on the Social Security to the U.S. Senate. In 2010 and 2011, he was nominated by President Barack Obama on three different occasions to serve on the Board of Governors for the Federal Reserve System. Even though chairman of the Federal Reserve Ben Bernanke had once been one of Diamond's students, each time opposition by Senate Republicans prevented confirmation. Eventually, Diamond withdrew his nomination.

Peter Arthur Diamond was born on April 29, 1940, in New York City. After attending public schools in the Bronx and Long Island, Diamond attended Yale University for his undergraduate studies. Even though he was studying math as a major, young Diamond was greatly influenced by not yet Nobel laureate Gérard Debreu, from whom Diamond had several classes. Diamond received a BA from Yale summa cum laude in 1960, and despite his interest in economics, he accepted an offer to study math at MIT for his graduate studies. Yet once at MIT it was suggested his fellowship be transferred to the economics department and Robert Solow was his adviser. Peter Diamond graduated from MIT with a PhD in 1963 with a strong interest in public finance, general equilibrium, and taxation.

In 1960, Diamond's research career in economics began as a research assistant to Nobel laureate-to-be Tjalling Koopmans (1975). Diamond's contributions to Koopmans's research led Koopmans to redesign his own plan. This led Diamond to be a coauthor with Koopmans and to Diamond's first publication in 1964. Diamond considered Koopmans as one of the major influences on and role models in his career.

Upon graduation from MIT in 1963, Diamond accepted a position at the University of California, Berkeley. After one year at UC Berkeley, Diamond returned permanently to MIT as a member of the faculty, rising through the ranks from associate professor to institute professor. From 1992 to 1997, Peter Diamond was the first Paul Samuelson Professor at MIT, relinquishing it in 1997 to become an institute professor. As a professor, Peter Diamond found invigorating the combination and supportive nature of teaching and research.

As an overseas fellow at Churchill College in Cambridge in 1964–65, Peter Diamond's research in public finance took a major leap forward while delivering a seminar on optimal taxation. At this time he met Nobel laureate-to-be James Mirrlees (1996) with recommendations on expanding Diamond's model from a one-consumer economy to a many-person economy. This meeting began a project that resulted in a paper on optimal taxation, not published till 1971, and the Diamond-Mirrlees efficiency theorem. Their theorem suggests taxes should not be imposed on intermediate goods and imports. The Diamond-Mirrlees collaborative partnership led to many additional papers throughout Diamond's career.

At the recommendation of Paul Samuelson, Diamond was invited to join the Panel on Social Security Financing, a consultant to the U.S. Senate Finance Committee. This invitation began Diamond's study of pensions and Social Security. A proponent of basis research and public policy analysis being supportive of each other, Diamond's professional interest in these areas made him well suited for this appointment.

Peter Diamond wrote many articles and books in his career with many collaborators and coauthors. Topics in his articles ranged from analyses of different social welfare programs to the U.S. Social Security system and Social Security Administration. In 2003, Diamond coauthored with Peter Orzag *Saving Social Security: A Balanced Approach*.

As a public finance economist, Diamond was focused on both the financial viability of a social program as well as the social benefit. This was reflected in his many writings on the Social Security system. Several of his recommendations included adjustments in the taxation of Social Security income as well as adjusting contribution amounts as life expectancy patterns change.

His career in public finance and work on Social Security did not go unnoticed by either his colleagues or the public. In 1978, he was named a fellow of the American Academy of Arts and Sciences and of the National Academy of Sciences in 1984. He was elected a fellow and served as president of the Econometric Society in 1968, and in 2003 held the prestigious office of American Economic Association president. In 2008, he was honored as the recipient of the Robert M. Ball Award for Outstanding Achievements in Social Insurance. In 2010, Peter Diamond received the ultimate honor, being awarded the Nobel Prize in Economic Sciences along with Dale T. Mortensen (Northwestern University) and Christopher A. Pissarides (London School of Economics). The focus of his prize-winning work was to determine equilibrium in labor markets.

*See also:* Arrow, Kenneth; Bernanke, Ben; Debreu, Gérard; Koopmans, Tjalling; Maskin, Eric; Mirrlees, James; Mortensen, Dale; Pissarides, Christopher; Samuelson, Paul; Solow, Robert

## Selected Works by Peter Diamond

Diamond, Peter A., and James A. Mirrlees. "Optimal Taxation and Public Production I: Production Efficiency." *American Economic Review* 61, no. 1 (1971): 8–27.

Diamond, Peter A., and James A. Mirrlees. "Optimal Taxation and Public Production II: Tax Rules." *American Economic Review* 61, no. 3, pt. 1 (1971): 261–78.

Diamond, Peter, and Peter R. Orzag. *Saving Social Security: A Balanced Approach*. Washington, DC: Brookings Institution Press, 2005.

## Selected Works about Peter Diamond

Debreu, Gérard. *Theory of Value: An Axiomatic Analysis of Economic Equilibrium*. New Haven, CT: Yale University Press, 1959.

Diamond, Peter A. "My Research Strategy." *Eminent Economists II: Their Work and Life Philosophies*. Edited by Michael Szenberg and Lall Ramrattan. New York: Cambridge University Press, 2011.

Diamond, Peter A. "Autobiography." Nobelprize.org. http://www.nobelprize.org/nobel_prizes/economics/laureates/2010/diamond.html (accessed April 2012).
Moscarini, Giuseppe, and Randall Wright. 2007. "An Interview with Peter Diamond." *Macroeconomic Dynamics* 11 (2007): 543–65.
"Peter Diamond." *Bloomberg News.* June 6, 2011. http://www.bloomberg.com/news/2011-06-06/nobel-laureate-peter-diamond-to-withdraw-his-nomination-as-a-fed-governor.html.

*David A. Dieterle*

## DRAGHI, MARIO

Born: September 3, 1947, in Rome, Italy; Italian; deficit financing, risk management, monetary policy; Major Works: *Public Debt Management: Theory and History* (coedited with Roger Dornbusch) (1990), *Transparency, Risk Management and International Financial Fragility: Geneva Reports on the World Economy 4* (with Francesco Giavazzi and Robert C. Merton) (2004).

Mario Draghi is an Italian banker and economist who succeeded Jean-Claude Trichet as president of the European Central Bank (ECB) on November 1, 2011. He served as governor of the Bank of Italy from 2006. Draghi was awarded the Knight Grand Cross of the Order of Merit of the Italian Republic in April of 2000. Draghi was named a fellow of Harvard University's Institute of Politics at the John F. Kennedy School of Government in 2001.

Mario Draghi was born on September 3, 1947, in Rome, Italy. He studied at the Massimiliano Massimo Institute, later graduating from La Sapienza University of Rome in 1970 with a degree in economics. In 1977, he received his PhD in economics from the Massachusetts Institute of Technology (MIT). He wrote his dissertation *Essays on Economic Theory and Applications* under the supervision of Franco Modigliani and Robert Solow.

Draghi began his career in academia with the Universities of Trento, Padua, and Venice from 1975 to 1981. He accepted a professorship at the University of Florence with the Cesare

Mario Draghi became president of the European Central Bank (ECB) in 2011. (AP/Wide World Photos)

Alfieri Faculty of Political Science where he remained until 1994. Concurrently, Draghi served as the Italian executive director of the World Bank till 1990.

Draghi's public service began when he became director general of the Italian Treasury in 1991. Beginning in 1993, Draghi chaired the Italian Committee for Privatisations. By 1997 and 1998, he had drafted legislation aptly known as "Draghi Law." The law sought to reform finance and corporate governance. From 1999 to 2001, Draghi chaired the Organisation of Economic Co-operation and Development's (OECD) Working Party No. 3 while chairing the European Economic and Financial Committee in 2000 and 2001. He was also a member of the G7 Deputies.

In 2002, Draghi moved from government to private investment banking with Goldman Sachs International, serving as vice chairman and managing director. In 2006, he was elected to oversee the Bank of Italy as governor. His duties included the governing and general councils of the European Central Bank and the board of directors of the Bank for International Settlements. During the subsequent five years, Draghi acted as chairman of the Financial Stability Board. Draghi was poised for perhaps the role of a lifetime as head of one of the world's most important central banks. He assumed his role as president of the European Central Bank on November 1, 2011.

Mario Draghi's rise as ECB's president was not without its challenges. Draghi was touted as a prospective suitor, but his early support from the French was delayed by their persistence to have a Frenchman replace Trichet. Another obstacle arose when questions surfaced concerning Draghi's prior affiliation with Goldman Sachs.

With an alarming debt crisis looming, Mario Draghi inherited a tough job. He took immediate action akin to the efforts of his U.S. counterpart, the Federal Reserve Bank's Ben Bernanke. Under Draghi's leadership, the ECB released a massive 490 billion euros to member institutions of the European Union intended to ease the credit crunch. Like Bernanke, Draghi authorized bond purchases to aid member nations. He also reversed the actions of his predecessor, a move some opposed given the recessive climate and doomsday forecasts.

Though his swift actions were largely favored, some critics believed Draghi's laissez-faire approach to the Greek loan defaults presented a windfall to those institutions insuring bad debts. Likewise, dissenters argued that the ECB and other central banks' additional round of debt financing would actually spark inflationary rises in key markets such as oil. As the European Central Bank's lead monetarist, his every action is adroitly followed and documented by the global press.

While presiding over ECB affairs, Draghi serves as chair of the European Systemic Risk Board. He has held other distinguished posts such as honorary trustee of the Brookings Institution in Washington, DC, and member of the board of trustees of Princeton University's Institute for Advanced Study. Draghi was an instrumental adviser to a number of banking institutions and corporate entities, which included Eni, Istituto per la Ricostruzione Industriale, Banca Nazionale del Lavoro, and IMI.

Draghi authored countless articles on a range of financial subject matter, specifically, international finance and monetary policy. Draghi functioned as editor of *Public Debt Management: Theory and History* with Rudiger Dornbusch, which was first published in 1990. In alliance with Francesco Giavazzi and Robert C. Merton, Draghi wrote *Transparency, Risk Management and International Financial Fragility: Geneva Reports on the World Economy 4* in 2004. This fourth installment examined government guarantees to banks and the inherent risks imposed on the respective government's financial picture.

Draghi has been decorated with a host of awards and honors. In 2000, he received the Knight Grand Cross of the Order of Merit of the Italian Republic. He was named a fellow of Harvard University's Institute of Politics at the John F. Kennedy School of Government in 2001. Draghi was awarded an honorary distinction in statistics in 2009 from the University of Padua. In 2010, he obtained an honorary MBA from the CUOA (University Center of Business Administration) Foundation in Vicenza, Italy.

*See also:* Bernanke, Ben; Merton, Robert; Modigliani, Franco; Solow, Robert; Trichet, Jean-Claude

**Selected Works by Mario Draghi**

Draghi, Mario. "Essays on Economic Theory and Applications." PhD diss., Massachusetts Institute of Technology, 1977.

Draghi, Mario, and Rudiger Dornbusch, eds. *Public Debt Management: Theory and History*. New York: Cambridge University Press, 1990.

Draghi, Mario, Francesco Giavazzi, and Robert C. Merton. *Transparency, Risk Management and International Financial Fragility: Geneva Reports on the World Economy 4*. London: Centre for Economic Policy Research, 2004.

**Selected Works about Mario Draghi**

"Mario Draghi." European Central Bank. http://www.ecb.int/ecb/orga/decisions/html/cvdraghi.en.html (accessed September 2012).

James, Harold. *Making the European Monetary Union*. Foreword by Mario Draghi and Jaime Caruan. Cambridge, MA: Harvard University Press, 2012.

Tamburello, Stefani. *Mario Draghi il Governatore: Dalla Banca d'Italia al vertice della Bce*. Diegaro di Cesena, Italy: Rizzoli Etas, 2011.

*Joy Dooley-Sorrells*

# DUFLO, ESTHER

Born: October 25, 1972, in Paris, France; French; development economics, social economics; Major Works: "The Experimental Approach to Development Economics" (with Abhijit V. Bannerjee) (2009), *Poor Economics: A Radical Rethinking of the Way to Fight Global Poverty* (2011).

Esther Duflo is a French economist with an international reputation for her pioneering work in development economics. An MIT economics professor, Duflo is noted for her work literally out in the field to discover and address causes and cures to poverty. She founded and was the first director of the Jameel Poverty Action Lab (J-PAL). She is credited for pioneering the study of development economics with the application of randomized control trials such as those conducted in medicine. Duflo explores the causes and cures of the microeconomic issues such as education, health, and finance in developing countries.

Esther Duflo was born on October 25, 1972, in France. She studied history and economics at the Ecole Normale Superieure in Paris, receiving her BA in 1994. During her time at Ecole Normale Superieure, she studied in Moscow, Russia, working with development economist Jeffrey Sachs. A year later in 1995, she earned her master's in economics from DELTA in Paris. She came to the United States to pursue her PhD in economics. She received her doctorate in economics from MIT in 1999.

Upon graduation, MIT appointed her an assistant professor of economics. Other than MIT, Duflo was a one-year visiting professor at Princeton University during the 2001–2 academic year and served a six-month leave at the Paris School of Economics in 2007. By age 29, she was a tenured associate professor. In 2005, Esther Duflo founded J-PAL at MIT and was named the Adbul Latif Jameel Professor of Poverty Alleviation and Development Economics. Through J-PAL, Duflo and her colleagues initiate research that evaluates the microeconomic issues of developing countries. J-PAL concerns itself with evaluating through randomized control trials social programs (health, education, finance) that directly impact the poverty-stricken people and families in less developed countries.

Esther Duflo's professional activities go beyond J-PAL. She serves on the board of the Bureau for Research and Economic Analysis of Development (BREAD), is a research associate for the National Bureau for Economic Research (NBER), and directs the Center of Economic Policy Research's development economics program. Duflo was the founding editor of the *American Economic Journal: Applied Economics*. She is also a coeditor for the *Review of Economics and Statistics* and the *Journal of Development Economics*, and a member of the Human Capital Research Programme for the International Growth Center.

Duflo's research incorporated field experiments in developing countries on several social fronts to identify causes so they could prescribe solutions. Her J-PAL teams investigated areas including the behavior involved in household decision making, educational issues such as school uniforms and absentee teachers, access (or lack of) to financial resources, financial decision making regarding health issues including immunizations. They also evaluated public policies as they applied to these microeconomic issues.

In 2011, Esther Duflo and Abhijit Banerjee (J-PAL cofounder and colleague) published *Poor Economics: A Radical Rethinking of the Way to Fight Global Poverty*. *Poor Economics* was awarded Business Book of the Year by both the *Financial Times* and Goldman Sachs. Duflo and Banerjerr addressed the small microeconomic questions of economic development. They revealed the results on a series of 18 countries' sets of data and topics researched using their pioneering randomized control trials methodology. Many of the causes and effects they revealed were counterintuitive, which raised the debate of effective prescriptions for developing countries.

Two topics they explored were microfinance and malnutrition. They launched a debate on the effectiveness of microfinance though they were still positive on it. Their observations and trials revealed that most individuals would trade, without hesitation, their small business for a factory job. They are "reluctant entrepreneurs." Duflo and Banerjee also found discrepancy with business funding in developing countries as medium-size businesses have limited access to financial resources. They also argued that the problem with the diet of malnourished people in different countries was not the quantity of food but the quality, an issue of nutrition and not hunger.

Esther Duflo has received countless honors and awards for her work including the John Bates Clark Medal in 2010. In 2009, Duflo was a John D. and Catherine MacArthur Fellow and was awarded the inaugural Calvo-Armengol International Prize. In 2005, she was honored as the *LeMonde*/Cercle des economistes (*LeMonde*/The Circle of economists) best young French economist. *Foreign Policy* magazine recognized Duflo as one of the top 100 intellectuals in 2008, and there were similar recognitions by *The Economist* and *Time* magazine. In 2009, Duflo became an American Academy of Arts and Sciences fellow. She was nominated by President Obama to serve as a member of the President's Global Development Council.

Esther Duflo has been labeled a left-of-center redistributionist in achieving global equity and prosperity. She has been criticized as an activist whose activism blurs her economics. She is unapologetic and views her role as vital to achieving a better future. Duflo has been a pioneering presence and driving force in furthering the use of field experiments as a methodology to identify solutions and advocate for the poor.

*See also:* Collier, Paul; Sachs, Jeffrey

## Selected Works by Esther Duflo

Banerjee, Abhijit V., and Esther Duflo. "The Experimental Approach to Development Economics." *Annual Review of Economics* 1 (2009): 151–78.

Banerjee, Abhijit V., and Esther Duflo. *Poor Economics: A Radical Rethinking of the Way to Fight Global Poverty*. New York: Public Affairs, 2011.

Duflo, Esther. *Expérience, science et lutte contre la pauvreté*. Paris: Fayard, 2009.

Duflo, Esther. *Le Développment Humain (Lutter contre la pauvrete*, vol. 1). Paris: Le seuil, 2010.

Duflo, Esther. *La polique de l'autonomie (Lutter contre la pauvrete*, vol. 2). Paris: Le seuil, 2010.

## Selected Works about Esther Duflo

Conley, Timothy G., and Christopher R. Udry. "Learning about a New Technology: Pineapple in Ghana." *The American Economic Review* 100, no. 1 (2010): 35–69.

"Esther Duflo Papers." MIT Economics. http://economics.mit.edu/faculty/eduflo/papers (accessed April 2012).

Parker, Ian. "Profiles—The Poverty Lab." *The New Yorker*. http://www.newyorker.com/reporting/2010/05/17/100517fa_fact_parker (accessed April 2012).

"Speakers Esther Duflo: Development Economist." TED—Ideas worth spreading. http://www.ted.com/speakers/esther_duflo.html (accessed April 2012).

*David A. Dieterle*

## DUPUIT, JULES

Born: May 18, 1804, in Fossano, France; Died: September 5, 1866, in Paris, France; French; political economy, marginal utility; Major Work: *On the Measurement of the Utility of Public Works* (*Annales des ponts et chausses*, vol. 8, 2nd series) (1844).

Jules Dupuit was the first economist to describe marginal utility. Using his definition of marginal utility, he was the also the first to provide a evidence for the demand curve. Dupuit used the term "relative utility" to describe the area above the price, and Marshall later built on this idea when he introduced the idea of consumer surplus, which describes the area above the demand curve (marginal utility curve). Dupuit has been considered economics' first public works economist. Dupuit died in 1866.

Jules Dupuit was born on May 18, 1804, in Fossano, Italy. His family emigrated to France when he was 10 years old. As a young man, he studied in Versailles. He went to study civil engineering at the Ecole Polytechnic. As a civil engineer, Dupuit received the Legion d'honneur for his work on France's system of roads. Dupuit continued his career in Paris, supervising Paris's construction of a new sewer system. As Dupuit continued his studies in civil engineering, he developed an interest in economics. He studied economics on his own, apart from his civil engineering career, so he was a self-taught economist.

In 1844 Dupuit published his classic, "On the Measurement of the Utility of Public Works," where he addressed the relationships between value, utility, price, and consumption. Dupuit examined utility as related to builing and maintenance costs for public works such as roads, canals, railways, and bridges. In this article, Dupuit first introduced the idea of a diminishing marginal utility curve. He showed that as the quantity of a good consumed rises, the user's marginal utility of the good declines. For example, as road tolls lower, more people will use the toll road or bridge. And conversely, as the usage increases, the willingness of the person to pay declines. The concept proposed by Dupuit converts into a downward-sloping demand function, leading him to describe the demand curve as a marginal utility curve.

Dupuit was the first economist to define the demand curve by using the defintion of marginal utility. Dupuit was also the first to provide a convincing explanation of why the demand curve is downward sloping. Many questioned Dupuit's reasoning, however, with some critics complaining about his use of marginal utility to define the demand curve. The concept of marginal utility is a microeconomic concept used to describe the action of an individual. However, Dupuit uses marginal utility to define an aggregate concept, market demand.

Dupuit also contributed to the devleopment of economics by defining the term "relative utility." Relative utility is the area under the demand curve (the marginal utility curve) and above the price. Dupuit used the idea to measure the public welfare on his bridge toll. He concluded that the public welfare would be maximized when the bridge toll is priced at zero. Dupuit's definition of relative utility is the same area as what Alfred Marshall later called consumer surplus. Dupuit's writings also included articles on monopoly and price discrimination.

Dupuit was a unique economic thinker in part because he was able to combine his economics background with his civil engineering training. His interdisciplinary research in many areas of public works is clearly evident. His research included, for example, an evaluation of the net economic benefit of Paris's public services. He analyzed functions for economic development, and once attempted to develop a paradigm for utility theory and measure the benefits of public works.

Other topics Dupuit researched in the area of public works included the development of tools for measuring groundwater flow. He simplified an equation to derive analytical solutions for groundwater flow. His assumption is known today as the Dupuit assumption.

Jules Dupuit died in Paris, France, on September 5, 1866.

*See also:* Marshall, Alfred

## Selected Works by Jules Dupuit

Dupuit, Jules. *Overview: Memory on the Circulation of Cars and Rolling Friction* [Overview: Memoire sur le tirage des voitures et sur le frottement de roulement] (1842). Whitefish, MT: Kessinger, 2010.

Dupuit, Jules. "On the Measurement of the Utility of Public Works." Translated by R. H. Barback from the *Annales des Ponts et Chauss Pes*, vol. 8, 2nd series, 1844.

Dupuit, Jules. *Theoretical and Practical Studies on the Movement of Water in the Channels* [Études théoriques et pratiques sur la mouvement des eaux dans les canaux] (1848). Paris: Dunod, 1863.

Dupuit, Jules. *Theoretical and Practical Treaty of Conduct and the Distribution of Waters* [Traité théorique et pratique de la conduite et de la distribution des eaux]. Cariliàn-Goeury et V. Dalmont, 1854.

Dupuit, Jules. "On the measurement of the utility of public works" [Reprint]. In *International Economic Papers*, no. 2. London: Macmillan, 1954.

## Selected Works about Jules Dupuit

Ekelund, Robert B., and Robert F. Hebert. "Dupuit and Marginal Utility: Context of the Discovery." *History of Political Economy* 8 (1976): 266–73.

Ekelund, Robert B., and Robert F. Hebert. *Secret Origins of Modern Microeconomics: Dupuit and the Engineers*. Chicago: University of Chicago Press, 1999.

Ubel, Peter A. *Free Market Madness: Why Human Nature Is at Odds with Economics—and Why It Matters*. Cambridge, MA: Harvard Business Press, 2009. (See the section "Water under the Bridge," 18–22.)

*Kathleen C. Simmons*

## EASTERLY, WILLIAM

Born: September 7, 1957 in Morgantown, West Virginia; American; economic development, growth in developing countries; Major Works: *The Elusive Quest for Growth: Economists' Adventures and Misadventures in the Tropics* (2001), *The White Man's Burden: Why the West's Efforts to Aid the Rest Have Done So Much Harm and So Little Good* (2006).

William Easterly is a professor of economics at New York University (NYU) and the codirector of NYU's Development Research Institute. His main fields of interest are economic development and growth, foreign aid, and the macroeconomics of developing countries. He authored two books: *The Elusive Quest for Growth* (Massachusetts Institute of Technology, 2001) and *The White Man's Burden* (Penguin, 2006); edited three books: *What Works in Development*, *Reinventing Foreign Aid*, and *The Limits of Stabilization*; and published more than 60 peer-reviewed academic papers. In 2008 and 2009, *Foreign Policy* magazine named him among the top 100 global public intellectuals.

William Russell Easterly was born in West Virginia on September 7, 1957 and raised in Bowling Green, Ohio. He received his BA from Bowling Green State University in 1979 and his PhD in economics from Massachusetts Institute of Technology (MIT) in 1985. He worked for 16 years as a research economist and senior adviser at the Macroeconomics and Growth Division at the World Bank. From 2001 to 2003, he worked at the Institute for International Economics and the Center for Global Development. Since 2003, he has been a professor of economics and codirector of the Development Research Institute at NYU. His work in the developing world has been mainly focused on Africa and Latin America, and it is widely reviewed by major media outlets.

In *The Elusive Quest for Growth* (2001), Easterly discusses the main factors behind the lack of developmental growth in Third World countries since World War II. He is specifically critical of governments and institutions such as the World Bank and the International Monetary Fund who try to implement various economics policies without understanding the culture and native people's financial incentives. He argues that without the financial motivation of local people, policies toward capital accumulation, education, and population control not only are useless but also, over time, add to corruption, high debt, and financial crisis in poor countries. The key, he discusses, is not in applying the planned theories of development economics but rather is in understanding the local economy, increasing the demand for product and services that help poor countries move forward, and enhancing poor countries' abilities to implement productive and profitable lines of market activities. In this case, the market would automatically determine the optimum level of important economic indicators, such as education and population size, that undeveloped countries are battling with.

In *The White Man's Burden* (2006), Easterly discusses two different approaches to providing aid to poor countries: a planner's approach versus a searcher's approach. According to Easterly, planners are those who think they already know the answers. Searchers acknowledge they do not know the answer. Searcher sees poverty as an intricate interdependence of social, historical, political, institutional, and technological factors. He argues that searchers offer a piecemeal problem-solving approach: collecting detailed information from the locals to first understand the culture and the problems, then applying different methods to solve the problems. Finally, searchers collect feedback from the community they are serving to analyze the method(s) used to find the optimum solution(s) to specific problems. Planners, however, measure the success of aid programs by the amount of money spent by the rich countries, not by their effectiveness in solving the locals' problems. Easterly submits that in the fight against global poverty, sometimes the best plan is to have no plan at all.

Easterly was the principal writer of the *Aid Watch* blog, a project of New York University's Development Research Institute. No longer active, the main idea behind the *Aid Watch* blog was to raise awareness of the aid programs because the authors believed that if more people watched and scrutinized the aid programs, more aid would reach the intended population.

Easterly's opponents criticize him for his rhetorical thrashing of those who he describes as ill-intended enemies of the poor. They argue that the ineffectiveness of Western-initiated developmental aid should encourage more dialogue and more scrutiny over the implementation of these programs to make them more effective, not dismiss such programs altogether as Easterly suggests.

Easterly has his detractors, who support the increase in international aid to poor countries while concurrently canceling their debt, but are critical of Easterly's pessimism and assert that Easterly disregards foreign aid even where it was successful in the past. Easterly's counterpoint, however, is that while for the past 50 years foreign aid to poor countries has increased dramatically, global poverty, especially in the areas that received the most amount of aid, has increased sharply as well. While others agree with Easterly regarding the ineffectiveness of past aid programs, they contribute this failure not to foreign aid but to an insufficient amount of foreign aid. Regardless, the majority of developmental economists agree that because of corruption among high-level officials in poor countries, most foreign aid did not reach the intended recipients.

William Easterly has written two books, coedited three others, and published more than 60 academic papers in peer-reviewed journals. His work has been addressed in many media outlets such as the *New York Times*, the *Wall Street Journal*, and the *Washington Post*, to name a few. He is one of the best-known development economists of the twenty-first century.

*See also:* Collier, Paul; Duflo, Esther; Ostrom, Elinor; Sachs, Jeffrey

### Selected Works by William Easterly

Easterly, William. *The Elusive Quest for Growth: Economists' Adventures and Misadventures in the Tropics.* Boston: MIT Press, 2001.

Easterly, William. *The White Man's Burden: Why the West's Efforts to Aid the Rest Have Done So Much Ill and So Little Good.* London: Penguin Group, 2006.

### Selected Works about William Easterly

"Development Research Institute at NYU." New York University. http://dri.fas.nyu.edu/object/WilliamEasterly.html (accessed March 2011).

Mishkin, Frederic S. *The Next Great Globalization: How Disadvantaged Nations Can Harness Their Financial Systems to Get Rich.* Princeton, NJ: Princeton University Press, 2006.

Sen, A. "The Man without a Plan." *Foreign Affairs* 85, no. 2 (2006): 171–78.

"William Easterly." The Brookings Institution. http://www.brookings.edu/experts/easterlyw (accessed October 2012).

*Elham Mahmoudi*

## EDGEWORTH, FRANCIS

Born: February 8, 1845, in Edgeworthstown County, Longford, Ireland; Died: February 13, 1926, in Oxford, England; Irish; political economy; Major Work: *Mathematical Psychics: An Essay on the Application of Mathematics to the Moral Sciences* (1881).

Francis Ysidro Edgeworth was an Irish-born political economist most noted for his work in economics and statistics. A prolific author, he was considered one of the best economists of his day. The first editor of *The Economic Journal*, his first and most important contribution to economics came in the publication of the book *Mathematical Psychics: An Essay on the Application of Mathematics to the Moral Sciences* (1881). In his book, Edgeworth introduces the economic ideas of indifference curves and the Edgeworth Box. The Edgeworth Box is a way to model how general equilibrium (quantity demand equals quantity supplied) might be reached in a simplified economy comprising two goods and two individuals. Edgeworth died in 1926.

Ysidro Francis Edgeworth was born on February 8, 1845, to a Spanish mother and Irish father. He later transposed his two first names and was called Francis or Frank by his family and friends. Home-schooled by tutors, Edgeworth later studied at Trinity College in Dublin and Balliol College in Oxford, graduating in 1869 and qualifying as an English barrister in 1877.

In his life and career, he made many contributions to the field of economics and statistics during the time when these sciences where coming into their own as fields of study in their own right. Edgeworth is remembered as a prolific author even if at times his striking originality is difficult to interpret. In his career, he held the Drummond chair at Oxford University and was considered among the best economists of his day.

He maintained extensive correspondence with his contemporary academic colleagues around the world and was the first editor of *The Economic Journal*, published by the Royal Economic Society. In the field of statistics, his work was recognized with a gold medal of the Royal Statistical Society in 1907 and he subsequently became president of the society in 1912–14.

His most important contribution to economics came in the publication of the book *Mathematical Psychics: An Essay on the Application of Mathematics to the Moral Sciences* (1881). He uses interesting and distinct metaphors in order to explain the problems he is setting out to understand if not solve. Specifically, he used electromagnetism as a metaphor to explain how energy arises with pleasure in humans and proceeds with a conception of man as a pleasure machine. Edgeworth envisioned society as a great aggregate of such machines, with collisions and compacts between them resembling electricity and magnetism fields.

Edgeworth attempted to determine the distribution of productive factors (land, labor, capital) that would be conducive to the highest aggregate of well-being. The conclusion of his philosophy here tends to support a hierarchical society of social rank rather than one of equality. He reasoned that the distribution of labor between those equally capable of work is equality, and generally those most capable of work will do more work and therefore suffer more fatigue. Understood this way, he considers that the highest and most capable of labor with education and improvement should advance the most. In practice, this conclusion of Edgeworth's would result in a society where the average issue of goods would be as large as possible for all segments of society above a determinate level of capacity, but zero for all sections below that degree.

*Mathematical Psychics* is also characterized by a style that has been called obscure, terse, and implicit, so that the reader is left to puzzle out every important sentence like an enigma. The book's ideas were only slowly adopted into the standard economic textbooks. *Mathematical Psychics* has nevertheless been influential in the history of economic thought.

One important concept widely used in economic analysis and first described and used in *Mathematical Psychics* is known as the indifference curve. This is a way to model the preferences of an individual or household when some combination of different goods results in the same utility. The indifference curve models how different combinations of goods are preferred by a particular individual while keeping the same level of satisfaction in all the combinations represented along the curve. This concept is applicable in many economic models and has been used widely in economic analysis. The indifference curve is equated with the marginal rate of substitution, which shows how much of one good a consumer is willing to give up for another good. This concept is relevant in microeconomic consumer theory and also plays a role in another key concept that was developed by Edgeworth, the "Edgeworth Box."

The Edgeworth Box models how general equilibrium might be reached in a simplified economy with two goods and two individuals. Edgeworth laid the theoretical groundwork for this analysis in his *Mathematical Psychics*. It has been further developed in future years by his successors, most notably Vilfredo Pareto.

The Edgeworth Box has proportions equal to the productive resources (land, labor, capital) of a country. The Box shows all of the ways those resources can be allocated to two industries who are producing two different goods, A and B. The lower-left origin on the Box is the origin for measuring allocations of factors for industry A. The upper-right corner origin on the Box is for industry B. Thus every point on the four sides of the Box denotes an allocation of the resources to the production of the two goods, A and B.

Indifference curves are drawn inside the box for each good, convex to their origin (lower-left or upper-right). The places where the indifference curves intersect represent where each individual could trade without feeling any worse off. Essentially, the model shows how general equilibrium is reached and predicts trade behavior based on the supposed indifference curves of two individuals.

Edgeworth's contributions to the field of economics cannot be understated. He helped shape the science into what it is today.

Francis Ysidro Edgeworth died on February 13, 1926, in Oxford, England.

*See also:* Bentham, Jeremy; Jevons, William Stanley; Pareto, Vilfredo

**Selected Works by Francis Edgeworth**

Edgeworth, Francis. *Mathematical Psychics: An Essay on the Application of Mathematics to the Moral Sciences.* London: C. Kegan Paul, 1881.

Edgeworth, Francis. "The Methods of Least Squares." *Philosophical Magazine* 16 (1883): 360–75.

Edgeworth, Francis. *New and Old Methods of Ethics.* Oxford: James Parker, 1877.

Edgeworth, Francis. *Papers Relating to Political Economy.* London: Ayers, 1925.

**Selected Works about Francis Edgeworth**

Barbé, Lluis. *Francis Ysidro Edgeworth: A Portrait with Family and Friends.* Translated by Mary C. Black. Northampton, MA: Edward Elgar, 2010.

Creedy, John. *Edgeworth and the Development of Neoclassical Economics.* Oxford: Basil Blackwell, 1986.

Price, L. L. "Francis Ysidro Edgeworth." *Journal of the Royal Statistical Society* 89 (1926): 371–77.

Stigler, Stephen M. "Francis Ysidro Edgeworth, Statistician." *Journal of the Royal Statistical Society Series A* 141, no. 3 (1978): 287–322.

*John E. Trupiano*

# EKELUND, ROBERT

Born: 1940 in Galveston, Texas; American; political economy, economic theory, economic history; Major Work: *A History of Economic Theory and Method* (with Robert F. Hébert) (2007).

Robert B. Ekelund Jr. contributed to economics through his extensive instruction and writings. Ekelund taught economics for more than 30 years at Louisiana State University, Texas A&M University, and Auburn University. Ekelund wrote dozens of books and journal entries on a variety of topics from economic and political theory, such as micro- and macroeconomics, mercantilism, and even the economics of the American Civil War and religion. His research and knowledge has been a major contribution to the economic community. He has been a contributor to both the Heartland Institute and the Mises Institute during his career. Much of the progression and development of economics over the past 40 years has been a result of his work and collaborations.

Robert Burton Ekelund Jr. was born in Galveston, Texas, in 1940. He attended St. Mary's University in San Antonio where he earned both his bachelor of business administration in economics and art history in 1962 and his master of arts in economics and history in 1963. Ekelund accepted a teaching position at Louisiana State University (LSU) following his graduation at St. Mary's. Teaching and studying, he earned a PhD in economics and political theory from LSU in 1967.

Bob Ekelund left LSU after accepting a teaching position with Texas A&M University in College Station, Texas, in 1967. At Texas A&M, Ekelund began his prolific writing career when he coauthored *A History of Economic Theory and Method* with colleague Robert F. Hébert in 1975. Ekelund and Hébert explained the growth and development of economic behavior dating back to ancient Greece and progressing through the late twentieth century. They explored how market behavior impacts modern economic theory through the use of mathematical and statistical analysis and inquiry. Comprehensive analysis and an easy-to-read writing style have made *A History of Economic Theory and Method* popular in the academic community as a textbook favorite. He and Hébert collaborated on several major contributions to the history of economic thought.

Ekelund moved from east Texas to east Alabama in 1977 when he accepted a position with Auburn University. He wrote a majority of his books and publications over the next 25 years while at Auburn. Ekelund's writings covered a wide array of topics from micro- and macroeconomics to the specifics of economics and how the subject relates to nineteenth-century France, the American Civil War, and even religion.

During his graduate studies, Ekelund developed an interest in the work of French engineer and economist Jules Dupuit. His fascination with Dupuit continued through his professional career. In 1999, Ekelund and Hébert cowrote *Origins of Modern Microeconomics: Dupuit and the Engineers*. They analyzed how the nineteenth-century French engineers used daily experiences to arrive at solutions and the use of that methodology with today's economic problems. Ekelund and Hebert were commended by the economic community for the dedication of their endeavors. Many of the sources from both before and after the French Revolution had yet to be translated and some were not accessible. Ekelund credits Dupuit as one of the founders of formal economic theory and reasoning.

After retiring from Auburn University in 2003 as the Catherine and Edward Lowder Eminent Scholar Emeritus, Ekelund continued to write. In 2004 while working with Mark Thornton, the two coauthored *Tariffs, Blockades, and Inflation: The Economics of the Civil War*. The authors investigate the American Civil War, interpreting data from the time period and organizing it into an interesting, easy-to-read format from the standpoint of contemporary economic theory. In 2006, he teamed up with Hébert and fellow economist Robert D. Tollison to write *The Marketplace of Christianity*. This book explores Christianity as an industry with intense competition dating back to the Protestant Reformation of the sixteenth century, making intriguing insights about religion and how it relates to economic concepts such as self-interest and individual choice. Ekelund provides interesting insights into a variety of topics, and his writing ability brings economic concepts to life in different contexts as exhibited in his books.

Ekelund's contributions to economic thinking are far-reaching and extensive. His teachings through both instruction and writing on economic and political theory are both inspired and influential from the Austrian-style economic perspective. His works are widely publicized and circulated throughout both the academic and economic arenas for both his expertise and his writing style.

*See also:* Dupuit, Jules; Hayek, Friedrich von; Mises, Ludwig von; Romer, Christina

## Selected Works by Robert Ekelund

Ekelund, Robert, and Leonardo Auernheimer. *The Essentials of Money and Banking.* Hoboken, NJ: Wiley, 1982.

Ekelund, Robert, and Robert F. Hébert. *Classics in Economic Thought.* New York: McGraw-Hill, 1996.

Ekelund, Robert, and Robert A. Hébert. *A History of Economic Theory and Method.* Long Grove, IL: Waveland Press, 2007.

Ekelund, Robert, and Robert F. Hébert. *Secret Origins of Modern Microeconomics: Dupuit and the Engineers.* Chicago: University of Chicago Press, March 1999.

Ekelund, Robert, Robert F. Hébert, and Robert D. Tollison. *The Marketplace of Christianity.* Cambridge, MA: MIT Press, 2006.

Ekelund, Robert, Robert F. Hébert, Robert Tollison, Gary Anderson, and Audrey Davidson. *Sacred Trust: The Medieval Church as an Economic Firm.* Oxford: Oxford University Press, 2003.

Ekelund, Robert, and Robert Tollison. *Mercantilism as a Rent-Seeking Society: Economic Regulation in Historical Perspective.* College Station: Texas A&M University Press, 1982.

Ekelund, Robert, and Robert Tollison. *Politicized Economies: Monarchy, Monopoly, and Mercantilism.* College Station: Texas A&M University Press, 1997.

## Selected Works about Robert Ekelund

Boumans, M. (1999). *Secret Origins of Modern Microeconomics: Dupuit and the Engineers Review.* Economic History Association. http://eh.net/book_reviews/secret-origins-modern-microeconomics-duputi-and-engineers (accessed February 2011).

Buchanan, James M., and Robert D. Tollison, eds. *The Theory of Public Choice—II.* Ann Arbor: University of Michigan Press, 1984.

Hammond, J. D. (2007). "Review of *The Marketplace of Christianity.*" Economic History Association. http://www.eh.net/book_reviews/marketplace-christianity (accessed February 2011).

Rowley, Charles K., and Friedrich Schneider, eds. *The Encyclopedia of Public Choice.* New York: Kluwer, 2004.

Surdam, D. G. (2004). *Tariffs, Blockades, and Inflation: The Economics of the Civil War.* Economic History Association. http://eh.net/book_reviews/tariffs-blockades-and-inflation-economics-civil-war (accessed February 2011).

*William S. Chappell*

# ELY, RICHARD

Born: April 13, 1854, in Ripley, New York; Died: October 4, 1943, in Old Lyme, Connecticut; American; economics, socialism, Christian socialism; Major Works: *French and German Socialism in Modern Times* (1883), *The Labor Movement in America* (1886), *Social Aspects of Christianity* (1888), *Hard Times: The Way In and the Way Out* (with Thomas William Lamont et al.) (1931).

Richard Ely was an economist and social reformer. He is credited as an intellectual guide for the Social Gospel movement, which is an attempt to apply Christian principles to social issues. His activities and writings also attracted a furious condemnation from a leading public official, which led to a trial over the question of academic freedom in universities. Ely died in 1943.

Richard Theodore Ely was born in Ripley, New York, in April 13, 1854. He was brought up in a strict Presbyterian household, though he transferred to the Episcopal Church in college at Columbia University. He earned his PhD in economics at Heidelberg University in Germany, where he came under the influence of German Historical economics. This school of thought emphasized an empirical, data-driven approach to economic questions, and criticized the Austrian and American tendencies toward abstract reasoning. The Historical School also led Ely to an evolutionary view of social development, in which communities and nations improve slowly over time through the efforts of individuals and organizations. Ely's writings emphasized progress; things were never good enough, nor were timeless laissez-faire policies sufficient for the governance of a nation.

After receiving his PhD, Ely joined the faculty at Johns Hopkins University in Maryland. He was constantly active in public life, seeking ways to apply economic reasoning to the problems the world faced. He helped organize the American Economic Association in 1885, was a member of the tax commissions of the city of Baltimore and the state of Maryland, became secretary of the Christian Social Union in 1889, and cofounded the American Institute for Christian Sociology in 1893. In 1892, he was hired by the University of Wisconsin.

Ely's writings are filled with calls for professors and other researchers to get involved in public life. Because he thought that the study of economics should use real data instead of abstract theories, he thought that professors should always be busy collecting information and processing it for the public interest. Furthermore, in order for such information to be useful, he thought that professors must work with government officials to put their studies into action. The theory that universities should be in close partnership with local, state, and national governments became known as the Wisconsin Idea.

Ely received a terrible shock in 1894 when the state superintendent of Wisconsin, Oliver E. Wells, wrote a letter to a national newspaper accusing Ely of teaching utopian, impracticable, and pernicious doctrines. His caustic remarks accused Ely of being a socialist who encouraged murderous anarchy. Thereafter followed a furious debate concerning (1) whether Ely was indeed a purveyor of dangerous ideas and (2) what were the limits of academic freedom in a state university. To take command of the situation, the board of regents of the University of Wisconsin called a trial for Richard Ely. They created a commission that was to investigate and pass judgment on the situation and on Ely himself.

The resulting investigation cast light onto important aspects of Ely's life and thought. First, the accusers had some of the facts of the case flatly wrong (they had mistaken one of Ely's students for Ely himself when the student went to meet with a union leader, and had misinterpreted some gossip about Ely's relationship with a local printer's union that printed his books). Second, Ely's philosophy could be characterized as progressive conservatism, a view that was quite conservative in its conception of most property rights and politics, but was not closed to Socialist demands concerning major industries that tended to be monopolistic. Indeed, while socialism at the time often referred to thoroughgoing Marxism, the socialism of Ely's mind corresponded more to the modern European policy in health care and national industries—but with a Christian twist. Ely was a lifelong believer that the teachings of Jesus could be used to guide government policy as it related to social welfare programs. He also thought, however, that society evolved in a sort of Darwinistic fashion, and that citizens should constantly try to find new ways to improve upon old traditions.

Ely was judged innocent of all charges by the commission. The commission released a ringing statement defending academic freedom in universities. Even if Ely did have radical views, they wrote, professors nevertheless ought to seek truth as best they could, even if what they found was not to society's liking.

Ely wrote many works on economic applications to social problems. He worked hard all throughout the Great Depression to find practical and theoretical solutions to what he called "Hard Times." He guided the social ministry of liberal Protestant churches. Ely was confident that mankind could create a better future, and there was no idea he would not sanction in order to achieve it.

Richard Ely died in Old Lyme, Connecticut, on October 4, 1943.

*See also:* Veblen, Thorstein

## Selected Works by Richard Ely

Ely, Richard. *Evolution of Industrial Society*. New York: Chatauqua Press, 1903.
Ely, Richard. *French and German Socialism in Modern Times*. New York: Harper & Brothers, 1883.
Ely, Richard. *The Labor Movement in America*. New York: Thomas A. Crowell, 1886.
Ely, Richard. *Recent American Socialism*. Baltimore: Johns Hopkins University Press, 1885.
Ely, Richard. *Social Aspects of Christianity, and Other Essays*. New York: Thomas A. Crowell, 1889.
Ely, Richard T., and George Ray Wicker. *Elementary Principles of Economics: Together with a Short Sketch of Economic History*. New York: Macmillan, 1921.
Ely, Richard Theodore, with Thomas William Lamont, William Arthur Berridge, American Federation of Labor, and American Association for Labor Legislation. *Hard Times: The Way In and the Way Out*. New York: Macmillan, 1931.

## Selected Works about Richard Ely

"Ely, Richard Theodore, 1854–1943." In *Dictionary of Wisconsin History*. Wisconsin Historical Society. http://www.wisconsinhistory.org/dictionary/index.asp?action

=view@term_id=1284&term_type_id=1&term_type_text=people&letter=E (accessed December 2011).
Fine, Sidney. "Richard T. Ely, Forerunner of Progressivism, 1880–1901." *The Mississippi Valley Historical Review* 37, no. 4 (March 1951).
Rolnick, Stanley R. "An Exceptional Decision: The Trial of Professor Richard T. Ely by the Board of Regents of the University of Wisconsin, 1894." *Arkansas Academy of Science* 1894: 198–203.
Schlabach, Theron F. "An Aristocrat on Trial: The Case of Richard T. Ely." *Wisconsin Magazine of History* 47, no. 2 (Winter 1963–64): 140–59.
Spiegel, Henry. *The Growth of Economic Thought*. Englewood Cliffs, NJ: Prentice-Hall, 1971.

*Stephen H. Day*

# ENGELS, FRIEDRICH

Born: November 28, 1820, in Barmen, Germany; Died: August 5, 1895, in London, England; German; socialism, Marxist; Major Work: *Manifesto of the Communist Party* (with Karl Marx) (1848).

Friedrich Engels was a nineteenth-century German philosopher and a father of Marxist theory. Alongside Marx, Engels was a key proponent and the main partner of Karl Marx in bringing communism and socialism to the forefront of economic thought. The son of an industrialist growing up in an upper-class lifestyle, young Engels befriended many of the workers and became familiar with their working and living conditions. Writing of these experiences led him to meet Karl Marx, his intellectual soul mate. Engels and Marx worked together to organize workers to join the Communist League in Belgium, Germany, and Prussia. In 1848, Engels and Marx published the *Communist Manifesto*. Engels would later become the main financial support of Marx's later works. Engels died in 1895.

Friedrich Engels was born on November 28, 1820, in Barmen, Germany, the son of a German industrialist who owned a number of textile companies. A rebellious young man, he was writing political tracts by the age of 18. As was required of all young German men, he served his mandatory military enrollment and completed it honorably. While serving in the military in Berlin, he became familiar with the works of Friedrich Hegel and embraced a leftist ideology. It was also here that his agnosticism would grow to militant atheism.

Young Engels persuaded his father to send him to a mill in Manchester in which the elder Engels was a partner. He told his father this would help further his knowledge of the family business. The elder Engels saw this as an opportunity to remove his son from exposure to the radical ideas in Germany and gladly sent him in 1842. En route, Engels and Marx would meet briefly for the first time. Neither was impressed with the other.

While Friedrich participated in the upper-class lifestyle enjoyed by the Manchester industrialists (he was particularly fond of fox hunting), he pursued his studies of the working men and women who were his employees. He frequented their clubs and their workers' meetings, even developing an ongoing relationship with one of the women who worked in his mill. His tours of the working-class slums and growing knowledge of their living and working conditions would result in the publication of *The Condition of the Working Class in England* in 1844.

Early that same year, Engels began contributing to a radical journal edited by Karl Marx. Upon leaving the family business to return to Germany, Engels went to Paris to meet Marx and this time found his intellectual soul mate. They began working together, and in January 1845, when Marx was expelled from France for his radical writings and ties to a radical organization, later to become the Communist League, both would end up in Belgium. In Brussels, Marx and Engels worked together to organize workers in Germany, joining the Communist League. The workers movement was already taking place in England and France, and both felt it was time for German workers to join ranks. It was while in Belgium that Engels and Marx would work on and publish their most famous collaboration, the *Manifesto of the Communist Party*. However, in 1848 revolution struck France and soon spread across much of Europe. Marx and Engels were expelled from Belgium, again for their radical writings and work with the Communist League. They returned to Germany.

While back in Prussia, Engels would continue working to organize workers and writing with Marx. Marx would lose his Prussian citizenship and again be expelled, but Engels would stay to take part in fighting against Prussian troops in an uprising against the government. When the Prussian army emerged as the winner, Engels would barely manage to escape into Switzerland. From there, he would rejoin Marx, this time in England.

While in England, Engels and Marx tried to resurrect the now defunct Communist League, but finances were stretched thin and Marx was beginning to work on *Das Kapital*. It is here that Engels would again play a crucial role in the development of economic theory, however, not as a writer or thinker but as a supporter. Engels would go back to work in the Manchester mills, providing funding for Marx and his family while the latter worked on his major work. Engels would also provide insights for Marx on economic and business matters, but his largest contribution was financial. But despite Engels's support, the Marx family continued to live in relative poverty. In 1869, Engels would sell his interest in his business and move to London to be near Marx. He and Marx would continue to work together for another 14 years, until Marx's death.

After Marx's death, Engels would continue to be a force in the workers movement. For the first five years, Engels spent much of his time with the pen. He wrote *The Origin of the Family, Private Property and the State*, a work in which he claimed that monogamy was a recent invention that kept women in a state of near slavery. He claimed that with the rise of communism, the institution would fall in an era of sexual freedom and that private property and the state would join monogamy as outmoded ideas. But he also spent much of his time editing volume 2 of *Das Kapital*.

Upon completing that work, Engels would visit the United States at about the same time of the publication of the American edition of *The Condition of the Working Class*. But while visiting, he did not address workers groups or tend to organize, opting to travel quietly, making notes as he traveled from place to place. Upon visiting New York City, he likened it to visiting Dante's Inferno.

Engels would return to England and spend much of the rest of his life editing the final volume of *Das Kapital*, which he would finish shortly before his death August 5, 1895 in London.

*See also:* Ely, Richard; Marx, Karl

### Selected Works by Friedrich Engels

Engels, Friedrich. *The Condition of the Working Class in England*. 1844 with preface written in 1892. Translated by Florence Kelley Wischnewetzky. London: Swan Sonnenschein, 1892.

Engels, Friedrich. *The Origin of the Family, Private Property and the State*. 1884. Translated by Ernest Unterman. Chicago: Charles H. Kerr, 1902.

Engels, Friedrich. *The Peasant War in Germany*. New York: International, 1926.

Engels, Friedrich. *Socialism: Utopian and Scientific*. London: Allen & Unwin, 1892.

Engels, Friedrich, and Karl Marx. *Manifesto of the Communist Party*. Moscow: Progress, 1848.

### Selected Works about Friedrich Engels

Carver, Terrell. *Friedrich Engels: His Life and Thought*. Basingstoke, UK: Macmillan, 1989.

Henderson, William Otto. *The Life of Friedrich Engels*. Vol. 1. Portland, OR: Frank Cass, 1976.

Henley, J. D. *The Life and Thought of Friedrich Engels: A Reintroduction*. New Haven, CT.: Yale University Press, 1991.

Hollander, Samuel. *Friedrich Engels and Marxian Political Economy*. Cambridge: Cambridge University Press, 2011.

Hunt, Tristram. *Marx's General: The Revolutionary Life of Friedrich Engels*. New York: Metropolitan Books, 2009.

*Timothy P. Schilling*

## ENGLE, ROBERT

Born: November 10, 1942, in Syracuse, New York; American; econometrics, Nobel Prize (2003); Major Work: *ARCH: Selected Readings* (1995).

Robert Engle published over 60 papers in a wide variety of economic, urban, tax, and statistical journals. Engle's most famous time series work and major breakthrough was the development of the ARCH model. This model was named for the concept of autoregressive conditional heteroskedasticity (ARCH). The model has become a major tool for researchers and financial analysts who use it in asset pricing and in evaluating portfolio risk. Robert Engle was the 2003 recipient of the Nobel Prize in economics.

Robert Fry Engle III was born on November 10, 1942, in Syracuse, New York. He later moved to the Philadelphia area where his father was a DuPont chemist and his mother a French teacher. Engle received his education in physics from Williams College and Cornell University. He was initially educated in physics (he studied quantum physics under Nobel laureate Hans Bethe) and planned to follow in his father's footsteps. During his senior year at Williams he took his first economics course. It was his love of this course that later proved to serve as a catalyst into the field of economics. After completing his master's in physics, Engle went on to study economics at Cornell, with a focus on time series econometrics. He received his PhD from Cornell in 1969.

Engle began teaching and researching at Massachusetts Institute of Technology (MIT) from 1969 to 1974. During this time, he became an associate professor and published six papers in various economic journals. It was his theory on band spectrum regression in 1970 (published in 1973, *International Economic Review*) that would lead him to attend the World Congress of the Econometric Society in Cambridge, England. It was here where he met Clive Granger and many other economists who would become lifelong friends and collaborators. Over the next five years, Engle collaborated to build a model for the city of Boston. In the process, he published some very elaborate statistical models in an area not typically known for its mathematical prowess. Wishing to work more with time series models, he left MIT to teach at the University of California, San Diego (UCSD) in 1975, where he began teaching as an urban economist.

During the 1970s and 1980s, Engle published over 60 papers in a wide variety of economic, urban, tax, and statistical journals. It is during his time at UCSD that Engle developed his most famous time series work and major breakthrough, the ARCH model. This model, named for the concept of autoregressive conditional heteroskedasticity (ARCH), has become a major tool for both researchers and financial analysts who use it in asset pricing and in evaluating portfolio risk. Where earlier models assumed the random error was constant over time, Engel's ARCH model was different. Its concept was that while most volatility is embedded in random error, its variance depends on previously realized random errors, with large errors followed by large errors and small by small. In financial market analysis, the investment returns of an asset are assessed against its risks. Based on the volatility of the stock price and its returns, Engel's techniques allowed researchers to test if and how volatility in one period was related to volatility in another. It was this model that in 2003 led to him receiving the Nobel Prize for Economics, which he shared with Clive W. J. Granger.

While at UCSD, Engle was coeditor of the *Journal of Applied Econometrics*. In addition, he also held associate editorships on several other academic journals. From 1990 to 1994, he was chair of the Department of Economics. He retired in 2003 from UCSD as professor emeritus and research professor.

Engle is considered an expert in time series analysis and has held a longtime interest in the analysis of financial markets. His interests included the economic topics of financial econometrics, equities, interest rates, exchange rates, and options. Engle's current position (accepted in 1999) is the Michael Armellino Professor in Management of Financial Services at the Stern School of Business, New York University. He has worked with Morgan Stanley and Salomon Brothers, and served on numerous committees and as a consultant to both countries and financial institutions. In addition to teaching, Engle lectures widely to both academic and practitioner audiences. Altogether he has more than 100 academic papers and three books to his credit. The Engle ARCH model has given way to many later versions with names such as GARCH, TARCH, GJR-GARCH,

NARCH, VGARCH, APARCH, FIGARCH, FIE-GARCH, STARCH, SWARCH, CES-GARCH, SQGARCH, component GARCH, etc. He is a fellow of both the American Academy of Arts and Sciences and the Society for Financial Econometrics (SoFiE), which he cofounded with Eric Ghysels.

*See also:* Granger, Clive

### Selected Works by Robert Engle

Engle, Robert. *Anticipating Correlations: A New Paradigm for Risk Management*. Econometric Institute Lectures. Princeton, NJ: Princeton University Press, 1999.

Engle, Robert. *ARCH: Selected Readings*. Advanced Texts in Econometrics. New York: Oxford University Press 1995.

Engle, Robert. "Prize Lecture: Risk and Volatility: Econometric Models and Financial Practice." Nobelprize.org. http://nobelprize.org/nobel_prizes/economics/laureates/2003/engle-lecture.html (accessed March 17, 2011).

Engle, Robert F., and Scott T. Weidman. *Technical Capabilities Necessary for Systemic Risk Regulation: Summary of a Workshop by National Research Council*. Washington, DC: National Academies Press, 2010.

Engle, Robert, and Halbert White, eds. *Cointegration, Causality, and Forecasting: A Festschrift in Honour of Clive W. J. Granger*. New York: Oxford University Press, 1999.

### Selected Works about Robert Engle

Engle, Robert F. "Autobiography." Nobelprize.org. http://nobelprize.org/nobel_prizes/economics/laureates/2003/engle.html (accessed March 17, 2011).

Bollerslev, Tim, Jeffrey Russell, and Mark Watson. *Volatility and Time Series Econometrics: Essays in Honor of Robert Engle*. New York: Oxford University Press, 2010.

Karier, Tom. "Robert Fry Engle III." In *Intellectual Capital: Forty Years of the Nobel Prize in Economics*, 272–74. Cambridge: Cambridge University Press, 2010.

*Carol Lynn Nute*

## FISCHER, STANLEY

Born: October 15, 1943, in Lusaka, Northern Rhodesia (now Zambia); American and Israeli; development economics, monetary policy; Major Work: *IMF Essays from a Time of Crisis* (2004).

Stanley Fischer became governor of the Bank of Israel in May 2005. From 2002 to 2005, Mr. Fischer served as vice chairman of Citigroup and president of Citigroup International. From 1994 to 2001, Stanley Fischer served as first deputy managing director of the International Monetary Fund, and was special adviser to the managing director in 2001 and 2002. In academia, Mr. Fischer was the Killian Professor and department chair of economics at Massachusetts Institute of Technology (MIT). Mr. Fischer also served the World Bank as vice president for development economics and chief economist from 1988 to 1990.

Stanley Fischer was born October 15, 1943 in Northern Rhodesia (Zambia). He earned his bachelor's and master's in economics at the London School of Economics from 1962 to 1966. In 1969, he earned his PhD in economics at MIT. He began his professional career at the University of Chicago as an assistant professor of economics. Fischer was a professor at the University of Chicago until 1973 when he returned to the MIT Department of Economics. He earned full professor in 1977. Fischer also held visiting professor positions at the Hebrew University in Jerusalem and Stanford's Hoover Institution.

As an author, Stanley Fischer has been widely published in development economics. He is also the coauthor of several textbooks and editor of several professional collections. In the market of college textbooks, he is the coauthor with Rudi Dornbusch and Richard Startz of *Macroeconomics*. He is also the coauthor of *Lectures in Economics* with Olivier Blanchard. With Rudiger Dornbusch and Richard Schmalensee, he coauthored *Economics* for McGraw-Hill.

Fischer has been editor for several selections of essays: *Securing Peace in the Middle East* in 1994 and *IMF Essays from a Time of Crisis* in 2004. He also authored *Indexing, Inflation, and Economic Policy* in 1986. From 1986 to 1994, Fischer served as editor of the *NBER Macroeconomics Annual*.

Mr. Fischer is a fellow of the Econometric Society and the American Academy of Arts and Sciences; a member of the Council on Foreign Relations, the G-30, and the Trilateral Commission; a Guggenheim fellow; and a research associate of the National Bureau of Economic Research. He has served on the boards of the Institute for International Economics, Women's World Banking, and the International Crisis Group, as well as on the international advisory board of the New Economic School, Moscow.

*See also:* Collier, Paul; Duflo, Esther; Sachs, Jeffrey

### Selected Works by Stanley Fischer

Fischer, Stanley. *IMF Essays from a Time of Crisis.* Cambridge, MA: MIT Press, 2004.
Fischer, Stanley. *Indexing, Inflation, and Economic Policy.* Cambridge, MA: MIT Press, 1986.
Fischer, Stanley, ed. *Securing Peace in the Middle East.* Cambridge, MA: MIT Press, 1994.
Fischer, Stanley, and Olivier Blanchard. *Lectures in Macroeconomics.* Cambridge, MA: MIT Press, 1989.
Fischer, Stanley, Rudi Dornbusch, and Richard Startz. *Macroeconomics,* 9th ed. New York: McGraw-Hill, 2004.

### Selected Works about Stanley Fischer

"Stanley Fischer." International Monetary Fund. http://www.imf.org (accessed January 2011).
"Stanley Fischer." http://www.iie.com/fischer/index.html (accessed January 2011).
"Stanley Fischer: The Israeli Economy." Bank of International Settlements. http://www.bis.org/review/r060620c.pdf (accessed January 2011).

*David A. Dieterle*

## FISHER, IRVING

Born: February 27, 1867, in Saugerties, New York; Died: April 29, 1947, in New York City; American; money, monetarism, inflation, interest, econometrics, index numbers; Major Works: "The Equation of Exchange, 1896–1910" (1911), "The Debt-Deflation Theory of Great Depressions" (1933).

Irving Fisher would shape the profession of economics. Irving early on showed a proclivity for mathematics and invention. His interest in mathematics was instrumental in making the study of economics more quantitative with a stronger mathematical foundation. Fisher developed and designed some of the first economic indexes—including the first weekly newspaper publication of a wholesale price index. His inventiveness would be manifested when he invented a rotary index card system, the Rolodex. Fisher died in 1947.

Irving Fisher was born on February 27, 1867, in Saugerties, New York. His father was a teacher and minister. Fisher went to Yale and studied a variety of topics, including science and philosophy. But his greatest concentrations were in the areas of mathematics and economics. He would receive his BA in mathematics in 1888. Despite there being no economics department at Yale, in 1891 Fisher was the first Yale student to receive a PhD in economics. As part of his dissertation, Fisher actually developed a price machine that used water and levers to show the circulation of money and capital throughout an economic system. Fisher would remain a member of the Yale faculty until his retirement in 1935.

It was Fisher's interest in mathematics that would help shape the profession. Through Fisher's influence, the study of economics became more quantitative with stronger mathematics-based research. Fisher is perhaps best known and remembered for two simple equations.

The first is the equation of exchange, which linked money supply to prices. It was well known that too much money led to rising prices. The relationship had been observed, commented on, and even exploited for centuries. What was missing was a sense of why and what constituted too much. Fisher would provide answers for those questions with his equation of MV = QP: money supply (M) multiplied by velocity (V) equals transactions (Q) times price level (P). The equation would tie the supply of money and its circulation to the production side of the economy—the exchange of goods and services at a price level. This equation has become instrumental in the development of modern central banking, and provides a foundation for the modern monetarist school.

Fisher's second important equation is the one that bears his name. The Fisher equation states that the nominal interest rate (the interest rate charged consumers or paid savers) is affected by the rate of inflation. By deducting the inflation rate from the nominal rate of interest, one can arrive at the real rate of interest to be paid. This is a truer measure of interest as it shows the amount of forgone real consumption that is necessary to service a debt. Thus only when inflation is zero is the nominal interest rate the same as the real interest rate. More importantly, this equation offers insights into how unanticipated inflation or deflation can impact the debtor-creditor relationship. Accelerating inflation can actually lower real interest rates below zero on longer-term debt bearing a fixed interest rate—effectively transferring wealth from the lender to the borrower. Likewise a significant reduction in inflation can result in the debtor paying a higher real rate of interest than was originally anticipated in an agreement. Thus it is the combination of the two equations that links price level changes to the perceived return on financial assets. This in turns becomes a factor in the boom-bust cycle.

This connection would manifest itself in his debt-deflation theory of the Great Depression. Fisher's debt-deflation theory was one of the first theories offered as a cause of the Great Depression. It would be discredited and discarded in favor of Keynes's view of the economy. Nevertheless, it is gaining favor once again as a tool for explaining the Great Recession that followed the collapse of the housing bubble in 2007.

Despite these important ideas, Fisher would unfortunately be remembered for some of his failures. Prior to the 1929 stock market crash and the onset of the Great Depression, Fisher was one of the best known and sought after economists in the United States. His pronouncements were as widely circulated as those of any other economist of his day. However, a few days before the crash, Fisher was assuring investors that stock prices were not overinflated but rather had reached a permanently high plateau. After the October crash, Fisher would spend the next few years trying to return a sense of confidence in the market, to no avail. He would lose a fortune, and when finally broke would sell his home to Yale University and rent it back from the school.

An early bout of tuberculosis made Fisher a lifelong advocate of healthy lifestyles. He was a vegetarian and a backer of Prohibition. He would also dedicate significant energy to the study and promotion of eugenics as well as being active in the movement.

Fisher was a cofounder of the American Econometrics Society in 1931 and its first president in 1932.

Irving Fisher died on April 29, 1947, in New York City.

*See also:* Friedman, Milton; Keynes, John Maynard; Tobin, James

**Selected Works by Irving Fisher**

Fisher, Irving. "The Debt-Deflation Theory of Great Depressions." *Econometrica* 1, no. 4 (1933): 337–57

Fisher, Irving. *Elementary Principles of Economics.* New York: Macmillan, 1912.

Fisher, Irving. "The Equation of Exchange, 1896–1910." *American Economic Review* (1911).

Fisher, Irving. "An International Commission on Cost of Living." *American Economic Review* (1912).

Fisher, Irving. *The Money Illusion.* New York: Adelphi, 1928.

Fisher, Irving. *The Nature of Capital and Income.* New York: Macmillan, 1906.

Fisher, Irving. *The Purchasing Power of Money: Its Determination and Relation to Credit, Interest and Crises.* New York: Macmillan, 1916.

Fisher, Irving. *The Rate of Interest.* New York: Macmillan, 1907.

Fisher, Irving. "A Remedy for the Rising Cost of Living: Standardizing the Dollar." *American Economic Review* (1913).

Fisher, Irving. *The Theory of Interest: As Determined by the Impatience to Spend Income and Opportunity to Invest It.* New York: Macmillan, 1930.

Fisher, Irving. "Will the Present Upward Trend of World Prices Continue?" *American Economic Review* (1912).

**Selected Works about Irving Fisher**

Allen, Robert Loring. *Irving Fisher: A Biography.* Hoboken, NJ: Wiley-Blackwell, 1993.

Fisher, Irving Norton. *My Father, Irving Fisher.* Chicago: Comet Press Books, 1956.

Formaini, Robert L. "Irving Fisher: Origins of Modern Central Bank Policy." Federal Reserve Bank of Dallas. *Economic Insights* 10, no. 1 (2005).

Thaler, Richard H. "Irving Fisher: Modern Behavioral Economist." *American Economic Review* (1997).

*Timothy P. Schilling*

# FOGEL, ROBERT

Born: July 1, 1926, in New York City; Died: June 11, 2013, in Oak Park, Illinois; American; cliometrics, economics theory, econometrics, Nobel Prize (1993); Major Works: *Railroads and American Economic Growth: Essays in Econometric History* (1964), *Time on the Cross: The Economics of American Negro Slavery* (1974), *Without Consent or Contract: The Rise and Fall of American Slavery* (1989), *Economic Growth, Population Theory, and Physiology: The Bearings of Long-Term Processes on the Making of Economic Policy* (1994).

Robert Fogel is an American economist historian and scientist. To Fogel, history, methodology, and economic theory are imperative for understanding the framework of institutions. Fogel is best known for being the leading advocate of cliometrics, a methodology of studying economic history that is the systematic application of economic theory, econometric techniques, and other formal or mathematical methods. This explains how items can be compared in terms of measurement as opposed to characteristics. In 1993 Fogel, with Douglass North, won the Nobel Prize in Economics for their work in cliometrics.

Robert William Fogel was born on July 1, 1926, in New York City. His parents were Jewish immigrants from Odessa in Russia. Even though they arrived penniless, Fogel's parents were able to save enough money to create several small businesses and encouraged their two sons to pursue education. Between 1932 and 1944, Fogel was educated at Stuyvesant High School, a public school that had attracted many gifted educators during the Depression. This atmosphere prepared him for a life in science. He attended Cornell University where he majored in history and minored in economics. He served as the campus president for a Communist organization, the American Youth for Democracy.

In 1948, he worked with the Communist Party as a professional organizer. By 1958, Fogel rejected communism and obtained his MA from Columbia University. By 1964, he received a PhD from Johns Hopkins University where he would later teach.

From his master's thesis, "The Union Pacific Railroad: A Case in Premature Enterprise" (1960), Fogel wrote his first work. The book focused on the economic public policy explaining how the building of the railroad went forward even though it was a young, unprofitable enterprise. Fogel asserted that government intervention was inevitable, leading to increasing issues in the government-business relationship. Fogel included an analysis of congressional debate bills prior to the acts of 1862 and 1864 to show that, even though government wanted to establish this rail line, there was great concern about how government ought to be involved, as this had not been government's normal role. Through the example of Union Pacific, Fogel showed the complex and unavoidable relationship between private investment and public economic policy.

In his first study involving cliometrics, Fogel wrote *Railroads and American Economic Growth: Essays in Econometric History* (1964). His purpose was to show, quantitatively, that the economic growth of the United States during the nineteenth century was minimal, despite the growth of railroads. The book consists of four separate yet connected essays: "The Interregional Distribution of Agricultural Products," "The Intraregional Distribution of Agricultural Products," "Railroads and the 'Take-Off' Thesis: The American Case," and "The Position of Rails in the Market for American Iron, 1840–1860: A Reconstruction." Fogel's arguments refuted the long-standing beliefs of the railroads' significant contribution to economic growth in the nineteenth century. Fogel asserts the railroad industry accounted for less than a 3 percent change in per capita income. Fogel had created a new series of outputs to demonstrate the ability to bring those estimates in conjunction with important issues and questions of the day. He brought to light counterfactual arguments such as what the world would be like if the railroad had not been invented. This helped changed the way historians would conduct research for future analysis.

Fogel's most controversial yet popular work is *Time on the Cross: The Economics of American Negro Slavery* (1989). This is a two-volume quantitative study of American slavery that was coauthored with Stanley Engerman. Originally, most economists had believed that slave labor was less efficient than free agricultural labor. However, once high-tech statistics and econometrics were calculated, the opposite was actually discovered. This resulted in new studies on the topic to show the real impact of this phenomenon. Fogel and Engerman argue that because the plantation owners rationally organized their production to maximize their profits, slavery was advantageous. In order to study slavery, demographics about the subject had to be examined because the health and longevity of slaves was a factor in measuring productivity.

This study led to another research project about the improvements in life expectancy from 1710 and beyond because the coauthors realized that little was known about the trends in mortality in the United States before the 1890s. Not only were the results of slavery on the southern economy controversial in itself, but the new methods Fogel and Engerman had used to determine it were also a topic of debate. Convincing his colleagues that using current technology to re-create the thousands of variables needed to interpret the old facts in new ways would take some time and patience.

Fogel won several National Science Foundation grants, a Ford Faculty research fellowship, a Fulbright grant, and the Exxon Educational Foundation grant. The National Institutes of Health have supported his research on life expectancy and aging over the past decade and a half. He was named the Indispensable Person in health research for his work on the economics of health and health care by the Alliance for Aging Research.

Fogel serves as the Charles R. Walgreen Distinguished Service Professor of American Institutions. He is also the director of the Center for Population Economics at the University of Chicago's Booth School of Business.

In 1993 Fogel, along with Douglass North, won the Nobel Prize in Economic Sciences.

Robert Fogel died on June 11, 2013, in Oak Park, Illinois.

*See also:* North, Douglass

## Selected Works by Robert Fogel

Fogel, Robert. *Economic Growth, Population Theory and Physiology: The Bearings of Long-Term Processes on the Making of Economic Policy*. Washington, DC: National Bureau of Economic Research, 1994.

Fogel, Robert. *The Escape from Hunger and Premature Death, 1700–2100: Europe, America, and the Third World*. New York: Cambridge University Press, 2004.

Fogel, Robert. *Forecasting the Cost of U.S. Health Care in 2040*. Washington, DC: National Bureau of Economic Research, 2008.

Fogel, Robert. *Railroads and American Economic Growth: Essays in Econometric History*. Baltimore: Johns Hopkins Press, 1964.

Fogel, Robert. *Three Phases of Cliometric Research on Slavery and Its Aftermath*. Chicago: R. W. Fogel, 1975.

Fogel, Robert. *The Union Pacific Railroad: A Case in Premature Enterprise*. Baltimore: Johns Hopkins Press, 1960.

Fogel, Robert. *Without Consent or Contract: The Rise and Fall of American Slavery.* New York: Norton, 1989.

Fogel, Robert, and Stanley L. Engerman. *Time on the Cross: The Economics of American Negro Slavery.* Boston: Little, Brown, 1974.

Fogel, Robert W., Roderick Floud, Bernard Harris, and Sok Chul Hong. *The Changing Body: Health, Nutrition, and Human Developments in the Western World since 1700.* New York: Cambridge University Press, 2011.

### Selected Works about Robert Fogel

Fishlow, Albert. *Quantitative Economic History: An Interim Evaluation. Past Trends and Present Tendencies.* Chicago: University of Chicago, Department of Economics and Graduate School of Business, 1970.

Lyons, John S., Louis P. Cain, and Samuel H. Williamson, eds. *Reflections on the Cliometric Revolutions: Conversations with Economic Historians.* New York: Routledge, 1980.

Miller, Joseph C., ed. *Slavery and Slaving in World History: A Bibliography.* Vol. 1, *1900–1991.* New York: M.E. Sharpe, 1977.

*Samantha Lohr*

## FRIEDMAN, MILTON

Born: July 31, 1912, in Brooklyn, New York; Died: November 16, 2006, in San Francisco, California; American; monetary policy, price theory, public policy, monetary history, Nobel Prize (1976); Major Works: *A Theory of the Consumption Function* (1957), *Capitalism and Freedom* (1962), *A Monetary History of the United States, 1867–1960* (1971).

Milton Friedman is considered one of the most influential economists of the twentieth century for his abilty to explain and defend the merits of free markets and individual freedom. Friedman was also considered the embodiment of the Chicago School of economics with an emphasis on monetary policy, free markets, and less government intervention. Friedman was instrumental in the economic policies of President Ronald Reagan and Prime Minister Margaret Thatcher. Milton Friedman won the Nobel Prize in Economics in 1976 and President Reagan honored him with the Presidential Medal of Freedom in 1988. Friedman died in 2006.

Milton Friedman was born in Brooklyn, New York, on July 31, 1912. Growing up in New Jersey in the home of immigrant Hungarian parents, young Friedman graduated from the public high school when he was 15, a month before his 16th birthday. He was destined for college, but the untimely death of his father during his senior year narrowed his college direction to Rutgers University. Financing his own education, along with a small scholarship, Friedman graduated from Rutgers University in 1832. Originally a mathematics major planning on becoming an acturary, he became interested in economics. Friedman graduated from Rutgers with double majors in mathematics and economics.

Encouraged to pursue graduate work in economics, Friedman accepted a scholarship to the University of Chicago. His early experiences at the University of Chicago framed his economics and research philosophies. During this time at the University of Chicago, he met the woman who would become his wife and lifelong

U.S. economist Milton Friedman, a champion of the free-market economy, has had a profound impact on twentieth-century economic thought through his many books and years of teaching. He was awarded the Nobel Prize in economics in 1976 for his contribution to understanding monetary policy. (University of Chicago News Office)

working professional partner, Rose. After one year at the University of Chicago, Friedman recieved a fellowship to Columbia University. Even though he returned to the University of Chicago after only one year at Columbia, he received his PhD in economics from Columbia in 1946.

In 1935, Friedman was recruited by his friend W. Allen Wallis to Washington, DC, to join him on the National Resources Committee. Friedman's role on the committee was to continue earlier work on a consumer budget study. It was this work on the consumer budget study that became the basis for one of the two key components for his later groundbreaking work, *Theory of the Consumption Function*.

In 1937, Friedman accepted a position with the National Bureau of Economic Research (NBER). At NBER he worked with Simon Kuznets, publishing *Incomes from Independent Professional Practice*. Kuznets and Friedman introduced the concepts of permanent and transitory income. They also initiated a debate among Washington bureaucrats asserting that the incomes of physicians were higher than dentists due to the monopoly power of physicians. For Friedman, this study also provided the second key component to his own later work on the consumption function.

Friedman continued his work in Washington during World War II. From 1941 to 1943, Friedman directed his efforts on tax policy at the U.S. Treasury. In 1943, he joined his friend Wallis again, this time at Columbia University applying his mathematical and statistical expertise on military tactics, design, and metals. After one year at the University of Minnesota, Friedman returned to the University of Chicago in 1946. He would remain at the University of Chicago till his retirement from active teaching in 1977. Another close friend, Arthur Burns, who was directing NBER, persuaded Friedman to rejoin NBER. Friedman remained with NBER till 1981.

In 1953, Friedman wrote "The Methodology of Positive Economics." He argued that the validity of economic theories should be based on the ability to predict human behavior. He followed this in 1957 with his classic, *A Theory of the Consumption Function*. Friedman's case was that it was necessary to think of individuals making rational spending and saving decisions over a lifetime. The basis was a return to his earlier work with Kuznets and the permanent-income hypothesis. His thesis in *A Theory of the Consumption Function* was also a return to classical economic thinking, which had been replaced in the middle of the twentieth century by the economic philosophies of John Maynard Keynes.

Friedman's launching of the Money and Banking Workshop at the University of Chicago set the academic and research foundation for his next target in economic research: monetary policy. The research and publications that originated from the workshop highlighted the Chicago School of economics' emphasis on the role of monetary policy as the key determinant to inflation and business cycles.

Friedman's work explaining the role of the money supply and monetary policy on an economy earned him an international reputation. His monetary policy theories were highlighted in 1969 with *The Optimum Quantity of Money and Other Essays*. The workshop provided the environment for many contributors and researchers to generate significant work on monetary policy. Through his work with the workshop and NBER, he began a collaboration with economic historian Anna J. Schwartz. In 1971, they wrote the classic *A Monetary History of the United States, 1867–1960*.

Another groundbreaking accomplishment in economic theory for Milton Friedman came when he suggested that the popular inflation-unemployment rate trade-off was not necessarily a long-run trade-off as most assumed. In 1967, while he acknowledged a short-run trade-off, he asserted that government intervention to keep inflation high to promote low unemployment would eventually fail, with ultimately both unemployment and inflation rising. This argument would later be proven correct in the 1970s and the ensuing period that became known as stagflation.

In 1976, Milton Friedman was awarded the Nobel Prize in Economics for his scientific work on consumption, monetary history, and stabilization policy. In 1988, Milton Friedman received both the Presidential Medal of Freedom from President Reagan and the National Medal of Science. Earlier in 1986 he had received the Japanese government's Grand Cordon of the First Class Order of the Sacred Treasure.

After his retirement from active teaching, he became involved in public affairs and public policy. He assisted presidential candidates Barry Goldwater, Richard Nixon, and Ronald Reagan as an economic adviser during their campaigns. He would later serve as an economic adviser to both presidents Nixon and Reagan. He also began writing columns for the popular news magazine *Newsweek* promoting the virtues of individual freedom and markets unfettered from government intervention.

In 1981, he served on President Reagan's Economic Policy Advisory Board. Friedman is given significant credit for the economic philosophies of President Reagan and Prime Minister Margaret Thatcher in the 1980s and later decades of the twentieth century. Friedman was viewed as the opposition to the popular theories of John Maynard Keynes that dominated economic thought and political economic policy from post–World War II through the 1970s.

Milton Friedman's popularity with the general public reached its pinnacle in 1980 with the release of the popular 10-part series, *Free to Choose*. Coauthored with his wife, Rose, the series was accompanied by a book of the same name. The book was the nonfiction bestseller in 1980, a rare occurrence for one with the high academic stature of Milton Friedman. Since its release, the series and book have been translated into 14 languages and the series can be seen in many foreign countries.

Milton Friedman concluded his career at the University of Chicago as the Paul Snowden Russell Distinguished Service Professor Emeritus of Economics. He also served the Hoover Institution at Stanford University as a senior research fellow.

Milton Friedman died on November 16, 2006, in San Francisco, California.

*See also:* Burns, Arthur; Keynes, John Maynard; Kuznets, Simon

## Selected Works by Milton Friedman

Friedman, Milton. *Capitalism and Freedom*. Chicago: University of Chicago Press, 1962.

Friedman, Milton. *Essays in Positive Economics*. Chicago: University of Chicago Press, 1966.

Friedman, Milton. *Money Mischief: Episodes in Monetary History*. Reprint ed. Orlando, FL: Harcourt Brace, 1991.

Friedman, Milton. *The Optimum Quantity of Money and Other Essays*. New York: Macmillan, 1969.

Friedman, Milton. *Price Theory*. Piscataway, NJ: Aldine, 1976

Friedman, Milton. *A Theory of the Consumption Function*. Princeton, NJ: Princeton University Press, 1957.

Friedman, Milton, Leonard J. Savage, and Gary Becker. *Milton Friedman on Economics: Selected Papers*. Chicago: University of Chicago Press, 2007.

Friedman, Milton, and Rose Friedman. *Free to Choose: A Personal Statement*. Orlando, FL: Harcourt, 1980.

Friedman, Milton, and Rose Friedman. *The Tyranny of the Status Quo*. Orlando, FL: Harcourt, 1984.

Friedman, Milton, and Anna Jacobson Schwartz. *A Monetary History of the United States, 1867–1960*. Princeton, NJ: Princeton University Press, 1971.

## Selected Works about Milton Friedman

Ebenstein, Lanny. *Milton Friedman: A Biography*. Basingstoke, UK: Palgrave Macmillan, 2007.

Ebenstein, Lanny. *The Indispensable Milton Friedman: Essays on Politics and Economics*. Washington, DC: Regnery, 2012.

Friedman, Milton. "Autobiography." Nobelprize.org. http://nobelprize.org/nobel_prizes/economics/laureates/1976/friedman-autobio.html (accessed March 20, 2011).

Friedman, Milton, and Rose Friedman. *Two Lucky People: Memoirs*. Chicago: University of Chicago Press, 1998.

Lindbeck, Assar, ed. *Nobel Lectures, Economics 1969–1980*, Singapore: World Scientific, 1992.

*David A. Dieterle*

## FRISCH, RAGNAR

Born: March 3, 1895 in Oslo, Norway; Died: January 31, 1973, in Oslo, Norway; Norwegian; econometrics, Nobel Prize (1969); Major Work: "Sur un problem d'economie pure" [On a problem in pure economics] (1926).

Ragnar Frisch was a pioneer in econometrics and a founding member of the Econometric Society. He is considered one of the founders of economics as a quantitative science. Frisch has been credited for coining the terms "econometrics," "microeconomics," and "macroeconomics." Frisch was the first to make the distinction between static and dynamic analysis. In collaboration with Frederick Waugh, the Frisch-Waugh theorem was developed. Frisch is most noted for his work on business cycles and large-scale econometric models on topics of economic planning and national income accounting. Frisch's other areas of economic research included business cycles, time series, and production theory. In 1969, Ragnar Frisch was the first recipient of the Nobel Prize in Economics, along with colleague Jan Tinbergen. Frisch died in 1973.

Ragnar Anton Kittil Frisch was born in Oslo, Norway, on March 3, 1895. His father was a successful silversmith in Oslo. As was customary, the family expected young Ragnar to continue in the family business. Yet with help from his mother, he began his studies in economics at the University of Oslo, even while continuing his silversmith apprenticeship. He graduated from Oslo University in 1919 and passed his apprenticeship exams in 1920. He returned to his father's business, becoming a partner with his father.

However, the academic world interrupted his silversmith career. In 1921, Frisch accepted a fellowship to Oslo University to study mathematics and economics in France and England. At the conclusion of his fellowship, Frisch's interest in continuing his academic studies saw an end to his career as a silversmith. In 1925, he began a teaching career at Oslo University. In 1926 he completed the requirements for the PhD in mathematics. Aside from a visiting professorship to Yale in 1930, he continued teaching at Oslo University till his retirement in 1965.

Following the publication of two articles about probability theory, his first article on one of the topics that would consume his career, the science of economics, came in 1926. In this article, Frisch argued the theoretical basis of economics should be as quantified as other sciences. He began his own initiative to this end later in 1926 when he published "Sur un problem d'economie pure." Frisch was a strong advocate of econometrics and mathematical tools as the way to an enhanced understanding of economics. He carried his initiative for a more mathematical economics foundation forward into his lectures on production theory.

In 1927, Frisch took his thesis to the United States when he accepted a fellowship from the Rockefeller Foundation. In the United States, he introduced his advanced mathematical and statistical economics methods. While in the United States, Frisch met Wesley Mitchell, who had published a book on business cycles. Mitchell adopted Frisch's notions and is credited for promoting Frisch. Following the unexpected death of his father and selling of the family business, Frisch published a series of articles on time series in 1927 and 1928.

When Frisch resumed his academic career, Oslo University promoted Frisch to associate professor of statistics and economics. He received full professor in 1931. In 1929, Frisch published his first essay implementing econometric modeling, "Correlation and Scatter in Statistical Variables." He followed that article with "Statics and Dynamics in Economic Theory," introducing economic analysis. In 1932, with funding from the Rockefeller Foundation, he launched the Institute of Economics at Oslo University, becoming its director of research. The institute was later named the Ragnar Frisch Center for Economic Research in his honor.

In 1933, Frisch and colleague Frederick Waugh presented a new view of the standard regression model. In what became known as the Frisch-Waugh theorem, they introduced an equivalency between how the coefficients in a standard regression model are determined.

Frisch continued his efforts promoting the quantitative foundations of economics when in 1930 he became one of the founders of the Econometric Society. The goal of the Econometric Society was to promote studies that bring together quantitative and theoretical economics so it is similar to the natural sciences. He was editor of *Econometrica*, the official journal of the Econometric Society, from 1933 to 1955. The Econometric Society honored Ragnar Frisch with the Frisch Medal. Named in his honor, the award is given every two years to the author of the best published paper in *Econometrica*.

After World War II, Frisch promoted quantitative analysis to address postwar global issues. He developed several planning and growth models that were used by the Norwegian government. He asserted that econometrics could be implemented to engage in rational investigation, evaluate moral outcomes, bring change, and be used as a prediction tool.

In 1969, Ragnar Frisch and Jan Tinbergen were awarded the first Nobel Prize in Economic Sciences. The award was bestowed on them for their pioneering work in econometrics. It was appropriate that the inaugural Nobel Prize recipient be a Norwegian economist. Prior to his Nobel honor, in 1961 the Accademia Nazionale dei Lincej awarded Frisch the Antonio Feltrinelli prize. Frisch was especially proud of this award as the Accademia was a very famous and ancient Italian society with Galileo as one of its early members.

Ragnar Frisch died on January 31, 1973, in Oslo, Norway.

*See also:* Tinbergen, Jan

## Selected Works by Ragnar Frisch

Frisch, Ragnar. "Correlation and Scatter in Statistical Variables." *Nordic Statistical Journal* 1 (1929): 36–102.

Frisch, Ragnar. *Economic Planning Studies*. New York: Springer, 1975.

Frisch, Ragnar. *New Methods of Measuring Marginal Utility* (1932). London: Porcupine Press, 1978.

Frisch, Ragnar. *The Occurrence Test*. Institute of Economics. Oslo: University of Oslo, 1952.

Frisch, Ragnar. *Planning for India: Selected Explorations in Methodology*. Kolkata, India: Asia, 1960.

Frisch, Ragnar. "Sammenhengen mellem primærinvestering og reinvestering" [The relationship between primary investment and reinvestment]. *Statsøkonomisk Tidsskrift* 41 (1927): 117–52.

Frisch, Ragnar. "Statikk og dynamikk i den økonomiske teori" [Statics and dynamics in economic theory]. *Nationaløkonomisk Tidsskrift* 67 (1929): 321–79.

Frisch, Ragnar. "Sur un problème d'économie pure" [On a problem in pure economics]. *Norsk Matematisk Forenings Skrifter* 1, no. 16 (1926): 1–40.

Frisch, Ragnar. *Theory of Production*. Skokie, IL: Rand McNally, 1965.

## Selected Works about Ragnar Frisch

Arrow, Kenneth J. "The Work of Ragnar Frisch, Econometrician." *Econometrica* 28, no. 2 (1960): 175–92.

Bjerkholt, Olav, and Ariane Dupont-Kieffer, eds. *Problems and Methods of Econometrics: The Poincaré Lectures of Ragnar Frisch, 1933*. New York: Routledge, 2009.

Bjerkholt, Olav, and Duo Qin, eds. *A Dynamic Approach to Economic Theory: The Yale Lectures of Ragnar Frisch*. New York: Routledge, 2010.

Frisch, Ragnar. "Ragnar Frisch—Autobiography." In *Nobel Lectures, Economics 1969–1980*. Edited by Assar Lindbeck, 6–9. Singapore: World Scientific, 1992.

Tinbergen, Jan. "Ragnar Frisch's Role in Econometrics: A Sketch." *European Economic Review* 5 (1974): 3–6.

*David A. Dieterle*

# G

## GAIDAR, YEGOR

Born: March 19, 1956, in Moscow, Union of Soviet Socialist Republics; Died: December 16, 2009, in Odintsovo, Moscow Oblast, Moscow, Russia; Russian; shock therapy, economist, diplomat; Major Work: *Collapse of an Empire: Lessons for Modern Russia* (2007).

Yegor Gaidar is considered the mastermind behind the controversial implementation of shock therapy to the Russian economic system following the dissolution of the Soviet Union. He favored rapid market liberalization to prevent a return to Stalinist economic practices. Gaidar helped draft the Belovezh Accords, which provided the framework for the dissolution of the Soviet Union. In the later years, his writings expressed concern for the lack of diversity in the modern Russian economy and fear that current economic policies will leave the state vulnerable to economic collapse. Gaidar died in 2009.

Yegor Timurovich Gaidar was born on March 19, 1956, in Moscow, Union of Soviet Socialist Republics. He came from a Bolshevik family. His grandfather, Arkady Gaidar, was a vice admiral in the Red Army and his father, Timur Gaidar, was a high-ranking officer in the Soviet Navy and foreign correspondent for the Soviet political newspaper *Pravda*.

Gaidar graduated from Moscow State University in 1978 with a degree in economics and completed his graduate studies in 1980. His graduate thesis, supervised by economist Stanislav Shatalin, explored the concept of price mechanism.

In 1980, Gaidar took a research position at the Academy of Sciences Institute of Systems Analysis at the Soviet Academy of Sciences. In 1983, he joined a commission advising General Secretary Yuri Andropov on economic reform. In 1987, he was made head of the economy section of the journal *Kommunist* and remained there until 1990 when he took the same position at *Pravda* where his father had been a foreign correspondent. The following year Gaidar briefly worked as head of the Institute of Economic Politics within the Soviet Academy of Sciences until the collapse of the Soviet Union.

Disillusioned with Soviet economic policies prior to the fall of the state, he argued that these policies were inefficient and posed a danger to the long-term economic interests and development of the Soviet Union. Most concerning to Gaidar was the financial support of the nonenergy sectors with energy revenues. Gaidar cautioned that because fluctuations in energy revenues have proven themselves volatile in the past, these policies would leave the entire Soviet economy vulnerable to instability. For Gaidar, the collapse of the Soviet economic system was not a question of if but of when and how.

Gaidar helped draft the Belovezh Accords, which officially dissolved the Soviet Union, establishing the Commonwealth of Independent States. With the establishment of the Russian state in 1991, Gaidar was appointed by Boris Yeltsin as minister of finance and economics assigned the task to reform the Russian economy. Gaidar claimed that Russia had two options: return to Stalinist-style economic policies or implement a free-market economy. He implemented a drastic economic program known as shock therapy. Shock therapy calls for an immediate and rapid liberalization of an economic market, opening space for free trade that would allow the market to set consumer prices. Understanding the potentially unfavorable consequences in the implementation of this program, Gaidar proclaimed himself a political kamikaze, prepared to sacrifice his political career should the program fail.

Gaidar posited that the shock would remedy the artificial values the previous Communist regime placed on goods and currency. Although he knew it would be uncomfortable in the short term, it was a necessary action for long-term Russian economic interests. The consequences of Gaidar's shock therapy included depleted savings accounts, massive bankruptcies, and empty food shelves. For the first time since prior to the Soviet Union, the nation was facing the possibility of mass starvation, riots, and revolution. Politicians and citizens blamed Gaidar for the economic crisis and the instability of the state's treasury.

With the passing of time, most Russian economists laud the bold decisions of Gaidar and now credit him with averting another Bolshevik-style revolution in Russia. Gaidar was elected to the Russian Duma as head of the Union of Right Forces in 1999. The Union of Right Forces was a party uniting most of Russia's fractured liberal leaders. Under immense pressures and duress, however, he resigned from the party in October of 2008.

In his postpolitical career, Gaidar was outspoken about modern Russian policies mimicking Soviet policies of the 1980s that led to the economic crisis of the early 1990s. In *Collapse of an Empire: Lessons for Modern Russia* (2007), Gaidar cautioned the modern Russian government that their economic policy of propping up nonenergy sectors with energy revenues, like the previous policies of the Soviet Union, would leave the Russian state vulnerable to energy market fluctuations. He prescribed strengthening nonenergy sectors of the economy to withstand the economic consequences if one sector would weaken.

Gaidar's criticisms of Russian policies were not without controversy. In a trip to Ireland, he excused himself from the stage shortly after beginning his speech and immediately collapsed in the hallway. His death was surrounded in conspiracy that the alleged 2006 poisoning contributed to his sudden 2009 illness and eventual death.

Gaidar died on December 16, 2009, in Odintsovo, a city located in the Moscow Oblast, at the age of 53 from a pulmonary edema.

*See also:* Engels, Friedrich; Marx, Karl; Sachs, Jeffrey

### Selected Works by Yegor Gaidar

Gaidar, Yegor. *Collapse of an Empire: Lessons for Modern Russia.* Washington, DC: Brookings Institution Press, 2007.
Gaidar, Yegor. *Days of Defeat and Victory.* Moscow: Vagrius, 1996 (English translation, 1999).
Gaidar, Yegor. *The Economics of Russian Transition.* Cambridge, MA: MIT Press, 2002.
Gaidar, Yegor. *State and Evolution: Russia's Search for a Free Market.* Seattle: University of Washington Press, 2003.
Gaidar, Y., and K. O. Pöhl. *Russia Reform/International Money.* Cambridge, MA: MIT Press, 1995.

### Selected Works about Yegor Gaidar

BBC World News. "Yegor Gaidar: The Price to Pay." Last modified December 16, 2009. http://news.bbc.co.uk/2/hi/8416497.stm (accessed August 2012).
Kavanagh, K., ed. *A Dictionary of Political Biography.* Oxford: Oxford University Press, 1998.
Millar, James R., ed. "Yegor Gaidar." *Encyclopedia of Russian History.* 4 vols. New York: Macmillan Reference USA, 2003.
Wilson, Dick. "On Yegor Gaidar." *Dissent Magazine*, Spring/Summer 2009.
"Yegor Gaidar." *The Economist.* http://www.economist.com/node/15125467 (accessed August 2012).
Yergin, D., and J. Stanislaw. *The Commanding Heights: The Battle for the World Economy.* New York: Free Press, 1998.

*Nevena Trajkov*

## GALBRAITH, JOHN KENNETH

Born: October 15, 1908, in Dunwich Township, Ontario, Canada; Died: April 29, 2006, in Cambridge, Massachusetts; American; general economics, economic policy; Major Works: *American Capitalism: The Concept of Countervailing Power* (1952), *The Great Crash of 1929* (1954), *The Affluent Society* (1958).

John Kenneth Galbraith was quite possibly the most widely read economist of the mid-twentieth century. He authored over 30 books. His most widely read, *The Affluent Society* published in 1958, became a popular read for the general population as well as academics. Galbraith is credited with penning economics phrases that are now part of the economics and political lexicon including conventional wisdom, countervailing power, and of course the affluent society. Galbraith was known for his writing style of addressing the economics topics and issues of the day as part of everyday life and not as an esoteric science. Galbraith died in 2006.

John Kenneth Galbraith was born on October 15, 1908, in Ontario, Canada, and raised on a small farm in Dunwich Township in Ontario. Of Scottish descent, his father was a farmer and schoolteacher who had a major influence on young Galbraith's early views of politics and his liberal philosophy. He attended Ontario Agricultural College (OAC), taking courses to be a farmer. While at OAC, he became more interested in the economics of farming than in farming itself. He completed his undergraduate work at the University of Toronto and went on to complete his

Perhaps the best known and most widely read of all U.S. economists, John Kenneth Galbraith is noted for his biting critiques of the American economy. (Getty Images)

master's and doctorate in agricultural economics at the University of California, Berkeley, in 1934.

Galbraith's writing notoriety started early in his academic career while at the University of California, Berkeley. This early success led him to Harvard where he joined the faculty as an instructor in 1934. In 1937, he received a fellowship to attend Cambridge University and study under John Maynard Keynes. During the Depression, the theories of Keynes were dominating both the economic and political landscapes. This one year under Keynes was to be the turning point in Galbraith's career. Yet he admits that his economic philosophy was also influenced by Thorstein Veblen.

Returning to Harvard from Cambridge, he remained at Harvard only one more year. In 1939, Galbraith joined the economics faculty at Princeton University. He also became an American citizen. However, with the outbreak of World War II, Galbraith joined President Roosevelt's administration, becoming an administrator in the Office of Price Administration. As administrator of wage and price controls, he gained a contentious reputation with industry. He resigned his post in 1943.

After holding various positions both in and out of government including a brief term as a writer for *Fortune* magazine, which introduced the United States to both John Maynard Keynes and his U.S. protégé, John Kenneth Galbraith, he returned to Harvard in 1949. This began what was to become his period of famous lectures and even more famous writings.

In 1952, Galbraith wrote *American Capitalism: The Concept of Countervailing Power*. In *American Capitalism*, he submitted the idea that U.S. economic power was concentrated between corporations on one side and unions on the other. These countervailing forces kept the U.S. economy in equilibrium. Also in 1952, Galbraith wrote *A Theory of Price Control*. In 1954, Galbraith wrote *The Great Crash of 1929*, suggesting that the same errors made in 1929 were being made in 1955. He went so far as to testify to the U.S. Senate that another "crash" was likely to occur.

His influence reached its zenith in 1958 when *The Affluent Society* was published. With *The Affluent Society*, Galbraith became a global success. He suggested that U.S. businesses had overproduced, leading consumers to overspend without thought to solving the social issues of the day. He went on to predict inflationary and recessionary dynamics with the overemphasis on private goods and with public goods being the trade-off.

One area where Galbraith was ahead of his time was in thinking about economic progress and its impact on the environment. He blamed advertising for frivolous spending at the expense of addressing environmental concerns as well as the social benefits to society. Along with several other writers of the 1950s, Galbraith began to change the public views of an economic system that would best suit a postwar United States.

Beyond his work in the Roosevelt administration, John Kenneth Galbraith also had a significant influence in the later political arena. An avowed political liberal, he was influential in shaping the ideas and views of the Democratic Party in the 1950s and 1960s. He advised presidential candidate Adlai E. Stevenson and eventual president John F. Kennedy on the Keynesian view of how to best deal with the economy. He was also instrumental in devising and promoting President Lyndon Johnson's Great Society program. During this period he was also a speechwriter for Roosevelt, Kennedy, and Johnson. Galbraith served as ambassador to India under President Kennedy.

John Kenneth Galbraith was not without his critics. As popular as he was with the general public, the economic academic community regarded his writings as often too simplistic to be highly regarded. Others regarded his blatant liberal political views as interfering with his economic objectivity. One area where his ideas were later disputed was advertising. As he submitted in *The Affluent Society*, he blamed advertising as the cause of an overly consumption-oriented economy. This notion was later countered by Nobel laureates Gary Becker and George J. Stigler using mathematical proofs that advertising was indeed informative to the consumer and not leading them to undesired consumption.

In 1967, Galbraith called for a new class of policy decision makers in *The New Industrial State*. In 1973, Galbraith wrote *Economics and the Public Purpose*. He called for an increase in central planning, socialism, increasing tax progressivity, more public housing and medical care, along with nationalizing some corporations who serve the federal government. In 2004 at the age of 95, Mr. Galbraith published *The Economics of Innocent Fraud*, a short book that questioned much of standard economic wisdom.

John Kenneth Galbraith received many awards, the most prestigious of which was the Medal of Freedom, which he received twice, first in 1946 from President Harry Truman and again in 2000 from President Bill Clinton. In 2001, Galbraith received India's Padma Vibhushan, its second-highest civilian award. In Canada, he was conferred the Officer of the Order of Canada in 1997 and in Dutton, Ontario, the library was renamed the John Kenneth Galbraith Reference Library. In 2010 posthumously, he was the first economist to have his popular works included in the Library of America series.

John Kenneth Galbraith died on April 29, 2006, in Cambridge, Massachusetts.

*See also:* Becker, Gary; Keynes, John Maynard; Stigler, George; Veblen, Thorstein

### Selected Works by John Kenneth Galbraith

Galbraith, John Kenneth. *The Affluent Society*. Boston: Houghton Mifflin, 1958.
Galbraith, John Kenneth. *American Capitalism: The Concept of Countervailing Power*. Boston: Houghton Mifflin, 1952.
Galbraith, John Kenneth. *The Good Society*. New York: Houghton Mifflin, 1996.
Galbraith, John Kenneth. *The Great Crash of 1929*. New York: Houghton Mifflin, 1954.
Galbraith, John Kenneth. *A Life in Our Times*. Boston: Houghton Mifflin, 1981.
Galbraith, John Kenneth. *The New Industrial State*. Boston: Houghton Mifflin, 1967.
Galbraith, John Kenneth. *The Scotch*. New York: Houghton Mifflin, 1964.
Galbraith, John Kenneth. *A Theory of Price Control*. Cambridge, MA: Harvard University Press, 1952.

### Selected Works about John Kenneth Galbraith

Parker, Richard. *John Kenneth Galbraith: His Life, His Politics, His Economics*. New York: Farrar Straus Giroux, 2005.
Stanfield, J. R. *John Kenneth Galbraith*. London: Macmillan, 1996.
Stanfield, J. R., and J. B. Stanfield. *Interviews with John Kenneth Galbraith*. Jackson: University Press of Mississippi, 2004.

*David A. Dieterle*

# GEORGE, HENRY

Born: September 2, 1839, in Philadelphia, Pennsylvania; Died: October 29, 1897, in New York City; American; political economy, editor, publisher, social reformer; Major Work: *Progress and Poverty: An Inquiry into the Cause of Industrial Depressions, and of Increase of Want with Increase of Wealth: The Remedy* (1886).

Henry George was a political economist who promoted the reforms of taxation and trade to benefit society as a whole. He developed his philosophy from his life experience without formal education or class privilege. His ideas were embraced by vast numbers of followers worldwide and are taught in "Georgist" schools of economics today. George argued that taxes and the government banking system favored the few at the expense of the masses and demanded social justice for citizens without regard to race and sex. He believed he had found a method of spreading wealth and dedicated his life to sharing it with the world. George died in 1897.

Henry George was born on September 2, 1839, to Richard S. H. George and Catherine Pratt Valliance George in Philadelphia, Pennsylvania. The second of 10 children, he quit school at 15 to work in an office and aboard a ship bound for India and Australia. He later wrote about seeing small numbers of wealthy Indians compared to the majority of citizens. Upon his return home, George learned to set type. When the printing business declined, he was hired to work aboard a ship sailing to California. When he arrived on the West Coast, he worked as a typesetter before joining his cousin's mining store in British Columbia on the Frazer River.

In 1858, his enthusiasm for gold prospecting waned and he returned to San Francisco. After a time of struggling financially, he found a job as a newspaper printer and writer. A speaker he heard on the topic of protectionism challenged his thinking about the negative impact of protectionism on individual prosperity. The editor of two small newspapers, George began to promote the benefits of free trade. The tariffs supported by protectionists kept prices for goods high. He saw that tariffs enriched a few at the expense of the majority. George found growing support for his viewpoint and was encouraged to run for a state office. He lost the election but was gaining a following for his ideas.

His writing promoted free trade, and then another idea stirred his conscience: land use reform. The common folks, barely eking out a living, outnumbered the few land speculators who were enriched by railroad and other developments. The seed of his best-known work, *Progress and Poverty*, began with a magazine article, published on September 18, 1877.

A year and a half later in 1879, George completed his first book and self-published the first 500 copies. The thesis of the book was that it was immoral to charge and collect rents on raw land that individuals had not created. George submitted that what nature provided could not be owned by individuals. People would own only what they themselves produced. George concluded that poverty was caused by the private ownership of land, which resulted in wealth for a small minority. He observed that land values depended on someone's need for the land and believed that this policy threatened democracy.

A single tax on land, not on improvements to land, was the only tax morally justified in George's view. He believed that all other taxes should be abolished and that since landowners did nothing to create the value of the land they owned, they should not extract increasingly higher rent from laborers. He concluded that the land's value was created by the need of someone to use it. Common workingmen found a hero in Henry George, and they rallied around him. Additional volumes of his book were printed and eventually sales surpassed all other volumes except for the Bible. At 42 years old, George became world famous and a popular public speaker on the topic of political economy. Europeans and Australians invited him to speak.

Renowned European economist Alfred Marshall debated George, who was considered a leader inspiring great societal changes beyond the United States. Proponents of land reform arose, empowered by the Henry George movement. He was warmly welcomed by the British and the Irish working class and social reformers. The well-known scientist Alfred Russell Wallace touted the significance of *Progress and Poverty*. George's public policy influences were popular as far away as Australia and New Zealand.

Politicians and union leaders desired his affiliation. The United Labor Party, a sector of Democrats who opposed the Tammany Hall political machine, supported his candidacy for mayor of New York City in 1886. They presented a petition signed by over 30,000 New Yorkers that helped convince George to run. He lost to Democrat Abram Stevens Hewitt and beat Republican Theodore Roosevelt.

Although George was maligned as a Socialist and a Communist, he participated in political campaigns to spread his message and appeal for broadened support of his ideology. As editor of the New York-based paper *The Standard*, George continued to educate the populace about the morality of his brand of economics. He published *The Condition of Labor*, *The Science of Political Economy*, and *Protection or Free Trade*, which became a part of the Congressional Record of 1890.

He used every opportunity to spread his message, traveling and debating.

In George's final campaign for mayor of New York, in 1897, he represented his former affiliation, renamed the Party of Thomas Jefferson. He was in poor health but decided to press on. The campaign would allow him to influence more people to consider his views on economic practices that he was convinced would alleviate the suffering of the impoverished.

Henry George's ideas are still discussed and debated today. In many cities, Schools of Henry George exist to continue teaching his philosophy of economics. Because he was one of the common folk with no formal education and no influential family, and because of his moral basis to fight for equality, justice, and fairness, the appeal of his policies endures.

Henry George died days before the election on October 29, 1897, in New York City.

*See also:* Marshall, Alfred

## Selected Works by Henry George

George, Henry. *The Condition of Labor: An Open Letter to Pope Leo XIII*. New York: United States Book, 1891.

George, Henry. *The Land Question*. New York: Doubleday, Page, 1912.

George, Henry. *Progress and Poverty: An Inquiry into the Cause of Industrial Depressions, and of Increase of Want with Increase of Wealth: The Remedy*. New York: D. Appleton, 1886.

George, Henry. *Protection or Free Trade*. New York: Doubleday, Page, 1886.

George, Henry, Francis Amasa Walker, William Saunders, and Francis George Shaw. *Social Problems, A Perplexed Philosopher*. New York: Doubleday, Page, 1911.

## Selected Works about Henry George

Cottler, Joseph. *Champions of Democracy*. Boston: Little, Brown, 1936.

Formaini, Robert L. "Henry George Antiprotectionist Giant of American Economics." *Economic Insights* 10, no. 2 (2005):1–4.

George de Mille, Agnes. "Who Was Henry George?" http://www.progress.org/books/george.htm (accessed March 30, 2011).

"Labour Land Campaign." Australian School of Social Science. http://www.labourland.org/lvt/what_is_lvt.php (accessed March 30, 2011)

Post, Louis. *The Prophet of San Francisco*. Honolulu, HI: University Press of the Pacific, 1904 (reprinted by the Minerva Group, 2002).

*Cynthia Blitz Law*

# GRANGER, SIR CLIVE

Born: September 4, 1934, in Swansea, Wales; Died: May 27, 2009, in San Diego, California; Welsh; financial economics, Nobel Prize (2003); Major Work: "Co-integration and Error Correction: Representation, Estimation, and Testing" (with Robert Engle III, 1987).

Sir Clive Granger was a Welsh-born economist whose career spanned from Nottingham, Wales, to San Diego, California. He finished his career as the professor emeritus at the University of California, San Diego. Professor Granger specialized in using applied statistics and time series analysis in economics. In 2003, Clive William John Granger was awarded the Nobel Prize with Robert Engle. The two were cited for their fundamental discoveries in the analysis of time series data. Their contribution to economics changed how economists analyzed financial and macroeconomic information and data. Granger died in 2009.

Clive William John Granger was born in Swansea, Wales, on September 4, 1934. His parents moved the family to England where he grew up. While in his early school years, Granger exhibited an interest and talent in mathematics. At the University of Nottingham, Granger received his BA and PhD, both in mathematics specializing in statistics. Interested in times series analysis as a graduate student, Granger began his professional interests early.

Only 23, Granger joined the University of Nottingham faculty as a junior lecturer in 1956. In 1959, after receiving his PhD, Granger accepted a Harkness fellowship from the Commonwealth Fund to attend Princeton University and participate in the Econometric Research Project of Oskar Morgenstern. His first book resulted from this work in 1964, *Spectral Analysis of Economic Time Series* with Michio Hatanaka. An article published in *Econometrica* in 1966 based on the same research introduced new methods in time series analysis. His paper in 1969 published in *Econometrica* introduced his concept of Granger causality. The Granger causality test is a statistical hypothesis test to determine whether onetime series are useful for forecasting. Granger argued that a set of tests could reveal causality.

Granger's interest expanded to forecasting in 1968. In 1977, he and his postdoctoral student Paul Newbold wrote a book that became a standard in series forecasting. The two later wrote a second paper, which led to a reevaluation of at the time accepted methods of empirical and economic methodology.

In 1974, Granger began the second phase of his career when he accepted a position at the University of California, San Diego (UCSD). Although a new academic environment, Granger's research on time series continued, now collaborating with colleague Robert Engle along with several other UCSD colleagues. It was, however, his work with Engle on developing the concept of cointegration that brought the most recognition. In 1987, they published a paper on cointegration titled "Co-Integration and Error Correction: Representation, Estimation, and Testing" in *Econometrica*, which resulted in their Nobel Prize in 2003. Cointegration, briefly defined, involved several variables combining to create a joint variable that would return to a long-run static point. The use of this joint variable then allows more traditional statistical and forecasting methods to be used.

Granger's major contribution focused on the relationships between different financial or economic variables over time. His work addressed the idea that traditional statistical methods could be misleading if the variables vary at different times without some return to a long-run static point.

In Granger's later career, he used time series methods to work on the Amazon rain forest, building a deforestation forecast model. He published those results in 2002. He also was a visiting eminent scholar at the University of Melbourne and Canterbury University.

Along with being recognized with the Nobel Prize, Granger also was awarded the honor of knight bachelor by Queen Elizabeth II in 2005. Granger was a fellow of the Econometric Society and a corresponding fellow of the British Academy. In 2004, he was voted into the 100 Welsh Heroes. In 2005, the building housing the economics and geography departments at the University of Nottingham was named the Sir Clive Granger Building in honor of his receiving the Nobel Prize.

Sir Clive Granger died on May 27, 2009, in San Diego, California.

*See also:* Engle, Robert

### Selected Works by Sir Clive Granger

Engle, Robert F., and C. W. J. Granger. "Co-Integration and Error Correction: Representation, Estimation and Testing." *Econometrica* 55, no. 2 (1987): 251–76.

Granger, Clive. "An Introduction to Long-Memory Time Series Models and Fractional Differencing." *Journal of Time Series Analysis* 1 (1980): 15–30.

Granger, Clive, and Michio Hatanaka. *Spectral Analysis of Economic Time Series*. Princeton, NJ: Princeton University Press, 1964.

Granger, Clive, and Oskar Morgenstern. *Predictability of Stock Market Prices*. Lexington, MA: Heath, 1970.

Granger, Clive, and Paul Newbold. *Forecasting Economic Time Series*. Salt Lake City, UT: Academic Press, 1977.

### Selected Works about Sir Clive Granger

Frängsmyr, Tore. "Clive W. J. Granger: The Sveriges Riksbank Prize in Economic Sciences in Memory of Alfred Nobel 2003." In *Les Prix Nobel*. Stockholm: Nobel Foundation, 2004.

Granger, C. W. J., L. Andersen, E. Reis, D. Weinhold, and S. Wunder. *The Dynamics of Deforestation and Economic Growth in the Brazilian Amazon*. Cambridge: Cambridge University Press, 2002.

Harms, Philipp. "Interview." *Study Center Gerzensee Newsletter*, July 2003.

O'Connor, Anahad. "Clive Granger, Economist, Dies at 74." *New York Times*. http://www.nytimes.com/2009/05/31/business/31granger.html (accessed January 2011).

Phillips, Peter C. B. "The ET Interview: Professor Clive Granger." *Econometric Theory* 13 (1997): 253–303.

*David A. Dieterle*

# GREENSPAN, ALAN

Born: March 6, 1926, in New York City; American; monetary policy, chairman of the Federal Reserve System, 1987–2006; Major Work: *The Age of Turbulence: Adventures in a New World* (2007).

Alan Greenspan served an unprecedented five terms as chairman of the Federal Reserve System (the Fed). While chairman, he experienced the stock market crash of 1987, fallout from the savings and loan (S&L) scandal, a record increase in the market, followed by the bursting of the dot-com and housing bubbles. He is a fiscal conservative, believing in free-market economics. He believes in creative destruction, that is, allowing some companies to fail, freeing resources for newer companies.

Alan Greenspan was born in Washington Heights, New York City, on March 6, 1926. He received training at the Juilliard School in 1943 (clarinet) before enrolling at New York University (NYU) in 1944, receiving his bachelor of science (1948) and master of arts (1950). His pursuit of a PhD from NYU was interrupted by his work experience, but he would earn the degree in 1977.

Greenspan began his career in 1950 with the National Industrial Conference Board. He would gain political attention for his research of the Defense Department's use of metal, twice published in the *Business Record*. In 1953, he formed a partnership with William Townsend called the Townsend-Greenspan

Alan Greenspan in the Board of Governor's room in Washington, DC, where he served as chairman of the Federal Reserve from 1987 to 2006, an unprecedented five terms. (AP/Wide World Photos)

Company. During this time he met Objectivist and author Ayn Rand. He was greatly influenced by her views. He would write several articles in the 1960s for Rand's *The Objectivist Newsletter* and she would include essays by him in her collection called *Capitalism: The Unknown Ideal*.

Greenspan's first political post was in 1967, working as a volunteer economic and domestic policy adviser for Richard Nixon's 1968 presidential campaign. He worked on the Commission on an All-Volunteer Armed Force that worked to abolish the draft in 1970. Just before President Nixon resigned in 1974, Greenspan became chairman of the Council of Economic Advisers, serving as an economic adviser to the president. He remained on the council through Gerald Ford's administration, helping to devise policies to fight inflation and unemployment. In 1980, he helped Ronald Reagan's campaign. He served on the Economic Policy Board and later worked to overhaul Social Security.

President Reagan appointed Greenspan chairman of the Fed in 1987. He inherited a national situation that had seen vast increases in the stock market and a tripling of the federal deficit under Reagan, plus an increase in inflation, measured by the Consumer Price Index (CPI). When he increased interest rates in September 1987, the stock market experienced its largest single-day drop (508 points) on Black Monday, October 19. The Fed responded by buying billions of dollars of treasury securities (increasing liquidity), encouraging lending by the Fed's member banks. The markets began to stabilize by November and growth resumed in the first quarter of 1988.

Greenspan continued his role as chairman of the Fed into the George H. W. Bush administration, though his relationship with the president was more strained under a difficult economy. Greenspan worked with the Resolution Trust Corporation to resolve issues with the S&L scandals of the late 1980s, which resulted in the federal government being saddled with about $87 billion in losses, less than expected. The recession continued into the 1990s despite the Fed lowering interest rates. The administration wanted rates cut lower, but Greenspan believed that the short-term benefit would quickly lead to a long-term inflation problem. Bush reappointed Greenspan as chairman of the Fed in 1991.

Under President Clinton, Greenspan encouraged passage of a 1993 budget that would begin to reverse the trend of steadily rising national debt. Greenspan believed this was necessary to encourage businesses to invest more and allowed the Fed to lower rates to sustain long-term growth. Following pressure by Congress to allow more transparency, Greenspan agreed to announce immediate moves of the Federal Open Market Committee. The Fed raised interest rates a quarter point in 1994 as a preemptive strike against inflation, the first increase in five years. The stock market would grow amid the dot-com boom of the late 1990s and Greenspan warned of irrational exuberance in investing. He believed the boom would not last long. Clinton reappointed Greenspan in 1996 and 2000 under a strong economy. As the dot-com bubble was bursting in 2000, Greenspan believed that the growing surplus of the federal budget should be used to pay down the national debt and that "triggers" should be implemented to prevent a reversal in the surplus.

Under George W. Bush, following the attack on 9/11 and in response to recession, the Fed cut interest rates several times to stimulate the economy. Greenspan disagreed with the president's plans to continue to cut taxes to stimulate the economy, figuring it was more important to control the deficit, and was displeased with the president's unwillingness to veto spending bills.

Greenspan is often criticized for politicizing the Fed. Despite being a libertarian Republican, he often praised both parties when they acted in a fiscally conservative manner. He also received criticism for the economic downturn of the 2000s, with many claiming his monetary policy was too lax. Since finishing his record fifth term as Fed chairman, Greenspan has accepted some fault for the problems related to the economy that could be linked to the Fed.

*See also:* Burns, Arthur; Volcker, Paul

## Selected Works by Alan Greenspan

Greenspan, Alan. *The Age of Turbulence: Adventures in a New World.* New York: Penguin Press, 2007.

Greenspan, Alan. *A History of the Federal Reserve, 1913–1951.* Vol. 1. Chicago: University of Chicago Press, 2004.

## Selected Works about Alan Greenspan

Kahaner, Larry. *The Quotations of Chairman Greenspan: Words from the Man Who Can Shake the World.* Holbrook, MA: Adams Media, 2000.

Martin, Justin. *Greenspan: The Man behind the Money.* Cambridge, MA: Perseus Books, 2001.

Sheehan, Frederick. *Panderer to Power: The Untold Story of How Alan Greenspan Enriched Wall Street and Left a Legacy of Recession.* New York: McGraw-Hill, 2010.

Woodward, Bob. *Maestro: Greenspan's Fed and the American Boom.* New York: Simon & Schuster, 2000.

*Joseph Lee Hauser*

## HAAVELMO, TRYGVE

Born: December 13, 1911, in Skedsmo, Norway; Died: July 28, 1999, in Oslo, Norway; Norwegian; economic forecasting, econometrics, and economics theory, Nobel Prize (1989); Major Works: "The Statistical Implications of a System of Simultaneous Equations" (1943), "The Probability Approach in Econometrics" (1944).

Trygve Haavelmo was a pioneer in the field of economic forecasting, introducing mathematical-statistics methods to economic analysis and breaking ground for a new area of economics research. He is noted for establishing econometrics as a separate science. Trygve Haavelmo was awarded the Nobel Prize in Economics in 1989. Haavelmo died in 1999.

Trygve Magnus Haavelmo was born on December 13, 1911, in Skedsmo, Norway. He received his undergraduate degree in political economy in 1933 and his PhD in economics in 1946, both from the University of Oslo. In 1933, while a graduate student in economics at Oslo, he went to work for Ragnar Frisch (winner of the Nobel Prize, 1969) at the Frisch Institute for approximately four years. The institute had obtained a grant from the Rockefeller Foundation, and its students, assistants, and others worked on mathematical-statistical experiments and empirical studies research. Haavelmo was involved in a number of Frisch's empirical studies, and this foundational research had a great influence on him. He briefly taught statistics at the University of Aarhus (1938–39). It was Haavelmo's use of statistics to forecast economic trends that would later lead to the development of the subfield of econometrics by Frisch.

Haavelmo was in the United States when World War II began and remained there for six and a half years. While in the United States, Haavelmo received a Rockefeller Foundation fellowship (1940–42) and became a student, though unregistered. He visited and studied at a number of universities including Princeton, Harvard, and University of California, Berkeley. Unable to return to Norway due to the war, he delivered his dissertation at Harvard in 1941 under the title "On the Theory and Measurement of Economic Relations." He later changed the title to "The Probability Approach in Econometrics," which was later published in 1944 in the American periodical *Econometrica*. It was this work and another ("The Statistical Implications of a System of Simultaneous Equations," also published by *Econometrica* in 1943) that would become his two most significant works noted in his 1989 Nobel Prize announcement.

These works by Haavelmo, an avid outdoorsman and pipe smoker, founded econometrics as a separate discipline. The first contended that economic development is determined by the interaction of a multitude of economic relations and that economic laws are not strictly rigorous, while the second studied the effects of the statistical impact of simultaneity in economic models. During his final four years in the United States, Haavelmo worked for Nortraship in New York, the Norwegian government in Washington, DC, and briefly for one year for the Cowles Commission in Chicago.

He returned to Norway in 1947 where he worked for a year at the Norwegian Economic Planning Administration. Haavelmo later became a professor of economics and statistics at his alma mater, the University of Oslo, from 1948 until his retirement in 1979. As a professor, Haavelmo began to research economic theory. It was his skill in statistical methods that would lead to bridging the gap between theory and data in economics. The "Haavelmo distribution" as some authors call it noted that the joint distribution of all the observable random variables for the entire sample period is what matters. He also felt it was important to establish the statistical adequacy of a statistical model before using the associated statistical results. Another methodological approach he incorporated was to select a statistical model in view of both the theory and the structure of the data so that the set of priori admissible theoretical models could be narrowed down.

During his time at Oslo, Haavelmo wrote two books. The first, *A Study in the Theory of Economic Evolution* (1954), was a study of the possible reasons for economic underdevelopment of a country in relation to other countries. His second, *A Study in the Theory of Investment* (1960), introduced theories on the demand for real capital and on lethargy in the adjustment of real capital. Both of these works pioneered additional research, numerous theories, and empirical studies. He was also the president of the Econometric Society in 1957. Haavelmo also studied economics from an environmental perspective.

Trygve Haavelmo died on July 28, 1999, in Oslo, Norway.

*See also:* Frisch, Ragnar

### Selected Works by Trygve Haavelmo

Haavelmo, Trygve. "Multiplier Effects of a Balanced Budget." *Econometrica* 14, no. 2 (April 1946): 156–58.

Haavelmo, Trygve. "The Probability Approach in Econometrics." *Econometrica* 12, Suppl. (July 1944): iii–vi, 1–115.

Haavelmo, Trygve. "The Role of the Econometrician in the Advancement of Economic Theory." *Econometrica* 26, no. 3 (July 1958): 351–57.

Haavelmo, Trygve. "The Statistical Implications of a System of Simultaneous Equations." *Econometrica* 11, no. 1 (January 1943): 1–12.

Haavelmo, Trygve. *A Study in the Theory of Economic Evolution*. Amsterdam: North Holland, 1954.

Haavelmo, Trygve. *A Study in the Theory of Investment*. Chicago: University of Chicago Press, 1960.

### Selected Works about Trygve Haavelmo

Economics Institute. "LN-11 Trygve Haavelmo from Frisch's Laboratory to Cowles Commission." University of Oslo. http://www.uio.no/studier/emner/sv/oekonomi/ECON4950/v11/undervisningsmateriale/LN-11%20Presentation-1.pdf (accessed July 2011).
Haavelmo, Trygve. "Autobiography." Nobelprize.org. http://nobelprize.org/nobel_prizes/economics/laureates/1989/haavelmo-bio.html (accessed June 2011).
Vane, Howard R., and Chris Mulhearn. *Trygve Haavelmo, James J. Heckman, Daniel L. McFadden, Robert F. Engle and Clive W. J. Granger*. London: Edward Elgar, 2009.

*Carol Lynn Nute*

## HABERLER, GOTTFRIED VON

Born: July 20, 1900, in Purkersdorf, Vienna, Austria-Hungary (now in Austria); Died: May 6, 1995, in Washington, DC; Austrian; Major Works: *The Theory of International Trade* (1933), *Prosperity and Depression* (1937).

Gottfried von Haberler was an Austrian-born economist, best known for being a proponent of free-market principles in national economic policies and international trade. Particularly during the 1930s and 1940s, he was a vocal critic of government intervention in the economy, in spite of this having gained favor as a response to the worldwide depression. Haberler died in 1995.

Gottfried von Haberler was born on July 20, 1900, in Purkersdorf, Vienna, Austria. He entered the University of Vienna in 1918, receiving his bachelor's degree in 1925. He continued his education at the University of Vienna, earning doctorates in law and economics. While living in Austria in the 1920s and 1930s, he was a member of the Mises-Kreis, a circle of economists, sociologists, and philosophers who regularly participated in private seminars. This group, organized by the Austrian economist Ludwig von Mises, is considered an important formative influence in Haberler's life.

While in Vienna during the 1920s, Haberler worked as a librarian at the Chamber of Commerce. Ludwig von Mises also worked at the Chamber of Commerce, as an economist. After studying in England and the United States, he taught economics and statistics at the University of Vienna from 1928 to 1936. He also worked as a consultant to the League of Nations in Geneva, Switzerland, for two years.

His first book, *The Meaning of Index Numbers* (1927), was an Austrian work that showed that statistical aggregates hide the essential relative price relationships in the market. His second book, *The Theory of International Trade* (1931), included a refutation of protectionism and demonstrated Haberler's belief that international trade can provide high living standards and economic efficiency. "Money and the Business Cycle" was presented at the University of Chicago in 1932. The paper is an exposition of the Austrian theory of the trade cycle. It analyzes the Federal Reserve's (the Fed) attempt to stabilize price levels and argues that the Fed's actions helped contribute to the Great Depression.

Haberler's most important contributions to economic theory are in the areas of business cycles and international trade. In 1933, he presented a modern reformulation of the argument from classical economics that free trade and international division of labor maximize social productivity and the standard of living for all nations participating.

Haberler moved to the United States and taught at Harvard University as a professor in economics from 1936 to 1971. He became well known primarily for his scholarship on international trade, and his major work, *The Theory of International Trade* (1933), is considered a classic in economics. An important notion was his reformulation of the theory of comparative costs in terms of opportunity cost. He introduced the production substitution curve—now known as the production possibility frontier—which provided a framework for analyzing the effects of multiple variables in the process of production. This led to other findings in the area of international trade.

In an early revised edition of his book *Prosperity and Depression* (1937), Haberler included a critique of the Keynes theory of the liquidity trap. Haberler's argument held that prices are more flexible than Keynes suggested. This theory became well known and was to be called the "Pigou effect."

In a 1937 study, published and sponsored by the League of Nations, Haberler surveyed existing literature on business cycle theory and constructed his own analysis of the causes and nature of cyclical phenomena. In this study, he included emphasis on the role of changes in the supplies of money and credit, combined with price and wage-rate rigidities imposed by government interventions in the market process.

Haberler repudiated his earlier support for an international gold standard in the early 1950s. At that time, he began to advocate a system of national fiat currencies linked to one another by flexible exchange rates. When describing the issue of stagflation, which became an economic issue during the 1970s, he identified the political pressure exerted by unions, for the purpose of maintaining high wages, as the initiating cause of inflationary recession.

Haberler is also known for having broadened the mathematical basis for the theory of comparative advantage. Theories of comparative advantage try to identify the benefits countries may gain from free trade, taking into consideration the possibility that one country's costs may be higher than the other for a given product.

Following his retirement from Harvard as Galen L. Stone Professor of International Trade in 1971, Haberler became a resident scholar at the American Enterprise Institute, a research group that focuses on free-market approaches to public policy issues.

Gottfried von Haberler died on May 6, 1995, in Washington, DC.

*See also:* Keynes, John Maynard; Mises, Ludwig von; Pigou, A.C.

## Selected Works by Gottfried von Haberler

Haberler, Gottfried von. *Inflation, Its Causes and Cures: With a New Look at Inflation*. Washington, DC: American Enterprise Institute for Public Policy Research, 1966.

Haberler, Gottfried von. "Money and the Business Cycle." In *Gold and Monetary Stabilization*. Edited by Quincy Wright, 43–77. Chicago: University of Chicago Press, (1932).

Haberler, Gottfried von. *Prosperity and Depression*. Geneva: League of Nations, 1937.
Haberler, Gottfried von. *A Survey of International Trade Theory*. Princeton, NJ: Princeton University Press, 1961.
Haberler, Gottfried von. *The Theory of International Trade*. Translated by Alfred Stonier and Friedrich Benham. London: William Hodge, 1933.

**Selected Works about Gottfried von Haberler**

Baldwin, Robert E. "Gottfried Haberler's Contributions to International Trade Theory and Policy." *Quarterly Journal of Economics* 97 (1982): 141–48.
Bradsher, Keith. "Gottfried Haberler, Resolute Free-Market Economist, Dies at 94." *New York Times*, May 9, 1995. http://www.nytimes.com/1995/05/09/obituaries/gottfried-haberler-resolute-free-market-economist-dies-at-94.html (accessed November 2011).
Ebeling, Richard. "Between Mises and Keynes: An Interview with Gottfried von Haberler (1900–1995)." *The Austrian Economics Newsletter* 20, no. 1 (2000).
Ebeling, Richard. "Gottfried Haberler, RIP." *Free Market* 13, no. 7 (1995). http://mises.org/freemarket_detail.aspx?control=238&sortorder=authorlast (accessed February 2012).
Gillis, Malcolm. "Gottfried Haberler: Contributions upon Entering His Ninth Decade." *Quarterly Journal of Economics* 97 (1982): 139–40.
Koo, Anthony K. C. *Selected Essays of Gottfried Haberler*. Cambridge, MA: MIT Press, 1986.
Salerno, Joseph T. "Biography of Gottfried Haberler (1901–1995)." Ludwig von Mises Institute. http://mises.org/about/3232 (accessed February 2012).

*Diane Fournier*

# HARROD, SIR ROY

Born: February 13, 1900 in London, England; Died: March 9, 1978, in Holt, Norfolk, England; English; Keynesian, macroeconomics; Major Works: *Towards a Dynamic Economics* (1948), "Price and Cost in Entrepreneurs Policy" (1939), "Essay in Dynamic Theory" (1939).

Sir Roy F. Harrod is known as a pioneer in the economics of dynamic growth, emphasizing the importance of determining the factors to economic growth rather than the quantities of equilibrium growth rates. Harrod developed his ideas in collaboration with U.S. economist E. D. Domar; their work is now known as the Harrod-Domar model of economic growth. Their model has been applied to the problems of economic development. Harrod administered and taught economics at Christ Church, Oxford. He is also noted for his work on inductive logic, his role on the Statistical Staff and as personal adviser to Winston Churchill during World War II, and his unofficial service to Harold MacMillan when he was prime minister. He was knighted in 1959. Harrod was a close colleague of John Maynard Keynes, whose official biography he published in 1951. Harrod died in 1978.

Henry Roy Forbes Harrod was born on February 13, 1900, in London, England. Having parents who were both educated and writers, he was given the opportunity to study at New College in Oxford where he majored in classic literature, ancient history, and philosophy. Harrod spent a term at King's College, Cambridge, where he came in contact with John M. Keynes. Keynes had a great influence on his scientific research on economic problems. Harrod's career at Christ Church,

Oxford, was interrupted by World War II service (1940–42) under Frederick Lindemann (later Lord Cherwell) as an adviser to Winston Churchill.

Harrod was most productive following World War II when his contributions to the theory of economics reached its peak. Harrod's first major accomplishment was the publication of his theory of growth in *Towards a Dynamic Economics* (1948). This publication drew on the concepts of growth dynamics he had developed in the 1930s and 1940s, and it later became known as the Harrod-Domar model. In essence, Harrod demonstrated that abrupt changes in specific economic variables can have long-term effects. For example, he showed that if savings were permanently high, there was a positive impact on long-term investment prospects. His main innovation was to suggest that there is a "warranted" rate of growth, or an equilibrium growth path that would achieve greatest prosperity and equilibrium across an economy. The Harrod-Domar model suggests that there is no natural reason for an economy to have balanced growth. It was the precursor to the exogenous growth model.

Another of Harrod's valuable contributions to economic theory is his extensive work on the theory of the firm with the publication of his important articles "Price and Cost in Entrepreneurs' Policy" (1939) and "Essay in Dynamic Theory" (1939). In these articles, he asserted that entrepreneurs' goals are best served by seizing the largest possible market share, setting prices so low as to deter competition and avoid overcapacity, and thereby maximizing profits in the long run. These conclusions are different from those suggested by the book *Oxford Studies in the Price Mechanism* (1951), which concluded that entrepreneurial decisions on future investments are not determined by the interest rate to any material degree and seek the added margin considered adequate for their average or total production costs, rather than maximum profits.

Harrod developed his contribution to the international monetary theory and money theory during World War II and the postwar period. In his 1969 *Money*, he discussed his view of the role of money in a market economy and analyzed individual monetary theories. He argued that the use of money as the means of exchange has consequences for macroeconomic trends. When money is used as the means of exchange, it becomes necessary to analyze changes in the money supply in terms of larger trends, not just in terms of microeconomic categories (like the production costs of gold or silver).

In the area of international monetary relations, Harrod's contribution caught the attention of the professional community in the aftermath of World War II. In collaboration with Keynes, he called for the establishment of special institutions that would, in one way or another, coordinate the development of the world financial system. These ideas led to the birth of the Bretton-Woods system, the International Monetary Fund, and the World Bank.

In his work on the inflation theory, Harrod advocated an increase in the price of gold in order to increase international liquid assets. In his book *Reforming the World's Money* (1965), he concluded that the price of gold is the key problem due to its inability to keep up with growth of other prices; therefore he advocated a major increase in the price of gold in order to avert a possible international monetary crisis.

In addition to his interest in postwar-era economics, Harrod had a keen interest in the problems of economic growth in Great Britain. Harrod was a fervent opponent of the elimination of import barriers, which he believed would restrict Britain's market and hinder its entry into the common European market. Unlike other renowned Keynesians, he insisted on the need to keep inflation low in order to keep control of cost inflation, which he considered the critical inflation component in Great Britain. In defense of this view, he published *Towards a New Economic Policy* (1967).

Harrod died on March 9, 1978, in Holt, Norfolk, England.

*See also:* Arrow, Kenneth; Galbraith, John Kenneth; Keynes, John Maynard

## Selected Works by Sir Roy Harrod

Harrod, Roy. "An Essay in Dynamic Theory." *Economic Journal* 49 (1939): 14–33.

Harrod, Roy. "Imperfect Competition, Aggregate Demand and Inflation." *The Economic Journal* 82, no. 325, Special Issue: In Honour of E. A. G. Robinson (March 1972): 392–401.

Harrod, Roy. *The Life of John Maynard Keynes*. London: Macmillan, 1951.

Harrod, Roy. "Price and Cost in Entrepreneurs' Policy." *Oxford Economic Papers* 2 (May 1939): 1–11.

Harrod, Roy. *Towards a Dynamic Economics: Some Recent Developments of Economic Theory and Their Application to Policy*. London: Macmillan, 1948.

Harrod, Roy. *Towards a New Economic Policy*. Manchester, UK: Manchester University Press, 1967.

Harrod, Roy. *The Trade Cycle: An Essay*. Oxford: Oxford University Press, 1936.

## Selected Works about Sir Roy Harrod

Ahmad, Syed. "Harrod on Domar's Theory of Growth." *The Economic Journal* 71 (1961): 449–51.

Besomi, Daniele. *The Making of Harrod's Dynamics*. New York: St. Martin's Press, 1999.

Besomi, Daniele. "Roy Harrod and Traditional Theory." *The European Journal of the History of Economic Thought* 4 (1997): 92–115.

Besomi, Daniele. "On the Spread of an Idea: The Strange Case of Mr. Harrod and the Multiplier." *History of Political Economy* 32 (2000): 347–79.

Brown, Henry Phelps. "Sir Roy Harrod: A Biographical Memoir." *The Economic Journal* 90 (1980): 1–33.

"Roy F. Harrod." In *The Concise Encyclopedia of Economics*. Edited by David R. Henderson. The Library of Economics and Liberty. http://www.econlib.org/library/Enc/bios/Harrod.html (accessed February 2012).

"Roy F. Harrod." The School of Cooperative Individualism. http://www.cooperativeindividualism.org/harrodbio.html (accessed February 2012).

Tatemoto, Masahiro. "Sir Roy F. Harrod on Internal and External Balances." *International Economic Review* 1 (1960): 217–22.

Weintraub, E. Roy. "Roy F. Harrod and the Interwar Years." *History of Political Economy* 37 (2005): 133–55.

*Ninee Shoua Yang*

## HARSANYI, JOHN

Born: May 29, 1920, in Budapest, Hungary; Died: August 9, 2000, in Berkeley, California; Hungarian-American; game theory, utilitarian ethics, Nobel Prize (1994); Major Work: *Games with Incomplete Information Played by Bayesian Players: The Basic Model* (1967).

John Harsanyi is best known for his contributions to the economic field of game theory. Game theory uses mathematics to predict outcomes in areas of labor negotiations, international political situations, and price wars. He contributed to game theory by explaining how to construct games where players have incomplete information; these became known as Bayesian games. His work in game theory has been used widely to explore real-life conflicts in business, management, and international relations. He won the Nobel Memorial Prize in Economics in 1994, sharing it with John F. Nash and Reinhard Selten. Harsanyi died in 2000.

John Charles Harsanyi was born on May 29, 1920, in Budapest, Hungary, to Catholic parents of Jewish ancestry. Although baptized Catholic and a lifelong practicing Catholic, Harsanyi was still considered a Jew by the authorities. After graduating from the prestigious Lutheran Gymnasium high school and winning the countrywide high school mathematical competition, he wanted to study mathematics and philosophy. However, he decided to work as a pharmacology student in order to defer his military service. He worked in his father's pharmacy and earned a degree in pharmacy in 1944 from University of Budapest. When Hungary was occupied in March 1944, the German army sent him to serve in a labor unit. During transportation he escaped and found refuge in the cellar of a Catholic Jesuit monastery until the war ended. He later learned that his friends in the labor unit who did not escape were killed at the concentration camp.

After World War II ended, Harsanyi returned to the University of Budapest and earned his PhD in psychology and sociology. He taught briefly at the Institute of Sociology at the University of Budapest, where he met Anne Klauber, a student who later became his wife. Harsanyi was forced to quit his teaching post because of his strong and outspoken anti-Marxist views. Concerned about his safety and academic future under communism in Hungary, he and Anne illegally escaped to Austria, crossing the border through an unguarded marshy area. After several months in Austria, they secured an Australian immigration permit. They arrived in Sydney, Australia, on December 30, 1950, and got married on January 2, 1951.

In Australia, Harsanyi's Hungarian degrees were not recognized so he worked manual-labor jobs while attending the University of Sydney. Fascinated by the mathematical aspects of economics, Harsanyi earned a master's degree in economics in 1953. He became a lecturer in economics at the University of Queensland in Brisbane and wrote significant papers on game theory. At the time, game theory was virtually unknown in Australia, and Harsanyi felt isolated from other game theory contributors. Importantly, Harsanyi won a Rockefeller fellowship, allowing him to come to the United States in 1956 to earn a PhD in economics from Stanford University. He wrote his dissertation on game theory working under the supervision of Kenneth Arrow, a future Nobel recipient.

After receiving his Stanford degree, Harsanyi's student visa expired and he returned to teach at the Australian National University in Canberra from 1958 to 1961. With the help of colleagues, he returned to the United States and taught at Wayne State University in Detroit from 1961 to 1963. Harsanyi accepted a visiting professorship at University of California, Berkeley, Haas School of Business in 1964 and was appointed to full professor in 1965 where he remained until his retirement in 1990. He also held a joint appointment in the Economics Department beginning in 1966.

Another area of interest for Harsanyi was moral philosophy. He promoted utilitarianism, or the thesis that utility accounts for moral goodness. In other words, actions are morally good insofar as they bring about the greatest happiness for the greatest number of people. His contributions continue to be essential to the understanding, development, and utilization of game theory in social, economic, and political competitive situations.

John Harsanyi was awarded the Nobel Prize in 1994 with John Nash and Reinhard Selten for their work on game theory. Harsanyi was also a member of the National Academy of Sciences, a fellow of the American Academy of Arts and Sciences and the Econometric Society, and a distinguished fellow of the American Economic Association.

John C. Harsanyi died on August 9, 2000, of a heart attack in Berkeley, California.

*See also:* Arrow, Kenneth; Nash, John; Selten, Reinhard

## Selected Works by John Harsanyi

Harsanyi, John. *Essays on Ethics, Social Behavior, and Scientific Explanation.* Dordrecht, Netherlands: D. Reidel, 1976.

Harsanyi, John. "Games with Incomplete Information Played by Bayesian Players I: The Basic Model." *Management Science* 14 (1967): 159–82.

Harsanyi, John. "Games with Incomplete Information Played by Bayesian Players II: Bayesian Equilibrium Points." *Management Science* 14 (1968): 320–34.

Harsanyi, John. "Games with Incomplete Information Played by Bayesian Players III: The Basic Probability Distribution of the Game." *Management Science* 14 (1968): 486–502.

Harsanyi, John. *Papers in Game Theory.* Dordrecht, Netherlands: D. Reidel, 1982.

Harsanyi, John. *Rational Behavior and Bargaining Equilibrium in Games and Social Situations.* Cambridge: Cambridge University Press, 1977.

Harsanyi, John C., and Reinhard Selten. *A General Theory of Equilibrium Selection in Games.* Cambridge, MA: MIT Press, 1988.

## Selected Works about John Harsanyi

Breit, William, and Barry T. Hirsch. *Lives of the Laureates: Eighteen Nobel Economists.* 4th ed. Cambridge, MA: MIT Press, 2004.

Harsanyi, John C. "Autobiography." Nobelprize.org. http://www.nobelprize.org/nobel_prizes/economics/laureates/1994/harsanyi-autobio.html (accessed April 2012).

Harsanyi, John C., Anne Klauber and Marion Ross. *Nobel Laureate John Harsanyi: Oral History Transcript: From Budapest to Berkeley, 1920–2000.* Charleston, SC: Nabu Press, 2000.

"John Harsanyi." In *The Concise Encyclopedia of Economics*. Edited by David R. Henderson. The Library of Economics and Liberty. http://www.econlib.org/library/Enc/bios/Harsanyi.html (accessed April 2012).

Scheib, Ariel. "John Harsanyi." Jewish Virtual Library. http://www.jewishvirtuallibrary.org/jsource/biography/harsanyi.html (accessed April 2012).

Selten, Reinhard. *Rational Interaction: Essays in honor of John C. Harsanyi*. Berlin: Springer, 1992.

University of Berkeley Haas School of Business. "Nobel Laureate John C. Harsanyi, UC Berkeley Economist and Game Theory Pioneer, Dies at 80." http://www.haas.berkeley.edu/news/harsanyi.html (accessed April 2012).

*Jean Kujawa*

## HAYEK, FRIEDRICH VON

Born: May 8, 1899, in Vienna, Austria; Died: March 23, 1992, in Freiburg, Germany; Austrian, naturalized English citizen; economic theorist, trade cycle theory, monetary theory, credit policy, Nobel Prize (1974); Major Works: *Profits, Interest and Investment* (1939), *The Pure Theory of Capital* (1941), *The Road to Serfdom* (1944), *The Constitution of Liberty* (1960).

Friedrich von Hayek was one of the most influential economists of the twentieth century. He not only made many important theoretical contributions in his field but blazed new paths in political theory, history, philosophy, and theoretical psychology as well. His acceptance of the Nobel Prize in Economics in 1974 was for his penetrating work during the 1920s and 1930s in the area of business and trade cycle theory and the effects of monetary and credit policy. Hayek's prodigious output and legacy have helped to revived interest and respect in Austrian and neo-Austrian economics. Hayek died in 1992.

Friedrich August von Hayek was born May 8, 1899 in Vienna, Austria, the eldest of three sons of August von Hayek and Felicitas née von Juraschek, Hayek. Not only was Hayek's father a medical doctor and later a professor of botany at the University of Vienna, but his brothers Heinz and Erich were later to become Austrian professors as well of anatomy and chemistry, respectively. In 1917, at the age of 19, Hayek served in an Austro-Hungarian artillery battery on the Italian front during World War I. After the war, Hayek entered the University of Vienna, receiving his doctorate in law in 1921 and a second doctorate in political economy in 1923. At university, Hayek attended the *Privatseminars* of Ludwig von Mises, later leading to a lifelong friendship and association. After attending New York University as a postgraduate research student in 1923–24, Hayek returned to Vienna and joined Mises at the temporary *Abrechnungsamt*, or Office of Accounts, as a legal consultant. In 1927, with Hayek as its first director, he and Mises founded the Austrian Institute for Business Cycle Research in Vienna. In 1928, invited to a London Conference on Economic Statistics, Hayek met John Maynard Keynes for the first time. They would later become friends as well as fierce intellectual critics of each other's economic positions.

In 1929, Hayek was appointed to his first academic post as a privatdozent in economics and statistics at the University of Vienna and authored his first book

During the last half of the twentieth century, the free-market, limited-government philosophy of Austrian economist Friedrich von Hayek stood in stark contrast to the theories of John Maynard Keynes. (Bettmann/Corbis)

entitled *Geldtheorie und Konjunkturtheorie*, published in 1933 in English as *Monetary Theory and the Trade Cycle*. Seeing a connection between business cycles, and capital and monetary theory, Hayek saw the market as an unplanned, spontaneous order that coordinates the activities of all factors of production. Lionel Robbins invited Hayek to speak at the London School of Economics in 1931, leading to Hayek's publication of *Prices and Production* that explained in greater detail his theory of underconsumption. Artificial increases in the money supply by central banks led Hayek to conclude that distortions between short- and long-term interest rates could create only "mal-investment." In that same year, Hayek assumed the Tooke Chair as professor of economic science at the London School of Economics, a position that he held for 19 years. Between 1931 and 1937, Hayek was engaged in a number of anti-Keynesian critiques and essays, culminating in his 1938 work entitled *Collectivist Planning: Critical Studies on the Possibilities of Socialism*. He never, however, waged nor planned a full-scale refutation of *The General Theory of Employment, Interest and Money*, something he regretted later in life. In 1938, he became a naturalized British citizen. During these years, his most significant works included: *Profits, Interest and Investment* (1939); *The Pure Theory of Capital* (1941), which delved into the complex nature of capital as it relates to economic booms and slumps; *The Road to Serfdom* (1944); and *Individualism and Economic Order* (1948). There was no work that took Hayek and the publishing industry more by surprise than *The Road to Serfdom*. Its unlikely success put Hayek back into the spotlight, warning his readers how the "ideal" of planning popular in Great Britain at the time could quickly turn into a totalitarian nightmare. Originally intended for a British audience, the condensed *Reader's Digest* version gained him an audience in the United States and established him as the world's most celebrated classical liberal economist. In 1947 following the devastation of World War II, Hayek, anxious to revive classical liberalism in Europe, convened the first meeting of like intellectuals at Mont Pèlerin in the Swiss Alps, known later as the Mont Pèlerin Society.

In 1950, Hayek was appointed professor of social and moral science and member of the Committee on Social Thought at the University of Chicago. Over the next 12 years, Hayek produced some of his best and most diverse writings. These included: *John Stuart Mill and Harriet Taylor: Their Friendship and Subsequent Marriage* (1951), *The Counter-Revolution of Science: Studies on the Abuse of Reason* and *The Sensory Order* (1952), *Capitalism and the Historians* (1954), and *The Constitution of Liberty* (1960), published on the 100th anniversary of the publication of John Stuart Mill's *On Liberty*. In this work, Hayek developed his view of the proper role of government, and his famous essay, "Why I Am Not a Conservative," was placed in the postscript.

In 1962, after 31 years out of his native Austria, Hayek left the University of Chicago and assumed a professorship at Freiburg University. In 1967, he published *Studies in Philosophy, Politics, and Economics*, dedicated to the philosopher Karl Popper. This work, unlike earlier studies, highlighted Hayek's outstanding breadth of intellectual knowledge. Although fighting ill-health and irrelevance, Hayek published the first volume of his trilogy *Law, Legislation and Liberty: Rules of Order* in 1973.

In 1974, reinvigorated after being awarded, along with Swedish economist Gunnar Myrdal, the Nobel Prize, he completed the final two volumes of *Law, Legislation and Liberty*, subtitled *The Mirage of Social Justice* (1976) and *The Political Order of a Free People* (1979). By the late 1970s, as inflation ravaged the industrialized world and standard Keynesian prescriptions appeared to be ineffective, Hayek again found himself in great demand after 30 years, speaking extensively about free-market solutions to packed lecture halls throughout the world. Approaching the age of 90, Hayek wrote his final book entitled *The Fatal Conceit: The Errors of Socialism* (1988). This strong critique of socialism would nearly coincide with the dissolution in 1989 of the former Soviet superstructure that was based on a collectivist foundation.

Friedrich von Hayek died on March 23, 1992, in Freiburg, Germany, at the age of 93.

*See also:* Keynes, John Maynard; Mill, John Stuart; Mises, Ludwig von; Myrdal, Gunnar; Robbins, Lionel

### Selected Works by Friedrich von Hayek

Hayek, Friedrich von. *The Constitution of Liberty*. London: Routledge, 1960.
Hayek, Friedrich von. *The Fatal Conceit*. Chicago: University of Chicago Press, 1988.
Hayek, Friedrich von. *Profits, Interest and Investment and Other Essays on the Theory of Industrial Fluctuations*. London: Routledge, 1939.
Hayek, Friedrich von. *The Pure Theory of Capital*. London: Jarrold and Sons, 1941.
Hayek, Friedrich von. *The Road to Serfdom*. Chicago: University of Chicago Press, 1944.

### Selected Works about Friedrich von Hayek

Caldwell, Bruce. *An Intellectual Biography of F. A. Hayek*. Chicago: University of Chicago Press, 2004.
Ebenstein, Alan. *Friedrich Hayek: A Biography*. New York: St. Martin's Press, 2001.
Ebenstein, Alan. *Hayek's Journey*. New York: Palgrave Macmillan, 2003.
Hayek, F. A. *Hayek on Hayek: An Autobiographical Dialogue*. Edited by Stephen Kresge and Leif Wenar. Chicago: University of Chicago Press, 1994.

*Joseph A. Weglarz*

## HAZLITT, HENRY

Born: November 28, 1894, in Philadelphia, Pennsylvania; Died: July 8, 1993, in Fairfield, Connecticut; American; economics, literary criticism; Major Works: *A New Constitution Now* (1942), *Economics in One Lesson* (1946), *The Failure of the "New Economics": An Analysis of the Keynesian Fallacies* (1959).

Henry Hazlitt was a journalist, writer, public intellectual, and determined supporter of free market and Austrian economics. Over his career, he wrote for several of the United States' leading newspapers and magazines, proving to be an eloquent expositor of the sometimes arcane arguments of his classical liberal heroes. Henry Hazlitt was a rare personality in the field of economics, having never earned a college degree. Nevertheless, he had an amazing talent for clearly and persuasively communicating complex ideas. Hazlitt died in 1993.

Henry Stuart Hazlitt was born November 28, 1894 in Philadelphia, Pennsylvania. His father, Stuart Hazlitt, died shortly after Henry was born. He was sent to Girard College, which was (and still is) a home and school for disadvantaged children. His mother remarried when he was nine, and the family moved to Brooklyn, New York. Henry sought to attend university to become a psychologist, but financial considerations led him to attend night classes at City College. Though the tuition was free, taking classes came with an opportunity cost. When his mother's second husband died, he quit college to support her.

Initially, Hazlitt went from job to job unable to stay employed. In 1915 at the age of 20, he got a job with the *Wall Street Journal* as a stenographer. At about the same time he wrote his first book, *Thinking as a Science*. In 1916, he joined the *New York Evening Post*. He served in World War I with the Army Air Services and when the war ended he went back to being a newspaper columnist.

Hazlitt's most enduring work is *Economics in One Lesson*. The lesson itself is only five pages long and is explained in the chapter "The Lesson." He asserts that economics can be reduced to a single sentence. The art of economics consists in looking not merely at the immediate but at the longer effects of any act or policy, tracing the consequences of a policy to the consequences to all groups. The rest of the book proceeds to show how a lack of thinking through the side effects of policies impacts all kinds of real-life situations. He was critical of minimum wage laws, government price fixing, protectionism, stimulus spending, and make-work programs. He goes on to explain the role of prices and profits in coordinating economic activity, writing that the economy is like a giant machine made up of thousands of smaller machines. Each machine has its own self-correcting mechanisms and tampering with the machine risks jamming or breaking it.

As an adherent of the Austrian School of economic thought, he deplored inflation. He became friends with Ludwig von Mises, who was a fugitive from Nazi-dominated Austria. Mises had experienced the post–World War I hyperinflation in Austria firsthand, and he promoted the view that inflation was a greater evil than unemployment—an opinion that was difficult to sell in an era when the United States was suffering from the Great Depression and the accompanying deflation. Hazlitt was one of Mises's few supporters at the time. Through Hazlitt, Mises's anti-Keynesian, anti-inflation, and pro-free-market views appeared in the nation's newspapers every week.

Hazlitt's uncompromising support for free enterprise occasionally got him into trouble with his editors. Throughout the 1930s, Hazlitt used his column to criticize the New Deal. In the 1940s, his target became the Bretton Woods conference, a post–World War II effort to create a global money system based on the U.S. dollar. He regarded it as inflationary, and wrote as much in the *New York Times*. His editor indicated that Hazlitt was embarrassing the *Times* by writing against Bretton Woods when 43 governments were in favor of it. Hazlitt departed soon after this incident for employment at *Newsweek*.

By the end of his life, Hazlitt had written and edited for the *New York Evening Mail*, the *New York Sun*, *The Nation*, the *New York Times*, and *Newsweek*. He was also instrumental with start-up journals such as *The American Mercury* and *The Freeman*. He was a prolific author, writing 18 books over the course of his life in addition to thousands of newspaper and magazine articles. Not limiting himself to economics, he also wrote book reviews and literary critiques.

Henry Hazlitt died on July 8, 1993, in Fairfield, Connecticut, at the age of 98.

*See also:* Hayek, Friedrich von; Mises, Ludwig von

## Selected Works by Henry Hazlitt

Hazlitt, Henry. *Economics in One Lesson*. New York: Harper & Brothers, 1946.
Hazlitt, Henry. *The Failure of the "New Economics": An Analysis of the Keynesian Fallacies*. Princeton, NJ: Van Nostrand, 1959.
Hazlitt, Henry. *The Foundations of Morality*. Princeton: NJ: Van Nostrand, 1964.
Hazlitt, Henry. *Man vs. the Welfare State*. New Rochelle, NY: Arlington House, 1969.
Hazlitt, Henry. *A New Constitution Now*. New York: Whittlesey House, McGraw-Hill, 1942.
Hazlitt, Henry. *A Practical Program for America*. Binghamton, NY: Books for Library Press, 1932.

Hazlitt, Henry. *Thinking as a Science.* New York: Dutton, 1916.
Hazlitt, Henry. *The Way to Will-Power.* New York: Dutton, 1922.
Hazlitt, Henry. *What You Should Know about Inflation.* Princeton, NJ: Van Nostrand, 1960.

### Selected Works about Henry Hazlitt

Greaves, Bettina Bien. "Remembering Henry Hazlitt." The Freeman: Ideas on Liberty. http://www.thefreemanonline.org/features/remembering-henry-hazlitt/.
Hazlitt, Henry. "An Interview with Henry Hazlitt." Ludwig von Mises Institute. August 31, 1983. http://mises.org/journals/aen/aen5_1_1.asp (accessed February 2012).
LewRockwell.com. "Henry Hazlitt." http://www.lewrockwell.com/archives/fm/9-93.html (accessed April 2012).
Rockwell, Llewellyn H., Jr. "Biography of Henry Hazlitt (1894–1993)." Ludwig von Mises Institute. http://mises.org/page/1453/Biography-of-Henry-Hazlitt-18941993 (accessed February 2012).
Uchitelle, Louis. "Henry Hazlitt, 98, a Journalist Who Concentrated on Economics." *New York Times.* http://www.nytimes.com/1993/07/10/obituaries/henry-hazlitt-98-a-journalist-who-concentrated-on-economics.html?scp=1&sq=Henry%20hazlitt&st=cse (accessed April 2012).

*Stephen H. Day*

## HECKMAN, JAMES

Born: April 19, 1944, in Chicago, Illinois; American; labor economics, econometrics, Nobel Prize (2000); Major Work: *Handbook of Econometrics* (2007).

James Heckman is another in a long line of University of Chicago professors who were recipients of the Nobel Prize in Economics, winning the prize in 2000. Earlier, Heckman also received the John Bates Clark Medal in 1983. Heckman is one of the preeminent econometricians in economics. His economic models focus on a variety of economic topics: life cycle skill, inequality, behavioral, labor, social programs, income distribution, and regulation.

James Joseph Heckman was born on April 19, 1944, in the Hyde Park area of Chicago. Growing up in Chicago and Kentucky, Heckman attended high school in the Denver area of Lakewood. While in high school he was introduced to the distinguished experimental physicist Frank Oppenheimer. A cattle rancher in Colorado, Oppenheimer introduced Heckman to physics, experimental science, and linking theory and evidence. Heckman has credited this relationship and these early experiences as a major experience in his intellectual development. Even though he moved on to economics in favor of physics, his ability to bring theory and evidence was to serve him well in the field of econometrics.

Heckman's interest in economics was spawned at Colorado College reading the works of Adam Smith and David Ricardo, and Paul Samuelson's *Foundations of Economic Analysis.* Heckman completed his doctoral work at Princeton University in 1971 and began his career at Columbia University. While at Columbia, Heckman was invited to join the National Bureau of Economic Research (NBER). Heckman was in his intellectual element at NBER, surrounded by a group of high-powered empirical scholars. The empirical environment was very exciting to a young Heckman. At NBER he was able to hone his econometric skills; data and theory were the priority for all the scholars at NBER. Heckman's research career and topics were formed during his time at NBER and Columbia.

In 1973, Heckman left Columbia and returned to the place of his birth, accepting an offer to return to Chicago and joining the faculty at the University of Chicago. Heckman found the environment at the University of Chicago intellectually stimulating and demanding. During his career at the University of Chicago, he developed a prestigious list of collaborators at the university for both research and publishing, directing the University of Chicago's Economics Research Center and the Center for Social Program Evaluation at the Harris Graduate School of Public Policy Studies. Heckman also holds the Henry Schultz Distinguished Service Professor in Economics endowed chair. In addition, Heckman is the professor of science and society in University College Dublin and a senior research fellow at the American Bar Foundation. In 1991, the American Bar Foundation approached Heckman to research the impact of law on the economy.

While Heckman had many areas of research, one area that received public attention was his work on early childhood education. At NBER, Heckman took a special interest in researching the investments in early childhood programs and impact of such programs. He determined that early intervention can make a difference in the life skills development of young children. Heckman's focus was on noncognitive skills of determination, social skills, and motivation, which lead to success.

Heckman devoted his career to the development of scientific foundations to evaluate economic policies. Specializing in models that focused on individuals and disaggregated groups, he was able to create new econometric models to address the special topics of his research. Heckman is especially recognized for his work in labor economics as well as his work on the effectiveness of early childhood education programs. Policy makers have new understandings in areas of education, labor markets, civil rights, and job training because of the econometric modeling developed by Heckman.

Beyond the 2000 Nobel Prize in Economics, Heckman is one of most honored and prized economists of the late twentieth century. He won the prestigious John Bates Clark Medal in 1983. In 2005, Heckman was honored with the Jacob Mincer Award from the Society of Labor Economists and the Ulysses Medal from the University College Dublin. He has been granted prestigious fellow status of the Econometric Society, American Statistical Association, Society of Labor Economists, International Statistical Institute, and American Association for the Advancement of Science.

*See also:* Ricardo, David; Samuelson, Paul; Smith, Adam

## Selected Works by James Heckman

Heckman, James. "Assessing Clinton's Program on Job Training, Workfare, and Education in the Workplace." NBER Working Paper No. 4428. August 1993.

Heckman, James. *Law and Employment: Lessons from Latin American and the Caribbean.* Chicago: University of Chicago Press, 2004.

Heckman, James. "Schools, Skills, and Synapses." *Economic Inquiry* 46, no. 3 (2008): 289–324.

Heckman, James, and Alan B. Krueger. *Inequality in America: What Role for Human Capital Policies?* 1st ed., vol. 1. Cambridge, MA: MIT Press, 2004.

Heckman, James J., and Edward E. Leamer, eds. *Handbook of Econometrics*. 1st ed., vol. 6A. Amsterdam: Elsevier, 2007.

Heckman, James, and Burton Singer, eds. *Longitudinal Analysis of Labor Market Data*. Cambridge: Cambridge University Press, 2008.

**Selected Works about James Heckman**

Cassidy, John. "Interview with James Heckman." *The New Yorker*, January 14, 2010. http://www.newyorker.com/online/blogs/johncassidy/2010/01/interview-with-james-heckman.html (accessed December 2010).

Heckman, James J. "Microdata, Heterogeneity and the Evaluation of Public Policy." In *Nobel Lectures, Economics 1996–2000*. Edited by Torsten Persson, 25–318. Singapore: World Scientific, 2003.

Heckman, James. "Autobiography." Nobelprize.org. http://nobelprize.org/nobel_prizes/economics/laureates/2000/heckman-autobio.html (accessed December 2010).

Vane, Howard R., and Chris Mulhearn, eds. *Trygve Haavelmo, James J. Heckman, Daniel L. McFadden, Robert F. Engle and Clive W. J. Granger*. London: Edward Elgar, 2009.

David A. Dieterle

# HEILBRONER, ROBERT

Born: March 24, 1919, in New York City; Died: January 4, 2005, in New York City; American; history of economic thought, economic systems; Major Works: *The Worldly Philosophers* (1953), *Teachings from the Worldly Philosophers* (1996).

Robert Heilbroner was an American economist who wrote extensively on the history of economic thought. His book *The Worldly Philosophers* is one of the best-selling nontextbook economics books in history and has been credited for many academics' decisions to become economic historians. Considered a Socialist, his professional interests extended the economic spectrum from Adam Smith to Joseph Schumpeter. Heilbroner died in 2005.

Robert Louis Heilbroner was born on March 24, 1919, in New York City. His father was a wealthy German-Jewish entrepreneur, a partner in one of the leading men's clothing stores of the time. Robert received his secondary education at the Horace Mann School. At the time, it was affiliated with Columbia University and considered an entry point for Ivy League education.

In the autumn of 1936, Heilbroner would enter Harvard. The timing was fortuitous. John Maynard Keynes had written *The General Theory of Employment, Interest and Money* the previous year, and the economics department, although divided at the time, would eventually become one of the leading centers of Keynesian economics in the United States. During his sophomore year, Heilbroner would be assigned Thorstein Veblen's *Theory of the Leisure Class*. As a result, Heilbroner became interested in the history of economic thought.

During World War II, Heilbroner would serve in the Office of Price Control working with John Kenneth Galbraith. He would also spend time in the U.S.

Army serving in the Pacific. After World War II, he worked as a freelance writer. It was during this postwar period that he would take a course in the history of economic thought under Paul Lowe at the New School of Social Research. This marked the beginning of his career as an academic and public intellectual. He would write what is perhaps his signature work, *The Worldly Philosophers*, in 1953, well before completing his graduate and postgraduate studies. *The Worldly Philosophers* is among the best-selling economics books of all time.

Heilbroner would receive his doctorate from the New School in 1963 and would be appointed the Norman Thomas Professor of Economics at the school in 1971. He would spend his career there teaching mostly the history of economic thought. Interestingly enough, Robert Heilbroner was considered a Socialist in his views. Nevertheless, his primary academic interests were Adam Smith and Joseph Schumpeter. This is not surprising as Heilbroner was fascinated with the economic process as a way to provide order on the material aspects of society, essentially seeing economics as a way to interpret and solve societal issues. He agreed with Smith that the invisible hand promoted growth; but without proper social norms, growth also had great potential for creating problems. His view, unusual at the time but commonplace now, was that to truly understand Smith one had to read *The Theory of Moral Sentiments* as well as *The Wealth of Nations*. Heilbroner's classification of economic systems as traditional, market, and command is still used by educators. Its value is enhanced because it is not as politically charged as other ways used to describe economic systems.

Robert Heilbroner was also recognized as a leader by his peers. He served on the executive committee of the American Economic Association and as a vice president in 1984. He was also the first recipient of the Scholar of the Year award by the New York Council for the Humanities, as well as a recipient of the Association for Evolutionary Economics' Veblen-Commons Award in 1994, a fitting recognition given his early interest in Veblen.

Upon the publication of his biography, *A Future of Capitalism*, Heilbroner influenced the growth of economic history as a science of study. More than a few historians of economic thought credit Heilbroner for economic history and economic thought as their career choice. Heilbroner's first major work was an entry point for many and remains a foundation upon which many careers have been built.

Robert L. Heilbroner died in New York City on January 4, 2005.

*See also:* Galbraith, John Kenneth; Schumpeter, Joseph; Smith, Adam; Veblen, Thorstein

**Selected Works by Robert Heilbroner**

Heilbroner, Robert. "Analysis and Vision in the History of Modern Economic Thought." *Journal of Economic Literature* (September 1990): 1097–1114.

Heilbroner, Robert. *Behind the Veil of Economics: Essays in the Worldly Philosophy*. New York: Norton, 1988.

Heilbroner, Robert. "Do Machines Make History?" *Technology and Culture* 8 (July 1967): 335–45.

Heilbroner, Robert. *The Economic Problem*. Upper Saddle River, NJ: Prentice Hall, 1968.
Heilbroner, Robert. *An Inquiry into the Human Prospect*. New York: Norton, 1974.
Heilbroner, Robert. *The Limits of American Capitalism*. New York: Harper & Row, 1966.
Heilbroner, Robert. *The Making of Economic Society*. 11th ed. (1st ed.1963). Upper Saddle River, NJ: Prentice Hall, 2001.
Heilbroner, Robert. *Marxism: For and Against*. New York: Norton, 1980.
Heilbroner, Robert. *The Nature and Logic of Capitalism*. New York: Norton, 1985.
Heilbroner, Robert. *Teachings from the Worldly Philosophers*. New York: Norton, 1996.
Heilbroner, Robert. *21st Century Capitalism*. New York: Norton, 1993.
Heilbroner, Robert. *The Worldly Philosophers*. 7th ed. (1st ed. 1953). New York: Simon & Schuster, 1999.
Heilbroner, Robert, and Aaron Singer. *The Economic Transformation of America: 1600 to the Present*. 4th ed. New York: Harcourt Brace Jovanovich, 1998.

### Selected Works about Robert Heilbroner

Blaug, Mark, and Paul Sturges, eds. *Who's Who in Economics: A Biographical Dictionary of Major Economists, 1700–1980*. Cambridge, MA: MIT Press, 1983.
"Robert Heilbroner." Cambridge Foreign Speakers, 1970–1990. Vol. 2. http://www.harvardsquarelibrary.org/cfs2/robert_heilbroner.php.
Carroll, Michael C. *The Future of Capitalism: The Economic Vision of Robert Heilbroner*. Rome: St. Martin's Press, 1998.
Madrick, Jeff. "Robert Heilbroner, 1919–2005." *Challenge* 48, no. 3 (May–June 2005): 5–13.

*Timothy P. Schilling*

## HELLER, WALTER

Born: August 27, 1915, in Buffalo, New York; Died: June 15, 1987, in Seattle, Washington; American; Keynesian, Council of Economic Advisers (1961–64); Major Work: *Monetary vs. Fiscal Policy* (with Milton Friedman) (1968).

Walter Heller is best known from his time working on the Council of Economic Advisers under Presidents Kennedy and Lyndon Johnson from 1961 to 1964. He also was influential in the reconstruction of the West German economy after World War II while working as a tax adviser to the U.S. military government in Germany in 1947 and 1948. Heller returned to an earlier post with the University of Minnesota's Economics Department and retired a year before his death. Heller died in 1987.

Walter Wolfgang Heller was born on August 27, 1915, in Buffalo, New York, to German immigrant parents. He moved with his family first to Washington State, before settling in Milwaukee from age six on. He received his BA in economics from Oberlin College in Ohio in 1935. He would complete an MA degree in 1938 and a PhD in 1941 from the University of Wisconsin while studying finance and taxation. He focused on state income tax laws for his dissertation, which he studied by touring 31 states, the District of Columbia, and Canada over the course of a year.

Heller would spend the next almost 20 years varying his work experience between government work and the education field, while becoming an expert on taxation. Between 1941 and 1945, he worked in tax research as a senior analyst in the Department of the Treasury. From 1945 until 1960, he was an associate professor at the University of Minnesota, missing time on occasion to perform various government jobs. In 1947, he spent a year in Germany as chief of finance for the U.S. military government in Germany, and would spend a year in Germany in 1951 to study German fiscal problems.

Heller's work in the 1950s would acquaint him more with the U.S. government. During Eisenhower's administration, Heller appeared before Congress on several occasions to encourage more federal spending on education and other programs, while also encouraging Congress to raise taxes. In 1952, he began to consult the United Nations on issues of encouraging growth and development of under developed countries. From 1955 to 1960, he was an economic adviser and consultant to the governor of Minnesota and the Department of Taxation. In a 1957 article, he criticized the Committee for Economic Development's plan to create flexible tax rates and expenditures to adjust for inflation and deflation as a plan that failed to adequately consider short-run economic forecasts. In 1960, he assisted the nation of Jordan in reforming their taxation and fiscal policies.

Heller was sought out by President-elect Kennedy in 1960 to become the chairman of the Council of Economic Advisers. One of the main tasks for Heller would be to implement strategies to help the country get out of a slight recession that it had been in for about six months, though Heller linked the problem to a recession that the nation had not fully recovered from that was from 1957–58. Kennedy's main focus was to use the Employment Act of 1946, which stated that the federal government should enact fiscal policy to maintain high employment and also created the Council of Economic Advisers, to its fullest potential.

Heller viewed the problem of recession as not being recovered until the nation's gross national product continued to rise above previous levels and not just bounce back to what it was before. To do this, he was not concerned with a balanced budget but rather wanted to see more economic growth and unemployment down to around 4 percent, as opposed to the 7 percent in March 1961. One way he would attack this problem would be through adjusting tax rates to eliminate loopholes and tax advantages for certain groups and lowering the tax range from 20–91 percent to 14–60 percent.

While working with Kennedy, Heller believed it was important to use forecasting tools to estimate how the economy was going to work. He also believed in the federal government's power to correct small problems with inflation and unemployment as needed through spending more. He supported cutting taxes in 1962 to pick up the lagging economy, a measure that was supported by Kennedy and promised to be enacted when it was necessary. The actual cut in taxes did not occur until February 1964, after Kennedy's assassination.

Heller maintained his position initially as Lyndon Johnson finished Kennedy's term, but he would resign by the end of 1964. Early in the year, Heller realized cutting taxes was leading to higher inflation and reversed his position, calling for a tax increase, especially as U.S. involvement in Vietnam increased. Johnson did not take his advice. His decision to leave his post, however, is attributed more to his own personal circumstances and not his disagreement with Johnson. He returned to teaching at the University of Minnesota.

One of Heller's most well-known books is a record of his debate with Milton Friedman at New York University in 1968, *Monetary vs. Fiscal Policy*, which was a friendly give-and-take between a supporter of monetary policy and the Keynesian. Heller also contributed to the *Wall Street Journal* and *Time* magazine. His ideas about the use of tax cuts to stimulate the economy would be embraced by Republicans in the 1980s, specifically by Ronald Reagan and "supply-side economists." He had been called an "educator of presidents."

Walter Heller died on June 15, 1987, in Seattle due to a heart attack at the age of 71.

*See also:* Keynes, John Maynard

### Selected Works by Walter Heller

Heller, Walter. *The Economy: Old Myths and New Realities*. New York: Norton, 1976.
Heller, Walter. *New Dimensions of Political Economy*. Cambridge, MA: Harvard University Press, 1966.
Heller, Walter, ed. *Perspectives on Economic Growth*. New York: Random House, 1968.
Heller, Walter W., and Milton Friedman. *Monetary vs. Fiscal Policy*. New York: Norton, 1969.

### Selected Works about Walter Heller

"Heller, Walter W(olfgang)." *Current Biography Yearbook, 1961 Edition*. Edited by Charles Moritz. New York: H. W. Wilson, 1962.
Kilborn, Peter T. "Walter Heller, 71, Economic Adviser in 60's, Dead." *New York Times*, June 7, 1987. http://www.nytimes.com/1987/06/17/obituaries/walter-heller-71-economic-adviser-in-60-s-dead.html?pagewanted=all&src=pm (accessed September 2011).
Stein, Herbert. *The Fiscal Revolution in America*. Chicago: University of Chicago Press, 1969.

*Joseph Lee Hauser*

## HICKS, SIR JOHN

Born: April 8, 1904, in Warwick, England; Died: May 20, 1989, in Blockley, Gloucestershire, England; English; welfare economics, labor theory, general equilibrium theory, international trade, Nobel Prize (1972); Major Works: *Value and Capital* (1939), *Contribution to the Theory of the Trade Cycle* (1950), *Capital and Growth* (1965).

Sir John Hicks was a British economist noted for his work in the areas of labor, value theory, international trade, and general economic equilibrium theory. His ideas changed over time to reflect new developments. As a result, his research interests were wide-ranging and diverse. Along with Kenneth Arrow, he was the 1972 recipient of the Nobel Prize in Economics. John Hicks became Sir John Hicks when he was knighted in 1964. Hicks died in 1989.

John Richard Hicks was born in April 8, 1904 in Warwick, England. His father was a journalist at a local newspaper. He was educated first at Clifton College and then at Oxford, with much of his education financed by mathematical scholarships. While at Oxford, he drifted away from mathematics to pursue interests in history and literature, joining the new school of philosophy, politics, and economics, even though he would graduate with only a second-class degree in 1925.

Upon graduation, Hicks received a temporary lecturer position at the London School of Economics (LSE) focusing on labor economics and industrial relations. His timing was fortunate, as he arrived shortly before Lionel Robbins became head of the department. As a result, he spent time at the LSE concurrent with Robbins, Friedrich von Hayek, Nicolas Kaldor, and Ursula Webb, who would become his wife. While there he published *The Theory of Wages* in 1932, in which he developed the relationship between capital and labor, concluding that labor-saving technology need not necessarily reduce labor's share of national income.

In 1935, Hicks was offered a position at Cambridge, where he would remain for three years. While at Cambridge, he would publish an article in *Econometrica* that would be instrumental in the acceptance of Keynesian economics. Hicks would develop the IS-LM model, which demonstrated graphically how an economy could be in equilibrium but at less than full employment.

Hicks left Cambridge in 1938 to accept a position at the University of Manchester, where he would remain for eight years. His book *Value and Capital* (1939) was one of the pioneering works on general equilibrium theory, a significant contribution to modern microeconomics. At about the same time, he published two articles on welfare economics. This was a new direction for Hicks. In "The Foundations of Welfare Economics" in the *Economic Journal*, and "The Valuation of Social Income" in *Econometrica*, Hicks resurrected Alfred Marshall's idea of consumer surplus and provide an argument to demonstrate how trade benefits to one group can offset losses to another group. The Hicks Compensation Criteria provided insights for policy makers regarding the efficacy of policies. But Hicks's work demonstrated that, even if costs went uncompensated, a policy could be advocated and implemented based on size of the benefits. This approach is fundamental when introducing gains from trade and combating arguments against trade barriers.

In 1946, Hicks returned to Oxford and held a number of positions there until his retirement in 1965. He remained at Oxford as a research fellow from retirement until 1971. During this time he shifted his focus again, this time to issues of growth and development. For example, he published *Contribution to the Theory of the Trade Cycle* in 1950, building on the work of Roy Harrod and solving some stability problems.

The problem of capital dominated much of Hicks's later work. In 1965, he published *Capital and Growth*, where he developed a flexprice/fixprice taxonomy to explain problems in some equilibrium models. The flexprice view assumes that prices move instantaneously to react to changes in markets, as is characteristic of perfectly competitive models. Fixprice recognizes the "sticky price" problem inherent in other types of markets. Hicks's taxonomy helped economists understand how to reconcile capital issues during the transition from one equilibrium point to another as economies grow. The search for a time factor would lead him to publish *A Theory of Economic History* in 1973.

In 1972, Hicks was the corecipient of the Nobel Prize in Economics with Kenneth Arrow. They were jointly recognized for their pioneering work in welfare economics and equilibrium theory. Hicks would confess to mixed feelings for being honored for ideas that he felt he had moved beyond. Hicks also received a number of honors including degrees bestowed by the Universities of Glasgow, Manchester, and Warwick, and the Technical University of Lisbon. His honorary posts include fellowship in the British Academy in 1946, the Swedish Academy in 1948, and the American Academy in 1958; president of the Royal Economic Society from 1960 to 1962; and knighthood in 1964.

Sir John Hicks died on May 20, 1989, in Blockley, Gloucestershire, England.

*See also:* Arrow, Kenneth; Hayek, Friedrich von; Kaldor, Nicolas; Marshall, Alfred; Robbins, Lionel

**Selected Works by Sir John Hicks**

Hicks, John. *Capital and Growth*. Oxford: Oxford University Press, 1965.
Hicks, John. *Contribution to the Theory of the Trade Cycle*. Oxford: Clarendon Press, 1950.
Hicks, John. *Money, Interest and Wages: Collected Essays on Economic Theory*. Cambridge, MA: Harvard University Press, 1982.
Hicks, John. *Theory of Wages*. New York: Macmillan, 1932.
Hicks, John. *Value and Capital*. Oxford: Clarendon Press, 1939.

**Selected Works about Sir John Hicks**

Blaug, Mark, and Paul Sturges, eds. *Who's Who in Economics: A Biographical Dictionary of Major Economists, 1700–1980*. Cambridge, MA: MIT Press, 1983.
Hicks, John. "Autobiography." The NobelPrize.org. http://www.nobelprize.org/nobel_prizes/economics/laureates/1972/hicks-autobio.html (accessed February 2012).
"John R. Hicks." In *The Concise Encyclopedia of Economics*. Edited by David R. Henderson. The Library of Economics and Liberty. http://www.econlib.org/library/Enc/bios/Hicks.html (accessed February 2012).

*Timothy P. Schilling*

# HILFERDING, RUDOLF

Born: August 10, 1877, in Vienna, Austria; Died: February 2, 1941, in a Nazi prison camp; German; Marxist ideologue; Major Work: *Finance Capital: A Study of the Latest Phase of Capitalist Development* (1910).

Rudolf Hilferding was one of the leading Marxist proponents of the early twentieth century. Identified as a member of the "Austro-Marxist" group, Hilferding was responsible for the early popularization of Karl Marx's economic ideology. A member of the German Parliament, the Social Democrat also served as German minister of finance. Following his exile to France, he was arrested and imprisoned by the Nazis. Hilderfing died in 1941.

Rudolf Hilferding was born on August 10, 1877, in Vienna, Austria, the son of a wealthy Jewish businessman. Pursuing a career in medicine, Hilferding earned a doctorate in medicine, practicing as a pediatrician in Vienna. Even though medicine was his career, economics and politics were never far from his thoughts. In 1901, he joined the Austrian Social Democratic Party. A year later he joined the German Social Democratic Party (SDP) and moved to Berlin to work for the German Democratic newspaper *Die Neue Zeit*. In Berlin he also taught economic history and economics.

In 1904, Hilferding wrote an article for *Die Neue Zeit* that became his classic. The article was a "Response to Böhm-Bawerk's Criticism of Marxist Economics, Karl Marx and the Close of His Systems." The response challenged Eugen von Böhm-Bawerk's, another Viennese, criticism of Karl Marx's economic ideas. Hilferding was considered the main Marxist voice to oppose Böhm-Bawerk's Austrian pro-market, anti-Marx position. The two participated in a series of debates, the Crises Debate, debating Marx's theories.

From 1904 to 1910, Hilferding wrote a series of books on Karl Marx's economic ideas. Two of his books include *Marx's System* in 1904 and *Finance Capital* in 1910. In *Finance Capital*, Hilferding analyzed capital development from a Marxist perspective of imperialism as capitalism's late stage.

Prior to World War I, Hilferding was a leader and teacher in the German SDP. Hilferding supported Germany's involvement in World War I. This view was directly contrary to his SDP. Given his medical background, he was drafted into the medical service of the Austro-Hungarian Army. By the end of World War I, in 1918, Hilferding had reversed his views on the war. He became a member of the more radical Independent Socialist Party.

Following the war, Hilferding became editor-in-chief of *Die Freiheit* from 1918 to 1922. *Die Freiheit* was the daily newspaper of the Independent Social Democratic Party. In 1919, he also became a German citizen.

Hilferding at this time climbed the leadership ladder to become of the leaders of the SDP. In 1923, he was appointed minister of finance under Chancellor Gustav Stresemann and again in 1928 under Chancellor Hermann Muller.

When Adolf Hitler came to power in 1933, Hilferding's life was changed forever. As both a leader of the Socialist Party and a Jew, it was imperative for him to go into exile. He first moved to Denmark and then to Switzerland and ultimately in 1938 ended up living in France.

In 1932, Hilferding was instrumental in the publication of "National Socialism and Marxism." While in exile he continued to write and promote Marxism. From 1933 to 1936, he was editor of the Karlovy Vary (a city in what is now the Czech Republic) *Journal of Socialism*.

Like his writing, Hilferding's organizational pursuits did not stop while in exile. In 1934, he was on the Board of Sopade, a social-democratic exile organization. In 1938, following the German invasion of Czechoslovakia, Sopade moved its headquarters to Paris, France. Hilferding disguised his identity at this time by changing his name to "Richard Kern." When he was in France, his identity was discovered and the Vichy government captured him and turned him over to the Gestapo (secret police).

Rudolf Hilferding died in a Paris prison on February 2, 1941. It is assumed he died from injuries inflicted by the Gestapo but definitive circumstances were never uncovered.

*See also:* Engels, Friedrich; Marx, Karl

### Selected Works by Rudolf Hilferding

Hilferding, Rudolf. "Parliamentarianism and the General Strike." *The Social Democrat*, November 1905.

Hilferding, Rudolf, and T. B. Bottomore. *Finance Capital: A Study of the Latest Phase of Capitalist Development.* Oxford: Routledge and Kegan Paul, 1910.

Hilferding, Rudolf, and Paul M. Sweezy, eds. *Böhm-Bawerk, Eugen. Karl Marx and the Close of His System: Böhm-Bawerk's Criticism of Marx* (1904). London: Porcupine Press, 1984.

### Selected Works about Rudolf Hilferding

"Rudolf Hilferding, 1877–1941." Bernard Schwartz Center for Economic Policy Analysis. New School for Social Research. http://www.newschool.edu/nssr/het/profiles/hilferd.htm (accessed March 2, 2011).

Smaldone, William. *Rudolf Hilferding: The Tragedy of a German Social Democrat.* De Kalb: Northern Illinois University Press, 1998.

Wagner, F. Peter. *Rudolf Hilferding: Theory and Politics of Democratic Socialism.* Revolutionary Studies. Amherst, NY: Prometheus Books, 1996.

*David A. Dieterle*

## HOBBES, THOMAS

Born: April 5, 1588, in Wiltshire, England; Died: December 4, 1679, in Hardwick, England; English; political economy, social contract theory; Major Work: *Leviathan* (1651).

Thomas Hobbes is best known as a political philosopher whose views on government would influence both the monarchy in England and the democracy of the United States. His role in economics is sometimes characterized as anything from overly minimal to being called the father of political economy. While he never wrote specifically on economics, his view of man's relationship to his country and the country's role in promoting society opened up a world of connections to economic issues. Hobbes died in 1679.

Thomas Hobbes was born on April 5, 1588, in Wiltshire, England. His father was a vicar, but it was mostly his uncle who provided for him to enter Oxford at age 14. He studied scholastic logic and physics, graduating with a bachelor of arts in 1607. He served as a tutor for the Cavendish family, which allowed him to travel around England and throughout Europe. His service as tutor to the wealthy Cavendish family and later other well-to-do families opened up doors of opportunity to study and formulate his own philosophy.

Hobbes was influenced by several people while working as a tutor. He was an acquaintance of Francis Bacon, who had an influence on Hobbes's pessimistic view that knowledge meant power. Hobbes was also fascinated by the mathematical field of geometry, seeing the proofs as groundwork for his later methods of philosophy. The idea of linking geometrical proofs with natural philosophy was proposed to Hobbes by Galileo in 1636.

Hobbes began his writing on political topics during the period in English history that featured much turmoil over the role of the king and Parliament. His writings mostly favored the king and were against democracy. The latter was a major purpose of his translation of Thucydides in 1628. In 1640, he published *Elements of Law, Natural and Politic*, which angered many in England because it supported the authority of the king, causing Hobbes to flee to Europe. He wrote *De Cive* in 1642 in Europe on the theme of the church-state relationship.

Hobbes's most famous work, *Leviathan*, was published in 1651 while in exile during the turmoil of the English Civil War. While almost half of Leviathan was about religion, it did give new insight into the idea of social contract theory and absolute government. According to Hobbes, the idea of a social contract presented in *Leviathan* dealt with the twin issues of power and death. Because men fear death, they are willing to give up power to a government in order to secure their life. In this kind of situation the leader must be absolute, but the government can take on multiple forms of structure. Therefore a democracy run by the people and an absolute monarchy can both be examples of a social contract so long as they provide order.

Following *Leviathan*, Hobbes continued working out his philosophical ideas through a planned trilogy that dealt with the body (*De Corpore*, published 1655), man (*De Homine*, published 1657), and a more complete explanation of his thoughts on politics (which was never published). The first work of the trilogy was met with great criticism as Hobbes unsuccessfully attempted to square the circle.

Unfortunately, *De Homine* ended up being his last philosophical book published while he was alive because of controversy surrounding his 1656 book, *Questions Concerning Liberty, Necessity, and Chance*. This book dealt with religious issues over free will in man and led to many debates with both religious and secular scholars. His *Leviathan* was condemned in the House of Commons in 1666 and almost condemned by the House of Lords. He was forbidden to publish more philosophical literature from then on.

Hobbes did not write explicitly on economics, but the potential for economic application was present in his writing. Hobbes has been credited with influencing Adam Smith and other economic philosophers such as the Physiocrats and Bernard Mandeville. He wrote eloquently about the power of human free will to accomplish its goals. His emphasis on the self-interest inherent in men led to others to expand on the role self-interest plays in economics. Despite Adam Smith's emphasis on free markets and Hobbes's emphasis on the importance of the state, both would agree that the state's main role was for peace and common defense, which would allow for something of a free-market system in Hobbes's work.

Toward the end of his life, Hobbes was relegated either to writing works that would not be published until after his death or to writing nonphilosophical works. He wrote his autobiography in Latin verse in 1672 and produced a new translation of Homer's *Iliad* and *Odyssey* into English rhyme in 1674. He wrote a history of the English Civil War, *Behemoth*, in 1668, but it would not be published until 1682 after his death.

Thomas Hobbes died on December 4, 1679, in Hartwick, England.

*See also:* Smith, Adam; Quesnay, François

### Selected Works by Thomas Hobbes

Hobbes, Thomas. *Behemoth: Or the Long Parliament*. London: Unwin Brothers, 1682.
Hobbes, Thomas. *De Corpore*. London: Andrea Crook, 1655.
Hobbes, Thomas. *The Elements of Law: Natural and Politic* (1640). London: Thornton, 1888.
Hobbes, Thomas. *The Elements of Law Natural and Politic. Part I: Human Nature; Part II: De Corpore Politico: with Three Lives* (1640). Edited by John C. A. Gaskin. London: Oxford University Press, 2008.
Hobbes, Thomas. Leviathan. 3rd ed. (1651). London: George Routledge & Sons, 1887.
Hobbes, Thomas. *Man and Citizen: De Homine and De Cive* (1657). Edited by Bernard Gert. New York: Anchor Books, 1972.

### Selected Works about Thomas Hobbes

Malcolm, Noel. *Aspects of Hobbes*. New York: Oxford University Press, 2002.
Missner, Marshall. *On Hobbes*. Belmont, CA: Wadsworth, 2000.
Rogers, G. A., and Ryan, Alan, eds., *Perspectives on Thomas Hobbes*. New York: Oxford University Press, 1991.
Taylor, Quentin. "Thomas Hobbes, Political Economist: His Changing Historical Fortunes." *The Independent Review* 14, no. 3 (Winter 2010): 415–33.
Winborne, Warner R. "Modernization and Modernity: Thomas Hobbes, Adam Smith, and Political Development." *Perspectives on Political Science* (Winter 2008): 41–49.

*Joseph Lee Hauser*

## HOBSON, JOHN

Born: July 6, 1858, in Derby, England; Died: April 1, 1940, in Hampstead Village, London, England; English; economic philosopher, imperialism, rent theory; Major Works: *The Physiology of Industry* (1889), *The Industrial System* (1909), *Imperialism* (1902).

John Hobson was a nineteenth-century writer and literature professor turned economic philosopher. Popularly known as John Atkinson Hobson or J. A. Hobson, he was one of the most ardent critics of the economic imperialism of the late nineteenth and early twentieth centuries. Besides his critiques of imperialism, Hobson also wrote on the economic topic of rent theory. Hobson died in 1940.

John Atkinson Hobson was born on July 6, 1858, in Derby, England. John attended Lincoln College in Oxford. He was a teacher of English literature. After brief teaching assignments of English literature and the classics, Hobson moved to London in 1887. Hobson's interest in economics began when he was introduced to Henry George and his one-tax philosophy as well as the economic philosophies of several groups as England experienced an economic depression. During this time he became acquaintances with the Fabians, who would later begin the London School of Economics.

However, it was Hobson's collaboration with businessman Albert Mummery that sparked his interest in economic philosophy. In 1889, Hobson and Mummery published *Physiology of Industry* in which they introduced their theory of underconsumption. Hobson and Mummery's theory of underconsumption countered the prevailing thrift theory of the day being advocated by the classical economists of the day and J. B. Say. His anticlassical views were not well received by the professional economic community and he was soon discredited for his bold stand.

Hobson joined the staff of the Manchester *Guardian* to cover the Second Boer War in South Africa. While on assignment in South Africa, Hobson formed his strong anti-imperialism and antiwar views regarding the Second Boer War. He viewed the war as a capitalistic plot by South African miners to increase profits.

Upon his return to England, he strongly opposed the war—so much so that he wrote a series of books opposing imperialism. In 1900, he wrote the *War in South Africa* and in 1901 the *Psychology of Jingoism*. Then, in 1902 Hobson wrote what is considered his signature book, *Imperialism*. In *Imperialism*, Hobson submitted that the incentive for a country's imperialism was the search for new markets and opportunities for expansion to other countries. Hobson's imperialistic theories launched him to the forefront of nineteenth-century economic thought. He influenced later theorists and philosophers such as Leon Trotsky and Vladimir Lenin.

A second area of economics Hobson expounded on was the area of rent theory. Several works of Hobson's included *Problems of Poverty* in 1891, *Evolution of Modern Capitalism* in 1894, and in 1896 *Problem of the Unemployed*.

Hobson's next seminal work in 1909, *The Industrial System*, argued that misallocation of income redistribution was the result of too much saving and not enough consumption. Hobson supported nationalization of monopolies and taxes as methods to solve this surplus condition.

The antiwar views Hobson developed as a result of his experiences in South Africa led him to oppose the World War I when it broke out in Europe. His opposition led him to join several antiwar political organizations. In 1919, Hobson joined the Independent Labour Party, a Socialist-leaning political party in England. He began to write on reforming the capitalistic system in England. He penned articles in the Socialist publications the *New Leader*, the *New Statesman*, and the *Socialist Review*.

Hobson was not without his critics. His Marxist theories on imperialism were severely criticized on several fronts. He was criticized for his definition and defense of imperialism, for not giving trade and trading power its credit, and for his lack of understanding of the sources of the mercantilist economic philosophy. Hobson was also criticized for his emphasis on the Industrial Revolution as the road to imperialism as opposed to the mercantilist era of exploration. He was also criticized for his idealistic views on foreign policy in the early twentieth century.

Hobson published his autobiography, *Confessions of an Economic Heretic*, in 1938.

John Hobson died in Hampstead Village, London, England, on April 1, 1940.

*See also:* George, Henry; Keynes, John Maynard; Say, Jean-Baptiste; Veblen, Thorstein

### Selected Works by John Hobson

Hobson, John. *Problems of Poverty: An Inquiry into the Industrial Condition of the Poor*. London: Methuen, 1891.
Hobson, John. *Evolution of Modern Capitalism: Study of Machine Production*. London: Walter Scott, 1894.
Hobson, John. *Problem of the Unemployed: An Inquiry and a Policy*. London: Methuen, 1896.
Hobson, John. *The War in South Africa: Its Causes and Effects*. London: James Nesbitt, 1900.
Hobson, John. *Psychology of Jingoism*. London: Grant Richards, 1901.
Hobson, John. *Imperialism: A Study*. New York: James Potts, 1902.
Hobson, John. *The Industrial System: An Inquiry into Earned and Unearned Income*. London: Longmans, Green, 1909.
Hobson, John. *Veblen*. London: Wiley, 1937.
Hobson, John. *Confessions of an Economic Heretic*. London: Allen & Unwin, 1938.
Mummery A. F., and J. A. Hobson. *The Physiology of Industry: Being an Exposure of Certain Fallacies in Existing Theories in Economics*. London: John Murray, 1889.

### Selected Works about John Hobson

Brailsford, H. N. *The Life-Work of J. A. Hobson*. Oxford: Oxford University Press, 1948.
"John Hobson: Imperialism, 1902." In *Modern History Sourcebook*. Fordham University. http://www.fordham.edu/halsall/mod/1902hobson.asp (accessed September 2011).
Wood, Robert D., and John C. Wood, eds. *John A. Hobson: Critical Assessment of Leading Economists*. London: Taylor & Francis, 2003.

*David A. Dieterle*

## HOLLANDER, SAMUEL

Born: April 6, 1937, in London, England; English/Canadian/Israeli; economic history; Major Work: *Studies in Classical Political Economy* series (1973, 1979, 1985, 1997).

Samuel Hollander is one of the most influential authors in the field of economic thought. Hollander is a citizen of Britain, Canada, and Israel. Hollander has authored many books and articles that have been considered some of the most influential works in economic history. Hollander's *Studies in Classical Political Economy* is one of the classics of economic history and thought. His comprehensive studies include Adam Smith, David Ricardo, Thomas Malthus, and John Stuart Mill. His historical interpretations were often quite controversial. While Hollander had his detractors, he also had key supporters, including Lionel Robbins.

Samuel Hollander was born on April 6, 1937, in London, England. He studied at the London School of Economics and Princeton University, receiving his PhD from Princeton University in 1963. His career began in Canada at the University of Toronto. In 1967, he became a Canadian citizen.

Hollander has written influential and controversial works on Adam Smith, David Ricardo, Thomas Malthus, John Stuart Mill, and Alfred Marshall. Hollander's most controversial theory was his view that the economic theories of neoclassical economists Alfred Marshall and Leon Walras were derived from the earlier ideas of David Ricardo. Hollander began his prolific writing career publishing a book on the increased efficiency of the DuPont rayon plants. His most significant work was a series of *Studies in Classical Political Economy*. The series consisted of two volumes, which included *The Economics of Adam Smith* (1973), *The Economics of David Ricardo* (1979), *The Economics of John Stuart Mill* (2 vols., 1985), and *The Economics of Thomas Robert Malthus* (1997). As a comprehensive series on the central characters of political economy and classical economics, Hollander often presents a thought-provoking reinterpretation of the contemporary thought. Hollander wrote *Classical Economics* in 1987.

In 2000, Hollander moved to Israel and joined the faculty of the Economics Department at Ben-Gurion University in Beersheba, Israel. That same year he became a citizen of Israel.

Samuel Hollander has received many honors and prizes throughout his career. In 1976, he was bestowed the position of fellow of the Royal Society of Canada. In 1998, Canada made Hollander an officer of the Order of Canada honor. The Order of Canada is equivalent to knighthood in England. It is the highest honor given by the Governor General-in-Council. In 2000, the Canadian government awarded Samuel Hollander the Queen Elizabeth II 50th Anniversary Medal.

Hollander's career also included a very extensive and excellent teaching résumé. Hollander accepted visiting appointments in Italy, United Kingdom, Japan, Australia, New Zealand, Holland, and France.

*See also:* Marshall, Alfred; Ricardo, David; Robbins, Lionel; Walras, Leon

### Selected Works by Samuel Hollander

Hollander, Samuel. *Classical Economics*. Oxford: Blackwell, 1987.

Hollander, Samuel. *The Economics of Adam Smith*. 2 vols. Studies in Classical Political Economy. Toronto: University of Toronto Press, 1973.

Hollander, Samuel. *The Economics of David Ricardo*. Studies in Classical Political Economy. Toronto: University of Toronto Press, 1979.

Hollander, Samuel. *The Economics of John Stuart Mill*. Studies in Classical Political Economy. Toronto: University of Toronto Press, 1985.

Hollander, Samuel. *The Economics of Karl Marx: Analysis and Application*. Cambridge: Cambridge University Press, 2008.

Hollander, Samuel. *The Economics of Thomas Robert Malthus*. Studies in Classical Political Economy. Toronto: University of Toronto Press, 1997.

Hollander, Samuel. *Jean-Baptiste Say and the Classical Canon in Economics: The British Connection in French Classicism*. London: Routledge, 2005.

Hollander, Samuel. *John Stuart Mill on Economic Theory and Method: Collected Essays III*. London: Routledge, 2000.

Hollander, Samuel. *The Literature of Political Economy: Collected Essays II*. London: Routledge, 1998.

Hollander, Samuel. *Ricardo—The "New View": Collected Essays I*. London: Routledge, 1995.

Hollander, Samuel. *The Sources of Increased Efficiency: A Study of DuPont Rayon Plants*. Cambridge, MA: MIT Press, 1965.

### Selected Works about Samuel Hollander

Blaug, Mark. *Who's Who in Economics*. 3rd ed. London: Edward Elgar, 1999.

Robbins, Lionel. *A History of Economic Thought: The LSE Lectures*. Edited by Steven G. Medema and Warren J. Samuels. Princeton, NJ: Princeton University Press, 1998.

Young, Jeffrey T. "From Adam Smith to John Stuart Mill: Samuel Hollander and the Classical Economists." In *Historians of Economics and Economic Thought: The Construction of Disciplinary Memory*. Edited by Steven G. Medema and Warren J. Samuels, 129–62. London: Routledge, 2001.

David A. Dieterle

## HOPPE, HANS-HERMANN

Born: September 2, 1949, in Peine, West Germany; German; Austrian economist; Major Works: *Handeln und Erkennen* (1976), *Democracy: The God That Failed* (2001).

Hans-Hermann Hoppe is one of the leading advocates for the Austrian School of economic thought in the United States. Hoppe is a distinguished fellow of the Ludwig von Mises Institute. He is founder and president of the Property and Freedom Society and served as editor-at-large for the *Journal of Libertarian Studies*. Hoppe is a mentor of Austrian economics philosopher Murray Rothbard. Hoppe specialized in applying Austrian School principles to debates about monarchy versus democracy, government policy and the behavior of elected officials, and time preference choice between current and future consumption. Professor Hoppe is professor emeritus of economics at the University of Nevada, Las Vegas.

Hans-Hermann Hoppe was born on September 2, 1949, in Peine, West Germany. Hoppe attended the University of Saarlandes and Goethe University in Frankfurt. His doctoral work began under the advising of avid promoter of Marx Jürgen Habermas. He earned his doctorate in 1974 from Goethe University. In 1976, he left West Germany for the United States, accepting a postdoctoral fellowship at the University of Michigan. Returning to West Germany in 1978, he completed additional graduate work at the University of Goethe, earning his "Habilitation" before teaching in West Germany and Italy. In 1986, he returned to the United States to study Austrian School economic thought with Murray Rothbard, later accepting a position at the University of Nevada, Las Vegas.

One of Hoppe's focuses is the behavior of government officials. Hoppe argues government officials have monopoly power and exert that power to increase their own personal power and wealth, creating political elite. In *Democracy: The God That Failed* (2001), Hoppe makes the argument that elected officials in a democracy do not have an incentive to maintain the value of a country but in fact have an incentive to exploit its resources for their own benefit. He draws the analogy of elected officials as "renters," not "owners," of a country's resources and consequently behave as such. This is contrasted to a country that has a dynasty with an incentive to maintain, and grow, a country's resources for future generations. This argument parallels closely those arguments of his mentor, Murray Rothbard.

Hoppe expands his argument to make the case against monopolies, including the monopolies of government. Monopolies, as a market structure, have absolute barriers of entry. Applying this idea to governments, Hoppe asserts that a government monopoly produces a product with a price higher and quality lower than what might be attained in a free-market structure. As a result, Hoppe proposes a free market for government services.

Hoppe received notable attention when he lectured on the Austrian School of economics view of time preference. During one of his lectures he submitted that family lifestyle preference was a significant variable in the preference choices between current consumption and saving for future consumption. Challenged by one of his students who filed a complaint with the university, Hoppe became somewhat of a national figure for academic freedom. Defended by such groups as the ACLU, the student newspaper, and the board of regents, Hoppe was eventually exonerated.

In May 2006, he founded the Property and Freedom Society. The international society was founded to promote the "Austro-Libertarianism" philosophy earlier represented by Ludwig von Mises, Frédéric Bastiat, and Hoppe's American mentor, Murray Rothbard. The inaugural meeting of the society was held in Bodrum, Turkey.

Hoppe was awarded the Frank T. and Harriet Kurzweg Award in 2004 and the Gary G. Schlarbaum Prize in 2006.

Hans-Hermann Hoppe retired from the University of Nevada, Las Vegas, in 2009 and holds the professor emeritus status.

*See also:* Bastiat, Frédéric; Böhm-Bawerk, Eugen von; Mises, Ludwig von; Rothbard, Murray

## Selected Works by Hans-Hermann Hoppe

Hoppe, Hans-Hermann. *Democracy: The God That Failed*. New Brunswick, NJ: Transaction, 2001.

Hoppe, Hans-Hermann. *Economic Science and the Austrian Method*. Auburn, AL: Ludwig von Mises Institute, 1995.

Hoppe, Hans-Hermann. *The Economics and Ethics of Private Property: Studies in Political Economy and Philosophy*. Boston: Kluwer Academic, 1993.

Hoppe, Hans-Hermann. *Eigentum, Anarchie und Staat*. Opladen, Germany: Westdeutscher Verlag, 1987.

Hoppe, Hans-Hermann. *Handeln und Erkennen: Zur Kritik des Empirismus am Beispiel der Philosophie David Humes*. Bern, Germany: Herbert Lang, 1976.

Hoppe, Hans-Hermann. *Kritik der kausalwissenschaftlichen Sozialforschung*. Opladen, Germany: Westdeutscher Verlag, 1983.

Hoppe, Hans-Hermann. *Praxeology and Economic Science*. Auburn, AL: Ludwig von Mises Institute, 1988.

Hoppe, Hans-Hermann. *A Theory of Socialism and Capitalism*. Boston: Kluwer Academic, 1989.

**Selected Works about Hans-Hermann Hoppe**

Hans-Hermann Hoppe. "Hans-Hermann Hoppe." http://www.hanshoppe.com/about/ (accessed September 2011).

"Interview with Hans-Hermann Hoppe." http://www.youtube.com/watch?v=19WEQFqw-8M (accessed September 2011).

"Hoppe's Ten Lecture Seminar, 'Economy, Society, and History.'" The Ludwig von Mises Institute. http://mises.org/media.aspx?action=category&ID=66 / (accessed September 2011).

"Professor Who Was Accused of Making Derogatory Remarks in Class Wants UNLV to Clear His Record." *Chronicle of Higher Education*, February 14, 2005. http://chronicle.com/free/2005/02/2005021406n.htm (accessed September 2011).

"U. of Nevada Reverses Professor's Reprimand." *Chronicle of Higher Education* 51, no. 26 (March 4, 2005): A10.

*David A. Dieterle*

## HORNICK, PHILIPP WILHELM VON

Born: January 23, 1640, in Frankfurt, Germany; Died: October 23, 1714, in Passau, Germany; Austrian; mercantilist, lawyer, scholar; Major Work: *Austria Over All, If She Only Will* (1684).

Philipp Wilhelm von Hornick is known as a radical Austrian mercantilist who laid out one of the clearest statements of mercantile policy in his work *Austria Over All, If She Only Will* (1684). Hornick asserted that natural resources, rather than money, constitute the wealth of a nation. Thus national consumption should be sustained by goods produced domestically, allowing for limited imports (raw materials excepted). He believed that people should be willing to pay twice the price for the home product because the money remained in the country, for whatever goes out stays out. As an Austrian by birth, he entreated Austria to become self-sufficient and independent of other countries. Hornick died in 1712.

Philipp Wilhelm von Hornick was born on January 23, 1640, in Frankfurt, Germany. Upon receiving his doctorate in law in 1661, he returned to Vienna to practice law for some years. Motivated by legalism and nationalism, in 1682 he published two tracts on public law, in which he renounced the French claims to Germany territory. He wrote in a time when his country was constantly threatened by Turkish invasion. In 1690, he became a civil servant of the cardinal of Passau, by whom he was later appointed privy councilor.

As a champion of mercantilism, he believed that a nation's wealth is determined by the amount of gold it accumulates for its monarch. Hornick differentiated between private and public economies by developing "nine principal rules" of public economy in his book *Austria Over All, If She Only Will*. Most of these rules involved ensuring maximum production of national necessities at home. In essence, Hornick advocated maximizing the utility of domestic land, whether it be for farming, mining, or industrial production; he thought this would ensure optimal employment of the population.

Other principal rules laid out in Hornick's book recommend minimal dependence on foreign nations and full exploitation of domestic natural resources. He asserted that all raw materials should be used for domestic manufacture only. Imports of a good should never be brought into a country if that good can be supplied domestically. He did make an exception for raw materials that were cheaper and could be imported for finishing in the home country. Although he encouraged the exportation of finished goods in exchange for gold and silver, he thought imports should be purchased with other goods, not with gold or silver.

Mercantile policy resulted in the "Golden Triangle," a trade route between Europe, Africa, and the United States. Along this trade route, boats would load up on copper, beads, guns, and ammunition and sail to Africa. Once in Africa, traders would barter goods for slaves. Slaves were then taken to the United States to be traded for raw materials like sugar, cotton, and tobacco, which then returned to England. What Hornick failed to foresee is that as the quantity of gold in a country increases, it becomes less rare and therefore less valuable. In other words, quantity affects prices and vice-versa; consequently, mercantilism actually led to the depreciation of domestic gold reserves.

Similarly to Thomas Mun, who was also a mercantilist, Hornick presented his mercantile arrangements as if they were a series of mathematical deductions that followed natural business laws, thereby leading both men to patriotic conclusions. While Mun denounced the Dutch invasion of English markets, Hornick rejected French claims to German lands and resources. They advocated for protectionist government, encouraging exports and discouraging imports through subsidies and tariffs.

Although Hornick and Mun were both mercantilists, Hornick offered a far more focused discussion of political economy in his publications. Mun, by contrast, meandered from piety to profit and back again in his book *England's Treasure by Foreign Trade*. Hornick's book was very popular for a generation or more. It went through 12 editions because he offered something Mun had not: a definite program based on principles and scientific management.

Philipp Wilhelm von Hornick died on October 23, 1714, in Passau, Germany.

*See also:* Mun, Thomas; Quesnay, François

## Selected Works by Philipp Wilhelm von Hornick

Hornick, Philipp Wilhelm von. "Austria Over All, If She Only Will." In *Early Economic Thought: Selections from Economic Literature Prior to Adam Smith*. Edited by Arthur Eli Monroe, 221–43. Cambridge, MA: Harvard University Press, 1924.

### Selected Works about Philipp Wilhelm von Hornick

Ekelund, Robert B., and Robert F. Hebert. *A History of Economic Theory and Method.* Long Grove, IL: Waveland Press, 1997.

Magnusson, Lars. *Mercantilism: The Shaping of an Economic Language.* London: Routledge, 1994.

Magnusson, Lars. *Mercantilist Theory and Practice: The History of British Mercantilism.* London: Pickering & Chatto, 2008.

"Mercantilism." In *The Concise Encyclopedia of Economics.* Edited by David R. Henderson. The Library of Economics and Liberty. http://www.econlib.org/library/Enc/Mercantilism.html (accessed February 2012).

"Mercantilism." The History of Economic Thought. http://www.econlinks.uma.es/Escuelas/mercant.htm#mercant (accessed February 2012).

Mun, Thomas. "A Discourse of Trade from England unto the East-Indies (1621)." Farnborough, England: Gregg International Publishers, 1971.

Mun, Thomas. *England's Treasure by Forraign Trade.* Oxford: Blackwell, 1664.

*Ninee Shoua Yang*

## HUANG, QIN SHI

Born: 259 BCE in the Zhao region, China; Died: 210 BCE; Chinese; standardized currency, weights and measures; Major Work: unified China, led construction of Great Wall of China, Lingqu Canal, Epang Palace.

Qin Shi Huang, with his adviser, Li Si Huang, dismantled the feudal system and ambitiously and aggressively expanded his father's kingdom sixfold. He unified the country in significant ways. He initiated structural institutions that created a period of prosperity he enjoyed until his death. Qin Shi Huang died at the age of 49.

Qin Shi Huang, born to King Zhuangxiang of Qin and Lady Zhao, was the first emperor of China at the age of 13. His father died in 246 BCE, after ruling only three years. In the Warring States period (246 BCE–221 BCE) of China's history, Huang conquered the neighboring regions in succession: Zhao, in 228 BCE (the earthquake of 229 BCE contributed to its fall); Han, in 226 BCE; Wei, in 225 BCE; Chu, in 223 BCE; Yan, in 222 BCE; and lastly, Qi (now known as Shandong Province, Guangdong Province, and Vietnam). Huang's decision to standardize the axle and cart sizes led to the construction of a massive network of roads that carried soldiers throughout the country. The farmers in this agrarian society benefited from the improved roads because the system created trade opportunities. Another institution Huang established was the standardization of currency, the Ban liang coin and weights and measures.

Huang relocated 100,000 families to tax and pay for the new capital, Xiangyang. He built a palace at Epang. He instituted numerous reforms, including for example a program to collect every sword and dagger from each household, melt them down, and recast them into the Twelve Bronze Giants. The country was reorganized as 40 districts, led by governors selected on merit, because Huang no longer recognized heredity succession. Districts were directly under governors, counties reported to districts, and units of 100 families were the bottom of the hierarchy.

More construction enhanced trade and transport of military supplies. In 214 BCE, Huang began work on a 34-kilometer canal to unite north and south China. The Linqu Canal connected the Xiang River, which fed the Yangtze River, and the Li Jiang River, which fed the Pearl River.

The Chinese currency was now one type, because all other currencies were declared void, as were regional scripts, as Huang also declared there would be one Chinese language. As everyone adjusted, it was a boon for trading. The emperor also practiced traditional Chinese medicine, which held that all things comprise five elements: earth, wood, metal, fire, and water. The emperor's element was water. For the superstitious Huang, this meant he would honor all the symbols of his time leading under the water element: the color black, the cardinal direction, north, the winter season, and the number six. He even required all wagon axles to be standardized to six feet, and hats were to be made six inches high and no more.

Retaliation was a major problem in Huang's regime and he escaped many assassination attempts. When he grew frustrated with the Xiongnu nomads' constant invasions from the north, he initiated construction of the Great Wall. Hundreds of thousands of men linked existing walls and constructed new ones on precarious, rocky cliffs—an enduring feat of engineering. Huang and his chancellor, Li Si, formulated elaborate methods of avoiding assassins because they made many enemies.

Huang's legalistic approach ended the period of the Hundred Schools of Thought of Confucius and like-minded philosophers. The emperor took steps to burn books on all topics except for astrology, agriculture, medicine, divination, and history, and had philosophers buried alive. Because he feared evil spirits and live enemies, Huang moved among his 200 palaces in underground tunnels. A meteor fell in Donjun in 211 BCE and someone inscribed upon it that Huang's death was imminent. When no one confessed to the deed, the emperor ordered execution for the entire community. He then had the stone completely obliterated.

The legacy of Qin Shi Huang was strong leadership and a unified world power more than 2,000 years ago.

All his life, Huang searched for the secret to immortality. Ironically, Huang died in 210 BCE when he took some mercury pills that he thought would achieve it. Huang's second-eldest son succeeded him because the first son had political loyalties in conflict with him and Li Si. To ensure a smooth transition, Huang's death was kept secret for two months, the time it took to travel to the capital, Xiangyang.

*See also:* Xiaochuan, Zhou

## Selected Works by Qin Shi Huang

Unpublished documents.

## Selected Works about Qin Shi Huang

Buwei, Lu. *The Annals of Lu Buwei*. Translated by John Knoblock and Jeffrey Riegel. Palo Alto, CA: Stanford University Press, 2000.

Lewis, Mark Edward. *The Early Chinese Empires: Qin and Han.* Cambridge, MA: Harvard University Press, 2007.

Ren, Changhong, and Jingyu Wu. *Rise and Fall of the Qin Dynasty.* Singapore: Asiapac Books, 2000.

*Cynthia Blitz Law*

## HUME, DAVID

Born: April 26, 1711, in Edinburgh, Scotland; Died: August 25, 1776, in Edinburgh, Scotland; Scottish; moral philosophy; Major Works: *A Treatise of Human Nature* (1739), *Essays, Moral and Political* (1741), *The History of England from the Invasion of Julius Caesar to the Revolution of 1688* (1757–62), *Dialogues Concerning Natural Religion* (1779).

David Hume is considered an Enlightenment author, but he did not believe in natural law and natural rights, like John Locke, Jean-Jacque Rousseau, or Adam Smith. Hume advocated utilitarianism, the idea that goodness is the same as usefulness. He is remembered as an extreme skeptic. He held no belief as sacred but instead attempted to test every theory by observation. Hume died in 1776.

David Hume was born on April 26, 1711 in Edinburgh, Scotland. His father died when he was very young. Hume entered the University of Edinburgh at the exceptionally young age of 11, and though he started his studies with the intent to become a lawyer, he quickly found that he had a passion for philosophy. From an early age, Hume seems to have taken questions of morality, life after death, free will, the existence of God, and other philosophical issues very seriously; he pursued these questions in his studies and writing for the rest of his life.

Hume was a lifelong writer and philosopher. He published his first book, *Treatise of Human Nature*, when he was 28. Hume challenged the notion that humans are guided by reason. Instead, he argued that people are driven by their desires, that they consistently seek to maximize their own happiness, and that a person's sense of "self" is simply a combination of sensations and choices. He drew a sharp distinction between the "is" of science and the "ought" of morality. The book was not well received at the time, to Hume's acute embarrassment, but has since come to be recognized as one of the most important works of philosophy ever written.

His subsequent work was taken more seriously, but it also made him a notorious figure since it contained antireligious sentiment. Perceiving him to be an atheist, church leaders successfully denied his application to be a professor of moral philosophy at the University of Edinburgh and the University of Glasgow. Hume secured employment as secretary to a Scottish general, actually taking part in an attempted attack on French Canada that, sidetracked, was diverted to France itself. He made his fortune when his eight-volume *History of England from the Invasion of Julius Caesar to the Revolution of 1688* proved to be a major success. He was able to devote the rest of his life to writing.

Hume's economic thought was dominated by utilitarianism; he believed that economic and social policies should be directed at producing the most possible value for the most number of people. From this starting point he defended private property, not on the basis of natural rights (like John Locke), but simply because of utility; resources are scarce, and people use these resources most efficiently when they own them privately. Hume argued that if resources were unlimited, then private property would cease to be useful.

Hume pointed out flaws in the theory of mercantilism, an idea that discouraged free trade in favor of state-supported monopolies. He responded to mercantilist claims that nations should seek to attract as much gold as they could through exports by arguing that this goal was impossible. If too much money was traded to one country, then prices in that country would rise due to inflation. This would cause people in that country to seek to buy imports from other countries that did not have an inflation problem. Therefore, in the long run, trade between nations would tend to balance. Furthermore, he pointed out that trade promotes the economic development of a country, but it also improves human capital, that is, the skills and knowledge of the population. It makes people become more aware of the world, which in turn makes them more dynamic, imaginative, and productive. He went on to say that countries need not fear the economic development of their neighbors, as if one nation can flourish only at the expense of another. Rather, the economic growth of a trading partner makes for a more prosperous community of nations. Rich nations and poor nations have nothing to lose and everything to gain from trade. He even made the outrageous claim that trade could bring happiness and wealth to France—this was not a popular statement in eighteenth-century Britain! But Hume had made his point. To this day economists still believe voluntary trade benefits both sides.

David Hume, like John Locke, was a link in the chain from political liberalism to modern economic thought. He was friends with Adam Smith, and no doubt shared with Smith his arguments against mercantilism and toward an economic philosophy driven by the decisions of individuals rather than the needs of the state. Hume's philosophy was first practical, and while this might not have won him the trust of the Church of Scotland, his writings have secured him a place among the most important of the world's philosophers.

David Hume died on August 25, 1776, in Edinburgh, Scotland.

*See also:* Locke, John; Smith, Adam

### Selected Works by David Hume

Hume, David. *Dialogues Concerning Natural Religion.* 2nd ed. (1779). Edited by Richard H. Popkin. Indianapolis, IN: Hackett, 1998.
Hume, David. *Essays, Moral and Political.* Edinburgh: R. Fleming and A. Alison, 1741.
Hume, David. *The History of England from the Invasion of Julius Caesar to the Revolution of 1688.* 8 vols. Edinburgh: Lackington, Allen, 1805.
Hume, David. *A Treatise of Human Nature.* Oxford: Clarendon Press, 1739.

### Selected Works about David Hume

Baier, Annette C. *The Pursuits of Philosophy: An Introduction to the Life and Thought of David Hume.* Cambridge, MA: Harvard University Press, 2011.
Copley, Stephen, and Andrew Edgar, eds. *Selected Essays by David Hume.* Oxford World Classics. New York: Oxford University Press, 2008.

Graham, Roderick. *The Great Infidel: A Life of David Hume.* Edinburgh, Scotland: Birlinn, 2006.

Townsend, Dabney. *Hume's Aesthetic Theory: Sentiment and Taste in the History of Aesthetics* Routledge Studies in Eighteenth-Century Philosophy. London: Routledge, 2001.

*Stephen H. Day*

## HURWICZ, LEONID

Born: August 21, 1917, in Moscow, Russia; Died: June 24, 2008, in Minneapolis, Minnesota; Polish, naturalized U.S. citizen; mechanism design theory, game theory, mathematical economics, microeconomics, Nobel Prize (2007); Major Works: "The Theory of Economic Behavior" (1945), "The Design of Mechanisms for Resource Allocation" (1973), "But Who Will Guard the Guardians?" (2007).

Leonid Hurwicz is considered a pioneer in the field of mechanism design. Mechanism design, similar to game theory, is a complex, highly quantitative approach to strategic decision making. Today, his theories are required courses for students of economics at every American college and university. His methodology for analyzing the interactions of institutions and markets was groundbreaking and relevant to solving economic, political, and social problems. Hurwicz was awarded the Nobel Prize in 2007. He died in 2008.

Hurwicz was born to Jewish parents in Moscow, Russia, on August 21, 1917, between the Kirensky and Bolshevik Revolutions. In 1938, he earned a law degree from the University of Warsaw and left to study at the London School of Economics. He was unable to extend his visa in Great Britain the following year. In August 1939, shortly before Hitler's armies invaded Poland, he traveled to Switzerland to study at the Graduate Institute of International Studies. There he learned that his parents and brother had been arrested and sent to a Soviet prison camp in the Arctic. By 1940, he found a safe haven with cousins in Chicago, Illinois, where his family were eventually able to join him.

Hurwicz studied and taught at the Massachusetts Institute of Technology (MIT) with Paul Samuelson and at the University of Chicago, where he collaborated with Kenneth Arrow, Oskar Lange, Tjalling Koopmans, and Jacob Marschak. Walter Heller urged him to accept a position at the University of Minnesota where Daniel McFadden was one of his graduate assistants. At the University of Minnesota he taught economic theory, public economics, welfare economics, mechanisms and institutions, mathematical economics, comparison and analyses of systems, and techniques of economic organizations. Retiring from the University of Minnesota, Leonid Hurwicz was the regent's professor emeritus at the University of Minnesota.

Leonid Hurwicz's career centered on his fascination and the challenges of determining whether individual needs could be met within societal goals, specifically if the same information was available to all parties, and if so, were agreements (contracts) enforceable. Hurwicz explored topics related to economic institutions and social choice.

He observed structural similarities of public and private institutions including ministries, governments, and corporate headquarters' departments, divisions, and bureaucratic organizational levels. He investigated whether there was a way he could measure efficiency of centralized and decentralized allocations. In his search for efficient outcomes of societal problems, Hurwicz considered how institutions met the needs of citizens, how public entities share information to make decisions, and how organizations use and protect limited resources. Hurwicz observed that competition for incentives or incentive compatibility in open markets influenced the allocation of resources. Hurwicz identified and accounted for strategic decision-making processes for resource allocation. Incentives could be applied when no one person or group stepped up to advocate for a best possible outcome for all players. In cases where government entities played the role of intervener, they established a new regulation to precipitate a market resolution when the market seemed stuck.

Game theory is quantitative strategic decision making. Hurwicz, pioneering a form of game theory known as mechanism design, recognized players who followed the rules and players who, in their self-interest, bent or broke the rules. His mechanism design model factored in both kinds of players.

In private life, Hurwicz tested his theories on available information and compatibility of competing personal interests. He initiated walking subcaucuses at the 1968 Democratic Convention, where he was a delegate for Senator Eugene McCarthy. He was a member of the Democratic Party Platform Committee. This method of information gathering and influence sharing is still used today.

Public policy makers and economists used mechanism design theory to mitigate inequities in the delivery of health care, insurance, government regulation in the telecom and digital fields, traffic management, and mediation. The theory is used when justice departments set up "sting" operations to catch public servants guided by self-interest over the public interest. Hurwicz concluded that corruption was preventable. To resolve a dispute in a win-win situation was an efficient application of mechanism design.

Leonid Hurwicz was awarded the Nobel Prize in Economics in 2007 with Eric Maskin and Roger Myerson. In 1990, Hurwicz received the National Medal of Science.

Leonid Hurwicz died June 24, 2008 at the age of 90 in Minneapolis, Minnesota, eight months after receiving the Nobel Prize.

*See also:* Arrow, Kenneth; Engels, Friedrich; Heller, Walter; Koopmans, Tjalling; Lange, Oskar; Marx, Karl; Maskin, Eric; Myerson, Roger; Samuelson, Paul

**Selected Works by Leonid Hurwicz**

Hurwicz, Leonid. "The Theory of Economic Behavior." *American Economic Review* 35, no. 5 (1945): 909–25.

Hurwicz, Leonid. "The Design of Mechanisms for Resource Allocation." *The American Economic Review* 63, no. 2 (May 1973): 1–30.

Hurwicz, Leonid. "But Who Will Guard the Guardians?" *American Economic Review* 98, no. 3 (June 2007): 577–85.

**Selected Works about Leonid Hurwicz**

Bauer, Ann. "Leonid Hurwicz's Game." *Twin Cities Business*, March 1, 2008. http://tcbmag.com/Leadership/Leaders/Leonid-Hurwicz-s-GameBiography (accessed October 2012).

Groves, Theodore, Roy Radner, and Stanley Reiter, eds. *Information, Incentives, and Economics Mechanisms: Essays in Honor of Leonid Hurwicz*. Minneapolis: University of Minnesota Press, 1987.

Hurwicz, Leonid. "Prize Lecture: But Who Will Guard the Guardians?" NobelPrize.org. http://nobelprize.org/nobel_prizes/economics/laureates/2007/hurwicz-lecture.html (accessed July 2011).

"Leonid Hurwicz." http://jewishvirtuallibrary.org/source/biography/Hurwicz.html (accessed July 2011).

Lohr, Steve. "Three Share Nobel in Economics for Work on Social Mechanisms." *New York Times*, October 16, 2007. http://www.nytimes.com/2007/10/16/business/16nobel.html?scp=3&sq=&st=myt (accessed July 2011).

*Cynthia Blitz Law*

## IRWIN, DOUGLAS

Born: October 31, 1962, in East Lansing, Michigan; American; trade policy, protectionism, tariffs, wages, infant industry; Major Works: *Against the Tide: An Intellectual History of Free Trade* (1996), *Free Trade under Fire* (2002).

Douglas Irwin is an American economist best known for his publications on American trade policy. Irwin dismisses protectionist policies and holds that economies that promote free trade will experience higher economic growth than those that limit it. Protectionist policies are paradoxical. They seek to encourage the purchase of domestic goods by restricting or restraining import products, but they inadvertently produce a stagnate or shrinking economy with declining levels of employment. Restricted trade agreements and high trade tariffs limit the growth potential and expansion of domestic businesses by denying them potential customers in states where trade agreements are void or tariffs are too high.

Douglas Alexander Irwin was born on October 31, 1962, in East Lansing, Michigan. He completed a Bachelor of Arts degree in political science from the University of New Hampshire in 1984, graduating magna cum laude. The following year, Irwin completed a master of arts in economics from Columbia University and continued on at Columbia to earn a doctorate of philosophy in economics in 1988, graduating with distinction.

In addition to holding academic appointments at prominent institutions such as Dartmouth College and the University of Chicago, Irwin also worked as a research associate at the National Bureau of Economic Research, was an editor of the publication *World Trade Review*, and was a regularly contributing author to the publication *The Economist*. Irwin served on the staffs of the Council on Economic Advisers and the Federal Reserve System Board of Governors.

The writings of Douglass Irwin argue that free trade is the catalyst for a growing economy and inherently promotes high levels of employment and national revenue. The implementation of protectionist policies that limit free trade such as tariffs and quotas are considered stifling to an economy's growth. Protectionist measures produce negative consequences in the areas of employment, the power of the consumer dollar, and the cost of production.

According to Irwin, protectionist policies are paradoxical in that while they seek to encourage the purchase of domestic goods, they inadvertently produce a stagnant or shrinking economy with declining levels of employment. Restricted trade agreements and high trade tariffs limit the growth potential of domestic businesses by denying them potential customers in states where trade agreements are void or tariffs are too high. Because business growth exists within a confined space, domestic economies are confined and will restrict additional workers from being added to the workforce.

Further compounding the effects of protectionist policies, Irwin argued, fewer employees in an economy yield a lower-paid and conservative consumer population. These effects lead to a declining economic sequence of lower demand for goods, lower business sales revenue, decreased product supply, higher prices, and lower purchasing power of the consumer dollar. All of this culminates in lower national tax revenues, leaving governments with less operating cash. These disastrous results led Irwin to a negative and skeptical stance toward protectionist policies, including fair-trade policies, infant industry protection, the privatization of U.S. trade, and even antidumping policies.

Contrary to protectionist views, Irwin advocates complete free trade and provides it as a prescription to grow the American economy. Free trade, he argues, not only expands the consumer base for domestic business but also provides healthy competition to domestic companies that benefit the American consumer. His strong preference for free trade stems from the principles found in Adam Smith's *The Wealth of Nations* as he argues that competition, regardless of its origins, ultimately leads to a strong economy and a wealthier government receiving higher tax revenues and therefore increasing its operating cash.

Irwin is currently the Robert E. Maxwell Professor of Arts and Sciences at Dartmouth College.

*See also:* Friedman, Milton; Krugman, Paul; Taussig, Frank

## Selected Works by Douglas Irwin

Irwin, Douglas. *Against the Tide: An Intellectual History of Free Trade*. Princeton, NJ: Princeton University Press, 1996.

Irwin, Douglas. *Free Trade under Fire*. Princeton, NJ: Princeton University Press, 2002.

Irwin, Douglas. *Peddling Protectionism: Smoot-Hawley and the Great Depression*. Princeton, NJ: Princeton University Press, 2011.

Irwin, Douglas A. "The GATT's Contribution to Economic Recovery in Post-War Western Europe." In *Europe's Postwar Recovery*. Edited by Barry Eichengreen, 127–50. Cambridge: Cambridge University Press, 1995.

## Selected Works about Douglas Irwin

Cato Institute. "Douglas Irwin, Advisor, Center for Trade Policy Studies." http://www.cato.org/people/douglas-irwin (accessed September 2012).

Dartmouth College. "Douglas A. Irwin." http://www.dartmouth.edu/~dirwin/bio.htm.

*Nevena Trajkov*

## JEVONS, WILLIAM STANLEY

Born: September 1, 1835, in Liverpool, England; Died: August 13, 1882, in Hastings, England; English; economic statistician, marginal utility theory; Major Work: *The Theory of the Political Economy* (1871).

William Stanley Jevons was one of the foremost writers of economics and logic in the nineteenth century. His writings and theories on the political economy were original and prominent. Jevons is most noted for his introduction of the concept of marginal utility theory of value and marginal analysis. Jevons may be considered one of the first environmental economists when he wrote about the British coal dependence in 1865 and introduced the Jevons paradox. Jevons was also later noted for his distinction between ordinal and cardinal utility. Jevons died in 1882.

William Stanley Jevons was born on September 1, 1835, in Liverpool, England. Jevons's father was a writer of legal and economic subjects and his mother was the daughter of famous historian William Roscoe. At the age of 15, his father sent him to the University College School. Early in his education Jevons actually preferred studying the sciences of chemistry and botany, and he excelled in both. After two years at University College School, he received an unexpected offer to take a position as an assayer in Australia. The thought of leaving England had never been in Jevons's mind, but financial problems in his father's firm in 1847 changed his thinking and in June of 1854, he left for Sydney.

It was in Australia that Jevons's interest in political economy flourished. After five years in his post as an assayer, Jevons resigned and returned to the University College School in 1859. He obtained a BA degree, and not long after taking his MA Jevons obtained a post to tutor at Owens College in Manchester, not far from Liverpool.

Jevons was one of the first political economists to value the use and application of mathematics to political economy. At Owens College Jevons began publishing, beginning with the piece "A General Mathematical Theory of Political Economy" (1862), which, written for the British Association, outlined the marginal utility theory of value. At the time, it was originally written as a letter and received little recognition, even after its full publication in the *Journal of Statistical Society* four years later.

Jevons wrote his first complete work in 1871 with *The Theory of Political Economy*. The theory of utility was the focal point of Jevons's thought on political economy. Jevons's main idea was that the degree of utility of a commodity is some continuous mathematical function of the quantity of the commodity available. His work was quickly developed by Austrian economist Carl Menger and Swiss economist Leon Walras. Although it was Gossen who should be credited with the discovery of the connection between value in exchange and final (or marginal) utility, Jevons's contribution cannot be ignored.

Of special note regarding Jevons's writing is the distinction between ordinal and cardinal utility, which he fails to acknowledge but with good reason. At the time of his writing this distinction did not exist. For a better understanding of his writing, it helps to know that his mathematics required the use of cardinal utility functions. Cardinal utility allowed Jevons to discuss the relative magnitude of utilities, unlike ordinal utility, which states that goods can be ranked and compared only according to which provides the most utility. Jevons strongly believed that his measurements of utility were relative, not a direct measure.

Although Jevons's work was essential in the development of such a key modern thought, his first recognition came through his writings on other practical economic questions. His next two books, *A Serious Fall in the Value of Gold* (1863) and *The Coal Question* (1865), placed Jevons on the face of applied economics and statistics. These works alone were sufficient to earn Jevons a reputation as one of the greatest economists, even in the absence of his more famous work, *The Theory of Political Economy*.

*The Coal Question* focused on Britain's dependence on coal. His ideas have even been revisited in modern times. Jevons introduced the counterintuitive idea we use today to improve energy efficiency. Jevons submitted that energy use will actually increase as energy efficiency measures are implemented that lead to reduced energy costs. This counterintuitive idea is now known as the Jevons paradox. Jevons also raised the question of sustainability as coal was stated as a finite, nonrenewable resource. As well as resource peaking, other topics that were central to this idea of sustainability were limits to growth, overpopulation, postglobal relocalization, energy return on energy input, taxation of the energy resources, and renewable energy alternative. The book remains at the foundation of energy depletion theory.

Jevons had a great impact in political economy, but his work in logic was on equal footing. *Pure Logic: Or the Logic of Quality Apart from Quantity* (1864) was his first small volume in this field. He simplified the principle of substitution of similars by explaining that "whatever is true of a thing is true of its like." He published *The Substitution of Similars* in 1869. It worked on the basis that the conclusion derivable from any given set of premises could be mechanically obtained. This was symbolized through the presentation of his "Logic Piano," a mechanical computer he built and presented in the same year alongside his new thought.

His works on logic went further in 1874 with his theory of induction, which appeared under the title of *The Principles of Science*. It was aimed to revive the theories of Whewell and address the criticisms made by John Stuart Mill. He developed the view that induction is simply an inverse employment of deduction. He also toyed with the general theory of probability and the relation between probability and induction. Jevons's work on this subject was different from the rest because of his knowledge of the various natural sciences. These enabled him to relieve the abstract character of logical doctrine by concrete scientific illustrations, often worked out in great detail.

William Stanley Jevons died from drowning on August 13, 1882, at Hastings, England.

*See also:* Menger, Carl; Mill, John Stuart; Walras, Leon

### Selected Works by William Stanley Jevons

Jevons, William Stanley. *The Coal Question: An Inquiry Concerning the Progress of the Nation, and the Probable Exhaustion of Our Coal-Mines* (1865). New York: Macmillan, 1906.
Jevons, William Stanley. *A Serious Fall in the Value of Gold.* London: E. Stanford, 1863.
Jevons, William Stanley. *The Substitution of Similars.* London: Macmillan, 1869.
Jevons, William Stanley. *The Theory of Political Economy.* London: Macmillan, 1871.

### Selected Works about William Stanley Jevons

Foster, John Bellamy. "Capitalism and the Curse of Energy Efficiency." *Monthly Review: An Independent Socialist Magazine* 62, no. 6 (2010): 1–13.
Heilbroner, Robert L. *Teachings from the Worldly Philosophy.* New York: Norton, 1996.
Maas, Harro. *William Stanley Jevons and the Making of Modern Economics.* Cambridge: Cambridge University Press, 2005.
Mosselmans, Bert. "William Stanley Jevons." Stanford Encyclopedia of Philosophy. http://plato.stanford.edu/entries/william-jevons/ (accessed March 2011).
Owen, David. "The Efficiency Dilemma." *New Yorker*, December 20, 2010, 78–83.

*John E. Trupiano*

## JOHNSON, HARRY

Born: May 26, 1923, in Toronto, Canada; Died: May 9, 1977, in Geneva, Switzerland; Canadian; international trade and finance, monetary policy; Major Works: "British Monetary Statistics" (1959), *Money, Trade and Economic Growth: Survey Lectures in Economic Theory* (1962).

Harry Johnson was a Canadian economist in the fields of international trade, international finance, and monetary policy after World War II. He was known for his ability to take opposing economic philosophical viewpoints. An avid proponent of free trade, Johnson was credited with the possibility theorem, the ability of a monopolistic country to levy a tariff without fear of retaliation. Johnson died in 1977.

Harry Johnson was born on May 26, 1923, in Toronto, Canada. Johnson received his BA and MA from the University of Toronto. He joined the Canadian armed forces and was stationed in England. After military service, he stayed in England earning BA and MA degrees from the University of Cambridge. While at Cambridge, he first heard John Maynard Keynes when Keynes presented a paper at the Political Economy Club.

Johnson earned his PhD from Harvard University in 1948. In 1949, Harry Johnson began his teaching career at Cambridge while still a student. He became a professor of economics at Manchester in 1956, and joined the economics faculty at the University of Chicago in 1959. Though retiring from the University of Chicago in 1977, Johnson interrupted his Chicago career to serve a span of eight years at the London School of Economics from 1966 to 1974.

In the field of international trade, Johnson was instrumental on several fronts. For one, he added significant contributions to expanding the knowledge base of the Hecksher-Ohlin theory of international trade.

Johnson also submitted that a country with a monopoly could impose a tariff on its imports without the concern of a successful retaliation tariff, even if one was instituted. This became known as the possibility theorem. Johnson did acknowledge the significant difference between theory and reality or practice, agreeing that even though it was possible, it was not likely.

His work also included efforts in international finance. Johnson was at the forefront of modern work on the balance of payments. In a 1958 paper, "British Monetary Statistics," he changed the way economists viewed a country's balance of payments. Prior to Johnson, the generally accepted method of determining a country's economic health was to look at nonmonetary factors such as consumption. Johnson for the first time introduced the idea of implementing a monetary approach to determine a country's balance of payments similar to those of Anna Schwartz's and Milton Friedman's efforts in the United States. During his time in England, Johnson contributed to monetary economics. While not completely successful, he broke new ground by establishing early attempts to measure the British money supply.

Having spent time in both England at the London School of Economics and the United States at the University of Chicago, Johnson became apt at converging the two prominent viewpoints of Keynes from England and the Chicago, monetarist, School from the United States. While his personal leanings were more to the Keynesian philosophy, his knowledge and use of monetarism were evident in his work. Johnson was, however, a devout proponent of free trade, personal freedom, and markets. Many of his lectures were critical of his native Canada for its protectionist policies, and he asserted that a freer Canada would have significant gains for the Canadian people.

Johnson was considered one of the most prolific writers in economics, if not the most prolific. It is noted that he contributed over 500 articles, over 40 books, and other publications to the economics body of knowledge. At one point during his career, he was the second most quoted economist, second only to Paul Samuelson. He was, however, not without his critics who contended he would often rewrite the same article.

Harry Johnson was bestowed many honors and awards. Of special significance for Johnson was being named an Officer of the Order of Canada in 1976. A year later he was recognized by the American Economic Association as a distinguished fellow. Each year, the Canadian Economics Association presents a Harry Johnson Prize for the best article in the *Canadian Journal of Economics*.

Harry Johnson died of a stroke on May 9, 1977, in Geneva, Switzerland.

*See also:* Keynes, John Maynard; Samuelson, Paul; Schumpeter, Joseph

### Selected Works by Harry Johnson

Johnson, Harry. "British Monetary Statistics." *Econometrica* 26 (February 1959): 1–17.

Johnson, Harry. *The Canadian Quandary: Economic Problems and Policies*. Toronto: McGraw-Hill, 1963.

Johnson, Harry. *Essays in Monetary Economics*. 2nd ed. Cambridge, MA: Harvard University Press, 1969.

Johnson, Harry. *Further Essays in Monetary Economics*. London: Allen & Unwin, 1972.

Johnson, Harry. "The 'General Theory' after Twenty-five Years." *American Economic Review* 51 (May 1961): 1–17.

Johnson, Harry. "The Keynesian Revolution and the Monetarist Counter-Revolution." *American Economic Review* 61 (May 1971): 1–14.

Johnson, Harry. *Macroeconomics and Monetary Theory*. Hawthorne, NY: Aldine, 1972.

Johnson, Harry. *Money, Trade and Economic Growth: Survey Lectures in Economic Theory*. London: Allen & Unwin, 1962.

Johnson, Harry. "Optimum Tariffs and Retaliation." *Review of Economic Studies* 21, no. 2 (1953): 142–53.

### Selected Works about Harry Johnson

Corden, W. Max. "Johnson, Harry Gordon (1923–1977)." In *Oxford Dictionary of National Biography*. Oxford: Oxford University Press, 2004 (accessed September 2011).

Moggridge, David. *Harry Johnson: A Life in Economics*. New York: Cambridge University Press, 2008.

Tobin, James. *Harry Gordon Johnson: 1923–1977*. New York: Oxford University Press, 1980.

*David A. Dieterle*

# K

## KAHN, ALFRED

Born: October 17, 1917, in Paterson, New Jersey; Died: December 27, 2010, in Ithaca, New York; American; regulation and deregulation; Major Work: *The Economics of Regulation: Principles and Institutions* (1970).

Alfred Kahn led the U.S. economy of the late twentieth century into the era of deregulation. Kahn's career was highlighted by his efforts to deregulate what he considered the anticonsumer regulated industries of the U.S. economy. Appointed by President Jimmy Carter to head the Civil Aeronautics Board, Kahn was instrumental in deregulating the airline industry. Kahn's deregulation of the airline industry transformed air travel into a form of mass transportation with discount prices affordable by most everyone. Kahn was known for continually extolling the virtues of simpler wording to explain the law or economics. Kahn died in 2010.

Alfred Edward Kahn was born on October 17, 1917, in Paterson, New Jersey. The son of Russian Jewish immigrants, Kahn graduated from New York University when most his age (18) were graduating from high school. He continued his graduate studies in economics, beginning at New York University and ending at Yale, where he earned his doctorate in 1942. Kahn began his career in public service in the U.S. Justice Department, Antitrust Division. He served in the army during World War II.

Following World War II, he served as chair of the Economics Department at Ripon College before moving on to Cornell in 1947. At Cornell he returned to the department chair role for the Economics Department. He eventually became dean of the College of Arts and Sciences and a member of the Cornell board of trustees.

Kahn authored many books and articles in his academic career. His classic work was *The Economics of Regulation: Principles and Institutions*. *The Economics of Regulation* was a two-volume set in which he brought economics to the forefront of exploring the costs and benefits or regulation. Many of his works focused on the deregulation of industries.

Kahn reentered public service in 1974 when he chaired the New York Public Service Commission. Alfred Kahn was responsible for utility companies charging different rates for different times or seasons. Using marginal analysis theory, utilities changed their rate charge practices to charge higher rates during peak times when costs were higher. This created incentives for customers to pursue alternatives and use power during off-peak times when rates were lower. As a result, the utilities earned revenues based on costs and consumers saved by using the utilities during lower-cost, and consequently lower-priced, periods. Kahn is also credited with the telephone industry eliminating free telephone directory assistance. He also served the private sector as an expert on regulations and deregulation in the electricity, transportation, telecommunications, and utility industries.

His notoriety as a public servant reached national status when he joined the Carter administration as President Carter's economic adviser on inflation in 1978. With inflation rates as high as ever in the United States, President Carter appointed Kahn to head his Council on Wage and Price Stability. Tabbed the "inflation czar," Kahn called the job thankless and in 1980 he resigned after only 15 months in the position. He had even lamented that the only reason he was not fired was that no one else would take the job.

President Carter appointed Kahn as head of the Civil Aeronautics Board (CAB) in 1977. At the time of his appointment, the airlines industry was regulated from prices and routes down to the meals that would be served on a flight. This structure of the airline industry was viewed as very much to benefit the airlines at a cost to the consumers. Kahn went to work putting his economics and experience in deregulation to work on the industry. During 1977 and 1978, Kahn and the CAB deregulated the airline industry, freeing up routes, carriers, and prices. Under Kahn's leadership, the CAB did such a good job in deregulating the airline industry that they ceased to exist in 1978. Kahn has been labeled the "father of the airline deregulation," a label he did not cherish.

While Kahn took his work very seriously, he was noted for the quick quip or quote. He once used the word "depression" when describing a potential scenario for the U.S. economy. Being ever the economist and not the politician, he was admonished for using the "d" word. So when the same topic came up again, he changed the "d" word to "banana." However, after objections from the banana industry, addressing the same issue a third time he changed "banana" to "kumquat." He was also known for sarcastically asking if an economic or law statement could be made more complicated. This attitude played directly into his continual efforts to have legal and economic policies explained in simple, understandable language.

In 1980, Kahn returned to Cornell, continuing his role as dean of Cornell's College of Arts and Sciences. He was also the Robert Julius Thorne Professor Emeritus of Political Economy. In 1997, he received the L. Welch Pogue Award for Lifetime Achievement in Aviation.

Alfred Kahn died on December 27, 2010, in Ithaca, New York.

*See also:* Galbraith, John Kenneth; Samuelson, Paul

**Selected Works by Alfred Kahn**

Kahn, Alfred. *The Economics of Regulation: Principles and Institutions.* Cambridge, MA: MIT Press, 1970.
Kahn, Alfred. *Great Britain in the World Economy.* Surrey, UK: Ashgate, 1993.
Kahn, Alfred. *Lessons from Deregulation: Telecommunications and Airlines after the Crunch.* Washington, DC: Brookings Institution Press, 2004.

Kahn, Alfred. *Letting Go: Deregulating the Process of Deregulation: Temptation of the Kleptocrats and the Political Economy of Regulatory Disingenuousness.* East Lansing: Michigan State University Institute of Public Utilities, 1998.

Kahn, Alfred. *Whom the Gods Would Destroy, or How Not to Deregulate.* Washington, DC: American Enterprise Institute for Public Policy Research, 2002.

**Selected Works about Alfred Kahn**

"Alfred Kahn, Father of 1970s Airline Deregulation, Dies at 93." Bloomberg News. http://www.bloomberg.com/news/2010-12-28/alfred-kahn-who-oversaw-airline-industry-break-up-for-carter-dies-at-93.html (accessed March 2011).

"Economist Alfred Kahn, 'Father of Airline Deregulation' and Former Presidential Adviser, Dies at 93." http://news.cornell.edu/stories/Dec10/KahnObit.html (accessed March 2011).

McCraw, Thomas K. *Prophets of Regulation: Charles Francis Adams, Louis D. Brandeis, James M. Landis, Alfred E. Kahn.* Cambridge, MA: Harvard University Press, 1984.

Russell, George. "Flying among the Merger Clouds." *Time.* http://www.time.com/time/magazine/article/0,9171,962408-3,00.html (accessed March 2011).

*David A. Dieterle*

## KAHNEMAN, DANIEL

Born: March 5, 1934, in Tel Aviv, Israel; Israeli; behavioral economics, Nobel Prize (2002); Major Works: "Prospect Theory: An Analysis of Decisions under Risk" (with A. Tversky) (1979), *Thinking, Fast and Slow* (2011).

Daniel Kahneman was a psychologist by profession, yet won the 2002 Nobel Prize in Economics for his work in behavavioral economics. Working along his longtime friend and colleague Amos Tversky, the two were honored for their research in economic decision making. They focused specifically on how humans may think in terms of costs and benefits, yet often make decisions based on irrational decision-making analysis. Kahneman and Tversky blended psychology and economics to derive what became a basis for the field of behaviorial economics.

Daniel Kahneman was born on March 5, 1934 in Tel Aviv, Israel. Even though he was born in Israel his family resided in Paris. He was growing up in Paris when the Germans occupied the city. During World War II, his family moved several times throughout France to avoid the fate of so many other Jewish people. Young Kahneman's father, who had been temporarily interred by the Germans, died just weeks before VE Day. At the conclusion of World War II, young Kahneman, his mother, and his sister were able to leave France for Israel and begin a new life.

Following high school, as a young Jewish man in Israel Kahneman had choices to make regarding his college education and his Israeli military obligation. Kahneman was able to defer his military obligation to attend Hebrew University, graduating in two years with a degree in psychology and mathematics.

After graduation he was drafted to fulfill his military obligation. After one year he was assigned to the psychology section of the Defense Forces. Several assignments during this time in the military became an influential foundation for his future career as a psychologist. During one assignment when he and his colleagues were being asked to make predictions on the future performance of young soldiers, they found their predictions not very accurate. This led Kahneman to create the term "illuson of validity." Twenty years later he was to introduce this term to the world of psychology. A second such experience that influenced his future career was an exercise where the psychologists would make very broad-based predictions of future performance based on very limited behavioral knowledge. A third military experience that strongly influenced Kahneman's future was the challenge of designing an interview process for determining the fitness of combat recruits. The system was a combination of statistical analysis and clinical interviews. The results were impressive, achieving predictive success at a rate three times the past rate. These challenges were the seeds of Kahneman's and Tversky's future work on the psychology of intuitive prediction.

In 1958, Kahneman went to the United States to attend the University of California, Berkeley (UC Berkeley). Receiving his PhD in 1961 from UC Berkeley, Kahneman returned to Israel. He joined the faculty of the psychology department at the Hebrew University. Kahneman set himself on the pursuit of becoming a better researcher. During his early years at Hebrew University he established a research lab, developed several research models, and assisted in developing additional training models for the Israeli military. His published research career began with his 1965 sabbatical.

In 1965 while on sabatical at the University of Michigan, Kahneman and a graduate student colleague Jackson Beatty began a series of experiments on mental effort. After several publishing successes with Beatty, Kahneman moved on, continuing his research on mental effort at Harvard. He returned to Hebrew University in 1967 a trained researcher.

During the 1967–68 academic year, Kahneman met Amos Tversky. Tversky's field of judgment and decision making intrigued Kahneman. Following a discussion on their personal experiences and the errors they each had made in predicting, the two decided to study the intuitions of experts, beginning what would become a lifelong professional duo. Kahneman and Tversky had a collaborative relationship that far transcended their professional lives. From 1971 to 1981, Kahneman and Tversky published eight journal articles. In 1971 and 1972 the "dynamic duo," as they became known to their colleagues, did considerable research and writing on judgment and decision making at the Oregon Research Institute (ORI). In 1972, Kahneman published *Attention and Effort*, his single most significant contribution to psychology.

Following his research and work at ORI, Kahneman's career took another major turn in 1972 when he and Tversky published an article in *Science* journal. The article, read by a small group of economists and philosophers, was interpreted as a critique on the rationality model of human behavior. Surprisingly to Kahneman, the article became the standard critical response to the rational agent model of decision making. The *Science* article had many critics, yet they collaboratively pressed forward in their study of decision making.

Kahneman continued his research in judgment and decision making with Tversky. In 1975, they presented a paper on what they originally labeled "value theory." In 1978, they published "Prospect Theory" in *Econometrica*. Interestingly, they did not publish in *Econometrica* to necessarily impact or influence the science of economics. Their focus was on impacting the field of decision making and *Econometrica* was the most respected and well-known professional journal for decision-making publishing. As a result, however, publishing the prospect theory in *Econometrica* did influence economics. Kahneman's entrance into the field of behavioral economics was about to be complete.

Kahneman and Tversky completed prospect theory while at Stanford University's Center for Advanced Studies in 1977–78. While at Stanford, Kahneman met a young economist named Richard Thaler. The integration of the prospect theory into economic theory became the basis for Kahneman's collaborations with Thaler. Through the collaborative efforts with Thaler, Kahneman's work now focused on the behavioral patterns of the economic human. Behavioral economics was born.

In 1984–85 Kahneman, now at the University of British Columbia, working with economists Thaler and Jack Knetsch expanded the field of behavorial economics. The focus of their work was on what they called "reference transactions," or making a decision based on the perception that someone has an entitlement to a particular outcome and the only fair transactions are those that uphold the entitlement. They created a series of experiments, vignettes, and surveys to support their thesis.

In 2002, Daniel Kahneman was awarded the Nobel Prize in Economics for his valuable contributions in integrating psycology into economics dealing with human judgment and irrational decision making. Besides the Nobel Prize in Economics, Daniel Kahneman has been the recipient of many awards and prizes in psychology. In 1982, he received the Distinguished Scientific Contribution Award of the American Psychological Association and in 2002 the Grawemeyer Prize. Both awards were jointly awarded with Amos Tversky. He was also honored with the Lifetime Contribution Award of the American Psychological Association in 2007.

After returning to his alma mater in 1986, in 1993 Kahneman accepted a position to teach at Princeton in both psychology and with the Woodrow Wilson School of Public Affairs and International Affairs. In 2011, Daniel Kahneman became known beyond the academic world to the general reader with his best-seller exploration of how we think, *Thinking, Fast and Slow*.

*See also:* Thaler, Richard

**Selected Works by Daniel Kahneman**

Kahneman, Daniel. *Attention and Effort*. Englewood Cliffs, NJ: Prentice-Hall, 1973.
Kahneman, Daniel. *Thinking, Fast and Slow*. New York: Farrar, Straus and Giroux, 2011.
Kahneman, Daniel, Thomas Gilovich, and Dale Griffin. *Heuristics and Biases: The Psychology of Intuitive Judgment*. Cambridge: Cambridge University Press, 2002.
Kahneman, Daniel, Ed Diener, and Norbert Schwarz. *Well-Being: The Foundations of Hedonic Psychology*. 1st ed. New York: Russell Sage Foundation, 2003.

Kahneman, D., J. Knetsch, and R. Thaler. "Experimental Tests of the Endowment Effect and the Coase Theorem." *Journal of Political Economy* 98, no. 6 (1990): 1325–48.

Kahneman, D., J. Knetsch, and R. Thaler. "Fairness and the Assumptions of Economics." *Journal of Business* 59 (1986): S285–S300.

Kahneman, D., J. Knetsch, J., and R. Thaler. "Fairness as a Constraint on Profit Seeking: Entitlements in the Market." *The American Economic Review* 76 (1986): 728–41.

Kahneman, D., and A. Tversky. "Choices, Values, and Frames." *American Psychologist* 39 (1984): 341–50.

Kahneman, Daniel, and Amos Tversky, eds. *Choices, Values, and Frames*. New York: Cambridge University Press and the Russell Sage Foundation, 2000.

Kahneman, D., and A. Tversky. "Prospect Theory: An Analysis of Decisions under Risk." *Econometrica* 47 (1979): 313–27.

Kahneman, D., and A. Tversky. "On the Psychology of Prediction." *Psychological Review* 80 (1973): 237–5l.

Kahneman, Daniel, Amos Tversky, and Paul Slovic. *Judgment under Uncertainty: Heuristics and Biases*. Cambridge: Cambridge University Press, 1982.

### Selected Works about Daniel Kahneman

Brockman, John. *This Will Make You Smarter: Daniel Kahneman and More*. Seattle, WA: Edge Foundation, 2012.

Kahneman, Daniel. "Autobiography." Nobelprize.org. nobelprize.org/nobel_prizes/economics/laureates/2002/kahneman-autobio.html (accessed March 22, 2011).

Vane, Howard R., and Chris Mulhearn. *James M. Buchanan, Gary S. Becker, Daniel Kahneman and Vernon L. Smith*. London: Edward Elgar, 2011.

Weiss, Beth. "Daniel Kahneman." Jewish Virtual Library. http://www.jewishvirtuallibrary.org/jsource/biography/kahneman.html (accessed March 22, 2011).

*David A. Dieterle*

## KALDOR, NICHOLAS

Born: May 12, 1908, in Budapest, Hungary; Died: September 30, 1986, in Papworth Everard, Cambridgeshire, England; Hungarian, naturalized English citizen; political economy, Keynesian economic theory, development economics; Major Work: *An Expenditure Tax* (1955).

Nicholas Kaldor was one of the leading economists of the Cambridge School, a school of thought that promoted the Keynesian economic philosophy. He was one of the few economists who changed views at the height of his career. Once an Austrian at the London School of Economics, he converted to Keynesian economic theory once the general theory emerged. While an Austrian he was a contributor to equilibrium theory and capital, but focused on welfare economics. Once a Keynesian, he altered his efforts to rates of interest and dynamics of speculation and the business cycle. Kaldor was known for his debate with Friedrich von Hayek. Kaldor died in 1986.

Nicholas Kaldor was born on May 12, 1908, in Budapest, Hungary. Nicholas attended the Model Gymnasium in Budapest. He began his study of economics at the University of Berlin. He graduated from the London School of Economics in 1930. In 1934, Kaldor became a naturalized citizen of England. He began his career as a lecturer at the London School of Economics in 1938. Kaldor moved his family to Cambridge during World War II and began a tenure with the National Institute of Economic and Social Research. In 1947 he moved once again, this time to Geneva, Switzerland, to direct research and planning at the Commission of Europe. In 1949, he returned to England to take a position of lecturer in the economics faculty at King's College of the University of Cambridge where he remained till his retirement in 1966 as professor.

Kaldor began his economics studies at the London School of Economics and the Austrian School. However, once John Maynard Keynes published his general theory, Kaldor became one of the theory's most ardent supporters, both in his development of economic theory and in his publications. He created the growth theory that became the main growth theory approach of the Cambridge School of economic thought. Kaldor's growth approach was the foundation of future economic philosophy for the neo-Ricardian and neo-Keynesian economic philosophies. As a leading voice for the new economic philosophy, Kaldor's focus shifted to the areas of growth theory and Veblen's theory of accumulation, and he was an unwavering critic of neoclassical economics.

Kaldor developed or was very influential in the development of several postwar economic theories. Following World War II, Kaldor shifted his professional focus once again to the development of developing countries and postwar reconstruction. As a consultant to several developing countries, Kaldor concentrated on growth, monetarism, equilibrium theory, and taxation. In 1955 Kaldor wrote *Expenditure Tax*, the early efforts proposing a value-added tax. His tax structure was implemented by two of his clients, India and Sri Lanka. Kaldor's tax plan was the basis for a value-added tax. In England, Harold Wilson's Labour government implemented such a tax under the term "selective employment tax." This tax was designed to tax service sector employment to subsidize the manufacturing sector. While the tax did not survive political scrutiny, it set the stage for future efforts to create a value-added tax base. Kaldor was also an economic policy adviser to the United Nations.

He was well known for the Kaldor-Hicks efficiency theory he developed with John Hicks in 1939, comparing the welfare of other countries. He was credited with the term "convenience yield" relative to commodity markets. In 1964, he addressed the issue of reserve currency with "commodity reserve currency" with Hart and Tinbergen. While his contributions to economics were in several different fields, his legacy is in his contributions to developing the Cambridge School and the later post-Keynesian and neo-Ricardian schools of economic thought.

In 1974, Kaldor was awarded a peerage as the City of Cambridge's Lord Kaldor of Newham. Kaldor retired in 1975, although he continued to lecture and provide advice on economic matters.

Nicholas Kaldor died on September 30, 1986, in Papworth Everard, Cambridgeshire, England.

*See also:* Hayek, Friedrich von; Hicks, John; Keynes, John Maynard; Robinson, Joan; Veblen, Thorstein

### Selected Works by Nicholas Kaldor

Kaldor, Nicholas. *Causes of Growth and Stagnation in the World Economy*. Cambridge: Cambridge University Press, 1996.

Kaldor, Nicholas. *Causes of the Slow Rate of Economic Growth of the United Kingdom: An Inaugural Lecture*. Cambridge: Cambridge University Press, 1966.

Kaldor, Nicholas. *Economics without Equilibrium: Arthur M. Okun Memorial Lectures, Yale University*. Armonk, NY: M.E. Sharpe, 1985.

Kaldor, Nicholas. *Essays on Economic Stability and Growth*. Tampa, FL: Free Press, 1960.

Kaldor, Nicholas. *Essays on Value and Distribution*. Tampa, FL: Free Press, 1960.

Kaldor, Nicholas. *An Expenditure Tax*. London: Allen & Unwin, 1955.

Kaldor, Nicholas. *Further Essays on Applied Economics*. Teaneck, NJ: Holmes & Meier, 1978.

Kaldor, Nicholas. *Further Essays on Economic Theory*. Teaneck, NJ: Holmes & Meier, 1978.

Kaldor, Nicholas. "Keynesian Economics after Fifty Years." In *Keynes and the Modern World*. Edited by David Worswick and James Trevithick, 1–48. Cambridge: Cambridge University Press, 1983.

Kaldor, Nicholas. *The Scourge of Monetarism*. Oxford: Oxford University Press, 1982.

Kaldor, Nicholas, A. G. Hart, and J. Tinbergen. "The Case for a Commodity Reserve Currency." United Nations Conference on Trade and Development. January 1964.

### Selected Works about Nicholas Kaldor

Harcourt, G. C. "Nicholas Kaldor, 12 May 1908–30 September 1986." *Economica* 55 (May 1988): 159–70.

King, John Edward. *Nicholas Kaldor*. Hampshire, UK: Palgrave Macmillan, 2009.

"Nicholas Kaldor Memorial Issue." *Cambridge Journal of Economics* 13, no. 1 (March 1989).

Setterfield, Mark. "History versus Equilibrium: Nicholas Kaldor on Historical Time and Economic Theory." *Cambridge Journal of Economics* 21, no. 3 (1997): 365–78.

Targetti, F. *Nicholas Kaldor: The Economics and Politics of Capitalism as a Dynamic System*. Oxford: Clarendon Press, 1992.

Thirlwall, A. P. *Nicholas Kaldor*. New York: New York University Press, 1987.

Turner, Marjorie Shepherd. *Nicholas Kaldor and the Real World*. Armonk, NY: M.E. Sharpe, 1993.

*David A. Dieterle*

## KALECKI, MICHAL

Born: June 22, 1899, in Lodz, Poland; Died: April 18, 1970, in Warsaw, Poland; Polish; macroeconomics, political economy; Major Work: *Proba teorii koniunktury* [An essay on the theory of the business cycle] (1937).

Michal Kalecki is referred to as one of the unsung heroes of macroeconomics. He predated Keynes by three years in writing about the principles commonly known as the Keynesian theory. Both economists worked independently but came to the same conclusion—that the capitalist economy is demand determined—and advocated government intervention to prevent down cycles in the economy. Kalecki did not receive earlier recognition because his essay was published in Polish and not immediately translated to English. Consequently, the English-speaking world was unaware of his writings. Kalecki died in 1970.

Michal Kalecki was born June 22, 1899, in Lodz, Poland. Kalecki was a self-taught economist. He finished a bachelor's degree in 1917 and entered the University of Warsaw to study civil engineering, completing only one year because of military duty from 1918 to 1921. Upon leaving the military, he entered the Polytechnic of Gdansk and continued there until 1924. Due to negative family financial circumstances, he left the Polytechnic before finishing his degree.

After five years of work at private companies utilizing his mathematical genius and writing for newspapers concerning topics in economics, Kalecki began work as an economist in 1929 with the Research Institute of Business Cycle and Prices (RIBCP). It was at the RIBCP in 1933 that Kalecki wrote his most famous paper concerning the theory of the business cycle. He quit in 1937 and left Poland.

During World War II, the Oxford Institute of Statistics (OIS) in England employed him during the period 1940 to 1945 writing reports for the British government. After leaving the OIS, he traveled and worked in Paris and Montreal. In July 1946, he returned to Poland to head the Central Planning Office of the Ministry of Economics but left after several months. He then was employed by the United Nations Secretariat in the economics department. He again returned to Poland in 1957, becoming the chairman of the Committee for Perspective Planning. His input was basically rejected and he left the position in 1959.

After 1959 he focused on research and teaching, particularly the economies of developing countries. His teaching career included appointments at the University of Oxford, University of Cambridge, London School of Economics, and Warsaw School of Economics. Michal Kalecki was an adviser to the governments of Cuba, India, Israel, Mexico, and Poland.

Kalecki in *Proba teorii koniunktury* ([An essay on the theory of the business cycle], 1933) arrived at similar conclusions as Keynes did in his *The General Theory of Employment, Interest and Money* in 1936. Kalecki published three years before Keynes.

Kalecki was an advocate of full employment and a more equitable distribution of wealth, much like Keynes. However, he disagreed with Keynes's view that capitalist economies are able to realize these goals. Kalecki held to a democratic, decentralized socialism. As a political economist, he developed a model of a "political business cycle." He favored central planning rather than laissez-faire capitalism. He was a reformer who favored socialism including government involvement in economic planning.

Kalecki and Keynes came from different schools of economic thought but arrived at the same conclusion. Kalecki's theory was based in Marxism. Keynes's theory was based in Marshallian theory. Both economists began their investigations seeking the cause of massive unemployment during the Great Depression. Kalecki's contributions helped create American post-Keynesian theory.

Kalecki was not fully appreciated by his fellow economists during his lifetime. There has been a renewal of interest in his writings with more of them being translated into English and published. By the time of his death in 1970, Kalecki's contributions were enormous to economic theory. It appears that even Kalecki himself did not fully appreciate his contributions to macroeconomic theory. In fact, he once stated that his influence was limited only to Israel where they did exactly the opposite of his recommendations.

Michal Kalecki died on April 18, 1970, in Warsaw at the age of 70.

*See also:* Keynes, John Maynard; Marx, Karl

### Selected Works by Michal Kalecki

Kalecki, Michal. *Essays on Developing Economies.* Brighton, UK: Harvester Press, 1972.
Kalecki, Michal. *Essays in the Theory of Economic Fluctuations.* New York: Farrar & Rinehart, 1939.
Kalecki, Michal. "Introduction to the Theory of Growth in a Socialist Economy." In *Selected Essays on the Economic Growth of the Socialist and the Mixed Economy*, 1–118. Cambridge: Cambridge University Press, 1972.
Kalecki, Michal. *Selected Essays on the Economic Growth of the Socialist and the Mixed Economy.* Cambridge: Cambridge University Press, 1972.
Kalecki, Michal. *Proba teorii koniunktury* [An essay on the theory of the business cycle]. Warsaw: Research Institute of Business Cycles and Prices, 1937.
Kalecki, Michal. "The Problem of Financing Economic Development." In *Essays on Developing Economies*, 1–22. Brighton, UK: Harvester Press, 1976.
Kalecki, Michal. "A Theory of the Business Cycle." *Review of Economic Studies* 4, no. 2 (1937): 77–97.
Kalecki, Michal, and Ignacy Sachs. "Forms of Foreign Aid: An Economic Analysis." *Social Science Information* 5, no. 1 (1966): 21–44.

### Selected Works about Michal Kalecki

Feiwel, George. *The Intellectual Capital of Michal Kalecki: A Study in Economic Theory and Policy.* Knoxville: University of Tennessee Press, 1975.
Kalecki, Michal, and Jerzy Osiatynski. *Collected Works of Michal Kalecki.* Vol. 5, *Developing Economies.* Oxford: Clarendon Press, 1993.
Robinson, Joan. 1976. *Michal Kalecki: A Neglected Prophet.* http://www.nybooks.com/articles/archives/1976/mar/04/michal-kalecki-a-neglected-prophet/ (accessed September 2011).
Sadowski, Zdzisław, and Adam Szeworski. *Kalecki's Economics Today.* New York: Routledge, 2004.
Sawyer, Malcolm. *The Legacy of Michal Kalecki.* Northampton, MA: Edward Elgar, 2000.

*Jean Kujawa*

# KANTOROVICH, LEONID

Born: January 19, 1912, in St. Petersburg, Russia; Died: April 7, 1986, in Moscow, Russia; Russian; optimal resource allocation, linear programming, mathematical economics, Nobel Prize (1975); Major Works: *The Mathematical Method of Production Planning and Organization* (1939), *The Best Uses of Economic Resources* (1965).

Leonid Kantorovich was known in the field of mathematical economics for his work on linear programing and his theory and techniques for optimal allocation of resources, for which he won a Nobel Prize in 1975. He worked as a scholar in Soviet Russia and applied his theories in industry under Stalin as part of the movement to modernize the nation. Kantorovich died in 1986.

Leonid Vitaliyevich Kantorovich was born on January 19, 1912, in St. Petersburg during the final years of the Russian Empire. During his formative years, he watched as his nation made the transition to communism, fighting a bloody civil war in the process. He obtained his PhD in mathematics from Leningrad State University at the young age of 18. While his interest was initially in the pure field of mathematics, he went on to teach at Leningrad University and in the Institute of Industrial Construction Engineering where he spent much of his time working on the development of functional analysis.

Kantorovich's first achievement involved the invention of a mathematical technique now known as linear programming. In 1938, he consulted as a professor at Leningrad for the Laboratory of the Plywood Trust attempting to maximize their use of resources. As it turned out, this economic problem was not unique, and his mathematical solution to involving linear functions was applicable across situations. For this work and for his research in *The Mathematical Method of Production Planning and Organization* and *The Best Uses of Economic Resources*, his first significant publications, Kantorovich was awarded the Stalin Prize in 1949. At a time when hybrid specialties such mathematics and economics were slow to gain recognition in the scientific community, the government accolades he received legitimized his work and caused others to take notice.

During this time Kantorovich was also enlisted for his mathematical ability in the World War II effort. Kantorovich was awarded a medal for defense of Leningrad for his work ensuring that supplies reached survivors of the siege over a terrain of ice-covered lakes. This application of his work points to the value that the state placed on his work as a method of advancing the Soviet industrial state during an era of struggle for economic, military, and political power in the USSR.

The crowning achievement of Kantorovich's career was the Nobel Prize in Economics for the work he pursued during the 1950s in improving theories on optimum allocation of resources. For this work, he was first awarded the Lenin Prize in 1965 and the Order of Lenin in 1967. International acclaim came years later in 1975 with his Nobel award, which he shared with his peer in the field, Tjalling Koopmans. During the 1950s, Stalin's five-year plan and collectivization policies represented an increased interest in government control of economic operations. Increased efficiency became a priority. Out of Kantorovich's work came his book *The Best Use of Economic Resources*, wherein he tackled the central economic problems of industry and management and the optimal conceptualization of these problems as they occur within industry, regional, and national economies.

From 1961 until 1971, Kantorovich continued his earlier work at the Siberian branch of the USSR Academy of the Sciences. He directed research at Moscow's Institute of National Economic Planning from 1971 until 1976 wherein he developed further evidence for the necessity of price systems to most efficiently allocate resources. In his later career, Kantorovich turned his attention to computer architecture.

Leonid Kantorovich died in Moscow, Russia, on April 7, 1986, at the age of 74.

*See also:* Koopmans, Tjalling

### Selected Works by Leonid Kantorovich

Kantorovich, Leonid. *The Best Uses of Economic Resources*. Cambridge, MA: Harvard University Press, 1965.

Kantorovich, Leonid. *The Mathematical Method of Production Planning and Organization*. Leningrad: Leningrad University Press, 1939.

### Selected Works about Leonid Kantorovich

Brezinski, Claude, and Luc Wuytack. *Numerical Analysis: Historical Developments in the 20th Century*. Amsterdam: Elsevier Science, 2001.

Kantorovich, Leonid. "Autobiography." Nobelprize.org. http://www.nobelprize.org/nobel_prizes/economics/laureates/1975/kantorovich-autobio.html (accessed September 2012).

Leifman, Lev J., ed. *Functional Analysis, Optimization, and Mathematical Economics: A Collection of Papers Dedicated to the Memory of Leonid Vital'evich Kantorovich*. New York: Oxford University Press, 1990.

Scheib, Ariel. "Leonid Kantorovich." Jewish Virtual Library. http://www.jewishvirtuallibrary.org/jsource/biography/kantorovich.html (accessed September 2012).

*Rebecca Kraft*

## KEYNES, JOHN MAYNARD

Born: June 5, 1883, in Cambridge, England; Died: April 21, 1946, in Firle, Sussex, England; English; macroeconomic theory; Major Works: *The Economic Consequences of the Peace* (1919), *Treatise on Probability* (1921), *Tract on Monetary Reform* (1929), *The General Theory of Employment, Interest and Money* (1936).

John Maynard Keynes, Baron Keynes of Tilton in the County of Sussex, was an English economist who impacted both political theory and modern economics. Keynesian economics promote a mixed economy dominated by the private sector but with a large role for government and the public sector. Keynesian economics argues that at the macroeconomic level the private sector is at times inefficient in its allocation of resources. When this occurs, the public sector needs to be actively involved in the fiscal and monetary policies to create stability of the business cycle. Keynes followed a legacy of successful nonconformists within his family and is revered as the father of macroeconomics. Keynes died in 1946.

John Maynard Keyes was born in Cambridge, England, on June 5, 1883. His father was a lecturer and the university's chief administrative official. His mother was an accomplished author, Cambridge's first woman councilor, and also its mayor. After enjoying an elite education at Eton College, Keynes completed his postsecondary studies at King's College in Cambridge and earned his degree in mathematics in 1905. He spent additional time studying under Alfred Marshall and Arthur Pigou and received a master's of arts in economics.

Keynes's early career started as a civil servant in London when he placed second on an examination, which cost him his desired job in the Treasury Department. He was appointed to a position in foreign affairs to the Royal Commission on Indian Currency and Finance, a bureau that extended advice on the administration of India, one of England's dominions at the time. Keynes accepted this foreign affairs job and learned how a government department operates. He soon developed an interest in Indian affairs and their currency; Keynes gained the attention of numerous government officials because he was able to apply economic theory to practical problems. His experience helped him write his first book in economics, *Indian Currency and Finance* (1913), a description of the Indian monetary system.

The ideas of twentieth-century British economist John Maynard Keynes still shape the economic policies of virtually every non-Communist nation. Considered by some the most influential person of the twentieth century. (Library of Congress)

In 1908, Keynes returned to Cambridge to teach economics. Tired of the slow-moving departments of the Indian Office, his attentions turned to writing. He composed an essay based on his experiences in government entitled "Recent Economic Events in India" (1919), which was his first major article in print. In addition to being a journalist and lecturer, Keynes was part of the acclaimed Bloomsbury Group of literary greats, including Virginia Woolf and Bertrand Russell. In 1911, Keynes was appointed the prestigious honor of editor of *The Economic Journal*. This was a significant accomplishment especially due to the fact that he had few publications at this time.

World War I put a hefty burden on the British economy, and in 1915 Keynes was offered a job at the British Treasury. He gladly accepted this offer to actively participate in the war effort. Keynes served as the Treasury's chief representative at the Paris Peace Conference of 1919 since his division had done much of the work on the preliminary reparations and war debts; however, its result was quite unfavorable to him. After returning to England, he resigned from this post and turned to writing a book. By the fall of 1919, Keynes had published *The Economic Consequences of the Peace*, which became an international best seller and a close foreshadowing of the immediate future. He predicted that the treaty's terms were too harsh and were aimed to cripple Germany instead of punishing them. Keynes's contention was that the provisions in the treaty would hamper Germany's postwar economy, Germany would eventually repudiate the treaty, and a rearming of Europe would ensue. Just as Keynes had suggested, the German economy experienced hyperinflation in 1923 and only a fraction of the reparations were ever received.

After 1929, the entire world was in a plummet and Keynes decided to take on the task of explaining and determining new ways to control trade cycles. This resulted in two books, *Tract on Monetary Reform* (1929) and *The General Theory of Employment, Interest and Money* (1936). Through these books, Keynes proclaimed that there needed to be both national and international programs that would lead to a cohesive monetary policy. He believed that a national budget should be used as a primary instrument in planning the national economy. Keynes asserted that policies were needed to regulate the ups and downs of the trade cycle. He firmly believed that it was the responsibility of government to regulate the levels of employment and investment. Keynes response to a depression or recession is government actions designed to encourage spending and discourage saving, and a key component is that the government's central bank should lower interest rates when prices are too high and raise interest rates when prices fall.

Keynes made other important contributions to economics, one focused on the disorganization caused by World War I and the other on the deterioration in the balance of trade between Europe and the United States. He continued to help the British government and became an unofficial adviser to Germany. Keynes worked with Roosevelt and other writers of the New Deal, contributing directly to its implementation. By the time World War II began, Keynes was a famous and accredited expert on economics. He assumed a primary role in establishing the Bretton Woods system, which would eventually lay foundations for the International Monetary Fund and the World Bank. He strongly supported William Beveridge's proposal for an expansion of Britain's social services, which led to the United Kingdom's National Health Service. Keynes occupied a seat in the House of Lords as a member of the Liberal Party and supported equal opportunities for women in business.

John Maynard Keynes suffered from several heart attacks before losing his life on April 21, 1946, in Firle, Sussex, England, due to heart failure. He was cremated and his ashes were scattered on the Downs above Tilton.

*See also:* Beveridge, William; Marshall, Alfred; Pigou, A. C.

### Selected Works by John Maynard Keynes

Keynes, John Maynard. *The Economic Consequences of the Peace*. New York: Harcourt, Brace & Howe, 1920.
Keynes, John Maynard. *The End of Laissez-Faire*. London: L & Virginia Woolf, 1926.
Keynes, John Maynard. *Essays in Persuasion*. New York: Macmillan, 1931.
Keynes, John Maynard. *The General Theory of Employment, Interest and Money*. New York: Macmillan, 1936.
Keynes, John Maynard. *How to Pay for the War*. New York: Harcourt, Brace, 1940.
Keynes, John Maynard. *Indian Currency and Finance*. London: Royal Economic Society, 1913.
Keynes, John Maynard. *A Revision of the Treaty*. London: Macmillan, 1922.
Keynes, John Maynard. *Tract on Monetary Reform*. London: Macmillan, 1929.
Keynes, John Maynard. *Treatise on Probability*. London: Macmillan, 1921.

### Selected Works about John Maynard Keynes

Maynardkeynes.org. "John Maynard Keynes." http://www.maynardkeynes.org/ (accessed March 2011).
Minsky, Hyman P. *John Maynard Keynes*. Columbia Essays on the Great Economists. New York: Columbia University Press, 1975.
Skidelsky, Robert. *John Maynard Keynes: 1883–1946: Economist, Philosopher, Statesman*. New York: Macmillan, 1980.
Skidelsky, Robert. *John Maynard Keynes*. Vol. 1, *Hopes Betrayed, 1883–1920*. New York: Viking Adult, 1986.
Skidelsky, Robert. *John Maynard Keynes*. Vol. 2, *The Economist as Savior, 1920-1937*. New York: Viking Adult, 1994.
Skidelsky, Robert. *John Maynard Keynes*. Vol. 3, *Fighting for Freedom, 1937–1946*. New York: Viking Adult, 2001.
Skidelsky, Robert. *Keynes: The Return of the Master*. New York: Public Affairs, 2009.

*Samantha Lohr*

## KHALDUN, IBN

Born: May 27, 1332 BCE/732 AH in Tunis; Died: March 19, 1406 BCE/808 AH in Cairo; theory of value, production theory, economic growth; Major Work: *The Muqaddimah: An Introduction to History* (1377).

Ibn Khaldun was a Muslim social scientist, historian, and philosopher living in the Maghreb (northern Africa) during the fourteenth century. He made significant intellectual contributions to sociology, historiography, the philosophy of history, and economics. He understood the mechanics of supply and demand, division of labor, and taxation, making his ideas a precursor to those of Adam Smith and other well-known economists. His description of *asabiyyah* (social solidarity or group cohesion) and his evaluation of the rise and fall of civilizations advanced ideas that still resonate with scholars today. Khaldun died in 1406.

Ibn Khaldun was born on May 27, 1332 BCE/732 AH in Tunis, in what we now call Tunisia, to an upper-class family. As a boy, he received training in the Qu'ran, poetry, rhetoric, and Islamic law, receiving his certification in these subjects. He also studied philosophy, mathematics, and logic under well-known scholars of the time, and read the works of influential Muslim thinkers, including Averroes and Avicenna. Although his career took him into politics, throughout his lifetime he studied and maintained contact with important thinkers of the era.

As a teenager, Ibn Khaldun lost his parents in the Black Death that came to Tunis from Sicily in 1348. Soon thereafter, he entered political life as a member of the elite, with his prosperity rising and falling based on the vagaries of political fortune and the leaders with whom he allied himself. He was jailed in one case of political intrigue, but eventually attained his goal of a ministerial position under Sultan Abu Salem, and later became prime minister under Abu Abdallah. His extensive experience under many different rulers throughout his lifetime contributed to his thinking on the personal qualities of strong leaders and the importance of the political circumstances to the advancement of a civilization. In 1375, he took refuge with a Berber group, staying in a fortress in what is now western Algeria. This was a productive time for Ibn Khaldun's writing, as he began his work on the history of the world, with the first volume, *The Muqaddimah*, being completed in 1377. He soon returned to Tunis to have access to scholarly texts to continue his project to explain the rise and fall of civilizations and develop his philosophy of history.

A keen observer of human action and group dynamics, Ibn Khaldun pursued an evidence-based evaluation of social, cultural, and historical phenomena. He believed that there were principles guiding economic, social, and political behavior, and that discovering these principles was the key to understanding economic development. In his theory of the rise and fall of civilization, he recognized cycles of progress, starting with subsistence rural societies that produce only what is necessary to survive as a self-sufficient group. As groups grow in size and move beyond subsistence, they develop political structures and gather in cities. With a larger population, societies are able to take advantage of technology and higher labor productivity resulting from what economists now call division of labor—the idea that a production process can be divided into separate tasks carried out by distinct laborers, thereby increasing total production. He argued that people desire luxuries, and even compete for markers of affluence in the more developed stage of civilization. Eventually, a combination of factors leads to the decline of a civilization according to Ibn Khaldun: extravagant spending, high taxation, corruption, and overpopulation that leads to famine and pestilence all contribute to an impoverished populace.

Ibn Khaldun's economic ideas resemble those of later scholars. His explanation of division of labor, price fluctuations, and profits resulting from supply and demand are similar to that of Adam Smith. Ibn Khaldun understood the expansion of production and profits due to increasing the size of the market, as described in Smith's *Wealth of Nations*. His views of the problems of overpopulation anticipate a later discussion of demographic crises in the work of Malthus. Like David Ricardo, he viewed labor as the source of value. In addition, he developed a rudimentary concept of a spending multiplier similar to that of John Maynard Keynes and argued for government involvement in the economy as Keynes did. And Ibn Khaldun's statement that higher tax rates may lead to lower revenues is a very early description of a mechanism that would generate a Laffer curve. Although Ibn Khaldun was quite influential during his time, his economic ideas lay dormant until nineteenth-century scholars recognized his contributions and the relevance of his work.

Ibn Khaldun died in Cairo on March 19, 1406 BCE/808 AH.

*See also:* Keynes, John Maynard; Laffer, Arthur; Malthus, Thomas; Ricardo, David; Smith, Adam

### Selected Work by Ibn Khaldun

Khaldun, Ibn. 1967. *The Muqaddimah: An Introduction to History*. 2nd ed. Edited by N. J. Dawood. Translated by Franz Rosenthal. Princeton, NJ: Princeton University Press.

### Selected Works about Ibn Khaldun

Boulaki, Jean David C. "Ibn Khaldun: A Fourteenth-Century Economist." *Journal of Political Economy* 79, no. 5 (1971): 1105–18.
Fromherz, Allen. *Ibn Khaldun: Life and Times*. Edinburgh, UK: Edinburgh University Press, 2010.
Haddad, L. "A Fourteenth-Century Theory of Economic Growth and Development." *Kyklos* 30 (1977): 195–213.
Weiss, Dieter. "Ibn Khaldun on Economic Transformation." *International Journal of Middle East Studies* 27, no. 1 (1995): 29–37.

*Kerry Pannell*

## KLEIN, LAWRENCE

Born: September 14, 1920, in Omaha, Nebraska; American; econometrics, Nobel Prize (1980); Major Works: *The Keynesian Revolution* (1947), *Economic Fluctuations in the United States, 1921–1941* (1950), *Econometric Model of the United States, 1929–1952* (with Arthur Stanley Goldberger) (1955), *The Economies of Supply and Demand* (1983).

Lawrence Klein is the leading figure in the mathematization of economics. Using the newly created power of computers, Klein pushed economics into ever more difficult calculations in an attempt to properly represent the complexity of the economy. His work was useful in predicting the effects of government policies in a time when macroeconomists were confident about the possibility of "steering" the economy through fiscal policy. He was awarded the Nobel Prize in 1980.

Lawrence Robert Klein was born in September 14, 1920 in Omaha, Nebraska. The Great Depression began when he was nine years old and continued throughout his teenage years. Klein studied mathematics at Los Angeles City College and economics at the University of California, Berkeley. He went on to earn his PhD in economics from the Massachusetts Institute of Technology in 1944, where he studied under Paul Samuelson. He then joined the research faculty at the University of Chicago. While in Chicago, he briefly joined the Communist Party, evidently not from sincere Marxist beliefs, but because the local Communist Party insisted that he join the Party if he was to deliver lectures to them on Marxist theory.

World War II was coming to an end at this time, and a common belief among economists was that the influx of soldiers returning from the war would create mass unemployment and perhaps sink the United States into another bout of the Great Depression. Klein drew up a mathematical model of the economy that contradicted this theory. Rather, wrote Klein, the purchasing power of the returning soldiers coupled with unsatisfied consumer demand during the war years would create an economic boom. He turned out to be correct, and this early example of the predictive powers of his models earned him fame among economists. He also established himself in the Keynesian tradition, not just because of his 1947 book, *The Keynesian Revolution*, but because his early analysis focused on total demand rather than supply or the level of money.

Klein taught at the University of Michigan from 1950 to 1954, but was denied tenure due to an unforeseen problem. His previous membership in the Communist Party had caught the attention of the House Un-American Activities Committee. Subsequently, Michigan denied him promotion and tenure. He then fled to England to the University of Oxford. In 1958, he returned to the United States for a post at the University of Pennsylvania, where he has remained for more than 50 years.

With the advent of computers, Klein deepened his use of models by starting a project called LINK, in which he attempted to create econometric models that included all the countries in the world. He also created the Brookings model and the Wharton econometric forecasting model. For these and other innovations, he earned the John Bates Clark Medal in 1959 from the American Economic Association and the Nobel Prize in Economics in 1980. Furthermore, he served as president of the Econometric Society, the Environmental Economics Association, and the American Economics Association. In 1976, Klein joined Jimmy Carter's economic task force during the presidential election, though he declined to take a job with the administration itself. In 1984, he joined W. P. Carey and Co. as director and chairman of the economic policy committee.

Klein did not remain dogmatically attached to Keynesian ideas. With the growing popularity of supply-side economics and monetarism in the early 1980s, he included the ideas of these challenges to Keynes in his models, noting that there are many important components to managing an economy. Nevertheless, his tendency to recommend government intervention as a key part of stabilizing the economy kept him firmly within the Keynesian tradition. The application of ultra-complex math has been criticized by some who think that no model is central part of the scientific side of economics, allowing economists to explain the movements of society in ever more detailed terms. Economics remains a thoroughly math-oriented field of study thanks in part to Lawrence Klein's technical genius.

*See also:* Keynes, John Maynard; Koopmans, Tjalling; Samuelson, Paul; Tinbergen, Jan

### Selected Works by Lawrence Klein

Bodkin, Robert G., Lawrence R. Klein, and Kanta Marwah. *A History of Macroeconomic Model Building*. Northampton, MA.: Edward Elgar, 1991.

Klein, Lawrence. *Economic Fluctuations in the United States, 1921–1941*. Hoboken, NJ: Wiley, 1950.

Klein, Lawrence. *The Economics of Supply and Demand*. Baltimore: Johns Hopkins University Press, 1983.

Klein, Lawrence. *The Keynesian Revolution*. New York: Macmillan, 1947.

Klein, Lawrence R., and Arthur Stanley Goldberger. *Econometric Model of the United States, 1929–1952*. Amsterdam: North-Holland, 1955.

### Selected Works about Lawrence Klein

Breit, William, and Barry T. Hirsch, eds. *Lives of the Laureates*. Cambridge, MA: MIT Press, 2004.

Klein, Lawrence. "Keynesianism Again: Interview with Lawrence Klein." *Challenge* 44, no. 3 (May 1, 2001): 6–16.

*Stephen H. Day*

## KNIGHT, FRANK

Born: November 7, 1885, in White Oak Township, McLean County, Illinois; Died: April 15, 1972, in Chicago, Illinois; American; political economy; Major Works: *Risk, Uncertainty, and Profit* (1921), *The Economic Organization* (1933), *The Ethics of Competition and Other Essays* (1935).

Frank Knight was a cofounder (along with Jacob Viner) of the Chicago School of economic thought based at the University of Chicago. Knight was a strong supporter of a competitive, largely unregulated economy as he believed any alternatives to this model would make life infinitely worse. In his book *Risk, Uncertainty, and Profit*, Knight famously distinguishes between "risk" and "uncertainty," and writes of the role of the entrepreneur in a theory of profit. Throughout his career Knight was known for his skepticism and belligerence, criticizing many ideas yet ultimately inspiring thoughtful discussion and action. Knight challenged any attempt to manipulate the economy or social engineering even throughout the New Deal years. Knight also significantly influenced those with whom he studied—even if they disagreed. He taught four future Nobel Memorial Prize winners in economics: Milton Friedman, George Stigler, James Buchanan, and Paul Samuelson. Knight died in 1972.

Frank Hyneman Knight was born in November 7, 1885, White Oak Township, McLean County, Illinois. He spent his early years working on the family farm and did not attend college until his early 20s. He attended several small southern schools before enrolling at the University of Tennessee, where he graduated with a bachelor's degree in the natural sciences and a master's degree in German. He then entered Cornell University in 1913 and earned his PhD. He completed his economics dissertation, "A Theory of Business Profit," in 1916, which was later revised and published as the book *Risk, Uncertainty, and Profit* in 1921. Knight worked at the University of Chicago as an instructor (as well as at Cornell) from 1917 to 1919, then as associate professor and professor at the University of Iowa (1919–28), finally committing to professorship at the University of Chicago from 1929 to 1952 and finally as professor emeritus (1952–72). He was the coeditor of the *Journal of Political Economy* from 1928 to 1945.

Knight's book *Risk, Uncertainty, and Profit*, published in 1921, is one of his most important contributions to economics. Knight explains why perfect competition would not necessarily eliminate profits because of "uncertainty," which he differentiated from "risk." "Risk" is a situation in which the probability of an outcome can be determined and insured against, such as car accidents or house fires. "Uncertainty," however, is an event whose probability is unknown and could arise from unpredictable changes in the economy. An alteration in resources, consumer preferences, or knowledge, for example, renders these uncertain elements uninsurable. Knight argued that even in long-run equilibrium, successful entrepreneurs would earn profits as a reward for making decisions in an uncertain environment.

Knight's 1933 book, *The Economic Organization* (originally a set of lecture notes), was written as a brief introduction to economics and ultimately adopted as a text for the introductory social sciences class for undergraduates at the University of Chicago. In it he explains the circular flow model and emphasizes that investments will be made until the returns to investments in each are equal at the margin.

Knight famously challenged A. C. Pigou's belief that traffic congestion justifies road taxation in his 1924 article, "Fallacies in the Interpretation of Social Cost." He writes that profits from private road ownership would ultimately help to reduce congestion. Knight advocates the free-market ideal of private ownership to eliminate the necessity of government intervention and promote efficiency.

Knight was a coeditor (with Jacob Viner) of the *Journal of Political Economy* from 1928 to 1945. He used his book reviews within this publication to illustrate his own opinions and to notably debate many prominent economists of his day such as Hayek, Mises, Pigou, Keynes, and Hutchison.

Knight was also known for his blending of economics and moral philosophy. In *The Ethics of Competition*, Knight argues that market organization does not ensure moral or ethical behavior. Knight believed that people did not always make consistent choices, nor always act out of self-interest. Social problems were the result of a failure in moral nature as opposed to structure or politics.

Knight was also a social philosopher. His strong belief in freedom led him to a forceful critique of social engineering and other liberal forms of social organization. Knight argued that social control by any well-intentioned group often led to a situation far worse than the original circumstances. As such, he opposed progressives, institutionalists, Keynesians, and Christians and any group interested in social control. Knight believed a liberal society needed continued questioning and discussion to ensure against tyranny and the continuation of individual freedom.

Always a skeptic, Knight ultimately maintained support for the market process. Individual freedom to make economic choices, however, in the end promoted the greatest satisfaction regardless of personal background or differences even using a flawed technique known as reason. Ultimately, Knight supported capitalism as imperfect but better than any other alternative.

Frank Knight was a significant presence at the University of Chicago. His skepticism, eclectic economics, and belief in individual freedom and moral philosophy paint a truly unique portrait of a highly influential economist. In addition to his teaching and editing duties, Knight was also a cofounder of the Committee of Social Thought at the University of Chicago during the 1940s. He was president of the American Economic Association in 1950 and earned a distinguished service award from the William Volker Fund in 1953. In 1957, he was awarded the Francis A. Walker Medal from the American Economic Association, which is given every five years to the living American economist who has made the greatest contribution to economics. He also was bestowed with the Great Living American Award from the U.S. Chamber of Commerce in 1959 and the Prize for Distinguished Service to Humanistic Scholarship from the American Council of Learned Societies in 1961.

Frank Knight died in Chicago, Illinois on April 15, 1972.

*See also:* Buchanan, James; Friedman, Milton; Hayek, Friedrich von; Mises, Ludwig von; Pigou, A. C.; Samuelson, Paul; Stigler, George; Viner, Jacob

### Selected Works by Frank Knight

Knight, Frank. *Risk, Uncertainty, and Profit*. Hart, Schaffner, and Marx Prize Essays, no. 31. Boston: Houghton Mifflin, 1921.

Knight, Frank. *The Economic Organization*. Chicago: University of Chicago, 1933.

Knight, Frank. *The Ethics of Competition and Other Essays*. New York: Harper & Bros.; London: Allen & Unwin, 1935.

### Selected Works about Frank Knight

Emmett, Ross B. *Frank H. Knight in Iowa City, 1919–1928*. London: Emerald Group, 2011.

Emmett, Ross B. *Frank Knight and the Chicago School in American Economics*. London: Routledge, 2009.

Skousen, Mark. *Vienna and Chicago, Friends or Foes?: A Tale of Two Schools of Free-Market Economics*. Los Angeles: Capital Press, 2005.

*Kathryn Lloyd Gustafson*

# KOOPMANS, TJALLING

Born: August 28, 1910, in Wijdemeren, Netherlands; Died: February 26, 1985, in New Haven, Connecticut; Dutch; comparative economics, Nobel Prize (1975); Major Works: "Statistical Estimation of Simultaneous Economic Relations" (1945), "On the Description and Comparison of Economic Systems" (1971).

Tjalling Koopmans was a Dutch-born comparative economist, and coawardee of the 1975 Nobel Prize in Economic Science, along with Leonid Kantorovich, for work in activity analysis. Koopmans's original publication was in the field of quantum mechanics (1934), where he described a subset of the Hartree-Fock method for describing closed-shell systems; this development continues to be referred to as Koopmans's theorem. Koopmans died in 1985.

Tjalling Charles Koopmans was born in Wijdemeren, Netherlands, on August 28, 1910. Koopmans studied mathematics and physics at Utrecht University. In 1933, he moved to Amsterdam to study mathematical economics under Jan Tinbergen. In 1940, Koopmans moved to the United States, working for the federal government in Washington, DC.

After transitioning to the field of economics and in work for the Cowles Commission for Research in Economics, Koopmans's "Statistical Estimation of Simultaneous Economic Relations" (1945) articulated two needs, one of which had not been met. He argued for complete systems of equations and variables in economic statistics, which had been lacking at the time. Economic theory had previously been informed by incomplete systems of equations, creating statistical problems when analyzing variables. These incomplete systems—particularly those systems that did not account for time lags—created jointly dependent sets of equations. Koopmans was not alone in this view, as he concurred with Trygve Haavelmo's contemporaneous work regarding the bias inherent from ignoring the existence of other relations, writing that "the sample of data from which we attempt to measure any one particular relation is conditioned by the fact that the other relations restricted the movements of some or all of the same variables in the same period" (1945, 462).

Koopmans continued involvement with the Cowles Commission for Research in Economics, renamed the Cowles Foundation after a 1955 change in institutional affiliation, included service as the organization's head thrice, from 1948 to 1955, 1961 to 1964, and 1965 to 1967. The Cowles school of thought—then and now—continued to be intended at building strong linkages between economic theory and the mathematics/statistics necessary to inform that theory, advancing the modern conceptualization of econometrics.

As a comparativist, Koopmans work sought the development of a general theory. Along with Montias (1971), he promoted a framework seeking an interdisciplinary approach to economic comparisons based upon the various arrangements made for distinct economic functions. This approach countered what the authors described as the traditional model of economic comparison that held the units of articulation to be the three prototypes of capitalism, socialism, and communism. The authors admitted that the knowledge to understand the detail and system complexity from all the necessary supporting disciplines was lacking.

In the citation for the 1975 Prize in Economic Science in Memory of Alfred Nobel in which Koopmans was a coawardee (with Leonid Kantorovich), the work of each was described as "contributions to the theory of optimum allocation of resources," through both improved methods and theorems. Given the language barrier and lack of exchange between their home countries, the work of Kantorovich was not widely known and Koopmans independently redeveloped and extended the model. There was some criticism of the selection of activity analysis theory as worthy of the Nobel Prize, as the theory drew the interest of scholars in many other disciplines and practitioners within the workplace.

Activity analysis did not just provide new insight into the necessary inputs and expected outputs of a production process; the analysis also tied these concepts into pricing systems. In fact, this work permitted the making of critical, direct deductions about optimal price systems. In his Nobel speech, Koopmans acknowledged the tension of developing a theory broader than simply the field of economics. Although the method had extensions both within and outside economics, he provided emphasis that the role of an economist was never to mandate how decisions were made, simply to inform and participate.

Tjalling Koopmans died on February 26, 1985, in New Haven, Connecticut.

*See also:* Haavelmo, Trygve; Kantorovich, Leonid; Tinbergen, Jan

**Selected Works by Tjalling Koopmans**

Koopmans, Tjalling. "Analysis of Production as an Efficient Combination of Activities." In *Activity Analysis of Production and Allocation: Proceedings of a Conference*. Edited by T. C. Koopmans, 33–97. Cowles Commission for Research in Economics Monograph No. 13. New York: Wiley, 1951.

Koopmans, Tjalling. "Statistical Estimation of Simultaneous Economic Relations." *Journal of the American Statistical Association* 40, no. 232 (1945): 448–66.

Koopmans, T. C., and J. M. Montias. "On the Description and Comparison of Economic Systems." In *Comparison of Economic Systems: Theoretical and Methodological Approaches*. Edited by A. Eckstein, 27–78. Berkeley: University of California Press, 1971.

**Selected Works about Tjalling Koopmans**

Karier, T. *Intellectual Capital: Forty Years of the Nobel Prize in Economics*. New York: Cambridge University Press, 2010.

Koopmans, Tjalling C. "Autobiography." Nobelprize.org. http://www.nobelprize.org/nobel_prizes/economics/laureates/1975/koopmans-autobio.html (accessed September 2011).

Koopmans, T. C. *Concepts of Optimality and Their Uses*. Nobel Memorial Lecture. December 11, 1975.

*Michael B. Becraft*

# KREGEL, JAN

Born: April 19, 1944, in Dallas, Texas; American; post-Keynesian economist, international economic development; Major Work: *Rate of Profit, Distribution and Growth: Two Views* (1971).

Jan Kregel is one of the most influential economists serving the United Nations on economic development of developing nations. He has advised the UN on developing nations' economic development in many different roles, including chief of the Policy Analysis and Development Branch of the Financing for the Development Office of the United Nation's Department of Economic and Social Affairs (UNDESA). He was the president of the UN General Assembly's Commission on Reform of the International Financial System, led the Policy

Analysis and Development Branch of the UN Financing for Development Office at the UN, and served as deputy secretary of the UN Committee of Experts on International Cooperation in Tax Matters. He is also the professor of development finance at Tallinn University of Technology.

Jan A. Kregel was born on April 19, 1944. Kregel received his doctorate from Rutgers University, though prior to completing his graduate work at Rutgers, he studied with Joan Robinson and Nicholas Kaldor at the University of Cambridge. Kregel joined the faculty at the Universita degli Studi di Bologna as a professor of political economy. He was the chair for political economy at the University of Bologna.

Professor Kregel developed a post-Keynesian methodology and paradigm. During the 1970s and 1980s, he focused his research on decision making under conditions of uncertainty, price theory, and price formulation. Using Keynes's general equilibrium theory on interest and money as a foundation, Kregel submitted that Keynes's analysis was basically a discussion on demand.

Critiquing Keynes, Kregel went on to submit his own proposal on market structure. Kregel's analysis provided a strong criticism of neoclassical price theory. He proposed an alternative, emphasizing that one's expectations of the future will help determine current prices.

Kregel's published works included over 130 articles as well as a series of books in post-Keynesian economic theory. His articles were published in scholarly journals including the *American Economic Review*, *Economic Journal*, *Journal of Economic Literature*, and *Journal of Post Keynesian Economics*. His works were translated and published in more than a dozen languages.

Jan Kregel has served the international community and the United Nations in many roles. He was high-level expert in international finance and macroeconomics in the New York Liaison Office of the United Nations Conference on Trade and Development (UNCTAD). In 2009, he became rapporteur of the president of the UN General Assembly's Commission on Reform of the International Financial System. He also held positions as director of the Policy Analysis and Development Branch of the UN Financing for Development Office and as deputy secretary of the UN Committee of Experts on International Cooperation in Tax Matters.

He continues to serve the *Trade and Development Report* of UNCTAD as a permanent adviser. Kregel is also a member of the Scientific Advisory Boards at the Italian International Economic Center in Rome and the Istituto per la Ricerca Sociale in Milan, Italy. Jan Kregel is a life fellow of the Royal Economic Society in London (UK). He has been elected a member of the Società Italiana degli Economisti and a distinguished member of the Asociación Nacional de Economistas de Cuba.

Kregel's teaching and research positions include universities around the globe. He has held positions in the United Kingdom, the United States, Belgium, France, Mexico, the Netherlands, and Germany. His teaching career has included positions at Johns Hopkins University's Paul Nitze School of Advanced International Studies (SAIS) from 1987 to 1990.

Kregel was also a visiting professor at the University of Missouri, Kansas City, where he is the distinguished research professor at the Center for Full Employmnet and Price Stability. He also is professor of development finance in the Talinn University of Technology. Kregel is also a senior scholar at Bard College's Levy Economics Institute, directing its program on Monetary Policy and Financial Structure.

In 2010, Kregel was honored with the Veblen-Commons Award. The award is presented for achievements in the field of economics by the Association for Evolutionary Economics.

*See also:* Collier, Paul; Kaldor, Nicholas; Robinson, Joan

**Selected Works by Jan Kregel**

Kregel, Jan. *Market Shock: An Agenda for Economic and Social Reconstruction of Central and Eastern Europe.* Ann Arbor: University of Michigan Press, 1992.
Kregel, Jan. *Rate of Profit, Distribution and Growth: Two Views.* Piscataway, NJ: Transaction, 1971
Kregel, Jan. *The Reconstruction of Political Economy.* London: Macmillan, 1973
Kregel, Jan. *The Theory of Capital.* London: Macmillan, 1976
Kregel, Jan. *The Theory of Economic Growth.* London: Macmillan, 1972

**Selected Works about Jan Kregel**

Levy Economics Institute of Bard College. "Jan Kregel." http://www.levyinstitute.org/publications/?auth=151 (accessed February 2011).
United Nations Department of Economic and Social Affairs. "Financing for Development." http://www.un.org/esa/ffd/ (accessed March 2011).

*Kathleen C. Simmons*

# KRUEGER, ANNE

Born: February 12, 1934, in Endicott, New York; American; international economics; Major Work: *Economic Policy Reform: The Second Stage* (2000).

Anne Krueger served the International Monetary Fund (IMF) as the first deputy managing director. An international economist, Krueger's early career was dedicated to understanding how international trade and payments impacted the global economy. This research was expanded to focus on a country's endowments of natural, labor, and capital resources, which led to her creating a trade model to understand this relationship. Krueger's research included the functioning of political regimes who had adopted restrictive trade policies. This interest in political regimes led to her further study in political economy, specifically the policy reform of developing countries.

Anne Osborn Krueger was born on February 12, 1934, in Endicott, New York. Krueger received her undergraduate degree from Oberlin College and her PhD from the University of Wisconsin. Following her time at the University of Wisconsin, Krueger took a position at the University of Minnesota. She also had a teaching appointment at Duke University before joining the faculty at Stanford University.

American economist Anne Krueger. She has been involved in developing international economic policy as a vice president and consultant for the World Bank and as director of the International Monetary Fund from 2001 to 2006. (AP/Wide World Photos)

Krueger joined the faculty at Stanford University as the Herald L. and Caroline L. Ritch Professor in Humanities and Sciences in the Department of Economics. At Stanford she was the founding director of Stanford's Center for Research on Economic Development and Policy Reform. She served Stanford's Hoover Institution as a senior fellow.

Early in her career she was dedicated to understanding how international trade and payments impacted the global economy. A component of her trade research focused on factor endowments. She expanded her research to focus on a country's endowments of natural, labor, and capital resources, which led to her creating a trade model to understand this relationship. An example of her efforts has been her continual criticism of U.S. sugar subsidies as a form of protectionism.

Her research on trade led to an increasing interest in political economy and policy reform in developing countries and the role of multilateral institutions in international trade. Krueger's research interests in policy reform in developing countries included the functioning of political regimes who had adopted restrictive trade policies.

In 1982, Krueger served the World Bank as its chief economist and vice president for economics and research. In September 2001, Krueger moved to the International Monetary Fund as the first deputy managing director, a position she held till 2006. Krueger also served the IMF as acting managing director for a time in 2004.

Upon leaving the International Monetary Fund, Krueger joined the faculty at Johns Hopkins University's School of Advanced International Studies as a professor of international economics.

Anne Krueger is a distinguished fellow and a past president of the American Economic Association. She is also a member of the National Academy of Sciences. Krueger is also a research associate of the National Bureau of Economic

Research (NBER). She has received many economic prizes and awards during her career.

*See also:* Collier, Paul; Duflo, Esther; Kregel, Jan

**Selected Works by Anne Krueger**

Krueger, Anne. *Economic Policy Reform: The Second Stage*. Chicago: University of Chicago Press, 2000.

Krueger, Anne. *Economic Policy Reform and the Indian Economy*. Chicago: University of Chicago Press, 2002.

Krueger, Anne. *A New Approach to Sovereign Debt Restructuring*. Washington, DC: International Monetary Fund, 2002.

Krueger, Anne. *The WTO as an International Organization*. Chicago: University of Chicago Press, 1998.

Krueger, Anne O., and Sajjid Z. Chinoy. *Reforming India's Economic, Financial, and Fiscal Policies*. Palo Alto, CA: Stanford University Press, 2003.

Krueger, Anne O., Jose Antonio Gonzales, Vittorio Corbo, and Aaron Tornell. *Latin American Macroeconomic Reform: The Second Stage*. Chicago: University of Chicago Press, 2003.

**Selected Works about Anne Krueger**

"Anne O. Krueger." Stanford University. http://scid.stanford.edu/peopleprofile/2705#bio (accessed January 2011).

"Anne Osborn Krueger." International Monetary Fund. http://www.imf.org/external/np/omd/bios/ak.htm (accessed January 2011).

*Kathleen C. Simmons*

# KRUGMAN, PAUL

Born: February 28, 1953, in Long Island, New York; American; neo-Keynesian, trade theory, economic geography, economies of scale, author, columnist, Nobel Prize (2008); Major Works: *Rethinking International Trade* (1990), "Does the New Trade Theory Require a New Trade Policy?" (1992).

Paul Krugman is one of the most admired and influential economists of modern times. Krugman is known for his work on international trade theory. Among his many notable contributions, Krugman showed that international trade flourishes where trading partners can take advantage of economies of scale and consumers' preference for diversity. His theory explained the persistence of international trade in the absence of distinct comparative advantage. His theory has been influential on research related to issues surrounding free trade, globalization, and worldwide urbanization. In 2008, Krugman won the Nobel Prize in Economics.

Paul Robin Krugman was born on February 28, 1953, in Long Island, New York. He was born into a Jewish family and grew up on Long Island in New York, graduating from John F. Kennedy High School in Bellmore. He received his BA in economics from Yale University in 1974 and PhD from the Massachusetts Institute of Technology (MIT) in 1977. During 1982 and 1983,

Krugman was the senior international economist for the President's Council of Economic Advisers under Ronald Reagan.

Prior to his appointment at Princeton in 2000, Krugman taught at Yale University, MIT, the London School of Economics, Stanford University, and the University of California, Berkeley. Krugman served as a consultant to the Federal Reserve Bank of New York, the World Bank, the International Monetary Fund, and the United Nations as well as to a number of countries including Portugal and the Philippines.

In contrast to traditional Ricardian trade theories, which assume that trade occurs mainly between economically unequal countries so some countries export agricultural products (e.g., Mexico) whereas others export industrial goods (e.g., the United States), Krugman's approach is based on the premise that trade occurs between relative equals as consumers demand a varied supply of goods that can lead to efficient economies of scale in industrial production. Consequently, a few countries that not only have similar conditions but also trade in similar products dominate the worldwide trade. Krugman first published his new trade theory, which deals with the analysis of trade patterns and location of economic activity, in 1979 in the *Journal of International Economics*. It has become the model of most international trade today, and in 2008 he was honored for his work with the Nobel Prize.

A proponent of globalized free trade in his theories for modern trade, Krugman formulated a model explaining how economies of scale plays a critical role in developing a comparative advantage for a country such as Sweden that both exports and imports cars (like the Volvo). For example, with a large domestic market for Volvo, Sweden becomes a leading exporter of Volvo to similar countries like the United States. Thereby, Sweden will gain more profits and even more production. This theory further helps explain why production is concentrated in just a few, large countries and why cities within those countries become densely populated, attracting workers and consumers.

Before the Enron scandal, Krugman served as one of the many economists on a panel that advised Enron on economic and political issues. He ended his affiliation with Enron when he accepted the offer to become a columnist at the *New York Times*. When news of the Enron scandal broke out, he disclosed his Enron affiliation to his *Fortune* readers and he emphatically denied all the charges of conflict of interest.

In addition to Krugman's reputation as a distinguished economist and nationally known columnist for the *New York Times*, he has written 20 books, including *Principles of Economics*, *The Return of Depression Economics and the Crisis of 2008*, and *The Conscience of a Liberal* (2007), and has published more than 200 scholarly articles. In 2003, he published his book *The Great Unraveling*, a collection of his columns, which went on to be a best seller. In recognition of his work, he received the John Bates Clark Medal from the American Economic Association, an award given every two years to the top economist under the age of 40.

Apart from his notoriety in academia, Krugman is an outspoken and vocal critic on issues of politics and the economy through his *New York Times* column and related blog, *The Conscience of a Liberal*, one of the most quoted and widely referred to blogs in the econoblogosphere.

*See also:* Mankiw, Gregory; Ohlin, Bertil; Ricardo, David; Samuelson, Paul; Stiglitz, Joseph

### Selected Works by Paul Krugman

Krugman, Paul. *The Conscience of the Liberal*. New York: Norton, 2007.
Krugman, Paul. "Does the New Trade Theory Require a New Trade Policy?" *The World Economy* 15 (1992): 423–42.
Krugman, Paul. *The Great Unraveling*. New York: Norton, 2003.
Krugman, Paul. "Increasing Returns, Monopolistic Competition, and International Trade." *Journal of International Economics* 9 (1979): 469–79.
Krugman, Paul. *Rethinking International Trade*. MIT Press, 1990.
Krugman, Paul. *The Return of Depression Economics*. New York: Norton, 1999.

### Selected Works about Paul Krugman

Jumo, K. S., and Rudiger von Arnim. "Trade Theory Status Quo Despite Krugman." *Economic & Political Weekly*, December 6, 2008.
Krugman, Paul. "Prize Lecture: The Increasing Returns Revolution in Trade and Geography." Nobelprize.org. http://www.nobelprize.org/nobel_prizes/economics/laureates/2008/krugman_lecture.pdf (accessed August 2012).
Krugmanonline.com. "Paul Krugman" (accessed October 2012).
Neary, J. Peter. "Putting the 'New' into New Trade Theory: Paul Krugman's Nobel Memorial Prize in Economics." *The Scandinavian Journal of Economics* 111 (2009): 217–50.
The Royal Swedish Academy of Sciences, "The Prize in Economic Sciences 2008." http://www.nobelprize.org/nobel_prizes/economics/laureates/2008/popular-economicsciences2008.pdf (accessed August 2012).

*Ninee Shoua Yang*

## KUZNETS, SIMON

Born: April 30, 1901, in Pinsk, Russia; Died: July 8, 1985, in Cambridge, Massachusetts; American; national income accounting, Nobel Prize (1971); Major Works: *National Income and Capital Formation* (1937), *Modern Economic Growth: Rate, Structure, and Spread* (1966), *Economic Growth of Nations: Total Output and Production Structure* (1971).

Simon Kuznets was a pivotal leader in transforming the field of economics from a largely speculative study to an empirical science. Economics was once viewed as a subsection of moral philosophy and Kuznets was influential in establishing it as an independent academic discipline. Kuznets was instrumental in devising classifications and subcategories for national income accounting to more accurately measure a nation's economic growth. He won the Nobel Prize in Economics in 1971. Kuznets died in 1985.

Simon Kuznets was awarded the Nobel Prize in 1971 for helping transform economics into a more exact science and providing the basis for the concept of gross national product. (UPI-Bettmann/Corbis)

Simon Smith Kuznets was born in Pinsk, Russia, on April 30, 1901. His education began as a child in Kharkov where he completed his primary schooling and gymnasium. Following his education he served for a short time in the Ukrainian government's Bureau of Labor Statistics and then emigrated to the United States in 1922. In the United States, Kuznets soon returned to his studies and distinguished himself with degrees from Columbia University, earning his BA in 1923, his MA in 1924, and his PhD in 1926.

Throughout his career Kuznets held a number of important academic and government positions. From 1930 to 1954, he was professor of economics and statistics at the University of Pennsylvania. In 1954, he moved on as professor of economics at Johns Hopkins University till 1960 when he left for Harvard, remaining at Harvard till 1971. He was a member of the research staff at the National Bureau of Economic Research (NBER) from 1927 to 1961. During his career, he authored over 200 papers and 31 books.

As an officer of the government, Kuznets made significant changes in the way government operations were carried out. He served in the Department of Commerce from 1932 to 1943 where he began his work in transforming the way the government collects economic statistics. He also served on the Bureau of Planning and Statistics of the War Production Board during World War II and was instrumental in establishing the Conference on Research in Income and Wealth in 1936. In 1947, he established its international counterpart, the International Association for Income and Wealth. He also advised the governments of China, Japan, India, Korea, Taiwan, and Israel on how to set up their economic statistical gathering operations.

During his life Kuznets made major contributions to many fields, most notably national income accounting. He was also influential in the fields of economic demography, the distribution of income, and the role of capital in economic growth. He had a significant impact on how government uses statistics to analyze economic growth and consumption.

The idea of measuring a nation's macroeconomy was introduced by John Maynard Keynes. A nation's economic growth can be measured in terms of its gross domestic product (GDP) or in terms of its gross domestic income (GDI). The measure known as GDP is the final value of purchases of all the goods and services produced in an economy during a given period of time, usually one year. The measure adds all the purchases of household consumption, business investment spending, and government spending with net exports. The second approach, GDI, measures total incomes earned by summing wages and salaries, rents, profits, interest, and other income.

The United States was in the midst of the Great Depression and policy makers were forced to use fragmentary and sketchy economic data to inform their policy decisions. President Roosevelt had to rely on incomplete stock indices, train freight statistics, and steel output levels. There was no clear picture by which policy makers could understand the economy as a whole. Kuznets was instrumental in breaking down into classifications and subcategories the U.S. national product and income accounts. These classifications allowed policy makers to get a bird's-eye view of the economy.

The U.S. national accounts to measure economic growth have become the foundation of modern macroeconomic analysis, allowing policy makers, economists, and the business community to analyze the impact of different plans, the impact of price shocks, and the impact of monetary policy on the economy as a whole and on specific parts of final demand, incomes, industries, and regions. The significance of Kuznets's work on national income accounts may be best portrayed by the fact that the U.S. Department of Commerce cited the development of national income accounting and product accounts as its "achievement of the century."

The result of these comprehensive standards developed and implemented by Kuznets shows that since their implementation economic fluctuations have been less severe. Recurring problems like bank runs, financial panics, and depressions have become far less painful than they were before World War II. The economy still has cyclical ups and downs, but the ability to measure the economy has resulted in a far more stable economic environment. Postwar prosperity in the United States is due in great part to the comprehensive data provided by the national accounts.

Simon Kuznets died on July 8, 1985, in Cambridge, Massachusetts.

*See also:* Friedman, Milton; Keynes, John Maynard

## Selected Works by Simon Kuznets

Epstein, Lillian, Elizabeth Jenks, and Simon Kuznets. *National Product since 1869.* New York: National Bureau of Economic Research, 1946.

Friedman, Milton, and Simon Kuznets. *Income from Independent Professional Practice.* New York: National Bureau of Economic Research, 1945.

Kuznets, Simon. *Economic Growth of Nations: Total Output and Production Structure.* Cambridge, MA: Belknap Press of Harvard University Press, 1971.

Kuznets, Simon. *Economic Growth and Structure: Selected Essays.* New York: Oxford & IBH, 1969.

Kuznets, Simon. *Modern Economic Growth: Rate, Structure, and Spread.* New Haven, CT: Yale University Press, 1966.

Kuznets, Simon. *National Income and Capital Formation.* New York: National Bureau of Economic Research, 1937.

**Selected Works about Simon Kuznets**

Fogel, Robert W. *Simon S. Kuznets 1901–1985: A Biographical Memoir.* Washington, DC: National Academy Press, 2001.

Kuznets, Simon. "Autobiography." Nobelprize.org. http://www.nobelprize.org/nobel_prizes/economics/laureates/1971/kuznets.html (accessed July, 2011).

Lundberg, Erik. "Simon Kuznets' Contribution to Economics." *The Swedish Journal of Economics* 73, no. 4 (December 1971): 444–59.

*John E. Trupiano*

# KYDLAND, FINN

Born: December 1, 1943, in Algard, Norway; Norwegian; business cycles, monetary policy, fiscal policy, labor economics, Nobel Prize (2004); Major Works: *Inflation Persistence and Flexible Prices* (2001), "Argentina's Recovery and 'Excess' Capital Shallowing of the 1990s" (2002), "Inflation Persistence and Flexible Prices" (with Robert D. Dittmar and William T. Gavin) (2005).

Finn Kydland is a notable economist whose primary interests are business cycles, monetary and fiscal policies, and labor economics. Kydland was awarded the 2004 Nobel Prize in Economics with his former adviser and fellow colleague, Edward C. Prescott. Their work in macroeconomics, particularly the time consistency of economic policy and the driving forces behind business cycles, has influenced the monetary and fiscal policies of several governments including the United Kingdom and New Zealand and helped to encourage the independence of many central banks.

Finn Erling Kydland was born on a farm in Algard, Rogaland County, Norway, on December 1, 1943. He was the only one in his elementary school full of farm children to go past elementary school. At 15, he left for Bryne and rented a room to go to Rogaland, the closest high school. He received high grades but was originally rejected by the Norwegian School of Economics and Business Administration (NHH). He taught mathematics to sixth and seventh graders while studying for a supplementary exam in economics, law, and business correspondence in English, German, and French. The following year, he attended NHH, receiving his BS in 1968. He then attended Carnegie Mellon where he obtained his PhD in 1973. He served as a professor of economics at NHH until 1978. In 1978, he taught at the Tepper School of Business of Carnegie Mellon University in Pittsburgh until 2004.

Kydland completed his earliest works, on economic fluctuations, while a student at the Graduate School of Industrial Administration (GSIA). There he studied under future Nobel laureate Robert Lucas Jr., who received the Nobel Prize for "Expectations and the Neutrality of Money," a paper he developed while teaching a class Kydland had taken. Kydland's first paper, "Duality in Fractional Programming," combined shipbuilding and mathematical programming and was published in *Naval Research Logistics Quarterly*. His second paper continued on with dual prices in conjunction with hierarchical linear programs and was published in *Management Science*. Kydland claimed that if the right instruments were assigned to the right targets, the economy would function quite well. If the target was incorrect, then problems would result and the economy would not function properly.

Kydland viewed fiscal and monetary policy makers as having different goals. Consequently, the target variables of the objectives functioned with different relative weights. Kydland saw fiscal policy makers as leaders and monetary policy makers as secondary. His theory was innovative because it was an alternative to the current symmetric noncooperative solution developed earlier by John F. Nash. This laid the foundations for his future work with Prescott.

Kydland and Edward C. Prescott together shaped dynamic economics. Together they explained how supply shocks are leading reasons for economic fluctuations. They were also able to show why the best government economic policies are often not implemented consistently over time. This helped them to explain microeconomic, supply-side influences on the business cycle, integrating theories of business cycles and of long-term economic growth. For example, Kydland and Prescott showed that political commitments to keep inflation low can lead investors to expect low inflation and unemployment rates. If policy makers decide, to the contrary, to reduce interest rates in order to take advantage of short-term gains in employment rates and general prosperity, they risk losing credibility. In fact, economic conditions may even worsen because of the discretionary policy.

Kydland's "Inflation Persistence and Flexible Prices" was published in 2005. His thesis was that when central banks follow an interest rate rule, then inflation will likely persist, even when prices are fully flexible. He argues that inflation persistence may result from any shock, whether persistent or not. Hence in equilibrium, the real driver behind the dynamics of inflation is the evolution of the spread between the real interest rate and the central bank's target.

Finn Kydland has been a fellow in the Econometric Society since 1992. He received the John Stauffer National Fellowship from Hoover Institution in 1982–83 and the Alexander Henderson Award of Carnegie Mellon in 1973. He is a member of the Norwegian Academy of Science and Letters, and he received the 2004 Nobel Prize in Economics. Since 2004, Kydland has served as a faculty member of the University of California, Santa Barbara, and has founded the Laboratory for Aggregate Economics and Finance. He is a senior research fellow at the IC2 Institute at the University of Texas, Austin, and is an adjunct professor at the NHH. Kydland also has served as a research associate for the Federal Reserve Banks of Dallas, Cleveland, and St. Louis.

*See also:* Lucas, Robert, Jr.; Nash, John; Prescott, Edward

### Selected Works by Finn Kydland

Dittmar, Robert D., William T. Gavin, and Finn E. Kydland. "Inflation Persistence and Flexible Prices." *International Economic Review* 46, no. 1 (February 2005): 245–61.

Kydland, Finn E. *Business Cycle Theory*. London: Edward Elgar, 1995.

Kydland, Finn E., David Backus, and Patrick J. Kehoe. *Relative Price Movements in Dynamic General Equilibrium Models of International Trade*. Issue 4243. Washington, DC: National Bureau of Economic Research, 1992.

Kydland, Finn E., and Edward C. Prescott. "Business Cycles: Real Facts and a Monetary Myth." In *The Rational Expectations Revolution: Readings from the Front Line*. Edited by Preston J. Miller, 307–34. Cambridge, MA: MIT Press, 1994.

Kydland, Finn E., and Edward C. Prescott. "Rules Rather than Discretion: The Inconsistency of Optimal Plans." *Journal of Political Economy* 85 (1977): 473–91.

Kydland, Finn E., and Edward C. Prescott. "Time to Build and Aggregate Fluctuations." *Econometrica* 50 (1982): 1345–70.

Kydland, Finn E., and Carlos Enrique Zarazaga. *Argentina's Recovery and Excess Capital Shallowing of the 1990s*. Dallas, TX: Federal Reserve Bank of Dallas, 2002.

### Selected Works about Finn Kydland

Badge, Peter. "Professor Dr. Finn E. Kydland." *Nobel Laureate Meetings at Lindau*. New York: Wiley VCH, 2008.

"Finn Kydland Wins Nobel Prize." https://econ.ucsb.edu/nobel/ (accessed April 2012).

Kydland, Finn. "Autobiography." Nobelprize.org. http://www.nobelprize.org/nobel_prizes/economics/laureates/2004/kydland-autobio.html (accessed April 2012).

*Samantha Lohr*

## LAFFER, ARTHUR

Born: August 14, 1940, in Youngstown, Ohio; American; fiscal policy, political economy; Major Works: *Foundations of Supply-Side Economics* (with Victor A. Canto, Douglas H. Joines, Paul Evans, Marc A. Miles, and Robert I. Webb) (1983), *End of Prosperity: How Higher Taxes Will Doom the Economy—If We Let it Happen* (with Stephen Moore and Peter J. Tanous) (2008), *Return to Prosperity* (with Stephen Moore) (2010).

Arthur Laffer is one of the few economists whose work became a namesake and foundation for a whole school of economic thought. The supply-side philosophy of economics laid the foundation for what was to become the Reaganomics of the 1980s. Supply-side economics underscored that lower tax rates would generate higher tax revenues. With this thesis, Laffer influenced business, government, and academic worlds. Laffer served the United States in several positions including consultant to Treasury Secretaries William Simon and George Shultz, chief economist for the Office of Budget and Management for George Shultz, and consultant to President Reagan's Economic Policy Advisory Board. Laffer was a founding member of the Congressional Policy Advisory Board. Arthur Laffer held academic positions at Pepperdine University, University of Southern California, and the University of Chicago.

Arthur Betz Laffer was born on August 14, 1940, in Youngstown, Ohio. After receiving his BA with a major in economics from Yale in 1963, he earned an MBA from Stanford University in 1965 and a PhD from Stanford in 1972. In 1967, he began his academic career by joining the faculty at the University of Chicago. In 1976, Laffer left for the University of Southern California where he was the Charles B. Thornton Professor of Business Economics. In 1984, he joined the faculty of Pepperdine University where he remained till 1987.

Laffer's career in the political arena began in 1970 when he served as chief economist for the Office of Budget and Management under U.S. Secretary of the Treasury George Shultz, a colleague of his at the University of Chicago. From 1972 to 1977, he served as a consultant to Treasury Secretary George Shultz as well as to U.S. Secretary of Treasury William Simon and Defense Secretary Ronald Rumsfeld. In the 1980s, Arthur Laffer's economic-political influence heightened when he served on President Reagan's Economic Policy Advisory Board from 1981 to 1989. His association with President Reagan began in 1980 as a member of then presidential candidate Ronald Reagan's Executive Advisory Committee. During the 1980s, he was also a consultant to UK Prime Minister Margaret Thatcher.

Arthur B. Laffer is a conservative economist and a leading theoretician of supply-side economics. His theory that lowering tax rates would result in economic expansion and higher revenues was a major influence in the economic program and policy of President Ronald Reagan. (AP/Wide World Photos)

Using the Laffer curve illustration as a teaching tool in his classes, he showed that at some level of tax rates, government would generate less revenue by creating disincentives to be productive through labor and more incentives to barter, participate in an underground economy, or just enjoy leisure. Consequently, these disincentives would then reduce tax revenues.

While this relationship between tax rates and tax revenues has become known as Laffer curve, Laffer himself never made any claim that the tax rates-tax revenues relationship was an original insight. He credited Ibn Khaldun and John Maynard Keynes as early architects. In the mid-1770s, both Adam Smith and David Ricardo made similar arguments.

Acceptance of the Laffer curve premise has not been universal. While there has been some research to identify tax rate ranges at which the tax rate-tax revenue relationship turns negative, there is also significant criticism of Laffer's illustration. Nobel laureates John Kenneth Galbraith and Paul Krugman both criticized Laffer's approach on the basis of equity and fairness. Others have criticized Arthur Laffer's description as too simplistic, while others attacked the theoretical, claiming the economy and consequently tax revenues would not totally be eliminated at a tax rate of 100 percent. Regardless of the criticisms, supply-side economics was the basis for the Kemp-Roth Tax Cut of 1981 and both the Economic Growth and

Tax Relief Reconciliation Act of 2001 and Jobs and Growth Tax Relief Reconciliation Act of 2003 (the "Bush tax cuts").

Arthur Laffer has authored several books and many articles on business economics and the political economy. In 1971, Laffer authored *Private Short-Term Capital Flows*. In 1983 Laffer—with Victor Canto, Douglas Joines, Paul Evans, Marc Miles, and Robert Webb—laid the foundations for supply-side economics with *Foundations of Supply Side Economics: Theory and Evidence*. As an author, Laffer is noted more for his recent works: *End of Prosperity: How Higher Taxes Will Doom the Economy—If We Let it Happen* (2009) with Stephen Moore and *Return to Prosperity* (2010) with Stephen Moore and Peter Tanous.

Laffer received many awards and honors during his career. In 1999, he was recognized as one of "The Century's Greatest Minds" for the Laffer curve. He received several Graham and Dodd Awards from the Financial Analyst Federation, the National Association of Investment Clubs Distinguished Service Award, and the Adam Smith Award.

*See also:* Galbraith, John Kenneth; Hayek, Friedrich von; Keynes, John Maynard; Khaldun, Ibn; Krugman, Paul; Ricardo, David; Smith, Adam

## Selected Works by Arthur Laffer

Canto, Victor A., Douglas H. Joines, Laffer, Arthur B., Marc A. Miles, and Robert I. Webb. *Foundations of Supply Side Economics: Theory and Evidence*. New York: Academic Press, 1983.

Laffer, Arthur. "The Ellipse: An Explication of the Laffer Curve in a Two-Factor Model." In *The Financial Analyst's Guide to Fiscal Policy*. Edited by Victor A. Canto, Charles W. Kadlec, and Arthur B. Laffer, 1–35. New York: Greenwood Press, 1986.

Laffer, Arthur. "The Laffer Curve: Past, Present, and Future by Arthur B. Laffer." June 1, 2004. Heritage Foundation: Leadership for America. http://www.heritage.org/research/reports/2004/06/the-laffer-curve-past-present-and-future.

Laffer, Arthur B., and Stephen Moore. *Return to Prosperity: How America Can Regain Its Superpower Status*. New York: Threshold Editions, 2010.

Laffer, Arthur B., Stephen Moore, and Peter J. Tanous. *End of Prosperity: How Higher Taxes Will Doom the Economy—If We Let it Happen*. New York: Threshold Editions, 2008.

## Selected Works about Arthur Laffer

"Arthur Laffer." Laffer Center for Supply-Side Economics. http://www.laffercenter.com/arthur-laffer/ (accessed April 2012).

"Dr. Arthur Laffer—Laffer Associates." CNBC. http://www.cnbc.com/id/24732335 (accessed April 2012).

"We Are All Keynesians Now." Jones College of Business, Middle Tennessee State University. http://frank.mtsu.edu/~berc/tnbiz/stimulus/laffer.html (accessed April 2012).

Wiggin, Addison, and Kate Incontrera. *I.O.U.S.A: One Nation. Under Stress. In Debt*. Hoboken, NJ: Wiley, 2008.

*David A. Dieterle*

## LAGARDE, CHRISTINE

Born: January 1, 1956, in Paris, France; French; international finance; Major Works: *Annales d'Economie Politique, N° 56/2008–2009* (2009), "Of Rules and Role Models" (2012).

Christine Lagarde, French lawyer and politician, was the first female minister of finance in France from 2007 to 2011. On July 5, 2011, she became the first woman leader of the International Monetary Fund (IMF) as managing director. Lagarde was named chevalier in the French Legion of Honor in July 2000. She has since been heralded as an influential leader, powerful businesswoman, and prominent centerpiece in international finance, as touted by her 2009 and 2011 top billings in *Forbes* as one of the most influential women in the world, in the *Wall Street Journal Europe* as best European executive woman, and as one of *Time* magazine's top 100 world leaders.

Christine Madeleine Odette Lagarde was born on January 1, 1956, in Paris, France. Her father (Robert Lallouette) was an English professor and her mother taught Latin. She completed her early years of study in Le Havre at the Lycée François 1er and Lycée Claude Monet. In 1973, at the age of 17, Lagarde moved to Washington, DC, to study at esteemed Holton-Arms, an all-girls college prep school in Bethesda, Maryland. During this time Lagarde interned for Representative William Cohen at the Capitol. She assisted his office during the beleaguered Watergate hearings, an experience that piqued her interest in politics. Lagarde earned a law degree in 1980 from the Université Paris X, specializing in antitrust and labor law. She went on to earn a master's degree in political science at the Institute of Political Studies at Aix-en-Provence in southern France.

Upon completion of her law degree, Christine Lagarde stayed on as a law lecturer at the Université Paris X. By 1981, Lagarde joined Baker & McKenzie, a Chicago-based international law firm with major operations in Asia and Europe. Lagarde's proven record in the legal specialties of antitrust and labor law and mergers and acquisitions boosted her to partner by 1987. In 1999 and 2002, Lagarde was chairman of the Global Executive Committee. By 2004, Lagarde was named chairman of the Global Strategic Committee.

Lagarde returned to France in June 2005 when she joined the ranks of French government as minister of foreign trade in President Jacques Chirac's cabinet. She maintained this position into Nicolas Sarkozy's presidency. He later named her minister of agriculture a month before designating her the new minister of finance. Known for her robust work ethic, Lagarde advocated for a lengthier than customary 35-hour workweek. In her ministerial role, Lagarde was instrumental in much-needed pension reforms. She was chair of the ECOFIN Council for six months in 2008. As a member and later chair of the G-20, she gained notoriety on the world stage for her part in managing the financial crisis, addressing weaknesses in international monetary policies, and instituting stronger financial regulation, supervision, and global economic governance.

Because Lagarde's background is in law rather than economics, she was an unlikely choice to lead the IMF. Her nomination was further complicated by developing countries seeking the post for one of their own. Lagarde campaigned for support in emerging nations such as India, Brazil, and China, to whom she promised an enhanced role in IMF relations and actions under her leadership. Though Agustin Carstens, the governor of Mexico's central bank, was her major adversary, he did not gain the backing of these nations. Eventually, Lagarde's expertise in European affairs, coupled with her ministerial experience, earned her the position. She is the 11th consecutive European to hold the position.

Lagarde serves as the chairman of the board of governors for the European Bank for Reconstruction and Development. She is a member of the board of governors at the EIB Group. She also works as a member of the board of governors at the European Investment Bank and the Inter-American Development Bank. Even with an impressive history and a cautious demeanor, the IMF chief is challenged by the European Union debt crisis, the precarious financial situation around the world, and the growing needs of developing nations.

With a number of personal "firsts" in top-ranked positions typically held by men, Lagarde lends her voice and power as an ally to women. Lagarde has been recognized for her contributions to the world of international finance and law. In July of 2000, Lagarde was named chevalier in the French Legion of Honor. She was named commander for the National Order of Agricultural Merit. In 2009, Christine Lagarde was ranked as the 17th most influential woman in the world by *Forbes* magazine, the 5th best European executive woman by the *Wall Street Journal Europe*, and one of *Time* magazine's top 100 world leaders. In 2011, Lagarde made *Forbes* magazine's list once again, this time as 8th and 39th on the World's 100 Most Powerful People list.

*See also:* Trichet, Jean-Claude

## Selected Works by Christine Lagarde

Lagarde, Christine. *Annales d'Economie Politique, N° 56/2008–2009*. Paris: Economica, 2009.

Lagarde, Christine. "Of Rules and Role Models." *IP Journal*, August 3, 2012. https://ip-journal.dgap.org/en/ip-journal/topics/rules-and-role-models (accessed October 2012).

## Selected Works about Christine Lagarde

"Challenges and Opportunities for the World Economy and the IMF." C. Peter McColough Series on International Economics. Council on Foreign Relations. July 26, 2011. http://www.cfr.org/international-finance/challenges-opportunities-world-economy-imf/p25546 (accessed October 2012).

"Christine Lagarde: Biographical Information." International Monetary Fund. http://www.imf.org/external/np/omd/bios/cl.htm (accessed September 2012).

"IMF's Lagarde: Rescuing Europe Will Take Years." Interview with Scott Pelley. *CBSNews*. October 2, 2012. http://www.cbsnews.com/8301-18563_162-57524856/imfs-lagarde-rescuing-europe-will-take-years/ (accessed October 2012).

Martel, Ned. "The Economy of Christine Lagarde." *Washington Post*, September 24, 2012. http://www.washingtonpost.com/politics/the-economy-of-christine-lagarde/2012/09/24/8d5c2b84-cd01-11e1-b7dd-ef7ef87186df_story.html (accessed September 2012).

*Joy Dooley-Sorrells*

# LANGE, OSKAR

Born: July 27, 1904, in Tomaszow Mazowiecki, Poland; Died: October 2, 1965, in London, England; Polish; socialism, market socialism; Major Work: *On the Economic Theory of Socialism* (with Benjamin Evans Lippincott and Fred Manville Taylor) (1938).

Oskar Lange was a Polish-born economist who after many years of teaching economics in the United States returned to Poland following World War II to establish socialism in his native land. Lange is most known for developing the earliest and most complete model of market socialism—an economic system where government ownership and a market price system would work together. He also served Poland in diplomatic roles. Lange died in 1965.

Oskar Richard Lange was born on July 27, 1904, in Tomaszow Mazowiecki, Poland. Lange studied law and economics in Poznań and Kraków, Poland, writing his PhD thesis (1928) on the topic of Polish business cycles. Lange worked at the Ministry of Labor in Warsaw during the period of 1926–27. As a lecturer Lange taught at the University of Krakow (1927–31, 1936), the Polish Free University of Warsaw (1937), the University of Michigan (1936), and the University of California and Stanford University (1937, 1937–38, respectively). He visited the United States from 1934 to 1937 under a Rockefeller grant, studying at both Harvard University and the University of Minnesota. He became a U.S. citizen in 1943.

After publishing *On the Economic Theory of Socialism* (1938), he taught at the University of Chicago until after World War II. Lange's varied experiences provided him an excellent understanding of both Marxist and Western economics. In 1944, Lange interviewed Joseph Stalin, supporting the newly formed Communist Polish government.

Lange believed that an economy run by the state was more efficient and superior to a free-market-based system, but he defended the role of market prices within centralized planning. The theory of market socialism relies on government ownership and control of firms. Yet the firms would sell their products in competitive markets. In developing his theory of market socialism, Lange relied on the concepts of efficiency suggested by Vilfredo Pareto and the general equilibrium theory developed by Leon Walras.

Lange proposed a centralized system of market socialism with three different decision-making levels. He proposed a central planning board (CPB), industrial ministries, and enterprises (firms and households). The CPB would initially set prices. Firms would act competitively and achieve the most efficient use of existing resources. A shortage or surplus in the markets would result and the CPB would then adjust prices to achieve the market equilibrium.

The CPB would also decide how to allocate social dividends (rent and profit). The state through the direction of the industrial ministries would control investment, direct the rate of growth, and set prices to control negative externalities. By directing savings and investment, Lange felt the state would be in a better position to reduce business fluctuations.

Lange's views were constantly challenged. Critics felt that Lange's model was simply unmanageable because the CPB would need such large amounts of information to make correct decisions. Since there was no ownership of capital by private individuals, there were really no incentives for mangers to produce efficiently. Later critics of market socialism continued to argue that both the lack of private property ownership and entrepreneurship opportunity were weaknesses of a market socialistic system; such a system would not allow incentives and rewards for innovation.

After World War II, Lange renounced his U.S. citizenship and became Poland's ambassador to the United States in 1945 and 1946. He then became Poland's delegate to the United Nations Security Council from 1946 to 1949. Lange fell out of political favor with the Communist Party and was recalled to Poland. In 1955, Lange became a professor at the University of Warsaw. His reputation in the West as an economist deteriorated as he continued his involvement with Stalin.

His work on market socialism still influences the work of economists today. In Poland there is a university named after him, the Wrocław University of Economics of Oskar Lange.

Oskar Lange died on October 2, 1965, in London, England.

*See also:* Hayek, Friedrich von; Mises, Ludwig von; Pareto, Vilfredo; Walras, Leon

## Selected Works by Oskar Lange

Lange, Oskar. "On the Economic Theory of Socialism, Part I, Part II." *The Review of Economic Studies*, 1936.

Lange, Oskar. *Papers in Economics and Sociology*. Translated and edited by P. F. Knightsfield. Oxford: Pergamon Press, 1970.

Lange, Oskar, and Antoni Banasinski. *Introduction to Econometrics*. Warsaw: Pergamon Press, PWN, 1978.

Lange, Oskar, Benjamin Evans Lippincott, and Fred Manville Taylor. *On the Economic Theory of Socialism*. Minneapolis: University of Minnesota Press, 1938.

## Selected Works about Oskar Lange

Friedman, Milton. "Lange on Price Flexibility and Employment: A Methodological Criticism." *American Economic Review* 36, no. 4 (1946): 613–31.

Kornai, Janos. "Socialism and the Market: Conceptual Clarification." http://www.madsociologist.net/resources/Socialism+and%2 (accessed September 2012).

Kowalik, Tadeusz, ed. *Economic Theory and Market Socialism: Selected Essays of Oskar Lange*. Economists of the Twentieth Century. London: Edward Elgar, 1994.

Kowalik, Tadeusz. "Lange, Oskar R." In *The New Palgrave: A Dictionary of Economics*. Vol. 3. Edited by John Eatwell, Murray Milgate, and Peter Newman, 123–29. Basingstoke, UK: Palgrave Macmillan, 1987.

Shleifer, Andrei, and Robert W. Vishny. "Politics of Market Socialism." *Journal of Economic Perspectives* 8, no. 2 (1994): 165–76.

*Jean Kujawa*

## LEONTIEF, WASSILY

Born: August 5, 1905, in Munich, Germany; Died: February 5, 1999, in New York; Russian-American; macroeconomics, input-output analysis, Nobel Prize (1973); Major Work: *Structure of American Industry, 1919–1929* (1941).

Wassily Leontief, a Russian-American economist, led the criticism of John Maynard Keynes's general theory during the 1930s. Leontief is associated with developing models of equilibrium and input-output analysis. Leontief's input-output model distinguished the many components of an economy and their interdependence on each other. His models broadened how the circular flow of economics was used to describe the relationships between inputs (land, labor, capital) and outputs (goods and services) in an economy. Wassily Leontief won the Nobel Prize in Economics in 1973 for his input-output modeling efforts. He was honored with awards from around the world. Leontief died in 1999.

Wassily Wassilyovich Leontief was born on August 5, 1905, in Munich, Germany. Wassily was a second-generation economist, following his father, Wassily Sr., in the profession. Wassily Jr. enrolled in the University of Leningrad at the age of 15, earned his master's at 19, and completed his PhD at the University of Berlin in 1928. The topic of his PhD dissertation paper was the circular flow of economic activity.

Wassily Leontief was an innovative American economist whose methods have had an international impact. He was also one of the first economists to take into account the impact of economic activity on environmental quality. (UPI-Bettmann/Corbis)

Leontief began his professional career in the Soviet Union at the University of Kiel, working at the Institute of World Economics. In 1930, he moved on to serve as an adviser for the Chinese Ministry of Railroads for a year before moving to the United States to join the National Bureau of Economic Research, and he joined Harvard University in 1932. When World War II broke out, Leontief was a consultant to the Office of Strategic Services. In 1946,

Wassily Leontief began a new era of his career with his appointment as professor at Harvard University. At Harvard, he established the Harvard Economic Research Project and was its director till 1973. He then established the Institute of Economic Analysis at New York University in 1975.

Continuing the work he began in his dissertation, Wassily Leontief was most noted for his study of input-output analysis. Leontief was expanding on the work of François Quesnay (*Tableau économique*) and Leon Walras (*Elements of Pure Economics*) in which both had developed earlier versions of the circular flow. Leontief's contribution was his ability to simplify and quantify the components of the circular flow.

The circular flow in its more complex form is an input-output model of general equilibrium analysis. Leontief's input-output analysis models showed how the components of an economy are interrelated. His models exhibited the dynamics of how a change in one sector of the economy will impact other sectors. This interdependence of economic sectors became a crucial component in understanding the consequences of policy decisions by governments. In 1941, continuing his work on the national accounting of an economy and input-output analysis, Leontief wrote his major work, *Structure of American Industry, 1919–1929*.

Doing work for the U.S. Bureau of Labor Statistics, Leontief was able to identify 500 different sectors of the economy. He created a quantitative measure for each one, thus creating a quantitative input-output analysis model for the entire economy. He is credited with being one of the first to use computers for mathematical modeling.

Wassily Leontief's contributions to economics go beyond his input-output models. In the area of international trade, in 1953 he founded what became known as the Leontief paradox. The Leontief paradox surmised that the United States was exporting labor-intensive goods rather than capital-intensive goods. The significance of this finding was that it was a reversal (a paradox) to the widely held international trade theory at the time that countries should produce and trade based on the relative scarcity of their resources. Yet the United States as a capital-intensive economy was trading internationally those goods that were labor-intensive.

In 1973, Wassily Leontief was awarded the Nobel Prize in Economics for his novel work on the input-output tables. Given specific assumptions, the tables he created can be used to approximate the changes necessary in the resources (inputs) needed when there is a change in the production of a final good. As stated before, Leontief's input-output tables showed how changes in one sector of the economy will influence changes in another sector, making an economy's sectors interdependent to each other.

Leontief was an ardent and vocal critic of John Maynard Keynes's general theory. In the 1930s, Leontief participated in debates on Keynes's general theory. Leontief was particularly critical of Keynes's methodology and definitions. Leontief criticized Keynes's definitions of aggregate demand and aggregate supply curves. Leontief's most serious criticism of Keynes was that he was proposing simplistic remedies for an interdependent, intricate, and complicated economy. He also questioned Keynes on his labor supply curve and his "liquidity preference." Leontief argued it prevented expansionary monetary policy for attaining full employment. Leontief expressed his doubts of Keynes's ideas in an article, "Implicit Theorising: A Methodological Criticism of the Neo-Cambridge School."

Along with the Nobel Prize in Economics in 1973, Wassily Leontief received many awards and honors from around the world. He received many honorary doctorates from universities around the world. In 1968, he was awarded the French Legion of Honor, the West German Bernhard-Harms Prize in Economics in 1970, and the Japanese Order of the Rising Sun in 1984. In 1980, Leontief was inducted into the Russian-American Hall of Fame, and in 1989 he was honored with the Society of the Optimate by the Italian Cultural Institute in New York. In 1995, the International House of New York honored Leontief with the Harry Edmonds Award for Life Achievement. While he received many honors and awards, one is named in his honor. Each year Tufts University's Global Development and Environment Institute awards an individual Leontief Prize in Economics.

Wassily Leontief died in New York City on February 5, 1999, at the age of 93.

*See also:* Keynes, John Maynard; Quesnay, François; Walras, Leon

### Selected Works by Wassily Leontief

Leontief, Wassily. *Essays in Economics: Theories, Theorizing, Facts, and Policies.* Piscataway, NJ: Transaction, 1966.
Leontief, Wassily. *Input-Output Economics.* New York: Freeman, 1951.
Leontief, Wassily. *The Structure of the American Economy, 1919–1929.* Cambridge, MA.: Harvard University Press, 1941.
Leontief, Wassily. *Studies in the Structure of the American Economy: Theoretical and Empirical Explorations in Input-Output Analysis.* White Plains, NY: International Arts and Sciences Press, 1953.
Leontief, Wassily. *Theories, Facts, and Policies: Essays in Economics.* Vol. 1. White Plains, NY: M.E. Sharpe, 1977.
Leontief, Wassily, Ann P. Carter, and Peter A. Petri. *The Future of the World Economy: A United Nations Study.* Oxford: Oxford University Press, 1977.
Leontief, Wassily, and Faye Duchin. *The Future Impact of Automation on Workers.* New York: Oxford University Press, 1986.

### Selected Works about Wassily Leontief

Dietzenbacher, Erick, and Michael L. Lahr, eds. *Wassily Leontief and Input-Output Economics.* Cambridge: Cambridge University Press, 2004.
Leontief, Estelle. *Genia and Wassily: A Russian-American Memoir.* Brookline, MA: Zephyr Press, 1987.
"Nobelist and Economist Wassily Leontief Dies." *Harvard University Gazette.* http://news.harvard.edu/gazette/1999/02.11/leontief.html (accessed September, 2011).
Surhone, Lambert M., Mariam T. Tenno, and Susan F. Henssonow, eds. *Wassily Leontief.* Beau Bassin, Mauritius: Betascript, 2011.
"Wassily Leontief—Father of the Input-Output Analysis Model." EconomyWatch. http://www.economywatch.com/economist/nassily-leontief.html (accessed September 2011).

*David A. Dieterle*

# LEWIS, SIR ARTHUR

Born: January 23, 1915, in Castries, Saint Lucia, British West Indies; Died: June 15, 1991, in Bridgetown, Barbados; industrial structure, economic development and growth, Nobel Prize (1979); Major Works: *Overhead Costs: Some Essays in Economic Analysis*, Volume 3 (1951), *The Principles of Economic Planning: A Study Prepared for the Fabian Society* (1952), *The Theory of Economic Growth* (1955), *Some Aspects of Economic Development* (1969), *Growth and Fluctuations, 1870–1913* (1978).

Sir Arthur Lewis was one of the most distinguished twentieth-century economists. Lewis is well known for his work in the field of development economics and history of the world economy. Lewis wrote many books and published influential articles. In 1979, he won the Nobel Prize in Economics for his significant contributions to economic development and growth. He shared the prize with an American economist, Theodore Schultz. He was the first person of African descent to win the Nobel Prize in categories other than literature or peace. Lewis died in 1991.

William Arthur Lewis was born on January 23, 1915, in a small city of Castries in the island country of Saint Lucia, which was a British colony at the time. Both his parents were schoolteachers and immigrated to Saint Lucia from Antigua to provide a better education for their five children. When Lewis was seven, he contracted an infectious disease and had to stay home for weeks. During the next three months, in order for him not to stay behind in school, his father taught him every day. He accelerated so much that upon his return to school, he had to shift from grade 4 to grade 6. He finished high school at age 14 and started working as a clerk in a civil service position. In 1932, he won a government scholarship to a British university. In 1937, Lewis became the valedictorian of his class and received his bachelor of commerce degree from London School of Economics (LSE). He then received a scholarship from LSE for a PhD in industrial economics. In 1948, at the age of 33, Lewis became a full professor at the University of Manchester. From 1957 to 1963, Lewis held various key administrative positions including UN economic adviser to the prime minister of Ghana, deputy managing director of the UN Special Fund, and president of University of West Indies. In 1963, he moved to Princeton University as a James Madison Professor of Political Economy. From 1970 to 1974, he moved to an administration position to establish the Caribbean Development Bank. Lewis came back to his professorship position at Princeton University until he passed away at age 76, in 1991. Lewis believed that his scholarly positions deepened his understanding of the economic problems of developing countries, and that his administrative roles expand his horizon regarding those issues. Throughout Lewis's career, he focused his research in three areas: (1) industrial economics, (2) history of world economy, and (3) development economics. He continued his research in the history of world economy and development economics until his death in 1991.

Lewis started his assistant lectureship under his adviser, Professor Arnold Plant, in the commerce department. Because of Plant's specialty in the area of industrial organization, Lewis was assigned to lecture and advised to choose his PhD thesis in this field. Lewis started by testing the dominant theories of industrial organizations against the available data of the time. In his research, he looked at the price structure where average cost per unit is higher than marginal cost. In theory, price should equal marginal cost. In reality, however, he found that this scenario would fluctuate between monopoly and bankruptcy. In addition, he paid particular attention to the time dimension aspect of demand. He suggested treating the fixed investment as a joint cost of different production outputs at different times, subject to total payment not exceeding total cost. He published his findings of British industrial organization in two books, *Overhead Costs* (1949) and *Principles of Economic Planning* (1950).

In 1945 Friedrich von Hayek, the acting chairman of the economics department at Manchester University, asked Lewis to lecture a course on the world economy between the two world wars. Four years later, Lewis published a book entitled *Economics Survey 1919–1939*, in which he summarized what he knew of the world economy during the mid-twentieth century. Lewis's book, however, did not investigate what led to a great depression after World War I and what led to a decade of prosperity after World War II. He accepted the fact that industrial recessions occur with varying intervals of 5 to 10 years. However, he could not explain what made the Great Depression so grave. He came to the conclusion that in 1929 many economic weaknesses happened together at once. He spent a good portion of his academic life attempting to answer a few unanswered questions regarding the nature of industrial fluctuations and determinants of the terms of trade between industrial and agricultural products. The result of his research was published in a book entitled *Growth and Fluctuations* (1978).

In 1948 Lewis, a full professor at Manchester University at the time, started to teach development economics with an emphasis on policy. Almost a decade later in 1955 he published *The Theory of Economic Growth* (1955). The main contribution of the book was the two-sector model, which analyzes the distribution of income in economy over a long period of time. Up to that point, the elasticity of supply of labor was considered to be zero, which means that any increase in investment ought to increase the demand for labor and therefore spike wages upward for all workers. Lewis, however, defined the elasticity of supply of labor infinite. According to his growth model, advancement in technology raises profits for only employers and a limited number of skilled workers. The result, therefore, would be a rise in national income without an enhancement in standard of living for the mass population. Because of the applicability of this model to many situations, this model drew attention of many economists around the world.

Sir William Arthur Lewis died on June 15, 1991, in Bridgetown, Barbados, and was sepulchered in Saint Lucia.

*See also:* Hayek, Friedrich von; Schultz, Theodore

### Selected Works by Sir Arthur Lewis

Lewis, Arthur. *Growth and Fluctuations, 1870–1913.* London: Allen & Unwin, 1978.

Lewis, Arthur. *Overhead Costs: Some Essays in Economic Analysis*. Vol. 3. London: Allen & Unwin, 1951.

Lewis, Arthur. *The Principles of Economic Planning: A Study Prepared for the Fabian Society*. London: Allen & Unwin, 1952.

Lewis, Arthur. *Some Aspects of Economic Development*. Accra: University of Ghana by the Ghana Publishing Corp., 1969.

Lewis, Arthur. *The Theory of Economic Growth*. Concord, Ontario, Canada: Irwin, 1955.

**Selected Works about Sir Arthur Lewis**

Breit, W., R. W. Spencer, and Trinity University. *Lives of the Laureates: Seven Nobel Economists*. Cambridge, MA: MIT Press, 1986.

Findlay, R. "On W. Arthur Lewis' Contributions to Economics." *The Scandinavian Journal of Economics* 82, no. 1 (1980): 62–79.

*Elham Mahmoudi*

## LIST, FRIEDRICH

Born: August 6, 1789, in Reutlingen, Germany; Died: November 30, 1846, in Kufstein, Austria; German; political economy; Major Work: *The National System of Political Economy* (1841).

Friedrich List was a German economist who promoted a national system of development to international trade. While influenced by Adam Smith, List had significant differences with Smith and other classical political economists of the time. List's theory of national economic system focused on the nation as a whole rather than on the individual. List promoted an economic system where the efficient production of resources created wealth, not the accumulation of goods. List believed a nation must first develop its domestic agricultural and manufacturing industries before it is capable of participating in international free trade. List died in 1846.

Georg Friedrich List was born on August 6, 1789, in Reutlingen, Germany. His father was a successful tanner, but List chose public service over joining his father in business. As a civil servant at 17, List rose to a ministry undersecretary in 1816. The following year he was selected to teach political economy at the University of Tubingen.

In 1818, he urged the abolishment of tariffs on trade between German states. He formed an organization of Frankfurt businessmen to promote this liberal idea. The political opposition to his ideas was very intense. It led to his resignation from his teaching post in 1819. Having been elected to the Wurttemberg Assembly in 1820, he was dismissed only two years later for his criticisms of the government. His expulsion from the Assembly forced List to leave Germany to avoid prison. After visiting France and England, he returned to Germany where he was arrested, expecting to fulfill his prison sentence. However, he could avoid prison if he left Germany, so in 1825 he left Germany for the United States.

In the United States, List located in Reading, Pennsylvania, farming and then becoming the editor of a German language newspaper. Influenced by Alexander Hamilton, List began to write and promote his ideas for a national economy. In 1827, he published *Outlines of American Political Economy*. In this publication, he returned to his early ideas when in Germany. He reasoned that a young national economy such as the United States needed tariffs to protect the new enterprises responsible for the early growth of the economy and stimulate new development. With the publication of *Outlines of American Political Economy*, List had now crossed over from businessman and journalist to political economist. Having gained a degree of financial independence with the discovery of coal on his land, List devoted more time to promoting his ideas and structure for a national economy. He also became an American citizen.

In 1832, List returned to Germany as U.S. consul to Baden and later Leipzig. In Germany, List became passionately involved in extending Germany's railroads. Following the mixed success of his efforts with the railroads, he completed his tenure as U.S. consul and in 1837 moved to France. In 1841, he wrote what would become his classic contribution to the study of the political economy, *The National System of Political Economy*.

List's work is marked by several disagreements with Adam Smith. For one, List submitted that the wealth of a nation was more dependent on the "productive forces" that would create the wealth as opposed to the wealth of goods accumulated. List argued that Smith had put too much emphasis on material wealth (accumulation of goods) and exchange of the wealth, and not enough emphasis on the productive side of an economy (accumulation of productive resources). List considered the productive resources more important to a national economy because they were investments in future development.

A second distinction between List and Smith has to do with their interpretations of productive labor. According to List, Smith had not done an adequate job crediting and promoting "mental labor" as a measure of wealth. This included the professions of the law, religion, the arts, science, and education. List also disagreed with Smith on the value of free trade. While Smith promoted free trade without limitation, List saw trade develop nationally and through definite stages of development.

List argued that national economies must progress through four stages of development. The first stage is when agriculture is the major domestic industry and manufactured goods are imported. In the second stage domestic manufacturing begins to increase, although the nation continues to import foreign manufactured goods. During the third stage domestic manufacturers are sufficiently large to provide for domestic consumption. And in the fourth stage agricultural products and large-scale productive resources are imported and there is large-scale exporting of manufactured products. Ultimately, the main idea of List's theory is that nations must first develop their agricultural and manufacturing industries to take care of their domestic needs as a prerequisite to participating in international trade.

Though List advocated a national economic system, he argued that too much government interaction would be more costly than beneficial. He was not for regulating all aspects of an economy and recognized that certain aspects of the economy needed to be worked out on their own.

List's writings on the development of a national economic system have been promoted and are highly influential among developing nations. His emphases on the importance of advances in transportation, education, law and order, and efficient government have created a framework for successful national development.

Friedrich List's *The National System of Political Economy* (*Das Nationale System der Politischen Okonomie*) is one of the classics of economic thought. It has been translated from its original German to English, French, Russian, Swedish, and Hungarian.

Friedrich List had little good fortune in his later days. He lost his property in the United States and his health was failing.

Friedrich List died in Kufstein, Austria, on November 30, 1846, by committing suicide.

*See also:* Smith, Adam

### Selected Works by Friedrich List

List, Friedrich. "The German Zollverein." *Edinburgh Review* 79 (1844): 105 et seq.
List, Friedrich. *The National System of Political Economy*. London: Longmans, 1928. First published in German (1841).
List, Friedrich. *Outlines of a New System of Political Economy*. Philadelphia: Lippincott, 1827.

### Selected Works about Friedrich List

Brinkmann, Carl. *Friedrich List*. Berlin: Duncker & Humblot, 1949.
Henderson, William O. *Friedrich List: Economist and Visionary*. London: Frank Cass, 1983.
Hirst, Margaret E. *Life of Friedrich List and Selections from His Writings*. London: Smith; New York: Scribner, 1909.
Streeten, Paul. "Unbalanced Growth." *Oxford Economic Papers New Series* 11 (1959): 167–90.

*Kathleen C. Simmons*

## LOCKE, JOHN

Born: August 29, 1632, in Somerset, England; Died: October 28, 1704, in Essex, England; English; political philosophy; Major Works: *Two Treatises on Government* (1690), *Some Considerations of the Consequences of the Lowering of Interest, and Raising the Value of Money: In a Letter Sent to a Member of Parliament* (1696).

John Locke was a political philosopher whose most enduring contributions were the development of Empiricism (the belief that knowledge comes from experience) and the idea of popular sovereignty (the belief that a government's right to rule comes from the people). His work also affected economics more directly in his rationale for private property, his belief that human beings are motivated by self-interest, and his advice to the British government on monetary theory. Locke died in 1704.

John Locke was born on August 29, 1632, in Somerset, England. John Locke would spend his life as a member of the intellectual middle class. He received an elite education as a result of his lawyer father's connections to a member of Parliament. Locke earned bachelor's and master's degrees in philosophy from Christ's Church College at Oxford College, and later a bachelor's degree in medicine. Locke had various careers such as lecturer in Greek, lecturer in rhetoric, and personal physician to the chancellor of the Exchequer.

In many ways, John Locke and his ideas were seen by the British government as a threat to the king. In 1682, Locke was forced to Holland in exile. Locke finished writing *An Essay Concerning Human Understanding* during his exile. During England's Glorious Revolution in 1688, John Locke returned to England, becoming a policy maker for the government of the American colonies.

It was in this role as secretary to the Council for Trade and Plantations that Locke was compelled to comment directly on economics, specifically monetary policy. His purely economic writings do not constitute his most important contributions to economic thought. These are contained in his writings on political philosophy, which included two ideas that would become central to a modern understanding of a market economy: private property and the utility of self-interest.

Locke's approach was starkly in contrast to historical Western notions of government at the time. The classical Greeks and Romans believed that government existed primarily to promote virtue. Medieval Christians saw government as an extension of God's rule over creation. Locke and other Enlightenment thinkers based their thinking on a notion of mankind's natural rights.

He began his analysis by envisioning a "state of nature," in which civilization did not exist and human beings lived unaffected by society, culture, or government. In such a world, mankind naturally possessed the rights of "life, liberty, and property." These rights were, however, insecure since people were likely to attack and enslave one another. Locke wrote that people voluntarily create governments with limited power in order to protect their natural rights. However, in doing so, they actually give up some of their rights since the government exists to prevent people from doing whatever they please. They surrender some rights in order to protect more important rights. Lastly, and perhaps most importantly, since the government is created by the people in order to protect their rights, the government is ultimately accountable to the people for its authority—a concept known as popular sovereignty.

In this analysis, Locke assumed that private property is a person's right. This was not the general belief in his time. Before Locke, most scholars had theorized that since the world belonged to God, people could not truly claim property as their own. To them, private ownership was regarded as a necessary evil in an imperfect world. Locke disputed this view, asserting that since people were entitled to enjoy the work of their hands, they were also entitled to possess the land that they developed by their own work—his theory could be called the "labor theory of property." For Locke, property was an indispensable measure of life and liberty.

Also implicit in his thinking was the view that people are motivated by self-interest. Locke did not emphasize duty as the classical thinkers had, or adherence to God's laws. Locke assumed that individuals make the choices that they think are most likely to improve their standard of living. The concept of individual self-interest, along with the belief in a person's right to private property, would become an important piece of the philosophical groundwork for later classical economists, most notably Adam Smith.

Lastly, Locke contributed to a growing body of practical economic thought in his role as a policy maker for the colonies of North and South Carolina. Locke argued that interest rates were linked to the supply of money, so they should not be changed arbitrarily. Such laws would not work as intended, but would simply interfere with trade and act as a subsidy to borrowers. Locke also argued against a view popular in the English government that asserted that coins should be made with smaller amounts of precious metals. Locke pointed out that this would simply cause merchants to demand more coins for the same quantity of goods since the value of money was determined in part by its scarcity. This last view makes him an early contributor to the quantity theory of money.

John Locke will be remembered among philosophers for his early contributions to the school of Empiricism and among political scientists for his writings on limited government, popular sovereignty, and natural rights. His thoughts on self-interest and private property found their way into the core of late eighteenth-century thought, clearing the way for Adam Smith and his seminal work, *The Wealth of Nations*. Without Locke's work, Smith's writings might have faced a much more difficult audience.

Prior to his death, four additional editions of *An Essay Concerning Human Understanding* were published. He occupied his time responding to critiques of his work and exchanging letters with Edward Stillingfleet. The series of correspondence was later published.

John Locke died in Essex, England, on October 28, 1704.

*See also:* Smith, Adam

## Selected Works by John Locke

Locke, John. *An Essay Concerning Human Understanding Volume I [&] Volume II*. London: T. Longman et al., 1796.
Locke, John. *Fundamental Constitutions of Carolina* (1670). Ann Arbor, MI: EEBO Editions, ProQuest, 2010.
Locke, John. *Some Considerations of the Consequences of the Lowering of Interest, and Raising the Value of Money: In a Letter Sent to a Member of Parliament*, 1696.
Locke, John. *Two Treatises on Government* (1690). Amherst, NY: Prometheus Books, 1986.

## Selected Works about John Locke

"John Locke—Biography." The European Graduate School. http://www.egs.edu/library/john-locke/biography/ (accessed March, 2011).
Locke, John. *The Selected Political Writings of John Locke*. Edited by Paul Sigmund. New York: Norton, 2005.
Woolhouse, Roger. *Locke: A Biography*. New York: Cambridge University Press, 2007.

*Stephen H. Day*

## LUCAS, ROBERT, JR.

Born: September 15, 1937, in Yakima, Washington; American; rational expectations, monetary theory, international trade, fiscal policy, and economic growth, Nobel Prize (1995); Major Works: "Expectations and the Neutrality of Money" (1972), *Lectures on Economic Growth* (2002).

Robert E. Lucas Jr. is an American economist who was awarded the Nobel Prize in Economics in 1995 for his pioneering work in econometrics and his contribution to the theory of rational expectations. Applying econometric hypothesis testing, Lucas correlated public policy decisions regarding fiscal and monetary policy at the macroeconomic level with the private microeconomic decisions made by individuals. Individuals, Lucas suggested, will use past experience and future predictions, i.e., rational expectations, in their microeconomic decision-making process, thus offsetting the macroeconomic policies. Lucas's arguments, which became known as the "Lucas Critique," were debated as the antithesis of John Maynard Keynes's government interventionist programs, which were the dominant theories and practices of the 1970s.

Robert Emerson Lucas was born on September 15, 1937, in Yakima, Washington. Growing up in Seattle, Washington, it was expected young Lucas would attend the University of Washington to study engineering. With his interest in history and not math, he attended the University of Chicago where he earned his AB in history in 1959. Lucas returned west and began his graduate work in history at the University of California, Berkeley, on a Woodrow Wilson doctoral fellowship. While at Berkeley, however, he changed from history to economics. Due to financial considerations, he returned to the University of Chicago to pursue economics, earning his PhD in 1964. While at Chicago, Lucas was introduced to two of his mentors, Paul Samuelson through his textbook and Milton Friedman through his classes. Having grown up in a family of New Deal political thinkers, the ideas of Milton Friedman were foreign to Robert Lucas the graduate student. Regardless of his political leaning, a reshaping began to take form for Mr. Lucas.

In 1963, Robert Lucas accepted a position at Carnegie Mellon University in their Graduate School of Industrial Administration. In 1974, he returned to the University of Chicago as a professor of economics. In 1980, Lucas was named the John Dewey Distinguished Service Professor.

Lucas's time at Carnegie Mellon was one of intense research and rapid formation of his beliefs regarding economic dynamics. In particular, Lucas devoted great energies to understanding tax structure and taxation of capital gains. During the early years of his career in the 1960s, Lucas promoted proposals to tax capital gains as ordinary income. Later in his career he advocated not taxing capital gains at all, in line with supply-side economics.

As much as Lucas enjoyed his time at Carnegie Mellon professionally, his return to the University of Chicago in 1974 was a homecoming. He found the University of Chicago environment exciting and conducive for teaching and research. Through his graduate teaching, he was able to address research issues in the areas of economic growth, international trade, along with fiscal and monetary policy.

Lucas researched and published in several areas of economics including labor economics, business cycles, investment theory, and economic growth. With Carnegie Mellon colleague Leonard Rapping, he researched labor economics (U.S. wages and employment from 1929 to 1958). With another Carnegie Mellon colleague David Cass, he researched Samuelson's overlapping generations model. In his 1988 publication "On the Mechanics of Economic Development," Lucas blended two fields of economic study, economic growth and economic development. He submitted that the same economic framework can apply to both fields. Prior to Lucas's work, the field of economic growth focused on developed countries while economic development focused on developing countries.

Lucas also challenged the Phillips curve, an inverse relationship between inflation and employment made famous by A. W. H. Phillips. Using rational expectations, Lucas argued that workers will eventually understand that the higher wages resulting from higher inflation do not equate to real income growth. As a result, unemployment will not fall as the Phillips curve assumes. Lucas's argument became known as the "policy ineffectiveness proposition" since individuals' rational expectations will neutralize any policy decisions, preventing economic growth.

Based on the number of Nobel laureates or Nobel laureates-to-be who would influence Lucas and vice versa, it should not come as a surprise that he was so successful in economics. Milton Friedman (1976) served on his University of Chicago thesis committee and was one of his professors; he credits Paul Samuelson's (1970) textbook for preparing him for his economics studies; Thomas Sargent (2011) was a colleague at Carnegie Mellon; and Edward Prescott (2004) was a graduate student of his at Carnegie Mellon. He would later write "Investment under Uncertainty" with Edward Prescott, which altered the view of rational expectations.

Robert Lucas was awarded the Nobel Prize in Economics in 1995 for his work on rational expectations and macroeconomic analysis. His Nobel lecture came from his paper with Edward Prescott, "Expectations and the Neutrality of Money" (1972), which Lucas considers the most influential of all his writings. To celebrate the paper's importance in macroeconomic theory, the Federal Reserve Bank of Minneapolis conducted a 25th Anniversary Conference on the paper in 1995. Lucas edited or coedited numerous economics journals. He also held the prestigious office of president for both the American Economic Association and the Econometric Society.

Robert Lucas is considered one of the economic revolutionaries through the second half of the twentieth century. He is one of the top 10 economists as reported by the *Research Papers in Economics* rankings. His work has influenced many economists, including Nobel laureates.

*See also:* Friedman, Milton; Keynes, John Maynard; Phillips, A. W. H.; Prescott, Edward; Samuelson, Paul; Sargent, Thomas

### Selected Works by Robert Lucas Jr.

Lucas, Robert, Jr. "Expectations and the Neutrality of Money." *Journal of Economic Theory* 4 (1972): 103–24.

Lucas, Robert, Jr. "Econometric Policy Evaluation: A Critique." *Carnegie-Rochester Conference Series on Public Policy* 1 (1976): 19–46.

Lucas, Robert, Jr. *Lectures on Economic Growth.* Cambridge, MA: President and Fellows of Harvard College, 2002.

Lucas, Robert, Jr. "On the Mechanics of Economic Development." *Journal of Monetary Economics* 22 (1988): 3–42.

Lucas, Robert, Jr. *Models of Business Cycles.* Oxford: Basil Blackwell, 1987.

Lucas, Robert, Jr. *Studies in Business-Cycle Theory.* Cambridge, MA: MIT Press, 1981.

Lucas, Robert, Jr. "Supply Side Economics: An Analytical Review." *Oxford Economic Papers* 42 (1990): 293–316.

Lucas, Robert, Jr. "Why Doesn't Capital Flow from Rich to Poor Countries?" *American Economic Review* 80 (1990): 92–96.

Stokey, Nancy L., and Robert E. Lucas. *Recursive Methods in Economic Dynamics.* Cambridge, MA.: Harvard University Press, 1989.

### Selected Works about Robert Lucas Jr.

Interview with Robert E. Lucas. The Region. Federal Reserve Bank of Minneapolis. June 1993. http://www.minneapolisfed.org/pubs/region/93-06/int936.cfm (accessed April 2012).

Lucas, Robert E. "Autobiography." Nobelprize.org. http://www.nobelprize.org/nobel_prizes/economics/laureates/1995/lucas-autobio.html (accessed April 2012).

Lucas, Robert E. "Prize Lecture: Monetary Neutrality." December 7, 1995. http://nobelprize.org/economics/laureates/1995/lucas-lecture.pdf.

Roberts, Russ. "Lucas on Growth, Poverty and Business Cycles with Bob Lucas." The Library of Economics and Liberty. http://www.econtalk.org/archives/2007/02/lucas_on_growth.html (accessed October 2012).

*David A. Dieterle*

# M

## MACHLUP, FRITZ

Born: December 15, 1902, in Wiener-Neustadt, Austria; Died: January 30, 1983, in Princeton, New Jersey; Austria-Hungarian, naturalized U.S. citizen in 1940; international monetary theory, information economics; Major Works: *Die Goldkernwahrung* [The gold bullion standard] (1925), *The Production and Distribution of Knowledge in the United States* (1962), *Knowledge: Its Creation, Distribution, and Economic Significance* (1980, 1982, 1983).

Fritz Machlup, an Austrian-American, is considered the father of the idea of the information economy. He was one of the first economists to explore the economics of invention, innovation, and knowledge. Austrian born and naturalized as a U.S. citizen after fleeing Nazi Germany, Machlup was a noted international economist specializing in monetary mechanisms, particularly the gold standard. Fritz Machlup's influence on the development of economics and economic theory was significant, as he made contributions in virtually every field of economics in areas of theory, policy, and methodology. Machlup died in 1983.

Fritz Machlup was born on December 15, 1902, in Wiener-Neustadt, Austria. Machlup studied under Friedrich von Weiser and Ludwig von Mises at the University of Vienna, earning his doctorate in 1923. He wrote his dissertation on the gold standard and it was published in 1925 as *Die Goldkernwahrung*, translated as *The Gold Bullion Standard*. His dissertation adviser was the "father of the Austrian School," Ludwig von Mises.

Machlup followed his father into the cardboard-manufacturing business, forming a paperboard corporation in Hungary in 1923. Machlup continued his interest in economics as a member of the Austrian Economic Society, serving as its treasurer and secretary. He was a participant in the Geistkreis, a seminar led by Austrian School leader Ludwig von Mises. In 1927, Machlup published a book on Europe's adoption of the gold standard. He also wrote on German war reparations, and in 1931 wrote a book on the stock market, *The Stock Market, Credit and Capital Formation*. Receiving a Rockefeller fellowship for the United States in 1933, Machlup spent time at several U.S. universities including Chicago, Stanford, and Harvard.

In 1935, Machlup accepted a professorship at the University of Buffalo, never to return to Austria professionally. While at Buffalo, he accepted visiting professorships at American University, Columbia, Cornell, Northwestern, Stanford, University of Michigan, Harvard, and University of California, Berkeley. He also was a visiting professor in Japan and Australia at the Universities of Kyoto, Doshisha, and Osaka in Japan and Melbourne University in Australia.

In 1947, Machlup joined the faculty of Johns Hopkins University as a professor of political economy. Machlup joined the faculty at Princeton in 1960 as the director of the International Finance Section and the Walker Professor of International Finance. In 1971, he continued living in Princeton, New Jersey, but left Princeton University and began a teaching tenure at New York University, remaining there till his death in 1983.

Having become a U.S. citizen in 1940, it was natural for Machlup to serve the U.S. government during World War II. He served as a U.S. Department of Labor special consultant for the Post War Labor Problems Division and also the Office of Alien Property. He later served the U.S. Treasury Department as well.

Machlup's areas of economic interest were quite varied. With his dissertation on the gold standard in 1925, the area of international finance, and specifically the gold standard and international monetary mechanisms, was always in the forefront of his work. During World War II, he wrote several papers on foreign exchange. He continued his work on international finance through the 1950s and 1960s. He attacked Keynes's foreign exchange multiplier approach.

On other economic fronts, Machlup was also a major contributor. Machlup supported the application of economic theory in research on industrial organization. He wrote two books on industrial organization to substantiate his point. In 1972, he published *Optimum Social Welfare* with coauthors Jan Tinbergen, Abram Bergson, and Oskar Morgenstern. He also revealed the problems of empirical research when questionnaires are used.

In the 1950s, Machlup began his study of the information economy, leading to a series of works on innovation and knowledge establishing him as the father of the information economy. In 1958, he published *The Economic Review of the Patent System*, followed by *The Production and Distribution Knowledge in the United States* in 1962. A decade later in 1970 he published *Education and Economic Growth*. Following the publishing of *Information through the Printed Word: Dissemination of Scholarly, Scientific, and Intellectual Knowledge* in 1978, Machlup began his magnum opus on the information economy with a three-volume compilation—*Knowledge: Its Creation, Distribution, and Economic Significance*—which was published in 1980, 1982, and 1983. He died before completing what was planned to be a 10-volume series.

To further study international monetary mechanisms and international crisis, in 1963 Machlup assembled a group of academics to study and develop solutions. The Bellagio Group published several books and articles with solutions on the problems facing the world's currency issues. The success of the Bellagio Group established Machlup as the intellectual face for addressing the international monetary issues of the 1960s, and reforming a monetary system on the verge of collapse. One position on which Machlup reversed himself was that of his long-standing support of the gold standard. He reversed his position on the gold standard knowing the position was considered politically not feasible for the time. While this led to an intellectual split with his mentor, Ludwig von Mises, Machlup was later instrumental in von Mises's publishing of *Human Action*, the

"Bible" of the Austrian School of economic thought. The Bellagio Group was the predecessor of the Group of Thirty advisory group.

Machlup died on January 30, 1983, in Princeton, New Jersey, shortly after finishing the third volume of *Knowledge: Its Creation, Distribution, and Economic Significance*.

*See also:* Miller, Merton; Mises, Ludwig von; Morgenstern, Oskar; Tinbergen, Jan

### Selected Works by Fritz Machlup

Machlup, Fritz. *Borsenkredit, Industriekredit Und Kapitalbildung Meilensteine Der Nationalokonomie*. New York: Springer, 2008.

Machlup, Fritz. *Die Goldkernwährung* (dissertation under Ludwig von Mises), 1925.

Machlup, Fritz. *The Economic Review of the Patent System*. Ann Arbor: University of Michigan Press and U.S. Government Printing Office, 1958.

Machlup, Fritz. *Education and Economic Growth*. Lincoln: University of Nebraska Press, 1970.

Machlup, Fritz. *Knowledge: Its Creation, Distribution, and Economic Significance*. Vol. 1. Princeton, NJ: Princeton University Press, 1980.

Machlup, Fritz. *Knowledge: Its Creation, Distribution, and Economic Significance*. Vol. 2. Princeton, NJ: Princeton University Press, 1982.

Machlup, Fritz. *Knowledge: Its Creation, Distribution, and Economic Significance*. Vol. 3. Princeton, NJ: Princeton University Press, 1983.

Machlup, Fritz. *Methodology of Economics and Other Social Sciences*. Waltham, MA: Academic Press, 1978.

Machlup, Fritz. *The Production and Distribution of Knowledge in the United States*. Princeton, NJ: Princeton University Press, 1962.

Machlup, Fritz. *The Stock Market, Credit and Capital Formation*. Auburn, AL: Ludwig von Mises Institute, 1931 (English translation, 1940).

Machlup, Fritz, and Kenneth Leeson. *Information through the Printed Word: The Dissemination of Scholarly, Scientific, and Intellectual Knowledge*. Santa Barbara, CA: Greenwood Press, 1978.

### Selected Works about Fritz Machlup

"Biography of Fritz Machlup (1902–1983)." Ludwig von Mises Institute. http://mises.org/about/3237 (accessed September, 2011).

Bitros, George, ed. *Selected Economic Writings of Fritz Machlup*. New York: New York University Press, 1976.

Dreyer, Jacob S., ed. *Breadth and Depth in Economics: Fritz Machlup—the Man and His Ideas*. Lanham, MD: Lexington Books, 1978.

"Fritz Machlup and the Infosphere." Caslon Analytics biographies. http://www.caslon.com.au/biographies/machlup.htm (accessed September 2011).

"Fritz Machlup: In Memoriam." http://www.cato.org/pubs/journal/cj3n1/cj3n1-2.pdf (accessed September 2011).

"Interview with Fritz Machlup." Ludwig von Mises Institute. http://mises.org/resources.aspx?Id=afa0fdca-c03f-4b5e-9d1c-1935af797751 (accessed September 2011).

*David A. Dieterle*

## MALTHUS, THOMAS

Born: February 14, 1766, in Surrey, England; Died: December 29, 1834, in Bath, England; English; economic principles, demographics; Major Work: *Principles of Political Economy* (1820).

Thomas Malthus is considered the father of demographic economics. He was the first to study the relationship between population growth and food production. He would become a friend of David Ricardo. They would spend much of their lives debating each other on everything from the Corn Laws to the nature of value. Malthus would be the first to use a demand schedule in his 1820 *Principles of the Political Economy*. Malthus died in 1834.

Thomas Robert Malthus was born on February 14, 1766, in Surrey, England, the son of an English gentleman. His father was a friend of Jean-Jacques Rousseau and David Hume. After being taught by his father and a number of tutors, Malthus entered Jesus College, Cambridge, in 1784. There he was ordained as a minister in 1788 and received his MA in 1791. As a result of debates with his father about the ideas of William Godwin and the Marquis de Condorcet, Malthus decided to write down his thoughts on the subject. The result was *An Essay on the Principles of Population* (1798).

British economist Thomas Malthus's theory on population growth and the inevitability of poverty created considerable controversy in Great Britain during the early nineteenth century. (National Library of Medicine)

In preparing this work, Malthus collected data on births, deaths, marriages, and longevity, making him one of the founders of the field of demographics. But Malthus was working on a bigger idea. Malthus noted that population had the capacity and tendency to outstrip food production. Indeed, it is the misunderstanding of this inverse population growth-food production relationship that most people link to his name. Critics of this relationship often point to Malthus as an example of economic predictions gone wrong as history has shown that food production and population can both grow geometrically. But the reality is he wrote in the dawn of the Industrial Revolution. He had no way of predicting the vast increase in productivity that would accompany the increase of capital and new technology.

But his view was larger than the simple inverse population-food production relationship. Malthus noted that despite past tendencies, humankind had not starved itself out. He attributed this to people choosing to change their behavior in the face of economic incentives such as higher food prices. The choices included choosing to marry later and to have fewer children. These choices ultimately helped to bring population back in line with food production, at which time prices would drop and create a different set of incentives. Then the new incentives would begin population growth on a track to outstrip food production again and the cycle would repeat.

In 1804, Malthus was married, which meant he had to give up his fellowship at Cambridge. In 1805, he was named professor of modern history and political economy at the East India College in Haileybury, becoming England's first academic economist. It was also during this decade that Malthus began to be interested in monetary economics. Around 1810, he read a number of papers on monetary issues by another economist named David Ricardo. He began a correspondence with Ricardo and they became friends on a number of levels. However, they would disagree on economic issues, such as the Corn Laws.

In 1814, Malthus became interested and involved in the debates over the Corn Laws. Initially, he sided with the free-traders, agreeing that the cheaper prices afforded by imports would help make food more affordable. Later he would switch sides, noting that foreign countries may place an export bounty on grain in periods of drought or famine, making food supplies in England subject to foreign political maneuvering. He felt that self-sufficiency in food would be guaranteed by encouraging domestic production—an example of the strategic industry argument for trade protection.

Malthus was the first among four to espouse a theory of rent in 1815. Unlike some predecessors who saw rent as a cost of production, Malthus saw rent as a deduction from surplus—a return on production. And while some disagreed on parts of his theory, his observation that land differed in quality and was scarce would be integrated into other theories of rent, most notably that by David Ricardo.

Malthus and Ricardo also differed in their views of value. Ricardo believed in a theory that ascribed value to a good based on the amount of labor needed to produce it—essentially a cost- or supply-based approach. But Malthus saw value as deriving from the amount of labor something could command, or the amount of work someone was willing to do to acquire a good or service. This view was more demand based and essentially depended on the amount of utility or satisfaction consumers believed they would receive from a good.

This would manifest itself more fully when he published his *Principles of Political Economy* in 1820. There, Malthus would be the first to use the idea of a demand schedule, thus drawing a relationship between prices and the amount of goods sought—essentially the willingness to buy at each price level. Prior to this, the relationship had been strictly one of price and the quantity sold as seen from the supply side of the transaction.

Finally, it was in his *Principles* that Malthus presented arguments against Say's law, stating that general gluts were possible, differentiating between the equilibrium of the long run and the cyclical swings of the short run.

Malthus was elected a member of the Royal Society in 1819. He became a member of the Political Economy Club in 1821. He became a royal associate of the Royal Society of Literature in 1824. He cofounded the Statistical Society of London in 1834. And his influence, despite criticisms, was significant and long-lasting, affecting scholars and intellectuals like Charles Darwin, Karl Marx, and John Maynard Keynes.

Thomas Malthus died on December 29, 1834, in Bath, England.

*See also:* Hume, David; Keynes, John Maynard; Marx, Karl; Ricardo, David; Say, Jean-Baptiste

### Selected Works by Thomas Malthus

Malthus, Thomas. *An Essay on the Principle of Population*. London: John Murray, Albemarle-Street, 1798.

Malthus, Thomas. *An Inquiry into the Nature and Progress of Rent*. London: John Murray, 1815.

Malthus, Thomas. *The Measure of Value Stated and Illustrated*. London: John Murray, 1823.

Malthus, Thomas. *Observations on the Effects of the Corn Laws*. London: J. Johnson, 1814.

Malthus, Thomas. *Principles of Political Economy*. London: John Murray, 1820.

### Selected Works about Thomas Malthus

Bonar, James. *Malthus and His Work*. Kila, MT: Kessinger, 2004.

Drysdale, Charles Robert. *Life and Writings of Thomas R. Malthus*. Charleston, SC: Nabu Press, 2010.

Hollander, Samuel. *The Economics of Thomas Robert Malthus*. Toronto: University of Toronto Press, 1997.

Peterson, William. *Malthus: Founder of Modern Demography*. Piscataway, NJ: Transaction, 1998.

*Timothy P. Schilling*

# MANKIW, GREGORY

Born: March 2, 1958, in Trenton, New Jersey; American; macroeconomics, public policy economics; Major Works: *Principles of Economics* (1st ed., 2000), *Intermediate Macroeconomics* (2010), *Macroeconomics and the Financial System* (with Laurence Ball) (2010).

N. Gregory Mankiw is one of the major contributors to new Keynesian economics theory. New Keynesian economic theory was developed in response to the criticisms of the traditional Keynesian model by new classical economic theorists. Through his writings and textbooks, he is considered one of the key interpreters of the neo-Keynesian theory to the general public. He also is a major contributor to the current macroeconomic policy debate and its development.

N. Gregory Mankiw was born in Trenton, New Jersey, on March 2, 1958, of Ukrainian parents. Professor Mankiw holds a BA in economics from Princeton

University and a PhD in economics from the Massachusetts Institute of Technology. Mankiw has been influenced throughout his career by many famous economists of differing viewpoints including John Maynard Keynes, Arthur Pigou, Stanley Fischer, and Milton Friedman.

Mankiw's research interests include the U.S. economy, entitlements, international trade policy, price adjustment, consumer behavior, financial markets, monetary and fiscal policy, and economic growth. Mankiw's interest and study of economics has led him to author several textbooks, write a daily blog, and receive many honors. He is Robert M. Beren Professor of Economics at Harvard University. His teaching includes the very popular Principles of Economics course. He is also a visiting research fellow at the American Enterprise Institute. From 2003 to 2005, he was chairman of President George W. Bush's Council of Economic Advisers. He also maintains a blog that is read widely across the country and the world (http://gregmankiw.blogspot.com).

He has authored several of the most popular textbooks used in high school and college economics courses including *Principles of Economics*, in its sixth edition; *Intermediate Macroeconomics*, in its seventh edition; and his newest text, with Laurence M. Ball, *Macroeconomics and the Financial System*, in its second edition. His academic papers are published in such journals as *American Economic Review*, *Journal of Political Economy*, and the *Quarterly Journal of Economics*. He is a frequent contributor to the *New York Times*, reflecting the views of the new Keynesian economics.

Mankiw's contributions to new Keynesian economics highlight the disagreement with new classical economics regarding the adjustment of wages and prices. Classical and monetarist theory says that in the short run, changes in the money supply affect employment and production levels. New classical economics theorizes that wages and prices are flexible, allowing markets to clear and regain their equilibrium (rebalancing demand and supply). New classical thinkers Robert Lucas Jr., Thomas J. Sargent, and Robert Barro criticized Keynesian theory (*The General Theory of Employment, Interest and Money*), saying that the Keynesian model does not explain the sluggish nature of wage and price changes to obtain equal demand and supply (market-clearing mechanism).

Through his writings and textbooks, Mankiw is one of the leading authors to interpret and explain the new Keynesian theory for the general public's understanding. Mankiw's writings are a response to the criticisms levied by the new classical economists regarding the initial market-clearing mechanism (prices determined by equal demand and supply) first proposed by John Maynard Keynes. The new Keynesian economics suggests that markets do not clear (where demand and supply are equal) quickly and that economic fluctuations are explained through models where wages and prices are not as mobile or flexible as the new classical economists contend. This new Keynesian model includes involuntary unemployment along with the important role of monetary policy to adjust supply-and-demand conditions when markets do not clear (which is assumed in the new classical thinking).

In the 1990s, a combination view emerged between the new classical and new Keynesian theorists. Mankiw's textbooks reflect this consensus view of a dynamic economy with inflexible components and market imperfections in the short run but ultimately a dynamic economy that adjusts in the long run.

Mankiw's awards include the Wolf Balleisen Memorial Prize in 1980 and the Galbraith Teaching Prize in 1991.

*See also:* Fischer, Stanley; Friedman, Milton; Keynes, John Maynard; Lucas, Robert, Jr.; Pigou, A. C.; Sargent, Thomas

### Selected Works by Gregory Mankiw

Ball, Laurence, and Gregory Mankiw. *Macroeconomics and the Financial System.* 2nd ed. New York: Worth, 2010.
Mankiw, Gregory. *Intermediate Macroeconomics.* 7th ed. New York: Worth, 2010.
Mankiw, Gregory. *Principles of Economics.* 6th ed. Boston: South-Western, 2011.
Mankiw, N. Gregory, and David Romer, eds. *New Keynesian Economics.* 2 vols. Cambridge, MA: MIT Press, 1991.

### Selected Works about Gregory Mankiw

"Gregory Mankiw." Harvard University Department of Economics. http://www.economics.harvard.edu/faculty/mankiw (accessed August 2011).
Mankiw, Greg. "Greg Mankiw's Blog: Random Observations for Students of Economics." http://gregmankiw.blogspot.com/index.html.

*Martha R. Rowland*

# MARKOWITZ, HARRY

Born: August 24, 1927, in Chicago, Illinois; American; finance economics, Nobel Prize (1990); Major Works: *Portfolio Selection: Efficient Diversification of Investment* (1959), *Mean-Variance Analysis in Portfolio Choice and Capital Markets* (with G. Peter Todd and William F. Sharpe) (1987).

Harry Markowitz is an American economist awarded the Nobel Prize in Economics in 1990. He is considered one of the major pioneers of mathematical formulation in portfolio theory for investing. The goal of mathematical formulation is to minimize risk for given expected returns and is widely used by investors today. He began his studies in economics at the University of Chicago and went on to work for many financial companies. His most famous work, *Portfolio Selection: Efficient Diversification of Investments*, was published in 1959.

Harry Max Markowitz was born on August 24, 1927, in Chicago, Illinois, as the only child of Morris and Mildred Markowitz. His parents, grocery store owners, were able to provide adequately, despite the conditions of the Great Depression. Growing up in Chicago, Markowitz's interests as a teenager included orchestra and reading, particularly the original works of philosophers such as David Hume and Charles Darwin. His interest in philosophy continued as he pursued it into his college years. After high school, he entered the University of Chicago where he earned his bachelor's degree in 1947. Upon completion of his bachelor's degree, Markowitz decided to study economics, with an interest in the "economics of uncertainty."

As Markowitz continued his graduate studies at the University of Chicago, he learned from several renowned economists including Milton Friedman and Jacob Marschak, and mathematician Leonard J. Savage. At the University of Chicago, he was invited to become a student member of the prestigious Cowles Commission for Research in Economics, under the leadership of Marschak. His paper "Portfolio Selection" was published in the *Journal of Finance* in 1952. Today, this model is one of the most widely used quantitative tools for investment analysis in portfolio selection diversification. He received his master's degree from the University of Chicago in 1950.

In 1952, Markowitz left the University of Chicago to work for the RAND Corporation on mathematical programming. He worked with George Dantzig to research and identify optimal mean-variance portfolios. While he did not work on portfolio selection at the RAND Corporation, the optimization techniques he learned from Dantzig are reflected in his later writings. In 1955, he received a PhD from the University of Chicago with a thesis on the portfolio theory.

During 1955–56, Markowitz was invited by James Tobin to return to the Cowles Foundation, located at Yale University, while on leave from RAND Corporation. He published a paper in 1956 about the critical line algorithm and also wrote his book on portfolio allocation, which was published in 1959 as *Portfolio Selection: Efficient Diversification of Investments*.

Markowitz has held various positions throughout his career, which have mostly focused on the application of computer methods and mathematics to problems of investments under uncertainty. In the early 1960s, he returned to the RAND Corporation to develop a programming language with Bernard Hausner called SIMSCRIPT, which was used to write economic analysis programs. Markowitz cofounded a computer software company, California Analysis Company Inc., with Herb Karr to offer training and support for SIMSCRIPT. In 1968–69, he was at the University of California, Los Angeles, and in 1969 joined Arbitrage Management Company. In 1972, he joined International Business Machines Corporation's (IBM) T. J. Watson Research Center and remained at IBM till 1983. In 1982, Markowitz became a faculty member of Baruch College of the City University of New York.

In 1989, Markowitz was awarded the von Neumann Prize in Operations Research Theory by the Operations Research Society of America and the Institute of Management Sciences. The award cited his works on portfolio theory, matrix techniques, and the development of SIMSCRIPT programming language as major contributions. Markowitz's work on sparse matrix techniques developed from his collaboration of work with Thomas Marschak and Alan Rowe at the RAND Corporation in the 1950s. Sparse matrix codes techniques, as a result of Markowitz's collaborations, are now largely standard in linear programming codes.

In 1990 while a professor at Baruch College of the City University of New York, Markowitz shared the Nobel Prize in Economics with Merton H. Miller and

William F. Sharpe. The award celebrated his theories for evaluating stock market risk and reward and for valuing corporate stocks and bonds.

Markowitz serves as the chief architect of an investment adviser company he cofounded, GuidedChoice. He also is an adjunct professor at the Rady School of Management at the University of California, San Diego. He continues to work on advisory boards for investment firms including Skyview Investment Advisors, LWI Financial Inc., Research Affiliates, and 1st Global.

*See also:* Friedman, Milton; Hume, David; Miller, Merton; Sharpe, William; Tobin, James

### Selected Works by Harry Markowitz

Markowitz, Harry. "Foundations of Portfolio Theory." *The Journal of Finance* 46, no. 2 (June 1991): 469–77.

Markowitz, Harry. "Portfolio Selection." *The Journal of Finance* 7, no. 1 (March 1952): 77–91.

Markowitz, Harry. *Portfolio Selection: Efficient Diversification of Investment*. New Haven, CT: Cowles Foundation for Research in Economics at Yale University, 1958.

Markowitz, Harry. "The Utility of Wealth." *Journal of Political Economy* 60, no. 2 (April 1952): 151–58.

Markowitz, Harry, William F. Sharpe, and Merton H. Miller, eds. *The Founders of Modern Finance: Their Prize-Winning Concepts and 1990 Nobel Lectures*. Charlottesville, VA: Research Foundation of the Institute of Chartered Financial Analysts, 1991.

Markowitz, Harry, G. Peter Todd, and William F. Sharpe. *Mean-Variance Analysis in Portfolio Choice and Capital Markets*. New York: Wiley, 1987.

### Selected Works about Harry Markowitz

Markowitz, Harry M. "Autobiography." Nobelprize.org. http://www.nobelprize.org/nobel_prizes/economics/laureates/1990/markowitz-autobio.html (accessed February 2012).

Markowitz, Harry, ed. *World Scientific Nobel Laureate Series*. Vol. 1, *Harry Markowitz*. Hackensack, NJ: World Scientific, 2008.

Markowitz, Harry, Edwin J. Elton, and Martin Jay Gruber. *Portfolio Theory, 25 Years After: Essays in Honor of Harry Markowitz*. Amsterdam: North-Holland, 1979.

Scheib, Ariel. "Harry Markowitz." Jewish Virtual Library. http://www.jewishvirtuallibrary.org/jsource/biography/markowitz.html (accessed March 2012).

*Sara Standen*

# MARSHALL, ALFRED

Born: July 26, 1842, in London, England; Died: July 13, 1924, in Cambridge, England; English; general equilibrium theory, marginal utility; Major Works: *The Economics of Industry* (with Mary Paley Marshall) (1885), *The Postulates of English Political Economy* (with Walter Bagehot) (1885), *Principles of Economics* (1890).

Alfred Marshall had far-reaching influence on the foundations of what is now called microeconomics, which ultimately led to the development of macroeconomics. Alfred Marshall introduced the supply-and-demand curves as we know them, noting that they go together like the blades of scissors, to arrive at the price point.

His insights were adopted by other members of his school, students, and professionals. These included A. C. Pigou, John Maynard Keynes, Joan Robinson, Jacob Viner, Milton Friedman, and George Stigler. Ironically, John Maynard Keynes would ultimately challenge his teacher and would change the foundations of economics. Marshall died in 1924.

Alfred Marshall was born on July 26, 1842, in London, England. Marshall was the son of a cashier at the Bank of England who originally chose the clergy as a career for his son. The father was very intense and refused to allow young Alfred to play chess because he believed it to be a waste of time. Alfred's father also thought mathematics was irrelevant for a budding clergyman. However, Marshall excelled in mathematics, and while attending Cambridge University he was drawn to the field of economics. In 1865, at the age of 23, Marshall was elected to a fellowship at St. John's College, Cambridge, and became a lecturer in moral sciences in 1868. Violating a tenet of the fellowship by getting married, he lost the fellowship after nine years. His first major work, *The Economics of Industry*, would be coauthored with his wife in 1879. He would become professor of political economy at Cambridge in 1885 and remain there until his retirement in 1908.

Alfred Marshall of Great Britain influenced generations of economists through his teaching at Cambridge University and his book *Principles of Economics*, including introducing supply-and-demand curves as we know them today. (Harlingue-Viollet)

In 1890, Marshall wrote his *Principles of Economics*, which would become the dominant text of the era, supplanting John Stuart Mill's work. Despite his own mathematical ability and his desire to make economics more rigorous, he strove to make his work understandable to the layman, relegating his calculations and computations to the footnotes and appendices of his work.

Alfred Marshall introduced the supply-and-demand curves as we know them, noting that they go together, like the blades of scissors, to arrive at the price point. This insight was important as it gave the demander (consumer) a role in determining the price. Many prior to Marshall had seen price as a function of cost alone and set largely by the supplier (producer).

That was not the only important idea to be derived from the supply-and-demand curves. It was Marshall who would develop the idea of consumer surplus and describe it as the triangle bounded by the market price and the demand curve. This measure showed the difference between the demander's willingness to buy and the market price, and it helps visualize the surplus value or utility that consumers receive in the market. Thus it is an important part of understanding the welfare received by market transactions.

The concept of elasticity, or the responsiveness of supply or demand to change in price, is also attributable to Marshall. Marshall showed that producers have some freedom to change prices without impacting revenue. Products that demonstrate lower price elasticity of demand tend to generate lower revenues when prices are lowered and higher revenues when prices are increased. This is because of the percentage change in demand relative to the percentage change in price. Conversely, a producer with a product with a high level of elasticity of demand may actually generate higher revenues by slightly reducing the price of the product. On the supply side, elasticity can provide insights into producers' ability to increase production when faced with changes in demand and, in turn, price.

One further contribution of Marshall was his recognition of time and its impact on decision making. Marshall divided time into three categories: immediate, short-term, and long-term. He believed that this division had a significant effect on decisions, particularly as they relate to elasticity, and surplus.

Thanks to these insights, Marshall became the face of what would later be called the neoclassical school of economics. Marshall and his fellow Cambridge economists would combine the classical works of Mill and Ricardo with other ideas, such as the marginalism developed by William Stanley Jevons. Additionally, it would be the neoclassical school that would help professionalize the field and develop it into a separate field of study in academia. In keeping with Marshall's views on the value of mathematics, the classical school would focus on the development of intuitive arguments. However, this would often lead to generalizations that would frustrate other economists in other schools, including the Austrian School.

Alfred Marshall died on July 13, 1924, in Cambridge, England.

*See also:* Jevons, William Stanley; Keynes, John Maynard; Mill, John Stuart; Pigou, A. C.; Ricardo, David; Robinson, Joan; Stigler, George; Viner, Jacob

## Selected Works by Alfred Marshall

Marshall, Alfred. *Elements of Economics of Industry: Being the First Volume of Elements of Economics.* London: Macmillan, 1909.
Marshall, Alfred. *Industry and Trade.* London: Macmillan, 1919.
Marshall, Alfred. *Money, Credit and Commerce.* London: Macmillan, 1923.
Marshall, Alfred. *Principles of Economics.* London: Macmillan, 1890.

Marshall, Alfred. *The Pure Theory of Foreign Trade: The Pure Theory of Domestic Values* (1879). London: London School of Economics and Political Science, 1930.

Marshall, Alfred, and Walter Bagehot. *The Postulates of English Political Economy.* London: Longmans, Green, 1885.

Marshall, Alfred, and Mary Paley Marshall. *The Economics of Industry.* London: Macmillan, 1885.

**Selected Works about Alfred Marshall**

"Alfred Marshall." In *The Concise Encyclopedia of Economics.* Edited by David R. Henderson. The Library of Economics and Liberty. http://www.econlib.org/library/Enc/bios/Marshall.html (accessed March 2012).

"Alfred Marshall." Scarlett History of Economic Theory and Thought. http://www.economictheories.org/2008/06/alfred-marshall-biography-economic.html (accessed March 2012).

Blaug, Mark, and Paul Sturges. *Who's Who in Economics: A Biographical Dictionary of Major Economists, 1700–1980.* Boston: MIT Press, 1983.

Bucholz, Todd G. *New Ideas from Dead Economists.* New York: New American Library, 1989.

Groenewegen, Peter. *Alfred Marshall, Economist, 1842–1924.* Hampshire, UK: Palgrave Macmillan, 2007.

*Timothy P. Schilling*

# MARX, KARL

Born: May 5, 1818, in Trier, Prussia (Germany); Died: March 14, 1883, in London, England; German; economic philosophy; Major Works: *The Communist Manifesto* (with Friedrich Engels) (1848), *Capital: A Critique of Political Economy* (1867).

Karl Marx used the study of economics to write harsh and systematic criticisms of capitalism, and by extension, the governments and societies that foster it. He proposed a completely new world order called communism, characterized by a stateless society and an equal distribution of resources. Marx's writings covered political philosophy, history, and economics. Marx died in 1883.

Karl Heinrich Marx was born May 5, 1818 in Trier, Prussia (present-day Germany). Karl's father, a lawyer and descendant of Jewish rabbis, had disavowed Judaism and converted to Lutheranism. Karl later rejected religion of any type, coining the famous dictum "Religion is the opium of the masses."

Marx studied law to please his father. However, he was more interested in philosophy, transferring to the University of Berlin and changing his studies to philosophy. He earned his doctorate in 1841. Upon graduation, Marx found a job in Cologne as a journalist for the Socialist newspaper *Die Rheinische Zeitung.* Prussia—indeed, most of Europe—was not tolerant of dissident ideas and Marx soon found himself expelled from Prussia. He spent most of the next decade moving from country to country, repeatedly exiled for his radical beliefs. In 1848, Marx penned his seminal *The Communist Manifesto,* in Brussels, Belgium. It was intended as an outline of doctrine for the small international Communist movement.

*The Communist Manifesto* (or in the original German, *Manifest der Kommunistische Partei*) begins with a sweeping statement that history of the existing society is a history of class struggles. Marx described human history as characterized by conflicts between the oppressed and the oppressors of social classes. To Marx, any and every idea, institution, religion, or belief serves to support the accumulation of wealth of the dominant social class.

Marx identified capitalism as the economic system that replaced feudalism. He credited capitalism with immense powers of production, and he described a shrinking, globalizing world that brings industrial workers—the proletariat—into closer association with one another as they crowd into cities to seek jobs. However, he also noted several "contradictions" within capitalism that would eventually spell doom for the system.

Marx submitted that shrinking profits force the capitalist bourgeoisie either to seek new markets for their products or to exploit their workers with increasing cruelty. Even though these techniques restore profits, the frenzy of exploitation causes overproduction followed by financial panics, recessions, and reduced profits. Eventually, the cycle begins all over again. According to Marx, capitalism also results in an increasing concentration of the proletariat into factories. This competition among workers reduces wages to the bare level of subsistence. This idea is similar to David Ricardo's iron law of wages. As workers become more like one another, they are more likely to band together to fight for a bigger share of the profits, even while resources are monopolized under fewer and fewer capitalists. The final result of this unstable equilibrium will be a revolution of the proletariat. Marx then predicts that the proletariat will overthrow the bourgeoisie and usher in a new social and political order. A brief period of socialism with the proletariat acting as the ruling class will exist, in which the government reorganizes society to achieve total equality. Once realized, the government will become irrelevant and wither away, making way for a classless state called communism.

Marx was the intellectual giant of the early Communist movement. As such, he was under constant pressure by his colleagues to write a full-length work that would show the economic necessity of the ideas enshrined in *The Communist Manifesto*.

Marx lived his years in poverty, supported mainly by his friend and cowriter, Friedrich Engels. Engels encouraged Marx to expand his work. In 1867, Marx published a more thorough analysis of capitalism, *Capital: A Critique of Political Economy*. He used many of the tools of economic analysis that were created by classical economists such as Adam Smith and David Ricardo. He begins with the concept of value and how commodities become valuable. For Marx, items are valuable according to the amount of labor that it takes to produce them. By adding capital resources to the production process, capitalists can reduce labor to that of a simple tool from which still more value, or surplus value, is obtained. His economic analysis merged the political and historical theories he described in *The Communist Manifesto*.

Soon after his death, the impact of his ideas gained such influence he has been called the most important thinker of the second millennium. His writings inspired revolutions in Russia, China, Cuba, North Korea, Vietnam, and Cambodia. By 1950, about a third of the world lived under a political system based on Marxist thought. Perhaps more importantly, Marxian methods have been introduced into every social science discipline. Marx's work taught later social researchers to use class analysis, which in turn opened the door for others to think in terms of oppressed cross sections of society. Ironically, Marxian analysis is used least in the field of economics. Marx's ideas continue to challenge a world still coming to terms with the implications of capitalism.

Karl Marx died on March 14, 1883, in London, England.

*See also:* Engels, Friedrich; Ricardo, David; Smith, Adam

### Selected Works by Karl Marx

Marx, Karl, and Friedrich Engels. *The Communist Manifesto* (1848). http://www.marxists.org/archive/marx/works/1848/communist-manifesto/index.htm (accessed December 23, 2010).

Marx, Karl. *Capital: A Critique of Political Economy.* Vol. 1 (1867). Chicago: Charles H. Kerr, 1906.

Marx, Karl. *Capital.* Vol. 2 (1885, published posthumously by Friedrich Engels). Chicago: Charles H. Kerr, 1907.

Marx, Karl. *Capital.* Vol. 3 (1894, published posthumously by Friedrich Engels). Chicago: Charles H. Kerr, 1909.

### Selected Works about Karl Marx

Berlin, Isaiah. *Karl Marx.* London: Fontana Press, 1995.

Berlin, Isaiah. *Karl Marx: His Life and Environment.* Oxford: Oxford University Press, 1978.

Engels, Frederick, "Marx-Engels Biography: Karl Marx." Marx and Engels Internet Archive. http://www.marxists.org/archive/marx/bio/marx/eng-1869.htm (accessed March 2011).

Wheen, Francis. *Marx's Das Kapital: A Biography.* Books That Changed the World. New York: Grove Press, 2008.

*Stephen H. Day*

## MASKIN, ERIC

Born: December 12, 1950, in New York City; American; political economy, game theory, property rights, Nobel Prize (2007); Major Works: *Economic Analysis of Markets and Games* (with P. Dasgupta, D. Gale, and O. Hart) (1992), *Recent Developments in Game Theory* (1999), *Planning, Shortage, and Transformation* (with A. Simonovits) (2000).

Eric Maskin is an economist and scholar, known for his work on mechanism design theory. He has held teaching positions in several American universities and is currently a professor of social science at the Institute for Advanced Study. He developed implementation theory, which is an economic theory for achieving specific economic or social goals. This theory resolves the problem that a mechanism usually admits multiple equilibria. Maskin was the first to develop conditions under which all equilibria are optimal and there are no inferior solutions. He was awarded the 2007 Nobel Prize in Economic Science with Roger B. Myerson and Leonid Hurwicz.

Eric Stark Maskin was born on December 12, 1950, in New York City. He grew up in a small town of fewer than a thousand residents called Alpine, New Jersey. He attended junior and senior high school in Tenafly, New Jersey, because Alpine did not have its own secondary schools. He became interested in calculus while a high school student at Tenafly High and went on to study mathematics at Harvard College. While at Harvard, Maskin studied math courses including algebra and analysis. He was particularly moved by a course taught by Kenneth Arrow on information economics. This course included information on a range of topics, including Leonid Hurwicz's work in mechanism design. After receiving his BA from Harvard, Maskin continued at Harvard to earn a master's degree and a PhD in applied mathematics.

He completed his PhD in 1976 with Kenneth Arrow as his adviser and held the position of research fellow at Jesus College, Cambridge University, from 1976 through 1977. After returning to the United States, Maskin was assistant professor of economics at the Massachusetts Institute of Technology (MIT) from 1977 to 1980. He became an associate professor at MIT from 1980 to 1981, then held the title professor of economics from 1981 to 1984. During this time, from 1980 to 1982, he was also overseas fellow at Churchill College, Cambridge University. Maskin became a professor of economics at Harvard from 1985 until 2000, when he became the Albert O. Hirschman Professor of Social Science, Institute for Advanced Study at Princeton University. This is a position he still holds, continuing scholarship on a variety of topics, but he is best known for his work on mechanism design theory.

In 2007 Maskin, Leonid Hurwicz, and Roger B. Myerson were awarded the Nobel Prize in Economics for their work on mechanism design theory. Mechanism design theory is a general view of how institutions translate inputs into an output or response while regarding the self-interest of the input institutions. Mechanism design begins with the desired outcome as the starting point and provides a way to develop an equitable distribution of income or technical innovation and a system that aligns private incentives with public goals. Maskin's work with Myerson on mechanism design theory, begun by Hurwicz, gives policy makers tools for structuring incentives and institutions to enhance social welfare. It allows policy makers to account for public goods that may not be accounted for in ordinary market transactions. Mechanism design theory can provide a framework for determining whether taxation is called for and then how best to design systems for revenue.

Maskin's contributions beyond mechanism design and implementation theory include the theory of income inequality, game theory, the study of intellectual property rights, and political economy.

*See also:* Arrow, Kenneth; Hurwicz, Leonid; Myerson, Roger

### Selected Works by Eric Maskin

Dasgupta, Partha, Douglas Gale, Oliver Hart, and Eric Markin, eds. *Economic Analysis of Markets and Games.* Cambridge, MA: MIT Press, 1992.

Maskin, Eric. *Recent Developments in Game Theory.* London: Edward Elgar, 1999.

Maskin, Eric, and András Simonovits, eds. *Planning, Shortage, and Transformation.* Cambridge, MA: MIT Press, 2000.

### Selected Works about Eric Maskin

"Eric S. Maskin—Faculty." IAS School of Social Science. http://www.sss.ias.edu/people#maskin (accessed December 2011).

Lohr, Steve. "Three Share Nobel in Economics for Work on Social Mechanism." *New York Times*, October 16, 2007.

Maskin, Eric S. "Autobiography." Nobelprize.org. http://www.nobelprize.org/nobel_prizes/economics/laureates/2007/maskin.html (accessed December 2011).

Tabarrok, Alex. "What Is Mechanism Design? Explaining the Research That Won the 2007 Nobel Prize in Economics." October 16, 2007. http://www.reason.com/archives/2007/10/16/what-is-mechanism-design (accessed December 2011).

*Diane Fournier*

# MCFADDEN, DANIEL

Born: July 29, 1937, in Raleigh, North Carolina; American; econometrics, economics of aging, consumer demand analysis, choice models and applications, consumer theory, Nobel Prize (2000); Major Works: *Urban Travel Demand: A Behavioral Analysis* (with Thomas A. Domencich) (1975), *Microeconomic Modeling and Policy Analysis: Studies in Residential Energy Demand* (with Thomas G. Cowing) (1984).

Daniel McFadden is the 2000 recipient of the Nobel Prize in Economics for his work on what is known as "discrete choice." McFadden is most known for his mathematics models relating to learning and choice. An econometrician, McFadden is regarded as one of the most influential economists in the world.

Daniel Little McFadden was born on July 29, 1937, in Raleigh, North Carolina. He attended rural public schools in North Carolina and was an avid reader. To avoid being suspended from North Carolina schools, McFadden moved to Minnesota to live with relatives. He entered the University of Minnesota at the age of 16 with an interest in science. McFadden received his BS in physics at the age of 19 and continued his education, pursuing a PhD at the University of Minnesota. His doctoral studies found him doing experiments on utilizing the prisoner's dilemma. This interest in mathematical model building and human behavior, and his growing interest in working with economists John Chipman and Leonid Hurwicz (future Nobel laureate) led McFadden to pursue his PhD in economics. He received his PhD in economics in 1962.

Following research experiences at Stanford and a year as a Mellon postdoctoral fellow at the University of Pittsburgh, McFadden accepted a teaching position at the University of California, Berkeley (UC Berkeley). McFadden began gaining a reputation as an econometrician on economic theory. His econometrics research pedigree was growing rapidly working with the likes of Kenneth Arrow, Peter Diamond, Dale Jorgenson, and Gérard Debreu, most of whom would become Nobel laureates. While at UC Berkeley, McFadden continued his interests in using mathematical modeling as an economics research tool and in choice behavior. By extension of these interests, his horizons were broadened to combining economic theory and measurement.

McFadden's research reflects his commitment to the inventive and creative use of mathematics and statistics. However, at the same time he constantly kept a focus on his models having an applied relevance for use by other economists. He credits Peter Diamond and James Heckman as two colleagues who were significant influences in his professional efforts. Both Diamond and Heckman were later to be Nobel laureates as well.

During the 1966–67 academic year, McFadden was a visiting professor at the University of Chicago. He also spent the 1976–77 year at Yale as the Irving Fisher Research Professor. In 1977, McFadden left UC Berkeley for MIT to join the likes of Robert Solow, Franco Modigliani, and Paul Samuelson. In 1986, McFadden became director of MIT's Statistics Research Center. However, in 1991 McFadden chose to return to UC Berkeley and start the Econometrics Laboratory on the Berkeley campus. He took one more visiting professorship in 1990, serving as the Fairchild fellow at the California Institute of Technology (Cal Tech).

McFadden's research focused on developing econometric tools that could be applied to economic theory, economic measurement, and economic analysis. He continued to show how these econometric tools applied to his interest in the area of choice behavior theory. McFadden's models have become known as the multinomial logit and random utility models for choice behavior. They have become widely used tools in the social sciences on such diverse topics as marriage, number of children, occupation choices, and even an automobile choice by a consumer.

McFadden's research crossed over to the discipline of psychology, specifically cognitive psychology. He was particularly interested in the research of Daniel Kahneman (Nobel laureate, 2002) and Amos Tversky on the implications of economic analysis. This led him to research on the aging and elderly in areas of financial planning, housing, and health services. One interesting finding of McFadden's was that the elderly tend to not sell their assets instead of generating income assuming they have longer to live.

In 2011, Daniel McFadden was appointed the Presidential Professor of Health Economics at the University of Southern California (USC). He also serves in the Department of Economics and the USC School of Policy, Planning, and Development. McFadden will continue his health care research with a special emphasis on consumer choice in health insurance and medical services.

In 1975, he won the John Bates Clark Medal and in 2000 the Erwin Plein Nemmers Prize.

*See also:* Akerlof, George; Debreu, Gérard; Diamond, Peter; Heckman, James; Kahneman, Daniel; Samuelson, Paul; Solow, Robert

### Selected Works by Daniel McFadden

McFadden, Daniel, and Thomas G. Cowing. *Microeconomic Modeling and Policy Analysis: Studies in Residential Energy Demand.* Salt Lake City, UT: Academic Press, 1984.

McFadden, Daniel, and Thomas A. Domencich. *Urban Travel Demand: A Behavioral Analysis.* Amsterdam: North-Holland, 1975.

McFadden, Daniel, and Melvyn A. Fuss. *Production Economics: Applications of the Theory of Production.* Amsterdam: North-Holland, 1978.

McFadden, Daniel, and Melvyn A. Fuss, eds. *Production Economics: A Dual Approach to Theory and Applications.* Contributions to Economic Analysis. Amsterdam: Elsevier Science, 1978.

McFadden, Daniel, and Charles F. Manski, eds. *Structural Analysis of Discrete Data with Econometric Applications.* Cambridge, MA: MIT Press, 1981.

### Selected Works about Daniel McFadden

"Daniel McFadden in Conversation with Michael Intriligator, UCLA." http://www.youtube.com/watch?v=lERmLAww3vU (accessed September 2011).

"Daniel McFadden, 1937–." New School for Social Research. http://www.newschool.edu/nssr/het/profiles/mcfadden.htm (accessed September 2011).

"Daniel McFadden—Presidential Professor of Health Economics." University of Southern California School of Policy, Planning, and Development. http://www.usc.edu/schools/sppd/faculty/detail.php?id=107 (accessed September 2011).

Economics Department. "Daniel L. McFadden." University of California, Berkeley, College of Letters and Science. http://elsa.berkeley.edu/econ/faculty/mcfadden_d.shtml (accessed September 2011).

McFadden, Daniel. "Autobiography." Nobelprize.org. http://www.nobelprize.org/nobel_prizes/economics/laureates/2000/mcfadden-autobio.html (accessed September 2011).

Miller, Frederic P., Agnes F. Vandome, and John McBrewster, eds. *Daniel McFadden.* Saarbrücken, Germany: VDM, 2010.

*David A. Dieterle*

## MEADE, JAMES

Born: June 23, 1907, in Bath, England; Died: December 22, 1995, in Cambridge, England; English; Keynesian, international economic policy, Nobel Prize (1977); Major Works: *The Theory of International Economic Policy* (2 vols., 1951, 1955).

James Meade is best known for being awarded the Nobel Prize in Economics in 1977 for his work on a theory of international trade. He shared the prize with Bertil Ohlin. He is credited with applying Keynesian economics to international trade and the flow of capital in the mid-twentieth century. Most of his working career was dedicated to teaching economics at Oxford and Cambridge Universities, and writing economics textbooks. Meade died in 1995.

James Edward Meade was born in Bath, England, on June 23, 1907. He enjoyed a classical education at Lambrook School and Malvern College between 1917 and 1926. He began studying at the School of Philosophy, Politics, and Economics at Oxford University in 1926. Due to his disgust at the high unemployment in Great Britain between the wars and to his belief that he knew how to fix it, he chose to study economics. In 1931, he began a one-year fellowship at Cambridge

University, where he became personally acquainted with John Maynard Keynes and other accomplished economists in a group known as the "Circus."

Meade returned to Oxford University in 1931 as a lecturer in economics and would continue to develop his interpretation of Keynesian economics. In 1936, he wrote one of the first textbooks to systematically explain Keynes's ideas from the *General Theory* (1936) in a textbook called *An Introduction to Economic Analysis and Policy*. In 1933, he married Margaret Wilson, and took his young family to Geneva in 1937 to work as editor of the *World Economic Survey* with the Economic Section of the League of Nations. Meade edited the seventh and eighth editions, which originally began in 1930 as *The Course and Phases of the World Depression*, put together by Bertil Ohlin.

Meade and his family left Geneva in 1940 fleeing the advancing German army and returned to England where Meade went to work in the Economic Section of the War Cabinet. His role during the war was to deal with any number of economic questions facing England. Along with Richard Stone in 1940–41, he was the first to create an account of the UK's national income and expenditures, which would be important for creating a workable economic policy. In 1944, he was a major contributor to the white paper titled *Economic Policy*, which led to the UK's commitment to low unemployment levels after the war as a matter of governmental obligation. At the end of the war, he was influential in discussions to establish an aborted International Trade Organization, which was supposed to work with International Monetary Fund (IMF) and the World Bank. However, the treaty to create the organization was not ratified, though the principles of the organization would be used to create the General Agreement on Tariffs and Trade (GATT) and the original intentions would be very similar to the current World Trade Organization (WTO). He became director in 1946 but resigned in 1947 over differences with other ministers who wanted to stick with wartime controls and rationing.

In 1947, James Meade began a 10-year tenure as professor of commerce at the London School of Economics (LSE). During this time, his writing career flourished, as he wrote his two-volume set *The Theory of International Economic Policy*, which began as a rewriting of his earlier *An Introduction to Economic Analysis and Policy*. Meade's Nobel award was due to his work in this series. The first volume, *The Balance of Payments* (1951), focused on the relationships of countries using the Keynesian economic model. It stated the need for countries to focus on using fiscal policy to maintain full employment (what he called internal balance) and using monetary policy to maintain a balance of payments equilibrium (external balance). Out of this work came *A Geometry of International Trade* (1952), which provided diagrams to solve problems associated with international economics.

The second volume, *Trade and Welfare* (1955), focused on international transactions and the general welfare of nations where perfectly competitive trade was not present. It stated that the nation's best welfare may result from allowing some trade barriers and not moving toward totally free trade. This was developed in the "theory of second best," which promoted trade barriers to result in higher economic welfare in general, although it might hurt some individuals. One point from these two volumes that would eventually lead to arguments for such devices as the European Union is the need for countries to be able to work together in some way to achieve balance. In order to avoid the problem of overdetermination between countries attempting their own ability to balance, some kind of cooperation is necessary.

In 1957, Meade left the London School of Economics to take the chair of political economy at Cambridge and continued his writing career. His major work during this time was a four-volume set called *Principles of Political Economy*, which focused on domestic economic issues. At Cambridge, he often failed to see eye to eye with other faculty members on Keynesian interpretation. His emphasis was on trying to create stable prices and full employment in a fair and efficient national system through the means of moderate reforms. His opponents in his department did not believe that the market could create these conditions, so they supported the use of sweeping government-led planning. This issue led to his resignation in 1968 to begin a senior research fellowship at Cambridge's Christ's College, which he held until 1974.

Meade worked in the 1970s studying the effects of direct taxation in the UK and maintained an influential role in the UK regarding economic policy for many years afterward. In 1978, he chaired a report known as "The Meade Report on Taxation," which identified the "poverty trap" that contributed to unemployment and also advocated a progressive tax on expenditures instead of income. He continued to write until the year of his death, with his final work being *Full Employment Regained?* (1995), which continued his emphasis on promoting full employment.

In one of his final works, the fictional tale of *Agathotopia* (1989), he describes a society that employs economics to create a society that is not perfect but still a "good place to live." This book emphasizes Meade's outlook on life that economics should be used to improve the conditions of all and not just to further the careers of economists.

James E. Meade died on December 22, 1995, in Cambridge, England.

*See also:* Keynes, John Maynard; Ohlin, Bertil

## Selected Works by James Meade

Meade, James. *Agathotopia: The Economics of Partnership*. Hume Paper No. 16. Aberdeen: Aberdeen University Press, 1989.

Meade, James. *Balance of Payments. Theory of International Economic Policy*. Vol. 1. New York: Oxford University Press, 1951.

Meade, James. *The Controlled Economy: Principles of Political Economy*. Vol. 3. Albany: State University of New York Press, 1972.

Meade, James. *Full Employment Regained?: An Agathotopian Dream*. New York: Cambridge University Press, 1995.

Meade, James. *A Geometry of International Trade*. London: Allen & Unwin, 1952.

Meade, James. *The Growing Economy: Principles of Political Economy*. Vol. 2. Chicago: Aldine, 1968.

Meade, James. *An Introduction to Economic Analysis and Policy*. Oxford: Clarendon Press, 1936.
Meade, James. *The Just Economy: Principles of Political Economy*. Vol. 4. Albany: State University of New York Press, 1976.
Meade, James. *A Neo-Classical Theory of Economic Growth*. New York: Oxford University Press, 1961.
Meade, James. *The Stationary Economy: Principles of Political Economy*. Vol. 1. London: Allen & Unwin, 1965.
Meade, James. *Trade and Welfare: Theory of International Economic Policy*. Vol. 2. New York: Oxford University Press, 1955.

**Selected Works about James Meade**

Corden, W. Max. "James Meade 1907–1995." *Economic Record* 217 (1996): 172–74.
Johnson, Harry. "James Meade's Contribution to Economics." *The Scandinavian Journal of Economics* 1 (1978): 64–85.
Meade, James E. (1907–95)." In *An Encyclopedia of Macroeconomics*. Edited by Brian Snowdon and Howard R. Vane. London: Edward Elgar, 2002.
Vane, Howard R., and Christ Mulhearn, eds. *Bertil G. Ohlin, James E. Meade and Robert A. Mundell: Pioneering Papers of the Nobel Memorial Laureates in Economics*. Vol. 10. Northampton, MA: Edward Elgar, 2010.

*Joseph Lee Hauser*

# MELTZER, ALLAN

Born: February 6, 1928, in Boston, Massachusetts; American; monetary policy; Major Works: *Money and the Economy: Issues in Monetary Analysis* (with K. Brunner) (1997), *A History of the Federal Reserve* (Vol. 1, 2003), *A History of the Federal Reserve* (Vol. 2, 2009).

Allan Meltzer is an economist and a professor of political economy at Carnegie Mellon University. He is the author of volumes 1 and 2 of *A History of the Federal Reserve* (2003 and 2009), and several other books. He has published more than 350 peer-reviewed academic papers and many newspaper articles. Meltzer held various key administrative positions such as the consultant on economic policy for the Congress, U.S. Treasury, Federal Reserve, and the World Bank. He was the cofounder and cochairman of the Shadow Open Market Committee from 1973 to 1999, and the director of many economic institutions such as the Commonwealth Foundation, Global Economic Action Institute, and Pittsburgh Economic Club. From 1999 to 2000, he served as the chairman of the International Financial Institution Advisory Commission. Meltzer has won quite a few prestigious awards and honors throughout his career.

Allan H. Meltzer was born February 6, 1928 in Boston, Massachusetts. He received his BA degree from Duke University in 1948. He then earned his MA and his PhD degrees in economics from the University of California, Los Angeles, in 1955 and 1958, respectively. In 1957, he started his academic career as an assistant professor at the Carnegie Institute of Technology, Graduate School of Industrial Administration. In 1964, Meltzer was promoted to full professorship and still teaches at the Carnegie Institute of Technology. Throughout his career, Meltzer has been a visiting professor at Ivy League institutions within the United States and abroad teaching political economics and monetary policy. Along with his academic career, Meltzer has held many key administrative positions at the Graduate School of Industrial Administration at the Carnegie Institute of Technology. In the period of 1966–69, Meltzer became the chairman of the PhD committee; in 1972–73, he was the acting dean; in 1981–82 and 1990–91, he was the chairman of the Dean Search Committee. From 1981 to 2000, Meltzer was a member of the Finance Committee of the board of trustees. Since 1975, Meltzer has written numerous newspaper articles in the *Los Angeles Times*, *Wall Street Journal*, and other respected newspapers. He has written more than 23 books and monographs and has published more than 300 peer-reviewed academic papers.

Allan Meltzer has won a great many awards such as the Irving Kristol Award from the American Enterprise Institute (2003), History Makers Award for Education from the John Heinz History Association (2003), Alice Hanson Jones award for the best book on North American Economic History (2004), and David Horowitz Award from the Bank of Israel and the Israeli Bankers Association (2004), just to name a few.

The Federal Reserve is one of the most powerful economic institutions in the world. Yet prior to the publication of Meltzer's colossal book, *A History of Federal Reserve* (2003 and 2009), not much was known about the institution. Allan Meltzer's book is one of the most critical analyses and revealing histories of the Federal Reserve ever published. Volume 1 of the book covers the history of the Federal Reserve from its origination in 1913 through the Treasury-Federal Reserve Accord of 1951. Volume 2 was published in two parts in 2009. One part of volume 2 covered the Federal Reserve's history from 1951 to 1986.

The documents and Minute notes of the Federal Reserve, which the book is based on, were not publicly available until during 1970s. Meltzer analyzed what the Federal Reserve did during its key turning points in history through careful review and analysis of the Minute notes, correspondence, and other internal documents. In the first volume, for instance, Meltzer explains the reasons behind the Federal Reserve's passive policies in the years that lead to the Great Depression. He brilliantly shows what actions of the Federal Reserve helped produce the sizable recession of 1937 and 1938. In addition, Meltzer examines the Federal Reserve's influence on international affairs, and its impact on the origination of the International Monetary Fund (IMF) and the World Bank.

The second volume of the book, published in two parts in 2009, covers the Federal Reserve's history from 1951 to 1986, when the great inflation in the United States ended. The second volume manifests the evolution and development of the Federal Reserve, from the Treasury to the most powerful financial and economical institution in the United States, during one of the most rapidly changing eras of the United States' history. Meltzer critically examines the gradual change of the Federal Reserve from a passive financial institute to a proactive economic think tank of the mid-1980s. The second volume of *A History of Federal Reserve*

(2009) ends with a prologue briefly discussing the 2007–9 financial and economic crises and the need for financial regulations. Academicians and policy makers alike benefit greatly from the rich and detailed history that Meltzer reveals in his book *A History of Federal Reserve* (2003 and 2009).

Allan Meltzer in his masterpiece, *A History of the Federal Reserve*, provided not only a detailed history of the Federal Reserve but also a history of the monetary policy and its political economy for more than seven decades starting from 1913. His effort to recognize trends and lessons learned from 1913 to 1987 is the best that has ever been done in understanding monetary policy and its economic and political consequences in the United States. Meltzer's insight magnifies the limitations of a central bank's monetary policy. He shows that in the United States, a failure to provide a consistent and transparent lender-of-last-resort policy during the history of the Federal Reserve has been the origin of many avoidable economic fluctuations. Meltzer brilliantly shows how personalities of key policy makers, their ideas, and politics have influenced the United States' monetary policy over time.

*See also:* Burns, Arthur; Greenspan, Alan; Volcker, Paul

### Selected Works by Allan Meltzer

Brunner, Karl, and Allan H. Meltzer. *Money and the Economy: Issues in Monetary Analysis.* Cambridge: Cambridge University Press, 1997.

Meltzer, Allan H. *A History of the Federal Reserve.* Vol. 1, *1913–1951*. Chicago: University of Chicago Press, 2003.

Meltzer, Allan H. *A History of the Federal Reserve.* Vol. 2. Chicago: University of Chicago Press, 2009.

### Selected Works about Allan Meltzer

"Arena Profile: Allan Meltzer." The Arena. http://www.politico.com/arena/bio/allan_meltzer.html (accessed May 25, 2011).

Carnegie Mellon Tepper School of Business. Meltzer Research. http://www2.tepper.cmu.edu/afs/andrew/gsia/meltzer (accessed May 25, 2011).

*Elham Mahmoudi*

# MENGER, CARL

Born: February 28, 1840, in Austrian Galicia, now in Poland; Died: February 26, 1921, in Vienna, Austria; Austrian; macroeconomics, microeconomics, political economy, marginal utility; Major Works: *Principles of Economics* (1871), *Investigations into the Method of the Social Sciences with Special Reference to Economics* (1883), *The Theory of Capital* (1888), *The Origin of Money* (1892).

Carl Menger is considered the father of the Austrian School of economics. While a reporter in Austria, Menger observed inconsistencies in the classical theories of price and value. Further pursuing a study of political economy, he worked out a system of thought that reconstructed the classical theory. Published as the *Principles of Economics*, Menger created the foundation for what would become the Austrian School of economics. Menger made significant contributions to the study of economics in his explanation of the origin of money. Menger died in 1921.

Carl Menger was born on February 28, 1840, in Austrian Galicia, which is now part of Poland. He was born into an old Austrian family that had been ennobled, but he dropped the title of "von" from his name. He had two brothers: Anton was an eminent Socialist author and fellow professor in the law faculty of the University of Vienna; and Max was a lawyer and Liberal deputy in the Austrian Parliament. Menger studied economics at the University of Prague and the University of Vienna from 1859 to 1863, receiving his doctorate of law from the University of Krakow in 1867.

Menger began his career as a newspaper journalist in 1876 reporting and analyzing market events. He worked at the *Lemberger Zeitung* in Lwow, Ukraine, followed by the *Weiner Zeitung* in Vienna. During this time Menger observed a contrast between the theory of price determination in classical economics and what market participants believed was truly the determinant of pricing in real-world markets. In 1870, Menger was given a civil service appointment in the press department of the *Ministerratspraesidium* (Austrian cabinet), followed by an appointment as a privatdozent (unpaid professor) in the faculty of law and political science at the University of Vienna. He was promoted to the position of professor extraordinarius in 1873.

Between 1876 and 1879 he served as a tutor to the crown prince, Rudolph von Hapsburg, and in 1879 Menger was appointed to the chair of political economy in Vienna's law faculty where he served as professor ordinarius. During his professorship he published *Investigations into the Method of the Social Sciences with Special Reference to Economics* (1883). His book along with several articles and pamphlets were widely criticized by German economists. He also served on a commission charged with reforming the Austrian monetary system during this time. He resigned his post in 1903.

During his time as a reporter, Menger observed incongruencies in the classical theories of price and value. He pursued a study of political economy and worked out a system of thought that would reconstruct classical theory. He published his theories as *Principles of Economics*, thereby creating the Austrian School of economics. Classical theorists had shown that price and production are determined by the universal law of supply and demand, determined by the interaction of all participants in an economy. However, the classical view recognized only the decisions and calculations of producers who were motivated by profit. This created a price theory in which only supply was explained as a determinant of monetary calculation by profit-motivated businessmen.

What was not considered were the nonmonetary values and preferences of the consumer, who Menger insists is the beginning and end of all economic activity. To Menger, the classical theory viewed consumer demand for goods treated as a given. Therefore prices were pushed toward equilibrium by the costs of production. Derived values of resources were also unexplained. This inconsistency created a "paradox of value."

Classical economics could not explain why life-sustaining products were priced very low compared to nonnecessity items. Menger resolved this by developing a comprehensive theory of the pricing process that places human action at the center. He used the law of marginal utility to refute the classical theory that price is determined by the cost of production, asserting instead that it is a result of satisfying consumers' wants.

Another important contribution Menger has made to the study of economics is his explanation of the origin of money. He published seven essays on the topics of monetary theory and currency reform from 1889 to 1893. He explains that although generally accepted mediums of exchange have been used in all ancient civilizations, the exact method and standard with which money was established is unrecorded. Menger rejected theories that assert that individuals or government leaders instituted this medium, instead suggesting that through the self-interested actions of individuals it emerged spontaneously.

Menger addresses the issue of salability in a barter economy. Different items have different levels of salability based on the availability of buyers wishing to purchase the item. With market experience, items would develop a standard value or true economic price in relation to other commonly traded goods. Goods that were most saleable would be traded more often because buyers recognized it as something that could be exchanged more readily for what they desired. Eventually, he claimed, certain goods became universally accepted in exchange by sellers of all other goods, thereby becoming a medium of exchange, or money.

The work of Carl Menger has influenced further development of economic theory in pricing, monetary policy, currency, and marginal utility by Eugen von Böhm-Bawerk, Friedrich von Wieser, Ludwig von Mises, and Friedrich von Hayek. Menger did not continue to publish after he resigned his professorship in 1903.

Carl Menger died in Vienna, Austria, on February 26, 1921.

*See also:* Böhm-Bawerk, Eugen von; Hayek, Friedrich von; Mises, Ludwig von

## Selected Works by Carl Menger

Menger, Carl. *Investigations into the Method of the Social Sciences with Special Reference to Economics*. Edited by Louis Schneider. Translated by Francis J. Nock. New York: New York University Press, 1985.

Menger, Carl. *The Origin of Money*. Charlotte, NC: Committee for Monetary Research and Education, 1892.

Menger, Carl. *Principles of Economics* (1871). Translated by James Dingwall and Bert F. Hoselitz. Arlington, VA: Institute for Humane Studies, 1976.

## Selected Works about Carl Menger

Caldwell, Bruce J., ed. *Carl Menger and His Legacy to Economics*. Durham, NC: Duke University Press, 1990.

"Carl Menger." In *The Concise Encyclopedia of Economics*. Edited by David R. Henderson. The Library of Economics and Liberty. http://www.econlib.org/library/Enc/bios/Menger.html (accessed August 2012).

Hayek, F. A. "Carl Menger (1840–1921)." In *The Collected Works of F. A Hayek*. Vol. 4, *The Fortunes of Liberalism: Essays on Austrian Economics and the Ideal of Freedom*. Edited by Peter G. Klein, 61–96. Chicago: University of Chicago Press, 1992.
Hicks, John, and Wilhelm Weber. *Carl Menger and the Austrian School of Economics*. Oxford: Clarendon Press, 1973.
Mises, Ludwig von. *The Historical Setting of the Austrian School of Economics*. New Rochelle, NY: Arlington House, 1969.

*Heather Isom*

## MERTON, ROBERT

Born: July 31, 1944, in New York City; American; finance economics, quantitative economics, Nobel Prize (1997); Major Works: "The Pricing of Options and Corporate Liabilities" (with Myron Scholes) (1970), "The Theory of Rational Option Pricing" (1973).

Robert Merton is best known for his work in finance. After receiving his PhD in economics from the Massachusetts Institute of Technology (MIT) in 1970, his collaboration with Fischer Black and Myron Scholes produced the now famous Black-Scholes option-pricing model. Myron Scholes and Robert Merton share the 1997 Nobel Prize in Economics for creating new methods in quantitative economics and their innovative work to determine the value of derivatives.

Robert C. Merton was born on July 31, 1944, in New York City. He began his studies in engineering at Columbia College where he received a BS in 1996. He started a PhD in applied mathematics at the California Institute of Technology. His interests, however, had turned to economics. He left the California Institute of Technology with an MS in applied mathematics in 1997. He began additional graduate work at MIT in 1967 in economics, receiving his PhD in 1970.

During his first year at MIT, at his adviser's (Harold Freeman) suggestion, Merton took Paul Samuelson's mathematical economics course. Merton became Samuelson's research assistant for the next two and a half years. Merton also was greatly influenced by Franco Modigliani who was part of MIT's Sloan School of Management faculty. When Merton completed his PhD, Modigliani helped him receive his first academic position, teaching finance at MIT. Merton taught at MIT from 1970 to 1988.

Moving to Harvard University in 1988, Merton was the George Fisher Baker Professor of Business Administration from 1988 to 1998. From 1998 through his retirement in 2010, Merton was the John and Natty McArthur University Professor at Harvard University. He is professor emeritus at Harvard Business School.

Merton's primary research interests are in financial engineering, financial innovation, and risk management. He is also interested in the following industries: banking, brokerage, financial services, insurance, investment banking, and retail financial services.

In the mid-1990s, Merton joined a hedge fund founded by John Meriwether, formerly of Salomon Brothers. As a board member of Long-Term Capital

Management (LTCM), Merton (and Myron Scholes) worked with Meriwether. Their goal was to use academic quantitative models and trader's knowledge and expertise to secure extraordinary returns for investors. LTCM went active in February 1994, raising over $1 billion from investors. In 1998, substantial losses to the fund led the Federal Reserve Bank of New York to organize a bailout of $3.625 billion by commercial and investment banks. LTCM was liquidated and closed in 2000.

Merton has received numerous honorary degrees. These include an MA from Harvard University in 1989 and a doctor of laws degree from the University of Chicago in 1991. He is a past president of the American Finance Association, a member of the National Academy of Science, and a fellow of the American Academy of Art and Science. He currently holds positions in many businesses and other organizations including Daedalus Software (chairman of the board); resident scientist at Dimensional Fund Advisors and Dimensional SmartNest LLC; member of the Quantitative Finance Advisory Board, Department of Applied Mathematics and Statistics, Stony Brook University; and member of the Board of Advisors, Santa Clara University Center for Innovation in Finance & Investment.

Awards received by Robert Merton in addition to the Nobel Prize include the Distinguished Finance Educator Award (2008) from the Financial Education Association; the First Annual Award for Foundational Contributions to Finance (2008) from the Owen School of Management at Vanderbilt University; the 2009 Robert A. Muh Award in the Humanities, Arts, and Social Sciences from MIT; the Tjalling C. Koopmans Asset Award from Tilburg University; the Award of Excellence for the Hall of Excellence from Hastings-on-Hudson High School; the Sigma Xi, Scientific Research Society, Life Member Award from Sigma Xi; the LECG Award for Outstanding Contributions to Financial Economics; and the 2010 Kolmogorov Medal from the University of London.

At the present time, Merton is the distinguished professor of finance in MIT's Sloan School of Management and is also a professor emeritus at Harvard Business School.

*See also:* Koopmans, Tjalling; Modigliani, Franco; Samuelson, Paul; Scholes, Myron

### Selected Works by Robert Merton

Black, Fischer, and Myron Sholes. "The Pricing of Options and Corporate Liabilities." *Journal of Political Economy* 81, no. 3 (1970): 637–54.

Merton, Robert C. "The Theory of Rational Option Pricing." *The Bell Journal of Economics and Management* 4, no. 1 (1973): 141–83.

### Selected Works about Robert Merton

Allen, Steve L. *Financial Risk Management: A Practitioner's Guide to Managing Market and Credit Risk.* Hoboken, NJ: Wiley, 2003.

Dunbar, Nicholas. *Inventing Money: The Story of Long-Term Capital Management and the Legends behind It.* New York: Wiley, 1999.

Merton, Robert C. "Autobiography." NobelPrize.org. http://nobelprize.org/nobel_prizes/economics/laureates/1997/merton.html (accessed July 2011).

"Robert C. Merton." Harvard Business School—Faculty and Research. http://drfd.hbs.edu/fit/public/facultyInfo.do?facInfo=pub&facId=6511 (accessed July 2011).

*Martha R. Rowland*

## MILL, JOHN STUART

Born: May 20, 1806, in London, England; Died: May 8, 1873 in Avignon, France; English; economic history, utility theory; Major Works: *Principles of Political Economy with Some of their Applications to Social Philosophy* (1848), *On Liberty* (1859), *The Subjection of Women* (1869), *Autobiography* (1873).

John Stuart Mill was an influential nineteenth-century British philosopher. Mill's father, James Mill, and Jeremy Bentham influenced Mill's interpretation of utilitarianism, which emphasized personal action toward the greatest possible happiness. Mill also greatly contributed to the advancement of economic thought. He authored *Principles of Political Economy* in 1848, which became the leading economics textbook for the next 40 years. Mill died in 1873.

John Stuart Mill was born on May 20, 1806, in London, England. James Mill, his father and author of the *History of British India* (1818), had a profound influence over him. Mill spent his childhood at home under the strict guidance of his father who served as his tutor. He learned Greek at age three and Latin at age eight. He read all nine books of Herodotus, Homer's *Iliad*, and Plato's six dialogues, in addition to an impressive array of others in their original language., He studied logic, math, and the basics of economic theory with works of Adam Smith and David Ricardo. Mill accompanied his father on daily walks where he was expected to provide a daily account of his learning. Mill's father used a Socratic method to question

English philosopher and economist John Stuart Mill was an early advocate of legal protection for animals. (Library of Congress)

the younger Mill's learning and understanding of particular writings and concepts. He was also held responsible for teaching his younger brothers and sisters, which he later admitted he disliked but that allowed him to learn more thoroughly and lastingly. In addition to his father, family friends David Ricardo and Jeremy Bentham also served to influence and educate Mill. In the spring of 1820, Mill studied in France with Bentham's brother, Sir Samuel Bentham, for one year, where he became a fluent speaker of French as well as a student of French thought and history.

His father's ambition was to mold a remarkable intellect to carry on his views of utilitarianism. Mill ultimately suffered the unhappy consequences of this imbalance of a life focused on study without emotional outlets. Fortunately, Mill eventually found recovery from his depression through reading Wordsworth's poetry.

Mill joined the East India Company in 1828 at the age of 17 to become an assistant examiner. He eventually headed the British company's relations with the Indian States and ultimately became chief of the examiner's office in 1856. Mill worked for the company for 38 years. Mill contributed to two newspapers, the *Traveler* and the *Morning Chronicle*, both edited by friends of his father. He also took part in regular discussions at his family home, in a newly formed reading society in English historian George Grote's home, and in the London Debating Society. This contact and discourse with others helped Mill begin to develop his own independent ideas and theories apart from his father's sphere of influence.

Mill's philosophy—influenced by John Locke, George Berkeley, David Hume, and Jeremy Bentham—takes a positive view of the world and assumes that people contribute to the progress of knowledge, individual freedom, and well-being. Mill believed strongly in the freedom of speech and considered it necessary in order to achieve development as a whole person. As long as individuals did not harm other individuals, Mill believed they ought to be free to do what they wished. Mill denounced slavery, promoted women's rights, and valued the environment.

In 1848, Mill wrote *Principles of Political Economy*, which became the leading economics textbook for the next 40 years. In it, he defends free markets with limited government intervention on utilitarian grounds. He felt that progressive taxes were unfair to those who worked hard and instead advocated the use of a flat tax. He continued to advance the ideas of Ricardo and Smith in writing on economies of scale, opportunity cost, and comparative advantage. His defense of free markets was not entirely consistent, in that he also believed in trade protectionism and regulation of work hours for laborers.

Mill married Mrs. Harriet Hardy Taylor in 1851. He had originally been introduced to her in 1830 while she was in a previous marriage. Mill credits Taylor's influence on his own intellectual and moral development. She helped Mill develop his expansive concept of the human good, conceived in utilitarian terms, in contrast to the more traditional ethic espoused by his father.

Mill retired from the India Company and became a member of Parliament during 1865–68. He called for women's suffrage and other voting reforms, although he believed that the more educated voters should receive more votes as they had a better understanding of the world around them. He will continue to be remembered for his lasting influence on the world of economics and philosophy.

John Stuart Mill died on May 8, 1873, in Avignon, France.

*See also:* Bentham, Jeremy; Hume, David; Locke, John; Ricardo, David; Smith, Adam

### Selected Works by John Stuart Mill

Mill, John Stuart. *Autobiography*. 1873. http://www.utilitarianism.com/millauto/ (accessed February 2012).
Mill, John Stuart. *On Liberty*. London: J. W. Parker, 1859.
Mill, John Stuart. *Principles of Political Economy, with Some of Their Applications to Social Philosophy*. 2 vols. London: John W. Parker, 1848.
Mill, John Stuart. *The Subjection of Women*. London: Longmans, Green, Reader and Dyer, 1869.

### Selected Works about John Stuart Mill

Heydt, Colin. *John Stuart Mill (1806–1873)*. October 24, 2006. http://www.iep.utm.edu/milljs/ (accessed February 2012).
"John Stuart Mill." In *The Concise Encyclopedia of Economics*. Edited by David R. Henderson. The Library of Economics and Liberty. http://www.econlib.org/library/Enc/bios/Mill.html (accessed October 2012).
"John Stuart Mill." n.d. Utilitarian.net. http://www.utilitarian.net/jsmill/ (accessed February 2012).
Mill, John Stuart. *Autobiography*. 1873. http://www.utilitarianism.com/millauto/ (accessed February 2012).
Wilson, Fred. "John Stuart Mill." Stanford Encylopedia of Philosopy. July 10, 2007. http://plato.standford.edu/entries/mill/ (accessed February 2012).

*Kathryn Lloyd Gustafson*

## MILLER, MERTON

Born: May 16, 1923, in Boston, Massachusetts; Died: June 3, 2000, in Chicago, Illinois; American; finance economics, Nobel Prize (1990); Major Works: "The Cost of Capital, Corporation Finance, and the Theory of Investment" (with Franco Modigliani) (1958), "Corporate Income Taxes and the Cost of Capital" (with Franco Modigliani) (1963).

Merton Miller was an active supporter of free-market solutions to economic problems in the traditional Chicago School of thought. He earned the Nobel Prize in Economics in 1990 with Franco Modigliani for their work in the theory of financial economics and the development of the Modigliani-Miller theorem. He spent most of his career, 1961–93, at the University of Chicago Booth School of Business where he was the Robert R. McCormick Distinguished Service Professor. Miller died in 2000.

Merton Howard Miller was born on May 16, 1923, in Boston, Massachusetts. His father, who was an attorney, encouraged his son to follow in his footsteps to Harvard University. Miller graduated with an AB magna cum laude in 1944 with a focus on economics.

Miller began his economics career working in the Division of Tax Research of the U.S. Treasury Department and then in the Division of Research and Statistics of the Board of Governors of the Federal Reserve System. In 1952, he attended Johns Hopkins University in Baltimore to work with faculty member Fritz Machlup and earn his doctorate in economics.

Miller spent the next year as a visiting assistant lecturer at the London School of Economics and then the Carnegie Institute of Technology. At the Carnegie Institute of Technology, Miller worked with fellow Nobel laureates Herbert Simon (1978) and Franco Modigliani (1985). It was here that he and Modigliani first published their joint corporation finance papers. Miller began his work at the University of Chicago in 1961 and remained there for the rest of his career. He was a visiting professor at the University of Louvain in Belgium during 1966–67.

Miller's work centers on corporate finance. He wrote or coauthored eight different books including the Modigliani-Miller theorem. The Modigliani-Miller theorem states that the value of a firm is independent of the firm's ratio of debt to equity. Investors can find their own balance between returns and risk. Consequently, firms do not need to differentiate between different stockholders' risk preferences. Corporate managers should instead focus on maximizing the firm's net wealth.

Using the Modigliani-Miller theorem as a basic model, Miller and Modigliani derived two invariance theorems now known as the MM theorems. If there is an optimal capital asset structure and dividend policy for firms, then this reflects the consequences of taxes or other specific market imperfections. These theorems are now used as the norm for comparison and analysis in corporate finance.

Miller became a fellow of the Econometric Society in 1975 and was president of the American Finance Association in 1976. In 1990, Miller became a public director of the Chicago Board of Trade. He also served as chairman of a special academic panel designed to study the Crash of October 19–20, 1987, for the Chicago Mercantile Exchange, and later became its director.

Merton Miller died on June 3, 2000, in Chicago, Illinois.

*See also:* Modigliani, Franco; Simon, Herbert

**Selected Works by Merton Miller**

Miller, Merton. *Financial Innovations and Market Volatility*. Chicago: Mid America Institute for Public Policy Research, 1988.

Miller, Merton. *Merton Miller on Derivatives*. New York: Wiley, 1997.

Miller, Merton H., and Eugene F. Fama. *The Theory of Finance*. Orlando, FL: Holt, Rinehart, and Winston, 1972.

Miller, Merton H., and Franco Madigliani. "Corporate Income Taxes and the Cost of Capital." *American Economic Review* 53 (June 1963): 433–43.

Miller, Merton H., and Franco Modigliani. "The Cost of Capital, Corporation Finance, and the Theory of Investment." *American Economic Review* 48 (June 1958): 261–97.

Miller, Merton H., and Charles W. Upton. *Macroeconomics: A Neoclassical Introduction*. Chicago: University of Chicago Press, 1974.

### Selected Works about Merton Miller

"Merton Howard Miller." Jewish Virtual Library. http://www.jewishvirtuallibrary.org/jsource/biography/MMiller.html (accessed February 2012).

"Merton H. Miller." In *The Concise Encyclopedia of Economics*. Edited by David R. Henderson. The Library of Economics and Liberty. http://www.econlib.org/cgi-bin/printcee.pl (accessed February 2012).

Miller, Merton H. "Autobiography." Nobelprize.org. http://www.nobelprize.org/nobel_prizes/economics/laureates/1990/miller-autobio.html (accessed February 2012).

University of Chicago, Graduate School of Business. *Merton Miller: A Giant of Modern Finance*. Summer 2000. http://www.chicagobooth.edu/magazine/sm00/features/miller-intro.htm (accessed February 2012).

*Kathryn Lloyd Gustafson*

## MIRRLEES, JAMES

Born: July 5, 1936, in Minnigaff, Scotland; Scottish; political economy, asymmetric information in economics, Nobel Prize (1996); Major Works: "Optimal Taxation and Public Production I: Production Efficiency" (1971), "Optimal Taxation and Public Production II: Tax Rules" (1971), *Economic Policy and Nonrational Behaviour* (1987), *Welfare, Incentives, and Taxation* (2006).

James Mirrlees is a Scottish economist awarded the Nobel Prize in Economics in 1996 with William Vickrey for their work on asymmetric information and incentives. Through his research on marginal income tax rates, Mirrlees was an early proponent of the flat tax, suggesting that all taxpayers pay the same marginal tax rate of 20 percent for optimal income tax rate efficiency. He also suggested that high-income earners should pay no tax, which later became a variation of supply-side economics. His work with Peter Diamond became known as the Diamond-Mirrlees efficiency theorem. In 1998, he was knighted for his contributions in the areas of political economy and economics.

James Alexander Mirrlees was born on July 5, 1936, in Minnigaff, Scotland. Graduating from Douglas Ewart High School in Newton Stewart as a brilliant math student in 1954, Mirrlees enrolled in Edinburgh University with the intention of preparing to be a math professor. His time at Edinburgh was influential in two ways. One, he again excelled in the math classroom. Two, through his cousin he was introduced to the world of philosophy. This philosophical influence was an important part of Mirrlees's later work in economics. Graduating from Edinburgh in three years, in 1957 he ventured to Cambridge University to pursue a second undergraduate degree in mathematics at Trinity College. With an interest in underdeveloped countries, Mirrlees pursued a degree in economics.

Mirrlees's professional career began while at Cambridge, where he served as a research assistant to future Nobel laureate Nicholas Kaldor. Also studying under the likes of Frank Kahn and future laureate Joan Robinson, his academic credentials grew. In 1963, Mirrlees received his PhD in economics from Cambridge University.

At the urging of Amartya Sen, Mirrlees went to India in 1962–63 as an adviser to the India Project as part of the Massachusetts Institute of Technology (MIT) Center for International Studies. After a summer at MIT, he and his wife moved to New Delhi, India. Returning to Cambridge in 1963, Mirrlees became a lecturer of economics at Cambridge University's Trinity College. In 1968, he left Cambridge to become the Edgeworth Professor of Economics at the University of Oxford. In 1995, he returned to the University of Cambridge as a professor of political economy. During his professorships at Oxford and Cambridge, he was an adviser to the Pakistan Institute of Development Economics, and a visiting professor at MIT on three different occasions in 1968, 1970, and 1976. He also served University of California, Berkeley, and Yale University in the same capacity, in 1986 and 1989 respectively.

While at Oxford, his most significant research interests took form. Mirrlees investigated problems generated by incomplete or asymmetrical information in economic transactions. One study of special significance, with William Vickrey, discussed the effects of asymmetrical information on the savings rate of an economy. Mirrlees also devoted much of his research to discovering the optimal marginal tax rate. Besides the academic and economic significance of the study, his research in this area became the basis for Mirrlees's Nobel Prize in Economics in 1996.

Mirrlees was also influential in the study of optimum income tax rates. As an adviser to the British Labour Party in the 1960s and 1970s, he assumed that high tax rates were most beneficial for the poor. However, his research led him, much to his own surprise and others', to the thesis that all taxpayers should pay a top marginal income tax rate of only 20 percent; i.e., they should pay a flat tax rate. Mirrlees took his income tax thesis one step further and suggested that the highest-income earners pay no income tax. He thought that a tax cut would incentivize high-income earners to work more, thus generating more wealth for the whole society. Mirrlees's additional tax research on consumption taxes with coauthor Peter Diamond concluded that small economies would be better off taxing consumption and not imports through tariffs.

Mirrlees research efforts also included studies of moral hazard, or the situation in which individuals (or companies) will take excessive risks, even beyond the risks they would take if granted immunity for the outcomes. For example, knowing that an insurance company will provide coverage for losses creates an environment of moral hazard. Mirrlees created a mathematical model for such environments, showing the optimal condition in which insurance markets will not become conducive to moral hazard. He showed that a combination of incentives and disincentives could align the insured's behavior with those who are uninsured and vice versa.

Once retired from the University of Cambridge, James Mirrlees was bestowed emeritus professor of political economy at the University of Cambridge and Trinity College fellow. He also divides his academic endeavors between the University of Melbourne, the Chinese University of Hong Kong, and the University of Macau. James Mirrlees was the lead of the UK tax system for the Institute of Fiscal Studies. He also is a member of Scotland's Council of Economic Advisers.

*See also:* Diamond, Peter; Kaldor, Nicholas; Robinson, Joan; Sen, Amartya; Stern, Nicholas; Vickrey, William

**Selected Works by James Mirrlees**

Diamond, Peter A., and James A. Mirrlees. "Optimal Taxation and Public Production I: Production Efficiency." *American Economic Review* 61, no. 1 (1971): 8–27.

Diamond, Peter A., and James A. Mirrlees. "Optimal Taxation and Public Production II: Tax Rules." *American Economic Review* 61, no. 3, Pt. 1 (1971): 261–78.

Mirrlees, James. *Economic Policy and Nonrational Behaviour.* Berkeley, CA: Institute of Business and Economic Research, 1987.

Mirrlees, James. "An Exploration in the Theory of Optimum Income Taxation." *Review of Economic Studies* 38, no. 2 (1971): 175–208.

Mirrlees, James. *Welfare, Incentives, and Taxation.* Oxford: Oxford University Press, 2006.

**Selected Works about James Mirrlees**

Institute for Fiscal Studies, ed. *Dimensions of Tax Design: The Mirrlees Review.* Oxford: Oxford University Press, 2010.

"James Mirrlees—Mathematics and Real Economics." Inaugural Conference at King's, Institute for New Economic Thinking. http://www.youtube.com/watch?v=-39znKX8kC8 (accessed October 2012).

"James A. Mirrlees." In *The Concise Encyclopedia of Economics.* Edited by David R. Henderson. The Library of Economics and Liberty. http://www.econlib.org/library/Enc/bios/Mirrlees.html (accessed April 2012).

Mirrlees, James A. "Autobiography." Nobelprize.org. http://www.nobelprize.org/nobel_prizes/economics/laureates/1996/mirrlees-autobio.html (accessed April 2012).

"Sir James Alexander Mirrlees." Institute for New Economic Thinking. http://ineteconomics.org/people/sir-james-alexander-mirrlees-fba (accessed April 2012).

*David A. Dieterle*

# MISES, LUDWIG VON

Born: September 29, 1881, in Lemberg, Austro-Hungarian Empire; Died: October 10, 1973, in New York City; American, naturalized U.S. citizen; trade cycle theory, monetary policy, credit policy analyst, economic epistemology; Major Works: *Theorie des Geldes und der Umlaufsmittel* (1912) translated as *The Theory of Money and Credit* (1934), *Die Gemeinwirtshaft* (1922) translated as *Socialism* (1936), *Nationalökonomie* (1940), *Human Action: A Treatise on Economics* (1949), *Theory and History* (1957).

Ludwig von Mises was one of the most influential Austrian economists of the twentieth century. He not only was the driving force and influence behind many contemporary Austrian-born economists, including Friedrich August von Hayek, Gottfried Haberler, Alfred Schütz, and Fritz Machlup, but also made important contributions in the areas of epistemology, history, political philosophy, trade cycle theory, and the economic effects of monetary and fiscal policy. Mises's output and influence laid the groundwork for a significant revival in Austrian and neo-Austrian economics. Mises died in 1973.

Ludwig von Mises was born on September 29, 1881, in the city of Lemberg, a part of the Austro-Hungarian Empire, to Arthur von Mises and Adele Landau. Mises attended the *Akademische Gymnasium* in Vienna from 1892 until 1900 studying the classics, classical languages, and the liberal arts. After a one-year military obligation with an artillery regiment near Vienna and the initial phase of his academic studies completed at the University of Vienna, Mises returned to his studies in 1903. It was in this year that he attended the lectures of Friedrich von Wieser and read *The Principles of Economics* by Carl Menger, the acknowledged founder of the Austrian School. He was also greatly influenced by the lectures (1905) and guidance of Finance Minister Eugen von Böhm-Bawerk, a second-generation Austrian economist who wrote *Capital and Interest*, a two-volume treatise on economics and the history of economic thought. Mises would attend his seminar until 1913. After obtaining a doctor of laws degree in 1906 and with the assistance of Böhm-Bawerk, Mises began work on a monetary treatise that was published in 1912 under the title *Theorie des Geldes und der Unlaufsmittel*, translated in 1934 as *The Theory of Money and Credit*.

This path-breaking work on monetary theory brought Mises significant recognition by integrating the theory of money and banking into the framework of Menger's theory of value and price. No longer was money simply seen as a numéraire or measure of value, nor as a historical accident, but rather as a natural commodity that has an integrative effect on the economic system. Unable to obtain a full professorship at an Austrian university, Mises taught as a privatdozent, an unsalaried position, at the University of Vienna in 1913 and was given the title of associate professor in 1918. After a short stint as a lawyer in Vienna, he obtained a full-time position in 1909 at the Austrian Chamber of Commerce as a *konzipist* or analyst, remaining there for the next 25 years. It was at this post that Mises conducted his famous *Privatseminar* that met regularly in his *Kammer* office throughout the 1920s.

During World War I, Mises saw action as a first lieutenant at the eastern front but was called back to Vienna after sustaining injuries and contracting typhoid fever in 1917. He later worked in the economics division of the Department of War in Vienna for the remainder of hostilities. From 1918 to 1920, he was director of the *Abrechnungsamt*, an office designed to reconcile various settlement questions arising from the Treaty of St. Germain. It was in this capacity that he first met and hired his lifelong friend and colleague, the Nobel Prize–winning economist Friedrich August von Hayek, as an assistant. His reflections on the political situation in Europe after the war prompted his *Nation, Staat und Wirtschaft* (1919), later translated as *Nation, State and Economy* (1983). The book contained an in-depth analysis of the various causes of the war, personal reminiscences, and observations about the economic challenges and political pressures facing a post–World War I Austria. It was followed in 1922 by another path-breaking work, *Die Gemeinwirtschaft*, translated in 1936 as *Socialism: An Economic and Sociological Analysis*. Mises not only laid out a cogent argument for the impossibility of Socialist economic calculation but also now became a leading critic of all forms of socialism. In 1926, Mises was instrumental in establishing the *Österreiches*

*Konjunkturforschungsinstitut*, or the Austrian Institute for Business Cycle Research, with Hayek as one of its major contributors. A successful private association from its inception, it became an important intellectual outlet for Austrian economic research on business cycle theory, predicting with great accuracy the banking crisis in Austria in 1931. In addition, his 1927 work *Liberalismus*, translated as *The Free and Prosperous Commonwealth* in 1962, signaled to his contemporaries his adherence to and advocacy of the free-market economy. In 1934, Mises joined the faculty of the Graduate Institute of International Studies in Geneva, Switzerland, as a professor of international economic relations.

In 1940, forced to leave his post because of the Nazi threat, Mises sought refuge in the United States, settling in New York City and obtaining U.S. citizenship in 1946. Unable to obtain a salaried teaching position at an American university, Mises accepted and held the position of visiting professor at the Graduate School of Business Administration at New York University from 1945 to 1969. Sponsored largely by the William Volcker Fund, Mises was able to reinstitute his seminars, continue his writing and research, and attract a new generation of students and scholars as he had earlier in Vienna.

Mises's most important work was *Human Action: A Treatise on Economics* (1949). This comprehensive 889-page treatise of economics grew out of his earlier work, *Nationalökonomie* (1940), and firmly established him as the primary spokesman for classical liberal thought in the United States. This work would later become a cornerstone document in the revival of the Austrian School, especially in the works of Murray N. Rothbard. During this period he also published *Bureaucracy* (1944), *Omnipotent Government* (1944), *Planning for Freedom and Other Essays and Addresses* (1952), and *The Anti-capitalist Mentality* (1956). In his last two significant works, *Theory and History* (1957) *and The Ultimate Foundation of Economic Science* (1962), Mises presented the epistemological case for capitalism.

Mises was the recipient of the William Volcker Fund Distinguished Service Award (1956), the Austrian Medal of Honor (1962), an honorary doctorate from New York University (1963), and an honorary doctorate in political science from the University of Freiburg (1964), and was a distinguished fellow of the American Economic Association (1969).

Ludwig von Mises died on October 10, 1973, in New York City at the age of 92.

*See also:* Böhm-Bawerk, Eugen von; Hayek, Friedrich von; Machlup, Fritz; Menger, Carl; Robbins, Lionel; Rothbard, Murray; Schumpeter, Joseph; Wieser, Friedrich von

## Selected Works by Ludwig von Mises

Mises, Ludwig von. *A Critique of Interventionism*. Stuttgart, Germany: Gustav Fischer Verlag, 1929.

Mises, Ludwig von. *The Historical Setting of the Austrian School of Economics*. New Rochelle, NY: Arlington House, 1969.

Mises, Ludwig von. *Human Action: A Treatise on Economics*. New Haven, CT: Yale University Press, 1949.

Mises, Ludwig von. *Liberalism: In the Classic Tradition*. 3rd ed. Translated by Ralph Raico. San Francisco: Cobden Press, 1927.

Mises, Ludwig von. *On the Manipulation of Money and Credit: Three Treatises on Trade-Cycle Theory*. Translated by Bettina Bien Greaves. Edited by Percy L. Greaves, Jr. New York: Free Market Books, 1978.

Mises, Ludwig von. *Planned Chaos*. Auburn, AL: Ludwig von Mises Institute, 1947.

Mises, Ludwig von. *Socialism: An Economic and Sociological Analysis*. London: Jonathan Cape, 1936.

Mises, Ludwig von. *Theory and History*. New Haven, CT: Yale University Press, 1957.

Mises, Ludwig von. *The Theory of Money and Credit*. London: Jonathan Cape, 1934.

Mises, Ludwig von. *The Ultimate Foundation of Economic Science*. New York: Van Nostrand, 1962.

### Selected Works about Ludwig von Mises

Butler, Eamonn. *Ludwig von Mises: Fountainhead of the Modern Microeconomics Revolution*. Aldershot, UK: Gower, 1988.

Greaves, Bettina Bien. *The Works of Ludwig von Mises*. Irvington-on-Hudson, NY: Foundation for Economic Education, 1969.

Hayek, Friedrich von, ed. *Toward Liberty: Essays in Honor of Ludwig von Mises on the Occasion of His 90th Birthday*. Menlo Park, CA: Institute for Humane Studies, 1971.

Hülsmann, Jörg Guido. *Mises: The Last Knight of Liberalism*. Auburn, AL: Ludwig von Mises Institute, 2007.

Kirzner, Israel M. *Ludwig von Mises*. Wilmington, DE: ISI Books, 2001.

Moss, Laurence S. *The Economics of Ludwig von Mises: Towards a Critical Appraisal*. Kansas City, MO: Sheed and Ward, Institute for Humane Studies Series in Economic Theory, 1974.

Sennholz, Mary, ed. *On Freedom and Free Enterprise: Essays in Honor of Ludwig von Mises*. Princeton, NJ: Van Nostrand, 1956.

*Joseph A. Weglarz*

# MODIGLIANI, FRANCO

Born: June 18, 1918, in Rome, Italy; Died: September 25, 2003, in Cambridge, Massachusetts; Italian; financial markets, Nobel Prize (1985); Major Work: *The Collected Papers of Franco Modigliani*, Volume 6 (2005).

Franco Modigliani has been recognized as being the most famous economist of Italian heritage. The son of a Jewish physician, his family fled Fascist Italy in 1939. He became a naturalized American citizen in 1946. A professor at the Massachusetts of Technology (MIT) at the time of his Nobel Prize in 1985, Modigliani was honored for his pioneering work on savings and financial markets. He developed several theories that have withstood the test of time including the Duesenberry-Modigliani hypothesis, the life cycle hypothesis, and the Modigliani-Miller theorem. Modigliani died in 2003.

Franco Modigliani was born in Rome, Italy, on June 18, 1918. In 1932, his father unexpectedly died, altering young Modigliani's life. The son of a physician (pediatrician), the family plan was for him to follow his father's path into medicine. Young Modigliani had other ideas, instead enrolling in the University of

Rome at the age of 17 to pursue a career in law. However, during his law studies he also developed an interest in economics. Modigliani won first prize in a national competition in economics and his interest in economics was firmly established. The Fascist political environment in Italy at the time necessitated that Modigliani leave Rome. Following a stay in Paris to complete his studies at the University of Rome, he immigrated to the United States in 1939.

In the United States, he continued his studies in economics at the New School for Social Research in New York. At the New School, Modigliani developed his solid foundations in mathematics and econometrics as well as economics. Modigliani credited much of his success to his early days at the New School learning empirical analysis and theory from Jacob Marschak. He received his doctorate from the New School in 1944.

In 1944, Modigliani published his first article in English, "Liquidity Preference and the Theory of Interest and Money" (*Econometrica* 12, no. 1). Following two years at Columbia University, Modigliani returned to the New School to lecture and research at the Institute of World Affairs. It was here where he made his first contribution to the study of savings. This research spawned the Duesenberry-Modigliani hypothesis.

In 1948, Modigliani moved to Chicago when he was awarded the political economy fellowship at the University of Chicago, including the opportunity to join the Cowles Commission for Research in Economics as a research consultant. He then joined the University of Illinois to lead a research endeavor on "expectations and business fluctuations." He remained on the University of Illinois faculty till 1952.

While his time at the University of Illinois was relatively brief, it was during this time in his career that many of his economic theories were developed. Modigliani and graduate student Richard Brumberg collaborated on two papers that were the early versions of what was to evolve into the life cycle hypothesis of saving. The life cycle hypothesis attempts to explain personal saving levels in an economy. The hypothesis explains that consumers' aim is to achieve a constant level of income during their lifetime. The life cycle can be briefly defined as describing one's saving behavior throughout life. People save during their working years so they can spend during their retirement years. While this notion by itself was not new, it was Modigliani who was able to create the quantitative model for use in economic research and ultimately as an economic theory.

This life cycle hypothesis has been the theoretical foundation for many economic empirical studies since its development, including many by Modigliani himself. He expanded its implications beyond the explanation of individual saving behavior to the savings behavior of an entire economy. Of major significance was his contribution that a key variable in the level of total savings in an economy is an economy's growth rate. An economy that is growing will have more savings, and vice versa. Modigliani also used the life cycle hypothesis studies to suggest that savings was also determined by the age distribution of a population and life expectancy where higher rates of economic growth favored younger ages. Modigliani's model led to new studies in both savings and consumption including studying the effect of pension systems on private savings.

In 1952, Modigliani joined the faculty at the Carnegie Institute of Technology (later named Carnegie-Mellon University). At Carnegie, Modigliani teamed with Merton Miller and they formulated the Modigliani-Miller theorem. The Modigliani-Miller theorem focused on determining the value of a firm. The core of the Modigliani-Miller theorem was that in determining the value of a firm, the type of financing to be instituted was not a significant factor. When certain conditions were met, whether the financing was with equity by buying shares or debt through borrowing, the type of financing was inconsequential in determining the final value. Later, Modigliani and Miller added a second theorem, asserting that a firm's dividend policy does not impact the value of the firm.

After a two-year stop at Northwestern University beginning in 1960, in 1962 Modigliani returned to MIT and the MIT Sloan School of Management and Department of Economics. Returning as a visiting professor, he later became an institute professor and received the James R. Killian Faculty Award in 1985. He was bestowed professor emeritus honors in 1988.

In 1985, Franco Modigliani was the recipient of the Nobel Prize in Economics. He was honored for his life's work regarding savings and later financial markets. Since 1969, there has been only one winner of Italian descent, Franco Modigliani.

Franco Modigliani died on September 25, 2003, in Cambridge, Massachusetts.

*See also:* Miller, Merton

## Selected Works by Franco Modigliani

Abel, Andrew, and Simon Johnson, eds. *The Collected Papers of Franco Modigliani*. Vol. 4, *Monetary Theory and Stabilization Policies*. Cambridge, MA: MIT Press, 1989.

Friedman, Milton, and Franco Modigliani. "The Monetarist Controversy: Discussion." *Monograph*, Federal Reserve Bank of New York, 1979.

Miller, Merton H., and Franco Modigliani. "Corporate Income Taxes and the Cost of Capital." *American Economic Review* 53 (June 1963): 433–43.

Miller, Merton H., and Franco Modigliani. "The Cost of Capital, Corporation Finance, and the Theory of Investment." *American Economic Review* 48 (June 1958): 261–97.

Modigliani, Franco. *The Collected Papers of Franco Modigliani*. Vol. 6. Cambridge, MA: MIT Press, 2005.

Modigliani, Franco. "The Monetarist Controversy: A Presentation." *Economic Review* Suppl. (Spring 1977): 5–11.

Modigliani, Franco, and Arun Muralidhar. "Rethinking Pension Reform." *Journal of Financial Transformation* 8 (2003): 8–9.

Modigliani, Franco, and Arun Muralidhar. *Rethinking Pension Reform*. Cambridge: Cambridge University Press, 2004.

## Selected Works about Franco Modigliani

Modigliani, Franco. *Adventures of an Economist*. Stamford, CT: Cengage Learning, 2001.

Modigliani, Franco. "Autobiography." Nobelprize.org. http://nobelprize.org/nobel_prizes/economics/laureates/1985/modigliani-autobio.html (accessed March 2011).

Modigliani, Franco. "Franco Modigliani." In *Nobel Lectures, Economics 1981–90*. Edited by Karl-Göran Mäler. Singapore: World Scientific, 1992.

David A. Dieterle

# MORGENSTERN, OSKAR

Born: January 24, 1902, in Gorlitz, Germany; Died: July 26, 1977, in Princeton, New Jersey; German, naturalized U.S. citizen; game theory; Major Works: *Theory of Games and Economic Behavior* (with John von Neumann) (1944), *The Question of National Defense* (1959), *On the Accuracy of Economic Observations* (1963), *Mathematical Theories of Expanding and Contracting Economies* (with G. L. Thompson) (1976).

Oskar Morgenstern was a German-born American economist. He began his studies at the University of Vienna, where he also taught before immigrating to the United States in 1938. He was a professor of economics at Princeton University until 1970 and New York University until 1977. He is most noted for his work with John von Neumann on using game theory to predict economic behavior. Morgenstern wrote many publications throughout his career on many topics including accuracy in economics, national defense, and business cycles. Morgenstern died in 1977.

Oskar Morgenstern was born in Gorlitz, Germany, on January 24, 1902. Oskar studied at the University of Vienna where he received his doctorate in 1925. To extend his studies, Morgenstern was awarded a three-year scholarship from the Rockefeller Foundation and came to the United States where he studied at Harvard and other institutions. He later wrote that the Rockefeller Foundation, which supported much of his work, was essential to his development. After returning to Austria in 1929, he began his work with the University of Vienna as a lecturer, later becoming a professor of economics. He remained there until 1938.

During his time in Vienna, he was part of the Austrian School of economics, a group of Austrian economists that met to discuss the economic issues in postwar Austria. In this group, Morgenstern met with economists such as Gottfried Haberler and Friedrich von Hayek while being mentored by Ludwig von Mises. In 1931, Morgenstern succeeded Hayek as manager of the Institute for Business Cycle Research, which was started by Morgenstern and his colleagues in the Austrian School. While manager, he published *The Limits of Economics*, in which he defended the view of the Austrian School, namely that governments should not organize markets.

While in Vienna, Morgenstern published numerous writings on economic forecasting, the economic conditions in Europe, business cycles, and currency. He also served as an adviser to the Austrian National Bank from 1932 to 1938 and to the Ministry of Commerce from 1936 to 1938. His influence in the Viennese economic community was considerable.

In 1938, Morgenstern went to the United States with help from the Carnegie Foundation for International Peace. He worked as a visiting professor of political economy at Princeton University. While Morgenstern was in the United States, Hitler and the Nazis were annexing Austria. Morgenstern remained in the United States, becoming a naturalized U.S. citizen in 1944. At Princeton University, he began to work with John von Neumann, with whom he would make his most famous contribution to economics, in the area of game theory.

In 1944, Morgenstern collaborated with von Neumann, a mathematician, to publish *Theory of Games and Economic Behavior*. Game theory uses mathematical calculation applied to strategic situations to analyze outcomes of individuals. The game is dependent on the actions of players who seek to maximize their own interest, while taking into consideration other players' self-interested behavior as well. In the 1950s, game theory was further developed by other economists. Their strategy would be applied to the social and behavioral sciences in areas such as military policy and political races, and even in the field of biology. Also with von Neumann, Morgenstern developed in 1947 the "Von Neumann-Morgenstern Utility," a model for measuring choice under uncertainty. In this model, four axioms of expected utility were applied to a rational decision maker to construct a weighted average of a probability.

Morgenstern was also widely known for his work on the validity and accuracy of economic data. In his 1950 book, *On the Accuracy of Economic Observations*, Morgenstern argued that economists rely on statistics and data as tools of predicting economic behavior, yet there are numerous errors and fallacies with the accuracy and validity in economic data. He suggested that these errors are caused by inadequate data collection and the likelihood of false and unclear classification in some examples. During the 1950s and 1960s, he wrote on various economic issues, also publishing *Prolegomena to a Theory of Organization* in 1951 and *The Question of National Defense and International Transactions and Business Cycles* in 1959. In 1970, Morgenstern retired from Princeton University.

Morgenstern accepted a position at New York University in 1970 as professor of game theory and mathematical economics, where he remained until his death. In 1976, he published *Mathematical Theory of Expanding and Contracting Economies* with Gerald L. Thompson.

Morgenstern died on July 26, 1977, in Princeton, New Jersey.

*See also:* Haberler, Gottfried von; Hayek, Friedrich von; Mises, Ludwig von

### Selected Works by Oskar Morgenstern

Morgenstern, Oskar. *On the Accuracy of Economic Observations*. Princeton, NJ: Princeton University Press, 1963.

Morgenstern, Oskar. *The Question of National Defense*. New York: Random House, 1959.

Morgenstern, Oskar, and G. L. Thompson. *Mathematical Theories of Expanding and Contracting Economies*. Lanham, MD: Lexington Books, 1976.

Morgenstern, Oskar, and John von Neumann. *Theory of Games and Economic Behavior*. Princeton, NJ: Princeton University Press, 1944.

### Selected Works about Oskar Morgenstern

Leonard, Robert. *Von Neumann, Morgenstern, and the Creation of Game Theory: From Chess to Social Science, 1900–1960.* New York: Cambridge University Press, 2010.

"Mises on Austrian Economics in Austria." Ludwig von Mises Institute. http://mises.org/etexts/misesaustrian.asp (accessed March 2012).

Weintraub, E. Roy, ed. *Toward a History of Game Theory.* Durham, NC: Duke University Press, 1992.

*Sara Standen*

## MORTENSEN, DALE

Born: February 2, 1939, in Enterprise, Oregon; American; labor economics, Nobel Prize (2010); Major Work: *Wage Dispersion: Why Are Similar Workers Paid Differently?* (2003).

Dale Mortensen is a contemporary theorist who specializes in labor economics with a focus on unemployment. His theories can be used to formulate and predict the impact of a variety of government influences on overall unemployment and wage distribution. Mortensen's professional pursuits led him to Northwestern University in 1965 and he remains there today. His expertise regarding labor markets has taken him to many parts of the world, and his theories earned him a Nobel Prize in 2010.

Dale Thomas Mortensen was born on February 2, 1939, in Enterprise, Oregon, a small community in Willowa County. He graduated from Wy'east High School in 1957 before attending Willamette University in Salem, Oregon, where he was a trailblazer in the economics department, which focused on economics via a mathematical approach. While at Willamette, his pursuits were limited to not only academic achievement but also leadership. Mortensen served as student body president during his senior year as he completed his bachelor of arts in economics in 1961. Following his time in Salem, Mortensen began working on his PhD at Carnegie Mellon University in Pittsburgh, Pennsylvania, which led him into his role in education and research. He earned his PhD in economics from Carnegie Mellon in 1967.

Mortensen began teaching at Northwestern University in Evanston, Illinois, in 1965 and he remains in that capacity today. Mortensen's upbringing and education led him into a career focused around labor markets and employment. He has worked in a variety of educational settings and promoted his theories throughout his career at numerous institutions and for several organizations.

The years of research on labor markets led Mortensen to write his most famous work, *Wage Dispersion: Why Are Similar Workers Paid Differently?*, which was published by MIT Press in 2003. The book gained wide praise from many of his contemporaries as it sought to use both theory and empirical data to explain labor markets theory. Much of his research on wage dispersion and distribution of earnings opened the eyes of many as experts try to assess the relationship between potential employees and employers. Several reviews, both domestic and abroad, also note that Mortensen's work was well written and inspired many to learn more about labor economics.

Mortensen's research and culminated in perhaps his most significant achievement: a Nobel Prize in Economics. The Royal Swedish Academy of Sciences awarded Mortensen and two other colleagues the Sveriges Riksbank Prize in Economic Sciences in Memory of Alfred Nobel in 2010. The committee selected Mortensen, Christopher Pissarides of the London School of Economics and Political Science in the United Kingdom, and Peter A. Diamond of the Massachusetts Institute of Technology for their analysis of markets, such as employment, where people looking for work are not being appropriately matched with those who are looking to hire these same workers. This is what is known as a search friction. Their extensive research on labor markets over the course of the past several decades helped explain how so many people can be unemployed while at the same time there are a tremendous number of job vacancies in the market. Much of their research focused on the impact of government regulation, monetary policy, and the overall involvement of government in the labor market, particularly the effect on employment data such as wages or job vacancies and the relationship between potential employees with their skill sets and the employers' need for labor. The Nobel Prize was awarded not only for the principal research conducted by Mortensen, Pissarides, and Diamond but for the predictive power of their theories.

Many experts in economics refer to their theory as the Diamond-Mortensen-Pissarides model, which is used to predict how unemployment benefits, interest rates, the efficiency or lack thereof of employment agencies, and other inputs can affect the labor market and employment. During our current global economic situation, this research and model is of particular interest. Their model would seem to suggest a positive correlation between increased unemployment benefits and longer periods of unemployment and longer search times for those who are currently seeking employment.

Dale T. Mortensen is well known for his work on labor economics, and though the crowning achievement in his remarkable career may be the Nobel Prize in Economics, he has been recognized by many other organizations and institutions as well. Mortensen served as a visiting professor or lecturer at several institutions, most notably at Aarhus University in Denmark. He has worked as a research associate of the National Bureau of Economic Research (NBER), a research fellow of the Institute for the Study of Labor (IZA), and a fellow of the Econometric Society, the American Academy of Arts and Sciences, the Society of Labor Economics, and the European Economic Association. He has also served in a plethora of other capacities for various committees, associations, and organizations. His remarkable efforts in labor economics have received much acclaim. He received the IZA Prize in Labor Economics in 2005 and the Mincer Prize from the Society of Labor Economics in 2007, and was named the American Economic Association distinguished fellow in 2008. Mortensen's expertise and efforts in his field provided the economic and academic community with a wealth of knowledge that will further assist in understanding the complexities of employment and labor.

*See also:* Diamond, Peter; Pissarides, Christopher

### Selected Works by Dale Mortensen

Burdett, Kenneth, and Dale T. Mortensen. *Equilibrium Wage Differentials and Employer Size.* Evanston, IL: Northwestern University, Center for Mathematical Studies in Economics and Management Science, 1989.

Mortensen, Dale. *Wage Dispersion: Why Are Similar Workers Paid Differently?* Cambridge, MA: MIT Press, 2003.

### Selected Works about Dale Mortensen

Mortensen, Dale T. "Autobiography." Nobelprize.org. http://www.nobelprize.org/nobel_prizes/economics/laureates/2010/mortensen.html (accessed June 2011).

Tremmel, Pat Vaughan. "Dale Mortensen Wins Nobel Prize." October 11, 2010. Northwestern University. http://www.northwestern.edu/newscenter/stories/2010/10/mortensen-nobel-economics.html (accessed June 2011).

*William S. Chappell*

## MUN, THOMAS

Born: June 17, 1571, in London, England; Died: July 21, 1641, in London, England; English; merchant, mercantilist; Major Work: "A Discourse of Trade from England unto the East Indies" (1621).

Thomas Mun, one of the first mercantilists, is known for his emphasis on the importance of the balance of trade for economic prosperity. As a proponent of the balance-of-trade theory, Mun believed that a healthy nation will sell a greater value of goods to foreigners than it consumes of foreign goods. Mun believed that gold was a stable measure of wealth, and that government should regulate trade to produce an excess of exports over imports in order to gain more gold for the country. During the economic depression of 1620, Mun was selected as a member of the great commission of trade set up in 1622 to make recommendations concerning economic policy. Mun died in 1641.

Thomas Mun was born on June 17, 1571, in London, England. He was the third son of an important London family. At a young age, he lost his father and his mother remarried. His stepfather was a director of the newly formed East India Company, where he later began his career in business by engaging in Mediterranean trade, primarily in Italy and the Levant (Turkey, Syria, and Lebanon area). He later settled in London, having amassed a large fortune. He is reported to have had commercial dealings with Ferdinand I, grand duke of Tuscany. Nothing specific is known of his education.

Mun came into public prominence in England during the economic depression of 1620. As the director of the East India Company, Mun was called on to defend the company's practice of exporting large amounts of silver while there was a silver shortage in the country. Many people in the country blamed the East India Company for the crisis because the company financed its trade by exporting £30,000 in bullion on each voyage.

In large part, Mun penned his first work in 1621 in defense of the East India Company's practices and it may have been made in self-interest. In *A Discourse of Trade from England unto the East Indies*, Mun argued that as long as England's total exports exceeded its total imports in the process of visible trade, the export of bullion was not harmful. In his argument, he pointed out that East Indian goods, when reexported, earned more silver than that originally exported to pay for them.

As one of the members of the commission of trade set up in 1622 to make recommendations concerning economic policy, Mun opposed successfully the advocates of two difference policies, each based on a distinct theoretical analysis of the mechanism of foreign trade. Out of this opposition, Mun composed his second book, *England's Treasure by Foreign Trade*, which he completed between 1626 and 1628 but was not printed till 1664 by his son. It was considered to be a direct repudiation of the arguments of Gérard de Malynes who believed that excessive export was intrinsic to a healthy foreign exchange and advocated exchange rate controls with a fixed exchange rate as presented in *The Maintenance of Free Trade* (1622).

In his second book, considered a classic of English mercantilism, Mun emphatically and formally defined the doctrine of the balance of trade. Mun asserted that foreign trade is governed by the demand for commodities, that the flow of goods rules the exchange rate, and that silver itself is merely another commodity. He was among the first to recognize the exportation of services as valuable trade, and made early statements strongly in support of capitalism.

Mun asserted that trade was the only way to increase England's treasure (i.e., national wealth). He suggested several courses of action in pursuit of this end: frugal consumption in order to increase the amount of goods available for export, increased utilization of land and other domestic natural resources to reduce import requirements, and lowering of export duties on goods produced domestically from foreign materials.

His recognition of the principle of elasticity of demand may be his most notable contribution to economic theory. Understanding that goods with inelastic demand command higher prices in the marketplace, Mun advocated exporting goods with inelastic demand to generate greater profits from international trade.

As a mercantilist, Mun believed that government should regulate trade to produce an excess of exports over imports in order to gain more gold. His position depended on the idea that the nation's holding of gold was the main measure of its wealth. Mun's view was later challenged by economists such as Adam Smith who showed that trade is self-regulating and that governments that seek to hoard gold or other hard currencies will make their countries worse off.

Mun's works on the theory of the balance of trade deeply influenced subsequent economic thought and were published in several editions. Laissez-faire economists such as John R. McCulloch, who saw Mun as a tentative exponent of freedom of trade, commended his practical liberalism.

Mun died on July 21, 1641, in London, England, at the age of 70.

*See also:* Quesnay, François; North, Dudley; Smith, Adam

### Selected Works by Thomas Mun

Mun, Thomas. "A Discourse of Trade from England unto the East-Indies (1621)." Farnborough, England: Gregg International Publishers, 1971.
Mun, Thomas. *England's Treasure by Forraign Trade*. Oxford: Blackwell, 1664.

### Selected Works about Thomas Mun

Gould, J. D. "The Date of *England's Treasure by Forraign Trade*." *Journal of Economic History* 15 (1955): 160–61.
Gould, J. D. "The Trade Crisis of the Early 1620's and English Economic Thought." *Journal of Economic History* 15 (1955): 121–33.
Hardy, Alfred L. "Thomas Mun." In *Dictionary of National Biography*, 1183–86. London: Smith, 1894.
Hinton, R. W. K. "The Mercantile System in the Time of Thomas Mun." *Economic History Review* Second Series 7 (1955): 277–90.
Malynes, Gérard de. *The Maintenance of Free Trade*. London: Sheffard, 1662.
Misselden, Edward. *Free Trade: Or, the Meanes to Make Trade Florish*. London: Waterson, 1622.
Spiegel, Henry William. *The Growth of Economic Thought*. Durham, NC: Duke University Press, 1992.
Supple, Barry E. *Commercial Crisis and Change in England, 1600–1642: A Study in the Instability of a Mercantile Economy*. Cambridge: Cambridge University Press, 1959.
Viner, Jacob. *Studies in the Theory of International Trade*. New York: Harper, 1937.

*Ninee Shoua Yang*

## MUNDELL, ROBERT

Born: October 24, 1932, in Kingston, Ontario, Canada; Canadian; international macroeconomics, exchange rates, currency, Nobel Prize (1999); Major Works: *The International Monetary System: Conflict and Reform* (1965), *Man and Science: The Science of Choice* (1968), *Monetary Theory: Interest, Inflation and Growth in the World Economy* (1971)

Robert Mundell is known as the man who invented the euro. He was a pioneer in the economic study of modern international economics. He long held the view that the gold standard could still be used with modern economies. He favored an international monetary system only if the currency is backed by a precious metal such as gold. Mundell was a prolific researcher and writer on monetary policy, inflation, and the economic theory of international economics. In 1999, Robert Mundell received the Nobel Prize in Economics for his work on monetary and fiscal policy within different exchange rate systems.

Robert A. Mundell was born on October 24, 1932, in Kingston, Ontario, Canada. He received his BA from the University of British Columbia (Vancouver) in 1953. He earned his PhD from the Massachusetts of Technology (MIT) in 1956 studying under the tutelage of Paul Samuelson. Influenced by Lionel Robbins and James Meade, he completed his dissertation while studying at the London School of Economics. In 1956 and 1957, he was a postdoctoral fellow in political economy at the University of Chicago.

Mundell began his academic teaching career at Stanford University. Following an appointment with the Johns Hopkins Bologna Center for Advanced International Studies in Italy, in 1961 he joined the International Monetary Fund (IMF). While at the IMF, Mundell devoted his study to the most efficient combination of fiscal and monetary policy for a country. The result was a paper, "Appropriate Use of Monetary and Fiscal Policy for Internal and External Stability." In the paper, Mundell presented a counterargument to the U.S. policies of easy money for long-term interest rates and a budget surplus to restrain pressures of inflation. This argument by Mundell led to a change in future U.S. policy.

A second area of research for Mundell while at the IMF was on the theory of inflation. Mundell showed that an increase in inflation would increase interest rates, but less than earlier theorized by Irving Fisher and Abba Lerner. This was to later be known as the Mundell-Tobin effect. His work in monetary theory also included efforts on balance-of-payments equilibrium.

After his tenure at the International Monetary Fund, he served as the initial Rockefeller Research Professor of International Economics at the Brookings Institution for two years. In 1966, Mundell joined the economics faculty at the University of Chicago. At the University of Chicago, he was editor of the *Journal of Political Economy* and spent his summers, till 1975, at the Graduate Institute of International Studies in Geneva, Switzerland. Robert Mundell also held professorships at University of Southern California, McGill University, University of Pennsylvania, and Columbia University.

Robert Mundell is a leading proponent for a modern gold standard. His gold standard of the future would have some fundamental differences from the gold standard of post–World War II. After World War II, the world currencies were pegged to the U.S. dollar and the dollar priced to gold. Mundell claims a repricing of gold by the United States in the 1970s would have served the global community well into the future. Instead, the United States abandoned the gold standard and begun a three-decade inflationary spiral.

Mundell is the author of over 100 articles and research papers focusing on economic theory of international economics. He was one of the first to write about a common currency for Europe and later worked on the development and creation of the euro. He was a major contributor to the history of the IMF with *The International Monetary System: Conflict and Reform* in 1965. His international macroeconomics model became the standard in the discipline. In 1997, he cofounded the *Zagreb Journal of Economics*.

Robert Mundell also had his critics. His advocating for a return to the gold standard in the early 1980s and to a modified fixed exchange rate system for the United States was considered insupportable by most of his colleagues in the economics profession. He was also highly criticized when he supported the "supply-side" theory of tax policy in the 1980s.

Since the 1960s, Robert Mundell has been a consultant and adviser to many international agencies, organizations, and countries. He has advised the IMF, World Bank, European Commission, Federal Reserve Board, as well as the United Nations. He has consulted and advised countries in Latin America and

Europe, and Canada. In the 1970s, he consulted with several committees and commissions of the European Union, which ultimately led to the establishment of the euro.

Robert Mundell was awarded the Nobel Prize in Economics in 1999 for his analysis of monetary and fiscal policy under different exchange rate regimes. During his illustrious career he also received the Guggenheim Prize (1971), the Jacques Rueff Medal and Prize (1983), the Docteur Honoris Causa from the University of Paris (1992), and an honorary professorship at Renmin University in China (1995). In 1997, he received the American Economic Association's Distinguished Fellow Award and became a fellow of the American Academy of Arts and Sciences the following year in 1998. A new university in China has been named in his honor: the Mundell International University of Entrepreneurship. The university is located in Zhongguancun, an area of Beijing that is known as the Silicon Valley of China.

For all his accomplishments, he himself considers most important his work in 1960 on a model that exhibits that under a floating exchange rate with perfect capital mobility, monetary policy becomes more powerful than fiscal policy. Yet if the exchange rate is fixed, the opposite is true. The model goes on to explain that if the country's exchange rate is fixed, its monetary and fiscal policies cannot be independent of each other, in the long run. Or if monetary policy is independent, the exchange rate system cannot be fixed. Mundell called this the "impossible trinity." This, he claims, caused the rush to flexible exchange rate systems in the 1970s.

*See also:* Fisher, Irving; Meade, James; Robbins, Lionel; Samuelson, Paul; Tobin, James

## Selected Works by Robert Mundell

Baldassarri, Mario, and Robert A. Mundell. *Building the New Europe: The Single Market and Monetary Unification*. New York: Macmillan, 1993.

Mundell, Robert. *International Economics*. New York: Macmillan, 1968.

Mundell, Robert. *Man and Economics: The Science of Choice*. New York: McGraw-Hill, 1968.

Mundell, Robert. *Monetary Theory: Interest, Inflation and Growth in the World Economy*. Santa Monica, CA: Goodyear, 1971.

Mundell, Robert A., Mario Baldassarri, and John McCallum. *Global Disequilibrium in the World Economy*. Rome: St. Martin's Press, Rome, 1992.

Mundell, Robert A., and Canadian Trade Committee. *The International Monetary System: Conflict and Reform*. Vol. 11, Issue 3. Ottawa, Ontario: Private Planning Association of Canada, 1965.

Mundell, Robert A., and Armand Clesse, eds. *The Euro as a Stabilizer in the International Monetary System*. Norwell, MA: Kluwer Academic, 2000.

Mundell, Robert, and Manuel Guitian, eds. *Inflation and Growth in China*. Darby, PA: DIANE, 1996.

Mundell, Robert, Jacques J. Polak, John M. Fleming, International Monetary Fund, and Columbia University, eds. *The New International Monetary System*. New York: Columbia University Press, 1977.

### Selected Works about Robert Mundell

International Monetary Fund. "People in Economics: Ahead of His Time." http://www.imf.org/external/pubs/ft/fandd/2006/09/people.htm (accessed August 2011).
Mundell, Robert A. "Autobiography." Nobelprize.org. http://www.nobelprize.org/nobel_prizes/economics/laureates/1999/mundell.html (accessed August 2011).
Wallace, Laura. "Nobel Laureate Robert Mundell: Ahead of His Time." USA Gold. http://www.usagold.com/gildedopinion/mundell.html (accessed August 2011).
*The Works of Robert Mundell*. http://robertmundell.net (accessed October 2012).

*David A. Dieterle*

## MURPHY, KEVIN

Born: 1958 in Los Angeles, California; American; econometrics, unemployment, economic growth, economic development; Major Works: *Social Economics: Market Behavior in a Social Environment* (with Gary Becker) (2000), *Measuring the Gains from Medical Research: An Economic Approach* (with Robert H. Topel) (2003).

Kevin Murphy is an American economist, widely known for utilizing economic principles to research social phenomena. Murphy is the George J. Stigler Distinguished Professor of Economics in the University of Chicago Department of Economics and Graduate School of Business. His research topics include addiction, war, unemployment, wage inequality, and medical issues. He is popular among his students and is known for wearing casual dress, including a collection of baseball hats.

Kevin M. Murphy was born in 1958 in the Los Angeles suburb Inglewood. He was the only son of an electrician who also enjoyed woodworking. He started working when he was 14, beginning by sorting soda bottles after school in an L.A. grocery store. He worked his way through the ranks at the store and continued working full-time while taking college classes at the University of California, Los Angeles. Murphy completed an AB in economics at the University of California in 1981. He worked as a research assistant at Unicon Research Corporation in Santa Monica, California, from 1979 to 1981. He then enrolled at the University of Chicago where he completed a PhD in economics in 1986. He joined the faculty of the University of Chicago Booth School of Business in 1984.

In 1997, Murphy was awarded the John Bates Clark Medal of the American Economic Association. The Clark Medal is awarded every two years to an outstanding economist under the age of 40. At the time of the award, he was recognized for his studies of wage inequality among white-collar and blue-collar workers. In researching that inequality, Murphy and his colleagues found that the increased demand for skilled labor rather than other factors, like increased international trade, caused growth in the wage inequality. Murphy was chosen as a MacArthur fellow in 2005. His selection was based on his work on social issues including unemployment, wage inequality, medical research, addiction, and economic growth.

Among Murphy's most prominent research is his work on the economics of addiction. He and his colleagues studied cigarette consumption and developed a model that explained how the cigarette industry managed to increase profits for manufacturers despite decreasing demand for their products.

Murphy has also looked at the value of education, researching the impact education has on health and choices for consumer goods. He and his colleagues have also studied the way the market responds to consumers who are educated. Murphy has explored the personal choices consumers make to improve longevity. For example, they may choose less-risky jobs and cars that are supposed to be safer.

Murphy's research has also included health care. In areas such as heart disease and cancer, he found that investments in basic health research and care result in great returns in economic value. Among his other health care research findings was the insight that increased longevity, much of it due to advances in medical research, added to the total wealth of the United States. One of the conclusions was that current expenditures in medical research are small relative to the value of potential gains.

Murphy has also tackled political topics from an economic perspective. For example, he and his colleagues studied the Iraq War. They found that the war was expensive for the United States, but that it was actually less expensive than the policy of containment of the Saddam Hussein regime had been.

In addition to his position at the University of Chicago, Murphy is employed as a faculty research associate for the National Bureau of Economic Research where he continues his research on the empirical analysis of inequality, unemployment, and relative wages.

Murphy is the George J. Stigler Distinguished Professor of Economics in the Department of Economics and Graduate School of Business. In addition to the books mentioned earlier, Murphy has written numerous articles that appeared in such publications as the *Journal of Law and Economics*, *Journal of Political Economy*, and *American Economic Review*.

*See also:* Arrow, Kenneth; Becker, Gary; Stigler, George

## Selected Works by Kevin Murphy

Murphy, Kevin, and Gary Becker. *Social Economics: Market Behavior in a Social Environment*. Cambridge, MA: Harvard University Press, 2000.

Murphy, Kevin M., Gary S. Becker, and Michael Grossman. "An Empirical Analysis of Cigarette Addiction." *American Economic Review* 84, no. 3 (1994): 396–418.

Murphy, Kevin, Gary S. Becker, and Michael Grossman; "The Market for Illegal Goods: The Case for Drugs." *Journal of Political Economy* 114, no. 1 (2006): 38–60. http://dx.doi.org/10.1086/427463.

Murphy, Kevin, Steven J. Davis, and Robert H. Topel. "War in Iraq versus Containment." In *Guns and Butter: The Economic Causes and Consequences of Conflict*. Edited by Gregory D. Hess, 203–70. Cambridge, MA: MIT Press, 2009.

Murphy, Kevin, and Robert H. Topel. *Measuring the Gains from Medical Research: An Economic Approach*. Chicago: University of Chicago Press, 2003.

### Selected Works about Kevin Murphy

Easton, John. "Murphy's Law." University of Chicago Magazine. December 14, 2011. http://magazine.uchicago.edu/0612/features/murphy-print.shtml (accessed March 2012).

Freiss, Steve. "The Cost of War: At What Price, War? Or, for That Matter, at What Price Peace?" Chicago Booth Magazine. http://www.chicagobooth.edu/magazine/vol29/issue01/cover.aspx?pf=y (accessed March 2012).

University of Chicago News Office. "Kevin M. Murphy Wins 1997 Clark Medal." March 14, 1997. http://www-news.uchicago.edu/releases/97/970314.murphy.shtml (accessed March 2012).

Welch, Finis. "In Honor of Kevin M. Murphy: Winner of the John Bates Clark Medal." *Journal of Economic Perspectives* 14 (Summer 2000): 193–204.

*Diane Fournier*

# MYERSON, ROGER

Born: March 29, 1951, in Boston, Massachusetts; American; mechanism design theory, game theory, incentive constraints, Nobel Prize (2007); Major Works: *Game Theory: Analysis of Conflict* (1991), *Probability Models for Economic Decisions* (2005).

Roger Myerson is an American academic best known in the fields of economics and political science for his work on game theory. His work has included models for conflict and cooperation. In particular he is applauded for his mechanism design theory. Myerson acknowledged that there are multiple equilibria (conditions of equality between demand and supply) in a model of a rational bargaining because in a given situation people can be satisfied with more than one outcome. To design a predictive model one must use the values of equity and efficiency to identify a focal equilibrium or an equilibrium on which players can agree. Myerson won the 2007 Nobel Prize.

Roger Bruce Myerson was born on March 29, 1951, in the suburbs of Boston. The climate of his childhood, like most Cold War children, was punctuated by the constant threat of nuclear war, which troubled him greatly. He was inspired to take action to end the Cold War by his father who was an applied engineering researcher and a proponent of higher education. On his father's suggestion, he became passionate about cultivating the wisdom necessary to improve relationships between nations.

Myerson completed his graduate studies in applied mathematics at Harvard in 1976. His doctoral thesis was entitled "A Theory of Cooperative Games," in which he argued there is no one outcome of a situation that would be preferred by all players. Instead, different alternatives are preferable for different people. Therefore to find an equitable bargain each player should receive compensation equivalent to his or her efforts.

During his early career at Northwestern University's Kellogg School of Management in the Managerial Economics and Decision Sciences Department, Myerson worked on perfecting an equitable bargaining solution. His early influences included John Nash, Thomas Schelling, and Reinhard von Neumann.

Myerson's first papers at Northwestern acknowledged that there are multiple equilibria in a model of rational bargaining because in a given situation people can be satisfied with more than one outcome. To design a predictive model one must use the values of equity and efficiency to identify a focal equilibrium or an equilibrium that players can agree satisfies their goals. This focal point can be determined through simple folkways or by a third party who is recognized as a neutral social leader. In this scenario, all players agree on a goal and one can predict the route they will take to achieve this goal. In 2001, Myerson moved to the south side of Chicago, joining the faculty at the University of Chicago.

An important early work, "Two-Person Bargaining Problems with Incomplete Information," was published in 1984 in the journal *Econometrica*. The article extended the Nash bargaining solution, solving the problem of two parties agreeing on an equilibrium. It also addressed the Shapley value, proposing the just allocation of resources according to the contribution of all players.

In the later 1980s, Myerson turned his attention to the creation of textbooks where microeconomic analysis had begun to recognize game theory. One such textbook, *Game Theory: Analysis of Conflict*, was published in 1991. In 2005, he published the textbook *Probability Models for Economic Decisions*.

His work on synthesizing game theory included consideration of markets with adverse selection. This gave rise to a version of Gresham's law. Gresham's law professes that bad or undervalued money will replace good or properly valued money. Using this analogy, Myerson suggested that bad types of game-playing behavior may be more common than good types in the market given the limited information that exists. Players may then choose what information to reveal.

Myerson saw this model as directly applicable to political systems, particularly electoral systems in constitutional democracies. Because the structure of these systems dictates the rules of play, these structures will determine the conduct of politicians. In particular, they will determine the exclusivity of political power. The more exclusive access to political office becomes, the more corrupt a government will tend to be. He also identified that significant incentives exist for politicians to compete at the center of the political spectrum where they are more likely to gain a greater political profit.

Myerson identified the distribution of constitutional powers as another factor in political decisions. For example, presidential veto powers and bicameral legislatures can decrease cooperation among political figures. Myerson has created mathematical theories that suggest political figures must be seen serving the greater public good while taking special care to provide for their base. He has also done extensive work to modify the pedagogy for probability models.

In the late 1990s, Myerson turned his political economic theories on historical events. Examining the history of the Weimar Republic, with the guidance of the most brilliant economists and political theorists of that era, he asked whether today's more advanced theories would aid in the development of a better constitutional design that eliminated the mistakes that existed in 1920s Germany. Those ideas that offered the most hope for the future related to analysis of strategic credibility. When his ideas were applied to the Iraq War, Myerson argued that the inability of the United States to place credible limits on the force it intended to use motivated potential adversaries to build up their own defenses. According to Myerson, had the United States understood the importance of a neutral third party in situations where each player guards private information, perhaps it would have chosen to enlist the help of the United Nations rather than pursuing unilateral solutions.

In 2007, Myerson was awarded the Nobel Prize in Economics for his contributions to mechanism design theory (game theory) and incentive constraints. He shared the prize with Russian-born American Leonid Hurwicz and American Eric Maskin.

Myerson continues in the economics department at the University of Chicago.

*See also:* Hurwicz, Leonid; Maskin, Eric; Nash, John; Schelling, Thomas

### Selected Works by Roger Myerson

Myerson, Roger. "Effectiveness of Electoral Systems for Reducing Government Corruption: A Game-Theoretic Analysis." *Games and Economic Behavior* 5 (1993): 118–32.

Myerson, Roger. *Game Theory: Analysis of Conflict.* Cambridge, MA: Harvard University Press, 1991.

Myerson, Roger. *Probability Models for Economic Decisions.* Pacific Grove, CA: Duxbury Press, 2005.

Myerson, Roger. "Two-Person Bargaining Problems with Incomplete Information." *Econometrica* 52 (1984): 461–88.

### Selected Works about Roger Myerson

Harms, William. "Roger Myerson Wins 2007 Nobel Memorial Prize in Economics." October 15, 2007. University of Chicago News Office. http://www-news.uchicago.edu/releases/07/071015.nobel.myerson.shtml (accessed September 2012).

Myerson, Roger. "Autobiography." Nobelprize.org. http://www.nobelprize.org/nobel_prizes/economics/laureates/2007/myerson.html (accessed October 2012).

*Rebecca Kraft*

## MYRDAL, GUNNAR

Born: December 6, 1898, in Gustav, Dalarna, Sweden; Died: May 17, 1987, in Danderyd, Sweden; Swedish; institutional economics, development economics, theory of money, Nobel Prize (1974); Major Works: *Monetary Equilibrium* (1939), *An American Dilemma: The Negro Problem and Modern Democracy* (1944), *The Political Elements in the Development of Economic Theory* (translated into English, 1954).

Gunnar Myrdal was a Swedish institutionalist economist, awarded the 1974 Nobel Prize in Economics (with Friedrich von Hayek) for his interdisciplinary approach to explaining economic phenomena. When a share of the 1982 Nobel Peace Prize was awarded to his wife Alva, he became part of the third husband-and-wife pairing of Nobel winners. In addition to the scholarship produced as an economist, Myrdal also served as a member of Swedish Parliament, was executive secretary of the United Nations Economic Commission for Europe from 1947 to 1957, and founded the Institute of International Economic Research in Stockholm. Myrdal died in 1987.

Karl Gunnar Myrdal was born on December 6, 1898, in Gustav, Dalarna, Sweden. Gunnar attended Stockholm University where he earned a law degree in 1923. He continued his education at the university and in 1927 earned his doctorate in economics.

Much of Myrdal's work was deemed controversial at the time of publication but gained broader acceptance later on. Reception of Myrdal was delayed also because he originally published in Swedish, and his texts were not immediately translated to other languages. For example, *The Political Elements in the Development of Economic Theory* was published in Swedish in 1930 but was not reprinted in English until 1954.

Gunnar Myrdal gained international fame for his 1944 study of race relations in the United States, *An American Dilemma*. (UPI-Bettmann/Corbis)

His work *Monetary Equilibrium* (1939) focused on what many defined as the key arguments for an expansive fiscal policy approach used by many governments today. Not only did this work outline a framework in which fiscal policy may be used, the work predated the much more commonly known *General Theory of Employment, Interest and Money* of John Maynard Keynes.

A self-described institutionalist and one of the founders of the Stockholm School, Myrdal refined his work and ideas over time. Of *The Political Elements in the Development of Economic Theory* (1954) and other early works, he later noted that the normative elements he had defined did not have the impact on an economy as initially imagined.

Myrdal's *An American Dilemma: The Negro Problem and Modern Democracy* (1944) was a study of African Americans beginning in 1870. Not only did the extensive work focus on economics, the author incorporated the other social sciences (history, sociology, political science) and gains the insight from other scholars in those fields to elicit a coordinative whole. The findings of this work suggested three interdependent types of causal factors to explain the experience of African Americans after the U.S. Civil War, of which economics were one, high moral standards of living a second, and discrimination the third, interacting as either vicious or virtuous cycles. One of Myrdal's key insights was that economic models alone could either be too simplistic and not representative of everyday life, or include factors from other disciplines that are difficult to conceptualize and quantify. The broad influence of this book is demonstrated by the U.S. Supreme Court's *Brown v. the Board of Education of Topeka* decision in 1954, which cited Myrdal's work and noted that the prior legal doctrine of "separate but equal" schools violated the Equal Protection Clause of the U.S. Constitution.

In the 1960s, Myrdal's focus turned to the poverty and underdevelopment within Asia. *Asian Drama: An Inquiry into the Poverty of Nations* (1968) provided background information upon which policy could be based, as the work presented two long-lasting implications. First, one could not pursue a solution to a problem until the current conditions were fully articulated. Second, the approach presented by Myrdal relied upon much more than the routine government expenditures traditionally seen as solutions to broader economic and social concerns. A later work, *The Challenge of World Poverty: A World Anti-poverty Program in Outline* (1970), reexamined existing models of trade theory given persistent—but at that point ignored or unexplained—differences in per capita income among trading partners. During his Nobel lecture, Myrdal focused on the use of aid from developed nations, land reform, and the choices made by developed nations and the citizens thereof, questioning at times the lack of interest in solving the global problems he perceived.

Myrdal was awarded the Nobel Prize in Economics in 1974 with coawardee Friedrich von Hayek. Myrdal was cited for his groundbreaking analysis of economic variations brought on by economic, social, and institutional interdependence and his work on the theory of money. Given that Myrdal and von Hayek had worked to develop original and conflicting viewpoints over the analyses for which they were awarded the Nobel Prize, the award to both in the same year was viewed as somewhat of a controversy among some theorists, including the awardee himself.

Gunnar Myrdal died on May 17, 1987, in Danderyd, Sweden.

*See also:* Cassel, Gustav; Hayek, Friedrich von; Keynes, John Maynard; Mises, Ludwig von

### Selected Works by Gunnar Myrdal

Myrdal, Gunnar. *Asian Drama: An Inquiry into the Poverty of Nations.* Vols. 1–3. New York: Twentieth Century Fund, 1968.

Myrdal, Gunnar. *The Challenge of World Poverty: A world Anti-poverty Program in Outline.* New York: Pantheon Books, 1970.

Myrdal, Gunnar. *Monetary Equilibrium.* London: W. Hodge, 1939.

Myrdal, Gunnar. *The Political Element in the Development of Economic Theory*. Cambridge, MA: Harvard University Press, 1954.

Myrdal, Gunnar, and Sissela Bok. *An American Dilemma: The Negro Problem and Modern Democracy*. Piscataway, NJ: Transaction, 1944.

## Selected Works about Gunnar Myrdal

Barber, William J. *Gunnar Myrdal: An Intellectual Biography*. Hampshire, UK: Palgrave Macmillan, 2007.

Brittan, S. "The Not So Noble Nobel Prize." *Financial Times*, December 19, 2003, 21.

"Gunnar K. Myrdal: Biography." Nobelprize.org. http://www.nobelprize.org/nobel_prizes/economics/laureates/1974/myrdal.html (accessed September 2011).

Karierk, Tom. *Intellectual Capital: Forty Years of the Nobel Prize in Economics*. New York: Cambridge University Press, 2010.

Lundberg, E. "Gunnar Myrdal's Contribution to Economic Theory." *The Swedish Journal of Economics* 74, no. 4 (1974): 472–78.

Reynolds, L. G. "Gunnar Myrdal's Contribution to Economics, 1940–1970." *The Swedish Journal of Economics* 74, no. 4 (1974): 479–97.

*Michael B. Becraft*

## NASH, JOHN

Born: June 13, 1928, in Bluefield, West Virginia; American; game theory, Nash equilibrium, mathematics; Major Works: "Equilibrium Points in N-Person Games" (1950), "The Bargaining Problem" (1950), "Non-cooperative Games" (1951), "Two-Person Cooperative Games" (1953).

John Nash is a mathematician who developed advanced studies of game theory that expanded their application to broad categories of political science, economics, business strategy, biology, and personal interactions. In 1994, he was awarded the Nobel Prize in Economics for his work in game theory with John Harsanyi and Reinhard Selten. Nash equilibrium is the most widely used and applied solution concept of game theory. Nash was the subject of the 2002 film *A Beautiful Mind*, which portrayed his struggle with paranoid schizophrenia.

John Forbes Nash was born on June 13, 1928, in Bluefield, West Virginia. He was raised in a highly intellectual environment and developed advanced mathematical skills as a child. Awarded the coveted George Westinghouse Scholarship, he began his undergraduate studies at Carnegie Institute of Technology (now Carnegie Mellon University) in chemical engineering. He did not care for the regimentation of the engineering classes or the quantitative analysis of the chemistry classes and changed to mathematics.

From an international economics course at Carnegie, he derived the idea for his paper "The Bargaining Problem" and ultimately his interest in game theory. By graduation he had progressed in his studies of mathematics and was awarded an MA degree in addition to the BS degree.

He was offered fellowships to both Harvard University and Princeton University for further studies in mathematics.

He chose Princeton because it was closer to home. During his graduate studies one of his discoveries led to "Noncooperative Games." He concurrently developed two theses, one in game theory and one based on his discovery relating to manifolds and real algebraic varieties.

His academic career began in 1950 at Princeton where he taught for one year. In 1951, he accepted a higher-paying position as a C.L.E. Moore instructor at the Massachusetts Institute of Technology (MIT) where he remained till 1959. During this time he solved a problem relating to differential geometry as well as developed the theorem known as the Nash embedding theorem.

He accepted the Alfred P. Sloan grant and returned to Princeton as a member of the Institute for Advanced Studies (IAS). While at IAS, he solved a problem involving partial differential equations. Unbeknownst to him, Ennio de Giorgi of Pisa,

Princeton University professor John Nash poses on the university's campus in Princeton, New Jersey, in 1994 when he was named the winner of the Nobel Prize in economics. (AP/Wide World Photos)

Italy, was also working on the problem and solved it prior to Nash. Had only one of the men solved this equation, it is speculated that he would have received the famous mathematics Field Medal.

John Nash made important contributions to game theory research. Game theory allows social scientists to evaluate interactive decision making when the outcome for one participant is dependent on the actions or strategies of all other participants. Nash introduced the distinction of identifying cooperative and noncooperative games. Cooperative games allow players to form binding enforceable agreements and make irrevocable threats to other players. Noncooperative games do not allow for such possibilities. The science of game theory can be applied broadly in the areas of experimental economics, behavioral economics, industrial organization, and political economy. Noncooperative games are accurate at understanding and predicting social interactions, voting behaviors, fair division, auction, mergers and acquisitions, corporate compensation plans, bargaining systems, oligopolies, and duopolies. Nash identified the equilibrium point in such games. It is a set of strategies and the corresponding pay-offs when no player may benefit by changing his strategy while other players leave their strategies unchanged.

A player would not choose to change his or her strategy for optimal outcome even after learning the strategies of other players. This is known as Nash equilibrium. Nash equilibrium is the most widely used and applied solution concept of game theory because it yields the most accurate insights into the workings of the social situation to which it is applied. In 1994, John Nash, with John Harsanyi and Reinhard Selten, received the Nobel Memorial Prize in Economic Sciences as a result of his game theory work as a graduate student at Princeton.

John Nash struggled with paranoid schizophrenia beginning in early 1959, which resulted in an involuntary hospital stay, his resignation from MIT, and an attempt to renounce his U.S. citizenship, seeking political asylum in France and East Germany. His experience was portrayed in Sylvia Nasar's 1998 movie *A Beautiful Mind*. He later spoke out against Nasar's false depiction that he recovered as a result of atypical antipsychotics when in fact he refused any medication after 1970. He credits his recovery to his decision to renounce his delusional hypotheses and to return to rational thought.

In addition to the Nobel Prize in 1994, Nash has been awarded the John von Neumann Theory Prize for his discovery of Nash equilibria (1978) and several honorary degrees and doctorates.

*See also:* Harsanyi, John; Selten, Reinhard

### Selected Works by John Nash

Nash, John. "The Bargaining Problem." *Econometrica* 18 (1950): 155–62.
Nash, John. "Equilibrium Points in *N*-Person Games." *Proceedings of the National Academy of Sciences* 36 (1950): 48–49.
Nash, John. "Non-cooperative Games." PhD thesis, Princeton University, 1950.
Nash, John. "Non-cooperative Games." *Annals of Mathematics* 54 (1951): 286—95.
Nash, John. "Two-Person Cooperative Games." *Econometrica* 21 (1953): 128–40.

### Selected Works about John Nash

Nash, John F., Jr. "Autobiography." Nobelprize.org. http://www.nobelprize.org/nobel_prizes/economics/laureates/1994/nash.html (accessed September 2012).
"National Cryptologic Museum Opens New Exhibit on Dr. John Nash." National Security Agency. 2012 press release. http://www.nsa.gov/public_info/press_room/2012/nash_exhibit.shtml (accessed September 2012).
Nisan, Noam. "John Nash's Letter to the NSA." February 17, 2012. Turing's Invisible Hand: Computation, Economics, and Game Theory. http://agtb.wordpress.com/2012/02/17/john-nashs-letter-to-the-nsa/ (accessed September 2012).

*Heather Isom*

# NORTH, DOUGLASS

Born: November 5, 1920, in Cambridge, Massachusetts; American; economic history, institutional economics, cliometrics, Nobel Prize (1993); Major Works: *The Economic Growth of the United States, 1790–1860* (1961), *Structure and Change in Economic History* (1981), *Institutions, Institutional Change and Economic Performance* (1990).

Douglass North is an American economist whose work in economic history and institutional economics earned him the 1993 Nobel Prize in Economics. North helped found the field of cliometrics (named after Clio, the muse of history), which applies economics and quantitative methods to the study of economic history. His interest in institutional economics shaped how the discipline views the role of institutions and property rights in economic growth. North was influential in understanding how people make choices. North was particularly interested in the way that individuals' ideas, beliefs, and prejudices influence their decision making, often in ways that hinder growth.

Douglass Cecil North was born on November 5, 1920, in Cambridge, Massachusetts. His mother was a strong believer in education, reflected by his early schooling experiences. He attended school in Lausanne, Switzerland, Ottawa, Canada, New York City, Long Island, and Choate Academy in Connecticut. He also developed a strong passion for photography, winning several awards in high school. Though he had been accepted at Harvard University, he followed his family to the West Coast when his father accepted a new position. He did his undergraduate work at the University of California, Berkeley (UC Berkeley). His academic record at UC Berkeley was only slightly above average, although he pursued a triple major in philosophy, political science, and economics.

While at Berkeley, North became a Marxist and a pacifist. He graduated from Berkeley and spent time pursuing photography, working with Dorothea Lange photographing migrant workers in California for the Farm Services Administration. When World War II broke out, North joined the Merchant Marines and became a navigator. He would even teach celo-navigation at the Maritime Service Officer School in Alameda, California.

North returned to Berkeley after the war for his graduate work in economics, graduating in 1952. By his own admission, he did not learn much theory there. It was during his first position at the University of Washington that the situation changed. As a result of his dissertation, North received a fellowship from the Social Science Research Council, which allowed him to go to the East Coast. There he attended classes taught by Robert Merton at Columbia, and Arthur Cole and Joseph Schumpeter at Harvard. North was invited to be a fellow at the National Bureau of Economic Research (NBER) where, from 1957 to 1958, he would work on a quantitative study of the U.S. balance of payments from 1790 to 1860. This would lead to his first major work, *The Economic Growth of the United States, 1790–1860*.

It was also during this time that North helped found the field of cliometrics (named after Clio, the muse of history), which applies economics and quantitative methods to the study of economic history. It was the result of a joint program of the NBER and the Economic History Association on the growth of the American economy. As a result of the program, two of North's former students, John Hughes and Lance Davis, both faculty members at Purdue University, held a conference for economic historians. That meeting would be a seminal moment in the field of cliometrics, and North would be involved in setting up a program at the University of Washington.

In the late 1960s, North turned his attention from American economic history to European economic history. Under the auspices of a Ford Foundation grant, North spent a year in Geneva studying European economic history. While there, North decided that neoclassical economics did not provide the proper tools for explaining the economic change in Europe from medieval times to the present.

In the area of institutional economics, one of the issues North confronted was the prevailing idea that institutions were always efficient. He found that this was not true for some economies and challenged the rationality postulate that provides the foundation for economic analysis. North and others found that individual ideas, beliefs, and prejudices were an important factor in shaping decisions, and that they could keep a society from developing efficient economic institutions that promoted growth. The result was that some societies would find themselves locked into dysfunctional institutions, actually providing a barrier to further development and growth.

By 1983, North was looking for a new environment to help him with his puzzles. He saw an opportunity when he was invited to join the faculty of Washington University in St. Louis. North established the Center in Political Economy, as well as the Center for New Institutional Social Studies to continue to study the effect of institutions on choice. North was convinced that understanding how people make choices when the conditions are uncertain was central to further research in human behavior.

In April 1985, he was appointed editor of the Cambridge series *The Political Economy of Institutions and Decisions*, editor of the *Journal of Economic History*, and president of the Economic History Association. North was elected to the American Academy of Arts and Sciences in 1987. In 1993, Douglass North along with Robert Fogel were awarded the Nobel Prize in Economics.

Douglass North's academic appointments have included the Peterkin Professor of Political Economics at Rice University in 1979 and the Pitt Professor at Cambridge University in 1981. North was also a visiting fellow at the Center for Advanced Studies in in Behavioral Sciences and the Hoover Institute at Stanford University. He was the Luce Professor of Law and Liberty at Washington University in 1983 and the Spencer T. Olin Professor of Arts & Sciences at Washington University in 1996.

*See also:* Fogel, Robert; Merton, Robert; Schumpeter, Joseph

## Selected Works by Douglass North

North, Douglass. *The Economic Growth of the United States, 1790–1860*. Englewood Cliffs, NJ: Prentice-Hall, 1961.

North, Douglass. *Institutions, Institutional Change and Economic Performance*. Cambridge: Cambridge University Press, 1990.

North, Douglass. *Structure and Change in Economic History*. New York: Norton, 1981.

North, Douglass. *Understanding the Process of Economic Change*. Princeton, NJ: Princeton University Press, 2005.

### Selected Works about Douglass North

Breit, William, and Barry T. Hirsch. *Lives of the Laureates*. Cambridge, MA: MIT Press, 2004.
"Douglass C. North." In *The Concise Encyclopedia of Economics*. Edited by David R. Henderson. The Library of Economics and Liberty. http://www.econlib.org/library/Enc/bios/North.html (accessed March 2012).
Hoover Institution Stanford University. "Douglass C. North, Bartlett Burnap Senior Fellow." http://www.hoover.org/fellows/10069 (accessed March 2012).
Mokyr, Joel, ed. *The Economics of the Industrial Revolution*. Lanham, MD: Rowman & Littlefield, 1985.
North, Douglass C. "Autobiography." NobelPrize.org. http://www.nobelprize.org/nobel_prizes/economics/laureates/1993/north-autobio.html (accessed March 2012).

*Timothy P. Schilling*

# NORTH, SIR DUDLEY

Born: May 16, 1641 in Westminster, England (now London); Died: December 31, 1691, in London, England; English; merchant, civil servant, economist; Major Work: *Discourses upon Trade: Principally Directed to the Case of the Interest, Coynage, Clipping, Increase of Money* (1691).

Sir Dudley North was one of the earliest proponents of free trade during the early U.S. era and is famed for the contribution to political economy he made in his *Discourses upon Trade*. Contrary to the older mercantilist view that trade was the exchange of goods not needed by the producing country, the *Discourses* insisted the entire world is essentially one global market. *Discourses* denounced sumptuary laws and legal restrictions on interest rates as harmful and ineffective. Though the *Discourses* preceded Adam Smith's doctrines and those of the free-trade school, it was free from the prejudices and fallacies of the mercantile system. North died in London in 1691.

Sir Dudley North was born on May 16, 1641, in Westminster, England (now in London), fourth son of Dudley, 4th Lord North. North engaged in foreign trade with the eastern Mediterranean, especially with Turkey, at an early age and spent a number of years serving as an agent for the Turkey Company in Constantinople (now Istanbul) and resided in Smyrna (now Izmir) from 1662 to 1680. He returned to England a wealthy man in 1680.

In England, North's experience in international commerce attracted the attention of the government. The influence of his brother Lord Guilford helped him secure an official post. During the Tory reaction under Charles II, he served as one of the sheriffs of the City of London with an express agenda of securing verdicts for the crown in state trials. He received a knighthood and was appointed a commissioner of customs and of treasury afterward.

Under James II, North was appointed a commissioner of customs. Having been elected a member of Parliament, he took the place of manager for the crown in all matters of revenue. After the Glorious Revolution (1688–89), he was called to account for his alleged unconstitutional proceedings in his office of sheriff. He retired a confirmed Tory shortly after the Revolution.

In 1691 North's most famous work, *Discourses upon Trade*, focused mainly on issues of interest, coinage, clipping, and increase of money, was published anonymously. For more than a century, his work remained neglected and forgotten until J. R. McCulloch edited and published it in the *Select Collection of Early English Tracts on Commerce*, printed by the Political Economy Club of London in 1856. It received more favorable notice during the economic discussions regarding the bank restriction and the Corn Laws debates. One particular group of liberals calling themselves "political economists" was drawn to the references made by North's brother Roger to the "Discourse."

In the *Discourses*, North meticulously and emphatically asserted the free-trade doctrine against the system of prohibitions that had gained strength by the Revolution. It was one of the earliest attempts to theorize as a whole the workings of a market economy in England with an emphasis, more so than the work of his predecessors, on the value of the home trade. There are two discourses in this work: one concerning "the abatement of interest" and the other on "coyned money."

According to North, wealth may exist independently of gold or silver, for its source is human industry, applied either to the cultivation of the soil or to manufactures. He maintained that the stagnation of trade arises not from want of money but either from a surplus of the home market, or a disturbance of foreign commerce, or from diminished consumption caused by poverty. Since trade is an exchange of surplus of goods among nations, he asserted, the export of money increases, instead of diminishing, the national wealth. He argued that nations are related to the world in just the same way as cities to the state or as families to the city. Unlike his colleagues of the time who were concerned about the problems of international money and bullion movements, North tried to exhibit the *structure* of the flow of trade and money in economic systems, both national and international, such that he was able to concentrate on the nature and significance of monetary *circulation* in the economy, rather than solely on money as such.

Concerning the discussion on interest rates, North emphasized the supply of savings as a key factor to determining interest rates. With John Locke, North argued that a low interest rate is a result not a cause of prosperous economic conditions, of the relative increase of capital, and cannot be brought about by arbitrary regulations, as had been proposed by Josiah Child and others. Thus North was largely keen on explaining the supply side of the loan markets, emphasizing the supply of savings or "stock." The demand side of the loan markets was perceived to be composed mainly of persons wishing to borrow for consumption expenditure.

In arguing in defense of free trade, North argued that the public benefits from trade without the interference of government or state regulations; when trade thrives, so does the public. Prices must be determined by the interaction of buyers and sellers because any forcible interference with them does harm instead of good. It is only due to peace, industry, freedom, and unimpeded economic activity that the wealth of people is increased, not due to state regulations. North was named by Wilhelm Roscher as one of that great triumvirate that in the seventeenth century raised the English school of economists to the foremost place in Europe, the other members of the group being Locke and Petty. North's works and views of things were closely related to those of Adam Smith's great work some 80 years later.

Sir Dudley North died on the December 31, 1691.

*See also:* Child, Josiah; Locke, John; Petty, William; Smith, Adam

### Selected Works by Sir Dudley North

North, Dudley. *Discourses upon Trade: Principally Directed to the Case of the Interest, Coynage, Clipping, Increase of Money* (1691). Ann Arbor, MI: EEBO Editions, 2011.

### Selected Works about Sir Dudley North

Grassby, Richard. *The English Gentleman in Trade: The Life and Works of Sir Dudley North, 1641–1691.* Oxford: Oxford University Press, 1994.

Letwin, William. "The Authorship of Sir Dudley North's Discourses on Trade." *Economica* New Series 18 (1951): 35–56.

McCulloch, John R. *A Discourse on the Rise, Progress, Peculiar Objects, and Importance of Political Economy: Containing an Outline of a Course of Lectures on the Principles and Doctrines of That Science.* Edinburgh: A. Constable, 1824.

*Ninee Shoua Yang*

## OHLIN, BERTIL

Born: April 23, 1899, in Klippan, Sweden; Died: August 3, 1979, in Åre, Sweden; Swedish; economist, politician, international trade, monetary policy, political economy, Nobel Prize (1977); Major Work: *Interregional and International Trade* (1933)

Bertil Ohlin was a well-known early twentieth-century economics professor, lecturer, and well-known politician in Sweden during the period of World War II. Awarded the Nobel Prize in 1977, Ohlin is famous for his work in international trade and monetary policy. He was professor at University of Copenhagen and Stockholm Business School. Ohlin became a member of the Swedish Parliament in 1938 and served as leader of the Liberal Party in Sweden. Ohlin died in 1979.

Bertil Gotthard Ohlin was born on April 23, 1899, in Klippan, a village in southern Sweden in an upper-middle-class family of seven children. He attended the University of Lund to study mathematics, statistics, and economics, the latter of which became his expertise. He obtained the degree fil kand, the equivalent of a bachelor of arts, after two years of study in 1917 under Smil Sommarin. Intrigued by the writing of Eli Heckscher about the economics of the world war, Ohlin decided to take up studies at the Stockholm Business School. He studied there for two years before moving to the philosophy department at Stockholm University under the teaching of Gustav Cassel and Gosta Bagge.

Ohlin became a member of the Political Economy Club, formed in 1918, a group of trained economists that met to discuss theories and opinions about scientific work in economics. In 1922, he visited Cambridge, England, with a stipend from the Swedish-American Foundation. The following year, Ohlin attended Harvard University where he received his MA in 1923. He returned to Sweden and received his doctorate degree under Cassel as adviser in 1924 from Stockholm University. Later that year he accepted the position of assistant professor at the University of Copenhagen with the aid of his teacher at Stockholm, Heckscher, in 1925. He taught there until 1930 when he moved back to Sweden to succeed Heckscher at the Stockholm School of Business where he would remain until 1965.

Ohlin's expertise led him to prepare a report titled *The Course and Phases of the World Economic Depression* for Geneva in late 1931. He also gave a lecture at the Nordic Economic Conference in 1931 about combining deficit financial and monetary policies to help remedy the world depression.

In 1933, Ohlin published his most well-known work, *Interregional and International Trade*. In this work, Ohlin discussed the international trade problem, expanding on the work of Heckscher's paper about foreign trade and distribution of income. Ohlin asserted in his work that trade between economies worked based on the price systems relative to the labor and capital resources of nations and its comparative advantages. According to Ohlin's work, nations will export goods that use relatively cheap and abundant resources, while importing goods in which capital and labor resources are relatively more scarce. Some economists believed he was exaggerating Heckscher's work, a claim that Ohlin disputed. Their ideas together became known as the Heckscher-Ohlin model, widely used by economists to analyze international trade.

By invitation, Ohlin delivered the Marshall Lectures at Cambridge in 1936. In his work, he encapsulated the Swedish theory of economics, making considerable connections to the work of John Maynard Keynes. Parts of his lectures were published in 1937 in the *Economic Journal* in an article titled "The Stockholm Theory of Saving and Investment." By 1938, Ohlin's political involvement accelerated by his membership into the Riksdag, the Swedish Parliament. As the climate of world war was erupting, his scope turned from scientific to political.

By 1944, Ohlin became leader of the Liberal Party, the opposition to the Social Democratic Party in Sweden. During his tenure as leader, he was a regular contributor of articles to leading Swedish newspapers. Ohlin served as the minister of trade from 1944 to 1945. His conviction with the Liberal Party did come into conflict with the more classical liberal views of his former teacher Heckscher. Ohlin asserted in his writings to Heckscher that among his motivations for loyalty to the Liberal Party were to help the poorest. He remained with the Liberal Party, which leaned to social reform measures, the opposite of free-market economics, but was not favorable to the nationalization of industry in Sweden. He remained a member of the Riksdag until 1970, afterward shifting his focus back to lecturing and scientific work in monetary theory and international economic problems.

Ohlin published nearly 1,200 articles during his career. He was awarded the Sveriges Riksbank Prize in Economic Sciences in Memory of Alfred Nobel in 1977 jointly with James E. Meade for their contributions to international trade and monetary policy.

Bertil Ohlin died on August 3, 1979, in Åre, Sweden.

*See also:* Cassel, Gustav; Keynes, John Maynard; Meade, James; Myrdal, Gunnar

## Selected Works by Bertil Ohlin

Ohlin, Bertil. *Interregional and International Trade.* Cambridge, MA: Harvard University Press, 1933.

Ohlin, Bertil. "Some Notes on the Stockholm Theory of Saving and Investment." 2 parts. *Economic Journal* 47 (March): 53–69; (June): 221–40. Reprinted in G. Haberler, ed., *Readings in Business Cycle Theory.* Philadelphia: Blakiston, 1951.

## Selected Works about Bertil Ohlin

Caplanova, Anetta. "Bertil Gotthard Ohlin." *BIATEC* 12 (2004): 20–23.

Carlson, Benny, and Lars Jonung. "Knut Wicksell, Gustav Cassel, Eli Heckscher, Bertil Ohlin, and Gunnar Myrdal on the Role of the Economist in Public Debate." *Econ Journal Watch* 3, no. 3 (2006): 511–50.

Findlay, Ronald, Lars Jonung, and Mats Lundahl. *Bertil Ohlin: A Centennial Celebration, 1899–1999.* Cambridge, MA: MIT Press, 2002.

Ohlin, Bertil. "Autobiography." NobelPrize.org. http://www.nobelprize.org/nobel_prizes/economics/laureates/1977/ohlin.html (accessed July 2012).

*Sara Standen*

## OKUN, ARTHUR

Born: November 28, 1928, in Jersey City, New Jersey; Died: March 23, 1980, in Washington, DC; American; neo-Keynesian, econometrics; Major Work: *Equality and Efficiency: The Big Tradeoff* (1975).

Arthur Okun is an American economist most noted for the economic law that bears his name. While a senior economist at the Council of Economic Advisers (CEA), Okun discovered the relationship between economic growth and changes in unemployment. He asserted that each point change in the unemployment rate equated to a change in real economic growth as measured by the gross national product (GNP) of between 2 and 3 percent. This inverse relationship applied with changes to either the unemployment rate or economic growth. A rise in one would create a decrease in the other and vice versa. Okun died in 1980.

Arthur Melvin Okun was born on November 28, 1928, in Jersey City, New Jersey. Okun received his BA and PhD degrees from Columbia University. He began his academic career when he accepted an offer to join the economics faculty at Yale University.

Early in his career Okun began public service when he became a member of President Kennedy's Council of Economic Advisers (CEA). Okun joined the CEA as an adviser in 1962 and served as a member till 1969. In 1968 and 1969 during President Johnson's administration, he chaired the CEA. While a senior economist there, Okun discovered a relationship between economic growth and changes in unemployment.

Based on data collected between World War II and 1960 when President Kennedy was elected, Okun provided President Kennedy the data necessary for him to make Keynesian-style tax cuts to boost a sagging economy. Okun asserted that a 1 percent decrease in the unemployment rate would create an approximate 3 percent increase in economic growth, measured as real gross national product (GNP). Conversely, a change in real GNP would create an opposite percentage change in the unemployment rate. While the evidence of the relationship convinced Kennedy to enact the tax cuts, the validity of the relationship over time the predictive relationship is now known as Okun's law.

As robust as Okun's law may be, Okun himself applied boundaries. One, the relationship applied only to the U.S. economy. Two, he asserted that its precision was accurate only when the unemployment rate was between a certain range of 3 to 7 percent. He was also careful to acknowledge there are many variables that cause economic growth. Okun was quick to point out that correlation between the two variables did not equate to causation between them. This correlation-causation has also been amended over time as Okun's law proves predictably strong.

Over time, Okun's boundaries have been revised. One, a smaller change in economic growth Okun's Law has been applied to other economies, most notably those of industrialized nations. Economists now assert that there is at least some causation to economic growth through lower unemployment. It has also been converted to the relationship between the unemployment rate and gross domestic product (GDP). This relationship fell to approximately a 2 percent growth in GDP for every 1 percent reduction in the unemployment rate.

As a stagnant economy continues to plague politicians and economists, research is beginning to question the modern reliability of Okun law's predictability. As the global economy develops and grows along with new technologies changing productivity variables, the economic growth-unemployment rate relationship and the ratios promoted by Okun face further research and scrutiny.

A second field in which Okun is noted is his work on wealth transfer. Using taxes as the transfer mechanism, he makes his case in *Equality and Efficiency: The Big Tradeoff* (1975). He admits both the inefficiency of such an action and the lack of incentives on both the poor and rich. For the inefficiency, he draws the analogy of a leaky faucet. Such things as administrative costs and lack of incentives provide shortcomings for the tax revenues to be completely transferred. He further acknowledges a complete lack of incentives on both the poor and rich. The poor lose the incentive to work by receiving the transfer of wealth and the rich have no incentive to work since a significant portion of their marginal dollar earned will be taxed away.

Fellow CEA member James Tobin labeled Okun's law as one of the most reliable regularities in macroeconomics. Arthur Okun also served as a Brookings Institution fellow from 1969 to 1980.

Arthur Okun died on March 23, 1980, in Washington, DC, of heart failure.

*See also:* Keynes, John Maynard

## Selected Works by Arthur Okun

Okun, Arthur M. *Equality and Efficiency: The Big Tradeoff*. Washington, DC: Brookings Institution Press, 1975.

Okun, Arthur M. *The Political Economy of Prosperity*. Washington, DC: Brookings Institution Press, 1970.

Okun, Arthur M. 1962. "Potential GNP: Its Measurement and Significance." Cowles Foundation Paper 190. New Haven, CT: Cowles Foundation, 1962.

Okun, Arthur M. *Prices and Quantities: A Macroeconomic Analysis*. Washington, DC: Brookings Institution Press, 1981.

## Selected Works about Arthur Okun

Abel, Andrew B., Ben S. Bernanke, and Dean Croushore. *Macroeconomics*. 6th ed. Boston: Pearson, 2008.

"Arthur M. Okun." In *The Concise Encyclopedia of Economics*. Edited by David R. Henderson. The Library of Economics and Liberty. http://www.econlib.org/library/Enc/bios/Okun.html (accessed September 2012).

Daly, Mary, Bart Hobijn, and Joyce Kwok. "Labor Supply Responses to Changes in Wealth and Credit." Federal Reserve Bank of San Francisco Economic Letter, 2009-05. January 30, 2009. http://www.frbsf.org/publications/economics/letter/2009/el2009-05.html.

Pechman, Joseph A., ed. *Economics for Policymaking: Selected Essays of Arthur M. Okun.* Cambridge, MA: MIT Press, 1983.

David A. Dieterle

## OLSON, MANCUR

Born: January 22, 1932, in Grand Forks, North Dakota; Died: February 19, 1998, in College Park, Maryland; American; group dynamics, public goods, labor; Major Works: *The Logic of Collective Action: Public Goods and the Theory of Groups* (1965), *The Rise and Decline of Nations: Economic Growth, Stagflation, and Social Rigidities* (1984), *Power and Prosperity: Outgrowing Communist and Capitalist Dictatorships* (2000).

Mancur Olson is best known for his work introducing the concept of the free-rider problem with public goods. Olson is remembered as an outstanding economic thinker with a keen ability to integrate ideas from sociology and political science into economic theory and make lasting contributions to how we study and understand our world. Olson died in 1998.

Mancur Lloyd Olson, Jr. was born on January 22, 1932, in Grand Forks, North Dakota. He studied as an undergraduate at North Dakota Agricultural College. From there he was awarded a Rhodes Scholarship and attended University College, Oxford. Upon returning to the United States, he then performed his doctoral work at Harvard University where he completed his widely recognized thesis, "The Logic of Collective Action" (1965). After finishing his doctoral work, Olson was hired at Princeton University in their economics department and later worked in the government under the Johnson administration in the Department of Health, Education, and Welfare for two years. After his stint in the government, Olson returned to academia at the University of Maryland where he spent the rest of his career.

Olson was a leader and pioneer in the study of group dynamics within a nation. An important concept that was first developed by Olson is known as the free-rider problem. Free riders are people who join a group and expect to gain the benefits that the collective action of the group yields, but are not willing to incur the costs associated with the work of the group. In his book *The Logic of Collective Action*, Olson shows that individuals can and will act in a self-interested manner that works contrary to the goals of collective action. For example, in a perfectly competitive market where there are many producers of a single identical good, it is in the collective interest of the producers to organize and raise the price of the product as high as possible in order to ensure higher profits for all. This is unlikely to happen because a single firm may well consider that it is in their self-interest not to join the price-setting collective action. If one producer refuses to join the group and sells at below market price, the result will be that they will gain the majority of market share. This explains how sometimes the individual self-interest of a firm can be opposed to the interest of collective action.

Another example of problems that can result from the dissymmetry between individuals and groups is that of people who seek benefits from collective actions, such as in the case of unions. All workers benefit from the higher wages and better working conditions that result from the collective bargaining actions of the union, including workers who are not members of the union. Since there is a cost associated with joining the union, the nonjoiners gain the benefits of membership without paying their dues. Nevertheless, people still do join unions, likely because they recognize that if too many people attempted to free ride, there would not be enough members to achieve their goals. One solution addressing the free-rider problem in the case of unions has been to pass legislation requiring membership, or to use selective incentives individuals will want, such as insurance, but can obtain only through membership.

Olson addresses the issue of mandatory union membership not from the perspective of rights as some of its critics do. He likens it to paying taxes or a military draft, not something we have constitutional protections from. Olson thinks the more relevant consideration is the question of how important a society considers the benefits of strong unions in a country.

In Olson's second book, *The Rise and Decline of Nations* (1984), Olson makes the counterintuitive claim that long-term political stability can have a negative impact on economic growth. He supports his claim by showing how small interest groups become entrenched within a political system, achieving successful lobbying efforts that result in inefficiencies for the rest of the economy. As opposed to larger interest groups where the free-rider principle is at work, smaller groups have the incentive to work and successfully lobby their interest. Their success secures certain political benefits for their groups, which stifle innovation and growth, limiting long-term growth. Olson called this idea institutional sclerosis. Using Japan and Great Britain after World War II as examples, they exhibited that surprising fast economic growth in those countries could be attributed, in part, to the clearing away of the old institutions that resulted from the war.

Olson was also concerned with the role of the government in fostering or blocking economic growth. While many had argued that the government was merely extracting benefits from citizens, Olson showed that even governments have an interest in ensuring at least minimal prosperity for its citizens. Olson's view was that government is not perfect, but it can do some things right if given proper incentives.

Mancur Olson died on February 19, 1998, in College Park, Maryland.

*See also:* Heckman, James; Kydland, Finn; Mortensen, Dale

### Selected Works by Mancur Olson

Olson, Mancur. *The Logic of Collective Action: Public Goods and the Theory of Groups.* Cambridge, MA: President and Fellows of Harvard College, 1965.

Olson, Mancur. *Power and Prosperity: Outgrowing Communist and Capitalist Dictatorships.* New York: Basic Books, 2000.

Olson, Mancur. *The Rise and Decline of Nations: Economic Growth, Stagflation, and Social Rigidities.* New Haven, CT: Yale University Press, 1984.

### Selected Works about Mancur Olson

Dixit, Avinash. "Mancur Olson—Social Scientist." *The Economic Journal* 109, no. 456 (1999): F443–F452.
Heckelman, Jac C. *Collective Choice: Essays in Honor of Mancur Olson*. Heidelberg, Germany: Springer-Verlag, 2010.
McLean, Iain. "The Divided Legacy of Mancur Olson." *British Journal of Political Science* 30, no. 4 (2000): 651–68.
McLean, Iain. "Obituary: Professor Mancur Olson." *The Independent*, March 2, 1998. http://www.independent.co.uk/news/obituaries/obituary-professor-mancur-olson-1147952.html (accessed August 2012).
Rowley, Charles K. *The Encyclopedia of Public Choice*. New York: Kluwer Academic, 2004.

*John E. Trupiano*

## OSTER, EMILY

Born: February 14, 1980, in New Haven, Connecticut; American; development economics, econometrics, health economics; Major Works: "Hepatitis B and the Case of the Missing Women" (2005), "Sexually Transmitted Infections, Sexual Behavior, and the HIV/AIDS Epidemic" (2005), "Hepatitis B Does Not Explain Male-Biased Sex Ratios in China" (with Gang Chen, Xinsen Yu, and Wenyao Lin) (2010).

Emily Oster is an American economist best known for her unorthodox analysis of data and her innovative use of economic tools. In 2002, she published her groundbreaking PhD dissertation, "Hepatitis B and the Case of the Missing Women," earning much publicity and notoriety. After later analysis she retracted her initial thesis in the publication "Hepatitis B Does Not Explain Male-Biased Sex Ratios in China" (2008), and her peers praised her response. Oster has also researched, published, and lectured extensively about HIV in Africa as well as other health and social issues. She is an associate professor at the University of Chicago Booth School of Business and remains a respected authority with great promise and potential within the profession.

Emily Fair Oster was born on February 14, 1980, in New Haven, Connecticut. Her parents, Sharon M. Oster and Ray C. Fair, are both Yale economists specializing in the regulation of business and business strategy and econometric models that show how the economy helps to determine elections. At a young age, Oster's parents noticed that she continued talking after they tucked her into bed. Young Oster became the subject of the book *Narratives of the Crib* (2006), wherein researcher Katherine Nelson analyzed the taped monologues of a two-year-old Oster. Her analysis offered insight into the psychology of early childhood. Oster went on to graduate magna cum laude with a BA in economics from Harvard in 2002. She continued on to earn her PhD in economics in 2006. She earned a Harvard graduate fellowship (2003–5) and then an International Security Program fellowship from the Belfer Center Kennedy School of Government (2005–6). In 2006, she was a Becker fellow as part of the Initiative on Chicago Price Theory at the University of Chicago. She began as an assistant economics professor at the University of Chicago in 2007, and then became an assistant professor in the Business School in 2009, before becoming associate professor in 2011.

Oster believes economics provides a powerful set of tools for understanding how the world works. In her dissertation "Hepatitis B and the Case of the Missing Women" (2005), Oster offered an explanation for why 100 million women were statistically missing from the developing world. Well-known economist Amartya Sen had previously claimed that this occurred due to poor medical care and sex-selected abortions. Oster's work analyzing medical data indicated that countries with higher hepatitis B infections produced more boys and accounted for 50 percent of the missing females. Later research from Avraham Ebenstien concluded that sex-selective abortion accounts for most of the male-heavy data for nonfirstborn children. Oster retracted her initial thesis in "Hepatitis B Does Not Explain Male-Biased Sex Ratios in China" (2010), which has been praised for demonstrating integrity within the profession.

Oster's continued work centered on HIV infections in Africa. She successfully questioned the known facts about AIDS to determine a more effective use of public policy. Oster compares health and mortality as an economic investment with costs and benefits. In places where mortality is low due to problems such as malaria and high maternal mortality, public policy campaigns to change personal behavior due to AIDS are unsuccessful. She advocates a more effective and multitargeted use of policy resources, rather than focusing singularly on pet projects such as the abstinence-oriented plan used in Uganda. In addition, she outlines the connection between exports and economic activity with increased new HIV infections, again suggesting that this knowledge can help policy makers make better use of their limited resources. Oster continues to investigate minority social issues such as the role of menstruation and school attendance for African females.

Oster is also noted for her innovative thinking and analysis of other atypical topics for economists such as Powerball lotteries, witchcraft, weather, and economic growth in Renaissance Europe. She has appeared in Ted Talks and worked since 2006 as a faculty research fellow for the National Bureau of Economic Research. Oster continues to write about numerous public policy issues with an emphasis on health and women's issues.

*See also:* Collier, Paul; Ostrom, Elinor; Sachs, Jeffrey; Sen, Amartya

### Selected Works by Emily Oster

Oster, Emily. "Hepatitis B and the Case of the Missing Women." *Journal of Political Economy* 113, no. 6 (December 2005): 1163–1216.

Oster, Emily. "Sexually Transmitted Infections, Sexual Behavior, and the HIV/AIDS Epidemic." *Quarterly Journal of Economics* 120, no. 2 (May 2005): 467–515.

Oster, Emily, Gang Chen, Xinsen Yu, and Wenyao Lin. "Hepatitis B Does Not Explain Male-Biased Sex Ratios in China." *Economics Letters* 107, no. 2 (May 2010): 142–44.

### Selected Works about Emily Oster

Leonhardt, David. "Recipe for Relevance in Economics: Add Sound Science - Business - International Herald Tribune." *New York Times*, January 9, 2007. http://www.nytimes.com/2007/01/09/business/worldbusiness/09iht-leonhardt.4151017.html?pagewanted=all (accessed August 2012).

Nelson, Katherine. *Narratives from the Crib*. Cambridge, MA: Harvard University Press, 2006.
TED Ideas Worth Spreading. "Emily Oster: Assumption-Busting Economist." http://www.ted.com/speakers/emily_oster.html (accessed August 2012).

*Kathryn Lloyd Gustafson*

## OSTROM, ELINOR

Born: August 7, 1933, in Los Angeles, California; Died: June 12, 2012, in Bloomington, Indiana; American; economic governance of common pool resources, individual choice theory, Nobel Prize (2009); Major Works: *Governing the Commons: The Evolution of Institutions for Collective Action* (1990), *Rules, Games, and Common-Pool Resources* (with Roy Gardner and James Walker) (1994), *Working Together: Collective Action, the Commons, and Multiple Methods in Practice* (with Amy R. Poteete and Marco A. Janssen) (2010).

Elinor Ostrom's research involved local public and private stakeholders at multiple levels managing common-pool resources. Her work was acknowledged by the Nobel committee in 2009. Along with Oliver Williamson, Ostrom was awarded the Nobel Prize in Economics in 2009. She was the first woman to receive this honor. Ostrom died in 2012.

Elinor Awan Ostrom was born on August 7, 1933. Growing up, her parents fed her from their vegetable garden and orchard, taught her to knit, and enrolled her in the nearby public school. She was a competitive swimmer and an accomplished member of her high school debate team. Following the majority of her peers at Beverly Hills High School, she decided she was going to be the first in her family to attend college. Holding jobs as a secretary, an assistant personnel manager, and graduate assistant, she acquired the funds she needed to attend the University of California, Los

Elinor Ostrom poses for a portrait after winning the 2009 Nobel Prize in economics, becoming the first woman to do so. Ostrom showed how common resources—forests, fisheries, oil fields or grazing lands—can be managed successfully by the people who use them, rather than by governments or private companies. (AP/Wide World Photos)

Angeles (UCLA). While at UCLA she earned her undergraduate degree in political science in 1954 (finished with honors in three years by attending year-round), a master's in 1962, and her PhD in 1965.

She wrote her dissertation on management of the groundwater industry in Southern California. In what was to become the introduction to her life's work, she studied the West Basin in Los Angeles County. This was her first common-pool resource problem. Because Garrett Hardin's classic article "The Tragedy of the Commons" had not yet been published, she was in a position to approach problems of the commons in her own way.

Ostrom was affiliated with Indiana University, Bloomington, since 1965 as a professor and cofounder of the Workshop in Political Theory and Policy Analyses. Her distinguished career includes the position of Arthur F. Bentley Distinguished Professor of Political Science and Senior Research Director of the Workshop at Indiana University. She was also the founding director of the Center for the Study of Institutional Diversity at Arizona State University, Tempe. Her topics in commons research were as diverse as forests, irrigation, and police departments.

For over a dozen years, Elinor Ostrom researched law enforcement delivery systems in six metropolitan areas. She concluded that large departments of 100 officers were no more efficient than small to medium cadres of 25 to 50 officers. Her long-term study included traffic, patrol, emergency response, and criminal investigators. She produced strong, empirical evidence that large, centralized institutions were not always more efficient than community organizations.

Based on her research, Ostrom concluded that it was indeed realistic to put the management of common resources in the hands of individuals and small groups without private property rights or centralized authority. Her findings defied popular assumptions that powerless, reasonable people were stuck in no-win situations in terms of commons management. She concluded that regime regulations or efforts to privatize to prevent waste and ruin of the commons often were not the best alternative. The empirical evidence indicated that multiple small governments operate effectively even though they lose some advantages gained from the opportunities presented by economies of scale.

In contrast to prevailing wisdom, Ostrom found that individuals and small parties could write their own rules and self-monitor to obtain maximum benefit from resources they shared in common. The widely held belief was that privatization was not the most favorable solution in many situations. She asserted that chaos and inefficiency were not certain outcomes without property rights as many traditional policy makers proclaimed. She warned that broken trust within public and private partnerships had more lasting detrimental effects on achieving efficient use of the commons. Ostrom contended that a complex system of large and small public bodies along with private individuals operating at all levels was the most beneficial strategy for optimizing the use of common-pool resources.

Along with husband Vincent Ostrom (also an Arthur F. Bentley Professor at Indiana University), in 1973 Ostrom founded the Workshop in Political Theory and Policy Analyses. The focus of the workshop was to encourage collaboration among social scientists. Researchers from multiple disciplines developed common methodologies for collecting, testing, and sharing data. The workshop schedules regular meetings for scientists worldwide with similar research interests.

Elinor Ostrom has many accolades to her credit. Most notable was being awarded the Nobel Prize in Economics in 2009. In addition to being a Nobel laureate, she was honored with the John J. Carty Award for the Advancement of Science by the National Academy of Science in 2004 and the Johan Skytte Prize in Political Science in 1999. She was recognized as an honorary fellow for the International Institute of Social Studies in 2002, and received the James Madison Award by the American Political Science Association in 2005 and the William H. Riker Prize in Political Science in 2008. She has served as president of the American Political Science Association and the Public Choice Society.

*See also:* Williamson, Oliver

## Selected Works by Elinor Ostrom

Ostrom, Elinor. *Governing the Commons: The Evolution of Institutions for Collective Action.* Cambridge, MA: Cambridge University Press, 1990.

Ostrom, Elinor, Roy Gardner, and Jimmy Walker. *Rules, Games, and Common-Pool Resources.* Ann Arbor: University of Michigan Press, 1994.

Poteete, Amy R., Marco A. Janssen, and Elinor Ostrom. *Working Together: Collective Action, the Commons, and Multiple Methods in Practice.* Princeton, NJ: Princeton University Press, 2010.

## Selected Works about Elinor Ostrom

Aligica, Paul Dragos. "Rethinking Institutional Analysis: Interviews with Vincent and Elinor Ostrom." Arlington, VA: Mercatus Center, George Mason University, 2003.

Droste, Nils. *Regime Effectiveness of Climate Protection: Adapting Elinor Ostrom's Institutional Design Principles.* Norderstadt, Germany: GRIN Verlag, 2010.

"Elinor Ostrom—Biographical." Nobelprize.org. http://nobelprize.org/nobel_prizes/economics/laureates/2009/ostrom.html (accessed July 2011).

*Cynthia Blitz Law*

## PARETO, VILFREDO

Born: July 15, 1848, in Paris, France; Died: August 19, 1923, in Lausanne, Switzerland; Italian; income distribution, equilibrium analysis, quantitative economics; Major Works: *Cours d'économie politique* (1896, 1897), *Trattato di sociologia generale* (1916) and the English edition *The Mind and Society* (1935).

Vilfredo Pareto was an Italian economist who developed many mathematical formulas used in economics today. Educated as a civil engineer, Pareto was an advocate of free trade. His economic ideas reflected those of Leon Walras and the Lausanne School of economics, which held the view economics was a mathematical science. His theories addressed a wide range of topics in both economics and sociology. Two of his most lasting ideas were the Pareto principle and Pareto optimality. The Pareto principle held that 80 percent of a country's wealth was held by 20 percent of the country's population. Pareto optimality asserted that the resources of a society are not optimally allocated if at least one person can still be made better without diminishing the wealth of others. Pareto died in 1923.

Vilfredo Pareto was born on July 15, 1848, in Paris, France. Vilfredo was born of an Italian father and a French mother. He graduated from the Polytechnic University of Turin with an engineering degree in 1870. His early fascination with equilibrium analysis seemed to have begun while a student, evidenced by his thesis on the equilibrium analysis of solid bodies. Following graduation he worked as a civil engineer for the Italian Railway Company. He began his teaching career in 1886 at the University of Florence in economics and management. In 1893, he joined the economics faculty at the University of Lausanne where he taught until his retirement.

Pareto, along with Leon Walras, is considered one of the key figures of the Lausanne School of economic analysis. The Lausanne School of economic thought is based on general economic equilibrium theory and the advanced application of mathematical formulas to economics.

Vilfredo Pareto was noted for many theories in economics. Using complex mathematical formulas to identify historical patterns of wealth distribution, he created the law of income distribution. He also is credited with beginning welfare economics through his Pareto optimality theory, which he developed in 1906. Pareto optimality postulated that the resources of a society are not optimally allocated if at least one person can still be made better without diminishing the wealth of others. The optimality Pareto was striving for in his theory was efficiency. According to Pareto, optimality was reached when all outcomes have been achieved except the one that makes someone else worse off. This definition of optimality, and associated mathematical formula, is the basis for much of the social policy and welfare economics of today.

Pareto has been considered by some to have initiated microeconomics. In 1906, Pareto wrote *Manual of Political Economy*. This work uses the study of equilibrium to solve individual economic problems and relies on the previous work of Francis Edgeworth on indifference curves. In it Pareto created the theory of the consumer and theory of the producer, and replaced utility theory with his Pareto optimality theory. Pareto optimality has been used to identify perfectly competitive markets as the most optimum market structure to distribute wealth.

A second major contribution of Pareto is now known as the Pareto principle. Pareto researched the distribution of income in different countries and concluded that a small percentage of a population own a large percentage of the wealth. In his *Cours d'économie politique* (1896, 1897), Pareto expanded on his law of income distribution. He argued that the distribution of income, regardless of country or era, followed a similar pattern that could be interpreted in a mathematical formula. Using mathematics, Pareto suggests that 80 percent of a country's wealth is owned by only 20 percent of the country's people. This 80/20 ratio of income distribution became known as Pareto's law. The ratio was later expanded to include other input/output ratios (such as in management) and was expanded to the 80/20 Pareto principle or 80/20 Pareto rule.

Pareto is credited for several other ideas basic to economics. He was critical of the economic concepts of marginal analysis and utility. The sociological element of his studies was evident in his explanations of human behavior and consumer preferences. He contended that humans make economic decisions based more on what they want than what will make them better off. Pareto's ideas about human behavior were the foundation for the later work of Daniel Kahneman and others known as behavioral economics.

Crossing over both disciplines, Pareto was also a vigorous critic of Karl Marx, particularly Marx's theory of class struggle between the laborers and the capitalists. Pareto asserted that the struggle between these two classes was only one of many different struggles between different groups.

Pareto later directed his studies more to sociology as his interest in human behavior expanded. He also argued that the field of economics devoted too little time to the subject and was too narrow in its scope when it did consider human behavior as an economic action.

In 1916, he published *Trattato di sociologia generale*. Pareto expanded on his sociology and study of human behavior, explaining that people act on sentiment and justify their sentimental decisions later. He labeled the decisions of sentiment as "residues" and the explanations as "derivations." His idea that human decisions are based on emotion conflicted with the notion of the rational decision-making process asserted by economics. *Trattato di sociologia generale* was first published in English using the title *Mind and Society*. Italian Fascist Benito Mussolini claimed that the lectures and theories of Pareto while he was a student at the Lausanne University were a significant influence on his ideas (Mussolini 1925, 14).

Another theory of Pareto's was that a society had two elites: a governing elite and a nongoverning elite. What made this theory so fascinating in later years was his contention that one of the elite factions is progressive, the other one is conservative, and in strong societies they alternate in holding power. Pareto contended that as the power-holding elite used up its goodwill with the people, the other elite would rise. Pareto asserted that the power holding between the two elites was both cyclical and predictable. This theory led Pareto to the conclusion that all political classifications were labels for different elite positions to obtain power.

After his death, Pareto's legacy was solidified in the 1930s and 1940s. John Hicks, Maurice Allais, and Paul Samuelson all popularized Pareto's work on consumer preferences and welfare economics. His welfare economics theories became the foundation for the welfare economics movement of the mid-twentieth century with such economists as Harold Hotelling and Oskar Lange.

Vilfredo Pareto died in Lausanne, Switzerland, on August 19, 1923.

*See also:* Allais, Maurice; Hicks, John; Kahneman, Daniel; Lange, Oskar; Marx, Karl; Samuelson, Paul; Walras, Leon

### Selected Works by Vilfredo Pareto

Pareto, Vilfredo. *Cours d'économie politique professé à l'université de Lausanne*. 3 vols. F. Rouge, 1896.

Pareto, Vilfredo. *Manual of Political Economy* (1927). Translated by Ann S. Schwier. Fairfield, NJ: Augustus M. Kelley, 1971.

Pareto, Vilfredo. *Trattato di Sociologia Generale* [Treatise on general sociology] (1916, rev. French trans. 1917); published in English by Harcourt, Brace in a four-volume edition. Edited by Arthur Livingston under the title *The Mind and Society*. New York: Harcourt Brace, 1935.

### Selected Works about Vilfredo Pareto

Alexander, James. "Pareto: The Karl Marx of Fascism." *Journal of Historical Review* 14, no. 5 (1994): 10–18.

Bridel, Pascal, ed. *Editing Economists and Economists as Editors: Papers Given at a Conference held at . . . Walras Pareto University of Lausanne*. Geneva: Librarie Droz, 1992.

Cirillo, Renato. *The Economics of Vilfredo Pareto*. London: Cass, 1978.

Lyttelton, Adrian. *Italian Fascisms: From Pareto to Gentile*. New York: Harper & Row, 1973.

Mussolini, Benito. *My Autobiography*. New York: Charles Scribner's Sons, 1928.

David A. Dieterle

## PASINETTI, LUIGI

Born: September 12, 1930, in Zanica, Bergamo, Italy; Italian; neo-Ricardian economics, theory of value and distribution, Kaldorian theory of growth, structural economic dynamics; Major Works: *Growth and Income Distribution: Essays in Economic Theory* (1974), *Lectures on the Theory of Production* (1977), *Essays on the Theory of Joint Production* (1980), *Structural Change and Economic Growth: A*

*Theoretical Essay on the Dynamics of the Wealth of Nations* (1981), *Keynes and the Cambridge Keynesians: A "Revolution in Economics" to Be Accomplished* (2007).

Luigi Pasinetti is an emeritus professor of economics at the Catholic University of Milan, Italy. He is the author of numerous economic books and many academic papers. He was a visiting professor in many top-ranking universities around the globe such as Columbia University and University of Southern California in the United States, Kyoto University in Japan, and University of Sydney in Australia. Throughout his career, he has been a member of many professional economic organizations and received many awards and honors including the Invernizzi Prize for Economics (1997), honorary fellow of Gonville and Caius, Cambridge (1999), honorary president of European Society for the History of Economic Thought (2002), and St. Vincent Prize for Lifelong Activity in Economic Sciences (2002).

Luigi Lodovico Pasinetti was born in September 12, 1930 in Zanica, Italy. In 1954, he received his BA in economics from the Catholic University of Milan with a dissertation titled "Econometric Models and Their Application to Trade Cycle Analysis." He won many scholarships for his graduate study, and decided to pursue his PhD at University of Cambridge in England. The University of Cambridge, at the time, was the center of the Keynesian revolution. Joan Robinson, Nicholas Kaldor, Richard Kahn, and Piero Sraffa were among the Cambridge Keynesians, who were actively producing new economic ideas. Pasinetti entered Cambridge as a new research student and almost immediately started his major contributions. In 1963, he earned his PhD in economics from Cambridge with a dissertation titled "A Multi-sector Model of Economic Growth." He also studied at Harvard University and Oxford University. In 1964, he became a full professor of political economy. He has also taught and lectured both in Cambridge, England, and in Milan, Italy.

In 1960, Pasinetti published his first paper, titled "A Mathematical Formulation of the Ricardian System." In this paper, he provided a mathematical explanation and proof of the Ricardian theory. His work in this area was the logical continuation of Sraffa's and Kaldor's works. In 1951, Sraffa published an important economic paper about the works of Ricardo. Later, in 1956, Kaldor published another paper covering the history of distribution theories from Ricardo to Keynes. Neither of these papers, however, examined the Ricardian model mathematically. Pasinetti's paper became a classical economic paper because, for the first time, it expressed the Ricardian model using the mathematical equations.

In 1962, Pasinetti published another paper on income distribution. He criticized Kaldor's distribution model and mathematically proved that Kaldor had made a logical mistake. In his model, Kaldor neglected the workers' income by assuming that society's total profit comes only from the capitalists. Pasinetti proved that although in the long run the saving propensity of a worker does not have any effects on the rate of profit in an aggregate economy, it presents the distribution rate of profit between workers and capitalists. In his paper, Pasinetti argued that Kaldor's original paper on income distribution was too general. Pasinetti's paper opened the door for new findings in this area.

In 1966, Paul Samuelson and Franco Modigliani, who were at the Massachusetts Institute of Technology (MIT), published a detailed paper arguing against Pasinetti's income distribution theorem. According to the Samuelson-Modigliani model, the workers' saving rate would surpass the capitalists' rate of saving. Therefore, in the long run, capitalists would disappear and the whole economy would be owned by the workers. Pasinetti along with Joan Robinson and Kaldor challenged the theorem of the two MIT economists. While Kaldor used the National Accounts data from the United States and England to empirically disprove the Samuelson-Modigliani theory, Pasinetti pointed out the logical flaw of their analysis. Pasinetti argued that the Samuelson-Modigliani model was based on extreme and sometimes contradictory assumptions and that it had no significant implications.

Pasinetti's income distribution model cannot define the workers' exact rate of profit. It can, however, determine its upper and lower limits. The mathematical model shows that workers' contribution is less than what they gain, through profit, in exchange for their work. This conclusion was an important contribution to the economic theories of income distribution and income inequality. During the 1970s and 1980s, economists such as Salvadori and Steedman enhanced the original model by relaxing most of the original assumptions and adding more complications to the model. The original findings of the model, however, still hold, and the additional contributions made Pasinetti's original income distribution model even more applicable.

Pasinetti made two major contributions to the theory of capital. First, in 1966 he published an article opposing David Levhari and Paul Samuelson to show that reswitching is possible at the aggregate level. Reswitching is an economic term, which means that it is possible for the same method of production to be the most profitable one at various rates of profit. Pasinetti concluded that one cannot make a connection between change in the rate of profit and change in the quantity of capital per person. Second, in 1969, in his infamous paper titled "Switches of Technique and the Rate of Return in Capital Theory," Pasinetti showed that the economic concept of rate of return on capital, which was introduced by Irving Fisher and later used by Robert Solow, does not have any significant economic implications.

In 1975, Pasinetti published one of his most successful books, *The Lectures on the Theory of Production*. In his book, Pasinetti analyzes the theory of production from a macroeconomic perspective, investigating, at a theoretical level, the production and distribution of wealth, as a flow rather than as a stock, in the society. This book, like many of his other books, has become one of the international textbooks in macroeconomics and has been translated in many languages such as French, German, and English.

*See also:* Kaldor, Nicholas; Modigliani, Franco; Robinson, Joan; Samuelson, Paul; Sraffa, Piero

## Selected Works by Luigi Pasinetti

Pasinetti, Luigi. *Essays on the Joint Theory of Production*. London: Macmillan, 980.
Pasinetti, Luigi. *Growth and Income Distribution: Essays on Economic Theory*. Cambridge: Cambridge University Press, 1974.

Pasinetti, Luigi. *Keynes and the Cambridge Keynesians: A Revolution in Economics to Be Accomplished.* Cambridge: Cambridge University Press, 2007.

Pasinetti, Luigi. *Lectures on the Theory of Production.* London: Macmillan, 1977.

Pasinetti, Luigi. *Structural Change and Economic Growth: A Theoretical Essay on the Dynamics of the Wealth of Nations.* Cambridge: Cambridge University Press, 1981.

### Selected Works about Luigi Pasinetti

Beaud, M., and Dostaler G. *Economic Thought since Keynes: A History and Dictionary of Major Economists.* London: Edward Elgar, 1995.

Blaug, Mark. *Great Economists since Keynes: An Introduction to the Lives and Works of One Hundred Modern Economists.* New York: Wheatsheaf, 1985.

Catholic University of Milan. "Luigi Pasinetti." http://docenti.unicatt.it/eng/luigi_lodovico_pasinetti (accessed February 2012).

*Elham Mahmoudi*

# PETTY, SIR WILLIAM

Born: May 26, 1623, in Romsey, Hampshire, England; Died: December 16, 1687, in London, England; English; political economist, pioneer in statistics; Major Work: *Treatise of Taxes and Contributions* (1662).

Sir William Petty was knighted by Charles II in 1661. He organized the Royal Society of London and became one of its original members. As a member of the Royal Society he was a regular contributor on the history of trades and technology, his main contributions being in the area of "political arithmetic" or statistics. In 1662 he wrote his most famous work, *Treatise of Taxes and Contributions*, contributed to the political economy. He examined the role of the state in the economy and briefly the labor theory of value. Petty wrote a great deal about taxation, how to implement its direct collection. Petty died in 1687.

William Petty was born on May 26, 1623, in Romsey, Hampshire, England. Although the son of a poor rural cloth worker, Petty would prove to be very resourceful at using both his education and his friends in order to advance into proper English society. Petty received his education from the Universities of Leiden, Paris, and Oxford where he studied medicine and was initially educated as a physician. Petty had many interests including languages, chemistry, math, music, and medicine.

Throughout his life Petty made many important friends. Many, like him, were followers of and influenced greatly by Baconian thought. It was his circle of friends and colleagues that helped him achieve numerous great appointments at such early ages.In 1648, he was made a fellow of Brasenose College in Oxford, and later there became a professor of anatomy. In 1651, by the time he was 28, he was a professor of music at the Gresham College in London, a new college dedicated to the experimental and mechanical arts. In 1652, he became a physician for the army in Ireland. It was here where he met Henry Cromwell and later served him as clerk of the council at Dublin.

Working under Cromwell, it was Petty who took over surveying all the despoiled Irish land that Cromwell was giving to soldiers as payment for their services. In due time, Petty would become a wealthy large landowner in Ireland, initially accumulating over 100,000 acres. He returned to London in the late 1650s and served as a member of Parliament.

The Royal Society of London for Improving Natural Knowledge was an opportunity for Petty to further himself politically and economically. He contributed regularly to its studies of the history of trades and technology. His main contribution, political arithmetic, or statistics, was his applied view of the Baconian social world. As a scientist, Petty considered himself an inventor, and one of his inventions, the double-hulled ship, came to realization.

Sir William Petty, seventeenth-century British economist. (The Print Collector/StockphotoPro)

In 1662, he wrote his most famous work that contributed to the political economy. This work, *Treatise of Taxes and Contributions*, examined the role of the state in the economy and briefly the labor theory of value. Petty wrote a great deal about taxation, how to implement its direct collection. He also consistently maintained the importance of the quantitative science of the economies, and many of his writings repeat this theme.

By the time of his death, Petty would more than double his land to over 250,000 acres. It was this ownership that caused him to return to Ireland numerous times to defend lawsuits over his lands. He moved back to Ireland in 1666 for 20 years, but visited London often. Many of Petty's writings were printed posthumously. *The Political Anatomy of Ireland* and the *Political Arithmetick* are two works of Petty's that are considered by some to be the origins of eighteenth-century statistics. They are both Petty's attempts to calculate the population of various cities.

Sir William Petty died on December 16, 1687, in London, England.

*See also:* Locke, John; North, Sir Dudley

## Selected Works by Sir William Petty

Petty, William. *The Economic Writings of Sir William Petty*. 2 vols. (Essays from 1662 to 1682). Edited by Charles Henry Hull. Reprinted by Augustus M. Kelley, 1963.

Petty, William. *The Political Anatomy of Ireland*. London: D. Browne, 1691.
Petty, William. *Political Arithmetick*. London: Peacock Hon. Mortlock, 1690.
Petty, William. *Political Survey of Ireland*. 2nd ed. London: D. Browne, 1719.
Petty, William. *Quantulumcunque* (1695). Reprinted as *Sir Petty His Quantulumcunque Concerning Money to the Lord Marquess of Halyfax, anno. 1695*. Ann Arbor, MI: Proquest, EEBO Editions, 2011.
Petty, William. *Several Essays on Political Arithmetic*. London: D. Browne, 1755.
Petty, William. *Treatise of Taxes and Contributions*. London: Obadiah Blagrave, 1685.

**Selected Works about Sir William Petty**

Aubrey, John. "A Brief Life of William Petty." http://socserv2.socsci.mcmaster.ca/~econ/ugcm/3ll3/petty/pettyl (accessed September, 2011).
Bevan, Wilson Lloyd. "Sir William Petty: A Study in English Economic Literature." *Publications of the American Economic Association* 9, no. 4 (1894).
Hull, Charles H. "Petty's Place in the History of Economic Theory." *Quarterly Journal of Economics* (1900).
McCormick, Ted. *William Petty and the Ambitions of Political Arithmetic*. Oxford: Oxford University Press, 2009.

*Carol Lynn Nute*

# PHELPS, EDMUND

Born: July 6, 1933, in Evanston, Illinois; American; economic systems, wealth accumulation, Nobel Prize (2006); Major Works: "The Golden Rule of Accumulation" (1961), *Political Economy* (1985).

Edmund Phelps's research has focused on the dissemination of information, technological innovation, and entrepreneurial endeavors as well as the relationship between unemployment and inflation. Over the course of his career, his contributions have been valuable in several contexts and areas, reshaping models and expectations within the economic community. Much of Phelps's more recent work is centered on the effects of capitalism.

Edmund Strother Phelps Jr. was born in Evanston, Illinois, on July 6, 1933, at the tail end of the Great Depression. He lived in the Chicago area until he was six years old, when his family moved to Hastings-on-Hudson, New York, to find employment. Even from an early age, Phelps had a curiosity in economics. His family cultivated this curiosity in their everyday lives with ongoing discussion and dialogue. He gained a further appreciation of economics in his formative early college years at Amherst College in Massachusetts. Phelps continued his studies and earned his bachelor of arts in 1955 and attained his PhD from Yale University in 1959. Following graduation, he worked for RAND Corporation in Los Angeles in 1959 and then at Yale University and the Cowles Foundation where he completed some remarkable research during the 1960s on economic growth. Phelps worked at the University of Pennsylvania from 1966 until 1970 before moving back to New York and joining the faculty at Columbia University in 1971.

Phelps published "The Golden Rule of Accumulation: A Fable for Growthmen" in 1961. The economic-themed fable brought him great praise from the international economic community. This initial fame and recognition brought with it higher expectations for substantial additional contributions to the economic community.

Phelps collaborated with many of his contemporaries while at the University of Pennsylvania and then later at Columbia. His work at the University of Pennsylvania focused on analyzing the Phillips curve. The Phillips curve was an established measurement of the trade-off between inflation and unemployment. His approach from the microeconomic perspective on unemployment and wage inflation had not yet been investigated and researched. Phelps emphasized how current policy decisions impact stabilization policy in the future. His work showed the generational impact one group may have on future groups and how significant analysis of the importance of human capital leads to growth and subsequently advances in technology. Phelps worked on a sequential model to explain the process in a systematic format.

In the 1980s Phelps authored a textbook, *Political Economy*. While complex by comparison, it was adopted by some economics departments in universities both domestically and abroad. Phelps was introduced into other circles and afforded the opportunity to work with many brilliant scholars in countries in Europe and even Russia among others. His prominence in popularity continued to flourish through the 1980s and 1990s.

Columbia's Center on Capitalism and Society was founded in 2001 by Phelps and his former student Roman Frydman to focus on capitalism. The center, comprising many economists and experts, is designed to conduct research on the dynamics of modern economics and promote capitalism to a public who is often misinformed about the very nature of their own economic system. The center believes that capitalism when properly administered in a democracy promotes growth through innovation, inclusion, and unlimited opportunities. As a result of recent economic challenges, the center is currently attempting to restructure the financial sector to promote economic stability during potential struggles and downturns.

In 2001, many of Phelps's contemporaries honored him with a Festschrift conference just three weeks after 9/11. The resulting book (*Knowledge, Information, and Expectations in Modern Macroeconomics: In Honor of Edmund S. Phelps* [2003]) is divided into four sections focusing on various areas of his tireless and extensive work in the field of economics.

Phelps has served as a consultant for the U.S. Treasury Department, U.S. Senate Finance Committee, and Federal Reserve Board. In addition, he also holds several honorary doctorates from colleges and universities around the world. Phelps's work in the micro foundations of macroeconomics has benefited the economic community in a global context.

For his work challenging the concept of the Phillips curve and efforts exploring the short-term and long-term effects of economic policy, the Royal Swedish Academy of Sciences awarded Edmund Phelps the Nobel Prize in 2006. In addition to his Nobel Prize, Phelps was elected fellow of the National Academy of Sciences in 1982, distinguished fellow of the American

Economic Association in 2000, and chevalier of the Legion of Honor in 2008, along with winning the Premio Pico della Mirandola for humanism and the Kiel Global Economy Prize.

Phelps works at Columbia University as the McVickar Professor of Political Economy and is director of the Center on Capitalism and Society.

*See also:* Phillips, A. W. H.

### Selected Works by Edmund Phelps

Phelps, Edmund. *Fiscal Neutrality toward Economic Growth.* New York: McGraw-Hill, 1965.

Phelps, Edmund. "The Golden Rule of Accumulation." *The American Economic Review* 51, no. 4. (1961): 638–43.

Phelps, Edmund. *Golden Rules of Economic Growth.* New York: Norton, 1966.

Phelps, Edmund. *Political Economy.* New York: Norton, 1985.

Phelps, Edmund. *Seven Schools of Macroeconomic Thought: The Arne Ryde Memorial Lectures.* Oxford: Oxford University Press, 1990.

Phelps, Edmund. *Studies in Macroeconomic Theory.* Vol. 1, *Employment and Inflation.* Maryland Heights, MO: Academic Press, 1980.

Phelps, Edmund. *Studies in Macroeconomic Theory.* Vol. 2, *Redistribution and Growth.* Maryland Heights, MO: Academic Press, 1980.

Phelps, Edmund S., and Jean-Paul Fitoussi. *The Slump in Europe: Reconstructing Open Economy Theory.* Boston: Blackwell, 1988.

### Selected Works about Edmund Phelps

Aghion, Phillipe, Roman Frydman, Joseph Stiglitz, and Michael Woodford, eds. *Knowledge, Information, and Expectations in Modern Macroeconomics: In Honor of Edmund S. Phelps.* Princeton, NJ: Princeton University Press, 2003.

"Edmund Phelps." Columbia University Economics. http://www.columbia.edu/~esp2/ (accessed June 30, 2011).

Phelps, Edmund. "Autobiography." NobelPrize.org. http://www.nobelprize.org/nobel_prizes/economics/laureates/2006/phelps.html (accessed July 2011).

Phelps, Edmund. "A Life in Economics." Columbia University. http://www.columbia.edu/~esp2/autobio1.pdf (accessed July 2011).

*William S. Chappell*

# PHILLIPS, A. W. H.

Born: November 18, 1914, in Dannevirke, New Zealand; Died: March 4, 1975, in Auckland, New Zealand; New Zealander; economic growth, Phillips curve; Major Works: "A Simple Model of Employment, Money and Prices in a Growing Economy" (1961), "Employment, Inflation and Growth" (1962).

A. W. H. Phillips was a leading twentieth-century New Zealand economist who spent most of his academic career at the London School of Economics (LSE). Phillips was noted for his work on the relationship between the level of unemployment and the rate of wage inflation, illustrated by what would become known as the Phillips curve. Using his engineering knowledge, Phillips also designed and built the MONIAC hydraulic economics computer in 1949. Phillips was appointed to the prestigious Tooke Professorship in Economics at the London School of Economics in 1958 and to a research professorship at the Australian National University in 1967. Phillips died in 1975.

Alban William Housego "A. W." "Bill" Phillips was born on November 18, 1914, in Dannevirke, New Zealand. Having a father who experimented with technology, he had an adventurous youth traveling through Australia (where he ran an outback movie theater) and South East Asia. At the age of 15, he left school to become an apprentice engineer for the Public Works Department. For the next 10 years, he worked at various jobs in New Zealand, Australia, and Britain. However, his civilian life was interrupted by World War II, which he joined. He later was captured and held as a Japanese prisoner of war. During the war Phillips was an armaments officer in Singapore and was awarded an MBE (Military Division) for outstanding courage while under attack.

With his fascination with the interactions of sectors across the economy and his engineering training, in 1949 he developed a hydraulic model of the macroeconomy, the MONIAC (Monetary National Income Analogue Computer). It was initially known as the "Phillips Machine." The model consisted of flows of water from one container to another, representing monetary flows—e.g., from consumption to income and thence, via an accelerator mechanism, to investment. "Leakages" to imports were included, and multiple models were built to represent multiple countries—interlinked by pipes. It was very well received and Phillips was soon offered a teaching position at the LSE.

Having worked on modeling the national economic processes of the British economy with his MONIAC, he published his own work on the relationship between inflation and unemployment, illustrated by the "Phillips curve" in 1958. The curve had been described as the most influential and productive macroeconomic idea in the postwar era. Phillips observed that there is a trade-off between a strong economy and low inflation. In years when the unemployment rate was high, wages tended to be stable, or possibly fall. Conversely, when unemployment was low, wages rose rapidly leading to inflationary pressures.

Following this publication, two other notable economists, Paul Samuelson and Robert Solow, wrote an influential article describing the possibilities suggested by the Phillips curve in the context of the United States. Although the Phillips curve has changed substantially over time, it remains an important feature of macroeconomic analysis of economic fluctuations; e.g., while it has been observed that there is a stable short-run trade-off between unemployment and inflation, this has not been observed in the long run.

He made several other notable contributions to economics, particularly relating to stabilization policy. He asserted that not only is it crucial to have the right policies but also they have to be implemented at the right time. The right policy implemented at the wrong time can make the economy worse. However, the subtlety and wisdom of Phillips's stabilization exercises were largely overlooked, as both monetarists and the Phillips curve Keynesians competed for policy influence.

With a profound distaste for such policy manipulation, he gradually abandoned macroeconomics for Chinese economic studies.

After the 1968 student riots in London, Phillips returned to Australia for a position at Australian National University and later at University of Auckland, which allowed him to devote half his time to Chinese studies. He became one of the first Western economists to turn his attention to Chinese developments with the anticipation of the rise of the Chinese economy despite its then perilous state. Although he did not become an academic until 1950 at the age of 36, his contributions have been significant and lasting.

A. W. H. Phillips died on March 4, 1975, in Auckland, New Zealand.

*See also:* Keynes, John Maynard; Samuelson, Paul; Solow, Robert

### Selected Works by A. W. H. Phillips

Phillips, A. W. H. "Employment, Inflation and Growth." *Economica* 29 (1962): 1–16.

Phillips, A. W. H. "Mechanical Models in Economic Dynamics." *Economica* 17 (1950): 283–305.

Phillips, A. W. H. "The Relation between Unemployment and the Rate of Change of Money Wage Rates in the United Kingdom, 1861–1957." *Economica* 25 (1958): 283–99.

Phillips, A. W. H. "A Simple Model of Employment, Money and Prices in a Growing Economy." *Economica* 28 (1961): 360–70.

Phillips, A. W. H. "Stabilisation Policy in a Closed Economy." *The Economic Journal* 64 (1954): 290–323.

Phillips, A. W. H. "Stabilisation Policy and the Time Form of Lagged Response." *The Economic Journal* 67 (1957): 265–77.

### Selected Works about A. W. H. Phillips

Bollard, Alan E. "Man, Money and Machines: The Contributions of A. W. Phillips." *Economica* 78 (2011): 1–9.

Gordon, Robert J. "The History of the Phillips Curve: Consensus and Bifurcation." *Economica* 78 (2011): 10–50.

Hally, Mike. *Electronic Brains: Stories from the Dawn of the Computer Age*. Washington, DC: Joseph Henry Press, 2005.

Laidler, David. "Phillips in Retrospect." A review essay on *A. W. H. Phillips: Collected Works in Contemporary Perspective*. Edited by Robert Leeson. Cambridge: Cambridge University Press, 2000. Available at http://economics.uwo.ca/faculty/laidler/workingpapers/phillips.pdf.

Leeson, Robert. *The Life and Legacy of A. W. H. Phillips*. Perth, Western Australia: Murdoch University, 1995.

Phillips, A. W. H., and A. R. Bergstrom. *Stability and Inflation: A Volume of Essays to Honour the Memory of A. W. H. Phillips*. Hoboken, NJ: Wiley, 1978.

"Phillips Curve." In *The Concise Encyclopedia of Economics*. Edited by David R. Henderson. The Library of Economics and Liberty. http://www.econlib.org/library/Enc/PhillipsCurve.html (accessed March 2012).

*Ninee Shoua Yang*

# PIGOU, A. C.

Born: November 18, 1877, in Ryde, Isle of Wight, England; Died: March 7, 1959, in Cambridge, England; English; classical economics, neoclassical economics, welfare economics, public finance; Major Works: *Wealth and Welfare* (1912), *Unemployment* (1914), *The Theory of Unemployment* (1933).

A. C. Pigou is a British economist best remembered for the development of welfare economics and public finance. Welfare economics refers to the study of maximizing economic value to benefit society as a whole. In this direction, he defined the economic concept of externalities before it was part of the economics lexicon. He also studied public finance, which investigates the impact of taxation and other government interventions in the economy. A star student of Alfred Marshall, Pigou rose from lecturer to professor and chair of political economy at Cambridge University. As professor, his star student was John Maynard Keynes. Pigou died in 1959.

Arthur Cecil Pigou was born in November 18, 1877 on the Isle of Wight. His father was an army officer and his mother came from a line of Irish government officials. Pigou won a scholarship to Harrow, a prestigious private school, from which he continued on to Cambridge where he began his studies in history. After taking classes from renowned economists Alfred Marshall and Henry Sidgwick, however, he was convinced instead to study political economy. He became Marshall's star student, and upon graduation was promptly hired as a lecturer. When Marshall retired in 1908, Pigou took his place as chair of political economy. Pigou always remained devoted to the teachings of his mentor, often telling his students "it's all in Marshall." Pigou's most famous student, John Maynard Keynes, would be less kind to his instructor. During World War I, Pigou used his summer vacations to serve in the front lines with the Ambulance Corps of the British Army. His wartime experience affected him deeply, and may have been what set him on the course from being a jovial man of society to an enigmatic recluse.

Pigou first developed his concept of economic welfare early in his career with the publication of *Wealth and Welfare* in 1912. "Welfare" refers to the benefits that society gets as a result of people's decisions. It is not to be confused with the study of government welfare programs, though it might sometimes include them. However, the decisions of individual economic actors can also damage social welfare. The key is to get the most benefit at the least cost to society. Adam Smith had famously stated in *The Wealth of Nations* that when people pursue their own interests, markets will tend to make decisions beneficial for society. But Pigou noted that this is not always the case, because people's choices may involve "external" costs and/or benefits. Pigou's idea came to be known later as "externalities," a term Pigou did not use. An externality is a cost or benefit that is "external" to the one who makes a particular decision. Externalities can be both negative and positive. Pollution is an example of a negative externality, while education is a positive externality.

Pigou wrote that externalities might be a good place for the government to get involved. The government could put a tax on negative externalities and a subsidy on positive externalities. The effect of these actions would be to encourage the "right" or "optimal" amount of, for example, toy making and education. These have come to be known as Pigovian taxes and subsidies. Pigou had introduced a systematic way to study the social impact of personal choices, and a framework for deciding whether or not government action was necessary in a certain situation. This framework is still in use, though it has received an interesting and serious challenge by Ronald Coase and other economists who point out that government action can produce externalities of its own.

Pigou's relatively uncontroversial life received a sudden shock when his former student, John Maynard Keynes, published the famous *General Theory of Employment, Interest and Money* (1936). Keynes used Pigou as the foil for his book, casting him and his classical predecessors as oblivious, out of touch, and uncaring to the plight of people in the real world. Pigou had indeed written that long-term unemployment was impossible as long as wages were permitted to fall. Keynes said that wages would not fall, and that the real problem was low overall demand—so the classical theory was pointless. Pigou was deeply offended, and responded with countertheories of his own. He and Keynes, however, were polite to each other in personal conversation.

Though Pigou remained at Cambridge, he spent more and more time in his apartment, venturing out only to deliver lectures. His reclusive habits (especially compared with Keynes's charm and dash) made him less than popular on campus. However, it was undeniable that his ideas, especially the ones having to do with economic welfare and public finance, had great promise. It was not long before his theories were used as the basis for determining whether or not the government should get involved in a matter and what the subsequent public policy might be. Laws that tax and regulate pollution and other externalities are directly affected by the pioneering work of A. C. Pigou.

Arthur Cecil Pigou died in Cambridge, England on March 7, 1959.

*See also:* Coase, Ronald; Keynes, John Maynard; Marshall, Alfred

### Selected Works by A. C. Pigou

Pigou, A. C. *The Economics of Welfare*. Vol. 1. New York: Macmillan, 1924.
Pigou, A. C. *Industrial Fluctuations*. New York: Macmillan, 1927.
Pigou, A. C. *The Political Economy of War*. New York: Macmillan, 1921.
Pigou, A. C. *The Theory of Unemployment*. New York: Macmillan, 1933.
Pigou, A. C. *Unemployment*. New York: Williams and Norgate, 1914.
Pigou, A. C. *Wealth and Welfare*. New York: Macmillan, 1912.

### Selected Works about A. C. Pigou

"Arthur Cecil Pigou." In *The Concise Encyclopedia of Economics*. Edited by David R. Henderson. http://www.econlib.org/library/Enc/bios/Pigou.html (accessed December 22, 2011).
Cassidy, John. "An Economist's Invisible Hand." *Wall Street Journal*, November 28, 2009. http://online.wsj.com/article/SB10001424052748704204304574545671352424680.html (accessed December 2011).

Collard, David. "A. C. Pigou, 1877–1959," In *Pioneers of Modern Economics in Britain.* Edited by D. E. O'Brien and John R. Presley, 105–39. London: Macmillan, 1981.

Pressman, Steven. "Arthur Cecil Pigou." In *Fifty Major Economists.* Edited by Steven Pressman, 143–48. New York: Routledge, 2006.

Spiegel, Henry. *The Growth of Economic Thought.* Englewood Cliffs, NJ: Prentice-Hall, 1971.

*Stephen H. Day*

## PISSARIDES, CHRISTOPHER

Born: February 20, 1948, in Nicosia, Cyprus; English; labor market adjustment, unemployment, wage inequality, Nobel Prize (2010); Major Work: "Job Creation and Job Destruction in the Theory of Unemployment" (with Dale Mortensen) (1994).

Christopher Antoniou Pissarides, a British Cypriot economist, is considered one of the pioneers of match theory approach to unemployment theory. Pissarides formulated economic modeling to show what happens to a person who loses his or her job and analyzed how assorted economic factors and government policy decisions impact the duration of unemployment among idle workers. In 2010, Pissarides became the first Cypriot citizen to win the Nobel Prize in Economics. He was jointly honored with Peter A. Diamond and Dale T. Mortensen for their work on the economics of unemployment, especially job flows and the effects of being out of work. In 2002, Pissarides earned election to the British Academy, and from 2009 he also served on the executive committee of the European Economic Association.

Christopher Antoniou Pissarides was born on February 20, 1948, in Nicosia, Cyprus. Growing up in a well-off Cypriot family, he was sent to England to study at the University of Essex, where he received a BA (1970) and an MA (1971) in economics. Pissarides went on to earn his PhD in 1973 at the London School of Economics (LSE). Following graduation he worked briefly at the Central Bank of Cyprus and the University of Southampton. In 1976, he took a lecturer position at the LSE, where he is currently a professor of economics and the director of the research program on Technology and Growth at the Centre for Economic Performance.

Upon winning the Nobel honor he noted that the liberal attitudes of the 1960s, the student political activity at Essex, and the invasion of his home in Cyprus by the Turkish Army in July of 1974 had left an indelible mark on him. Pissarides wrote that July 14, 1974, was a pivotal point in which his life was forever altered. It was also during his undergraduate study at Essex that he met Dale Mortensen, with whom he later collaborated frequently and was jointly awarded the Nobel Prize in 2010.

The Mortensen-Pissarides model that resulted from the paper "Job Creation and Job Destruction in the Theory of Unemployment" is regarded as Pissarides's most influential contribution in modern macroeconomics and has highly enriched research on unemployment as an equilibrium phenomenon, on labor market dynamics, and on cyclical adjustment. It has become part of the core of most graduate economics curricula throughout the world. This paper built on the previous individual contributions that both authors had been making in the previous two decades; it was published in the *Review of Economic Studies* in 1994. Policy makers have also been using this model to help them better understand unemployment and job flows.

As a result of his research, he calls for low, limited-time unemployment benefits. An extended unemployment period can lead to loss of skills and sense of belonging in the labor force. Pissarides's main concern is that longer or more lucrative payments encourage higher unemployment and longer out-of-work times. In particular, his research shows that the more intensely job seekers looked for employment, the more jobs companies will offer because of the ease with which they can fill those positions.

In the course of his research, Pissarides helped develop the concept of matching functions, which explains the flows from unemployment to employment at a given moment of time, and pioneered the empirical work on its estimation. More recently, Pissarides has done research on the importance of structural change and economic performance as indicators of the strategies required to stimulate economic growth.

Given his main research interests in search theory and unemployment, Pissarides has lectured widely and written extensively on unemployment and labor market policy issues. His book *Equilibrium Unemployment Theory* (1990; 2nd ed. 2000) became a standard reference in the literature of the macroeconomics of unemployment. His other publications include: *Labour Market Adjustment: Microeconomic Foundations of Short-Run Neoclassical and Keynesian Dynamics* (2009), *Short-Run Equilibrium Dynamics of Unemployment, Vacancies and Real Wages* (1985), and *Labour Market Adjustment* (1976).

In addition to teaching at the LSE, he has been a consultant at the World Bank, the European Commission, and the Organisation for Economic Co-operation and Development (OECD). He is a fellow of the Econometric Society, a member of Council of the Royal Economic Society, a research fellow of CEPR and IZA, and a member of the Monetary Policy Committee of the Central Bank of Cyprus. He currently holds the Norman Sosnow Chair in Economics at the Economics Department at the London School of Economics.

*See also:* Arrow, Kenneth; Diamond, Peter; Hicks, John; Keynes, John Maynard; Mortensen, Dale

**Selected Works by Christopher Pissarides**

Mortensen, Dale, and Christopher Pissarides. "Job Creation and Job Destruction in the Theory of Unemployment." *Review of Economic Studies* 61 (1994): 397–415.

Pissarides, Christopher. *Equilibrium Unemployment Theory*. Cambridge, MA: MIT Press, 2000.

Pissarides, Christopher. "Job Matchings with State Employment Agencies and Random Search." *Economic Journal* 89 (1979): 818–33.

Pissarides, Christopher. *Labour Market Adjustment.* New York: Cambridge University Press, 1976.
Pissarides, Christopher. "Short-Run Equilibrium Dynamics of Unemployment, Vacancies, and Real Wages." *American Economic Review* 75 (1985): 676–90.

### Selected Works about Christopher Pissarides

"Christopher Pissarides." London School of Economics and Political Science. http://www2.lse.ac.uk/aboutLSE/keyFacts/nobelPrizeWinners/pissarides.aspx (accessed August 2012).

Pissarides, Christopher A. "Autobiography." Nobelprize.org. http://www.nobelprize.org/nobel_prizes/economics/laureates/2010/pissarides.html (accessed August 2012).

"Prize in Labor Economics 2005 awarded to Dale Mortensen and Christopher Pissarides." IZA Prize in Labor Economics. http://www.iza.org/en/webcontent/prize/history/prize2005/iza_prize (accessed August 2012).

Rampell, Catherine. "Shared Nobel Economics Prize for Market Analysis." *New York Times*, October 11, 2010. http://www.nytimes.com/2010/10/12/business/economy/12nobel.html?_r=2 (accessed August 2012).

*Ninee Shoua Yang*

## PRESCOTT, EDWARD

Born: December 26, 1940, in Glens Falls, New York; American; macroeconomics, business cycles, econometrics, Nobel Prize (2004); Major Works: "Rules Rather than Discretion: The Inconsistency of Optimal Plans" (with Finn Kydland) (1977), "Time to Build and Aggregate Fluctuations" (with Finn Kydland) (1982).

Edward Prescott is a U.S. economist who won the Nobel Prize in 2004 with Finn E. Kydland. Prescott is noted as one of the premier econometricians in the United States. The Nobel Prize was awarded to Prescott for his research on the time consistency of economic policy as related to business cycles, a topic in dynamic macroeconomics. Prescott is currently the Shinsei Bank Visiting Professor at New York University.

Edward Christian Prescott was born on December 26, 1940, in Glens Falls, New York. He graduated from Swarthmore College in 1962 with a major in mathematics. Prescott studied operations research at Case Western Reserve University where he received his master's degree in 1963. In 1967, Prescott earned his PhD in economics from Carnegie Mellon University.

Prior to graduating from Carnegie Mellon, Prescott began his academic career at the University of Pennsylvania in Philadelphia. At the University of Pennsylvania, Prescott expanded his interest in economic modeling through the encouragement of his colleague Lawrence Klein, a 1980 Nobel laureate in economics. It was this new interest that was to expand his field and vision of economics. Another colleague Prescott credits for his development as an econometrician is Ned Phelps. With Phelps's help, Prescott tackled problems in how to relate macroeconometric models to economics.

Edward Prescott was awarded the 2004 Nobel Prize in economics for his research on the time consistency of economic policy as it related to business cycles. (AP/Wide World Photos)

In 1970, Prescott took a leave to serve as a Brookings economic policy fellow. He was assigned to the U.S. Department of Labor. In 1969, Prescott published "Investment under Uncertainty" with Bob Lucas Jr., a University of Chicago economist who would later receive the Nobel Prize in 1995. In preparation for this paper, Prescott came to the conclusion that market failures can disappear if advantageous trades are allowed to occur and not be constrained. This conclusion has been the basis for many of Prescott's later works. He also credits Gérard Debreu's earlier works as providing a stimulus to his work and a writing style he wished to emulate.

Prescott stayed at the University of Pennsylvania till 1971. In 1971, he returned to his alma mater, Carnegie Mellon. During his time at the Graduate School of Industrial Administration (now Tepper School of Business) at Carnegie Mellon University, Prescott met a new graduate student named Finn Kydland. In 1977, Prescott and Kydland published "Rules Rather than Discretion: The Inconsistency of Optimal Plans." They explored the roles of goals and purpose in economic planning and policy as a "trigger" for a desired response from the economy. They investigated the question of whether or not the best monetary approach for central banks is a policy of exacting numerical targets or a more discretionary approach.

Prescott was selected as a Ford Foundation Research Professor while at the University of Chicago as a visiting professor in 1978. While in Chicago, he also was a visiting professor at Northwestern University. In 1980, Prescott moved to the University of Minnesota and stayed there till 2003. While at the University of Minnesota, Prescott also served as an economist for the Federal Reserve Bank of Minneapolis.

Realizing they left several questions unanswered in their first paper, Prescott and Kydland wrote a second paper, "Time to Build and Aggregate Fluctuations," in 1982. The paper outlined an econometric model to investigate changes in consumption, employment, investment, labor productivity, and output between the end of World War II and 1980. In this paper, they argued that supply shifts caused by technology improvements created both short-term business cycle variations and long-term improved living standards. For their work on the two papers, Prescott and Kydland were awarded the 2004 Nobel Prize in Economics.

Prescott is also known for an econometric model designed to level disparities in time series, the Hodrick-Prescott Filter. In 2003, Prescott moved to Arizona State University. A year later he accepted the Maxwell and Mary Pellish Chair in Economics at the University of California, Santa Barbara. In 2006, he returned to the eastern United States to accept the position of Shinsei Bank Visiting Professor at New York University.

In 2011, Edward Prescott was identified as one of the most influential modern economists. His later efforts and writings have focused on the negative effects that taxes and tax policies are having on the European economy.

Along with his Nobel Prize in Economics, Prescott also received the Carnegie Mellon Alexander Henderson Award in 1967, the designation of fellow in the Econometric Society in 1980, and the Ewin Plein Nemmers Prize in Economics from Northwestern University in 2002. In 2008, Edward Prescott was recognized by the United States' National Academy of Sciences.

*See also:* Debreu, Gérard; Klein, Lawrence; Kydland, Finn E.; Lucas, Robert, Jr.

## Selected Works by Edward Prescott

Kehoe, Timothy J., and Edward C. Prescott, eds. *Great Depressions of the Twentieth Century.* Minneapolis, MN: Federal Reserve Bank of Minneapolis, 2007.

Kydland, F., and E. C. Prescott. "Rules Rather than Discretion: The Inconsistency of Optimal Plans." *Journal of Political Economy* 85, no. 3 (1977): 473–92.

Kydland, Finn, and Edward C. Prescott. "Time to Build and Aggregate Fluctuations." *Econometrica* 50, no. 6 (1982): 1345–70.

Lucas, Robert E., Jr., and Edward C. Prescott. "Investment under Uncertainty." *Econometrica* 39, no. 5 (1971): 659–81.

Mehra, Rajnish, and Edward C. Prescott. "The Equity Premium: A Puzzle." *Journal of Monetary Economics* 15, no. 2 (1985): 145–61.

Prescott, Edward C. "Why Do Americans Work So Much More than Europeans?" *Federal Reserve Bank of Minneapolis Quarterly Review* 28, no. 1 (July 2004): 2–13.

Prescott, Edward C., and Rajnish Mehra. "Recursive Competitive Equilibrium: The Case of Homogeneous Households." *Econometrica* 48, no. 6 (1980): 1365–79.

## Selected Works about Edward Prescott

"Edward C. Prescott: W. P. Carey Chaired Professor." Minneapolis Federal Reserve Bank. http://www.minneapolisfed.org/research/prescott/ (accessed October 2011).

Prescott, Edward C. "Autobiography." Nobelprize.org. http://www.nobelprize.org/nobel_prizes/economics/laureates/2004/prescott-autobio.html (accessed September 2011).

"Prescott on the Estate Tax." *Greg Mankiw's Blog: Random Observations for Students of Economics*. http://gregmankiw.blogspot.com/2006/06/prescott-on-estate-tax.html (accessed September 2011).

Vane, Howard R., and Chris Mulhearn, eds. *James Tobin, Franco Modigliani, Finn E. Kydland and Edward C. Prescott*. London: Edward Elgar, 2010.

*David A. Dieterle*

## QUESNAY, FRANÇOIS

Born: June 4, 1694, in the village of Méré, France; Died: December 16, 1774, in Versailles, France; French; Physiocrat; Major Work: *The Tableau Oeconomical: An Attempt towards Ascertaining and Exhibiting the Source, Progress, and Employment of Riches* (1758).

François Quesnay is considered the founder of the economic philosophy called the Physiocratic system, and leader of economic thinkers during the Enlightenment called Physiocrats. The Physiocrats assumed that society was subject to natural laws. They believed that an economy's force came from the economy's agriculture. The Physiocrats proposed the propositions that led to the basic elements of capitalism. They promoted deregulation and reduced taxes. Quesnay and the Physiocrats are also credited with deriving the term "laissez-faire." Quesnay was elected to the Academy of Sciences and earned the nickname as the "modern Socrates." Quesnay died in 1774.

François Quesnay was born on June 4, 1694, in Méré, France. Méré is located outside Versailles. Quesnay grew up in a lower-middle-class home. He father was a country lawyer and did not earn much money as a rural lawyer. Growing up, it appears that Quesnay was a slow learner, not learning to read until he was 12 years old. Even though he was orphaned at 13, his desire to read and learn led him to study and become self-educated in medicine. When he was 24 he began a medical practice in the village of Mantes, France.

Quesnay's skills quickly developed a solid reputation and he gradually climbed to performing medical services to local aristocrats. Quesnay wrote many articles on surgery, which increased his medical reputation. Through his writings, he elevated surgery into a medical science. In 1749, Quesnay became the personal physician of the King Louis XV's mistress, the Madame de Pompadour, and eventually became a resident of Versailles.

In 1756, at the age of 60 Quesnay developed an interest in economics. Based on his rural background, he wrote several articles on farming for the *Encyclopedia* of Diderot. Quesnay based his writings on the works of Richard Cantillon, Marchal de Vauban, and Pierre de Boisguilbert.

In 1766, Quesnay wrote what became his most famous work, *Tableau economique*. This writing depicted the income flows between the different economic sectors. This work and the income flows concept became the founding document of the Physiocratic thinkers.

In *Tableau économique*, he detailed a circular-flow diagram of the economy. Quesnay's circular flow was an attempt to understand and explain the causes of

The originator of the physiocracy school of economics, François Quesnay was one of the most influential economists of the eighteenth century. Quesnay and the Physiocrats are credited with deriving the term "laissez-faire." (Meek, Ronald, *The Economics of Physiocracy*)

economic growth. The diagram illustrated what was produced by producers and how consumers spent money. In the *Tableau*, his defined "sterile" classes were both the producers and also consumed everything they produced. According to Quesnay, production and consumption were equal so there was no surplus production to carry over to the next economic period.

Quesnay emphasized the role of the agricultural sector. The wealth of a nation, Quesnay argued, lies in the size of its net product. According to Quesnay, only the agricultural sector could produce a surplus that could then be used for further economic growth the following year. He concluded that both industry and manufacturing were "sterile." Quesnay used the term "sterile" to mean these economic sectors were unproductive relative to future economic growth.

Quesnay constructed the "Table" to fit his belief of the economy, not the reverse. As a result, there are inconsistencies in his Table so it would illustrate the story that best suited his thinking that industry and manufacturing were zero-surplus economic sectors.

Quesnay's thesis that manufacturing was a "sterile" economic sector for economic growth has not held up over time. However, he was proved correct in his criticism of mercantilism. Quesnay was very critical of the mercantilist doctrines of Louis XV's finance minister, Jean-Baptiste Colbert. Quesnay asserted that the French government used mercantilist policies to protect French manufacturers from foreign competition, increasing prices of manufactured goods. Quesnay believed that the French court supported manufacturing and industry more than agriculture.

As a product of the Enlightenment, Quesnay promoted eliminating many of the medieval rules that governed the production of agricultural products. This, according to Quesnay, would permit the economy to find what he called its own "natural state." Quesnay defined the natural state of the economy as the balance in the circular flow between income of the economic sectors and the net product. Drawing on his medical background, Quesnay compared the circular flow to the circulation of human blood and the human body's ability to maintain a stable, continuous condition.

Quesnay and the Physiocrats advocated freer trade for French companies with major tax reform and deregulation leading to a freer French economy. Quesnay's attacks on the mercantilist French economic system and advocating his tax and regulation reforms were ultimately more acceptable than his economic theories on economic "sterility" of the manufacturing industry.

Quesnay and the Physiocrats promoted private property, property rights, and the merits of free choice for an individual to be at the heart of any economic system. In addition, however, a central authority (i.e., government) must assert itself to protect those rights. Quesnay credits Locke for many of his views on private property and liberty.

Quesnay's works were the foundation on which Adam Smith wrote *An Inquiry into the Nature and Causes of the Wealth of Nations*, culminating the fight against the mercantilist economic systems.

François Quesnay died on December 16, 1774, in Versailles at the age of 80.

*See also:* Cantillon, Richard; Colbert, Jean-Baptiste; Smith, Adam

## Selected Works by François Quesnay

Quesnay, François. *The Tableau Oeconomical: An Attempt towards Ascertaining and Exhibiting the Source, Progress, and Employment of Riches.* London: Printed for W. Owen, 1766.

## Selected Works about François Quesnay

Blaug, Mark. *François Quesnay (1694–1774)*. London: Edward Elgar, 1991.
Hishiyama, Izumi. "The Tableau Iconomique of Quesnay: Its Analysis, Reconstruction, and Application." *Kyoto University Economic Review* 30, no. 1 (1960): 1–46.
Sauvy, Alfred, ed. *François Quesnay et la physiocrats*. 2 vols. Paris: Institute National d'Études Demographiques, 1958.
Vaggi, Gianni, and John Eatwell. *The Economics of François Quesnay*. Durham, NC: Duke University Press, 1987.

*David A. Dieterle*

## REICH, ROBERT

Born: June 24, 1946, in Scranton, Pennsylvania; American; political economy; Major Works: *The Next American Frontier* (1983), *The Work of Nations: Preparing Ourselves for 21st-Century Capitalism* (1991), *Supercapitalism: The Transformation of Business, Democracy, and Everyday Life* (2007).

Robert Reich is a political economist, author, professor, and political commentator. He is currently Chancellor's Professor of Public Policy at the Richard and Rhoda Goldman School of Public Policy at the University of California, Berkeley. He has served in the administrations of Presidents Ford and Carter and was the secretary of labor under President Clinton from 1993 to 1997. Reich also worked on then President-Elect Obama's transition advisory board. He has written extensively on industrial policy and contributes regularly to National Public Radio, several forms of social media, and television programs.

Robert Bernard Reich was born in Scranton, Pennsylvania, on June 24, 1946. He began his life with Fairbanks disease, or multiple epiphyseal dysplasia, a rare congenital disorder that can stunt growth. As an adult, he is 4 feet and 10½ inches tall. Reich earned his AB summa cum laude from Dartmouth College in 1968 and his MA from Oxford University in 1970 where he was a Rhodes Scholar. He continued on to earn his JD from Yale University in 1972 where he was an editor of the *Yale Law Journal*. He married Clare Dalton in 1973. After graduating, Reich clerked for a federal judge and then went to work for his former law school professor Robert H. Bork, who was then U.S. solicitor general in the Ford administration. He then was the policy planning director for the Federal Trade Commission from 1976 to 1981. Reich next became a professor of business and public policy at the John F. Kennedy School of Government at Harvard University from 1981 to 1993. He served as President Clinton's secretary of labor from 1993 to 1996 when he left to spend more time with his teenage sons.

Reich made many lasting changes in his role as the secretary of labor with the Clinton administration. He implemented the Family and Medical Leave Act; headed the administration's successful effort to increase the minimum wage; secured worker pensions; started job-training programs, one-stop career centers, and school-to-work initiatives; and led a national fight against U.S. sweatshops and illegal child labor around the world. In 2008, *Time* magazine named him one of the 10 most successful cabinet secretaries of the century.

Reich explores industrial policy, the practice of using government intervention as a solution to a troubled American economy, throughout many of his published works. While teaching at Harvard, Reich authored many works including *The Next American Frontier* and *The Work of Nations: Preparing Ourselves for 21st-Century Capitalism*. In *American Frontier*, Reich promotes industrial policy, or more governmental power, over more conservative Keynesian thought. He also discusses the failure of "paper entrepreneurialism" to promote the American economy. He writes that business managers are maneuvering company assets and production figures to achieve profit instead of advancing production. He also advocates moving from simple product manufacturing to a skilled and flexible labor force. He argues that government promotion of human capital, tax incentives and loans for companies who train the unemployed, and the elimination of tax incentives for industries planning mergers would promote a positive influence on the American economy in light of foreign competition.

Reich promotes the global market and individual education in *The Work of Nations*. He advises the United States to open its doors to global trade and invest in education, or human capital, for unskilled American workers. In his book *Locked in the Cabinet*, Reich candidly writes of his years serving as the labor secretary in the Clinton White House. Reich clearly illustrates his frustrations in trying to represent the common worker within the Washington bureaucracy and his ultimate decision to return to teaching. In *Supercapitalism: The Transformation of Business, Democracy, and Everyday Life*, Reich advises corporations to make quality products and services with an underlying theme of corporate social responsibility.

Reich has had a significant partnership with the Democratic Party. He served as a summer intern for Senator Robert Kennedy in 1968, coordinated Eugene McCarthy's 1968 presidential campaign, and worked as an adviser to Democratic presidential candidates including Walter Mondale (1984) and Michael Dukakis (1988). He was a member of the governing board of Common Cause in Washington, DC (1981 to 1985), a member of the board of directors for Business Enterprise Trust (1989 to 1993), and trustee for Dartmouth College from 1989 to 1993.

He also founded the periodical *American Prospect* and served as the host of the PBS television programs *Made in America* and *At the Grass Roots*. He continues to cohost the television series *The Long and the Short of It* and regularly contributes to National Public Radio, the *New York Times*, *The New Yorker*, the *Los Angeles Times*, the *Boston Globe*, the *Washington Post*, the *Observer*, and *Business Week*.

He was the contributing editor of *The New Republic* from 1982 to 1992 and chair of the editorial board of *American Prospect* in 1990. His book *The Next American Frontier* won the Louis Brownlow Book Award from the National Academy of Public Administration in 1983. In 2002, he unsuccessfully ran for governor of Massachusetts. In 2003, the former Czech president awarded Reich the Vaclav Havel Foundation VIZE 97 Prize for his work in economics and politics. He continues to work as a political commentator on television programs such as *Hardball with Chris Matthews*, *This Week with George Stephanopoulos*, CNBC's *The Kudlow Report*, and APM's *Marketplace*.

*See also:* Keynes, John Maynard

**Selected Works by Robert Reich**

Reich, Robert. *Locked in the Cabinet*. New York: Knopf, 1997.
Reich, Robert. *The Next American Frontier*. New York: Times Books, 1983.
Reich, Robert. *Supercapitalism: The Transformation of Business, Democracy, and Everyday Life*. New York: Knopf, 2007.
Reich, Robert. *The Work of Nations: Preparing Ourselves for 21st-Century Capitalism*. New York: Knopf, 1991.

**Selected Works about Robert Reich**

"Arena Profile: Robert B. Reich." Politico. http://www.politico.com/arena/bio/robert_b_reich.html (accessed September 2010).
Kelly, Michael. *Things Worth Fighting For: Collected Writings*. New York: Penguin Press, 2004.
Leibovich, Mark. "The True Measure of a Man." *Washington Post*, March 14, 2002, C01.
Reich, Robert. "Robert Reich." http://www.robertreich.org (accessed September 2011).
"Robert Reich Profile." CNBC. http://www.cnbc.com/id/24730820/ (accessed September 2010).

*Kathryn Lloyd Gustafson*

# REISMAN, GEORGE

Born: January 13, 1937, in New York City; American; Austrian economics, economic theory, political economy, economic history, money and banking; Major Works: *The Government against the Economy* (1979), *Capitalism: A Treatise on Economics* (1996).

George Reisman was a born scholar, curious about how the world operates and eager to learn as much as possible from original sources. Reisman founded a magazine called *Freeman*, promoting free markets, laissez-faire capitalism, and what he called the rational concept of rights. Reisman developed his ideas about economics combining the British classical and Austrian schools of thought. Reisman's view and writings were highly influenced by Adam Smith, David Ricardo, John Stuart Mill, Jean-Baptiste Say, Carl Menger, Eugen von Böhm-Bawerk, and Friedrich von Hayek. Reisman is a professor emeritus of economics at Pepperdine University.

George Gerald Reisman was born on January 13, 1937, in New York City. Reisman graduated from Columbia University with a BA in economics and from New York University (NYU) a PhD in economics studying under Ludwig von Mises. Reisman met a like-minded student, Murray Rothbard, with whom he founded The Circle Bastiat in 1955 at NYU. The group met regularly to discuss morality and philosophy. The Objectivist Movement, founded by the controversial author and philosopher Ayn Rand, captured his imagination and he spent several years under her tutelage.

Reisman's work and writings focus on what he calls a rational concept of rights. He compares this to a needs or entitlement concept of rights, which he asserts is a predominant philosophy of our culture. The rational concept of rights is where people seek their own happiness, respecting and without interfering in someone else pursuing his or her rights to happiness. Cooperation is voluntary and is accomplished by trading. We have rights to buy from willing sellers, and sell to willing buyers, of our own free will. Government's primary role is to protect rights of individuals against others taking unfair advantage of them, stealing from them, and doing physical harm to them.

Reisman developed his ideas about economics by combining the British classical and Austrian schools of thought. Adam Smith, David Ricardo, John Stuart Mill, Jean-Baptiste Say, Carl Menger, Eugen von Böhm-Bawerk, and Friedrich von Hayek were some of his most influential economic thinkers. Böhm-Bawerk informed his views on capital and interest, cost, and value. Laissez-faire capitalism, an economic structure where entrepreneurs operate with little government intervention, is the correct path to a financially healthy nation, according to Reisman.

Objectivists such as Reisman argue that individuals have rights to be employed by a willing employer, a right to purchase health insurance from a free market of providers, and a right to buy or build a home. He further asserts that to insist one be given a job, a home, or care violates rights of the individuals from whom these demands are made.

Reisman asserts that when a society claims rights to housing, education, medical care, and/or jobs, they expect the government to coerce citizens to provide these things. Reisman emphasizes that when citizens expect "free" or nearly free services, the demand will eventually become unsustainable. To claim a right to something for no reason, he thinks, is a contradiction and a violation of his rational concept of rights. Some of Reisman's examples of violations of rational rights include the minimum wage laws, zoning laws, arbitrary building codes, tariffs on imported construction goods, and medical licensing boards.

Professor Reisman distinguishes random spending from saving money to purchase cars and homes at a later date. Consuming these high-ticket products impacts employment and manufacturing, which stimulates our economy. According to Reisman savings, not traditional consumption, represents most spending. He adds this productive savings to an equation that includes investment and consumption, which represent elements of national economic health and vigor.

Reisman opposes environmentalism. He objects to activists who prefer to preserve the intrinsic value of every aspect of nature rather than advance the quality of life for individuals through technology and innovation.

Reisman claims that historically technologies evolve when they are unencumbered by government bureaucracy. "Green" energy resources develop as carbon-based resource users seek to improve efficiency and profitability. As a result, Reisman criticized California's legislation to reduce greenhouse gas emissions without any technology or technology plan in place to replenish the needed energy. An absence of ready, affordable noncarbon technology would be, Reisman declares, disastrous for California's economy.

Reisman is troubled by the widespread lack of knowledge and understanding of fundamental economic principles that drive our private enterprise market system.

Professor Reisman writes a blog on current economic and political topics. A senior fellow at the Goldwater Institute, he critiques and offers constructive comments on how to approach problems from the private enterprise perspective. He asserts that the United States is the world's most prosperous nation due to its free-market, capitalist economic system. He analyzes current political and economic issues and formulates measured responses perhaps not considered by influential policy makers.

George Reisman retired from Pepperdine University in 2005.

*See also:* Böhm-Bawerk, Eugen von; Hayek, Friedrich von; Menger, Carl; Mill, John Stuart; Mises, Ludwig von; Ricardo, David; Rothbard, Murray; Say, Jean-Baptiste; Smith, Adam

### Selected Works by George Reisman

Reisman, George. *Capitalism: A Treatise on Economics.* Ottawa, IL: Jameson Books, 1996.
Reisman, George. *The Government against the Economy.* Ottawa, IL: Caroline House, 1979.
Reisman, George. "Our Financial House of Cards and How to Start Replacing It with Solid Gold." LewRockwell.com. March 26, 2008. http://www.lewrockwell.com/reisman/reisman44.html (accessed October 2012).
Reisman, George. *Production vs. Consumption.* Laguna Hills, CA: Jefferson School of Philosophy, Economics, and Psychology, 1991.
Reisman, George. "The Growing Abundance of Natural Resources and the Wastefulness of Recycling." In *Rational Readings on Environmental Concerns.* Edited by Jay H. Lehr, 631–36. New York: Van Nostrand Reinhold, 1992.

### Selected Works about George Reisman

"George Reisman." Ludwig von Mises Institute. http://www.mises.org/ (accessed July 2012).
Reisman, George. "George Reisman's Blog on Economics, Politics, Society, and Culture." http://georgereismansblog.blogspot.com/.
Woods, Thomas. *33 Questions about American History You're Not Supposed to Ask.* New York: Crown, 2007.

*Cynthia Blitz Law*

# RICARDO, DAVID

Born: April 18, 1772, in London; Died: September 11, 1823, in Gloucestershire, England; English; classical school, monetary economics, economic rent, theory of value, comparative advantage; Major Works: *An Essay on the Influence of a Low Price of Corn on the Profits of Stock Showing the Inexpediency of Restrictions on Importation; with Remarks on Mr. Malthus's Two Last Publications* (1815), *On the Principles of Political Economy and Taxation* (1817).

David Ricardo was a British economist considered one of the classical economists. After reading Adam Smith, Ricardo began writing on the benefits of converting currency to gold. Ricardo was an early proponent that an economy's money supply and price level (inflation) are positive related. While he was an early writer on the concept of economic rent, David Ricardo is probably most famous for his expansion of Adam Smith's idea of absolute advantage with his introduction of comparative advantage and expanding on Smith's benefits of trade. Ricardo died in 1823.

David Ricardo was born in April 18, 1772 in London. His father was a Jewish stockbroker who had originally come from Holland. After attending school in London and Amsterdam, Ricardo joined his father's brokerage firm. Ricardo formed his own stock firm and become very successful. In 1814, at the age of 41, he retired from business worth more than $40 million in today's dollars. At his death in 1823, his estate would today be worth more than $100 million.

Ricardo became interested in economics after reading the works of Adam Smith in his early 20s. He would often discuss his ideas with his friend James Mill, who encouraged him to write. Ricardo began by writing articles and tracts about currency issues. In this area, Ricardo was a bullionist, arguing for the convertibility of currency to gold. He held that it was because the notes were not convertible, that they had been overissued and inflation had resulted. He was, in that respect, an early proponent of the quantity theory of money, which proposes a positive relationship between an economy's money supply and the price level (inflation).

Ricardo also dismissed the idea that surplus is simply what is left over after a country consumes what it produces of goods and services. He entered into a long correspondence and friendship, debating the idea with Thomas Malthus. Ricardo was a believer in Say's law, in that he believed that production automatically creates a market for consumption; hence a general glut is impossible.

Ricardo drew extensively on Malthus's work in his writings about rent. Ricardo saw rent not just as a return for the use of natural resources but as an unearned surplus. By this he meant that rent was a residual, arising from the difference between the gross outputs of the land minus all of the production costs. This residual had no impact on the future supply of land; and differences in rent simply arose from differences in the land—fertility, access to water, and climate. Thus because the output of varying types of land would be same (i.e., a bushel of corn grown on inferior land fetches the same price as a bushel grown on very fertile land), producers would bid up the price of better land, benefiting the landowner rather than the producer.

In 1815, Ricardo wrote "An Essay on the Influence of a Low Price of Corn on the Profits of Stock." In this work, he would describe what would perhaps become one of his most enduring ideas in economics, the concept of comparative advantage.

Prior to this essay, the general belief was that gains from trade arose from absolute advantage—that nations prospered because they had an advantage in the production of a good or service that other nations could not match. Therefore trading the good allowed the nation to increase its wealth. But Ricardo demonstrated that a nation did not have to have an absolute advantage in anything in order to trade profitably and grow. It needed a comparative advantage. This meant that as long as a nation had a lower opportunity cost in the production of a good than another nation, the first nation could trade profitably even if the other nation had an absolute advantage.

It was the recognition and application of a lower opportunity cost that provided the comparative advantage and allowed the nation to trade on terms that resulted in growth. If all nations specialized in those products for which they had comparative advantage, then unhindered trade would result in all nations trading and becoming better off.

Ricardo used this idea to argue against the Corn Laws, which set up barriers to imported grain to the benefit of English growers. He argued that reducing the trade barriers not only would make grain more affordable to the poor but would shift England's resource use to areas where it had a comparative advantage and result in greater wealth, although perhaps at the expense of English landowners.

Ricardo also contributed to the debate about value. Through most of his work, he remained a proponent of the labor theory of value, which held that the relative natural prices of goods reflected the amount of labor necessary to produce them. However, he realized early on that capital usage also was a factor in profitability and, in turn, the level of wages. This led him to develop two explanations: one based on an assumption that firms employ capital in approximately the same proportion to labor; the other based on the existence of a single commodity that represented the average capital per worker, which would allow an explanation of price and wage variation based on variances from the average amount of capital per worker.

Ricardo's masterpiece was his *On the Principles of Political Economy and Taxation* (1817). It is not a particularly easy read, but it is significant for its breadth and understanding.

What is particularly amazing about Ricardo's work is that it was done without the benefit of the mathematics that is such an integral part of today's economics.

David Ricardo died on September 11, 1823, in Gloucester, England.

*See also*: Malthus, Thomas; Mill, John Stuart; Say, Jean-Baptiste; Smith, Adam

## Selected Works by David Ricardo

Ricardo, David. *An Essay on the Influence of a Low Price of Corn on the Profits of Stock Showing the Inexpediency of Restrictions on Importation; with Remarks on Mr. Malthus's Two Last Publications*. London: John Murray, 1815.

Ricardo, David. *The High Price of Bullion: A Proof of the Depreciation of Bank Notes*. London: John Murray, 1810.

Ricardo, David. *On the Principles of Political Economy and Taxation*. London: John Murray, 1817.

Ricardo, David. *On Protection in Agriculture*. London: John Murray, 1822.

Ricardo, David. *Plan for the Establishment of a National Bank*. London: John Murray, 1824.

## Selected Works about David Ricardo

Gootzeit, Michael. *David Ricardo*. New York: Columbia University Press, 1975.

Henderson, John P., David Ricardo, John Bryan Davis, Warren J. Samuels, and Gilbert B. Davis. *The Life and Economics of David Ricardo*. Hingham, MA: Kluwer Academic, 1997.

Weatherall, David. *David Ricardo: A Biography*. Boston: Martinus Nijhoff, 1976.

*Timothy P. Schilling*

# RIVLIN, ALICE

Born: March 4, 1931, in Philadelphia, Pennsylvania; American; fiscal policy, monetary policy; Major Works: *Systematic Thinking for Social Actions* (1971), *Reviving the American Dream: The Economy, the States, and the Federal Government* (1993).

Alice Rivlin is an economist who has devoted her career to public service for the American people. She served as the first director of the Congressional Budget Office (February 1975 to August 1983) during the Carter and Reagan administrations. She was also the 30th director of the Office of Management and Budget (October 1994 to April 1996), this during the Clinton administration. She then became the vice chairman of the Federal Reserve from June 1996 through July 1999. President Barack Obama appointed Rivlin to his National Commission on Fiscal Responsibility and Reform in 2010. Rivlin has also worked for the Brookings Institution throughout her career. She is currently a visiting professor at the Georgetown Public Policy Institute along with her work on the National Commission of Fiscal Responsibility and Reform.

Alice Mitchell Rivlin was born on March 4, 1931, in Philadelphia, Pennsylvania. She began her studies at Bryn Mawr College with a focus on history. She took a first-year summer course in economics with Reuben Zubrow at Indiana University and decided that economics would be more useful. She graduated in 1952, writing her senior thesis on the economic integration of Western Europe, even discussing the European monetary union. She then moved to Paris where she held a junior position working on the Marshall Plan. She was later rejected from the public administration program at Harvard because she was of

American economist, Alice Rivlin. She has spent at least half of her career either serving a U.S. president or on the board of the Federal Reserve. (AP/Wide World Photos)

marriageable age and consequently was considered a poor student risk. She then applied to Radcliffe College's (Harvard University) economics program where she earned her PhD in economics in 1958. She is married to economist Sidney G. Winter, who is a professor at the University of Pennsylvania. She is a frequent contributor to newspapers, television, and radio, and has written numerous books.

Instead of an academic career, Rivlin ultimately focused on policy work instead as she saw this as an avenue to improving people's lives. In her book *Systemic Thinking for Social Change*, Rivlin examines how systemic analysis has positively contributed to social action programs like education, health, manpower training, and income maintenance and where it falls short due to inadequate data or methods. Rivlin ultimately endorses widespread implementation of social experimentation and acceptability of the federal government with the requirement of comprehensive, reliable performance measures.

In *Reviving the American Dream*, Riven discusses how to foster faster growth rates in average incomes over the long run. She states that this is necessary to restore confidence in the United States as a place where people who work hard can expect to do better than their parents did. Specifically, Rivlin proposes a common tax for states to be collected on a uniform basis and rate across the country and shared by the states on a formula basis. She advocates that this policy would encourage interstate commerce and ultimately promote growth. She also writes that state tax policy should shift away from tax breaks and move toward improving services as this would encourage an aggressive effort for states to improve their infrastructure and their education systems to attract business.

Rivlin not only is an economist but was also at the forefront of female representation within the profession. Rivlin recounts that her years as a graduate student at Harvard in the 1950's were not always smooth sailing. She taught mixed-gender economics classes but initially was assigned only women tutees. When wanting to allow a swap of students with a male colleague for a research project, a senior tutor objected to the switch on the grounds that a female tutor would make male students feel second class. In addition, Rivlin did not teach introductory economics in the spring of her second year due to the birth of her child. The man who picked up the class in the spring announced that since a woman could not adequately teach economics, all work and grades previously given would not count. Fortunately, the department chair intervened and Rivlin's students were able to keep their prior grades. She has maintained that she has never worried about being the only woman (or one of the few) in her government positions as people eventually realized she was competent and not self-conscious about her gender.

Rivlin is also the director of Brookings Institution's Greater Washington Research Project. President Lyndon Johnson appointed Rivlin to serve as assistant secretary for planning and evaluation at the U.S. Department of Health, Education, and Welfare (1968–69). She was the founding director of the Congressional Budget Office (CBO) during 1975–83, where she was known to criticize Reaganomics as head of the CBO. In 1983, she won a MacArthur Foundation "genius" award. She was a senior fellow for economic studies at the Brookings

Institution from 1983 to 1993. Under President Clinton, she served as deputy director of the Office of Management and Budget and then as the first female director from 1994 to 1996.

From 1996 to 1999, she served as a governor of the Federal Reserve (Fed) and the Fed's vice chair. She was also chair of the District of Columbia Financial Responsibility and Management Assistance Authority from 1998 to 2000 where she helped rescue the District of Columbia from bankruptcy. She has taught at Harvard University, George Mason University, and The New School Universities. She has served as president of the American Economic Association and is currently a member of the board of directors of the New York Stock Exchange. She is the author or coauthor of 16 books and numerous articles and papers.

*See also:* Bernanke, Ben; Burns, Arthur; Volcker, Paul

**Selected Works by Alice Rivlin**

Rivlin, Alice. *Reviving the American Dream: The Economy, the States and the Federal Government*. Washington, DC: Brookings Institution Press, 1993.

Rivlin, Alice. *Systematic Thinking for Social Actions*. Washington, DC: Brookings Institution Press, 1971.

**Selected Works about Alice Rivlin**

Edison, Hali J. "An Interview with Alice Rivlin." American Economic Association. 1998. http://www.aeaweb.org/committees/cswep/awards/rivlin.php (accessed September 24, 2010).

Levy, David. "Interview with Alice Rivlin." The Region: Minneapolis Fed Magazine Profile, June 1, 1997. http://www.minneapolisfed.org/publications_papers/pub_display.cfm?id=3638 (accessed September 24, 2011).

Woodward, Bob. *The Agenda: Inside the Clinton White House*. New York: Simon & Schuster, 1994.

*Kathryn Lloyd Gustafson*

## ROACH, STEPHEN

Born: September 16, 1945, in Los Angeles, California, American; global economics; Major Works: *This China Is Different: A Collection of Essays on China's Growing Stature in the World Economy* (2002), *The Next Asia: Opportunities and Challenges for a New Globalization* (2009).

Stephen Roach is a senior fellow and lecturer with the Jackson Institute and Yale's School of Management. In addition to his academic position in economics, Roach has written books, journal articles, and pieces for the news media. A former senior research associate at the Federal Reserve Bank in Washington, DC, he was chief economist for the financial services company Morgan Stanley. He is considered an expert on global economics specializing in Asia.

Stephen S. Roach was born September 16, 1945, in Los Angeles, Californiia. He began his studies in engineering in 1963 at the University of Wisconsin. During his third semester, he decided to change majors and transferred to the College of Letters and Science at Wisconsin, exploring several majors before deciding to study economics. He completed a bachelor's degree in economics in 1968. He then enrolled at New York University where he earned a master's degree and a PhD in economics.

After completing his graduate work, Roach served in a senior capacity on the research staff of the Federal Reserve Board in Washington, DC, from 1972 to 1979. After that, Roach held a position as a research fellow at the Brookings Institution in Washington, DC. Roach then joined Morgan Stanley in 1982. In more than 25 years with the financial firm, he held senior positions including the chief economist. In this role he headed up the firm's global team of economists in New York, London, Frankfurt, Paris, Tokyo, Hong Kong, and Singapore. He was appointed chairman of the firm's Asia businesses in 2007, a position he held until 2010. He remains the nonexecutive chairman of Morgan Stanley Asia.

Stephen Roach addresses a plenary session during the 2006 World Economic Forum in Davos, Switzerland. Roach is considered one of the foremost thought leaders on the Chinese economy. (AP/Wide World Photos)

In addition to his position at Morgan Stanley, Roach is currently a senior fellow and senior lecturer with the Jackson Institute and Yale University's School of Management. Roach's research includes a broad range of topics, with most recent emphasis on globalization, productivity and the macro paybacks of information technology, and the emergence of China. His most recent book, *The Next Asia: Opportunities and Challenges for a New Globalization*, provides an assessment of Asia's potential to provide a new source of growth for a postcrisis global economy. The book consists of 70 of his essays, focusing on five Asian issues including the state of the world after the financial crisis, Asia's role in globalization, the process of rebalancing the Chinese economy, a new pan-regional structure for integration and competition, and a discussion of the risk in U.S.-China trade tensions.

Considered a contemporary economist thought leader and expert on the Chinese economy, the media and economic community are attentive to Roach's views on the modern Chinese economy. Roach has called the 2008–9 global recession an important wake-up call for Asia's old-mode economy. For an economy that has been in growth mode for the past 25 years, the recession strongly suggested the need to find a new growth model for the future. He emphasizes that the new growth model must be sustainable, integrated, coordinated, and balanced. According to Roach, the new Asian economy must have a more domestic-economy orientation. Roach has also suggested that the Great Recession of 2008–9 was the result of a too unbalanced global economy.

In addition to his teaching post at Yale, Roach also makes regular appearances in the news media as an expert on global economics. His work has appeared in academic journals, in books, in congressional testimony, and on the op-ed pages of the *Financial Times*, the *New York Times*, the *Washington Post*, and the *Wall Street Journal*.

*See also:* Roubini, Nouriel; Sachs, Jeffrey

### Selected Works by Stephen Roach

Roach, Stephen. *This China Is Different: A Collection of Essays on China's Growing Stature in the World Economy*. New York: Morgan Stanley, 2002.

Roach, Stephen. *The Next Asia: Opportunities and Challenges for a New Globalization*. Hoboken, NJ: Wiley, 2009.

### Selected Works about Stephen Roach

Steinberger, Michael. "A Dark View of the Street; Spotlight Shines on Skeptic Who Sees a Long Slowdown." *New York Times*, May 17, 2001. http://www.nytimes.com/2001/05/17/business/a-dark-view-of-the-street-spotlight-shines-on-skeptic-who-sees-a-long-slowdown.html?ref=stephensroach (accessed March 2012).

"Wiley Announces the Launch of *Stephen Roach on The Next Asia* by Morgan Stanley's Asia Chairman." Morganstanley.com. September 10, 2007. Web November 17, 2011. http://www.morganstanley.com/about/press/print/2858cd77-a936-11de-b891-79e6260f77e0.html (accessed March 2012).

*Diane Fournier*

## ROBBINS, LIONEL

Born: November 22, 1898, in Sipson, Middlesex, England; Died: May 15, 1984, in London, England; English; history of economic thought, macroeconomics, economics of war and peace; Major Works: *An Essay on the Nature and Significance of Economic Science* (1932), *The Great Depression* (1934).

Lionel Robbins was a British economist. Unlike many of his contemporaries, he was not an advocate of the Marshallian view, which was dominant during his education. He would attack Marshall's idea of the representative firm in the 1920s, arguing that the idea was of no help in understanding equilibrium in the firm or an industry. While some would think this would make him a ready convert to the upcoming Keynesian revolution, he would later find fault with those views as well. Robbins died in 1984.

Lionel Charles Robbins was born on November 22, 1898, in Sipson, Middlesex, England. Prior to going to university, Robbins served in the military in World War I. He returned with a desire to help change the world. Robbins received his education at the London School of Economics (LSE). He then served as a lecturer at the New College at Oxford, but would return to the London School of Economics to become chair of the economics department in 1929. He held that post until his retirement in 1961.

While at the London School, Robbins did much to raise its visibility. Bringing Friedrich von Hayek to the school as a faculty member was a start. He would also welcome a number of other notable economists during his tenure, including John Hicks and Nicholas Kaldor. But he continued in his own research to challenge the common consensus and develop different ways of looking at problems. In his 1932 work, *Essay on the Nature and Significance of Economic Science*, he drafted the definition of economics that later became the standard. He viewed economics as a theorist: he saw economics as founded on logical deduction. Robbins was also antiempirical and skeptical about the use of statistics and data. Yet he also believed strongly that the field was and should be positive (describing things as they are), instead of normative (emphasizing how things should be), an interesting paradox.

Another of his more significant works from the 1930s was *The Great Depression*. Robbins defended the view of the Austrian School that the Depression was caused by undersaving (or overconsumption), a view that coincided with Hayek's. Prior to the publication, while serving on the five-member Economic Advisory Council, he opposed import restrictions and public works projects as means to alleviate the downturn. This would label him as a strong opponent to the Keynesian school being developed at rival Cambridge. It would not be until after World War II and the publication of his work *The Economic Problem in Peace and War* that he would advocate the policies of full employment through management of aggregate demand.

Robbins is renowned as a historian of economic thought. While he experimented in this area as early as the 1930s with a work on William Stanley Jevons, his contributions expanded beginning in the 1950s with *The Theory of Economic Policy in English Classical Political Economy*; a work on Robert Torrens, *The Theory of Economic Development in the History of Economic Thought in the Late 1960s*; and the publication of *A History of Economic Thought: The LSE Lectures*. This publication was a collection of his lectures on the LSE history of economic thought, published posthumously in 1998. Robbins was a strong believer that the history of economic thought needed to be covered in mainstream academic journals and should not be relegated to a separate field.

Robbins was generally viewed as an anti-Socialist and anti-interventionist. As chairman of the Committee on Higher Education in the early 1960s, however, he advocated for government subsidization to any qualified candidate who sought a university or college education. The result was a massive expansion of higher education in Great Britain through the 1960s and 1970s.

He was made a life peer as Baron Robbins in 1959. Upon his retirement from the London School of Economics in 1961, Robbins became chairman of the

*Financial Times*, a post he would hold until 1970. Robbins received many honorary degrees from Oxford, Exeter, Sheffield, Columbia, and Penn, among many others. He was president of the British Academy from 1962 to 1967 and trustee of the National Gallery from 1952 to 1974. In 1954 and 1955, he was president of the Royal Economic Society and chairman of the UK Committee on Higher Education from 1961 to 1964. He was made chancellor of Stirling University in 1968 and held this post till 1978.

Lionel Robbins died on May 15, 1984, in London, England.

*See also:* Hayek, Friedrich von; Hicks, John; Jevons, William Stanley; Kaldor, Nicholas; Keynes, John Maynard

### Selected Works by Lionel Robbins

Robbins, Lionel. *An Essay on the Nature and Significance of Economic Science*. London: Macmillan, 1932.

Robbins, Lionel. *The Great Depression*. New York: Macmillan, 1934.

Robbins, Lionel. *A History of Economic Thought: The LSE Lectures*. Edited by Steven G. Medema and Warren Samuels. Princeton, NJ: Princeton University Press. 1998.

Robbins, Lionel. *The Theory of Economic Development in the History of Economic Thought: Being the Chichele Lectures for 1966*. New York: Macmillan, 1968.

### Selected Works about Lionel Robbins

Blaug, Mark, and Paul Sturges. *Who's Who in Economics: A Biographical Dictionary of Major Economists, 1700–1980*. Cambridge, MA: MIT Press, 1983.

Howson, Susan. *Lionel Robbins*. Cambridge: Cambridge University Press, 2011.

"Lionel Robbins." In *The Concise Encyclopedia of Economics*. Edited by David R. Henderson. The Library of Economics and Liberty. http://www.econlib.org/library/Enc/bios/Robbins.html (accessed March 2012).

*Timothy P. Schilling*

## ROBERTSON, SIR DENNIS

Born: May 23, 1890, in Lowestoft, Suffolk, England; Died: April 21, 1963, in Cambridge, England; English; banking policy, industrial fluctuations; Major Works: *A Study of Industrial Fluctuation* (1915), *Banking Policy and the Price Level* (1926).

Sir Dennis Holme Robertson was an English economist who taught at Cambridge and London Universities. He played a major role in the development of economic theory with respect to monetary and business cycle theory and policy during the twentieth century. Robertson was an early supporter of and regularly collaborated with John Maynard Keynes, as well as A. C. Pigou and R. G. Hawtrey, although he later famously critiqued some of Keynes's ideas. Robertson was noted for his first-rate mind and his unique ability to present abstract economic analysis in highly readable form. Robertson died in 1963.

Dennis Holme Robertson was born in Lowestoft, Suffolk, England, on May 23, 1890. He was the son of a Church of England clergyman and the youngest of six children. He graduated from Eton where he earned many honors, including captain of the school. In 1908, he began his successful amateur acting career by playing the part of the White Queen in Lewis Carroll's *Alice through the Looking Glass*, which set the stage for many references in his future published works. He continued on to Trinity College, Cambridge, in 1912 where he read classics and economics and graduated with first-class honors. Robertson was commissioned into the 11th Battalion, London Regiment in 1914 during World War I, where he eventually served in Egypt and Palestine, and was awarded the Military Cross. He was also selected as a fellow of Trinity College at the same time. Robertson eventually became a reader in economics at Cambridge University in 1930 and then ultimately was made a fellow of the British Academy in 1932. He taught at London University from 1938 to 1944 where he also worked for the Treasury handling financial relations between Great Britain and the United States. In 1944, he returned to Cambridge as a professor of political economy until his retirement in 1957. Robertson also played an active part in the postwar Bretton Woods Monetary Conference.

Robertson published prolifically within his profession. He wrote his first book in 1915 at the age of 22 while in his third year of economic studies. In *A Study of Industrial Fluctuation*, he examines the trade cycle with a focus on the interaction between invention and investment, with support for government intervention and avoiding inflation. In his 1922 successful textbook *Money*, Robertson wrote of monetary forces. Specifically, he maintained that government policy should work to maintain price stability and that bank deposits were essential to the money supply. Within his *Banking Policy and Price Level* book from 1926 and works collected in his *Economic Fragments* (1931), Robertson lays the foundation for period analysis, which became very helpful to future economists.

Robertson's *Banking Policy* centers on monetary theory that included many insights from Knut Wicksell and the Stockholm School. He also brought real factors, like savings and investment, into focus where monetary variables once dominated. This work foreshadows some of Keynes's later work in his historic *General Theory of Employment, Interest and Money*. In his own later works, Robertson built a theory of saving and investment that many speculate was more sophisticated than the later Keynes model. In 1937, Robertson engaged Keynes in a now famous debate over this savings-investment relationship in the *General Theory*, which ultimately led to the end of his association with Keynes.

Robertson was known for including many quotations from Lewis Carroll's *Alice in Wonderland* throughout his writing. He has also been critiqued at times for clumsy mathematics and confusing terminology. Yet it is notable that within *A Study of Industrial Fluctuation*, Robertson apologizes in his introduction, stating, "In the ordinary course of events the essay would have undergone considerable overhauling before publication ... But the pressure from other duties [World War I] has prevented me from undertaking the task; and it became clear that unless publication was to be indefinitely delayed, the work must be published substantially as it stood" (Robertson 1926, vii).

Robertson became a fellow of Eton College in 1948. From 1944 to 1946, Robertson served as a member of the Royal Commission on Equal Pay. He also became a companion of the Order of St. Michael and St. George in 1944. He was the president of the Royal Economic Society from 1948 to 1950. In 1953, he earned knighthood. From 1957 to 1958, he worked as a member of the Council on Prices, Productivity and Incomes and also retired from his Cambridge chair. Robertson earned honorary degrees from many universities including London, Manchester, Durham, and Sheffield as well as from Harvard, Columbia, Amsterdam, and Louvain.

Sir Dennis Robertson died of a heart attack on April 21, 1963, in Cambridge, England.

*See also:* Keynes, John Maynard; Pigou, A. C.; Wicksell, Knut

**Selected Works by Sir Dennis Robertson**

Robertson, Dennis. *Banking Policy and the Price Level* (1926). London: P. S. King and Son, 1932.

Robertson, Dennis. *A Study of Industrial Fluctuation* (1915). London: Routledge, 1997.

**Selected Works about Sir Dennis Robertson**

Fletcher, Gordon. "In Search of Dennis Robertson: Through the Looking Glass and What I Found There." http://www.liv.ac.uk/managementschool/research/working%20papers/wp200621.pdf (accessed September 2011).

Fletcher, Gordon. *Understanding Dennis Robertson: The Man and His Work*. Northampton, MA: Edward Elgar, 2000.

Hutchinson, Terence Wilmot. *A Review of Economic Doctrines, 1870–1929*. Oxford: Clarendon Press, 1966.

Presley, J. R. *Robertsonian Economics: An Examination of the Work of Sir D. H. Robertson on Industrial Fluctuation*. New York: Holmes and Meier, 1979.

Seligman, Ben B. *Main Currents in Modern Economics: Economic Thought since 1870*. Piscataway, NJ: Transaction, 1990.

*Kathryn Lloyd Gustafson*

# ROBINSON, JOAN

Born: October 31, 1903, in Willesden, England; Died: August 5, 1983, in Cambridge, England; English; imperfect competition, socialism, Keynesianism; Major Works: *Economics of Imperfect Competition* (1933), *The Theory of Unemployment* (1933), *Essay on Marxian Economics* (1942), *The Accumulation of Capital* (1956), *Essays in the Theory of Economic Growth* (1964).

Joan Robinson was a remarkably complex economist. Robinson's 1933 *Economics of Imperfect Competition* confronted the prevailing neoclassical economic models of the day. For example, she was a major critic of models suggesting that equilibrium could be identified. As a lecturer at Cambridge, Robinson was an early disciple of John Maynard Keynes. Robinson later promoted the work of Karl Marx and, sympathetic to social revolutions, she was supportive of Chinese and North

Korean communism. Robinson enjoyed lively debate, often treating fellow professors as students. Robinson died in 1983.

Joan Robinson was born Joan Maurice on October 31, 1903, in England to a wealthy and distinguished family. Even during her growing years, her thoughts were dominated by questions about how to create a more just and equal society. She studied at Cambridge under A. C. Pigou, and after graduation married economist Austin Robinson. They moved to India in 1926 so Austin could work as a tutor to a maharajah. They returned to England in 1929 so Austin could take a position at Cambridge. Not having a job, Joan sought to continue her work in economics by writing articles and a book.

The book *Economics of Imperfect Competition* (1933), expressed her belief that current "neoclassical" economic methods (as expressed by Marshall, Walras, and Pigou) did not reflect reality. Their methods were organized around the pursuit of ideal equilibrium situations, which, she argued, are illusory. Furthermore, their models assumed perfect competition, as if all products were the same and a business could be opened or shut down instantly. In her book, Robinson suggested more realistic assumptions.

Unlike many (perhaps most) economists, Robinson was not content to make minor improvements on economic theory. In her view, the reality of imperfect competition did not simply require small modifications to current economic theory but completely undermined it. She insisted that economists abandon the old models and seek out a brand-new way of looking at the world. Her 1933 book established her as a serious and innovative economist, and she secured a position as a lecturer at Cambridge in 1934.

At Cambridge, Robinson came under the influence of John Maynard Keynes, who was also at Cambridge at the time. In Keynes's *The General Theory of Employment, Interest and Money* (1936), Robinson saw a way to completely do away with the old Marshallian view of economics. She became Keynes's greatest supporter, and considered her own theory of imperfect competition as the way to destroy the old system. She thought that Keynes's theory of aggregate demand could become the groundwork for a new one. She was enormously disappointed, however, when Keynes himself did not seem to think his ideas were as revolutionary as she did. When Keynesianism began to be used by neoclassical economists all over the world, Robinson dismissed them as "bastard Keynesians" and counted such development as a severe missed opportunity.

Desperate for fresh ideas, she turned to Karl Marx, studying his work and writing a short book called *Essays on Marxian Economics* (1942). She found Marx's questions about the development of capitalism and the distribution of income to be promising, but in the end decided that his methods were not much better. The book did not make her popular, for she gained the enmity of both Marxists (for finding fault with Marx) and mainstream economists (for making it seem like Marx was worth studying).

Robinson was sympathetic to the various Socialist revolutions that occurred around the world, and deeply hostile to American foreign and domestic policy, in particular the arms race with the Soviet Union. She was not impressed with

Soviet communism either. Instead, she was highly optimistic about Chinese and North Korean communism. She took several trips to China, the first being in 1953. She was also encouraged by the possibility of a social experiment by comparing North and South Korea, and was convinced that Communist North Korea would be far more successful than the capitalistic South.

She was an ardent follower of John Maynard Keynes, and seemed to consider herself more of a Keynesian than he was. She desperately desired a more just society, but cared nothing for feminism. She might have been the most important economist not to have been awarded the Nobel Prize. Yet she herself dismissed her own most important work as flawed. She claims to have lost interest in the groundbreaking *Imperfect Competition* soon after she wrote it, and much preferred *The Accumulation of Capital* (1956).

Joan Robinson died in Cambridge, England, in 1983.

*See also:* Keynes, John Maynard; Marshall, Alfred; Marx, Karl; Pigou, A. C.; Sraffa, Piero

### Selected Works by Joan Robinson

Robinson, Joan. *The Accumulation of Capital*. London: Macmillan, 1956.
Robinson, Joan. *Economic Heresies: Some Old-Fashioned Questions in Economic Theory*. New York: Basic Books, 1971.
Robinson, Joan. *Economics of Imperfect Competition*. London: Macmillan, 1933.
Robinson, Joan. *Essay on Marxian Economics*. London: Macmillan, 1942.
Robinson, Joan. *Essays in the Theory of Economic Growth*. London: Macmillan, 1964
Robinson, Joan. *Introduction to the Theory of Employment*. London: Macmillan, 1937.
Robinson, Joan. *The Theory of Unemployment*. London: Macmillan, 1933.

### Selected Works about Joan Robinson

Beaud, Michael, and Gilles Dostaler. *Economic Thought since Keynes*. Aldershot, UK: Edward Elgar, 1995.
Cicarelli, James, and Julianne Cicarelli. "Joan Robinson (1903–1983)." In *Distinguished Women Economists*, 160–64. Westport, CT: Greenwood Press, 2003.
Rima, Ingrid Hahne. *The Joan Robinson Legacy*. London: M.E. Sharpe, 1991.
Turner, Marjorie Shepherd. *Joan Robinson and the Americans*. Armonk, NY: M.E. Sharpe, 1989.

*Stephen H. Day*

# ROMER, CHRISTINA

Born: December 25, 1958, in Alton, Illinois; American; economic history, monetary policy, fiscal policy; Major Works: *Reducing Inflation: Motivation and Strategy* (coedited with David H. Romer) (1997), "Do Tax Cuts Starve the Beast?: The Effect of Tax Changes on Government Spending" (with David H. Romer) (2009), "The Macroeconomic Effects of Tax Changes" (with David H. Romer) (2010).

Christina Romer has been a Class of 1957-Garff B. Wilson Professor of Economics at the University of California, Berkeley, since 1997. She has also been a codirector of the Program in Monetary Economics at the National Bureau of Economic Research from 2010 to the present and from 2003 to 2008 with programs in Monetary Economics, Economic Fluctuations and Growth, and the Development of the American Economy. She served as the chair of the Council of Economic Advisers for Barack Obama from January 2009 to September 2010 during one of the worst economic crises in American history. She is regarded as a premier Great Depression academic and has published numerous articles collaborating with her husband—economist David Romer—a Herman Royer Professor in Political Economy at the University of California, Berkeley.

Christina Duckworth Romer was born on December 25, 1958, in Alton, Illinois. She graduated with a bachelor's degree in economics from the College of William and Mary in 1981 and earned her PhD from the Massachusetts Institute of Technology (MIT) in 1985. She was an assistant professor of economics and public affairs at the Woodrow Wilson School at Princeton University until 1988 when she moved to the University of California, Berkeley. It was during her time at MIT that she met and married her husband and fellow notable economist, David H. Romer. In 2009, Romer was chair of the Council of Economic Advisers in the Obama administration. She worked with economist Jared Bernstein to coauthor the administration's plan for recovery from the 2008 recession.

Romer's early work with pre–World War II gross national product figures cast doubt on Nobel laureate Simon Kuznets's prior calculations, which supported the idea that government economic policy shortened U.S. recessions while lengthening expansions. Romer noted that pre–World War II recessions were longer than postwar downturns but that the severity of economic fluctuations on both sides of the Great Depression are roughly equal; thus the perceived stabilization of the postwar economy due to government policy was not strongly supported with data.

Romer's work also illustrated that fiscal or monetary policy error can also add to economic downturns. Specifically, Romer has argued that fiscal policy stimulus packages (change in taxes and spending) have not helped the U.S. economy recover from previous recessions. She explains that during the New Deal, for example, taxes were raised as quickly as government spending increased, giving fiscal policy just a minor role in the recovery. Romer writes that it was accidental monetary policy (the devaluation of the dollar and introduction of European capital) that helped the United States into recovery from the Great Depression.

Romer also analyzed the forecasting ability of the Federal Open Market Committee (FOMC) and compared it to that of the Federal Reserve (Fed) staff. She ultimately determined that the FOMC added very little extra value to the forecasting data. She writes that while monetary policy making has improved since World War II, the FOMC could have made better decisions if it had fully used the forecasting expertise of the Fed staff economists. The FOMC, as a representative for the American people, should use their comparative advantage in making value judgments about which outcomes or path is best given the situation.

Romer's work often shows that simply looking at correlation can mislead one to infer causation. In her work, she uses additional data and details from history to achieve a fuller picture of causation. In 2009, Romer researched the history of tax changes. She isolated the tax change decisions that would test her hypothesis that cutting taxes would ultimately shrink the size of government. Her conclusion indicates that tax cuts are usually associated with increases in government spending and that tax increases cause the economy to contract. Romer and her husband wrote in "Do Tax Cuts Starve the Beast?" that their research results "provide no support for the hypothesis that tax cuts restrain government spending; indeed, the point estimates suggest that tax cuts may increase spending. The results also indicate that the main effect of tax cuts on the government budget is to require subsequent legislated tax increases" (2009, 139).

Romer's numerous published articles and commitment to her profession are notable. She resigned from the White House Council of Economic Advisers in September of 2010 to allow her son to spend his high school years in one place. She remains active within the economics community working with an impressive number of organizations. She was vice president of the American Economic Association in 2006 and active on other committees for this group starting in 2001. She was an academic consultant (December 1991 and September 2006) and later visiting scholar for the board of governors of the Federal Reserve System from 1991 to 1993 and in 2004. She served on the program and nominating committees for the Economic History Association and on the editorial boards of the *American Economic Journal: Macroeconomics* (2007–8), *Review of Economics and Statistics*, (1994–2002), and the *Journal of Economic History* (1994–97). She has received numerous grants from the National Science Foundation and the Social Science Research Council. She also held training seminars on the Great Depression for the International Monetary Fund in 2002, 2003, and 2005. In addition, her fellowships include the John Simon Guggenheim Memorial Foundation Fellowship (1998–99), the Alfred P. Sloan Research Fellowship (1989–91), the National Bureau of Economic Research Olin Fellowship (1987–88), the Alfred P. Sloan Doctoral Dissertation Fellowship (1984–85), and the American Academy of Arts and Sciences Hellman Fellowship (2004). She also earned an honorary doctor of public service from the College of William and Mary in 2010 and a Distinguished Teaching Award from the University of California, Berkeley, in 1994.

*See also:* Kuznets, Simon

**Selected Works by Christina Romer**

Romer, Christina D. "Lessons from the Great Depression for 2009." Paper presented at the Brookings Institution, Washington, DC, March 9, 2009. http://www.brookings.edu/~/media/Files/events/2009/0309_lessons/20090309_romer.pdf (accessed September 2011).

Romer, Christina D., and David H. Romer. "Do Tax Cuts Starve the Beast? The Effect of Tax Changes on Government Spending." *Brookings Papers on Economic Activity* 1 (2009): 139–200.

Romer, Christina D., and David H. Romer. "The Macroeconomic Effects of Tax Changes: Estimates Based on a New Measure of Fiscal Shocks." *American Economic Review* (June 2010): 763–801.

Romer, Christina D., and David H. Romer, eds. *Reducing Inflation: Motivation and Strategy.* Chicago: University of Chicago Press for NBER, 1997.

**Selected Works about Christina Romer**

"Christina Romer." University of California, Berkeley. http://elsa.berkeley.edu/~cromer/index.shtml (accessed September 2011).

Clement, Douglass. "Interview with Christina and David Romer." The Region: Minneapolis Fed Magazine Profile, June 25, 2008. http://www.minneapolisfed.org/pubs/region/08-09/romers.pdf (accessed September 24, 2011).

Rampell, Catherine. "The New Team—Christina D. Romer." *New York Times*, November 25, 2008. http://www.nytimes.com/2008/11/25/us/politics/25web-romer.html (accessed September, 2011).

*Kathryn Lloyd Gustafson*

# ROMER, PAUL

Born: 1955 in Denver, Colorado; American; endogenous growth theory, technological change, development economics, urban systems; Major Works: "Increasing Returns and Long-Run Growth" (1986), "Growth Based on Increasing Returns Due to Specialization" (1987), "Endogenous Technological Change" (1990), "Idea Gaps and Object Gaps in Economic Development" (1993), "New Goods, Old Theory, and the Welfare Costs of Trade Restrictions" (1994).

Paul Romer is an American economist who established new growth theory within the field of economics and is famous for developing models that explain endogenous technological change in a model of long-run economic growth. In the course of his ongoing career, he has taught at New York University, Stanford University, the University of Chicago, the University of Rochester, and the University of California, Berkeley, and was given a Distinguished Teaching Award at Stanford in 1999. He was named one of the 25 most influential Americans in 1997 by *Time* magazine. In 2000 he founded Aplia, a company that produces online pedagogical resources for college students. As a faculty member currently at New York University, he continues to work on growth and technological change, but from the new perspective of urbanization in developing countries.

Paul M. Romer was born in 1955 in Denver, Colorado. He received his bachelor of science degree in physics from the University of Chicago in 1977 and went on to get his PhD from the University of Chicago in 1983. His thesis expanded on growth theory developed by Robert Solow, Kenneth Arrow, and others by explicitly incorporating the idea of increasing returns via the accumulation of knowledge in a competitive economic system. This model demonstrated that increasing human capital, the knowledge derived from education and training, is the way to generate increasing growth rates of gross domestic product per capita in the long run.

Continuing his work on technology and growth while a faculty member at the University of Rochester in the 1980s, Romer produced his most important work to date: his 1990 *Journal of Political Economy* paper "Endogenous Technological Change." By integrating the choice of doing research into the model, Romer allows economic agents to decide to contribute to future growth by using their human capital to expand technology. This model explains why we see rising human capital, physical capital, and technological progress increase together in economies that already have high levels of human capital. Romer also argues that opening up the economy to international markets enhances the human capital, so expanding trade can produce growth in the long run as well.

Named one of *Time* magazine's most influential Americans for 1997, Romer is a thinker who looks for important practical problems and applies economics to solve those problems. In 2000 he founded Aplia, a company that provided online pedagogical resources to enhance student engagement with their economics textbook material. The company grew rapidly, branching into a wide variety of disciplines, and he sold the company to Cengage Learning in 2007.

In 2011, Paul Romer joined the Department of Economics at New York University's Stern School of Business. He continues to work on the economics of technical change, but from a new angle. As head of the Urbanization Project at New York University, he is pursuing the idea that urbanization in the twenty-first century provides opportunities for social progress through the adoption of innovative technology and the development of norms promoting tolerance and inclusion within a framework based on choice. He believes that linking choice to urban development via charter cities (similar to special economic or administrative zones) will provide the kind of social and economic dynamism that will enhance people's well-being.

*See also:* Solow, Robert

**Selected Works by Paul Romer**

Romer, Paul. "Are Nonconvexities Important for Understanding Growth?" *American Economic Review* 80 (May 1990): 97–103.

Romer, Paul. "Endogenous Technological Change." *Journal of Political Economy* 98 (October 1990): S71–S102.

Romer, Paul. "Growth Based on Increasing Returns Due to Specialization." *American Economic Review* 77 (May 1987): 56–62.

Romer, Paul. "Idea Gaps and Object Gaps in Economic Development." *Journal of Monetary Economics* 32 (1993): 543–73.

Romer, Paul. "Increasing Returns and Long-Run Growth." *Journal of Political Economy* 94 (1986): 1002–37.

Romer, Paul. "New Goods, Old Theory, and the Welfare Costs of Trade Restrictions." *Journal of Development Economics* 43 (1994): 5–38.

Romer, Paul. "What Parts of Globalization Matter for Catch-Up Growth?" *American Economic Review* 100 (May 2010): 94–98.

### Selected Works about Paul Romer

Bailey, Ronald. "Post-Scarcity Prophet." *Reason* 33, no. 7 (2001): 52–61.
"Paul Romer: Why the World Needs Charter Cities." TED Talks. http://www.ted.com/talks/paul_romer.html (accessed November 4, 2012).
"TIME's Twenty-Five Most Influential Americans." *Time*, April 21, 1997.

*Kerry Pannell*

## ROSEN, SHERWIN

Born: September 29, 1938, in Chicago, Illinois; Died: March 17, 2001, in Chicago, Illinois; American; labor economist; Major Works: "Hedonic Prices and Implicit Markets: Product Differentiation in Pure Competition" (1974), *Studies in Labor Markets* (1981).

Sherwin Rosen was an economist and professor of labor economics and industrial organization. Rose published over 80 journal articles and contributed several book chapters. He was known for his work on hedonic prices in the market, on the skew of earnings and wages, and on earnings and education. He served in several academic capacities including department chairman at the University of Chicago. Rosen died in 2001.

Sherwin Rosen was born on September 29, 1938, in Chicago, Illinois. As an undergraduate, Rosen attended Purdue University in West Lafayette, Indiana. He studied engineering and received his bachelor of science in 1960. Sherwin's interest in economics landed him at the University of Chicago for graduate work. Having failed the general core exam, Milton Friedman advised him not to pursue economics as a field, but accounting perhaps. However, Rosen rejected this advice and completed his PhD in 1966 under the supervision of Gregg Lewis at the University of Chicago.

Rosen's teaching career began at the University of Rochester in 1964. It was here that Rosen published one of his most famous articles on hedonic pricing, "Hedonic Prices and Implicit Markets: Product Differentiation in Pure Competition" (1974), arguing that goods are valued on their utility-bearing characteristics. The market responds to heterogeneous demands of consumers, including consumer demand for income, for goods with certain characteristics, and for other preferences. In 1975, Rosen was named Kenan Professor of Economics. He also spent time as a visiting professor at Harvard while at the University of Rochester. He left in 1977 and returned to the University of Chicago. He spent summers at the Hoover Institution of Stanford University.

Despite offers to go elsewhere, he identified with the school of thought in Chicago and would remain there until his death. At the University of Chicago, Rosen became the Edwin A. and Betty L. Bergman Distinguished Service Professor in 1983. He was chairman of the economics department from 1988 to 1994.

In Rosen's article published in 1981, "The Economics of Superstars," he focused on the high wages of performers to explain the skew in wage distribution. He theorized that high wage earnings of performers are so much higher than performers of the same ability because of the marginal cost in production and consumption. Rosen's further work with Edward Lazear introduced tournament theory to explain differences in individual wages, explaining for example why CEOs make significantly higher salaries than vice presidents.

Rosen made major contributions in the area of labor economics with his collaboration with Robert Willis. In their article "Education and Self-Selection" (1979), they provided important insights regarding the relation of earnings to education. In their evaluation, individuals who attend college perform better in occupations that require college degrees, yet are not proficient at jobs that required only a high school diploma. Likewise, individuals who did not attend college are good at jobs that require only a high school diploma. The paper confirmed Rosen's view that heterogeneity is imperative and schooling choice is made in the context of comparative advantages for individuals.

Additionally, Rosen wrote on the potato paradox of the famine in Ireland, discrediting the view that potatoes are a "Giffen good." A Giffen good is a good that violates the law of demand: as price increases so does the quantity demanded. In his paper "Potato Paradoxes" (1999), he argued that supply and demand could in fact be applied to the potato problem as with any normal good. Rosen explains that the idea that potatoes were a Giffen good was caused by mistakes in expectations that farmers would oversave potatoes for future planting, i.e., that farmers would treat potatoes as a capital good as opposed to a consumption good. Rosen's work spanned other areas including risk, segmentation of the labor market, and housing.

Rosen published 80 articles and contributed chapters for various books. In 1997, he was recognized by and accepted into the National Academy of Sciences. The following year, he was elected to serve as president for the American Economic Association. Two posthumous publications came out after his death, *Markets and Diversity* (2004) and "The Engineering Labor Market" (with Jaewoo Ryoo) (2004).

After his death, the Society of Labor Economists recognized his work by establishing the Sherwin Rosen Prize for Outstanding Contributions in the Field of Labor Economics.

Sherwin Rosen died on March 17, 2001, in Chicago, Illinois.

*See also:* Friedman, Milton

### Selected Works by Sherwin Rosen

Lazear, Edward P., and Sherwin Rosen. "Rank and Order Tournaments as Optimal Labor Contracts." *Journal of Political Economy* 89, no. 5 (1981): 841–64.

Rosen, Sherwin. "The Economics of Superstars." *American Economic Review* 71 (1981): 845–58.

Rosen, Sherwin. "Hedonic Prices and Implicit Markets: Product Differentiation in Pure Competition." *Journal of Political Economy* 82, no. 1 (1974): 34–55.

Rosen, Sherwin. "Potato Paradoxes." *Journal of Political Economy* 107, no. 6, part 2: Symposium on the Economic Analysis of Social Behavior in Honor of Gary S. Becker (December 1999): S294–S313. Chicago: University of Chicago Press, 1999.

Rosen, Sherwin. *Studies in Labor Markets*. Chicago: University of Chicago Press, 1981.
Willis, Robert J., and Sherwin Rosen. "Education and Self-Selection." *Journal of Political Economy* 87, no. 5 (1979): S7–S36.

**Selected Works about Sherwin Rosen**

Emmett, Ross B. *The Elgar Companion to the Chicago School of Economics*. Cheltenham, UK: Edward Elgar, 2010.
Lazear, Edward P. "Sherwin Rosen September 29, 1938–March 17, 2001." In *Biographical Memoirs*. Vol. 83, 176–95. Washington, DC: National Academy of Sciences, 2003.
Maler, Karl-Goran, and Jeffrey R. Vincent, eds. *Handbook of Game Theory with Economic Applications: Game of Chess*. Amsterdam: Elsevier, 2000.

*Sara Standen*

# ROTH, ALVIN

Born: December 19, 1951, in New York City; American; game theory, experimental economics, market design, Nobel Prize (2012); Major Works: "The Evolution of the Labor Market for Medical Interns and Residents: A Case Study in Game Theory" (1984), *Game-Theoretic Models of Bargaining* (1985), *Two-Sided Matching: A Study in Game-Theoretic Modeling and Analysis* (with Marilda Sotomayor) (1990), "Predicting How People Play Games: Reinforcement Learning in Experimental Games with Unique, Mixed Strategy Equilibria" (with Ido Erev) (1998), *The Need for (Long) Chains in Kidney Exchange* (with Itai Ashlagi, David Gamarnik, and Michael A. Rees) (2012).

Alvin Roth received the 2012 Nobel Prize in Economics for his research in game theory, experimental economics, and market design. Roth is best known for his pioneering work in creating the kidney transplant market. Along with his research on the effectiveness of organ transplant markets, he was personally involved as the cofounder of the New England Program for Kidney Exchange. Roth has been recognized for his market design efforts with the New York and Boston public schools. Roth led a team who designed selection procedures for matching high school freshmen to high schools in both New York and Boston public schools. Roth was awarded the Nobel Prize jointly with Lloyd Shapley.

Alvin Eliot Roth was born on December 19, 1951, in the Queens borough of New York City. He graduated with a major in operations management from Columbia University in 1971. He received his master's in 1973 and doctorate in 1974 from Stanford University. Alvin Roth began his career at the University of Illinois. In 1982, he moved on to the University of Pittsburgh as the Andrew W. Mellon Professor of Economics. Roth joined the faculty at Harvard University Business School in 1998, becoming the George Gund Professor of Economics and Business Administration in the Department of Economics.

Roth's research has been varied including game theory, experimental economics, and market design. Market design may be his most unique contribution to economics as he explored the unfamiliar field of the transplant organ market. In 1984, he wrote on the transplant organ market and the National Resident Matching Program (NRMP) in "The Evolution of the Labor Market for Medical Interns and

Residents: A Case Study in Game Theory" (1984). His 1984 conclusion asserted the program was effective for single individuals but less certain regarding married couples. He later was involved in the redesigning of the NRMP to be more acceptable and receptive to married couples.

Roth was later to become personally involved in transplant organ market exchange as a cofounder of the New England Program for Kidney Exchange. The Exchange matched couples to provide organ access to those whose partner was not compatible to be a donor. The Exchange aligned couples when a match was compatible with one of the other couples. Legislation in the federal National Organ Transplant Act has necessitated exchanges to occur as simultaneous exchanges.

Another focus for Roth was public education in New York City and Boston. Prior to Roth's work, New York City schools assigned freshman students to schools through rankings of schools submitted by students. Schools selected students based on the information provided by each student's list. The result was a less than optimal fairness selection process for the students. Roth and his team created a procedure based on matching student incentives with the schools. Their program designed a procedure creating incentives for the students to be truthful in their selection process. This allowed the district officials to better match the student with a high school. The process was implemented in 2004.

Roth and his team re-created a similar program for Boston schools in 2004. Boston's original program had the potential of being more random than New York's with a student being assigned to a school not even on his or her initial choice list. The final version of the Boston plan was implemented in 2006 as a modification of the New York plan. The public school systems of Denver and Chicago also later incorporated Roth's market design.

Alvin Roth is a member of the National Bureau of Economic Research (NBER) and a fellow of the American Academy of Arts and Sciences. He has served the American Economic Association and has been a member of the Econometric Society.

In 2012, Alvin Roth was awarded the Nobel Prize in Economics with Lloyd Shapley for their work in designing markets where price has not served as a clear allocating mechanism between a buyer and seller, including Roth's prominent work in the organ-transplant market and student-school matching markets for major city public school systems. Besides organ transplant matching, Roth has also designed systems in the medical field to match doctors with hospitals.

Prior to winning the Nobel Prize, Roth was awarded the Frederick W. Lancaster Prize for his contribution to operations research and management sciences. The honor was based on his two-sided matching work in game theory with Marilda Sotomayor in 1990.

*See also:* Shapley, Lloyd

### Selected Works by Alvin Roth

Ashlagi, Itai, David Gamarnik, Michael A. Rees, and Alvin E. Roth. *The Need for (Long) Chains in Kidney Exchange.* Cambridge, MA: National Bureau of Economic Research, 2012.

Erev, Ido, and Alvin E. Roth. "Predicting How People Play Games: Reinforcement Learning in Experimental Games with Unique, Mixed Strategy Equilibria." *American Economic Review* 88, no. 4 (1998): 848–81.

Kagel, J. H., and Alvin E. Roth, eds. *Handbook of Experimental Economics*. Princeton, NJ: Princeton University Press, 1997.

Roth, Alvin. "The Evolution of the Labor Market for Medical Interns and Residents: A Case Study in Game Theory." *Journal of Political Economy* 92 (1984): 991–1016.

Roth, Alvin, ed. *Game-Theoretic Models of Bargaining*. New York: Cambridge University Press, 1985.

Roth, Alvin, ed. *Laboratory Experimentation in Economics: Six Points of View*. New York: Cambridge University Press, 1987.

Roth, Alvin, ed. *The Shapley Value: Essays in Honor of Lloyd S. Shapley*. New York: Cambridge University Press, 1988.

Roth, Alvin. "What Have We Learned from Market Design?" *Innovation Policy and the Economy* 9, no. 1 (2009): 79–112.

Roth, Alvin E., Tayfun Sönmez, and M. Utku Ünver. "Kidney Exchange." *The Quarterly Journal of Economics* 119, no. 2 (May 2004): 457–88.

Roth, Alvin, and Marilda A. Sotomayor. *Two-Sided Matching: A Study in Game-Theoretic Modeling and Analysis*. New York: Cambridge University Press, 1990.

Wallis, C. Bradley Wallis, Kannan P. Samy, Alvin E. Roth, and Michael A. Rees. "Kidney Paired Donation." *Nephrology, Dialysis, Transplantation* 26, no. 7 (July 2011): 2091–99.

**Selected Works about Alvin Roth**

Harvard Business School. "Working Knowledge—The Thinking That Leads, Alvin E. Roth." http://hbswk.hbs.edu/faculty/aroth.html (accessed October 2012).

Harvard Business School, Faculty and Research. "Alvin E. Roth, George Gund Professor of Economics and Business Administration." http://www.hbs.edu/faculty/Pages/profile.aspx?facId=6594 (accessed October 2012).

National Bureau of Economic Research. "Alvin E. Roth." https://www.nber.org/people/alvin_roth (accessed October 2012).

Rampell, Catherine. "2 from US win Nobel in Economics." *New York Times*, October 16, 2012. http://www.nytimes.com/2012/10/16/business/economy/alvin-roth-and-lloyd-shapley-win-nobel-in-economic-science.html?_r=0 (accessed October 2012).

David A. Dieterle

# ROTHBARD, MURRAY

Born: March 2, 1926, in New York; Died: January 7, 1995, in New York City; American; libertarian economics; Major Works: *Man, Economy, and State* (1962), *Power and Market: Government and the Economy* (1970), *The Case against the Fed* (1994).

Murray Rothbard is best known as a libertarian author and educator influential in shaping the political and economic philosophies of the early Libertarian Party. He taught for over 20 years at the Polytechnic Institute of New York and finished his teaching career at the University of Nevada, Las Vegas. He is known for his anarchistic and conservative thought and was heavily influenced by his former teacher, Ludwig von Mises. He wrote over 20 books and contributed numerous articles for publication. Rothbard died in 1995.

Murray Newton Rothbard was born on March 2, 1926, in New York City. He received all of his formal college education at Columbia University, receiving a BA in 1945, an MA in 1946, and a PhD in economics in 1956. In the early 1950s, Rothbard spent considerable time at Ludwig von Mises's seminars at New York University, which helped foster his later libertarian views. Von Mises and Aristotle shaped Rothbard's understanding of natural law and helped convince him that government involvement usually violated natural principles. He was involved with a group in the mid-1950s in New York called Circle Bastiat, which allowed him to cross paths with other libertarians like Ralph Raico, George Reisman, and Ronald Hamowy. During this time, he also met Ayn Rand, and shared with her his views on the importance of the human right to property and self-ownership. In the mid-1950s, Rothbard was also influential at the Foundation for Economic Education.

Rothbard's writing career began in the 1940s while he was teaching at City College in New York. Most of his early work involved writing essays for *Faith and Freedom* and the *National Review* and working for the Volker Fund, which sought out young libertarians. His first major work was the two-volume *Man, Economy, and State*, published in 1962. This publication established his overarching economic principles and defended the idea that individuals use scarce resources to achieve different ends, based on their different values. It also promoted the free-market system and put down government interferences. In a 1970 companion to this book, *Power and Market*, Rothbard spoke out about taxation, focusing more on the total amount of taxes individuals pay than on the method of that payment. Throughout his writing, he targeted big government, especially the Federal Reserve and the money and banking system, such as in *What Has Government Done to Our Money?* (1963) and *The Case against the Fed* (1984).

Much of Rothbard's writings involved economic interpretations of history. *The Panic of 1819* focused on the first major financial crisis in the United States and placed blame on the National Bank, which was the forerunner to the Federal Reserve. *America's Great Depression* (1963) blamed the Depression on the Federal Reserve and credit inflation. It also criticized Hoover's handling of the Depression as an unnecessary expansion of government that paved the way for the massive expansion under the New Deal. In the late 1970s, he wrote a four-volume history, *Conceived in Liberty*, which approached early American history from a libertarian perspective, and gave his views on how the American market began.

Beginning in the late 1960s, Rothbard worked on two different libertarian-centered journals, *Left and Right* with Leonard Liggio and *Libertarian Forum* with Karl Hess. He was involved with the latter until 1984. In 1973, Rothbard published *For a New Liberty: The Libertarian Manifesto*, which outlined his main ideas for libertarianism. Included was his idea of a rights-based anarchist society, describing the problems of the "international anarchy" that he observed in the contemporary world. Rothbard would use this work and his 1982 book, *The Ethics of Liberty*, to distance his views from von Mises's utilitarian ethics and from Robert Nozick and F. A. Hayek's minimal state libertarianism.

Rothbard was influential in the formation of the new Libertarian Party in 1970s, even though he was not involved from the outset. Advocacy organizations and think tanks, such as the Cato Institute and the Center for Libertarian Studies, as well as the *Journal of Libertarian Studies* all began under his guidance. Beginning in 1982 until his death, he was vice president of the Ludwig von Mises Institute, which gave him an outlet for activism. Tension with the rest of the libertarian movement began in the 1970s, as Rothbard clashed with Cato president Ed Crane, until Rothbard left the Libertarian Party in 1989. Following his break with the Libertarian Party, Rothbard began a new movement called paleolibertarianism with fellow von Mises Institute colleague Llewellyn Rockwell Jr., which linked libertarianism with cultural conservatism.

Murray Rothbard died on January 7, 1995, in New York City of a heart attack.

*See also:* Bastiat, Frédéric; Hayek, Friedrich von; Mises, Ludwig von

### Selected Works by Murray Rothbard

Rothbard, Murray. *The Case against the Fed*. Auburn, AL: Ludwig von Mises Institute, 1994.

Rothbard, Murray. *Conceived in Liberty*. Vol. 1, *American Colonies in the 17th Century*. New Rochelle, NY: Arlington House, 1975.

Rothbard, Murray. *Conceived in Liberty*. Vol. 2, *Salutary Neglect*. New Rochelle, NY: Arlington House, 1975.

Rothbard, Murray. *Conceived in Liberty*. Vol. 3, *Advance to Revolution*. New Rochelle, NY: Arlington House, 1976.

Rothbard, Murray. *Conceived in Liberty*. Vol. 4, *The Revolutionary War*. New Rochelle, NY: Arlington House, 1979.

Rothbard, Murray. *Man, Economy, and State: A Treatise on Economic Principles*. Princeton, NJ: Van Nostrand, 1962.

Rothbard, Murray. *Power and Market: Government and the Economy*. Menlo Park, CA: Institute for Humane Studies, 1970.

### Selected Works about Murray Rothbard

Frohnen, Bruce, Jeremy Beer, and Jeffrey O. Nelson, eds. *American Conservatism: An Encyclopedia*. Wilmington, DE: ISI Books, 2006.

Gordon, David. *The Essential Rothbard*. Auburn, AL: Ludwig von Mises Institute, 2007.

Hamowy, Ronald, ed. *The Encyclopedia of Libertarianism*. Los Angeles: Sage, 2008.

Raimondo, Justin. *An Enemy of the State: The Life of Murray N. Rothbard*. Amherst, NY: Prometheus Books, 2000.

Romano, Richard, and Melvin Leiman, eds. *Views on Capitalism*. Beverly Hills, CA: Glencoe, 1975.

Stout, David. "Murray N. Rothbard, Economist and Free-Market Exponent, 68." *New York Times*, January 11, 1995.

*Joseph Lee Hauser*

# ROUBINI, NOURIEL

Born: March 29, 1959, in Istanbul, Turkey; American; macroeconomics, economic systems, emerging economies; Major Works: *Political Cycles and the Macroeconomy* (with Alberto Alesina and Gerald Cohen) (1997), *Bailouts or Bail-Ins? Responding to* the *Financial Crises in Emerging Economies* (with Brad Setser) (2004), *Crisis Economics: A Crash Course in the Future of Finance* (with Stephen Mihm) (2010).

Nouriel Roubini is a professor of economics and international business at the Stern School of Business at New York University. He is most widely known for being among the few economists to predict the financial downturn in the United States in 2007 that resulted in a recession. Many colleagues were skeptical and some even laughed at his prediction in 2006 when unemployment and inflation were relatively low. But his words proved to be prophetic when the housing market crashed and unemployment soared in the years that followed.

Nouriel Roubini was born on March 29, 1959, in Istanbul, Turkey. He lived in Italy from 1962 until 1983, interrupted by a one-year program of undergraduate studies in Jerusalem, Israel, at the Hebrew University of Jerusalem. He earned a BA in economics in 1982 at Università L. Bocconi in Milan, Italy, graduating summa cum laude. He earned a PhD in economics from Harvard University in Cambridge, Massachusetts, in the United States in 1988. His fields of specialization were international economics and macroeconomics.

While a student at Harvard, Roubini worked as a summer intern at the International Monetary Fund, a research assistant at the National Bureau of Economic Research, and a consultant at the United Nations University in Helsinki, Finland. After graduation from Harvard, Roubini was a consultant for the World Bank in Washington, DC, and a visiting scholar at the International Monetary Fund.

He was an associate editor for the *Journal of International Economics* and the *Journal of Development Economics*. In 1988, he joined the faculty of Yale University as an assistant professor of economics. He stayed at Yale until 1995, when he became an associate professor in the Department of Economics at the Stern School of Business at New York University.

In 2000, he served as the senior adviser to the undersecretary for international affairs at the U.S. Treasury Department, where he worked on a variety of issues, including the Asian and global economic crises. He is the chairman and cofounder of Roubini Global Economics, LLC.

Roubini has published several books and more than 70 papers on global economic topics, and his views are cited in various news sources.

He is best known for having predicted the 2007 financial crisis. In his statements before a group of economists at the International Monetary Fund, he predicted the demise of the housing market and the series of events that would culminate in the deep recession. When others suggested it would come to an end, Roubini insisted it would get worse, which it did. Such pessimistic predictions earned him the nickname "Dr. Doom."

Since then he has been sought after in both public and privates spheres. His views have been widely cited in the media and he has been a commentator on various business news programs.

*See also:* Reich, Robert; Rivlin, Alice; Roach, Stephen; Romer, Christine

### Selected Works by Nouriel Roubini

Alesina, Alberto, Nouriel Roubini, and Gerald Cohen. *Political Cycles and the Macroeconomy*. Cambridge, MA: MIT Press, 1997.

Roubini, Nouriel, and Stephen Mihm. *Crisis Economics: A Crash Course in the Future of Finance*. New York: Penguin Press, 2010.

Roubini, Nouriel, and Brad Setser. *Bailouts or Bail-Ins? Responding to the Financial Crises in Emerging Economies*. Washington, DC: Institute for International Economics, 2004.

Roubini, Nouriel, and Marc Uzan. *New International Financial Architecture*. Vol. 1. London: Edward Elgar, 2005.

### Selected Works about Nouriel Roubini

Bloomberg TV. "Roubini Says 2013 'Storm' May Surpass 2088 Crisis." http://www.bloomberg.com/video/roubini-says-2013-storm-may-surpass-2008-crisis-HCAjTp9VTD~gm6Ux8jnQvQ.html.

EconoMonitor. "Nouriel Roubini." http://www.economonitor.com/nouriel.

Nimh, Stephen. "Dr. Doom." Profile. *New York Times Magazine*, August 17, 2008. http://www.nytimes.com/2008/08/17/magazine/17pessimist-t.html?pagewanted=all (accessed January 2012).

*Diane Fournier*

## SACHS, JEFFREY

Born: November 5, 1954, in Detroit, Michigan; American; environmental sustainability, economic development, globalization; Major Works: *The End of Poverty* (2005), *Common Wealth* (2008), *The Price of Civilization* (2011).

Jeffrey Sachs is an American academic in the field of political economics best known for his work on developing international economies and alleviating poverty while promoting sustainability with respect to our environment. He has worked to effect change in economic policy and well-being in developing countries across the world. His work transforms the theoretical into the practical, and his writing is recognized by both scholars and the general public. He writes a monthly newspaper column appearing in over 80 countries. Sachs is widely considered the leading international economic adviser of his generation.

Jeffrey D. Sachs was born on November 5, 1954, in the Detroit, Michigan, suburb of Oak Park. He completed his undergraduate degree at Harvard University in 1976 and continued his education there, obtaining his MA and PhD in economics at the age of 28. He then spent the next 22 years of his career as a professor of economics at Harvard, most recently as the Galen L. Stone Professor of International Trade. He also served as Harvard's director of the Center for International Development. During his early years as a student and then professor at Harvard, he concentrated mostly on the problems of the developing world.

A turning point in Sachs's career took place after attending a lecture on Bolivia's problem of hyperinflation. Sachs was invited to visit Bolivia to explore the problem further. From the moment he arrived in the South American country, his worldview was altered and priorities shifted. He later wrote he found the world more interesting than just mathematical equations. This prompted Sachs to help the Bolivian government tighten its budget in an effort to take on less new debt while simultaneously negotiating debt forgiveness. Sachs determined that countries cannot be coerced to repay debts without political and civil consequences. He also advised the Bolivian government to implement shock therapy fiscal and monetary policies to quickly eliminate the burgeoning monetary chaos.

Shock therapy policies were first championed by Milton Friedman. Shock therapy was a process of using fiscal and monetary policies to combat the overinvolvement of government in the economy. While Friedman's model promoted rapid privatization of all public industries, Sachs's model did not see government programs as the villains. Sachs's model claimed that a quick shock to a nation's monetary system could jump-start development in a very short period of time.

Professor Jeffrey Sachs is director of the Earth Institute. He is also director of the UN Millennium Project and adviser on the Millennium Development Goals, the internationally agreed goals to reduce extreme poverty, disease, and hunger by the year 2015. (Bruce Gilbert)

After his work in Bolivia, Sachs was invited as a special adviser to many nations and organizations around the world. He worked with Poland to transition from a command to a capitalist economy after the fall of communism. Using the same method of shock therapy, the nation was able to achieve great success. When he worked with other Eastern European nations to achieve the same goal, success was not always clearly achieved. Russia saw devastating effects when he helped them take the same course of action. In Asia, he helped rapidly developing nations such as India and China design economically and environmentally sustainable development solutions. In Africa, he has focused his attention on eradicating communicable diseases, which prevent citizens from contributing as productive members of society.

Some of the most important work of Sachs's career has been in conjunction with the United Nations where he has served as special adviser under UN Secretaries General Ban Ki-Moon and Kofi Annan. From 2002 to 2006, he was director of the UN Millennium Project. The Millennium Declaration signed in 2002 asserts that every individual has the right to dignity, freedom, equality, and a basic standard of living that includes freedom from hunger and violence while encouraging tolerance and solidarity. The purpose of developing the Millennium Goals is to create practical ideas to improve infrastructure and increase social, economic, and political rights, improving quality of life. The project dedicates the resources of the UN to eight goals with 21 targets to be met by the year 2015. In this role, Sachs has been able to implement his theories focused on debt reduction and the link to poverty elimination. By convincing the G8 to provide funds to the World Bank and International Monetary Fund, the UN has been able to help the poorest countries channel their money into health and education initiatives rather than paying off debt. Funding for the project has come in the form of aid from the many developed UN member nations. While the goals are considerable and obstacles numerous, Sachs maintains the optimistic conviction that extreme poverty can be eliminated worldwide.

Sachs left Harvard in 2002 to become the director of the Earth Institute at Columbia University and serve as their distinguished Quetelet Professor of Sustainable Development. In this role, he creates and promotes large-scale efforts to mitigate human-induced climate change. Through the Earth Institute, he works with developing nations to simultaneously develop their economy while protecting their environment. He also founded a not-for-profit group aimed at ending extreme poverty, the Millennium Promise Alliance.

He has twice been named as one of *Time* magazine's 100 most influential leaders. He has been called the most important economist in the world by the *New York Times*.

He currently continues to serve as the director of the Earth Institute at Columbia University and as the distinguished Quetelet Professor of Sustainable Development.

*See also:* Collier, Paul; Duflo, Esther; Friedman, Milton; Schultz, Theodore

**Selected Works by Jeffrey Sachs**

Sachs, Jeffrey. *Common Wealth*. New York: Penguin Press, 2008.
Sachs, Jeffrey. *The End of Poverty*. New York: Penguin Press, 2005.
Sachs, Jeffrey. *The Price of Civilization*. New York: Random House, 2011.

**Selected Works about Jeffrey Sachs**

The Earth Institute Columbia University. "Full Bio: Jeffrey D. Sachs." http://www.earth.columbia.edu/articles/view/1770 (accessed October 2012).
PBS. "Commanding Heights." http://www.pbs.org/wgbh/commandingheights/lo/story/index.html.
Saporito, Bill. "Jeffrey Sachs." *Time*, March 6, 2005.

*Rebecca Kraft*

# SAMUELSON, PAUL

Born: May 15, 1915, in Gary, Indiana; Died: December 13, 2009, in Belmont, Massachusetts; American; macroeconomics, author, Nobel Prize (1970); Major Work: *Economics: An Introductory Analysis* (first published 1948).

Paul Samuelson is probably one of the most referenced and decorated of contemporary economists. Economic historians have referred to him as the "father of modern economics," and the *New York Times* once referred to him as the foremost academic economist of the twentieth century. He authored the best-selling college economics textbook of all time, *Economics: An Introductory Analysis*. In 1970, Paul Samuelson was the first U.S. economist to receive the Nobel Prize in Economics. Samuelson died in 1994.

Paul Anthony Samuelson was born on May 15, 1915, in Gary, Indiana. He received his bachelor of arts degree in 1935 from the University of Chicago. Paul Samuelson went on to Harvard University where he was awarded his PhD in

1941. His early economic influences at Harvard were noted economists Wassily Leontief, Joseph Schumpeter, and Alvin Hansen. At the age of 21, while a doctoral student at Harvard, Samuelson wrote his first published article, "A Note on the Measurement of Utility."

In 1940, Samuelson accepted a position as assistant professor at the Massachusetts Institute of Technology (MIT) where he would remain till his retirement. Paul Samuelson was more than the author, and later coauthor, of the most widely used college textbook in history. During his tenure at MIT, Samuelson worked in the fields of international trade, welfare economics, consumer theory, applying nonlinear dynamics to economic analysis, and public-private choice allocation. In each of these areas, Samuelson has been credited for adding to the body of economic knowledge. In terms of economic philosophy, Professor Samuelson referred to himself as a "right wing ... New Deal economist," i.e., a Keynesian.

In 1938, he introduced a way to measure consumer choices and satisfaction-witnessing consumer behavior. This became known as the revealed preference theory. In 1941, he with economist Wolfgang Stolper developed the Stolper-Samuelson theorem in trade theory. This theorem proposed, under certain conditions, that when a resource is scarce trade will lower real wages and thus protectionism will raise real wages. Stolper-Samuelson would submit that trade between developed and developing countries lowers the wages of the unskilled labor in the developed country that is competing with the lower unskilled wages in the developing country. The Stolper-Samuelson theorem was influential in the later international trade models.

Another area of economics in which Samuelson was recognized was in the area of public finance where he is credited for his efforts in resource allocation between public and private goods and services.

One thing that set Samuelson apart from other economists of his time was his use and application of mathematical analysis. In 1947, Samuelson published *Foundations of Economic Analysis*. Samuelson illustrated the importance of mathematics to the science of economics. In 1948, he published the first edition of what was to become the best-selling, most widely used economics textbook in history, *Economics: An Introductory Analysis*. Since the first edition in 1948, "Samuelson" has been translated into over 40 languages since 1948. Many consider it the most influential economics textbook since World War II. The Keynesian approach Samuelson presents had a great influence on the embracing of John Maynard Keynes's theories in the United States.

From 1941 to 1945 during World War II, Paul Samuelson served on the National Resources Planning Board, the War Production Board, as well as the Office of War Mobilization and Reconstruction. Following the war, he served in various government positions till 1960. In 1960–61, he was a member of the National Task Force on Economic Education. Samuelson served as an adviser to Presidents John F. Kennedy and Lyndon B. Johnson, and was a consultant to the U.S. Treasury, the Bureau of the Budget, the Council of Economic Advisers, and the Federal Reserve Bank. Samuelson wrote a weekly column for *Newsweek* magazine along with Chicago School economist Milton Friedman, where they represented opposing sides: Samuelson took the Keynesian perspective, and Friedman represented the Monetarist perspective.

Paul Samuelson was the first economist to introduce the idea of "cost-push" inflation. Cost-push inflation is the inflation caused by general rise in resource prices, which includes wages. As the cost of resources increases, price increases follow. In 1960, Samuelson was particularly sensitive to and expressed concern about the issue during periods that even when full employment had not yet been reached, the future effects of the high employment were visible in the economy.

Along with his Nobel Prize in 1970, Paul Samuelson was the honoree of the David A. Wells Prize in 1940 from Harvard University and the John Bates Clark Medal by the American Economic Association in 1947. Paul Samuelson was a member of the editorial board of the Econometric Society and was their past-president in 1951. He was elected president of the International Economic Association in 1965.

Paul Samuelson described himself as a "generalist" whose true interests were in teaching and research. Paul Samuelson is not the only economist in the family. His nephew is Harvard professor and former presidential economic adviser Larry Summers.

Paul Samuelson died on December 13, 2009, at the age of 94.

*See also:* Hicks, John; Keynes, John Maynard; Leontief, Wassily; Schumpeter, Joseph; Summers, Lawrence

## Selected Works by Paul Samuelson

Samuelson, Paul. *Economics: An Introductory Analysis*. New York: McGraw-Hill, 1948.

Samuelson, Paul, and William A. Barnett, eds. *Inside the Economist's Mind: Conversations with Eminent Economists*. Malden, MA: Blackwell, 2007.

Samuelson, Paul, Robert L. Bishop, and John R. Coleman, eds. *Readings in Economics*. New York: McGraw-Hill, 1955.

Samuelson, Paul, Robert Dorfman, and Robert Solow. *Linear Programming and Economic Analysis*. Santa Monica, CA.: RAND Corporation, 1958.

## Selected Works about Paul Samuelson

Brown, Edgar Cary, and Robert Solow. *Paul Samuelson and Modern Economic Theory*. New York: McGraw-Hill, 1983.

"Paul A. Samuelson: Biography." Nobelprize.org. http://www.nobelprize.org/nobel_prizes/economics/laureates/1970/samuelson-bio.html (accessed September, 2011).

Szenberg, Michael, Aron A. Gottesman, and Lall Ramrattan. *Paul A. Samuelson: On Being an Economist*. New York: Jorge Pinto Books, 2005.

Weinstein, Michael M. "Paul Samuelson, Economist, Dies at 94." *New York Times*, December 14, 2009. http://www.nytimes.com/2009/12/14/business/economy/14samuelson.html (accessed September, 2011).

Wong, Stanley. *The Foundations of Paul Samuelson's Revealed Preference Theory: A Study by the Method of Rational Reconstruction*. Oxford: Routledge & Kegan Paul, 1978.

*Dave Leapard*

## SARGENT, THOMAS

Born: July 19, 1943, in Pasadena, California; American; macroeconomics, monetary policy, global economy, time series econometrics, Nobel Prize (2011); Major Works: *Rational Expectations and Econometric Practice* (with Robert E. Lucas Jr.) (1981), *Macroeconomic Theory* (1987), *Dynamic Macroeconomic Theory* (1987), *The Big Problem of Small Change* (with François R. Velde) (2002), *Recursive Macroeconomic Theory* (with Lars Ljungqvist) (2004), *Robustness* (with Lars P. Hansen) (2007).

Thomas Sargent is one of the most influential American economists of the twenty-first century. In 2011, he was ranked among the top 20 most cited economists in the world. He has published many significant books and more than 170 peer-reviewed journal articles. Sargent is one of the founders of the freshwater economics movement, which is associated with the Chicago School of economics and closely related to the neoclassical thought that emphasizes the benefits of free markets and real business cycle. Sargent has won many prestigious awards. In October 2011, he and Christopher Sims won the Nobel Prize in Economics for their breakthrough research in macroeconomics and work on the long-term cause-and-effect relationship between policy and the economy.

Thomas J. Sargent was born on July 19, 1943, in Pasadena, California. He earned his BA from the University of California, Berkeley, in 1964 and his PhD in economics from Harvard University in 1968. Following graduation in 1968, he became a first lieutenant and captain of the U.S. Army and served as a staff member and an acting director of economics division. Two years later, he became an associate professor of economics at the University of Pennsylvania, and then from 1971 to 1978, he taught at the University of Minnesota. In 1975, he became a full professor.

Since then he has been a research adviser to many economic institutions such as the National Bureau of Economic Research, Brookings Panel on Economic Activity, the Federal Reserve Bank of Minneapolis, and the Hoover Institute at Stanford University. He has also been a visiting professor at many prestigious universities such as the University of Chicago, Harvard University, and Stanford University. In 2002, he joined the faculty at New York University as the Berkeley Professor of Economics and Business.

Sargent is known as one of the central figures behind the development of the rational expectations model. The theory explains economic situations in which individuals' expectations influence future outcomes. The price of a stock, for instance, partially depends on what potential buyers and sellers think of its value in the future. Thus anticipations of value contribute to the creation (or destruction) of value. In his paper titled "Interpreting Economic Time Series," he suggests the theory and proceeds to makes it operational. Throughout his career, he conducted many historical studies in which he used the rational expectations theory to explain the results of important macroeconomic policy issues. Sargent extended the application of the rational expectations theory to analyzing economic systems.

Sargent was not the first economist to apply the thesis behind what he identified as rational expectations. Earlier economists such as Pigou and Keynes implemented the premise behind rational expectations to define the central point in determining business cycles. Later in the early 1960s, John Muth reintroduced a similar premise of rational expectations to economic theory. It was Thomas Sargent and other rational expectation economists who applied the label rational expectations, assuming people make logical economic decisions to primarily maximize their happiness or financial profits (utility). The concept of rational expectations has helped economists to explain a variety of situations in which speculation about future events is an important predictor of present actions.

One of Sargent's strength as an economist is his ability to integrate mathematical economics and economic history. In his paper titled "Some Unpleasant Monetarist Arithmetic," he argues that higher interest rates help reduce inflation not only by making credit more expensive but also by changing individuals' expectations regarding the Federal Reserve's actions in the future. However, he notes that the ability of central banks to influence inflation depends on specific circumstances. His conclusion is that government policies do not happen in a vacuum; people's responses to changes in interest rates or tax cuts can vary substantially. In part, reactions to a policy changes depend on expectations about how the government will perform in the future. Thus the effect could be substantially different from the predictions of traditional economic models.

Sargent has won many distinguished awards throughout his academic life. To begin, he was the Berkeley University medalist as the most distinguished scholar in his class of 1964. In 1979, the University of Chicago awarded him the Mary Elizabeth Morgan Prize for excellence in economics. In 1997, he was the recipient of the Erwin Plein Nemmers Prize in Economics from Northwestern University. In 2011, he won the National Academy of Sciences Award for his scientific reviewing and the CME Group-MSRI prize for his innovations in quantitative applications.

In 2011, at the age of 68, Thomas Sargent shared the Nobel Prize in Economics with the Princeton economist Christopher Sims. The prize was awarded to them for their independent but complementary work on the long-term cause-and-effect relationship between policy and the economy. Rational expectations are the centerpiece of Sargent's analytical research. He has been one of the most influential economists and a leader in the field of macroeconomics in recent economic history.

*See also:* Keynes, John Maynard; Pigou, A. C.; Sims, Christopher

## Selected Works by Thomas Sargent

Sargent, Thomas. *Dynamic Macroeconomic Theory*. Cambridge, MA: Harvard University Press, 1987.

Sargent, Thomas J. "Interpreting Economic Time Series." *Journal of Political Economy* 89, no. 2 (1981): 213–48.

Sargent, Thomas. *Macroeconomic Theory*. Vol. 2. San Diego, CA: Academic Press, 1987.

Sargent, Thomas J., and Lars P. Hansen. *Robustness*. Princeton, NJ: Princeton University Press, 2007.
Sargent, Thomas J., and Robert E. Lucas Jr. *Rational Expectations and Econometric Practice*. Vol. 1. Minneapolis: University of Minnesota Press, 1981.
Sargent, Thomas J., and Lars Ljungqvist. *Recursive Macroeconomic Theory*. Cambridge, MA.: MIT Press, 2004.
Sargent, Thomas J., and François R. Velde. *The Big Problem of Small Change*. Princeton, NJ: Princeton University Press, 2002.
Sargent, Thomas J., and Neil Wallace. "Some Unpleasant Monetarist Arithmetic." *Federal Reserve Bank of Minneapolis Quarterly Review* 5, no. 3 (1981): 1–17.

**Selected Works about Thomas Sargent**

Cowen, Tyler. "Thomas Sargent, Nobel Laureate." *MarginalRevolution*. October 10, 2011. http://marginalrevolution.com/marginalrevolution/2011/10/thomas-sargent-nobel-laureate.html (accessed October 2012).
Sargent, Thomas. "Prize Lecture: United States Then, Europe Now." Nobelprize.org. http://www.nobelprize.org/nobel_prizes/economics/laureates/2011/sargent-lecture.html (accessed October 2012).
Sent, Esther-Mirjam. *The Evolving Rationality of Rational Expectations: An Assessment of Thomas Sargent's Achievements*. Cambridge: Cambridge University Press, 1998.

*Elham Mahmoudi*

## SAY, JEAN-BAPTISTE

Born: January 5, 1767, in Lyon, France; Died: November 15, 1832, in Paris, France; French; general equilibrium, classical, political economy; Major Works: *Traité d'Economie Politique* (Treatise on political economy) (1803), *Catechism of Political Economy* (1817).

Jean-Baptiste Say is most famous for Say's law, which simply states: supply creates its own demand. While those were not his exact words, they do convey the essence of his response to the nineteenth-century Glut Controversy, a trade dispute England was having with Brazil. Say died in 1832.

Jean-Baptiste Say was born on January 5, 1767, in Lyon, France. His parents had recently returned to their homeland from Switzerland fleeing religious persecution. Say's father was a silk merchant, and he made sure that his son had an education that would prepare him for the business world. Say therefore received a modern education in both Lyon and London. He later worked in the offices of a Paris life insurance company after returning to France in 1787. His employer gave him a copy of Adam Smith's *Wealth of Nations*, which led him to become an economic disciple of Smith.

In 1789, the French Revolution broke out. The young Say took advantage of the general mood of progress to write articles and edit a journal in favor of a free press, republican ideals, and various mildly revolutionary topics. A common thread throughout his writings was the need for the population to be educated in the study of political economy (what is now economics).

In the midst of the Reign of Terror during the French Revolution, Say translated Benjamin Franklin's *Poor Richard's Almanac* into French. He wrote a laudatory biography of Franklin, who was something of a folk hero in revolutionary France. He also corresponded with Thomas Jefferson and considered emigrating to the United States.

When Napoleon Bonaparte became dictator of France, Say was made a member of the Tribunate (part of Napoleon's legislature) where he was given the task of reporting on the government's budget. His report stressed the need for clear accounting standards and for tax revenues to be collected before they were actually spent. These ideas drew Napoleon's disapproval. Say's economic writings lamented war, voiced suspicion of government bureaucrats, deplored slavery, and called for relaxing the restrictions on trade, all of which were features of the Napoleonic government. In 1802, perhaps because of these differences of opinion, Say was removed from his post, whereupon he left Paris and opened a cotton mill. His business was successful, and when not managing it, he spent his time writing.

Say did not write about just economics. In 1800, he published a short book called *Olbie*, which gave a picture of a utopian society. In it he espoused the belief (not uncommon at the time) that if a revolutionary society could overthrow monarchy and aristocracy, emphasize education, remain untempted by greed, and build a republic where morality was enforced by meddling neighbors, then a near-perfect society could exist. Wishing to popularize the economic theories of Adam Smith and expand the subject of political economy, he published his *Treatise on Political Economy* in 1804 and continued to release updated editions throughout his life. In 1821, Say was offered a position as professor at the Conservatoire National des Arts et Métiers. It was the first professorship in political economy ever created in France.

Say is most famous for Say's law, which in its simplest iteration is: supply creates its own demand. (There are several, sometimes conflicting, versions of Say's law.) Say did not actually write this, but it appropriately captures his contribution to a two-decade-long dispute known as the Glut Controversy. The question at hand was: why do markets collapse into recession? Certain philosophers had claimed that this was because of overproduction; producers had foolishly made more than people could consume. Say disagreed, pointing out that "each of us can only purchase the productions of others with his own productions ... the more men produce, the more they will purchase." Therefore there could be no "general glut," or total supply greater than total demand. Instead, wrote Say, recessions happen when there is a temporary imbalance of certain goods and services relative to other ones. People should produce *more* of the goods that are lacking in order to pay for the ones in relative abundance, rather than seeking through public policy to cut production. Markets would eventually correct themselves.

In response to Say, Simonde Sismondi and Thomas Malthus advanced theories claiming that there could indeed be a general oversupply. For instance, increased demand for money would mean that supply could exceed demand. Demand would be satisfied by the holding of real money balances rather than by products. Another of the critics' ideas was that production might exceed an equilibrium level at which producers could profitably operate their businesses. There might be demand for goods, but producers would go out of business trying to meet that demand. Other economists, mostly notably David Ricardo, agreed with Say.

The Glut Controversy was the central economic dispute of the early nineteenth century, eventually involving every major economist of the time. The dispute was not always edifying. Both sides tended to misrepresent, or simply misunderstand, each other's arguments. Eventually, a consensus emerged and remained for the rest of the nineteenth and early twentieth centuries. The consensus confirmed that Say was right. Supply did indeed create its own demand. This theory remained almost completely unchallenged until John Maynard Keynes chose a version of Say's law as the foil for his own theory of recessions.

Say was not available to defend his ideas. He died in 1832, almost a hundred years earlier. Though out of favor with many policy makers and economists, Say's law remains a cogent, if not quite sufficient, explanation for the tendency of markets to regulate themselves.

Jean-Baptiste Say died on November 15, 1832, in Paris, France.

*See also:* Keynes, John Maynard; Malthus, Thomas; Ricardo, David; Smith, Adam

### Selected Works by Jean-Baptiste Say

Say, Jean-Baptiste. *Catechism of Political Economy*. Translated by John Richter. London: Sherwood, Neely, and Jones, 1816.

Say, Jean-Baptiste. *England and the English People*. London: Sherwood, Neely, and Jones, 1816.

Say, Jean-Baptiste. *Treatise on Political Economy or the Production, Distribution, and Consumption of Wealth*. Translated by C. R. Prinsep. Boston: Wells and Lilly, 1803.

### Selected Works about Jean-Baptiste Say

Blaug, Mark. *Great Economists before Keynes*. Atlantic Highlands, NJ: Humanities Press International, 1986.

Palmer, R. R. *J.-B. Say: An Economist in Troubled Times*. Princeton, NJ: Princeton University Press, 1997.

Sechrest, Larry. "Biography of Jean-Baptiste Say: Neglected Champion of Laissez-Faire; J. B. Say: The Forgotten Early Austrian." Ludwig von Mises Institute. http://mises.org/page/1462/Biography-of-JeanBaptiste-Say-Neglected-Champion-of-LaissezFaire.

Sowell, Thomas. *Say's Law*. Princeton, NJ: Princeton University Press, 1972.

Spiegal, Henry. *The Growth of Economic Thought*. Upper Saddle River, NJ: Prentice-Hall, 1971.

*Stephen H. Day*

# SCHELLING, THOMAS

Born: April 14, 1921, in Oakland, California; American; game theory, conflict strategy, Nobel Prize (2005); Major Works: *Strategy of Conflict* (1960), *Arms and Influence* (1966).

Thomas Schelling was awarded the Nobel Prize in 2005 with Robert Aumann for his work in the field of game theory. Schelling served the U.S. government during World War II as an analyst and foreign policy adviser. During his academic career he was a pioneer in game theory. Schelling committed the bulk of his studies to conflict situations and how best to manage military conflicts and weapons deterrence. Consistent with the times, much of his work focused on the Cold War conflict between the United States and the Soviet Union. He wrote of the importance of both sides having a credible nuclear threat, which neither was likely to use, to serve as a deterrent.

Thomas C. Schelling was born in Oakland, California, on April 14, 1921. He earned his bachelor's degree in economics from the University of California, Berkeley, in 1944 and his PhD in economics from Harvard University in 1951. Prior to beginning his PhD work at Harvard University, he worked as an analyst with the U.S. Bureau of the Budget. Schelling worked on the Marshall Plan. He continued working in the government serving as a White House foreign policy adviser. Schelling moved into academia working as a faculty member at Yale University and then spent the majority of his career, over 30 years, at Harvard. At Harvard he worked in both the Department of Economics and International Affairs and the Kennedy School of Government. Over time, he consulted with presidential administrations from Kennedy to Nixon. After the invasion of Cambodia during the Vietnam War, Schelling led a group of Harvard faculty to meet with Nixon's national security adviser and express their opposition to the invasion and severed ties with the administration.

Schelling's book *The Strategy of Conflict* is one of the more influential books on weapons policy and military deterrence. In *The Strategy of Conflict*, Schelling proposed the rather unique idea that effective conflict strategies could be applied to any conflict situation. There are similarities in dealing with common everyday conflicts and large-scale, international military conflicts.

Schilling coined a now common game-theory term, focal point. This term has also come to be known as the Schilling point. The term refers to the solution to a problem where the players are not able to communicate with each other but must cooperate to reach the same point. The focal point is the point where both players believe they both are most likely to reach a common agreement or understanding.

Later in his career Schelling devoted his time to studying addictive behaviors. He was motivated to explore this area by his involvement with the National Academy of Sciences on Substance Abuse and Addictive Behavior. Schelling looked at the conflict between our rational and impulsive natures and the steps we take to try to manage the two and overcome addictions. He wrote numerous essays on the subject, many of which are included in his books *Choice and Consequence* (1984) and *Strategies of Commitment and Other Essays* (2005).

Schelling embarked on a new area of economic exploration when he was invited by President Carter to chair a committee on carbon dioxide pollution. Schelling himself admits that he knew very little on the subject at the time. However, he would go on to study the issue over a two-year period with the Carbon Dioxide Assessment Committee of the National Academy of Sciences. Schelling has stated that he believes that climate change will be to this century what nuclear arms control was to the twentieth century.

Schelling was awarded the Nobel Prize in Economics in 2005. He was a corecipient of the award as it was awarded to Schelling and Robert Aumann, though the two never worked together. Schelling was awarded the Nobel Prize for his specific work on the strategic decision-making (game theory) processes of why cooperation by individuals, organizations, and countries is successful in some cases and not successful in others.

Thomas Schelling is a distinguished professor of economics at the University of Maryland.

*See also:* Aumann, Robert; Nash, John

### Selected Works by Thomas Schelling

Schelling, Thomas. *Arms and Influence.* New Haven, CT: Yale University Press, 1966.
Schelling, Thomas. *Choice and Consequence.* Cambridge, MA: Presidents and Fellows of Harvard College, 1984.
Schelling, Thomas. *Strategies of Commitment and Other Essays.* Cambridge, MA: Harvard University Press, 2005.
Schelling, Thomas. *Strategy of Conflict.* Cambridge, MA: Presidents and Fellows of Harvard College, 1960.

### Selected Works about Thomas Schelling

Harford, Tim. "Lunch with the FT: Thomas Schelling and the Game of Life." http://timharford.com/2005/12/lunch-with-the-ft-thomas-schelling-and-the-game-of-life/ (accessed September 2012).
Kinsley, Michael. "A Nobel Laureate Who's Got Game." *Washington Post*, October 12, 2005. http://www.washingtonpost.com/wp-dyn/content/article/2005/10/11/AR2005101101336.html (accessed September 2012).
Schelling, Thomas. "Autobiography." Nobelprize.org. http://www.nobelprize.org/nobel_prizes/economics/laureates/2005/schelling-autobio.html (accessed September 2012).

*Andrew Probert*

# SCHOLES, MYRON

Born: July 1, 1941, in Timmins, Ontario, Canada; Canadian; financial markets, asset pricing, Nobel Prize (1997); Major Works: "The Market for Securities: Substitution versus Price Pressure and the Effects of Information on Share Prices" (1972), "Rates of Return in Relation to Risk: A Re-examination of Some Recent Findings" (with Merton Miller) (1972), "The Valuation of Options Contracts and a Test of Market Efficiency" (with Fischer Black) (1972).

Myron Scholes is a Canadian economist who was awarded the Nobel Prize in 1997. At the Massachusetts Institute of Technology (MIT), he worked closely with Robert Merton and Fischer Black, developing a new method in asset pricing, known as the Black-Scholes model. In 1995, Scholes was a founding member of Long-Term Capital Management (LTCM), a hedge fund that used the mathematical models of Scholes and others for selecting investments. LTCM went bankrupt when Russia defaulted, and the Federal Reserve was needed to save the financial markets. However, his influence in financial markets continued when he founded the investment firm Platinum Grove Asset Management in 2006 and was placed on the boards of the Chicago Mercantile Exchange and Dimensional Fund Advisors.

Myron S. Scholes was born in Timmins, Ontario, Canada, on July 1, 1941. In 1951, his family moved to Hamilton, Ontario. His formative years in Canada were characterized by hardships and a keen interest in economics. He was exposed to the stock market through watching investments his family made. When Scholes's uncle died, the family disputes that followed over the family business were his first exposure to the disagreements that contracts can evoke. As a teenager, he faced the death of his mother and the loss of his eyesight in a short period of time. At the age of 26, his eyesight was restored after a successful cornea transplant.

In the wake of his mother's death, Scholes wanted to stay near his family for his undergraduate work and became a student at McMaster University, graduating in 1962 with a bachelor's degree in economics. While at McMaster, Scholes read the works of future Nobel laureates George Stigler and Milton Friedman with great interest. Scholes would subsequently enroll at the University of Chicago where he earned his MBA in 1964 and his PhD in 1969.

After finishing his dissertation, Scholes accepted an academic position at the MIT Sloan School of Management where he met two people he would work closely with to develop the formula that would earn him a Nobel Prize in economics. Robert Merton and Fischer Black together with Scholes developed groundbreaking work in asset pricing, including their famous option-pricing model known as the Black-Scholes model.

The Black-Scholes model was a pioneering effort because never before had traders been able to value options precisely. The impact was that investors could significantly reduce their risk by hedging their bets in the options market. Options are investment vehicles that allow one the right, but not the obligation, to buy or sell a given security at a set price in the future. With this formula, firms and households could select an appropriate amount of risk by effectively redistributing it throughout the financial markets to those who are willing and able to assume it.

The first historical attempt to use advanced mathematics to model financial markets was in 1900 and is credited to French academician Louis Bachelier. The options contract had long been an object of study by academic financial mathematicians because of the fact that it can potentially eliminate all the downside risk of trading when used as a hedge against an adverse move in the market. Before the discovery of this mathematical model by Scholes and Black, options and derivatives contracts were much more obscure, mostly because traders were not able to accurately price them. Today, options contracts and derivatives are widely traded in financial markets.

In 1995, Scholes went on to become a founding member of hedge fund called Long-Term Capital Management (LTCM), which used proprietary mathematical models to guide investments. His reputation and notoriety as a Nobel Prize winner helped him attract vast amounts of capital from high-profile investors worldwide, as people were eager to have him invest their funds. In the first three years of LTCM, the company was widely successful and outperformed all other funds. It soon became clear, however, that certain underlying market conditions were developing for which the models at LTCM were insufficient. In 1997, the Asian financial crisis caused panic in the markets, and LTCM borrowed large sums of money to hold positions because their models predicted that markets would return to normal. They were able stay in business until August of 1998 when the highly improbable event of Russia defaulting on its foreign debt occurred. This caused a major swing in the market, which LTCM was not able to bear and subsequently brought their operations to an end. The result was a massive bailout by the Federal Reserve for fear that LTCM was so immersed in financial markets on such a large scale that that their default could lead to a freeze-up of the entire system. Scholes and his investors lost millions.

Scholes's contributions to financial economics opened markets to vast new opportunities and revolutionized how risk is managed by investors. His formula is used millions of times every day by traders as it continues to shape the development of financial markets in the world today.

*See also:* Friedman, Milton; Merton, Robert; Stigler, George

### Selected Works by Myron Scholes

Black, Fischer, and Myron Scholes. "The Valuation of Options Contracts and a Test of Market Efficiency." *Journal of Finance*, 27, no. 2 (1972): 399–417.

Miller, Merton, and Myron Scholes. "Rates of Return in Relation to Risk: A Re-examination of Some Recent Findings." In *Studies in the Theory of Capital Markets*. Edited by Michael C. Jensen, 47–78. Santa Barbara, CA: Praeger, 1972.

Scholes, Myron S. "Financial Infrastructure and Economic Growth." In *The Mosaic of Economic Growth*. Edited by Ralph Landau, Timothy Taylor, and Gavin Wright, 281–301. Palo Alto, CA: Stanford University Press, 1996.

Scholes, Myron. "Global Financial Markets, Derivative Securities and Systemic Risks." *Journal of Risk and Uncertainty* 12, nos. 2 and 3 (1996): 271–86.

Scholes, Myron. "The Market for Securities: Substitution versus Price Pressure and the Effects of Information on Share Prices." *Journal of Business*, 45, no. 2 (1972): 179–211.

Scholes, Myron. "Omega Has a Nice Ring to It." In *Capital Ideas Evolving*. Edited by Peter L. Bernstein, 110–24. Hoboken, NJ: Wiley, 2007.

Scholes, Myron S., and Mark A. Wolfson. *Employee Stock Ownership Plans and Corporate Restructuring: Myths and Realities*. No. w3094. Cambridge, MA: National Bureau of Economic Research, 1989.

### Selected Works about Myron Scholes

Johnson, David Cay. "A Tax Shelter, Deconstructed." *New York Times*, July 13, 2003.

Scholes, Myron S. "Autobiography." Nobelprize.org. http://www.nobelprize.org/nobel_prizes/economics/laureates/1997/scholes-autobio.html (accessed April 2012).

Vane, Howard R., and Chris Mulhearn. *The Nobel Memorial Laureates in Economics: An Introduction to Their Careers and Main Published Works*. London: Edward Elgar, 2005.

*John E. Trupiano*

# SCHULTZ, THEODORE

Born: April 30, 1902, in Arlington, South Dakota; Died: February 26, 1998, in Evanston, Illinois; American; human capital theory, agricultural economics, development economics, Nobel Prize (1979); Major Works: *Investment in Human Capital* (1961), *The Economics of Being Poor* (1993).

Theodore Schultz was noted for his achievements in agricultural and developmental economics. Schultz provides five major categories in which human capabilities could be improved including health initiatives, on-the-job training, formal education, study programs for adults (including extension), and population migration. Due to the significant increases in human capital resulting from education, this activity inherently would see a larger increase in overall investment. However, he suggests that the opportunity cost of seeking education is significant. Theodore Schultz won the Nobel Prize in 1979 with William Arthur Lewis. Schultz died in 1998.

Theodore William Schultz was born on April 30, 1902, in Arlington, South Dakota. He studied agriculture at South Dakota State College, then earned his MA (1928) and PhD (1930) degrees in agricultural economics from the University of Wisconsin.

Schultz joined the faculty of Iowa State College in 1930, where he remained until his 1943 departure for the University of Chicago. As a researcher, he began to explore agriculture on a global scale, leading the Technical Assistance for Latin America (TALA) project in the 1950s. He was president of the American Economic Association (AEA) in 1960; his address to that body became the work *Investment in Human Capital* in 1961.

Primary contributions of Schultz in agricultural economics was the recognition that much of the observed increases in farm productivity could not be explained by increases in capital or traditional factors of production, contrasting with the Marshall's accepted theory of diminishing returns. Initially, Schultz attributed these unexplained increases to specialization of communities and the advancement of technology and innovation. This pattern of increased productivity beyond the expectations of additional inputs was seen in both the United States as well as developing economies. He added "the quality of people as productive agents" as a contributing component of the model. Through these activities, agricultural agents could increase food production to accommodate any geometric increase in population.

In his 1960 AEA address, he outlined reasons for the lack of explicit analysis of investment in human capital, attentively describing that national output had increased at a far greater rate than that predicted by land, labor, and physical capital. The human capital concept he articulated challenged the idea that a unit of labor was interchangeable; each individual was invested with human capital with health and education impacting wage rates. Investments in human capital were any activities that created a positive rate of return for labor. The idea of human capital was not without controversy, as some observers objected to the conceptualization of individuals as assets that have a market (and marketable) value.

He cogently argued that the traditional model of helping developing nations was to build physical items rather than investing in the citizens of that nation. Schultz provides five major categories in which human capabilities could be improved including health initiatives, on-the-job training, formal education, study programs for adults (including extension), and population migration. Due to the vast comparative increases in human capital based upon education, this activity inherently would see a larger increase in overall investment. Simultaneously, he contributes the idea that the opportunity cost of seeking education is not a negligible figure.

In 1979, he was the coawardee of the Nobel Prize in Economics with William Arthur Lewis for pioneering economic development research in developing countries. His Nobel Prize lecture, *The Economics of Being Poor*, posits that individuals are concerned with improving living situations regardless of income or region of the world. Rather than contemplating the amount of farmland under development, the skills and knowledge of the farmworkers was a key to modernizing agriculture-based economies. He further expands on this idea by describing farmers as highly decentralized entrepreneurs consistently making adjustments to improve their returns based upon skills and knowledge, possibly imperceptible to experts.

Schultz realized that politically cities with industry were perceived as a better indicator of economic progress than improving the agricultural sector, despite many developing nations where agriculture was the predominant industry. He further felt that government interventions restricted the economic incentives that could be available to improve agriculture on a wider scale.

Theodore William Schultz died on February 26, 1998, in Evanston, Illinois.

*See also:* Duflo, Esther; Lewis, Arthur; Marshall, Alfred; Sachs, Jeffrey

## Selected Works by Theodore Schultz

Schultz, Theodore. *Agriculture in an Unstable Economy*. New York: McGraw-Hill, 1945.
Schultz, Theodore. "Diminishing Returns in View of the Progress in Agricultural Production." *Journal for Farm Economics* 14 (1932): 640–49.
Schultz, Theodore. *The Economic Organization of Agriculture*. McGraw-Hill, 1953.
Schultz, Theodore. *The Economic Value of Education*. New York: Columbia University Press, 1963.
Schultz, Theodore. *The Economics of Being Poor*. Cambridge, MA: Blackwell, 1993.
Schultz, Theodore. *Investment in Human Capital: The Role of Education and of Research*. New York: Free Press, 1971.
Schultz, Theodore. *Redirecting Farm Policy*. New York: Macmillan, 1943.
Schultz, Theodore. "Theory of the Firm and Farm Management Research." *Journal for Farm Economics* 21 (1939): 570–86.

## Selected Works about Theodore Schultz

Schultz, Theodore W. "Autobiography." Nobelprize.org. http://www.nobelprize.org/nobel_prizes/economics/laureates/1979/schultz-autobio.html (accessed August 2012).
"Theodore Schultz." In *The Concise Encyclopedia of Economics*. Edited by David R. Henderson. The Library of Economics and Liberty. http://www.econlib.org/library/Enc/bios/Schultz.html (accessed August 2012).
Vane, Howard R., and Chris Mulhearn, eds. *Simon S. Kuznets, Theodore W. Schultz, W. Arthur Lewis and Robert M. Solow*. London: Edward Elgar, 2010.

*Michael B. Becraft*

# SCHUMACHER, ERNST

Born: August 16, 1911, in Bonn, Germany; Died: September 4, 1977, in Switzerland; English; statistics, economic development; Major Works: *Small Is Beautiful: Economics as If People Mattered* (1973), *A Guide for the Perplexed* (1977).

Ernst Schumacher was a German-born English economist best known for his 1973 classic promoting a decentralized economy as most beneficial to the quality of life, *Small Is Beautiful*. An Oxford-educated Rhodes Scholar, Schumacher returned to England before World War II to avoid living in Nazi Germany. Interned for his German heritage during World War II, Schumacher became a significant presence in the British postwar rebuilding effort. A statistician and economist and protégé of John Maynard Keynes, Schumacher served the UK National Coal Board as its chief economic adviser for over 20 years. Schumacher died in 1977.

Ernst Friedrich "Fritz" Schumacher was born on August 16, 1911, in Bonn, Germany. Following his studies in Bonn and Berlin, Schumacher earned a Rhodes Scholarship to New College, Oxford. He earned his PhD in economics from Columbia University in the United States. As the Nazis took power in Germany, Schumacher chose to leave Germany and returned to England. During World War II, he was interned for his German heritage. During his internment he wrote a paper, "Multilateral Clearing," that gained the attention of John Maynard Keynes. Keynes arranged for Schumacher's release, and Ernst spent the remainder of World War II aiding Britain's war efforts.

At the conclusion of World War II, Schumacher was offered a teaching position at Oxford University. In 1950, Schumacher was appointed as chief economic adviser to the UK National Coal Board, a position he would retain till 1970. In his role with the Coal Board, he promoted coal as the commodity necessary to build England, and not oil. Schumacher is credited as the first economist to predict the growing scarcity of oil and the creation of the Oil Producing Exporting Countries (OPEC) cartel.

In 1955, Schumacher was an economic consultant to the government of Burma. While in Burma, he became very interested in their Buddhist beliefs and incorporated them into his economics, "Buddhist economics." Buddhist economics was based on the idea that individualism and good works can go hand and hand. He continued throughout other developing countries promoting production of local resources and developing independent economies. In 1966, he founded the Intermediate Technology Development Group to promote what has become known as appropriate technology.

Schumacher's writings, while few, were very influential. In 1973, in response to his visit to Burma and other developing countries, he wrote *Small Is Beautiful* to advocate and propose his self-contained appropriate technology for economic growth in the developing world. A collection of essays on humanist economics, Schumacher stressed the finite nature of our resources and the need for conservation. This line of thinking was at the heart of the early ecology movement, which added to his fame, both in England and internationally. *Small Is Beautiful* has been recognized as one of the 100 most influential books since World War II.

Schumacher's premise for a self-contained, appropriate technology economy in *Small Is Beautiful* is considered the remedy to globalization.

Again critiquing Western culture, this time materialism, he wrote *A Guide for the Perplexed* in 1977. Schumacher also wrote regularly for the *Times* of London newspaper and *The Economist* and *Resurgence* magazines. Schumacher's own philosophy was exhorted when he delivered the Gandhi Memorial Lecture in 1973 and honored Mahatma Gandhi for his economic thinking being more spiritual than material.

Ernst F. Schumacher died of a heart attack on September 4, 1977, in Switzerland.

*See also:* Keynes, John Maynard

### Selected Works by Ernst Schumacher

Schumacher, Ernst. *Future Is Manageable: Schumacher's Observations on Non-violent Economics and Technology with a Human Face*. New Delhi: Impex India, 1978.

Schumacher, Ernst. *Good Work*. Cape May, NJ: Cape, 1979.

Schumacher, Ernst. *A Guide for the Perplexed*. New York: HarperCollins, 1978.

Schumacher, Ernst. "Multilateral Clearing." *Economica* 10, no. 38. (1943): 150–65.

Schumacher, Ernst. *Small Is Beautiful: Economics as If People Mattered*. New York: Harper & Row, 1973.

### Selected Works about Ernst Schumacher

Etherden, Peter. "The Schumacher Enigma." *Fourth World Review*, 1999, 93.

Fager, Charles. "Small Is Beautiful, and So Is Rome: The Surprising Faith of E. F. Schumacher." *Christian Century* 94 (1977): 325.

Kirk, Geoffrey, ed. *Schumacher on Energy*. London: Sphere Books, 1983.

Kohr, Leopold. "Tribute to E. F. Schumacher." *The Schumacher Lectures*. Edited by Satish Kumar. New York: Harper & Row, 1980.

Schumacher, Ernst. *This I Believe and Other Essays*. Totnes, Devon, UK: Green Books, 1977.

Wood, Barbara. *E. F. Schumacher: His Life and Thought*. New York: Harper & Row, 1984.

*David A. Dieterle*

# SCHUMPETER, JOSEPH

Born: February 8, 1883, in Triesch, Moravia, Austria-Hungary; Died: January 8, 1950, in Taconic, Connecticut; Austrian; business cycles, economic development, entrepreneurship, evolutionary economics; Major Works: "The Common Sense of Economics" (1933), *Theory of Economic Development* (1934), *Business Cycles* (2 vols., 1939), *Capitalism, Socialism and Democracy* (1942), *History of Economic Analysis* (1964).

Joseph Schumpeter was an Austrian economist who developed a comprehensive theory about economic growth and business cycles that saw the entrepreneur as a major reason for economic growth and evolution. He was responsible for the term "creative destruction" as a way of describing economic growth. He was also a strong proponent of the use of mathematics in economics. Schumpeter died in 1950.

Joseph A. Schumpeter was born on February 8, 1883, in Triesch, Moravia (now the Czech Republic) in what was then Austria-Hungary. His father owned a factory, but he died while Schumpeter was still very young. Schumpeter would remain very close to his mother throughout the rest of her life. When she remarried, his stepfather was able to send him to a prestigious school, which would prepare him well for attending the University of Vienna.

While there, Schumpeter would study law and economics. He would also spend some time at Cambridge, Oxford, and the London School of Economics. In the area of economics, Schumpeter was a student of two of the leading members of the Austrian School, Friedrich von Weiser and Eugen von Böhm-Bawerk. Despite this, Schumpeter would not develop along the lines of that school choosing instead to follow a more classical line of inquiry in his work.

Harvard economist Joseph Schumpeter was one of the most talented economists of the interwar period. He was responsible for the term "creative destruction" as a way of describing economic growth. (Getty Images)

Upon leaving the University of Vienna, Schumpeter would take up a teaching post at the University of Czernowitz where he would be from 1909 until being offered a position at the University of Graz in 1911 at the age of 28. Schumpeter was the youngest professor in the entire Austro-Hungarian Empire.

In 1912, Schumpeter completed his first major work. His *Theory of Economic Development* was received to critical acclaim. But it would not receive wide recognition until it was translated into English in 1934. It was in the *Theory of Economic Development* that he would first address one of the areas that would make him a major figure in twentieth-century economics, the role of the entrepreneur. While entrepreneurs had been a subject of study throughout classical economics, Schumpeter made a clear distinction between the role of the entrepreneur and the role of the manager.

After World War I, the Austro-Hungarian Empire was dismantled. Austria, like its ally Germany, was in dire financial straits. Additionally, the winds of socialism were blowing across much of central Europe. In this climate, Schumpeter was appointed minister of finance for the new Austrian Republic in 1919. Unfortunately, his ideas were not popular and he would leave the post the next year. This was followed by a stint in banking, which was also not successful. In 1925, Schumpeter found himself at a low point. He enthusiastically accepted a position at the University of Bonn, in Germany. While at Bonn, his "Explanation of the Business Cycle" would be published in *Economica*. This was a precursor to his two-volume work, *Business Cycles*. That work would be published after he left Bonn in 1932, concerned about the rise of Hitler and the Nazi Party in Germany.

Schumpeter landed in the United States at Harvard. He would stay there until his retirement in 1949. It was at Harvard that the rest of his major works took shape. *Business Cycles* would be published in 1939. Schumpeter's theory began with a static analysis, assuming a period of stability. However, the stability would be punctuated by periods of upheaval. These booms represented eras of innovation that resulted in fundamental changes in production. Over time, the resulting changes led to periods of dynamic growth that were occasionally punctuated by downturns as the resources of the economy were reallocated. The innovation that caused this instability was generated, to a certain extent, by the entrepreneur working in an environment that allowed innovation to take place.

Schumpeter would follow that work with *Capitalism, Socialism and Democracy* (1942). It was in this work that two of his most famous ideas would become part of the public discussion. The first was his belief that, despite its superiority, capitalism would eventually be replaced by socialism. The success of capitalism would, in his view, lead to the rise of a large class of intellectuals. These same intellectuals would make their living from attacking the system that made their existence possible. But this work also built on some of his earlier work. The success of capitalism was due, in his view, in large part to the entrepreneur. It was here that second of his famous ideas from this book came into play.

According to Schumpeter, it was the entrepreneur who unleashed what he labeled creative destruction. Creative destruction disrupted the static situation that is represented by the circular flow diagram. This disruption causes the creation of new enterprises and the destruction of the old with resources being reallocated in the process. This was the cause of the underlying dynamism described in *Business Cycles*. Furthermore, the creative destruction was the connection between the microeconomics we see in studying the firm, and the macroeconomics we see in studying policy. It is the enterprise that creates change, which results in new policies, which change incentives, which lead to new enterprises.

Schumpeter held a number of roles of professional leadership during his career. He was a founding member of the Econometric Society in 1933, president of the American Economic Association in 1948, and chair of the International Economic Association in 1949. During his tenure at Harvard, Schumpeter would be able to count Paul Samuelson, Wassily Leontief, and James Tobin among those he worked with or influenced.

His last major work, *History of Economic Analysis*, was published by his wife in 1964, 14 years after his death.

Joseph Schumpeter died at his home in Taconic, Connecticut, on January 8, 1950.

*See also:* Böhm-Bawerk, Eugen von; Friedman, Milton; Hicks, John; Menger, Carl; Pareto, Vilfredo; Samuelson, Paul; Tobin, James; Walras, Leon; Wicksell, Knut; Wieser, Friedrich von

### Selected Works by Joseph Schumpeter

Schumpeter, Joseph. *Business Cycles.* 2 vols. New York: McGraw-Hill, 1939.
Schumpeter, Joseph. *Capitalism, Socialism and Democracy.* New York: Harper and Brothers, 1942.
Schumpeter, Joseph. "The Common Sense of Econometrics." *Econometrica* 1, no. 1 (January 1933): 5–12.
Schumpeter, Joseph. "Explanation of the Business Cycle." *Economica* 21 (December 1927): 286–311.
Schumpeter, Joseph. *History of Economic Analysis.* New York: Oxford University Press, 1964.
Schumpeter, Joseph. *Ten Great Economists.* New York: Oxford University Press, 1951.
Schumpeter, Joseph. *Theory of Economic Development.* Cambridge, MA: President and Fellows of Harvard College, 1934.

### Selected Works about Joseph Schumpeter

Blaug, Mark, and Paul Sturges. *Who's Who in Economics: A Biographical Dictionary of Major Economists, 1700–1980.* Cambridge, MA: MIT Press, 1983.
"Joseph Alois Schumpeter." In *The Concise Encyclopedia of Economics.* Edited by David R. Henderson. The Library of Economics and Liberty. http://www.econlib.org/library/Enc/bios/Schumpeter.html (accessed October 2012).
McCraw, Thomas. *Prophet of Innovation: Joseph Schumpeter and Creative Destruction.* Cambridge, MA: Harvard University Press, 2010.
Schulak, Eugen-Maria, and Herbert Unterköfler. "Joseph A. Schumpeter: Maverick and Enigma." Ludwig von Mises Institute. http://mises.org/daily/5857/Joseph-A-Schumpeter-Maverick-and-Enigma (accessed October 2012).
Swedberg, Richard. *Schumpeter: A Biography.* Princeton, NJ: Princeton University Press, 1992.

*Timothy P. Schilling*

## SCHWARTZ, ANNA

Born: November 11, 1915, in New York City; Died: June 21, 2012, in New York City; American; economic and financial history, banking policy, monetary policy, international economic policy, financial policy; Major Works: *The Growth and Fluctuation of the British Economy, 1790–1850: An Historical, Statistical, and Theoretical Study of Britain's Economic Development* (with A. D. Gayer and W. W. Rostow) (1953, 2nd ed., 1975), *A Monetary History of the United States, 1867–1960* (with Milton Friedman) (1963).

Anna Schwartz worked as an economist at the National Bureau of Economic Research since 1941. She has been praised for her contributions to economic history and her use of this insight to interpret current day events. She is best known for her collaboration with Nobel laureate Milton Friedman in their book *A Monetary History of the United States, 1867–1960*, which outlines the importance of the quantity of money—not interest rates—in influencing monetary policy and the economy as a whole. In addition, they critique the actions of the Federal Reserve during the banking panics of the 1930s. Her collaboration skills, her empirical rigor, and the longevity of her research define a woman who has significantly contributed to economics scholarship. Schwartz died in 2012.

Anna Jacobson Schwartz was born on November 11, 1915, in New York City. At age 18, she graduated from Barnard College and was elected to Phi Beta Kappa. One year later, she earned her master's degree in economics from Columbia University. Schwartz then married and started her family (including four children) all while continuing to work as a professional economist. She ultimately earned her PhD from Columbia in 1964.

In 1936, Schwartz worked briefly for the U.S. Department of Agriculture and then at the Columbia University Social Science Research Council. In 1941, she began her work in statistical research at NBER in which she has continued to the present. Eleven years later she began teaching at Brooklyn College and then Baruch College for a short time along with her work at the National Bureau. In 1967, she became an adjunct professor of economics for City University of New York, Graduate Division at Hunter College for several years. In 1969, she was adjunct at New York University, Graduate School of Arts and Sciences. Since then she has served on the board of editors of the *American Economic Review* (1972–78), the *Journal of Money, Credit, and Banking* (1974–75, 1984–2012), the *Journal of Monetary Economics* (1975–2012), and the *Journal of Financial Services Research* (1993–2012). Schwartz served as the president of the Western Economic Association from 1987 to 1988. She also was the honorary visiting professor of the City University Business School in London from 1984 to 2002.

Schwartz began her academic collaboration with Milton Friedman in 1948 at the suggestion of Arthur Burns. She had recently completed work on another collaboration project with Arthur D. Gayer and Walt Rostow, *The Growth and Fluctuation of the British Economy, 1790–1850*. Many have remarked that neither Friedman nor Schwartz could have completed *Monetary History* without the other. Notably, this collaboration was carried out between New York City, where Schwartz worked and lived, and Chicago, where Friedman worked and lived. The two did meet in New York or talk on the phone occasionally, but most correspondence, editing, and other writing activity for this work was carried out using the postal mail service.

Schwartz and Friedman state that their inspiration for *Monetary History* arose from the NBER program to study the cyclical behavior of different economic processes like transportation, inventory management, and consumption. This work illuminated the importance of fluctuations in the growth rate of the money stock and the business cycle and criticized the ineptness of the Federal Reserve during the Great Depression. Many note that this work's greatest effect has been to focus monetary policy on the goal of price stability.

Schwartz remained until her death in 2012 a founding member of the Shadow Open Market Committee created in 1973 to act as a watchdog over Federal Reserve policy. She has published numerous articles and publications over the course of her career—many in collaboration with Michael Bordo.

Schwartz continued her work at the National Bureau of Economic Research and as adjunct professor of economics at the Graduate School of the City University of New York till her death. She earned numerous honorary doctorates from prestigious schools such as Williams, Loyola, Emory, Rutgers, and London City University to name a few. She was the distinguished fellow of the American Economic Association in 1993, the honorary fellow of the Institute of Economic Affairs in 1997, and a fellow of the Academy of Arts and Sciences in 2007.

Anna Schwartz died on June 21, 2012, in Manhattan, New York City.

*See also:* Burns, Arthur; Friedman, Milton

### Selected Works by Anna Schwartz

Gayer, A. D., W. W. Rostow, and Anna Schwartz. *The Growth and Fluctuation of the British Economy, 1790–1850.* 2 vols., 2nd ed. Sussex, UK: Harvester Press, 1975.

Schwartz, Anna, and Milton Friedman. *A Monetary History of the United States, 1867–1960.* Princeton, NJ: Princeton University Press for NBER, 1963.

### Selected Works about Anna Schwartz

Bloomberg. "Anna Schwartz, Economist Milton Friedman's Co-author, Dies at 96." http://www.bloomberg.com/news/2012-06-21/anna-schwartz-economist-milton-friedman-s-co-author-dies-at-96.html.

Feldstein, Martin. "Anna Schwartz ar the National Bureau of Economic Research." *Journal of Financial Services Research* 18, no. 2/3 (2000.): 115–17 http://www.nber.org/feldstein/schwartz.html (accessed October 2012).

Ferguson, Tim. "Anna Schwartz, Monetary Historian, RIP." Forbes. http://www.forbes.com/sites/timferguson/2012/06/21/anna-schwartz-monetary-historian-rip (accessed October 2012).

Fettig, David. "Interview with Anna J. Schwartz." Federal Reserve Bank of Minneapolis. September 1, 1993. http://www.minneapolisfed.org/publications_papers/pub_display.cfm?id=3724 (accessed October 2012).

*Kathryn Lloyd Gustafson*

## SELTEN, REINHARD

Born: October 5, 1930, in Breslau, Germany (now Wroclaw, Poland); German; game theory, Nash equilibrium, multistage games, experimental economics, bounded rationality, Nobel Prize (1994); Major Works: *The Chain Store Paradox* (1974), *Game Theory and Economic Behaviour: Selected Essays*, Volume 1 (1999), *Game Equilibrium Models I: Evolution and Game Dynamics* (2010).

Reinhard Selten is a mathematician and economist who won the Nobel Prize in 1994 for his work in game theory, specifically by furthering and deepening the equilibrium equations of fellow Nobel winner John Nash. He is the only German to have won the Nobel Prize in Economics. Selten was also a leader in the field of experimental economics. Selten believed all economic theories should be supported by empirical evidence. He set up economics testing laboratories where he could see his ideas in action.

Reinhard Selten was born in Breslau, Germany (now Wroclaw, Poland), on October 5, 1930. His father, Adolf Selten, was an ethnic Jew, and as a result of his mixed heritage he faced discrimination from the Nazi regime. His father was forced to sell his small business, and Reinhard was not permitted to pursue an education past the age of 14. Many of the Seltens' Jewish relatives were killed during the Holocaust. Nevertheless, the family feared Soviet occupation even more than the Nazi threat, and when Red Army troops closed in on Breslau at the end of the war, the Selten family escaped on one of the last trains out of the city.

The family fled to Austria, and Selten worked briefly as a farm laborer before he was able to return to school. He studied math in college and graduate school. Rather than take astronomy, the standard minor for math students, he requested economics, and began to apply sophisticated mathematics to social questions. When he eventually visited a game theory conference at Princeton University in the United States, his career path was sealed.

Selten's work expanded on the idea of the Nash equilibrium, which posits that given rules and a perfect knowledge of opponents' choices in a given competitive situation, one can calculate the strategy that the game-players will choose. The Nash equilibrium works as sort of a snapshot of the strategic options that competitors face. Selten took it further. He explained that sometimes games unfold in stages, and while each stage has its own equilibrium (i.e., a best possible strategy), the game as a whole, what Selten called a "supergame," has its own equilibrium, which may in turn affect the equilibria of each stage, and even go back and change them.

The example he used was called the "chain store paradox." In this example, a chain store is the only store of its kind in a particular town, but there is another chain that is thinking about moving in. The original chain has a choice: should they lower their prices to such a point that the newcomers will be unable to make a profit, and therefore decide not to come? This would make sense because it would deter future competition, which could devastate the chain, but it would hurt their profits in this current stage. If a second competitor appears and the choice must be made a second time, cutting prices would still be a good strategy since the point is still to discourage *future* attempts at competition. But whenever the final stage of the "game" arrives, that is, when there is only one possible competitor remaining, then it would not be worth it to lower prices. The chain would accept the new competition. But this is where the paradox begins.

Reasoning backward, we see that if the store does not lower prices in the final stage, then the time *before* that final stage becomes the new final stage. Therefore they would opt a second time not to slash prices. This logic continues all the way back to the first stage. This led Selten to believe that the company would never cut prices in the first place. They will allow the competition to exist.

Selten was also a leader in experimental economics. He thought that all economic theories should be supported by empirical evidence, and to this end he set up economics testing laboratories where he could see his ideas in action. In the case of the chain store paradox, he found that companies in fact choose a middle road. They often allow come competition for a while, but at some point decide to retaliate and begin a price war. The explanation for this seemed to be simply that humans do not operate strictly according to the pure logic of game theory. There are instincts, emotions, and relationships to consider, even among competitors. These factors and the fact that people have imperfect information when making decisions led Selten to work in still another important area: the theory of bounded rationality. This theory holds that, while people are generally rational in their decision making, their rationality has limits. Even so, such tendencies can be modeled and predicted.

In 1994 Selten was awarded the Nobel Prize along with John Nash and John Harsanyi for their work in game theory. Selten is now a professor emeritus at the University of Bonn.

*See also:* Harsanyi, John; Nash, John

## Selected Works by Reinhard Selten

Selten, Reinhard. *The Chain Store Paradox.* Bielefeld, Germany: Institute for Mathematics, Wirtschaftsforschung and University of Bielefeld, 1974.

Selten, Reinhard. *Game Equilibrium Models I: Evolution and Game Dynamics.* Berlin: Springer, 2010.

Selten, Reinhard. *Game Theory and Economic Behaviour: Selected Essays.* Vol. 1. Cheltenham, UK: Edward Elgar, 1999.

Selten, Reinhard. *A Model of Oligopolistic Size Structure and* Profitability. Bielefeld, Germany: Institute for Mathematics, Mathematische Wirtschaftsforschung, University, 1977.

Selten, Reinhard. *Models of Strategic Rationality.* Berlin: Springer, 1988.

Selten, Reinhard. *Spieltheoretische Behandlung eines Oligopolmodells mit Nachfrageträgheit* [An oligopoly model with demand inertia]. Vol. 121. Geneva, Switzerland: Droz, 1965.

Selten, Reinhard, and John C. Harsanyi. *A General Theory of Equilibrium Selection in Games.* Cambridge, MA: MIT Press, 1988.

## Selected Works about Reinhard Selten

McCarty, Marilu Hurt. *The Nobel Laureates.* New York: McGraw-Hill, 2001.

O'Connor, J. J., and E. F. Robertson. "Reinhard Selten." School of Mathematics and Statistics, University of St. Andrews. http://www-history.mcs.st-and.ac.uk/Biographies/Selten.html (accessed July 2012).

"Reinhard Selten." In *The Concise Encyclopedia of Economics.* Edited by David R. Henderson. The Library of Economics and Liberty. http://www.econlib.org/library/Enc/bios/Selten.html (accessed July 2012).

Selten, Reinhard. "Autobiography." Nobelprize.org. http://www.nobelprize.org/nobel_prizes/economics/laureates/1994/selten-autobio.html (accessed July 2012).

*Stephen H. Day*

## SEN, AMARTYA

Born: November 3, 1933, in Santiniketan, West Bengal, India; Indian; social choice theory, economic welfare, developmental economics, Nobel Prize (1998); Major Works: *On Economic Inequality* (1973, 1977), *Poverty and Famines* (1981), *Choice, Welfare, and Measurement* (1982), *On Ethics and Economics* (1987), *Inequality Reexamined* (1992), *Development as Freedom* (1999), *Rationality and Freedom* (2002), *Identity and Violence: The Illusion of Destiny* (2007).

Amartya Sen is one of the most engaged economists of the twenty-first century. Sen has written more than 25 books (most of them translated into more than 30 languages) and published more than 250 journal articles. Sen is the first Indian to win the Nobel Prize in Economics. He is a professor of economics and philosophy at Harvard University, and was the master of Trinity College in Cambridge. He is well known for his work in the theory of social choice, welfare economics, theory of measurement, and moral and political philosophy.

Amartya Sen was born in November 3, 1933 to a well-known Bengali Hindu family in Santiniketan of West Bengal, India. His grandfather, Acharya Kshiti Mohan Sen, was a prominent professor of Sanskrit and medieval Indian literature and the second vice chancellor of Visva-Bharati University in India. His father was a professor of chemistry at Dhaka University (Dhaka was then part of India, and now it is the capital of Bangladesh). Sen earned his BA in economics from the University of Calcutta in 1953, and then after moving to England, in 1956, from Trinity College, in Cambridge. At the age of 23, after enrolling for a PhD in economics at Trinity College, he returned to India for two years and was immediately appointed the head of the department of economics at Jadavpur University in Calcutta, India. In 1959, Sen returned to Cambridge to finish his PhD. Upon completing his PhD in economics, he won a prize fellowship at Trinity College, which enabled him to study philosophy for four years.

Amartya Sen is the first Indian to win the Nobel Prize. In 1998 Sen was awarded the Nobel Prize in economics for his work on welfare economics and the underlying mechanisms of poverty. (Nobel Foundation)

Sen's work on social choice theory has been one of his most important contributions to economics. The theory of social choice is about the connection between individual values and preferences of a society as a whole. The field of social choice theory goes back to the eighteenth-century work of a French mathematician, Marquis de Condorcet. In the 1950s, Kenneth Arrow reintroduced the theory to the new generation of economic scholars. The main question in this theory is whether the collective choices of the society are based upon all its members' preferences. This topic is the basis for the welfare economics. Sen developed his measurement of economic welfare according to social choice theory.

Sen is also concerned about the measure of a society's success in connection with its members' preferences. He studied gross domestic product (GDP) or gross national product (GNP) to determine whether they are good measures of economic development and how best to measure poverty in a vastly diverse society. Sen argues that measures such as GDP or GNP cannot adequately evaluate economic well-being of a society mainly because they do not show how income is distributed between people and because social welfare depends on so many non-income-related factors. In 1976, Sen came up with a new measure of a poverty that takes into account individual's "relative deprivation." In 1989, he introduced a new measure of welfare for the Human Development Report of the United Nations Development Program, which instead of only looking at one absolute figure such as GNP would look at an array of factors influencing human well-being and possible opportunities.

Sen has introduced new ideas and has written numerous books about famines. In his book *Poverty and Famines* (1981), he examined famines in India, Bangladesh, and Africa. He showed that in most cases people starve to death when they do not have enough money to buy food, rather than when there is a sharp decline in a food supply. He also argued that people who suffer from poverty and starvation are not only the poorest of poor but also those who, for one reason or another, have lost their economic means of survival. In addition, Sen discovered that no famine had ever happened in a democracy. He argued that in a democratic government information spreads at a much faster speed. Therefore government and other social-welfare organizations can respond to disastrous situations like famines faster and more efficiently.

One of Sen's main influences is Adam Smith. Sen admires Smith because he was concerned about the distribution of economic means. In his book *Development as Freedom* (1999), Sen argues that development means letting people choose the kind of life they value. He points out that poverty, lack of education, and lack of economic opportunities are the main enemies of freedom and development because they deprive people from the means they need to choose what they value. As an alternative, freedom and economic development of a society should be measured based on the capabilities of its citizens.

Amartya Sen is a fellow of the British Academy, foreign honorary member of the American Academy of Arts and Sciences, and a member of the American Philosophical Society. Sen has received numerous international recognitions and awards such as the Bharat Ratna from the President of India, the Brazilian Ordem do Merito Cientifico, the presidency of the Italian Republic Medal, and the Eisenhower Medal. In 1998, Amartya Sen was awarded the Nobel Prize in Economics. In 2010, *Time* magazine listed Amartya Sen as one of the 100 most influential persons in the world.

*See also:* Arrow, Kenneth; Smith, Adam

### Selected Works by Amartya Sen

Foster, James, and Amartya Sen. *On Economic Inequality after a Quarter Century*. Oxford: Clarendon Press, 1997.
Sen, Amartya. *Development as Freedom*. New York: Alfred Knopf, 1999.
Sen, Amartya. *Identity and Violence: The Illusion of Destiny*. New York: Norton, 2007.
Sen, Amartya. *Inequality Reexamined*. Oxford: Clarendon Press, 1992.
Sen, Amartya. *On Economic Inequality*. Oxford: Clarendon Press, 1973.
Sen, Amartya. *On Ethics and Economics*. Oxford: Basil Blackwell, 1987.
Sen, Amartya. *Poverty and Famines: An Essay on Entitlement and Deprivation*. Oxford: Clarendon Press, 1981.
Sen, Amartya. *Rationality and Freedom*. Cambridge, MA: Harvard University Press, 2002.

### Selected Works about Amartya Sen

Kuklys, Wiebke. *Amartya Sen's Capability Approach: Theoretical Insights and Empirical Applications*. Berlin: Springer, 2005.
Morris, Christopher W., ed. *Amartya Sen*. Cambridge: Cambridge University Press, 2010.
Sen, Amartya. "Autobiography." Nobelprize.org. http://www.nobelprize.org/nobel_prizes/economics/laureates/1998/sen-autobio.html (accessed February 2012).
Walker, Melanie, and Elaine Unterhalter, eds. *Amartya Sen's Capability Approach and Social Justice in Education*. New York: Palgrave Macmillan, 2007.

*Elham Mahmoudi*

# SENIOR, NASSAU

Born: September 26, 1790, in Compton Beauchamp, Berkshire, England; Died: June 6, 1864, in Kensington, England; English; economic theory, public policy relating to labor, wages, rents, productivity, trade; Major Works: *An Outline of the Science of Political Economy* (1836, revised 1850), *Historical and Philosophical Essays in Two Volumes* (1865).

Nassau Senior's most significant contributions to economics were enhancements to David Ricardo's cost and productivity value theory and refinements to the economic principles of his contemporaries. He distilled economic philosophy to four basic theses: individuals are primarily motivated by wealth, the population is controlled by scarcity, labor enhances production, and technology produces diminishing returns. He approached the study of political economy as the method by which wealth was defined, created, and shared. Senior died in 1864.

Nassau William Senior, the son of Reverend John Raven Senior, vicar of Durnford, Wiltshire, and Mary Duke, daughter of the solicitor-general of Barbados, was born September 26, 1790, in Compton Beauchamp, England. He was educated at Eton and Magdalene College and earned a bachelor of arts degree in 1811. In 1819, Senior was admitted to the bar and eventually earned his master of arts degree in chancery in 1836. He was the first professor at Oxford to be named as the Drummond Chair of Political Economy (1825–30 and 1847–52).

Senior approached political economy more as an empirical science than as a social science. He supported Adam Smith, who also believed that men were motivated primarily by self-interest. It was with this lens that he scrutinized theories of popular economic philosophies. When he wrote about Smith's work, Senior expanded on Smith's theory of the division of labor and distinguished between the price of labor and the rate of wages. His economic perspective was that wages should be based on funds directly attributable to productivity. As productivity increases, funds would rise leading to an increase in wages.

One of Senior's most notable ideas was that capital accumulation is a cost of production. Senior referred to this phenomenon as abstinence. He stated that in waiting for a return on an investment, a capitalist abstained from using the capital for a period of time. Ricardo's theory of production value stated that capital, resources, and labor combined are greater than the cost of these production components. Senior identified previously unrecognized element among the costs of production: abstinence. He showed that capital, resources, labor plus abstinence combined were equivalent to production value. Further, he stated that conserving capital and saving it should be considered as a factor in production costs. Senior's expansion of Ricardo's theory secured a place for him in the history of economic theory.

History showed that Ricardo's production cost and value theory was valid. However, Senior disagreed with Ricardo's view on the relationship of rent to productivity, using agricultural property as an example. David Ricardo pointed out, however, that more fertile land could command a higher rent because it would produce more than less fertile parcels. Senior was more a theoretical thinker than a practical one, and could not prevail in this argument.

Senior reflected the popular opinion of Thomas Malthus and others when he wrote that the former version of poor laws encouraged indigent families to have several children (as each child brought an increase of funds) and recipients assumed an attitude of entitlement. In his 1834 report for the Poor Law Commission, Senior and Chadwick recommended that an independent commission administer the laws. Nassau Senior also defended the prevailing Malthusian belief that the poor needed moral and intellectual education to stimulate their productivity. No longer did society believe that there would always be poor people. The middle and upper classes had begun to think that poor individuals had simply made bad choices and could change their lot if they tried.

In his response to Thomas Malthus, preeminent demographer of the time, Senior disagreed that exponentially increasing population would deplete resources. A result of his study comparing earnings and productivity, Senior noted that wages could grow in relation to increased productivity levels. For incomes to rise and increase prosperity, either productivity would have to rise or numbers of dole recipients must fall. He was confident that the economy would grow in proportion with population and argued there was no need for concern in this matter, for man's desire to improve his financial standing would balance his urge to procreate.

Nassau Senior's careful examination of politics and economics appealed to lawmakers who applied his perspectives on practical matters and problems of the times. Senior advised government leaders to encourage economic prosperity and protect the impotent poor. Additional policies that Senior believed would develop a prosperous economy were promotion of free trade, including the precious metals market, and elimination of "poor laws." The early ones established a worker's right to employment and a tax burden on employers. He believed that the dole interfered with individuals' transitions to lives of economic independence.

Nassau Senior died on June 6, 1864, in Kensington, England.

*See also:* Malthus, Thomas; Ricardo, David; Smith, Adam

**Selected Works by Nassau Senior**

Senior, Nassau. *Historical and Philosophical Essays in Two Volumes*. London: Longman, Green, Longman, Roberts, & Green, 1865.

Senior, Nassau. *An Outline of the Science of Political Economy*. London: Allen & Unwin, 1836.

Senior, Nassau. *Political Economy*. 3rd ed. London: Richard Griffin, 1854.

Senior, Nassau. *Statement of the Provision for the Poor, and of the Condition of the Labouring Classes, in a Considerable Portion of America and Europe*. London: B. Fellowes, 1835.

**Selected Works about Nassau Senior**

Bloy, Marjie. "Village Life in the 1830s and 1840s." http://www.victorianweb.org/history/poorlaw/implemen.html (accessed March 2012).

"The Implementation of the Poor Law." http://www.victorianweb.org/ (accessed March 2012).

Murphy, Robert P. "The Abstinence Theory of Interest." Ludwig von Mises Institute. November 6, 2003. http://mises.org/daily/1369 (accessed March 2012).

Vaggi, Gianni, Peter D. Groenewegen, and Barry D. Smart. *A Concise History of Economic Thought: From Mercantilism to Monetarism*. New York: Palgrave Macmillan, 2003.

*Cynthia Blitz Law*

# SENNHOLZ, HANS

Born: February 3, 1922, in Brambauer, Germany; Died: June 23, 2007, in Grove City, Pennsylvania; American; Austrian economist and libertarian, educator and author; Major Works: *How Can Europe Survive?* (1955), *Inflation, or the Gold Standard* (1973), *Death and Taxes* (1976), *Money and Freedom* (1985).

Hans Sennholz is best known as an author and educator with a long tenure with small Grove City College (Pennsylvania) and long association with the Foundation for Economic Education. He authored 17 books and booklets during his life and published over 500 other essays and articles, including a website of essays and articles maintained over the last eight years of his life. His writings were influential in promoting a monetary policy that supported the gold standard, opposed

Keynesian economics, and opposed the use of the Federal Reserve and fractional reserve banking to influence and control the money supply. Sennholz died in 2007.

Hans F. Sennholz was born on February 3, 1922, in Brambauer, Germany. He grew up during the hyperinflation in Germany following World War I. During World War II, he lost both parents in separate incidents and his brother perished while serving with the German army in Russia. Sennholz was a member of the German Luftwaffe and spent time as a prisoner of war in the United States after being shot down over Egypt. He was able to study some in the United States while he was a prisoner thanks to some American relatives.

Sennholz returned to Germany following the war and continued his education, earning a master's degree at the University of Marburg in 1948 and a doctorate in political science from the University of Cologne in 1949. He immigrated to the United States in 1949 and earned his second PhD at New York University in 1955, under the tutelage of Ludwig von Mises. Von Mises would influence Sennholz's Austrian economic outlook to focus on the dysfunction of socialist economies and government intervention, the need for a return to the gold standard, and the importance of the profit-and-loss system for the free market.

Sennholz began his teaching career as assistant professor of economics at Iona College in New Rochelle, New York, from 1954 to 1956. Oil magnate and major donor J. Howard Pew recommended Sennholz to Grove City College (Pennsylvania) in 1955, where Sennholz would teach undergraduates from 1956 to 1992 and head the economics department. He insisted on teaching undergraduates because he regarded the young minds as malleable and held high regard for their passion. He also invested his time writing articles, books, and conducting a graduate program for International College in Los Angeles.

Sennholz's book writing career began with *How Can Europe Survive?* (1955). Sennholz favored unification as a free-market/capitalist system, but not as a welfare state. Though he acknowledged the peoples' desire for European unification, he argued that the only unity would involve free markets and the freedom of the individual, an arrangement that he thought unlikely. His next books would not be until 1969 with *The Great Depression* and the 1973 *Inflation, or the Gold Standard*, both minibooks that spoke out against Keynesian approaches to the economy and the negative effects of inflation.

In 1975, Sennholz edited and contributed to *Gold Is Money*, a collection of essays by noted economists in support of the gold standard. Sennholz's essay contribution was entitled "No Shortage of Gold," which argued that the gold standard would help businesses and that it was necessary to end monetary expansion policies. In his 1976 book, *Death and Taxes*, he gives reasons why government taxes, specifically inheritance taxes that attempt to equalize income and wealth, are not effective but rather harmful to society. Sennholz used his 1979 work, *Age of Inflation*, to point out the errors and dangers inherent in inflation and again call for a return to the gold standard to protect the value of the dollar. He also hoped to see the end of the Federal Reserve.

During the late 1970s, Sennholz met presidential hopeful Ronald Reagan after one of Reagan's speeches in Honolulu. There Reagan admitted to being influenced by Sennholz's work, which would provide Reagan justification for promoting free markets during his presidency. In 1985, Sennholz wrote *Money and Freedom*, which pointed out more flaws in the "money monopoly" of the Federal Reserve, but also pointed out flaws in the Friedmanite monetarist view. He thought that the popular supply-side economics supported by Reagan's administration were too close to Keynesian ideals. He concluded the book with another appeal to return to the gold standard.

In the 1990s, Sennholz concluded his career at Grove City College, retiring at the age of 70 and having been honored in 1990 with the Outstanding Teacher Award from the Pennsylvania Academy for the Profession of Teaching. He began a five-year service to the Foundation for Economic Education in 1992 as president, during which time he rescued the organization and made it profitable again.

Hans Sennholz died on June 23, 2007, in Grove City, Pennsylvania.

*See also:* Bastiat, Frédéric; Keynes, John Maynard; Mises, Ludwig von; Say, Jean-Baptiste

### Selected Works by Hans Sennholz

Sennholz, Hans. *The Age of Inflation*. Belmont, MA: Western Islands, 1979.
Sennholz, Hans. *Death and Taxes*. Washington, DC: Heritage Foundation, 1976.
Sennholz, Hans. *Debts and Deficits*. Spring Mills, PA: Libertarian Press, 1987.
Sennholz, Hans, ed. *Gold Is Money*. Westport, CT: Greenwood Press, 1975.
Sennholz, Hans. *The Great Depression: Will We Repeat It?* Spring Mills, PA: Libertarian Press, 1988.
Sennholz, Hans. *How Can Europe Survive*. New York: Van Nostrand Company, 1955.
Sennholz, Hans. *Inflation, or Gold Standard?* Lansing, MI: Bramble Minibooks, 1973.
Sennholz, Hans. *Money and Freedom*. Spring Mills, PA: Libertarian Press, 1985.
Sennholz, Hans. *The Politics of Unemployment*. Spring Mills, PA: Libertarian Press, 1987.

### Selected Works about Hans Sennholz

Boettke, Peter J. *The Elgar Companion to Austrian Economics*. London: Edward Elgar, 1994.
Robbins, John W., ed. *A Man of Principle: Essays in Honor of Hans F. Sennholz*. Grove City, PA: Grove City College, 1992.
Salerno, Joseph. "Biography of Hans Sennholz: Teacher and Theorist." Ludwig von Mises Institute. http://mises.org/about/3246 (accessed October 2012).
Sennholz.com. "Welcome to the Home Page of Hans F. Sennholz." http://www.sennholz.com/obit.html.

*Joseph Lee Hauser*

# SHAPLEY, LLOYD

Born: June 2, 1923, in Cambridge, Massachusetts; American; mathematics, game theory, Nobel Prize (2012); Major Works: "A Value for N-Person Games" (1953), "College Admissions and the Stability of Marriage" (1962), *Values of Non-atomic Games, Part II* (with Robert Aumann) (1969), "On Market Games" (with Martin Shubik) (1969).

Lloyd Shapley received the 2012 Nobel Prize in Economics for his work in the fields of mathematical economics and game theory. A Bronze-Star World War II veteran, Shapley is known for many mathematical economics and game-theory theorems that bear his name: Bondareva-Shapley theorem, Shapley value, Shapley-Folkman theorem, Gale-Shapley algorithm, and the Shapley-Shubik power index to name only a few. Shapley was also influential in the development of game theory. Shapley has been a professor and professor emeritus at University of California, Los Angeles (UCLA), since 1981.

Lloyd Stowell Shapley was born on June 2, 1923, in Cambridge, Massachusetts, the son of the distinguished astronomer Harlow Shapley. Shapley began his college studies at Harvard University but was interrupted when he was drafted during World War II. During World War II he was awarded the Bronze Star for breaking a Soviet weather code. Following the war he returned to Harvard, graduating in mathematics with his bachelor's degree in 1948. Shapley went to Princeton University, earning his PhD in mathematics in 1953 where he studied with fellow future Nobel laureate John Nash.

Shapley began his academic career by staying on at Princeton as an instructor. In 1954, Shapley left academia and rejoined the RAND Corporation where he had been a research mathematician in 1948 and 1949. At the RAND Corporation, Shapley worked on problems associated with matrix games, the Von Neumann-Morgenstern stable sets, and nonatomic games with Nobel laureate Robert Aumann. His early work on matrix games has been considered so comprehensive he left little room for future improvement. Shapley's work has significantly influenced economic theory on competition and utility theory.

Lloyd Shapley has been called one of the most prolific economic mathematicians. The theorems, algorithms, and game-theory solutions that bear his name are numerous. Besides his significant work with Robert Aumann on nonatomic games, his work included block voting with the Shapley-Shubik power index and the Bondareva-Shapley theorem addressing convex games. The Shapley value was introduced in 1953 as a solution concept in cooperative game theory. In cooperative game theory, the value assigns distributions of a surplus created by a coalition of players.

In 1962, Shapley and David Gale developed an algorithm on marriage matching. The Gale-Shapley algorithm was designed as a way to create a marriage market on how to pair individuals for marriage even if the individuals did not agree on what would make a good marriage.

In 2012, Lloyd Shapley, along with Alvin Roth, were awarded the Nobel Prize in Economics for their work in market design and game theory. They were noted for the applications of their research, especially in creating markets for the purpose of matching different individuals such as his work on matching marriage couples with the Gale-Shapley algorithm.

The 2012 Nobel Prize in Economics was one more honor for Shapley. Besides the Bronze Star and Nobel Prize, Lloyd Shapley was a fellow of the Econometric Society, American Academy of Arts and Sciences, and INFORMS (Institute for Operations and Management Sciences). In 1981, the year he left RAND Corporation for UCLA, he received the John von Neumann Theory Prize. In 1986, Shapley received an honorary PhD from Hebrew University of Jerusalem.

*See also:* Aumann, Robert; Edgeworth, Francis; Morgenstern, Oskar; Nash, John; Roth, Alvin

### Selected Works by Lloyd Shapley

Aumann, Robert, and Lloyd Shapley. *Values of Non-atomic Games, Part II: The Random Order Approach.* Fort Belvoir, VA: Defense Technical Information Center, 1969.

Gale, D., and L. S. Shapley. "College Admissions and the Stability of Marriage." *American Mathematical Monthly* 69 (1962): 9–14.

Shapley, Lloyd. "Stochastic Games." *Proceedings of National Academy of Science* 39 (1953): 1095–1100.

Shapley, Lloyd S. "A Value for N-person Games." In *Contributions to the Theory of Games.* Vol. 2. *Annals of Mathematical Studies.* Vol. 28. Edited by H. W. Kuhn and A. W. Tucker, 307–17. Princeton, NJ: Princeton University Press, 1953.

Shapley, Lloyd. *Values of Non-atomic Games.* Princeton, NJ: Princeton University Press, 1972.

Shapley, Lloyd, and Robert Aumann. *Values of Non-atomic Games.* Princeton, NJ: Princeton University Press, 1974.

Shapley, Lloyd, and Martin Shubik. "The Assignment Game I: The Core." *International Journal of Game Theory* 1 (1971): 111–30.

Shapley, Lloyd, and Martin Shubik. "On Market Games." *Journal of Economic Theory* 1 (1969): 9–25.

Shapley, Lloyd, and Martin Shubik. "A Method for Evaluating the Distribution of Power in a Committee System." *American Political Science Review* 48 (1954): 787–92.

### Selected Works about Lloyd Shapley

"Lloyd S. Shapley." Nobelprize.org. "http://www.nobelprize.org/nobel_prizes/economics/laureates/2012/shapley.html (accessed October 2012).

Lubin, Gus. "Alvin Roth and Lloyd Shapley Win the Nobel Prize for Economics." *Business Insider.* http://www.businessinsider.com/alvin-roth-and-lloyd-shapley-win-nobel-2012-10 (accessed October 2012).

Rampell, Catherine. "2 from US Win Nobel in Economics." *New York Times*, October 16, 2012. http://www.nytimes.com/2012/10/16/business/economy/alvin-roth-and-lloyd-shapley-win-nobel-in-economic-science.html?_r=0 (accessed October 2012).

Roth, A. E., ed. *The Shapley Value: Essays in Honor of Lloyd S. Shapley.* Cambridge: Cambridge University Press, 1988.

*David A. Dieterle*

# SHARPE, WILLIAM

Born: June 16, 1934, in Boston, Massachusetts; American; finance economics, asset pricing model, Nobel Prize (1990); Major Works: "Capital Asset Prices: A Theory of Market Equilibrium under Conditions of Risk" (1964), *Portfolio Theory and Capital Markets* (1970).

William Sharpe is an American economist who worked in both academia and the corporate world. An economist specializing in finance and asset pricing, he served both academia and the world of finance. A professor at Washington University, Stanford University, and University of California, Irvine, he was also a consultant for companies such as RAND, Wells Fargo, AT&T, United Technologies, and Merrill Lynch. Sharpe's capital asset pricing model (CAPM) explains the relationship between securities, prices, risks, and returns. For his work on CAPM, Sharpe was awarded the Nobel Prize in 1990.

William F. Sharpe was born on June 16, 1934, in Boston, Massachusetts. His father was in the National Guard and the family moved to Texas and then central California. Sharpe initially attended University of California, Berkeley, in 1951 but transferred after a year to the Los Angeles campus (UCLA) where he majored in business administration. He received his bachelor of arts degree with a major in economics in 1955 from UCLA and a master of arts degree in 1956, again with a focus on economics. While at UCLA he was influenced and befriended by two professors, Armen Alchian and Fred Weston.

After a brief stint in the army, Sharpe joined the RAND Corporation as an economist. While there he completed his doctorate degree at UCLA in economics in 1961. His dissertation explored a number of aspects of portfolio analysis and would prove foundational to his capital asset pricing model, a model expressing the relationship between risk and expected rate of return. Alchian served on his dissertation committee, but it was Weston who suggested he work with Harry Markowitz, who would later be named as cowinner of his Nobel Prize.

In 1961, Sharpe began teaching finance at the University of Washington (UW). There he continued to work on a generalization of the equilibrium theory that he started to develop in the final chapter of his dissertation. Using this information, in 1964 he published "Capital Asset Prices: A Theory of Market Equilibrium under Conditions of Risk" in the *Journal of Finance*. This article became the basis of his capital asset pricing model (CAPM). This model is built on the assumption that market participants seek to maximize their profits. His model explains the relationship between securities prices, risks, and returns. The uniqueness of the CAPM is the dual purpose of compensation: risk and the time value of money.

While at UW, Sharpe also wrote about the economics of computers and computer programming based on his work at RAND and continued to study extensions of the CAPM model. In 1966, he developed the Sharpe ratio, which determines whether a portfolio's return is due to smart investment decisions or to excess risk. This tool is very useful for determining whether a portfolio or fund's higher returns have too much additional risk.

He went on to the University of California, Irvine, from 1968 to 1970, when he left to begin his long-standing career at Stanford University Graduate School of Business. While there he wrote a number of textbooks and created the binomial option pricing procedure. Sharpe also worked as a consultant with both Merrill Lynch and Wells Fargo with the intent of putting into practice his ideas on financial economics. In fact, Sharpe took on a number of different roles to further his understanding of finance and economics and improve his research. In 1973, he was named the Timken Professor of Finance at Stanford. During the 1976–77 academic years, Sharpe was a member of a team studying issues of bank capital adequacy at the National Bureau of Economic Research.

In 1980, Sharpe became president of the American Finance Association. He was also named the recipient of the American Assembly of Collegiate Schools of Business award for his outstanding contributions to the field of business education. During this time he began to work on pension plan investment policies and asset allocation. In 1983, he helped to develop a program of international investment management at Stanford. Also during this time, he worked as a consultant to a number of equity funds. In 1986, he took a two-year leave from Stanford to found his own company now known as William F. Sharpe Associates. His firm performs research and develops procedures to help pensions, endowments, and foundations select appropriate asset allocations based on their circumstances and objectives. He published additional research based on the findings of his firm. Then in 1989, he became Timken Professor Emeritus of Finance at Stanford in order to devote more time to research and consulting at his firm. During this same year, he was the recipient of the Financial Analysts' Federation Nicholas Molodovsky Award for outstanding contributions to the finance profession.

In 1990, Sharpe was awarded the Nobel Prize in Economic Sciences for price formation of financial assets, his CAPM model. He shared the award with Harry M. Markowitz and Merton H. Miller. During the 1990s, his firm disbanded and in 1996 he established a new firm, Financial Engines Inc., which is a portfolio advising company. Sharpe is a pension consultant for several major firms including AT&T, United Technologies, Hewlett Packard, and Altria.

*See also:* Alchian, Armen; Markowitz, Harry; Miller, Merton

## Selected Works by William Sharpe

Alexander, Gordon, and William Sharpe. *Fundamentals of Investments.* New York: Prentice-Hall, 1989.

Sharpe, William. "Capital Asset Prices: A Theory of Market Equilibrium under Conditions of Risk." *Journal of Finance* 19, no. 3 (September 1964): 425–42.

Sharpe, William. *Investors and Markets: Portfolio Choices, Asset Prices, and Investment Advice.* Princeton, NJ: Princeton University Press, 2007.

Sharpe, William. *Portfolio Theory and Capital Markets.* New York: McGraw-Hill, 1970.

## Selected Works about William Sharpe

Daniells, Lorna M. *Business Information Sources.* 3rd ed. Berkeley: University of California Press, 1993.

Sharpe, William F. "Autobiography." Nobelprize.org. http://www.nobelprize.org/nobel _prizes/economics/laureates/1990/sharpe-autobio.html (accessed February 2012).

Vane, Howard R., and Chris Mulhearn. *Harry M. Markowitz, Merton H. Miller, William F. Sharpe, Robert C. Merton and Myron S. Scholes.* London: Edward Elgar, 2009.

*Carol Lynn Nute*

## SHILLER, ROBERT

Born: March 29, 1946, in Detroit, Michigan; American; behavioral economics, housing and real estate economics; Major Works: *Market Volatility* (1989), *Macro Markets: Creating Institutions for Managing Society's Largest Economic Risks* (1993), *Irrational Exuberance* (2000), *Subprime Solution: How the Global Financial Crisis Happened and What to Do about It* (2008), *Animal Spirits: How Human Psychology Drives the Economy and Why It Matters for Global Capitalism* (with George Akerlof) (2009).

Robert Shiller is an American economist who teaches at Yale University and the Cowles Foundation. His contributions to the economic community are varied and far-reaching. While providing valuable insight into a variety of economic fields such as financial markets, economic behavior, and others, his most recent contributions focus primarily on the stock market collapse of the early twenty-first century. His contributions include a direct analysis of the 2008–9 subprime lending crisis and economic systems, both of which played a pivotal role in the current economic environment.

Robert James Shiller was born in Detroit, Michigan, on March 29, 1946. He earned his bachelor of arts from the University of Michigan in 1967 and continued his studies at the Massachusetts Institute of Technology where he earned his PhD in 1972. His academic career includes time at the University of Pennsylvania and the University of Minnesota before accepting a position in the economics department at Yale University and the Cowles Foundation for Research in Economics in 1982. He now serves as the Arthur M. Okun Professor in Economics, professor of finance, and fellow at the International Center for Finance at the School of Management at Yale University.

His extensive study of the housing market has proved to be a valuable addition to the real estate industry. The Standard & Poor's Case-Shiller Home Price Indices track changes in the housing market by evaluating those changes based on a three-month average with a two-month lag time. The data are based off of the sales figures of specific single-family residences and condominiums at a variety of price points across 20 cities throughout the nation. These indices are produced and released each month by Fiserv Lending Services.

Much of Shiller's work has extended beyond the classroom and into the bookstores. *Market Volatility*, published in 1989, provided readers with an in-depth statistical analysis of markets and how they operate. *Irrational Exuberance* explored the stock market bubble of the late 1990s, culminating in the rapid decline near the turn of the century. In the book, Shiller claims that the rapid, extreme, and largely volatile stock market growth in the later part of the 1990s led to the overvaluation of technology-based stocks. He argues that the tremendous growth could potentially lead to an exponential catastrophic decline. His work proved to be largely correct as the economic environment rapidly changed as market instabilities prevailed and an economic decline plagued the global economy. The book was a great success, even becoming a *New York Times* best seller. This widespread popularity prompted Shiller and his publishers to develop and expand with a second edition in 2005. The second edition included his work on the housing and real estate markets, explaining how the extension of credit to borrowers would have a negative effect on the economy.

Shiller continued his exploration of the dire subprime lending situation through his work in the *Subprime Solution: How Today's Global Financial Crisis Happened, and What to Do about It*. The Princeton Review published this work in 2008. Shiller provided a brief history of how the subprime lending crisis emerged and he offered an aggressive, multifaceted remedy to resolve the crisis in the mortgage industry, including a substantial restructuring of the complex system. While some of Shiller's solutions are focused on the immediate and imminent crisis faced by many borrowers and home owners, he also emphasizes the long-term need for developing a complex system of safeguards and protective measures to prevent similar situations from arising again. He claimed that his solutions would promote further economic recovery and growth in the future as people strive to reclaim the American dream.

Shiller's contributions to economics are not limited to his writings; any estimation of his work must also take into account his career in the classroom and other economic associations, boards, and advisory councils. He has been a research associate for the National Bureau of Economic Research since 1980; he served as vice president of the American Economic Association in 2005, and he was president of the Eastern Economic Association from 2006 to 2007. He writes "Economic View" for the *New York Times* and "Finance in the 21st Century" for Project Syndicate. His career has provided much to the economic community in a variety of fields and specialties and his contributions to his area of expertise are immense and far-reaching.

Shiller is a professor at Yale University and the Cowles Foundation as the Arthur M. Okun Professor in Economics, and professor of finance and fellow at the International Center for Finance at the School of Management.

*See also:* Okun, Arthur M.

### Selected Works by Robert Shiller

Shiller, Robert. *Irrational Exuberance*. Princeton, NJ: Princeton University Press, 2000.
Shiller, Robert. *Macro Markets: Creating Institutions for Managing Society's Largest Economic Risks*. Cambridge: Oxford University Press, 1993.
Shiller, Robert. *Market Volatility*. Boston: MIT Press, 1989.
Shiller, Robert. *The New Financial Order: Risk in the 21st Century*. Princeton, NJ: Princeton University Press, 2003.
Shiller, Robert. *Subprime Solution: How the Global Financial Crisis Happened and What to Do about It*. Princeton, NJ: Princeton University Press, 2008.
Shiller, Robert, and George A. Akerlof. *Animal Spirits: How Human Psychology Drives the Economy and Why It Matters for Global Capitalism*. Princeton, NJ: Princeton University Press, 2009
Shiller, Robert, and Randall Kroszner. *Reforming U.S. Financial Markets: Reflections before and beyond Dodd-Frank*. Cambridge, MA: MIT Press, 2011.

### Selected Works about Robert Shiller

Blaug, Mark, and Howard R. Vane. *Who's Who in Economics*. 4th ed. London: Edward Elgar, 2003.

Grove, Lloyd. "The World of Robert Shiller." The Business Journals, UpStart Business Journal. May 2, 2008. http://upstart.bizjournals.com/views/columns/the-world-according-to/2008/05/02/Interview-With-Robert-Shiller.html (accessed July 2011).

Yale University. "Shiller Short Biography." http://www.econ.yale.edu/~shiller/bio.htm (accessed July 2011).

William S. Chappell

## SHULTZ, GEORGE

Born: December 13, 1920, in New York City; American; economist, public administration, public policy; Major Works: *Guidelines, Informal Controls and the Market Place (Study in Business)* (1966), *Turmoil and Triumph: My Years as Secretary of State* (1993), *Putting Our House in Order: A Guide to Social Security and Health Care Reform* (2008).

George Shultz served in several executive positions in the United States. He also worked as an economist, researcher, and political adviser, and he influenced American conservative policies for more than 50 years.

George Pratt Shultz was born on December 13, 1920, in New York City. He attended Princeton University, and directly following graduation, he joined the U.S. Marine Corp. He served during World War II and rose to the rank of captain. After the war he enrolled at the Massachusetts Institute of Technology (MIT), earning a PhD in industrial economics.

After his graduation from MIT, Shultz rose quickly to power and influence. He became a professor of economics at MIT and shortly thereafter served as an economic adviser to President Dwight Eisenhower. He returned briefly to MIT before moving to the University of Chicago in 1957, becoming dean of the university's Graduate School of Business in 1962. Chicago was the center for free-market ideas and for the new monetarist theories of Milton Friedman. Such ideas ran counter to the Keynesianism that was popular at the time and prepared Shultz for his later career as a Republican policy maker.

In 1969, Shultz was appointed to the administration of President Richard Nixon, first as secretary of labor, then as director of the Office of Management and Budget. Upon taking office, Shultz and the Nixon administration faced two major economic problems: the imminent failure of the gold standard and the threat of inflation.

After World War II, the Bretton-Woods conference had created a world monetary system in which the United States set a value for the dollar tied to the price of gold; other countries set the value of their money according to the dollar. As the demand for gold fluctuated, the United States was having trouble keeping up its end of the deal, and it became apparent to the administration that the Bretton-Woods gold standard had to end. But there was a problem with this.

Going off the gold standard was likely to make the dollar less valuable, which would in turn make inflation worse. Inflation was high when Shultz took office, and though it had been declining (falling from 6% to 5% in 1970), administration officials feared that it would go back up when the gold standard ended.

A tempting option presented itself: wage and price controls. John Connally, the secretary of the Treasury, recommended that Nixon simply mandate a 90-day freeze in wages and prices if Congress would allow it. George Shultz claimed to have opposed the idea—he noted later that "it's always much easier to get into something like that than to get out of it"—yet the freeze continued anyway.

Though the price freeze was initially popular, it ultimately failed to tame inflation, which would continue to be a problem until the early 1980s. Shultz later summarized that wage and price controls, even when instituted by the talents of Shultz, Richard Nixon, John Connally, Dick Cheney, and Don Rumsfeld, would not work. During Shultz's years in public life, he considered wage and price controls an ineffective public policy.

Shultz replaced Connally as secretary of the Treasury in 1972, but resigned from this office shortly before President Nixon himself resigned in the face of the Watergate scandal. Shultz spent the next eight years as a private citizen, working as president of Bechtel Corporation, the largest engineering company in the United States. As president, Shultz oversaw several major projects in the areas of hydroelectric power, steel factories, deep-waters ports, and other heavy industries.

In 1982, Shultz was called back to Washington, DC, by the administration of Ronald Reagan, this time to serve as secretary of state. In this capacity, he was in charge of foreign relations for the United States at a time when the Cold War was the central concern of American foreign policy. Shultz supported an increased nuclear presence in Europe in order to put pressure on the Soviet Union, even though an expansion of nuclear arms was extremely controversial. However, he also encouraged a dialogue with the Soviet leader, Mikhail Gorbachev.

While Shultz retired from government service in 1989 he did not retire completely. He remained active influencing policy in many capacities: as a scholar at the Hoover Institute, a board member of several companies, cochairperson of California's Economic Recovery Council, adviser to President George W. Bush, and other various policy-influencing organizations.

*See also:* Friedman, Milton; Reich, Robert; Romer, Christine

## Selected Works by George Shultz

Shultz, George, ed. *Guidelines, Informal Controls and the Market Place.* Studies in Business. Chicago: University of Chicago Press, 1966.

Shultz, George. *Turmoil and Triumph: My Years as Secretary of State.* New York: Scribner, 1993.

Shultz, George P., and John B. Shoven. *Putting Our House in Order: A Guide to Social Security and Health Care Reform.* New York: Norton, 2008.

### Selected Works about George Shultz

Manweller, Matthew, ed. *Chronology of the U.S. Presidency*. Santa Barbara, CA: ABC-CLIO, 2012.

Norris, Lloyd. "George Shultz on Politics and Budgets." *New York Times, Economix*, September 16, 2011. http://economix.blogs.nytimes.com/2011/09/16/george-shultz-on-politics-and-budgets/ (accessed October 2012).

PBS.org. "Interview with George Shultz conducted 10/2/00." Commanding Heights. http://www.pbs.org/wgbh/commandingheights/shared/minitextlo/int_georgeshultz.html (accessed October, 2012).

*Stephen H. Day*

## SIMON, HERBERT

Born: June 15, 1916, in Milwaukee, Wisconsin; Died: February 9, 2001, in Pittsburgh, Pennsylvania; American; economist, political scientist, sociologist, Nobel Prize (1978); Major Work: *Models of Man* (1957).

Herbert Simon was a twentieth-century economist, political scientist, psychologist, and sociologist. He spent his career as a faculty member of Carnegie Mellon University for 52 years, pioneering new departments. He is known for his research in the fields of economics, mathematics, computer science, and psychology. He received numerous awards and recognition over in his lifetime including the Nobel Prize in Economics and the National Medal of Science. Simon died in 2001.

Herbert Alexander Simon was born on June 15, 1916, in Milwaukee, Wisconsin, to Jewish parents. His father was a successful inventor and electrical engineer. As a young student, Simon developed an interest in economics and human behavior as he attended public school. He entered the University of Chicago in 1933 to study economics. He received his BA in 1936. That same year, he became a research assistant with Clarence Ridley in the field of municipal administration, which then led him to directorship of a study at the University of California, Berkeley, from 1939 to 1942.

In 1943, Simon earned his PhD in political science from the University of Chicago. He gained a teaching position in political science at the Illinois Institute of Technology in 1942 where he remained until 1949. Being in Chicago, Simon was a contributor to the Cowles Commission for Research in Economics. Simon's doctoral work became the focus of his publication *Administrative Behavior* in 1947. In his book, Simon applied the theory of behavior and cognitive process to organizational problem solving.

Simon left Chicago and joined the faculty of Carnegie Mellon University in 1949, then known as Carnegie Institute of Technology. He, along with G. L. Bach and William W. Cooper, worked to establish a graduate school for industrial administration. He teamed with David Hawkins from 1950 to 1955 to formulate and prove the Hawkins-Simon theorem, a quantitative approach to the input-output analysis of an economy. Simon's 1957 publication, *Models of Man*, presented mathematical models of human behavior social settings.

Over the course of his career, Simon received many awards and recognitions. For his research in decision making of organizations, Simon was awarded the Sveriges Riksbank Prize in Economic Sciences in Memory of Alfred Nobel in 1978. He was awarded the National Medal of Science in 1986. In 1994, he was inducted into the Chinese Academy of Sciences, an honor that had been given to only 14 scientists. He was given the Award for Outstanding Lifetime Contributions to Psychology from the American Psychological Association in 1993. Simon also received awards from the International Joint Conferences on Artificial Intelligence and the American Society of Public Administration in 1995.

In 1991, Simon published an autobiography of his life, *Models of My Life*, in which he describes his cross-disciplinary work in various fields of sciences.

Herbert Simon died on February 9, 2001, in Pittsburgh, Pennsylvania.

*See also:* Hicks, John; Koopmans, Tjalling; Meade, James; Modigliani, Franco; Samuelson, Paul

### Selected Works by Herbert Simon

Simon, Herbert. *Administrative Behavior: A Study of Decision-Making Processes in Administrative Organization.* New York: Free Press, 1957.
Simon, Herbert. *Models of Man: Social and Rational.* New York: Wiley, 1957.

### Selected Works about Herbert Simon

Augier, Mie, and James G. March, eds. *Models of a Man: Essays in Memory of Herbert A. Simon.* Cambridge, MA: MIT Press, 2004.
Crowther-Heyck, Hunter. *Herbert A. Simon: The Bounds of Reason in Modern America.* Baltimore: Johns Hopkins University Press, 2005.
Lewis, Paul. "Herbert A. Simon, Nobel Winner for Economics, Dies at 84." *New York Times*, February 10, 2001. http://www.nytimes.com/2001/02/10/business/herbert-a-simon-dies-at-84-won-a-nobel-for-economics.html (accessed October 2012).
Simon, Herbert A. "Autobiography." Nobelprize.org. http://www.nobelprize.org/nobel_prizes/economics/laureates/1978/simon-autobio.html (accessed July 2012).

*Sara Standen*

## SIMON, JULIAN

Born: February 12, 1932, in Newark, New Jersey; Died: February 8, 1998, in Chevy Chase, Maryland; American; macroeconomics, economic systems, environment; Major Works: *How to Start and Operate a Mail-Order Business* (1965), *The Resourceful Earth: A Response to Global 2000* (1984), *Theory of Population and Economic Growth* (1986), *Population and Development in Poor Countries* (1992), *The Ultimate Resource* (1996).

Julian Simon was an American economist, widely known for arguing against scholars who were concerned about humankind's overuse of natural resources. Considered an "optimistic economist," he wagered a famous bet on the matter and wrote on a range of topics, including mail-order business start-up, the environment and renewable resources, and population growth. Simon was a professor of business administration at the University of Maryland and a senior fellow at the Cato Institute, a conservative research organization. Simon died in 1998.

Julian Lincoln Simon was born on February 12, 1932, in Newark, New Jersey. As a recipient of the Navy ROTC Holloway Plan scholarship, he studied experimental psychology at Harvard University. Simon earned a BA in 1953, and also took several graduate courses while completing his bachelor's degree. After graduation from Harvard, he spent three years in the military, working as a line officer, a liaison officer, and a battalion legal officer. In 1956, he worked as an advertising copywriter for a firm in New York. He stayed in New York for another year working as an assistant promotion manager before beginning graduate work at the University of Chicago where he earned an MBA in 1959. In 1961, he obtained a doctorate in business economics at the University of Illinois.

After graduation, Simon started a mail-order and advertising agency called Julian Simon Associates. He later became an assistant professor of advertising at the University of Illinois in 1963. He went on to become an assistant and associate professor of marketing at Illinois. During this time in 1965, he published the first edition of his successful book *How to Start and Operate a Mail-Order Business*.

Among the topics he researched and wrote about was the effect of population growth. While many scholars warned of the negative impact humans have on their environment and the problems associated with population growth, Simon argued that humans bring benefits to the planet and that their material conditions would continue to improve. He noted rules, patterns of behavior, and institutions humans developed that lead to an increase of available resources. Many theorists of his generation were instead suggesting that more people brought more problems and put a strain on the earth and its resources.

In *The Resourceful Earth: A Response to Global 2000*, Simon sought to refute theorists who argued that population growth was having an adverse impact on the earth. In this, he introduced a progrowth paradigm to contrast the "limits to growth" ideas of other scholars. In this work, Simon and coauthor Herman Kahn offered a point-by-point analysis and response to the *Global 2000 Report to the President*. The contrast is quite remarkable. Where the *Report* suggests overcrowding and other environmental damage will rise, in the *Response*, Simon argues that living conditions will improve as, he believes, the historical and economic data suggest.

His most famous attack on this "limits to growth" movement involved a bet he wagered in 1980 with Paul Ehrlich, an economist at Stanford who wrote the 1968 book *The Population Bomb*. In this book, Ehrlich postulated that one-fifth of humans would die of starvation by 1985. Ehrlich and a few of his colleagues read an article Simon wrote for *Science* magazine called "Resources, Population, Environment: An Oversupply of False Bad News." In it, Simon challenged anyone to bet that the price of any natural resource would be lower, not higher, by an agreed-upon date. Ehrlich accepted the offer. The wager was set at $1,000 on five metals: chrome, copper, nickel, tin, and tungsten. During the next decade, the population grew and the store of metals did not increase, but the prices of the metals fell sharply. On the proposed date 10 years later, Simon won the wager.

Possibly his most popular work on the impact humans have on the planet is *The Ultimate Resource* (1981). In this book, Simon argued that the most valuable resource on the earth is people. He set out to prove that scholars are incorrect to think that the destruction and decline is inevitable. For works such as this, many described him as a "doomslayer." He also wrote multiple pieces on these topics for publications including *USA Today*, the *Washington Post*, the *New York Times*, the *Wall Street Journal*, the *Christian Science Monitor*, and other news media outlets.

Julian Simon died on February 8, 1998, in Chevy Chase, Maryland.

*See also:* Malthus, Thomas

### Selected Works by Julian Simon

Simon, Julian. *Economic Consequences of Immigration.* Oxford: Basil Blackwell, 1989.
Simon, Julian. *How to Start and Operate a Mail-Order Business.* New York: McGraw-Hill, 1965.
Simon, Julian. *Population and Development in Poor Countries: Selected Essays.* Princeton, NJ: Princeton University Press, 1992.
Simon, Julian. *Population Matters: People, Resources, Environment, and Immigration.* New Brunswick, NJ: Transaction, 1990.
Simon, Julian. *Theory of Population and Economic Growth.* Hoboken, NJ: Blackwell, 1986.
Simon, Julian. *The Ultimate Resource.* Princeton, NJ: Princeton University Press, 1996.
Simon, Julian L., and Herman Kahn. *The Resourceful Earth: A Response to Global 2000.* Hoboken, NJ: Blackwell, 1984.

### Selected Works about Julian Simon

Aligica, Paul Dragos. "Julian Simon and the 'Limits to Growth' Neo-Malthusianism." *Electronic Journal of Sustainable Development* 1, no. 3 (2009).
Codrington, Stephen. *Planet Geography.* Hong Kong: Solid Star Press, 2002.
Regis, Ed. "The Doomslayer." Wired.com. http://www.wired.com/wired/archive/5.02/ffsimon_pr.html (accessed February 2012).
Simon, Julian L. *A Life against the Grain: The Autobiography of an Unconventional Economist.* New Brunswick, NJ: Transaction, 2002.

*Diane Fournier*

## SIMONS, HENRY

Born: October 9, 1899, in Virden, Illinois; Died: June 19, 1946, in Chicago, Illinois; American; monetary theory, taxation; Major Works: *A Positive Program for Laissez Faire: Some Proposals for a Liberal Economic Policy* (1934), *Personal Income Taxation: The Definition of Income as a Problem of Fiscal Policy* (1938).

Henry Simons was an American economist who spent his teaching career at the University of Chicago. Simons is best known for defending free-enterprise solutions to revive the U.S. economy after the Great Depression. He proposed a modified laissez-faire role of government to protect and defend the free-market economy. Simons opposed monopoly power, and advocated clear monetary policy rules and price stability. He developed a definition of income for taxation purposes. He is remembered as an invaluable early contributor to the Chicago School theories of antitrust and monetary policy, and as an influential teacher responsible for teaching many famous Chicago economists including Milton Friedman and George Stigler. Simons died in 1946.

Henry Calvert Simons was born on October 9, 1899, in Virden, Illinois. His parents greatly valued higher education and sent him to the University of Michigan. In 1920, he received his AB from the University of Michigan and continued additional study at the University of Michigan and Columbia University. In 1921, he continued graduate work at the University of Iowa and taught there until 1927. He transferred to the University of Chicago to study with Frank H. Knight, who interested him in the Department of Economics. Simons completed his graduate work in economics at Chicago but never finished his dissertation to receive a PhD. He spent his entire career teaching and researching at the University of Chicago, first as a lecturer. In 1942, he was finally appointed an associate professor.

Simons published in 1934 his most famous work, *A Positive Program for Laissez Faire*, as University of Chicago Press Pamphlet No. 15. This work was published as the Great Depression was ending. Simons wanted to see a strong resurgence of private market activity and was unhappy with some of the policies being promoted that relied on what he considered excessive and unnecessary government intervention. In this pamphlet he outlined his major policy beliefs and continued throughout his career to expand, revise, and defend them. His positions addressed many economic issues. Simons promoted reforming the monetary system, a position later made famous by Milton Friedman. He promoted eliminating all monopoly power in a market that included large oligopoly corporations, applying antitrust laws to labor unions, instituting a federal incorporation law to limit corporate size, and government ownership of low-cost technology firms. He also addressed tax system reform including income tax equity. On international trade Simons would abolish all tariffs. Simons was not an enthusiast of advertising and marketing and would limit their use.

Simons believed in a laissez-faire economic philosophy but also believed government had an important but limited role to play. The government should protect the free-market forces as they operated to determine prices. For example, he wanted government to actively pursue antitrust activities against any type of monopoly—large corporations as well as labor unions. He was absolutely against any group obtaining an unfair amount of power, which would interfere with the efficient operation of a free-market economy. He did think that government could own and operate natural monopolies for reasons of low-cost production.

In addition to promoting conditions that encouraged competition, Simons believed in a role for government by establishing sound economic conditions using monetary policy necessary to protect the free markets. He believed there should be clear monetary policy rules to determine the supply of money or price-level stability. However, any monetary policy must allow for flexible prices and wages. He understood how the phases of the business cycle could be influenced by monetary policy and also recognized the importance of complementary fiscal and monetary actions.

Simons agreed with Irving Fisher, who recommended that banks establish a 100 percent reserve requirement rule for funds held on deposit. He believed that too much short-term borrowing or excessive speculation would contribute to financial instability and that there was danger in allowing the development of too much private credit. He felt the organization of the current central banking system needed to be thoroughly evaluated but believed some sort of central monetary control was needed. The ideas in his 1936 article "Rules versus Authorities in Monetary Policy" influenced the later works of Milton Friedman on monetary policy, and Hyman Minsky's theory of financial crises.

The ideas explained in *Personal Income Taxation* in 1938 discussed the concepts of progressive taxation. Simons felt strongly that other forms could also address the social goal of reducing inequality. Simons developed, along with Robert M. Haig, the Haig-Simons definition of income used for tax purposes: the sum of consumption plus the change in the value of assets owned. Debate on the U.S. federal tax system still relies on ideas proposed and clarified by Simons.

His life was cut short by an accidental overdose of sleeping pills. Henry Simons died in Chicago, Illinois, on June 19, 1946.

*See also:* Fisher, Irving; Friedman, Milton; Knight, Frank; Stigler, George

## Selected Works by Henry Simons

Simons, Henry. *Economic Policy for a Free Society*. Chicago: University of Chicago Press, 1948.
Simons, Henry. *Federal Tax Reform*. Chicago: University of Chicago Press, 1950.
Simons, Henry. *Personal Income Taxation: The Definition of Income as a Problem of Fiscal Policy*. Chicago: University of Chicago Press, 1938.
Simons, Henry. *A Positive Program for Laissez Faire: Some Proposals for a Liberal Economic Policy*. Public Policy Pamphlet, no. 15. Chicago: University of Chicago Press, 1934.
Simons, Henry. "Rules versus Authorities in Monetary Policy." *Journal of Political Economy* 44, no. 1 (1936): 1–30.

## Selected Works about Henry Simons

Director, Aaron. "Simons on Taxation." *University of Chicago Law Review* 14 (1946):15–20.
Friedman, Milton. "The Monetary Theory and Policy of Henry Simons." *Journal of Law and Economics* 10 (1967): 1–13.
"Guide to the Henry C. Simons Papers 1925–1962." Special Collections Research Center, University of Chicago Library. http://www.lib.uchicago.edu/e/scrc/findingaids/view.php?eadid=ICU.SPCL.SIMONS&q=citation (accessed September 2012).
Kasper, Sherryl D. *The Revival of Laissez-Faire in Twentieth Century Macroeconomics: A Case Study of Its Pioneers*. London: Edward Elgar, 2002.
Stigler, George. "Henry Calvert Simons." *Journal of Law and Economics* 17 (1974): 1–5.

*Jean Kujawa*

## SIMS, CHRISTOPHER

Born: October 21, 1942, in Washington, DC; American; econometrics, macroeconomic models, rational expectations, Nobel Prize (2011); Major Work: "Money, Income and Causality" (1972).

Christopher Sims, the Harold H. Helm '20 Professor of Economics and Banking at Princeton University, was awarded the Nobel Prize in Economics along with Dr. Thomas Sargent in October 2011. Sims's work centers on creating econometric models to determine cause and effect in the macroeconomy. Specifically, Sims developed a tool called vector auto regression to analyze how fiscal and/or monetary policy changes affect the greater economy. In addition, Sims's work centers on the relationship between budget deficits and monetary policy.

Christopher Albert Sims was born on October 21, 1942, in Washington, DC. Intellectual discussion was a large part of Sims's family and early years. Sims's grandfather, William Morris Leiserson, emigrated from Estonia and later became one of the first members of the U.S. National Labor Relations Board. His daughter Ruth, Sims's mother, headed the Connecticut League of Women Voters and was the first woman selectman of the town of Greenwich, Connecticut. Sims's father Albert worked in the U.S. State Department and as vice president of the College Board in New York. He later helped to start the Peace Corps under the Kennedy administration. Sims's uncles, Mark Leiserson, economist at Yale and then the World Bank, and Avery Leiserson, professor at Vanderbilt University, also encouraged lively discussion. Mark in particular urged Sims to study economics from the early age of 13.

Sims spent his early years in Germany where his father worked for the State Department. The family eventually returned to Greenwich, Connecticut, via a short stay in Virginia when Sims was 11. Sims graduated in 1959 from Greenwich High School where he earned perfect scores on his SATs; he still speaks fondly of his math teacher there. Sims majored in mathematics at Harvard University. He wrote his undergraduate thesis on information theory and then turned to economics during his senior year, graduating magna cum laude. Sims spent the first year of graduate study at University of California, Berkeley, returning to Harvard to earn his PhD and work as an assistant professor. In 1970, he left Harvard to work as an associate professor and then full professor at the University of Minnesota where he stayed for the next 20 years. Interestingly, Sims knew Thomas Sargent as a graduate student at Harvard, but it was at the University of Minnesota that the two began to influence each other as colleagues. After Sargent left Minnesota, Sims also left to become the Henry Ford II Professor of Economics at Yale from 1990 until 1999. In 1999, he joined the economics faculty at Princeton University as the Harold H. Helm '20 Professor of Economics and Banking.

Christopher Sims and Thomas Sargent won the Nobel Prize in Economics in October 2011. Their work centered on using empirical models to understand cause and effect between the economy and economic policy. In particular, they examined how future expectations influence present decisions. This model works for both public policy as well as private sector decision makers.

Sims developed a model called vector auto regression (VAR) to test cause-and-effect relationships such as the impact of increases in interest rates on the money supply or the consequences of tax cuts on growth and inflation. Central banks and governments use VAR as a specialized tool for financial analysis. Many look to this tool to help recover from global recession. In total, Sims wrote over 70 articles published in economics periodicals.

Sims has also been influential in integrating information theory with economic modeling, calling his discovery in these areas "rational inattention." The idea is that people have a limit on their capacity to process information. This limit is illustrated as sluggishness or a delay in the individual's behavior in the marketplace or in response to changes like monetary policy.

Sims was director of graduate studies for the Princeton Economics Department from 2003 to 2008 and has remained a visiting scholar for the International Monetary Fund since 2003. He served as a visiting scholar for the Federal Reserve Banks of Philadelphia (2000–2003), New York (1994–97, 2004–present), and Atlanta (most years since 1995), and consultant for the Federal Reserve Bank of Minneapolis (1983, 1986–87). He was a consultant for the Federal National Mortgage Association from 1999 to 2002. From 1987 to 1991, Sims was the director of the Institute for Empirical Macroeconomics in Minneapolis. He served as part of the editorial board of the *International Journal of Supercomputer Applications* from 1987 to 1989, as associate editor for the *Journal of Applied Econometrics* from 1986 to 1989, as associate editor for the *Journal of Business and Economic Statistics* from 1986 to 1993, and as part of the editorial board of the *Journal of Economics and Philosophy* from 1985 to 1994. Sims has an active role in the Econometric Society, serving as president in 1995.

*See also:* Arrow, Kenneth; Debreu, Gérard; Sargent, Thomas

### Selected Works by Christopher Sims

Sims, Christopher. "Comparing Interwar and Postwar Business Cycles: Monetarism Reconsidered." *American Economic Review: Papers and Proceedings* 70, no. 2 (1981): 250–57.

Sims, Christopher. "Macroeconomics and Reality." *Econometrica* 48 (1980): 1–48.

Sims, Christopher. "Money, Income and Causality." *American Economic Review* 62 (1972): 540–52.

Doan, Thomas, Robert B. Litterman, and Christopher Sims. *Forecasting and Conditional Projection Using Realistic Prior Distributions*. Washington, DC: National Bureau of Economic Research, 1983.

Sims, Christopher, ed. *Advances in Econometrics: Sixth World Congress*. Vol. 2. Economic Society Monographs. New York: Cambridge University Press, 1994.

### Selected Works about Christopher Sims

Irwin, Neil. "Americans Thomas Sargent and Christopher Sims Win Economics Nobel." October 10, 2011. http://www.washingtonpost.com/business/economy/americans-thomas-sargent-and-christopher-sims-win-economics-nobel/2011/10/10/gIQAOv7xZL_story.html (accessed April 2012).

Rolnick, Arthur J. "Interview with Christopher Sims." June 1, 2007. http://www.minneapolisfed.org/publications_papers/pub_display.cfm?id=3168 (accessed April 2012).

Sims, Christopher. "Prize Lecture: Statistical Modelling of Monetary Policy and Its Effects." Nobelprize.org. http://www.nobelprize.org/nobel_prizes/economics/laureates/2011/sims-lecture.html (accessed April 2012).

*Kathryn Lloyd Gustafson*

## SINGH, MANMOHAN

Born: September 26, 1932 in Gah, Punjab, India; Indian; public policy, global economics; Major Work: *India's Export Trends and Prospects for Self-Sustained Growth* (1964).

Manmohan Singh, an economist by training, is India's 14th prime minister since independence in 1947. Singh made the transition from academia to civil service in 1971, early in his career, and then to politics in 1991. Throughout his career in public sector, Singh has held many governmental positions such as economic adviser in the Commerce Ministry (1971), chief economic adviser in the Ministry of Finance (1972), secretary in the Ministry of Finance (1977), deputy chairman of the Planning Commission (1985), governor of the Reserve Bank of India (1982), adviser to the prime minister of India on economic affairs (1990), finance minister (1991), and finally prime minister of India (2004 to present). Singh is known as a man of integrity and has won many awards and honors throughout his career as a scholar and politician.

Manmohan Singh was born on September 26, 1932, in a village in the Punjab province of British India (undivided India) into a Sikh family. In 1947, at the time of dividing the country, Singh and his family moved to India. In 1948, Singh graduated from Punjab University and attended St. John's College at Cambridge University in England. In 1957, he graduated with a first-class honors degree in economics. In 1962, he earned his doctorate in economics from Oxford University. His doctorate dissertation was about India's export performance. Two years after his graduation from Oxford he published it in a book titled *India's Export Trends and Prospects for Self-Sustained Growth*. Singh had a brief academic career teaching at Punjab and Delhi School of Economics. Between 1987 and 1990, he served as secretary general of the South Commission in Geneva.

He started his civil service career in 1971 by taking a position of economic adviser in the Commerce Ministry. From 1971 to 1991, Singh held many governmental positions. Since 1991, Singh has been in the world of politics. Between 1991 and 1996, Singh was India's finance minister, where he had played an important role in an all-inclusive policy of economic reforms. Since the dawn of Singh's political career, in 1991, he has been a member of India's Upper House of Parliament. On May 22, 2004, after the general elections, Manmohan Singh became the first Sikh Prime Minister of India. Five years later, in 2009, he took the oath of office for a second term. Since the 2004 election, Singh has been the prime minister of India.

Between 1991 and 1996, while Singh was a member of India's Upper House of Parliament, he also became the finance minister. This was during Narasimha Rao's administration, and he supported Singh in his successful introduction and implementation of major economic reforms in India. Rao and Singh envisioned changing India's economy from socialism to capitalism. Up to that point, India was able to sustain a closed economy. However, by the early 1990s the country was rapidly going toward bankruptcy. In order to increase competition and productivity, Singh introduced a series of open-market policies.

Singh demolished the Licence Raj, an elaborate system of licenses and regulations that prohibited the spread of privatization. This opened the door for Foreign Direct Investment (FDI) and for privatization of public sector. In addition, a series of reforms in India's capital markets caused a sudden rise in foreign investment. First, the Security Laws of 1992 gave the Securities and Exchange Board of India (SEBI) a legal power to extensively regulate the security market. Two years later, in 1994, a computerized trading system of India known as the National Stock Exchange (NSE) officially started working, which successfully boosted India's other stock exchanges. As a result, between 1991 and 1996 international capital markets in India grew from a trivial amount of $132 million in 1991 to $5.3 billion. Meanwhile, other open-market policies such as reducing tariffs and increasing the upper limit of foreign capital in international joint ventures led India to be at the forefront of the global market.

Throughout his career in politics, Singh has remained a strong supporter of globalization. He has seen India's enormous labor market as a leverage to lift the country's economy by promoting commercial exports of India's goods and services around the world. Economic liberalization of India, which started in the 1990s while Rao was in office, has continued during Singh's administration. During his terms in office as prime minister, Singh has continued his predecessor's open-market and growth policies. As a result, India has enjoyed a long period of rapid economic growth. In 2007, India achieved its highest growth rate of 9 percent and became the second-fastest-growing economy in the world. Furthermore, in order to reduce extreme poverty, Singh has initiated a series of modernization programs such as improving India's infrastructure and highway systems, introducing the value-added tax system instead of sales tax, and investing, especially in rural areas, in health care and education.

Singh has won many awards and honors during his academic and public careers; among them are the Wright's Prize for the excellent performance at St. John's College in Cambridge University (1955), Padma Vibhushan, India's second-highest civilian honor (1987), and the Euro Money Award for Finance Minister of the Year (1993), to name a few. In 2010, *Newsweek* magazine named him as a world leader who earned the respect of other heads of state. However, in recent years, due to allegations of corruption since the start of his second term in 2009, Singh's public image has been tarnished.

*See also:* Bhagwati, Jagdish; Sen, Amartya

## Selected Work by Manmohan Singh

Singh, Manmohan. *India's Export Trends and Prospects for Self-Sustained Growth*. Oxford: Clarendon Press, 1964.

### Selected Works about Manmohan Singh

Ahluwalia, Isher Judge, and Ian Malcolm David Little. *India's Economic Reforms and Development: Essays for Manmohan Singh.* 2nd ed. Calcutta: Oxford University Press India, 2012.
BBC News. "Profile of Manmohan Singh." http://news.bbc.co.uk/2/hi/south_asia/3725357.stm (accessed August, 2012).
Venkateswaran, R. J. *Reforming Indian Economy: The Narasimha Rao and Manmohan Singh Era.* Noida, India: Vikas, 1996.
Yadav, Satish. *Manmohan Singh: A Profile.* Gurgaon, Delhi: Hope India, 2004.

*Elham Mahmoudi*

## SMITH, ADAM

Baptized: June 5, 1723 (exact birthdate unknown), in Kirkcaldy, Scotland; Died: July 17, 1790, in Edinburgh, Scotland; Scottish; moral philosophy, political economy (economic theory); Major Works: *The Theory of Moral Sentiments* (1759), *An Inquiry into the Nature and Causes of the Wealth of Nations* (1776).

Adam Smith is considered the father of modern economics. The theories contained in his seminal book, *The Wealth of Nations*, include division of labor, the importance of competition, the idea of the "invisible hand," and arguments for free trade. These concepts form much of the foundation of modern economic thought. Though Adam Smith is considered the founder of free-market economics, other ideas that he held, such as the labor theory of value, were used by later writers to form the foundation for socialism. For his part, Smith was a quintessential Enlightenment thinker. He believed in natural rights, natural law, and limited government. Theology had little place in his writings. He viewed the world, human society, and hence the economy as being governed by natural law that if left on its own would work smoothly, like a grand machine. Smith died in 1790.

Adam Smith was born in Kirkcaldy, Scotland, in 1723. His father, a lawyer and customs official, died shortly before his birth. He was raised by his mother, Margaret Douglas, with whom he had a close, lifelong relationship. At the age of seven, he was enrolled at the reputable Burgh School of Kirkcaldy where he studied classics and mathematics. He studied moral philosophy at Glasgow University and Oxford University. Upon graduating he sought an academic career, eventually becoming the professor of moral philosophy at Glasgow. He held this position for 13 years, during which time he assembled his lecture notes into a book entitled *The Theory of Moral Sentiments*, published in 1759. In *The Theory of Moral Sentiments*, Adam Smith argues that human morality originates through a natural desire to identify with the emotions of others.

Smith quit his position at Glasgow when he was offered a lucrative job as tutor to a Scottish duke. Though this job lasted only about two years, it provided Smith with a pension on which he could live for the next decade without having to worry about other employment.

*The Wealth of Nations* begins with the observation that "division of labor," or specialization, is essential for increasing the production of wealth. Division of labor occurs because human beings have a tendency to "truck, barter, and exchange one thing for another," that is, to trade. This causes people to become dependent on one another. Smith's fundamental insight is his explanation as to how this complex interdependence is organized: trade and division of labor occur because of individual self-interest, not from kindness or the designs of politicians. When each individual acts as he or she sees best, within the constraints of the law and in a competitive business environment, the economy organizes itself naturally, as if guided by an "invisible hand."

Trade was a controversial issue in the British Empire in Smith's time, and *The Wealth of Nations* was a powerful weapon for those who favored free trade. The book explained that division of labor was limited by the extent of the resources available to a market and that a greater division of labor, and therefore greater wealth, could be obtained by expanding the market through global trade. It also sharply criticized the ideas of mercantilism, which held that a country should attempt to accumulate gold by encouraging exports and discouraging imports. By showing the importance of trade, Smith gained great popularity among merchants, whose work had previously been considered distasteful.

While Smith's work legitimized the work of traders and capitalists, it asserted that an item receives its value from the work of the laborers who made it, called the labor theory of value. It assumes that there is a natural price for a certain commodity that is made up of the amount of work that went into producing it. However, this natural price is difficult to know, since the circumstances of the world can cause the actual price for which the item is sold to change. Smith explains that the sale price will gravitate to the natural labor price, even if they are not always exactly the same. In this analysis of value, Smith recognizes the importance of supply and demand (which had been described by earlier economic thinkers) but defers to the labor theory of value.

The labor theory has been rejected by economists, who now see value as something subjective and price as being determined by supply and demand. It gained adherents, however, in David Ricardo and Karl Marx. Marx built his entire economic philosophy on the labor theory and drew other parts of Socialist thought from elements of Smith's macroeconomic observations. Later economists used Smith's work in a different way, applying his concepts of supply and demand, competition, spontaneous order, market price, and voluntary trade to all areas of economic thought, eclipsing the indefensible-labor theory and turning economics into the versatile social science that it is today.

Adam Smith died on July 17, 1790, in Edinburgh, Scotland. His gravesite in Edinburgh has become a shrine and symbol of free markets, capitalism, and the strength and power of individual freedom.

*See also:* Marx, Karl; Quesnay, François; Ricardo, David

## Selected Works by Adam Smith

Smith, Adam. *An Inquiry into the Nature and Causes of the Wealth of Nations.* London: J. J. Tourneisen and J. L. Legrand, 1776.

Smith, Adam. *The Theory of Moral Sentiments*. London: A. Millar, A. Kincaid, and J. Bell, 1759.

### Selected Works about Adam Smith

Buchan, James. *The Authentic Adam Smith: His Life and Ideas*. New York: Norton, 2006.

Colander, David, and A. W. Coats, eds. *The Spread of Economic Ideas*. Cambridge: Cambridge University Press, 1989.

McKenna, Stephen. *Adam Smith: The Rhetoric of Propriety*. Albany: State University of New York Press, 2006.

Muller, Jerry Z. *Adam Smith in His Time and Ours: Designing the Decent Society*. Princeton, NJ: Princeton University Press, 1993.

Otteson, James R., and John Meadowcroft. *Adam Smith*. New York: Continuum International, 2011.

Phillipson, Nicholas. *Adam Smith: An Enlightened Life*. New Haven, CT: Yale University Press, 2010.

Rae, John. *Life of Adam Smith*. Charleston, SC: Nabu Press, 2010.

Shapiro, Michael J. *Reading "Adam Smith": Desire, History and Value*. Lanham, MD: Rowman & Littlefield, 2002.

*Stephen H. Day*

## SMITH, VERNON

Born: January 1, 1927, in Wichita, Kansas; American; microeconomics, experimental economics, Nobel Prize (2002); Major Works: *Experimental Economics: Induced Value Theory* (1976), *Papers in Experimental Economics* (1991), *Rationality in Economics: Constructivist and Ecological Forms* (2008).

Vernon Smith was the 2002 winner of the Nobel Prize for establishing laboratory experiments as a methodology for empirical economic analysis and study of alternative market mechanisms. Smith revolutionized the traditional view that controlled experiments of economic theory were not possible due to the difficulty of controlling other important factors. Smith was instrumental in the use of experimental economics to study air traffic and airport management, to study electricity and energy trading in the utility industry, and as an effective method in regulating property rights without government intervention.

Vernon L. Smith was born on January 1, 1927, in Wichita, Kansas. He was raised on a Kansas farm by his father, Vernon Chessman Smith, and his mother, Lulu Belle Lomax, under the difficult circumstances of the Great Depression. Years of struggle, unemployment, and finally foreclosure confirmed his mother's political commitment to socialism. His undergraduate studies included physics and electrical engineering, and in 1949 he received his BS in electrical engineering from the California Institute of Technology. He was motivated to pursue advanced studies of economics after recognizing the correlation between the principles of physics and economics in Samuelson's *Foundations* and the reasoning found in von Mises's *Human Action*. He went on to earn his MA in economics from the University of Kansas in 1952 and his PhD in economics from Harvard University in 1955.

Vernon Smith's diverse teaching career began in 1955 at Purdue University where he served until 1967. Smith served as a visiting assistant professor at

Stanford University in 1961–62, and as a tenured professor at Brown University in 1967–68 and University of Massachusetts from 1968 to 1975. In 1975, Smith moved to the University of Arizona where he remained until 2001, followed by George Mason University where he served as a professor of economics and law until 2008. In 2008, Vernon Smith joined the faculty as professor of economics and law at Chapman University upon founding the Economic Science Institute.

Smith began using experiments in his first year of teaching at Purdue as a tool to help make microeconomic theory more comprehensible to his undergraduate students. Through Smith's induced-value experiments, students experienced actual market conditions in which price equilibrium was achieved without the participants having any knowledge of the value conditions of the other participants. Smith also observed that the efficiency of achieving equilibrium increased over several trading periods, with subsequent periods experiencing a reduced standard deviation from the theoretical equilibrium price.

Smith's continued development of experimental methodology was articulated in *Experimental Economics: Induced Value Theory* (1976) and was further expanded six years later in the article "Microeconomic Systems as an Experimental Science" (1982). Smith identifies two distinct components of a microeconomic system: the environment and the institution. The environment consists of all the participants, commodities, and characteristics within the institution and cannot be altered by the agents. The institution is the system that specifies and administers the rules and laws created within the system. The goal of the experiment is to evaluate whether the incentives created by the institution create outcomes that are conducive to the established goals of the institution. He has authored more than 250 articles and publications.

Experimental economics has been utilized to solve economic problems such as determining slot allocations used by national airport management to determine the most efficient scheduling practices between air traffic. It has also been used to create new systems of electricity and energy trading that transformed the utility industry throughout the nation. Experimental economics has also been demonstrated to be effective at regulating private property rights without government intervention.

In 2002, Vernon Smith was awarded the Nobel Prize in Economics for establishing laboratory experiments as a methodology for empirical economic analysis and study of alternative market mechanisms. Smith revolutionized the traditional view that controlled experiments of economic theory were not possible due to the difficulty of controlling other important factors. The inability to empirically test traditional theory could potentially inhibit the development of economics due to the difficulty of determining the exact components or causes of success or failure of the theory. Observation of these components allows for new theories to emerge and undergo new testing.

Smith received the Friedrich-August-von-Hayek-Gesellschaft e.V. Award (2008) and the 1995 Adam Smith Award. The Vernon Smith Prize for the Advancement of Austrian Economics, sponsored by the European Center of Austrian Economics, is named after him.

*See also:* Hayek, Friedrich von; Mises, Ludwig von; Samuelson, Paul

### Selected Works by Vernon Smith

Smith, Vernon. "Behavioral Economics Research and the Foundations of Economics." *Journal of Socio-Economics* 34, no. 2 (March 2005): 135–50.

Smith, Vernon. "Economics in the Laboratory." *Journal of Economic Perspectives* 8, no. 1 (1994): 113–31.

Smith, Vernon. *Economics of Natural and Environmental Resources*. New York: Gordon and Breach, 1977.

Smith, Vernon. *Experimental Economics: Induced Value Theory*. Washington, DC: Department of Economic and Business Research, 1976.

Smith, Vernon. "Microeconomic Systems as an Experimental Science." *American Economic Review* 72, no. 5 (1982): 923–55.

Smith, Vernon. *Papers in Experimental Economics*. New York: Cambridge University Press, 1991.

Smith, Vernon. *Rationality in Economics: Constructivist and Ecological Forms*. New York: Cambridge University Press, 2008.

### Selected Works about Vernon Smith

Chorvat, T., and K. McCabe. "Law and Neuroeconomics." In *Supreme Court Economic Review*. Edited by F. Parisi and D. Polsby, 35–62. Chicago: University of Chicago Press, 2005.

Chorvat, T., and K. McCabe. "Lessons from Neuroeconomics for the Law." In *The Law and Economics of Irrational Behavior*. Edited by F. Parisi and V. Smith, 68–94. Palo Alto, CA: Stanford University Press, 2005.

Hoffman, E., and K. McCabe. "What Makes Trade Possible?" In *The Law and Economics of Irrational Behavior*. Edited by F. Parisi and V. Smith, 169–85. Palo Alto, CA: Stanford University Press, 2005.

*Heather Isom*

## SOLOW, ROBERT

Born: August 23, 1924, in New York City; American; macroeconomics, economic growth, unemployment, capital and interest, Nobel Prize (1987); Major Works: "Balanced Growth under Constant Scales of Return" (with Paul Samuelson) (1953), "A Contribution to the Theory of Economic Growth," (1956), *Capital Theory and the Rate of Return* (1963), *Nature and Sources of Unemployment in the U.S.* (1964), "Economics of Resources or Resources of Economics" (1974), *Growth Theory: An Exposition* (2000).

Robert Solow is an American economist who produced significant work in the area of economic growth, earning the Nobel Prize in Economics in 1987. The basis of Solow's work on economic growth was the publication "A Contribution to the Theory of Economic Growth." Solow reworked the earlier works of other economists claiming an economy could remain at full employment when wages are flexible. He spent his entire career at the Massachusetts Institute of Technology where his office was next to Paul Samuelson's.

Robert Merton Solow was born on August 23, 1924, in New York City. He was the oldest of three children. His grandparents were immigrants and he and his siblings were the first members of his family to attend college. Solow attended a public high school in New York and was a good student. From high school he received a scholarship and went on to attend Harvard in 1940 at the age of 16 where he chose to study sociology and anthropology. World War II would interrupt his education when he joined the U.S. Army in 1942 and serving in North Africa, Sicily, and Italy. He would receive his discharge in 1945 and return to Harvard to resume his education.

It was at this point that Solow became immersed in economics. He studied under Wassily Leontief who would become his friend and mentor as well as a teacher. Solow continued studying at Harvard, receiving his BA in 1947, his MA in 1949, and his PhD in 1951. He would continue working with Leontief to develop the first capital coefficients in an input-output model. He would also develop an interest in statistics and modeling, and on advice of Frederick Mosteller would spend 1949 and 1950 in a fellowship at Columbia University. While there, Solow would also work on his thesis for his PhD at Harvard.

The thesis would win the Wells Prize from Harvard, which carried publication in book form along with a $500 check. However, he was not satisfied with the thesis and the thesis would remain unpublished and the check uncashed. Just prior to starting his fellowship, Solow received and accepted an offer of an assistant professorship at the Massachusetts Institute of Technology (MIT) teaching econometrics and statistics. As luck would have it, he was given an office next door to Paul Samuelson, beginning a lifelong relationship of friendship and collaboration.

It was at MIT Solow would publish "A Contribution to the Theory of Economic Growth." This work would be the foundation that would result in his Nobel Prize. In it, Solow expanded on the previous work of Roy Harrod and Evsey Domar. Harrod and Domar independently presented models suggesting there was no reason for a balanced growth rate. The main criticism of their models was the assumption of fixed labor and capital. Solow would modify this approach with one that was more dynamic, allowing for flexible wage rates maintaining an economy could maintain full employment.

That same year, he published "Technical Change and the Aggregate Production Function" in the *Review of Economics and Statistics*. The work was significant because it showed that only half of economic growth could be explained by changes in the size of labor and capital endowments. The rest, he posited, was the result of innovation; this became known as the Solow residual.

The Solow paradox is also named for him. The paradox derives from a claim he made in the 1990s, when he stated that the productivity increase from computer use was showing up everywhere except in aggregate statistics. There have been numerous studies of the paradox and just as many theories for it. None have decisively explained it.

Solow served in a professional capacity and received a number of honors during his career. He received the John Bates Clark Medal in 1961 as the most promising young economist. Robert Solow received the Nobel Prize in 1987 and the National Medal of Science in 1999.

Solow served on the Council of Economic Advisers under President John Kennedy from 1961 to 1963. Solow was an Eastman Professor at Oxford

University in 1968 and 1969. He served as a member of the board of directors of the Federal Reserve Bank of Boston from 1975 to 1980, serving as its chairman in the last two years. He was named a visiting scholar of the Russell Sage Foundation in 1999 and 2000, becoming a permanent staff member in 2012. He has been awarded honorary degrees from the University of Chicago, Brown University, University of Warwick, Lehigh University, and Tufts University.

Solow has the professorial distinction of seeing three of his students follow him in receiving the Nobel Prize: George Akerlof, Peter Diamond, and Joseph Stiglitz.

Robert Solow retired from his post at MIT in 1995.

*See also:* Akerlof, George; Diamond, Peter; Galbraith, John Kenneth; Leontief, Wassily; Samuelson, Paul; Stiglitz, Joseph

**Selected Works by Robert Solow**

Arrow, Kenneth, Hollis Chenery, Bagicha Minhas, and Robert Solow. "Capital Labor Substitution and Economic Theory." *Review of Economics and Statistics* 43, no. 3 (August 1961): 225–50.

Solow, Robert. *Capital Theory and the Rate of Return*. Amsterdam: North Holland, 1963.

Solow, Robert. "A Contribution to the Theory of Economic Growth." *The Quarterly Journal of Economics* 70, no. 1 (February 1956): 65–94.

Solow, Robert. *Growth Theory: An Exposition*. 2nd ed. Oxford: Oxford University Press, 2000.

Solow, Robert. *Nature and Sources of Unemployment in the U.S.* Stockholm: Almqvist and Wicksell, 1964.

Solow, Robert. "Perspectives on Growth Theory." *The Journal of Economic Perspectives* 8, no. 1 (Winter 1994): 45–54.

Solow, Robert. "The State of Macroeconomics." *The Journal of Economic Perspectives* 22, no. 1 (Winter 2008): 243–46.

Solow, Robert, and Paul Samuelson. "Balanced Growth under Constant Scales of Return." *Econometrica* 21, no. 3 (July 1953): 412–24.

**Selected Works about Robert Solow**

Blaug, Mark, and Paul Sturgess. *Who's Who in Economics: A Biographical Dictionary of Major Economists, 1700–1980*. Cambridge, MA: MIT Press, 1983.

Hoover, Kevin D., and Mauro Boianovsky. *Robert Solow and the Development of Growth Economics*. Durham, NC: Duke University Press, 2009.

Horn, Karen Ilse. *Roads to Wisdom, Conversations with Ten Nobel Laureates in Economics*. London: Edward Elgar, 2009.

"Robert Merton Solow." In *The Concise Encyclopedia of Economics*. Edited by David R. Henderson. The Library of Economics and Liberty. http://www.econlib.org/library/Enc/bios/Solow.html (accessed July 2012).

Solow, Robert M. "Autobiography." Nobelprize.org. http://www.nobelprize.org/nobel_prizes/economics/laureates/1987/solow.html (accessed July 2012).

*Timothy P. Schilling*

## SOWELL, THOMAS

Born: June 30, 1930, in Gastonia, North Carolina; American; political economy, economics, author; Major Works: *Race and Economics* (1975), *Inside American Education* (1993), *Basic Economics* (2007), *The Housing Boom and Bust* (2009).

Thomas Sowell is an economist, author, professor, and syndicated columnist. He currently serves as the Rose and Milton Friedman Senior Fellow on Public Policy at the Hoover Institution of Stanford University. He has served as faculty at various institutions including Cornell University and University of California, Los Angeles. He has written extensively about politics, education, ethnic relations, and child development, and is the author of 40 books and numerous articles. He has a syndicated column that appears in numerous newspapers around the United States.

Thomas Sowell was born on June 30, 1930, in Gastonia, North Carolina. At the age of nine, he moved to Harlem, New York, with his family. He dropped out of high school as a teenager and began working various jobs. Sowell was drafted into the U.S. Marine Corps during the Korean War and served as a photographer. After his service, he attended classes at Howard University in Washington, DC, receiving high marks and earning him acceptance into Harvard University on recommendations from professors. At Harvard, much of Sowell's study was on German philosopher Karl Marx on whom he wrote his senior thesis. He received his bachelor's degree in economics in 1958. Sowell received his master's degree from Columbia University in 1959. In 1968, Sowell obtained his doctorate degree from the University of Chicago, studying under George Stigler and Milton Friedman.

Sowell's economic career began when he became a labor economist for the U.S. Department of Labor from 1960 to 1961. He taught at Howard University and Rutgers before accepting a position as an economic analyst at AT&T from 1964 to 1965.

From 1965 to 1970, Sowell was on the faculty at Cornell and Brandeis University. In 1972, Sowell was affiliated with the Urban Institute till 1974. He served on the faculty at the University of California, Los Angeles, and has served as a senior fellow at the Hoover Institution since 1980. When Ronald Reagan was elected president in 1980, he offered Sowell a cabinet position to assist in bringing a conservative voice among African Americans, but he declined. He served on the White House Economic Advisory Board for a one-meeting stint for Reagan, but quit because of the difficulty in traveling to Washington, DC, from California.

Sowell's writings span a range of topics including economics, political ideology, race relations, affirmative action, education, and child development. Known for his conservative and libertarian viewpoint, Sowell's writings have drawn criticism from liberal counterparts. Sowell's position on race and income is the theme of his 1975 publication, *Race and Economics*. In this book, he analyzed the relationship between blacks and wealth, drawing on factors from slavery, contrast to other ethnicities, as well as criticizing government policies directed toward blacks.

Also a strong critic of affirmative action, Sowell's 1990 book, *Preferential Policies: An International Perspective*, criticized the use of quotas in college admissions and employment. He asserted that such policies led to degraded standards and did not allow individuals to reach their full potential. In his 2004 publication, *Affirmative Action around the World: An Empirical Study*, compares the policy in recent U.S. history to those of other nations. His concluding arguments are that affirmative action policies have negligible effects on their intended groups and lower incentives for achievement. His work received critical reception, some arguing that affirmative action had gone too far beyond its purpose.

Aside from his writing on economics and policy, Sowell has taken to writing on child development and education. In his book *The Einstein Syndrome: Bright Children Who Talk Late* investigates the phenomenon of late-talking children, a follow-up to his earlier book *Late-Talking Children*. The research in his book argues that these children are misdiagnosed as autistic or with a disorder, but theorizing instead that they are developing other areas of the brain and not using functions of the brain for language development. In Sowell's book *Inside America's Education*, he is highly critical of the American educational system. He argues that the standards, practices and programs used in the educational institutions lack credibility and he calls for reform.

Sowell detailed his life story in his book *A Personal Odyssey*, published in 2001. He writes about his childhood and stages of life, as well as his education from growing up in the poor South, moving to Harlem, and eventually into the Ivy League at Harvard. He also accounts for the vast differences of wealth that he has experienced in his life in this personal story.

In addition to Sowell's books, he is a regularly syndicated columnist, writing for mass media. His column focuses on issues in the economy, affirmative action, government policy, and social issues, with a free-market viewpoint. It appears in over 150 newspapers in the United States and has been featured in *Newsweek*, *Forbes*, and the *Wall Street Journal*. His conservative opinions often draw criticism from liberals. Some of his essays were published in his work *Ever Wonder Why?: And Other Controversial Essays* in 2006.

Sowell was a recipient of the Francis Boyer Award, given by the American Enterprise Institute in 1990. He was awarded the National Humanities Medal in 2002 and the Bradley Prize in 2003.

Sowell serves as Rose and Milton Friedman Senior Fellow on Public Policy at the Hoover Institution of Stanford University.

*See also:* Friedman, Milton; Stigler, George

## Selected Works by Thomas Sowell

Sowell, Thomas. *Affirmative Action around the World: An Empirical Study*. New Haven, CT: Yale University Press, 2004.

Sowell, Thomas. *Basic Economics: A Common Sense Guide to the Economy*. 4th ed. New York: Basic Books, 2011.

Sowell, Thomas. *The Housing Boom and Bust*. New York: Basic Books, 2009.

Sowell, Thomas. *Inside American Education: The Decline, The Deception, The Dogmas*. New York: Free Press, 1993.

Sowell, Thomas. *Preferential Policies: An International Perspective.* New York: Morrow, 1990.

Sowell, Thomas. *Race and Economics.* New York: McKay, 1975.

**Selected Works about Thomas Sowell**

Quartey, Kojo A. *A Critical Analysis of the Contributions of Notable Black Economists.* Burlington, VT: Ashgate, 2003.

Sowell, Thomas. *A Personal Odyssey.* New York: Free Press, 2000.

"Thomas Sowell." tsowell.com. http://tsowell.com (accessed July 2012).

*Sara Standen*

# SPENCE, MICHAEL

Born: November 7, 1943, in Montclair, New Jersey; American; job market signaling model, Nobel Prize (2001); Major Work: *Market Signaling* (1974).

Michael Spence is perhaps most notable in the twenty-first century for his job market signaling model for which he, along with George Akerlof and Joseph Stiglitz, received the 2001 Nobel Prize in Economics. In *Market Signaling* (1974), Spence examined the information exchange between employees and employers. He argued that employees signal their skills to employers via their education credentials, and employers are willing to pay higher wages to more educated employees because they assume that greater education correlates with greater ability. His current work on economic policy in emerging markets, the economics of information, and the impact of leadership on economic growth led to his appointment of chairman of the independent Commission on Growth and Development (2006–10).

A. Michael Spence was born on November 7, 1943, in Montclair, New Jersey. Spence grew up in Canada during and after World War II until leaving for college in the United States. His father was a member of the War Time Prices and Trades Board based in Ottawa, the Canadian version of wartime price controls. Spence graduated from Princeton University in 1966 with a degree in philosophy and went on to study mathematics at Oxford University as a Rhodes Scholar before he received his PhD from Harvard University in 1972. Spence is also the former dean of the Stanford University Graduate School of Business and is a professor of economics at New York University's Stern School of Business.

Spence began his work on job market signaling in his doctoral thesis for which he was awarded the David A. Wells prize for outstanding doctoral dissertation at Harvard University in 1972. His market signaling model essentially led to more research and literature in the branch of contract theory. According to Spence, marketplace signals exist so that people with a high-quality product in the marketplace will have lower costs of emitting the signal than people with a low-quality product. In this model, Spence shows how qualified workers can signal their worth in the job market. The basic premise is that due to an information asymmetry during the hiring process, the worker knows more about his productivity than a potential employer knows. Since employers cannot sufficiently determine a worker's productivity by the interview alone, highly productive workers "signal" their productivity by getting formal education. For the model to work, it is not even necessary for education to have any intrinsic value because, Spence asserted, the education is less important for what particular knowledge that worker might have learned and more important as a signal of his or her inherent worth.

Spence's market signaling model was significant because it was new to the study of economic behavior. For instance, we send signals to other people by the clothes we wear, the cars we drive, the food we eat, the movies/TV we watch, the people we socialize with, or the work we do.

As chairman of the independent Commission on Growth and Development, a global policy group launched by the World Bank and focused on growth and poverty reduction in developing countries, Spence spent time studying the shifting patterns of economic activity in developing countries. Following the end of his chairmanship in 2010, he published his latest work based on this experience: *The Next Convergence: The Future of Economic Growth* (2011).

Michael Spence was awarded the 2001 Nobel Prize in economics along with George Akerlof and Joseph Stiglitz for developing ways to measure the power of information in a wide range of deals and investments. (AP/Wide World Photos)

According to Spence, the industrialized West had benefited much from economic growth before World War II, which led to enormous gaps in wealth and living standards between the West and the rest of the world. However, after the war this pattern of divergence reversed; emerging economies are reshaping the international order. He argued that although globalization has been critical to the rapid growth of emerging markets, it has also led to rising inequality in the rich countries, and they may respond by raising protectionist barriers, leading to frictions when the world tries to accommodate both rapidly growing emerging giants like India and China and slow-growing developed countries like the United States.

Spence discussed in detail the growth of the emerging markets, which he called the "dynamics of high-speed growth." According to Spence, "dynamics of high-speed growth" requires these emerging markets to invest at very high rates, increase the size of the modernizing parts of the economy, employ surplus labor which has little cost to them, and then sell into a global economy.

Spence emphasized the importance of the role of the government in the economy as opposed to a laissez-faire economy. He believes that the United States needs to spend more on unemployment insurance, industrial policy, and public infrastructure. He advocated for "enhanced coordinated oversight" and "global effective government" for the world economy and the replacement of the current hybrid of floating and fixed exchange rates with "a new hybrid."

Among his many honors, Spence was elected a fellow of the American Academy of Arts and Sciences in 1983; he was awarded the John Kenneth Galbraith Prize for excellence in teaching in 1978 and the John Bates Clark Medal in 1981 for a "significant contribution to economic thought and knowledge." He has served as member of the boards of directors of General Mills, Siebel Systems, Nike, and Exult, and a number of private companies. From 1991 to 1997, he was chairman of the National Research Council Board on Science, Technology, and Economic Policy.

Spence's contribution on market signaling helped lay the foundation for research in contract theory. His current research interests focus on the study of economic growth and development, dynamic competition, and the economics of information. He is a senior fellow at the Hoover Institution, a professor of economics at the Stern School at New York University, and the Philip H. Knight Professor Emeritus of Management in the Graduate School of Business at Stanford University.

*See also:* Akerlof, George; Stiglitz, Joseph

### Selected Works by Michael Spence

Spence, Michael. "Job Market Signaling." *Quarterly Journal of Economics* 87 (1973): 355–74.

Spence, Michael. *Market Signaling*. Cambridge, MA: Harvard University Press, 1974.

Spence, Michael. *The Next Convergence: The Future of Economic Growth in a Multispeed World*. New York: Farrar, Straus and Giroux, 2011.

### Selected Works about Michael Spence

A. Michael Spence. "Autobiography." Nobelprize.org. http://nobelprize.org/nobel_prizes/economics/laureates/2001/spence-lecture.html (accessed July 2011).

Badge, Peter. *Nobel Faces*. Weinheim, Germany: Wiley VCH, 2008.

Stanford Graduate School of Business. "A. Michael Spence." http://gsbapps.stanford.edu/facultyprofiles/biomain.asp?id=36072009 (accessed July 2011).

Vane, Howard R., and Chris Mulhearn. *James A. Mirrlees, William S. Vickrey, George A. Akerlof, A. Michael Spence and Joseph E. Stiglitz*. London: Edward Elgar, 2010.

*Ninee Shoua Yang*

## SRAFFA, PIERO

Born: August 5, 1898, in Turin, Italy; Died: September 3, 1983, in Cambridge, England; Italian; microeconomics, theory of the firm, value economics, history of economic thought; Major Works: "The Laws of Returns under Competitive Conditions" (1926), "Increasing Returns and the Representative Firm: A Symposium" (1930), "Works and Correspondence of David Ricardo" (with Maurice Dodd, 11 vols.) (1951–73), *Production of Commodities by Means of Commodities* (1975).

Piero Sraffa was an Italian economist of the early twentieth century. His work is significant because it challenged the dominant Marshallian view of the times regarding cost. Sraffa's view of production was more complex because of his observation that supply curves were interconnected and changes in one market could have significant impact on other markets. He also edited what many consider to be a definitive collection of David Ricardo's papers. Sraffa died in 1983.

Piero Sraffa was born on August 5, 1898, in Turin, Italy. He was the son of a notable professor of commercial law, and much of his early life was spent traveling around Italy to his father's teaching posts, including Parma and Milan as well as Turin. During his secondary school years, he was first exposed and attracted to socialism. This would be reinforced during his later education at the University of Turin where he would become acquainted with Antonio Gramsci, a founding member of the Communist Party in Italy. However, he would never become a formal member of either the Socialist or Communist parties.

During his studies in Turin, Sraffa was very interested in monetary economics. His 1920 dissertation focused on monetary inflation in Italy. Upon graduation he would be employed for a short time in an Italian bank. His practical experience with banking practices would later supplement his theoretical knowledge.

In 1921, Sraffa would travel to England to continue his studies at the London School of Economics (LSE). It was during this visit that he would first meet and develop a professional relationship with John Maynard Keynes. The following year, Sraffa would return to Italy where he was given a post setting up the Office of Labor Statistics by the Socialist government. He would resign that post when the Fascists came to power.

In 1922, Sraffa was invited by Keynes to submit an article to *The Economic Journal*, "The Bank Crisis in Italy." Initially there was some criticism about the article. The criticism intensified when Sraffa submitted a second article, this time to the *Manchester Guardian* (also at the invitation of Keynes) titled "The Present Situation of Italian Banks." The second article created even more controversy in Sraffa's home country and sparked protest from the prime minister, Benito Mussolini.

From 1924 to 1926, Sraffa held a post as professor of political economy at the University of Perugia. While there he published "On the Relationship between Cost and Quantity Produced," challenging the ideas that had underpinned Marshallian economics.

In 1926, he published (again at the invitation of Keynes) another article that ran counter to dominant economic thinking. Sraffa suggested, among other things, that imperfect competition may be the dominant market form, viewing perfect competition and monopolies as special cases. This insight provided a foundation for additional challenges to the Marshallian explanation of markets.

After spending 1926 and 1927 at the University of Cagliari, Sraffa received an invitation from Keynes to apply for a lecturer position at Cambridge. In 1930, he was given responsibility for editing the works of David Ricardo. At the time, this was not considered important, as Ricardo was not yet held in great esteem. Sraffa's meticulous work would result in the publication of an 11-volume set, published from 1955 to 1973. The papers were actually ready for publication in the 1940s. A large collection of Ricardo's papers were found in Ireland, which resulted in postponement as Sraffa incorporated the new material.

In 1931, Sraffa resigned his lectureship due to conflicts with his research. He was given the position of assistant director of research and librarian of the Marshall Library. Sraffa's closest intellectual colleague was probably Keynes. Sraffa became part of the group known as the Cambridge Circus that would offer comments and criticism to Keynes as he developed *The General Theory*. The group also included two of Sraffa's students, Joan Robinson and Richard Kahn. Both of them would credit Sraffa for their research despite coming to conclusions that differed from his.

Sraffa's greatest work would appear in 1960. The roots of *Production of Commodities by Means of Commodities* can be seen in some of his earliest work. His research continued for over 30 years. It was a reaffirmation of the classical school of thought on value and the firm and renewed focus on the circular flow model of the economy.

Sraffa was nominated as a fellow of the British Academy in 1954, and he would be awarded the gold medal by the Swedish Academy of Sciences (the precursor to the Nobel Prize) in 1961.

Piero Sraffa died on September 3, 1983, in Cambridge, England.

*See also:* Kalecki, Michal; Keynes, John Maynard; Ricardo, David; Robinson, Joan; Samuelson, Paul; Sen, Amartya

## Selected Works by Piero Sraffa

Robertson, D. H., Piero Sraffa, and G. F. Shove. "Increasing Returns and the Representative Firm." *The Economic Journal* 40, no. 157 (March 1930): 79–116.

Sraffa, Piero. "The Bank Crisis in Italy." *Economic Journal* 32, no. 126 (June 1922): 178–97.

Sraffa, Piero. "Dr. Hayek on Money and Capital." *Economic Journal* 42, no. 165 (March 1932): 42–53.

Sraffa, Piero. "The Laws of Returns under Competitive Conditions." *Economic Journal* 36, no. 144 (December 1926): 535–50.

Sraffa, Piero. *Production of Commodities by Means of Commodities*. Cambridge: Cambridge University Press, 1975.

Sraffa, Piero, ed., with the collaboration of M. H. Dobb. *The Works and Correspondence of David Ricardo.* 11 vols. Cambridge: Cambridge University Press, 1951–73.

**Selected Works about Piero Sraffa**

Blaug, Mark, and Paul Sturges. *Who's Who in Economics: A Biographical Dictionary of Major Economists, 1700–1980.* Cambridge, MA: MIT Press, 1983.

Chiodi, Guglielmo, and Leonardo Ditto, eds. *Sraffa or an Alternative Economics.* Hampshire, UK: Palgrave Macmillan, 2008.

Kurz, Heinz, and Neri Salvadori, eds. *The Legacy of Piero Sraffa.* Intellectual Legacies in Modern Economics. 2 vols. London: Edward Elgar, 2003.

Marcuzzo, Maria Christina. "Piero Sraffa at the University of Cambridge." *European Journal of the History of Economic Thought* 12, no. 3 (September 2005): 425–52.

Roncaglia, Alessandro. *Piero Sraffa: His Life, Thought and Cultural Heritage.* Routledge Studies in the History of Economics. Oxford: Routledge, 2000.

*Timothy P. Schilling*

# STERN, NICHOLAS

Born: April 22, 1946, in Hammersmith, England; English; political economy, climate economics, economic development, economies in transition, tax reform, public policy; Major Works: *Economic Development in Palanpur over Five Decades* (with Peter Lanjouw) (1998), "Making Development Work in Africa: Our Common Interest" (2005), *The Stern Review Report on the Economics of Climate Change* (2006).

Nicholas Stern focused on the economics of climate change, economic development and growth, economic theory, tax reform, public policy, and the role of the state and economies in transition. Stern's public service included serving the World Bank and the British government's Economic Service and Treasury. Prime Minister Tony Blair appointed Stern to lead the Commission for Africa, an organization of 17 African leaders. Stern's stance on climate change included the alarming view that Southern Europe would emerge as an extension of the Sahara Desert with Bangladesh and Florida being under water.

Nicholas Herbert Stern, born on April 22, 1946, in Hammersmith, England, is the son of the late Bert Stern and Marion Stern. Bert Stern, a Jew and German citizen, escaped to England after *Kristallnacht* in 1938. Young Nicholas was educated at the private institution Latymer Upper School. He earned a BA degree in mathematics from Peterhouse, Cambridge, and a PhD from the research college, Nuffield, Oxford.

Stern's academic career from 1970 to 1977 began at Oxford as a lecturer. At Warwick University, he became a professor from 1978 to 1987. In 1986, he began teaching at Oxford, where he earned the Sir John Hicks Professor of Economics.

From 1987 to 1993, Stern was director of Suntory and Toyota International Centres for Economics and Related Disciplines (STICERD). In addition to his work at Oxford and Warwick, he taught and did research at the Massachusetts Institute of Technology, the Ecole Polytechnique in Paris, the Indian Statistical Institutes in Bangalore and Delhi, and the People's University of China in Beijing. He was chief economist and senior vice president at the World Bank from 2000 to 2003.

In 2003, Gordon Brown hired Stern for the position second permanent secretary at Her Majesty's (HM) Treasury and head of Government Economic Service. In 2004, Prime Minister Tony Blair appointed Stern to lead the Commission for Africa, an organization of 17 African leaders. Stern's July 2005 report asked for G8 aid to be doubled and for existing debts to be extended.

During his time as chief economist of the European Bank for Reconstruction and Development, Stern was a visiting professor of economics at the London School of Economics and Political Science (LSE). He was the India Observatory director and the Asia Research Centre founder and director in 2007. His next position was IG Patel Professor of Economics and Government at the LSE.

Professor Lord Stern was adviser to the UK government on the economics of climate change and development from 2005 to 2007 and head of the Stern Review on the Economics of Climate Change. The seeds for the 700-page Stern Report were sown in meetings with the Africa Commission and the 2005 G8 conference in Gleneagles, Scotland. Instead of calculating risks of more predictable climate change, Stern examined changes that were most unlikely and could render the most damage.

He served as chair of the Grantham Research Institute on Climate Change and the Environment. Professor Lord Stern taught at College de France in 2010 and was named chair at the Centre for Climate Change Economics and Policy.

The alarming view of Stern's world with climate change includes southern Europe emerging as an extension of the Sahara Desert, and Bangladesh and Florida being under water. Stern's estimate of the cost or investment of managing greenhouse gas (GHG) emissions was an underestimate of $1 billion with a realistic forecast of $2–3 billion. Further, Stern suggested imminent world wars erupting due to mass migrations of people forced to relocate. Overall he expected widespread loss of crops, shortages of water supply, disease, and intense and erratic weather patterns. The plea expressed in the Stern Report is for a swift, decisive universal effort to stabilize GHG emissions in order to avert catastrophic repercussions.

Stern recommended that countries pay for environmental remediation efforts and establish low-carbon technologies, permits for carbon usage, and taxes on air, sea, and land shipping industries, and end subsidies of fossil fuel use. The most effective way of immediately slowing GHG emissions was energy efficiency—using insulation, efficient technology, and nonhydrocarbon energy. Stern's commission opined that the longer the world hesitated to act, the more costly and difficult the task to stabilize carbon emissions.

There were two significant responses to the report that impacted Nicholas Stern's career. One, it was the most influential research on the subject to reach a broad audience. Two, critics who acknowledged the phenomenon of global warming pointed out flawed reasoning in the argument. Dozens of report responses, both pro and con, were published on the LSE website.

Stern dedicated himself to promotion of international economies implementing "green" innovation and jobs with countries committed to low-carbon technologies. Stern saw this "green" industrial revolution as an opportunity for poverty reduction and wealth redistribution. He asserted that poorer nations suffered unfairly from the global-warming crisis. Economist Stern viewed costs as investments and forecast opportunities for growth, health, and prosperity for the planet as they aggressively implemented Stern Commission recommendations. He was acutely aware of the free-rider aspect to this campaign and understood the lack of support and inertia from a significant constituency.

In response to critics, Stern acknowledged that he erred in his use of discounting to forecast the future value of present assets. The projected costs determined the discount rates he used in his calculations. The uncertainties of climate change, and unknowns including timing, were valid concerns about the model.

Professor Lord Stern was honored and awarded many accolades in his career as a political economist: Econometric Society Fellowship (1978), the British Academy fellow (1993), and foreign honorary membership of the American Academy of Arts and Sciences (1998). Lord Nicholas Stern received the knight bachelor honor in 2004 for services in economics. His life peerage designation, granted on October 18, 2007, allowed him the privilege of a cross-bench position in the House of Lords. His complete title was Baron Stern of Brentford of Elsted in the County of West Sussex and of Wimbledon in the London Borough of Merton. He has numerous honorary fellowships and doctorates to his credit.

*See also:* Robbins, Lionel

## Selected Works by Nicholas Stern

Lanjouw, Peter, and Nicholas Stern. *Economic Development in Palanpur over Five Decades*. Oxford: Clarendon Press, 1998.

Stern, Nicholas. "Making Development Work in Africa: Our Common Interest." *Economie Publique* 17 (2005).

Stern, Nicholas. *The Stern Review Report on the Economics of Climate Change*. Cambridge: Cambridge University Press, 2006.

## Selected Works about Nicholas Stern

Adam, David. "Stern Consequences." *Guardian*, March 16, 2007. http://www.guardian.co.uk/politics/2007/mar/17/economy.greenpolitics (accessed October 2012).

Levitt, Steven D., and Stephen J. Dubner. *SuperFreakonomics*. Illustrated ed. New York: HarperCollins, 2009.

LSE, Grantham Research Institute on Climate Change and the Environment. "Professor Nicholas Stern (Lord Stern of Brentford)." http://www2.lse.ac.uk/GranthamInstitute/whosWho/Staff/NicholasStern.aspx (accessed October 2012).

O'Brien, John, ed. *Opportunities beyond Carbon*. Victoria, Australia: Melbourne University, 2009.

*Cynthia Blitz Law*

## STEUART, JAMES

Born: October 21, 1712, in Edinburgh, Scotland; Died: November 26, 1780, in Edinburgh, Scotland; Scottish; mercantilism, political economy, public policy/trade; Major Work: *Inquiry into the Principles of Political Oeconomy* (2 vols. 1767, 1770).

James Steuart was a mercantilist whose work contributed to the development of the classical and neoclassical schools of economics. Through travel experiences and his personal connections, he gained awareness that the most effective government programs were those that were specifically adapted to the country's morals, religions, geography, and culture. His major contribution to economic history was the first book on political economics, an *Inquiry into the Principles of Political Oeconomy*. Steuart described a political economy from a mercantilist perspective. He supported colonialism with restrictive trade rules, tariffs on imports, use of staple port monopolies, and bans on trade involving gold and silver to induce national stability and build wealth. Steuart died in 1780.

James Steuart was born on October 21, 1712, the only child of Sir James Steuart. His father served as the solicitor general for Scotland, appointed by Queen Anne and George I. His grandfather, Sir James Steuart, was lord advocate for William III, and his great-grandfather, Sir James Steuart, was provost of Edinburgh from 1648 to 1660. They descended from the Bonhill branch of the Stewart family.

Steuart attended North Berwick Elementary School until the age of 14. He continued his studies in language and the sciences at the University of Edinburgh. Hercules Lindsay, who later became a professor at Glasgow University, taught Steuart's civil law classes. He completed his studies in 1736, was admitted to the bar, and continued his education traveling Europe until 1740. In Rome, he met Prince Charles Steuart, the Duke of Ormand, and several Scottish expatriates, who persuaded him to join the Jacobite rebellion. Steuart seriously reconsidered his Whig allegiance.

Until 1763 Steuart lived in Italy and Angouleme. While in Europe, Sir James traveled and studied economies and policies of various governments. While in France he was heard praising the British Army. He was arrested and sent to a prison in Luxemburg. Friends came to his rescue by petitioning French authorities and he was released.

His major contribution to economic history was the first book on political economics. He supported Richard Cantillon's population-subsistence concept and discussed the diminishing returns of land value. Steuart's view was that independent countries thrive when they can make minor adjustments to general economic theories and systems to fit their own needs.

Miller and Cadell paid Steuart £500 to publish *Inquiry into the Principles of Political Oeconomy*. In his extensive book, Steuart described political economy from a mercantilist perspective. He supported colonialism with restrictive trade rules, tariffs on imports, use of staple port monopolies, and bans on trade involving gold and silver to induce national stability and build wealth. This viewpoint recognized values of commodities when they were traded.

Steuart believed that a sound economy satisfied the demands of suppliers within it and that trading produced profits. He concluded that a commodity's value is influenced by the labor required to produce or acquire it. He defined real profits as those that combined labor, effort, and skill, and relative profit as selling a commodity at a price above value. Steuart connected a long-run labor theory to supply-and-demand short-run price theory and suggested the concept of equilibrium.

Although mercantilism eventually lost its favor to free-market ideology in Great Britain and France in the 1800s, German philosophers and economists such as Karl Marx, Friedrich Engels, and Georg Wilhelm Friedrich Hegel focused on the value of labor and the concept of profit when they developed their economic theories. Britain's Corn Laws of 1815 that required significant tariffs on cereal/grain imports brought severe hardships to citizens. Tariffs prevented imports, and people had no choice but to pay the price of the local grain to make bread, their essential food staple. Landowners, who comprised the majority of Parliament, benefited from this trade restriction. The laws were repealed in 1846.

Centuries later, students of economics appreciated Steuart's argument against application of universal economic strategies without regard to the unique characteristics of individual nations. When he wrote about the presence of chaotic conditions under foreign leaders, perhaps he thought of the American Revolution. Sir James described the political and economic frustration of British colonies to prosper under the strict control of the monarchy. A proud Scotsman, who suffered exile in the effort to preserve Scottish political autonomy, Steuart experienced firsthand the effects of British colonialism. Adam Smith and David Hume were his contemporaries. Notably, Smith's antimercantilist *The Wealth of Nations*, published several years after Sir James's historic tome, included no discussion of his compatriot's work.

In the 1770s, Steuart helped Indian leaders with their monetary system and business with the East India Company. The local Indian province leadership awarded him for his assistance. Steuart's experience as a well-traveled scholar gave him insights into diverse political economies.

Steuart's most significant treatise was a systematic analysis of political economic policies. His work contributed to the development of the classical and neoclassical schools of economics. Through travel experiences and his personal connections, he gained awareness that the most effective government programs were those that were specifically adapted to the country's morals, religions, geography, and culture.

James Steuart died on November 26, 1780, in Edinburgh, Scotland.

*See also:* Cantillon, Richard; Hume, David; Smith, Adam

## Selected Works by James Steuart

Steuart, James. *Inquiry into the Principles of Political Oeconomy*. Vol. 1. Dublin: James Williams and Richard Moncriefe, 1770.

Steuart, James. *Inquiry into the Principles of Political Oeconomy.* Vol. 2. London: A. Millar and T. Cadell, 1767.

### Selected Works about James Steuart

Perera, P. Eardley. *Gethsemane of the Steuart Legacy: The Story of the James Steuart Trust.* Oxford: Perera, 1975.

Taylor, W. L. "A Short Life of Sir James Steuart: Political Economist." *South African Journal of Economics* 25 (1957): 290–302. doi: 10.1111/j.1813-6982.1957.tb02850.x

Tortasjada, Ramon, ed. *The Economics of James Steuart.* London: Routledge, 1999.

*Cynthia Blitz Law*

## STIGLER, GEORGE

Born: January 17, 1911, in Renton, Washington; Died: December 1, 1991, in Chicago, Illinois; American; microeconomics, price theory, economics of information, government regulation, Nobel Prize (1982); Major Works: *The Theory of Competitive Price* (1946), *The Organization of Industry* (1968).

George Stigler was a scholar, teacher, and author, and his contributions to the field were immense. Stigler's primary contributions to economics were in the fields of price theory, economics of information, government regulation, and organization of industry. Stigler wrote many articles and books during his tenure in academia. His emphasis on microeconomics and empirical data changed the direction of economic study during the second half of the twentieth century and even drove the development of new areas of exploration such as organization of industry, economics of information, and capture theory. Stigler died in 1991.

George Joseph Stigler was born in Renton, Washington, on January 17, 1911, the son of two European immigrant parents. Stigler attended public schools throughout grade school and upon graduation attended the University of Washington. Stigler earned his bachelor of arts in 1931 during the early part of the Great Depression. The challenging economic times led Stigler to apply for and receive a fellowship for graduate studies at Northwestern University in Illinois. He earned his master of business administration in 1932 before continuing his education at the University of Chicago during the mid-1930s. He earned his PhD in 1938.

While obtaining his education in Chicago, Stigler worked with and was greatly influenced by W. Allen Wallis and Milton Friedman. He was part of an economic movement during the 1930s and 1940s that altered the way that people viewed economic policy and decision making. Stigler taught at a variety of colleges and universities for over five decades including Iowa State College, University of Minnesota, Brown University, Columbia University, and the University of Chicago. Stigler held positions with several organizations including the Mont Pelerin Society, the American Economic Association, and the National Bureau of Economic Research.

*The Theory of Competitive Price* was one of Stigler's earliest works, published in 1942. Stigler wanted to know how the real world operated and used this book as inquiry into this realm as he tried to mesh price theory with authentic observation. His goal was to test theories with real-world data and research.

Stigler was one of 36 economists selected by F. A. Hayek to attend a meeting in Switzerland. Some of the most influential economic minds of the time in 1947 were selected to discuss the dangers facing the free-market system. The Mont Pelerin Society formed at this monumental meeting of academic elites to research, renew, and promote the key principles of a free society. Stigler served as president of the group from 1976 to 1978.

Stigler's most prized contribution to the field of economics is arguably his article "The Economics of Information." Stigler believed that information itself was largely overlooked and undervalued. His study of price dispersion and advertising changed that. As Milton Friedman explained, Stigler had a way of explaining his main points about familiar things in a unique and insightful manner. Stigler's study of information prompted many other scholars to follow and began a new discipline within economic circles.

Stigler's curiosity about how the real world worked guided much of his research. Government regulation and its effects were one of Stigler's curiosities. Stigler understood that government regulation was intended to help people, but there was a substantial lack of data and research on the topic. Stigler wanted to go beyond just the effects of regulation and understand its causes. He studied a variety of topics from the markets for electricity to securities. As a result of his data-driven studies, he developed a greater skepticism about the role of government in the economy. He claimed that government influence had little effect on prices and in fact harmed consumers and potentially created monopolies in some instances. This general idea is known as the capture theory. The businesses that benefit from regulation will capture more of the market than their competition will. Through regulation, he claimed, the government interfered with competition, therefore generating monopolies in the market. His work led to the emergence of public choice economics. His influential study gained considerable support in the economic community and led to the deregulation movement of the Carter administration in the late 1970s.

*The Organization of Industry*, a collection of 17 of Stigler's articles, was published in 1968. Stigler used empirical data to test theories related to various aspects of the organization of industry and other topics, most notably evaluating past economic policy and offering recommendations for future policy.

The Nobel Prize in Economics was awarded to George J. Stigler in 1982 for his comprehensive and exhaustive study of the causes and effects of government regulation.

George Stigler died on December 1, 1991, in Chicago, Illinois.

*See also:* Friedman, Milton; Hayek, Friedrich von

## Selected Works by George Stigler

Stigler, George. *Essays in the History of Economics*. Chicago: University of Chicago Press, 1965.
Stigler, George. *Memoirs of an Unregulated Economist*. New York: Basic Books, 1988.
Stigler, George. *The Organization of Industry*. Chicago: University of Chicago Press, 1968.

Stigler, George. *The Theory of Competitive Price*. New York: Macmillan, 1946.
Stigler, George. *The Theory of Price*. New York: Macmillan, 1952.

**Selected Works about George Stigler**

"George J. Stigler." In *The Concise Encyclopedia of Economics*. Edited by David R. Henderson. The Library of Economics and Liberty. http://www.econlib.org/library/Enc/bios/Stigler.html (accessed January 2012).

National Academies Press. "George Joseph Stigler." http://www.nap.edu/html/biomems/gstigler.html (accessed January 2012).

Rowley, Charles K., and Friedrich Schneider, eds. *The Encyclopedia of Public Choice*. New York: Kluwer, 2004.

Stigler, George J. "Autobiography." Nobelprize.org. http://www.nobelprize.org/nobel_prizes/economics/laureates/1982/stigler-bio.html (accessed January 2012).

*William S. Chappell*

# STIGLITZ, JOSEPH

Born: February 9, 1943, in Gary, Indiana; American; asymmetric information, taxation, international development, monetary theory, Nobel Prize (2001); Major Works: *Globalization and Its Discontents* (2001), *Making Globalization Work* (2006).

Joseph Stiglitz is a voracious scholar of economics specializing in the study of how to use multiple perspectives to a given problem to reach a reasoned solution. He was a member of the Clinton administration's Council of Economic Advisers from 1993 to 1995 and then chairman from 1995to 1997. He served as chief

Joseph Stiglitz was awarded the 2001 Nobel Prize for his analysis of markets with asymmetric information with George A. Akerlof and Michael Spence. (AP/Wide World Photos)

economist and senior vice president of the World Bank from 1997 to 2000. In 2001, he was awarded the Nobel Prize for his analysis of markets with asymmetric information with George Akerlof and Michael Spence. He was also the lead author of the 1995 report of the Intergovernmental Panel on Climate Change, which shared the 2007 Nobel Peace Prize. At Columbia University, Stiglitz holds appointments at the Business School, the Department of Economics, and the School of International and Public Affairs (SIPA).

Joseph E. Stiglitz was born on February 9, 1943 in Gary, Indiana. Stiglitz attended public school where he also learned the printing and electric trades. He thrived in his extracurricular activity of debate, which he states helped to shape his later interest in public policy. His most formative intellectual experiences include the period from 1960 to 1963 when he attended Amherst College on a full scholarship. His teachers favored the use of the Socratic seminar, which Stiglitz credits to helping him organize his thoughts and learn to ask useful questions. It was not until late during his third year when Stiglitz decided to leave the field of physics to pursue his studies of economics, putting his mathematical ability to use to solve social problems.

Stiglitz's decision to pursue economics led him to leave Amherst before earning his degree (although later Amherst gave him one) and immediately begin his graduate studies at the Massachusetts Institute of Technology (MIT) to avoid repetition of studies. Stiglitz lived off of $1 a day beyond his rent after his modest last-minute fellowship from MIT. He had four Nobel laureates as professors: Paul Samuelson, Robert Solow, Franco Modigliani, and Kenneth Arrow. He notably worked to edit Paul Samuelson's collected papers. During the summer he moved to the University of Chicago to work with Hirofumi Uzawa. Stiglitz later received a Fulbright fellowship to Cambridge for 1965–66. He later returned to Cambridge for a one-year appointment as an assistant professor at MIT where he worked on his PhD. Throughout his career, Stiglitz has also taught at Yale University, Oxford University, Princeton University, Stanford University, and Columbia University.

During the next few years, Stiglitz would continue to develop his new Keynesian ideas. His work laid the foundation for the study of asymmetric information including new ideas like adverse selection and moral hazard. When buyers and sellers have unequal knowledge about the markets, they may not use resources efficiently. According to Stiglitz, governments may then intervene as a third party to increase the information to all market participants to achieve a more efficient use of resources. He tempers this recommendation of government intervention with the need for a watchful eye on incentives of government's intervention so the buyers and sellers are both better off as a result of government's intervention. His continued work also centers on further development of macroeconomic and monetary theory, development economics and trade theory, public and corporate finance, theories of industrial organization and rural organization, and theories of welfare economics and of income and wealth distribution.

In 1992 Stiglitz joined the Clinton administration as a member and then chairman of the Council of Economic Advisers and was able to put his ideas into practice. His research on adverse selection and moral hazard helped him to create a self-titled "third way" for limited government intervention within the market when markets do not work well.

Stiglitz served as the senior vice president for development policy and the chief economist for the World Bank in 1997–2000. He ultimately left this job as he felt the World Bank and the International Monetary Fund (IMF) were using models that failed to incorporate advances in economic theory like his work on imperfect information and incomplete markets. He advocated the use of openness, broad consensus building, and widespread consultations with parliaments or civil society to assist countries in need. Stiglitz credits his time in Washington with the founding of his initiative for policy dialogue to enhance democratic processes for decision making in developing countries. He continues to advise foreign governments on a broad range of issues.

Stiglitz chaired the Commission on the Measurement of Economic Performance and Social Progress at the 2008 request of French president Nicolas Sarkozy. The president of the United Nations General Assembly appointed Stiglitz chair of the Commission of Experts on Reform of the International Financial and Monetary System in 2009. He has been a fellow of the Econometric Society since age 29 and is a member of the National Academy of Sciences.

In addition to his work at Columbia University, Stiglitz is the editor of *The Economists' Voice* journal and chairs the Brooks World Poverty Institute at the University of Manchester. He cochairs the Columbia University Committee on Global Thought. Stiglitz continues to publish an impressive number of economic works. At present, he has authored 54 books including several principles of micro- and macroeconomic textbooks. *Globalization and Its Discontents* has been translated into 35 different languages.

In 2011, *Time* magazine named Stiglitz one of the 100 most influential people in the world.

*See also:* Akerlof, George; Arrow, Kenneth; Modigliani, Franco; Samuelson, Paul; Solow, Robert; Spence, Michael

## Selected Works by Joseph Stiglitz

Stiglitz, Joseph. *Freefall: America, Free Markets, and the Sinking of the World Economy.* New York: Norton, 2010.
Stiglitz, Joseph. *Globalization and Its Discontents.* New York: Norton, 2002.
Stiglitz, Joseph. *Making Globalization Work.* New York: Norton, 2006.
Stiglitz, Joseph. *The Roaring Nineties.* New York: Norton, 2003.

## Selected Works about Joseph Stiglitz

Brown, Gordan. "Joseph Stiglitz." *Time*, April 21, 2011 (accessed February 2012).
"Joseph E. Stiglitz." In *The Concise Encyclopedia of Economics.* Edited by David R. Henderson. The Library of Economics and Liberty. http://www.econlib.org/library/Enc/bios/Stiglitz.html (accessed May 2012).

Stiglitz, Joseph. "Autobiography." Nobelprize.org. http://www.nobelprize.org/nobel_prizes/economics/laureates/2001/stiglitz-autobio.html (accessed February 2012).

Stiglitz, Joseph E. "Brief Biography of Joseph E. Stiglitz." http://www2.gsb.columbia.edu/faculty/jstiglitz/bio.cfm (accessed February 2012).

*Kathryn Lloyd Gustafson*

## STONE, SIR RICHARD

Born: August 30, 1913, in London, England; Died: December 6, 1991, in Cambridge, England; English; national accounts, social accounting, demand analyses, growth models, Nobel Prize (1984); Major Works: *Social Accounting and Economic Models* (1959), *National Income and Expenditure* (1961), *Demographic Accounting and Model-Building* (1971), *Towards a System of Social and Demographic Statistics* (1975).

Richard Stone was one of the most prolific economists of the twentieth century. Throughout his career he published numerous books and papers on economic theory and application. Stone's most noted contribution to economics was the development of systems of national accounts (SNAs). It not only is used in the analysis of economic activities of a nation, but also it has made it possible to track a nation's economic progress and to compare it with other nations. In 1984, Stone received the Nobel Memorial Prize in Economic Sciences for his major role in development of SNAs. Furthermore, his work on social accounting, SNAs' demographic and environmental applications, and demand analyses and growth models has been very influential in advancing economics theory and application. Stone died in 1991.

John Richard Nicholas Stone was born in London on August 30, 1913. He was the only child of Gilbert and Elsie Stone. Stone's father was a barrister who wanted his son to follow a career in law. From 1926 to 1930, Stone studied law at Westminster. In 1930, his father was selected as a high court judge in Madras, India; Stone took a year off from school and accompanied his father, spending a year in India.

Upon his return, in 1931, he started his undergraduate study in Gonville and Caius College in Cambridge, which was a well-known school for medicine and law. However, after two years he changed his major to economics, believing that the world would be a better place if economics were better understood. Since Gonville and Caius did not have an economist fellow, he was sent to study with Richard Kahn, Colin Clark, and Keynes at King's College. Stone received his BA degree in 1935 and immediately started working in a firm of Lloyds brokers in London. With his wife, they began writing about economic subjects in a monthly pamphlet called *Trends*. Although it was small and insignificant, it drew attention. In 1939, he was asked to join the staff of the Ministry of Economic Warfare.

In 1940, he was assigned a position in the Central Economic Information Service of the Offices of War Cabinet to help James Meade with a survey of England's economic situation. This was the start of an exceptionally fruitful research career in economics during which Stone developed the systems of national accounting, social accounting and its demographic and environmental applications, and finally demands analysis and growth.

During the early years of the 1940s, Stone and Meade helped Keynes to assess the current total resources of the nation against its total consumption, investments, and war expenses. The simplest form of Stone's SNA consists of four sections: production, consumption, accumulation, and foreign finance. Stone used the methods of double-entry to show that what is recorded as a cost in one section would be recorded as revenue in another section. Stone's SNA can be used not only to examine the levels of economic activities of each section of the national economy but also to monitor a nation's economy over time and to compare the economic progress of different nations. In 1944, Stone and Meade published *National Income and Expenditure*, which adopts methods of accounting in a national scale. After the war, based on Keynes's recommendation, Stone was appointed as the director of the newly established department of applied economics at Cambridge University. During the late 1940s and throughout the 1950s, Stone led the work in standardizing national accounting systems to be used internationally by United Nations and the Organization for European Economic Cooperation. Due to Stone's efforts, by the early 1960s the systems of national accounting were practically in use for international purposes.

Later, Stone added more depth to the systems of national accounting by adding a complex set of information known as social accounting to the basic version. Social accounting provides detailed input-output tables of accounting for subdivisions of the main sections of SNA. For instance, it breaks down the production by industry and provides detailed interlocking input-output accounts of all industries. The input-output tables were originally introduced by Wassily Leontief, the 1973 Nobel Prize–winning economist. It was Stone, however, who explained and applied the input-output tables to economic models of SNA. In 1959, Stone and his third wife, Giovanna Croft-Murray, wrote a book entitled *Social Accounting and Economic Models*, explaining the concept of social accounting.

In addition, Stone applied the concept of systems of national accounting to measure the demographic changes that occur over a given period. As with systems of national accounting, demographic accounts are also based on equality of inputs-outputs over a period. Demographic accounts, however, measure activities of different subpopulations or different socioeconomic groups. For instance, the population of a study can be divided based on race and ethnicity, educational attainments, or occupation. Stone's work in the area of demographic applications, titled *Demographic Accounting and Model-Building*, was published in 1971. Furthermore, in 1975 he published a paper called *Towards a System of Social and Demographic Statistics*.

Finally, in addition to his systems of national accounting and social and demographic analysis, Stone had a significant role in measuring consumer demand and in building growth models. In his consumer demand models, Stone related demand for goods and services to three factors: the consumer's income level, the price of the product, and the price index or a comparative price of a product. Stone analyzed the changes in consumer demand for a given product by measuring price and income elasticity. In 1945, Stone published a paper analyzing the consumer demand function entitled "The Analysis of Market Demand."

During the 1960s, Stone started developing mathematical growth models in which he united his demand analysis with the analysis of national accounting. The main purpose of his growth models was to forecast the future economic development. He summarized his mathematical growth models in his 1961 paper titled "An Econometric Model of Growth."

Stone was knighted in 1978 and was a recipient of the 1984 Nobel Prize. In 1980, he retired from Cambridge University but kept working on economic subjects.

Sir Richard Stone died December 6, 1991, in Cambridge, England.

*See also:* Keynes, John Maynard; Leontief, Wassily; Meade, James

### Selected Works by Richard Stone

Stone, Richard. *Demographic Accounting and Model-Building*. Paris: Organisation for Economic Co-operation and Development, 1971.

Stone, Richard. *Towards a System of Social and Demographic Statistics*. New York: United Nations, 1975.

Stone, Richard, and G. Croft-Murray. *Social Accounting and Economic Models*. Cambridge: Bowes and Bowes, 1959.

Stone, R., and G. Stone. *National Income and Expenditure*. Cambridge: Bowes and Bowes, 1961.

### Selected Works about Richard Stone

Pesaran, Mohammad H., and Geoffrey C. Harcourt. "Life and Work of John Richard Nicholas Stone." *The Economic Journal* 110, no. 461 (2000): F146–F165.

Pesaran, M. Hashem, and Sir Richard Stone. *An Interview with Professor Sir Richard Stone*. Cambridge: University of Cambridge, Department of Applied Economics, 1992.

Stone, Richard. "Autobiography." Nobelprize.org. http://www.nobelprize.org/nobel_prizes/economics/laureates/1984/stone-autobio.html (accessed August 2012).

*Elham Mahmoudi*

## SUMMERS, LAWRENCE

Born: November 30, 1954, in New Haven, Connecticut; American; public finance, labor economics, finance economics; Major Work: *Understanding Unemployment* (1990).

Lawrence "Larry" H. Summers began his economic political career as a domestic policy economist on the Council of Economic Advisers under President Reagan in 1982–83. During the 1980s, Larry Summers wrote or coauthored over 50 papers on debt, savings, taxes, stocks, the overall economy, and more. In 1987, he was awarded the Alan T. Waterman Award from the National Science Foundation. This award along with its $500,000 research grant is awarded every year to honor an exceptional young scientist or engineer from the United States whose work demonstrates originality, innovation, and a significant impact within one's field.

Lawrence Henry Summers was born on November 30, 1954, in New Haven, Connecticut, into a family of economics professors. His parents, Robert and Anita Summers, were both economics professors at the University of Pennsylvania, and two of his uncles—Paul Samuelson of the Massachusetts Institute of Technology (MIT) and Kenneth Arrow of Stanford University—were Nobel laureates. Summers spent most of his childhood in Penn Valley, a suburb of Philadelphia. Encouraged in early childhood to take part in family discussions of economic theory and current events, Summers followed his love of the topic and attended MIT where he received his bachelor of science in economics degree in 1975. He taught economics for three years at MIT and was named an assistant professor in 1979 and associate professor in 1982. As a graduate student, Summers attended Harvard University and received his PhD in economics in 1982. Summers went on to teach at Harvard and became one of its youngest tenured professors at the age of 28, returning to serve as the Charles W. Eliot University Professor.

In the 1990s, Summers wrote or coauthored over 50 papers and five books including *Understanding Unemployment* (1990). He left Harvard in 1991 and became the chief economist of the World Bank (1991–93). Later he became the U.S. deputy secretary of the Treasury (1995–99), and then the secretary of the Treasury (1999–2001). During his tenure as secretary, the U.S. economy experienced an unprecedented period of sustained economic growth. As a result, he is considered an expert on domestic economics and a leading authority on international finance. It was during his work with the Clinton administration that he recommended the deregulation of the derivatives contracts within the financial industry. Specifically, he endorsed the Gramm-Leach-Bliley Act, which removed the separation between investment and commercial banks, repealing the Banking Act of 1933, also known as the Glass-Steagall Act.

Summers is not without his critics, as some claim he ignored the 1990s stock bubble and later the housing bubble. He left the political limelight to become president of Harvard University from 2001 to 2006. While there, he wrote and edited a number of works including papers for the Brookings Institution and the *Harvard Business Review*, and cowrote a paper with Henry Kissinger for the Council on Foreign Relations. While at Harvard, he quarreled with a number of the faculty and resigned under pressure. After taking a year off, he returned as a professor of economics at Harvard's Kennedy School of Government.

Summers was an adviser to Barack Obama's presidential campaign and was later named director of the National Economic Council in 2009. As in President Clinton's administration, Summers held significant influence over economic policies in President Obama's administration. He frequently writes for a variety of news publications including the *Washington Post*, *Financial Times*, *Boston Globe*, and *Wall Street Journal*.

In 1993, Summers was awarded the John Bates Clark Medal for being an outstanding young American economist.

*See also:* Arrow, Kenneth; Samuelson, Paul

### Selected Works by Lawrence Summers

Summers, Lawrence. *Investing in All the People: Educating Women in Developing Countries.* Washington, DC: World Bank Publications, 1994.

Summers, Lawrence, ed. *Tax Policy and the Economy.* Multiple vols. Cambridge, MA: MIT Press, 1987–90.

Summers, Lawrence. *Understanding Unemployment.* Cambridge, MA: MIT Press, 1990.

Summers, Lawrence H., and Lawrence H. Goulder. *A General Equilibrium Analysis.* Cambridge, MA: National Bureau of Economic Research, 1987.

Summers, Lawrence H., and Lawrence H. Goulder. *Tax Policy, Asset Prices, and Growth: Understanding Unemployment.* Cambridge, MA: National Bureau of Economic Research, 1987, 1990.

Summers, Lawrence H., Timothy J. Hatton, and Alan M. Taylor. *The New Comparative Economic History: Essays in Honor of Jeffrey G. Williamson.* Cambridge, MA: MIT Press, 2007.

Summers, Lawrence H., and Henry Kissinger. *Renewing the Atlantic Partnership: Report of an Independent Task Force Report.* Washington, DC: World Bank Publications, 1994, 2004.

Summers, Lawrence H., C. K. Prahalad, and Rosabeth Moss Kanter. *Harvard Business Review on Leadership in a Changed World.* Cambridge, MA: Harvard Business School Press, 2004.

### Selected Works about Lawrence Summers

Bradley, Richard. *Harvard Rules: Lawrence Summers and the Battle for the World's Most Powerful School.* New York: HarperCollins, 2005.

Harvard Kennedy School. "Lawrence H. Summers." http://www.hks.harvard.edu/about/faculty-staff-directory/lawrence-summers (accessed October 2012).

Kinsley, Michael. *Creative Capitalism: A Conversation with Bill Gates, Warren Buffett, and Other Economic Leaders.* New York: Simon & Schuster, 2008.

"Lawrence Summers." *New York Times.* http://topics.nytimes.com/top/reference/timestopics/people/s/lawrence_h_summers/index.html (accessed October 2012).

MIT News. "Economist Lawrence Summers, MIT '75, named Harvard President." March 12, 2001. http://web.mit.edu/newsoffice/2001/summers.html (accessed February 2012).

*Carol Lynn Nute*

## SUNSTEIN, CASS

Born: September 21, 1954, in Concord, Massachusetts; American; law and economics, behavioral economics; Major Works: *After the Rights Revolution* (1990), *Risk and Reason: Safety, Law, and the Environment* (2002), *Worst-Case Scenarios* (2007), *Nudge: Improving Decisions about Health, Wealth, and Happiness* (with Richard H. Thaler) (2008).

Cass Sunstein is the administrator of the Office of Information and Regulatory Affairs (OIRA), part of the Office of Management and Budget. OIRA was created by Congress in the 1980 Paperwork Reduction Act and is an agency within the Executive Office of the President. Sunstein was nominated to the position by President Barack Obama and confirmed by the U.S. Senate. In this position, Sunstein and his colleagues review and collect information. They also develop and oversee the implementation of government policies in many areas, including statistical standards and the quality of information.

Cass Robert Sunstein was born on September 21, 1954, in Concord, Massachusetts. After graduation from Middlesex School in Concord, Massachusetts, in 1972, he attended Harvard University. He graduated from Harvard with his AB magna cum laude in 1975. He then attended Harvard Law School, obtaining his JD in 1978, graduating magna cum laude. During this time, he served as the executive editor of the *Harvard Civil Rights-Civil Liberties Law Review*.

After finishing law school, Sunstein worked as a law clerk. His first position was with Hon. Benjamin Kaplan of the Supreme Judicial Court of Massachusetts. Next he worked as law clerk for Hon. Thurgood Marshall of the U.S. Supreme Court. He then worked as an attorney-adviser in the Office of the Legal Counsel of the U.S. Department of Justice from 1980 through 1981.

Following the work in government, Sunstein entered academia. He joined the faculty of the University of Chicago Law School in 1981 and remained there until 2008. He held visiting professor positions at Harvard Law School and Columbia Law School before joining the faculty of Harvard Law School in 2008. He assumed the position of Feliz Frankfurter Professor of Law.

While at Harvard, Sunstein was also the director of the Program on Risk Regulation. The focus of the program was on how law and policy deal with some of the central hazards of the twenty-first century. Among the topics for study were climate change, terrorism, occupational safety, natural disasters, infectious diseases, and other high-consequence events that have a low probability of happening.

Sunstein has been a prolific writer. He has written hundreds of scholarly articles and more than 15 books. Topics cover many aspects of public law, including rights, judicial decision making, environmental and constitutional doctrine, the regulation of risk, and the relationship between the law and human behavior. He has also authored articles that appeared in newspapers and magazines such as the *Boston Globe*, the *New York Times*, the *Washington Post*, *Harper's*, and *The New Republic*. He has testified before congressional committees on many subjects and has been involved in the law reform activities of countries including Russia, South Africa, Poland, Ukraine, and China.

In the book *Nudge: Improving Decisions about Health, Wealth, and Happiness*, Sunstein studied legal questions using information from research on human behavior. He explored these issues in several areas, including family law, environmental protection, and the stock and mortgage markets.

In the position he currently holds as administrator at OIRA, Sunstein oversees extensive research and the implications of various governmental measures on society. He and his colleagues explore the costs and benefits of various governmental agencies' regulations. Data analysis may predict the number of lives saved or resources spent on a specific course of action designed to prevent a particular type of emergency, for example. Such analysis is applied to many sectors of society and influences policy decisions.

*See also:* Thaler, Richard

### Selected Works by Cass Sunstein

Sunstein, Cass. *After the Rights Revolution: Reconceiving the Regulatory State.* Cambridge, MA: President and Fellows of Harvard College, 1990.

Sunstein, Cass, ed. *Behavioral Law and Economics.* New York: Cambridge University Press, 2000.

Sunstein, Cass. *Free Markets and Social Justice.* New York: Oxford University Press, 1997.

Sunstein, Cass. *Risk and Reason: Safety, Law and the Environment.* New York: Cambridge University Press, 2002.

Sunstein, Cass. *Worst-Case Scenarios.* Cambridge, MA: President and Fellows of Harvard College, 2007.

Thaler, Richard H., and Cass R. Sunstein. *Nudge: Improving Decisions about Health, Wealth, and Happiness.* New Haven, CT: Yale University Press, 2008.

### Selected Works about Cass Sunstein

"Cass R. Sunstein." The Law School, University of Chicago. http://www.law.uchicago.edu/faculty/sunstein/ (accessed October 2012).

"Cass R. Sunstein: Administrator of the Office of Information and Regulatory Affairs at the Office of Management and Budget (since September 2009)." *Washington Post.* http://www.washingtonpost.com/politics/cass-r-sunstein/gIQAb1bBAP_topic.html (accessed April 2012).

Kysar, Douglas A. *Regulating from Nowhere: Environmental Law and the Search for Objectivity.* New Haven, CT: Yale University Press, 2010.

*Diane Fournier*

## SWEEZY, PAUL

Born: April 10, 1910, in New York City; Died: February 27, 2004, in Larchmont, New York; American; Marxian economist, journalist, capital accumulation; Major Works: *Theory on Capitalist Development* (1942), *Monopoly Capital* (with Paul A. Baran) (1966).

Paul Sweezy was regarded as one of the foremost Marxian economists. Sweezy believed he had identified three stages in the developmental process: monopolization, stagnation, and financialization. Sweezy argued that the monopolistic system of capitalism is very profitable for a small minority and generates large surpluses. The most popular and influential books written by Paul Sweezy were *The Theory of Capitalist Development* (1942) and *Monopoly Capital* (1966). The *Theory of Capitalist Development* is generally regarded as one of the foremost explanations of Marx's economic ideas. Sweezy helped create the *Monthly Review*, one of the preeminent Socialist periodicals in the United States. Sweezy died in 2004.

Paul Marlor Sweezy was born on April 10, 1910, in New York City. His father was a wealthy banker with J. P. Morgan. He received both his undergraduate and doctoral degrees in economics from Harvard University. He had an exceptional tenure at Harvard, as he was selected editor of the *Harvard Crimson* and graduated magna cum laude. Sweezy continued his journalistic bent as he started the academic journal *The Review of Economic Studies*, while working on his doctorate at Harvard. He later went on to start the *Monthly Review* magazine. He worked as an instructor at Harvard in the late 1930s, and by the 1940s Sweezy was regarded as one of the foremost Marxian economists.

In between his undergraduate and doctoral studies at Harvard, Sweezy spent a year studying at the London School of Economics. While there, he was affected by his exposure to Marxists and by the rise of Hitler and Nazism in Germany. Back at Harvard working on his doctorate, Sweezy was mentored by Joseph Schumpeter. The two were said to be close friends in spite of their philosophical differences. Sweezy was becoming a more determined Marxist while Schumpeter was a conservative economist. The two engaged in a now historic debate on Harvard's campus in 1946. The debate centered on the future of capitalism. His liberal leanings were put into action when he helped begin a Harvard teacher's union. Before obtaining tenure at Harvard, Sweezy resigned his teaching position. Typically, his resignation is attributed to his frustration with the administration's resistance toward more liberal philosophies.

After leaving Harvard, he spent the majority of his time engaged in researching and writing. In 1948, he went to work for Henry Wallace's presidential campaign. Wallace represented the far-left Socialist groups and lost by a significant amount. Sweezy felt Wallace's campaign was disadvantaged because voters were unaware of Socialist alternatives to the problems that most concerned them. It was partly in response to this experience that he helped to create the *Monthly Review*. For nearly half a century, Sweezy would head up the independent, Socialist magazine.

The *Monthly Review* would become one of the preeminent Socialist periodicals in the United States and continues today. The *Monthly Review* was considered a critical component in sustaining the Marxist left philosophy in the United States. The leftist ideologies of Sweezy and his involvement with the *Monthly Review* caught the attention of the House Un-American Activities Committee during the height of McCarthyism in 1954. Convicted for refusing to turn over notes for a lecture he had given at the University of New Hampshire, he received a jail sentence for "contempt," which was later overturned by the U.S. Supreme Court.

The most popular and influential books written by Paul Sweezy were *The Theory of Capitalist Development* and *Monopoly Capital*. *The Theory of Capitalist Development* is generally regarded as one of foremost explanations of Marx's economic ideas. The book was based on a number of lectures he had given at Harvard. *Monopoly Capital* focused on the problems of the concentration of capital among a few large monopolies. *Monopoly Capital* introduced the idea of stagnation. A central theme of both books is the concern for accumulation of wealth concentrated in the hands of large corporations and the stagnation created by the surplus created by the monopolies.

Sweezy hypothesized that large military expenditures would be required to absorb the surplus.

To manage the surpluses and keep prices from falling too low, monopolistic businesses will intentionally curtail production, resulting in stagnation. As a consequence, those with capital accumulated will look to alternatives for investment. Those alternative investments typically involve financial institutions with an incentive to create ever more complex instruments to accommodate the demand for investment opportunities.

Sweezy spent the majority of the 1970s and 1980s traveling and giving lectures. He was praised as the most noted American Marxist scholar.

Paul Sweezy died on February 27, 2004, in Larchmont, New York, at the age of 93.

*See also:* Marx, Karl; Schumpeter, Joseph

## Selected Works by Paul Sweezy

Baran, Paul A., and Paul Sweezy. *Monopoly Capital.* New York: Monthly Review Press, 1966.

Sweezy, Paul M. *The Theory of Capitalist Development.* Oxford: Oxford University Press, 1942.

## Selected Works about Paul Sweezy

Berg, Maxine, ed. *Political Economy in the Twentieth Century.* Lanham, MD: Rowman & Littlefield, 1990.

Simon, John. "Paul Sweezy: A Leading American Marxist Economist, He Founded the Socialist Magazine Monthly Review." *Guardian*, March 4, 2004. http://www.guardian.co.uk/news/2004/mar/04/guardianobituaries.obituaries (accessed October 2012).

Uchitelle, Louis. "Paul Sweezy, 93, Marxist Publisher and Economist, Dies." *New York Times*, March 2, 2004. http://www.nytimes.com/2004/03/02/business/paul-sweezy-93-marxist-publisher-and-economist-dies.html (accessed October 2012).

*Andrew Probert*

## TAUSSIG, FRANK

Born: December 28, 1859, in St. Louis, Missouri; Died: November 11, 1940, in Cambridge, Massachusetts; American; economist (trade theory), educator; Major Works: *The Tariff History of the United States* (1888), *Principles of Economics* (1911).

Frank Taussig was first and foremost a teacher who even in his later career continued to teach the introductory economics course at Harvard University. He wrote extensively, having published some 60 books and articles. He worked at Harvard his entire career except for brief periods of federal government service and recovery from a nervous breakdown. He acted as an adviser on commercial policy to President Woodrow Wilson. He was editor the *Quarterly Journal of Economics* for over 40 years. Taussig died in 1940.

Frank William Taussig was born on December 28, 1859, in St. Louis, Missouri. His father, William Taussig, was an immigrant from Prague in 1826. His father had a varied and successful career as a doctor and a businessman, fulfilling the American dream. Frank Taussig was one of three children. Taussig began at Harvard as a student in 1876, graduated in 1879, and then went on to earn his PhD from Harvard in 1883 as well as a law degree from Harvard in 1886. Frank Taussig was a member of the Harvard faculty starting in 1882, and he became professor of economics at Harvard from 1892 until his retirement in 1935.

Taussig spent his professional career researching, teaching, and writing in the field then called political economy. Over many years Taussig developed a version of neoclassicism, as the views and methods of "classical economics" (dating from the period between 1776 and 1848) were slowly being revised. Taussig was deeply influenced by Alfred Marshall, and his acceptance and promulgation of Marshallian doctrines led him to be regarded as the "American Marshall."

Taussig soon became highly influential in American economic thought. This was considerably due to his position at Harvard, his authorship of his famous two-volume 1911 textbook the *Principles of Economics*, which became one of the most widely used textbooks in the teaching of economics, and his role of editor of the *Quarterly Journal of Economics* from 1889 to 1890 and again from 1896 to 1935 (a period of over 40 years).

Taussig showed an early interest in the history of American tariff legislation while completing his PhD in economics. One of his notable books concerned American tariffs in 1888, with subsequent editions extending to the eighth edition in 1931 titled *The Tariff History of the United States*. This publication established Taussig's reputation as the first American authority in the tariff policy.

Taussig employed the Socratic method of teaching economics to his students and is reputed to have once complained to a colleague how he talked too much in class on any particular day. Taussig spent his entire life researching, teaching, and writing about principally what is now known as international trade policy. International trade (particularly tariff policy) was the area of his greatest contributions to economics. He was regarded as the foremost authority on tariffs for his professional career, and he has been identified as the creator of modern trade theory.

Taussig served a number of federal government agencies including chairman of the U.S. Tariff Commission from 1917 to 1919, the U.S. Treasury Department, the U.S. Food Administration serving on the Milling Committee and Meat Packing Committee, the Price Fixing Committee of the U.S. War Industries Board, and the President's Industrial Conference from 1919 to 1920. He served as a member of the U.S. Sugar Equalization Board, and at the request of President Woodrow Wilson was a participant in economic discussions following World War I in Paris.

After his retirement he continued to live in Cambridge. He passed away from a stroke on November 11, 1940. He is buried at Mt. Auburn Cemetery, in Cambridge, Massachusetts.

*See also:* Marshall, Alfred

**Selected Works by Frank Taussig**

Taussig, Frank. *Principles of Economics.* New York: Macmillan, 1911.
Taussig, Frank. *Some Aspects of the Tariff Question.* Vol. 13. Cambridge, MA: Harvard University Press, 1915.
Taussig, Frank. *The Tariff History of the United States.* Cambridge, MA: Ludwig von Mises Institute, 1888.
Taussig, Frank. *Wages and Capital: An Examination of the Wages Fund Doctrine.* New York: D. Appleton, 1896.

**Selected Works about Frank Taussig**

Bourne, Edward G. Review of *The History of the Present Tariff*, by Frank W. Taussig. *The New Englander and Yale Review* 45 (1886): 195.
Ely, Richard T. Review of *Principles of Economics*, by Frank W. Taussig. *American Economic Review* 2, (1912): 3.
Mussey, H. R. Review of *Some Aspects of the Tariff Question*, by Frank W. Taussig. *American Economic Review* 5 (1915): 4.

*Jean Kujawa*

# THALER, RICHARD

Born: September 12, 1945, in East Orange, New Jersey; American; behavioral finance, behavioral economics; Major Works: *Quasi-Rational Economics* (1991), *The Winner's Curse: Paradoxes and Anomalies of Economic Life* (1991), *Nudge: Improving Decisions about Health, Wealth, and Happiness* (2008).

Richard Thaler, an American economist, is one of the pioneering theorists in the field of behavioral finance and behavioral economics. He is the Ralph and Dorothy

Keller Distinguished Service Professor of Behavioral Science and Economics at the University of Chicago, Booth School of Business. He also serves the university as the director of the Center for Decision Research and teaches MBA courses in behavioral economics and managerial decision making.

Richard H. Thaler was born on September 12, 1945, in East Orange, New Jersey. Thaler received his bachelor's degree from Case Western Reserve University in 1967 and his master's from the University of Rochester in 1970. He pursued a doctorate degree at the University of Rochester, which culminated with his dissertation "The Value of Saving a Life: A Market Estimate," under the supervision of Sherwin Rosen. While pursuing the PhD, he worked as an instructor with the Graduate School of Management, then as program associate with the Rochester-Monroe County Criminal Justice Pilot City Program. He would accept an assistant professor's position upon graduation.

Early in his 20 years of research, from 1976 to 1977, Thaler partnered with ASPER and the U.S. Department of Labor as principal investigator in the research project "An Equalizing Difference Model of Employment." Thaler continued his inquiries in the 1983 project for the U.S. Department of the Navy, which explored descriptive choice models, followed by "Research in Psychology and Economics" for the Alfred P. Sloan Foundation. A seven-year research stint financed by the Alfred P. Sloan Foundation and Russell Sage Foundation furthered the study of behavioral economics titled "Continued Research in Psychology and Economics." Another example was the 1995 project, "Myopic Loss Aversion," sponsored by the National Science Foundation.

Widely recognized for his independent and collaborative research, Thaler has published a plethora of articles in revered journals such as the *American Economic Review, Journal of Finance, Journal of Political Economy*, and *University of Chicago Law Review*. Thaler was editor of the publication *Advances in Behavioral Finance* (1992) and a successive volume by the same name in 2005.

In the leading-edge *Nudge: Improving Decisions about Health, Wealth, and Happiness* (2008), Thaler and coauthor Cass Sunstein offered forward-thinking answers to society's most perplexing conundrums. Thaler's other major works include *Quasi-Rational Economics* (1991) and *The Winner's Curse: Paradoxes and Anomalies of Economic Life* (1991). The content of *The Winner's Curse* was expertly distilled from his "Anomalies" columns previously published in the *Journal of Economic Perspectives* from 1987 to 1990.

His research questioned established economic theories by exposing inconsistencies from actual case studies. Thaler ingeniously morphed his findings into a fresh perspective ideal for the everyday consumer. A resurgent thread in Thaler's work is the view of economics through a human lens whereby he projects people as emotional creatures rather than hardwired, data-driven machines. Consequently, Thaler submits that humans are inclined to behave or make decisions based on a combination of factors such as emotion or attachment even if irrational. The humanist element of his research and writings has led to the emerging acceptance of behavioral economics. Thaler's attempts to narrow the gap between the worlds of psychology and economics is evidenced in a recent collaborative effort titled

*Deal or No Deal?: Decision Making Under Risk in a Large-Payoff Game Show*, where Thaler and others illustrate the distinctive role of psychology in the economic choices of game show contestants.

Thaler served as a research economist for the Public Research Institute and the Center for Naval Analyses, and as professor of economics at Cornell University Johnson Graduate School of Management. He was a visiting professor and scholar at several distinguished institutions including Cornell, the Massachusetts Institute of Technology, the Russell Sage Foundation, and Stanford University's Center for Advanced Study in Behavioral Sciences. He currently serves as director of the Center for Decision Research, University of Chicago, a position he previously held for six years.

In 2009, he began writing a column for the *New York Times* on an assortment of economic-minded and finance-related themes to address challenging issues plaguing the United States. Most notably, Thaler infused the earlier notions of Thomas Hazlett to craft a solution to the nation's monstrous deficit in his piece "Selling Parts of the Radio Spectrum Could Help Pare US Deficit." Thaler proposed a strategy for the Federal Communications Commission (FCC) to leverage existing broadcast frequency as an income channel for the United States to cut national spending and strengthen future technological prospects.

In May of 2012, Thaler was chosen as the Nicholas Molodovsky Award recipient by the CFA Institute, a worldwide membership organization of investment professionals. Thaler is the founder of Fuller & Thaler Asset Management, which applies research-driven methods to wealth creation and management.

Richard Thaler maintains a conversation on behavioral economic topics in a grant-funded lecture series for the National Bureau of Economic Research with Robert Shiller.

*See also:* Kahneman, Daniel; Rosen, Sherwin; Sunstein, Cass

### Selected Works by Richard Thaler

Thaler, Richard, ed. *Advances in Behavioral Finance*. New York: Russell Sage Foundation, 1993.

Thaler, Richard. *Advances in Behavioral Finance*. Vol. 2. Roundtable Series in Behavioral Economics. Princeton, NJ: Princeton University Press, 2005.

Thaler, Richard. *Quasi-Rational Economics*. New York: Russell Sage Foundation, 1991.

Thaler, Richard H. "Toward a Positive Theory of Consumer Choice. In *Choices, Values, and Frames*. Edited by Daniel Kahneman and Amos Tversky, 269–89. Cambridge: Cambridge University Press, 2000.

Thaler, Richard. "The Value of Saving a Life: A Market Estimate." PhD dissertation, University of Rochester, 1974.

Thaler, Richard. *The Winner's Curse: Paradoxes and Anomalies of Economic Life*. New York: Free Press, 1991.

Thaler, Richard, and Cass R. Sunstein. *Nudge: Improving Decisions on Health, Wealth, and Happiness*. New Haven, CT: Yale University Press, 2008.

### Selected Works about Richard Thaler

Cassidy, John. "Interview with Richard Thaler." *The New Yorker*, January 21, 2010. http://www.newyorker.com/online/blogs/johncassidy/2010/01/interview-with-richard-thaler.html (accessed October 2012).

Chicago Booth, University of Chicago School of Business. "Richard H. Thaler." http://www.chicagobooth.edu/faculty/bio.aspx?person_id=12825835520 (accessed October 2012).

Van Overtveldt, Johan. *The Chicago School: How the University of Chicago Assembled the Thinkers Who Revolutionized Economics and Business.* Chicago: Agate, 2007.

*Joy Dooley-Sorrells*

## THUNEN, JOHANN

Born: June 24, 1783, in Jever, Germany; Died: September 22, 1850, in Tellow, Germany; German; economic theory of location, economic rent, diminishing returns; Major Works: *The Isolated State* (Vols. 1 [1826], 2 [1850], and 3 [1867].

Johann von Thunen was a farmer and economist in early nineteenth-century Germany. In his book *The Isolated State* (1826), he outlines the most efficient and profitable use of crops and animals with respect to their proximity to market. He is known for his ability to combine mathematical theory with practical application. He is also cited for introducing concepts like economic rent, diminishing returns, opportunity cost, and marginal-productivity theory of wages. Thunen died in 1850.

Johann Heinrich von Thunen was born on June 24, 1783, in Jever, Germany. He studied national economy in Goettingen in 1803. In 1809, he purchased his a farm, Tellow Manor, in Mecklenburg-Schwerin where he applied his studies of national economics to his estate.

Thunen created a mathematical formula to determine the best use of land. It is important to note that his model was created before industrialization. His model assumes a theoretical town that is isolated and located in the center of a fertile plain. The only transportation available is horse-drawn wagon. All the land is equally fertile and lacks any distinct individual advantage or obstructions like mountains or rivers. Outside the fertile plain lies a wilderness, leaving the town to draw all resources from within (no international trade). Thunen constructed the following equation to maximize profits for farmers:

$L = Y(P - C) - YDF$.

$L$ = location or land rent
$Y$ = yield per unit of land
$P$ = Per unit market price of crop
$C$ = cost to produce crop
$D$ = distance to market
$F$ = freight rate or transport cost.

In short, economic rent, or von Thunen rent, is measured as the location of a resource.

He also used a series of ever-larger rings to illustrate his idea of profit maximization and location theory. For example, Thunen would locate ranching or grazing animals on the outermost ring as they can walk themselves to market and leave horticulture and dairy products in the first ring as they are more perishable and need a closer proximity to the city. The second ring would consist of forestry to produce timber and firewood necessary for fuel and building materials. Grains would be in the third ring as they last longer and are easier or lighter to transport than wood. Goods with larger transportation costs or shorter lives are on the inner rings, and durable goods or goods that can move themselves are located on the outer rings. His model illustrates least-cost location for each resource within the isolated state.

Thunen also studied wage rates trying to determine their natural rate. He wrote of the basic theory of marginal productivity in which an employer will hire a worker only as long as their work is valued (through their wages) as greater than or equal to the value of the product produced (product price).

Thunen's agricultural models have been adapted to modern land use patterns and improving technology. Transportation costs continue to influence location decisions for manufacturing as well as spatial analysis.

Economic peers laud the method in which Thunen explained his ideas. His use of a simplified model or state, mathematical formulas, and an abstract-deductive format for writing was noteworthy in his time. The University of Rostock granted Thunen an honorary doctorate in 1830.

Johann Heinrich von Thunen died on September 22, 1850, in Tellow, Germany.

*See also:* Dupuit, Jules; Jevons, William Stanley; Marshall, Alfred; Wicksteed, Philip

### Selected Works by Johann Thunen

Thunen, Johann. *The Isolated State*. Vols. 1, 2, and 3 (1826, 1850, 1867).
Thunen, Johann von. *Isolated State: An English Edition of Der isolierte Staat*. Edited by Peter Geoffrey Hall. Translated by Carla M. Wartenberg. Oxford: Pergamon Press, 1966.

### Selected Works about Johann Thunen

Crosier, Scott. *Johann-Heinrich von Thünen: Balancing Land-Use Allocation with Transport Cost*. http://www.csiss.org/classics/content/9 (accessed August 2012).
Schumacher, H. *Johann Heinrich von Thunen*. Ann Arbor: University of Michigan Library, 1883.

*Kathryn Lloyd Gustafson*

## THUROW, LESTER

Born: May 7, 1938, in Livingston, Montana; American; global economy, income distribution; Major Works: *The Zero-Sum Society: Distribution and the Possibilities for Economic Change* (1980), *Head to Head: The Coming Battle among Japan, Europe, and America* (1992), *Building Wealth: The New Rules for Individuals, Companies and Nations in a Knowledge-Based Economy* (1999).

Lester Thurow is a global economist, author, and professor. He is currently the Jerome and Dorothy Lemelson Professor of Management and Economics Emeritus at the Sloan School of Management at the Massachusetts Institute of Technology (MIT). He served as dean of the school from 1987 to 1993. Thurow has served as a staff economist for President Lyndon Johnson. He has written several books on the global economy and the distribution of income. He also has contributed as a columnist for news magazines.

Lester Carl Thurow was born in Livingston, Montana, on May 7, 1938. Thurow earned his BA from Williams College in 1960 in political economy. As a Rhodes Scholar, he received his MA in philosophy, politics, and economics from the Balliol College at Oxford University in 1962. Thurow earned his PhD in economics from Harvard University in 1964.

After serving as a staff economist for President Lyndon Johnson's Council of Economic Advisers, Thurow taught at Harvard from 1966 to 1968. Since 1968, Thurow has served on the faculty of MIT. From 1987 to 1993, Thurow served as dean for the Sloan School of Management.

His academic work has focused on global economy, the distribution of income and wealth, and public economic policy. In his book *The Zero-Sum Society: Distribution and the Possibilities for Economic Change* (1980), Thurow argued that the economic turnaround needed from a slow-growing economy will not take place until the zero-sum theory in macroeconomics is applied, meaning members of society will have to face taxation for government economic actions to work. His following book, *Dangerous Currents: The State of Economics* (1983), critiqued academic economics as the only reliable tool for government policy.

Thurow's advocacy for the U.S. economy to change from an individual capitalism to a more communitarian form of capitalism is the basis of his 1992 *New York Times* best seller, *Head to Head: The Coming Battle among Japan, Europe, and America*. He calls on government to play a leading role to help businesses become efficient in developing new processes and skill development to stay competitive in the global economy, with regard to Europe and Japan as economic superpowers. Further writing on globalization is the topic of Thurow's 2003 book, *Fortune Favors the Bold: What We Must Do to Build a New and Lasting Global Prosperity*. In this work, Thurow asserts that companies that want to succeed in the global changing economy must take bold financial risks.

In addition to his books, Thurow has contributed as a columnist and editor. He has written articles for the *Boston Globe* and *USA Today*. He served on the editorial board for the *New York Times* and on the board of economists for *Time*. Thurow has appeared on the television program *Nightly Business Report*, as well as been featured on *60 Minutes*. He is a board of director member for companies including Analog Devices and E-Trade. Thurow is a member of the American Academy of Arts and Sciences and served as vice president for the American Economic Association in 1993.

*See also:* Krugman, Paul; Samuelson, Paul

## Selected Works by Lester Thurow

Thurow, Lester. *Building Wealth: The New Rules for Individuals, Companies and Nations in a Knowledge-Based Economy*. New York: HarperCollins, 1999.

Thurow, Lester. "Changing the Nature of Capitalism." In *Rethinking the Future*. Edited by Warren G. Bennis and Rowan Gibson, 228–50. London: Nicholas Brealey, 1996.

Thurow, Lester. *Dangerous Currents: The State of Economics*. New York: Random House, 1983.

Thurow, Lester. "Growing Older." In *Aging: Concepts and Controversies*. Edited by Harry R. Moody, 334–39. Thousand Oaks, CA: Pine Forge Press, 2010.

Thurow, Lester. *Head to Head: The Coming Economic Battle among Japan, Europe, and America*. New York: Morrow, 1992.

Thurow, Lester. *The Zero-Sum Society: Distribution and the Possibilities for Economic Change*. New York: Basic, 1980.

**Selected Work about Lester Thurow**

Jahnke, Art. "2010: Interview with Lester Thurow We Can Shape the Global Economy." CIO. December 15, 2003. http://www.cio.com/article/32034/2010_Interview_with_Lester_Thurow_We_Can_Shape_The_Global_Economy (accessed July 2012).

*Sara Standen*

## TINBERGEN, JAN

Born: April 12, 1903, in The Hague, Netherlands; Died: June 9, 1994, in The Hague, Netherlands; Dutch; econometrics, business cycle, economic policy, Nobel Prize (1969); Major Works: *Statistical Testing of Business-Cycle Theories: Business Cycles in the United States of America, 1919–1932* (1939), *Business Cycles in the United Kingdom, 1870–1914* (1951), *Economic Policy: Principles and Design* (1964).

Jan Tinbergen was an innovative Dutch economist who combined mathematics, statistics, and economic theory to develop new models in econometrics. In 1969, he shared the first Nobel Prize in Economics in memory of Alfred Nobel with Ragnar Frisch for his work developing and applying models to analyze the economic process. Tinbergen died in 1994.

Jan Tinbergen was born on April 12, 1903 in The Hague, Netherlands, as the eldest of five children. His parents, Dirk Tinbergen and Jeannette van Eek, were both schoolteachers. He attended the Hogere Burgerschool in The Hague, which allowed middle-class Tinbergen to begin studies in 1921 at the University of Leiden after passing extra exams in Greek and Latin. Tinbergen's teacher Paul Ehrenfest proved a positive influence as Tinbergen studied mathematics and theoretical physics. He also started a social democratic student club and newspaper, which published his first works on unemployment and the economic depression of the 1920s. Tinbergen continued his doctorate studies under Ehrenfest, writing his thesis titled "Minimization Problems in Physics and Economics" in 1929. This was one of the first examples of mathematical modeling. It was here that Tinbergen worked with many revered thinkers such as Albert Einstein.

Dutch legislation allowed Tinbergen, who was a conscientious objector, to join the Central Bureau of Statistics in 1929. He remained associated with the bureau until 1945 when he became the director of the Central Planning Bureau (1945–55). During 1936–38, he worked for the League of Nations as a business-cycle research expert. In 1933, Tinbergen also became a professor of economics at the Netherlands School of Economics, Rotterdam, and taught there until 1973. Along with Ragnar Frisch, in 1969 Tinbergen was awarded the first Nobel Prize in Economics for his work creating the first macroeconomic models. His brother Nikolaas, a zoologist, also won the Nobel Prize for physiology in 1973 and brother Luuk became famous for the scientific study of animal behavior.

In 1936, Tinbergen developed the first national and fully inclusive macroeconomic model for the Netherlands' economy. He later constructed an econometric model of the United States and the United Kingdom, as well as for other countries. His work served as the groundwork for his business cycle theory and strategies for economic stabilization. This application of mathematics and economics was especially useful for monetary policy. The Dutch government would later use these ideas as the foundation for their economic plans.

Tinbergen developed the idea that government must have equal numbers of policy instruments and targets to achieve their economic goals. A target might be the unemployment or inflation rate and an instrument might be some form of monetary policy. This notion of economic thought is now an underlying assumption for current economists.

Tinbergen also is known for his principle of wage ratios. The Tinbergen Norm states that if the maximum and minimum pay rates within a company exceed 1:5, the company will not work to its fullest potential.

In later years, Tinbergen continued to spotlight the need to help impoverished countries. From 1965 to 1972, Tinbergen worked as the chairman of the United Nations Committee for Development Planning where he was able to advise various developing countries such as the United Arab Republic, Turkey, Venezuela, Surinam, Indonesia, and Pakistan to name several. He also advised international organizations such as European Coal and Steel Community, the International Bank for Reconstruction and Development, and the United Nations Secretariat. He was a member of the Royal Academy of Science and honorary doctor of 15 universities. In 1992, he received the Four Freedoms Award for his humanitarian efforts to encourage economic assistance to developing nations.

Jan Tinbergen died on June 9, 1994, in The Hague, Netherlands.

*See also:* Frisch, Ragnar

## Selected Works by Jan Tinbergen

Tinbergen, Jan. *Business Cycles in the United Kingdom, 1870–1914.* Amsterdam: North Holland, 1951.

Tinbergen, Jan. *Economic Policy: Principles and Design.* Amsterdam: North Holland, 1964.

Tinbergen, Jan. *Statistical Testing of Business-Cycle Theories: Business Cycles in the United States of America, 1919–1932.* Geneva, Switzerland: League of Nations, Economic intelligence service, 1939.

## Selected Works about Jan Tinbergen

"Jan Tinbergen." In *The Concise Encyclopedia of Economics.* Edited by David R. Henderson. The Library of Economics and Liberty. http://www.econlib.org/library/Enc/bios/Tinbergen.html (accessed August 2012).

The Nobel Foundation. "Jan Tinbergen." http://www.nobel-winners.com/Economics/jan_tinbergen.html (accessed August 2012).

Piazzo, Diego. *Conversations with Great Economists: Friedrich A. Hayek, John Hicks, Nicholas Kaldor, Leonid V.Kantorovich, Joan Robinson, Paul A. Samuelson, Jan Tinbergen.* New York: Jorge Pinto Books, 2009.

Tinbergen, Jan. "Prize Lecture." Nobelprize.org. http://www.nobelprize.org/nobel_prizes/economics/laureates/1969/tinbergen-lecture.html (accessed August 2012).

*Kathryn Lloyd Gustafson*

## TOBIN, JAMES

Born: March 5, 1918, in Champaign, Illinois; Died: March 11, 2002, in New Haven, Connecticut; American; macroeconomics, monetary policy, neo-Keynesian economics, portfolio theory, Nobel Prize (1981); Major Works: *Essays in Economics* (vols. 1–4, 1987–96), *Full Employment and Growth* (1996).

James Tobin was an American economist who spent his long career explaining and developing John Maynard Keynes's *General Theory of Employment, Interest and Money*, leaving a legacy as an essential neo-Keynesian. Tobin was a strong advocate of government intervention in the economy to avoid recessions and stabilize output. He made numerous significant economic contributions, including his portfolio theory, which won him the 1981 Nobel Prize in Economics. Other notable contributions by Tobin included the Tobin's q, the Tobin tax, and the Tobin model. Tobin died in 2002.

James Tobin was born on March 5, l918, in Champaign, Illinois. His father was the publicity director for the University of Illinois athletics department, and Tobin attended University High School run by the University of Illinois College of Education. Tobin graduated summa cum laude in economics from Harvard University in 1939 and stayed to complete his MA degree in 1940. His doctoral studies were interrupted by working at the Office of Price Administration and Civilian Supply and the War Production Board in Washington, DC, prior to World War II. Following the attack on Pearl Harbor, Tobin enlisted in the U.S. Navy. After serving on the USS *Kearny* destroyer for four years, he returned to Harvard and finished his PhD in 1947. He remained at Harvard as a junior fellow until 1950.

In 1950, he began his career at Yale University, becoming a full professor in 1955 and in 1957 received the honor of becoming the Sterling Professor of Economics. He formally retired in 1988 but stayed at Yale to continue working on his theories.

Tobin became interested in the subject of economics for two reasons: he enjoyed the intellectual challenge, and he wanted to use economics for comprehending the world events. Tobin saw economics as a means to prevent such human misery from reoccurring. Tobin's fundamental concern was how economic policies affected people's lives. He believed that the federal government could use fiscal and monetary measures to benefit society. At Harvard as a young freshman, he quickly became a convert to the new theories of Keynes. He spent the remainder of his life explaining and developing theoretical supports to Keynesian economics. He wrote extensively as a pioneer in the development of macroeconomics.

Besides his treasured teaching at Yale in New Haven, Tobin also served as director of the Cowles Foundation for Research in Economics from 1955 to 1961 and again in l954–65. Tobin occasionally left his professorial post at Yale, commonly as a visiting professor at another academic institution or as a consultant, but one significant departure from academics was serving on the Council of Economic Advisers at the express request of newly elected President John F. Kennedy during l961–62. That Council produced what was called the Economic Report of l962, which was dubbed by the media as the "new economics." Tobin himself described this report as a comprehensive account of the theories and practices for economic growth.

Nobel Prize winner James Tobin notifies his son by telephone in 1981 to tell him that he has been awarded the Nobel Prize in economics. (AP/Wide World Photos)

Tobin was author or editor of 16 books and over 400 articles concerning economics. The topics ranged from econometrics to macroeconomics, monetary theory, monetary policy, fiscal policy, public finance, and portfolio theory and asset markets. Tobin is remembered for his work in financial analysis, especially the portfolio theory, which explained that investors should balance portfolios with both low- and high-risk assets to minimize risk. Tobin described his portfolio theory as not putting all of one's investment eggs in a single basket.

It was accepted monetary policy that interest rates could influence capital investment. Tobin felt, however, that there was another important consideration. He developed Tobin's q, a measure to predict whether there will be an increase or decrease in capital investment. The q was a mathematical ratio between the market value of an asset and the cost to replace it. If the ratio is greater than one, new investment will be profitable. If less than one, new investment in similar equipment will not be profitable. Tobin suggests that at this point companies tend not to invest in new plants and equipment but decide instead to purchase existing companies.

Another Tobin idea is the Tobin tax. The Tobin tax is a small tax on currency transactions in international markets to reduce short-term currency speculation. He felt that such a tax would help stabilize exchange markets without being a burden on free trade. Today, his tax idea is often proposed as a way to raise revenue. He also developed a regression to analyze spending decisions called the Tobin model, an econometric model investigating dependent variables within a model.

Tobin served in many professional associations and received numerous awards beyond the Nobel Prize in 1981. He was awarded the John Bates Clark Medal in 1966 and was president of the American Economic Association in 1971. Tobin will be remembered through his prolific research and publications as one of the most influential macroeconomists of the twentieth century, especially his lifelong contributions in explaining and elaborating on the theories of Keynes.

James Tobin died on March 11, 2002, in New Haven, Connecticut.

*See also:* Heller, Walter; Keynes, John Maynard; Markowitz, Harry; Okun, Arthur; Solow, Robert

### Selected Works by James Tobin

Tobin, James. *Asset Accumulation and Economic Activity: Reflections on Contemporary Macroeconomic Theory.* New Haven, CT: Yale University Press, 1979.

Tobin, James. *Essays in Economics.* Vols. 1–4. New Haven, CT: Yale University Press, 1987–96.

Tobin, James. *Full Employment and Growth.* London: Edward Elgar, 1996.

Tobin, James. "A General Equilibrium Approach to Monetary Theory." *Journal of Money, Credit, and Banking* 1, no. 1 (1969): 15–29.

Tobin, James. "Liquidity Preference as Behavior towards Risk." *Review of Economic Studies* 25, no. 1 (1958): 65–86.

Tobin, James. *World Finance and Economic Stability: Selected Essays of James Tobin.* London: Edward Elgar, 2003.

Tobin, James, and Stephen S. Golub. *Money, Credit, and Capital.* New York: Irwin/McGraw-Hill, 1998.

### Selected Works about James Tobin

"James Tobin." In *Lives of the Laureates, Seven Nobel Economists.* Edited by William Breit and Roger Spencer. Cambridge, MA: MIT Press, 1986.

"James Tobin—Autobiography." July 15, 2012. Nobelprize.org. http://www.nobelprize.org/nobel_prizes/economics/laureates/1981/tobin-autobio.html (accessed August 2012).

"James Tobin—Prize Lecture: Money and Finance in the Macro-Economic Process." July 8, 2012. Nobelprize.org. http://www.nobelprize.org/nobel_prizes/economics/laureates/1981/tobin-lecture.html (accessed August 2012).

*Jean Kujawa*

## TRICHET, JEAN-CLAUDE

Born: December 20, 1942, in Lyon, France; French; monetary policy, public administration; Major Works: unpublished papers and speeches.

Jean-Claude Trichet is a former president of the European Central Bank (ECB). He was instrumental in establishing the euro system and the European Central Bank when it began in 1999. In the 1970s, Trichet was France's general inspector of finance. He became France's director of the Treasury Department in 1987. Trichet was France's head central banker as governor of the Bank of France in 1993. He served as president of the European Central Bank from 2003 to 2011.

Jean-Claude Trichet was born on December 20, 1942, in Lyon, France. He obtained a degree in civil engineering from the École des Mines de Nancy in 1964. In 1966, he graduated from the University of Paris with a degree in economics and certificate in political studies.

Trichet began his career as an engineer before joining the French government in 1971. Prior to becoming president of the European Central Bank, Trichet held positions in several French government agencies including the general inspector's office, the Treasury Department in which he held several positions, and Economic Affairs. In 1987, he became director of the Treasury Department and in 1993 began his first term as governor of the Bank of France, France's central bank.

Jean-Claude Trichet's tenure as director of the French Treasury was marred with scandal in 2002. Labeled the Credit Lyonnais Affair, several banking officials including Trichet were charged with fraud for manipulating financial reports to suppress the real business health of the Credit Lyonnais. The reports were presumably altered to hide the actual losses on some property investments by Credit Lyonnais. The French government was the majority owner of Credit Lyonnais, and with public monies emergency funding was supplied and the crisis was averted. Trichet was cleared of any wrongdoing in 2003. If any legal charges had been brought against Trichet and had he been convicted, he would not have been eligible for the ECB presidency.

Trichet was an active participant in the euro system's development and the launching of the European Central Bank in 1999. Prior to his appointment as governor for the Bank of France, he served as chairman of the European Monetary Committee in 1992 and 1993. As governor, he was also served as governor for the Bank of International Settlements and for the World Bank, furthering his experience and expertise in international banking. In 1994, he chaired the Council of the European Monetary Institute, and in 2003 as chairman of the Group of Ten Governors was a leading choice for president of the European Central Bank.

Jean-Claude Trichet's term as president of the ECB began with expectations that he was a much better and more experienced policy maker and consensus builder than his predecessor, Wim Duisenberg. Trichet had a new single-currency region consisting of a wide diversity of countries. One of Trichet's early successes was in 2004 when he was able to slow the appreciation of the euro without a significant rise in interest rates.

Trichet was often faced with conflicts between what he thought was best for the euro region versus what each country thought was best for their own situation. This conflict was especially noticeable in 2004 when Trichet apparently felt a rate cut was warranted. In his transparent fashion of management, he made it known to the press and public only to have it denounced and rejected in the bank's meeting. The politics of the Eurozone had won over the region's economic interests. Not only did his credibility take a hit but so did the ECB's.

Debate and discussions over the Common Agriculture Policy (CAP) was another example of the European Union (EU) interest clashing with the interests of each sovereign nation member. Established in 1957 well before the EU came into being, the direct subsidies and revenues generated through the tariffs imposed on non-EU goods as part of CAP have long been a valuable source of revenue to EU countries. Thus each attempt to revise or even repeal the subsidies or tariffs from CAP is met with stiff opposition.

In 2011, Jean-Claude Trichet stepped down as president of the European Central Bank.

*See also:* Bernanke, Ben; Draghi, Mario; Lagarde, Christine

### Selected Works by Jean-Claude Trichet

Unpublished papers and speeches.

### Selected Works about Jean-Claude Trichet

Business Insider. "Jean-Claude Trichet." http://www.businessinsider.com/blackboard/jean-claude-trichet#ixzz26uD5oUL5 (accessed October 2012).

Edmond Israel Foundation. "Biography of Jean-Claude Trichet, Recipient of the Vision for Europe Award 2008." http://www.ei-foundation.lu/vision/08bio_trichet.htm (accessed October 2012).

Organisation for Economic Co-operation and Development Staff. "Transparency Is the Key to Stability, Trichet Says." In *Sustainable Development and the New Economy: Forum Highlights, 2001*, 49. Paris: OECD, 2001.

David A. Dieterle

# TULLOCK, GORDON

Born: February 13, 1922, in Rockford, Illinois; American; public choice theory, rent seeking theory; Major Works: *The Calculus of Consent: Logical Foundations of Constitutional Democracy* (with James Buchanan) (1962), *The Social Dilemma: The Economics of War and Revolution* (1974), *The Economics of Special Privilege and Rent Seeking* (1989).

Gordon Tullock is considered one of the leaders and forward thinkers of the twenty-first-century classical economists. His contributions in the field of classical economics are both impressive and often understated. Tullock's interdisciplinary study of behavioral economics and political theory helped initiate a new focus in economics. His ideas launched a new journal, *Public Choice*, and inspired additional study and research by a new group of economists who became known as the Public Choice Society.

Gordon Tullock was born on February 13, 1922, in Rockford, Illinois. He attended public schools in Rockford before enrolling at the University of Chicago in 1940. He completed the initial two-year program in only a year. He barely took one economics course, a course taught by Henry Simons. His progress was interrupted in 1943, however, when he was drafted into the U.S. Army. Tullock was deployed for a brief stint to Europe before being reassigned as a clerk. As the war came to a close, Tullock's unit was demobilized and he was sent home.

Upon returning home, Tullock continued his studies at the University of Chicago where he earned his law degree in 1947. Following a brief experiment in law, where Tullock experienced moderate success in the courtroom, he accepted a position as an officer with the Foreign Service. The Foreign Service took him to Asia for a decade and from 1947 until 1956. He held positions in China, Hong Kong, and Korea. During this time, he also pursued Chinese studies at Yale and Cornell. During this turbulent time in Asia, Tullock learned a substantial amount about the government and its inner workings. Tullock resigned from the Foreign Service upon his return to the United States in 1956.

Tullock served as research director for the Princeton Panel, a subsidiary of the Gallup organization. By this time, Tullock had already published in several journals. In 1958–59, he secured a postdoctoral fellowship at the Thomas Jefferson Center for Political Economics at the University of Virginia where he met future Nobel laureate James Buchanan, another classical economist who would be influential in his life. Tullock's seminal paper on applying theory and analysis to majority voting propelled Tullock into a new realm of critical thinkers.

With the publication of *The Calculus of Consent* with Buchanan in 1962, Tullock combined the behavioral economics of choice with political theory. This type of unconventional combination of ideas sparked several other efforts as well. In 1966, Tullock launched a journal called *Papers in Non-Market Decision Making*, which would later be known as *Public Choice*. The journal later inspired a series of monthly meetings, which became a group known as the Public Choice Society. Tullock served the society as its president. Tullock first introduced the idea of rent seeking during this time. Rent seeking is the manipulation of information through lobbying or other means to redistribute existing wealth as opposed to creating new wealth.

Tullock spent over five decades in university settings. He went from the University of Virginia to Rice University and then to Virginia Polytechnic Institute, now known as Virginia Tech. Along with colleague Charles Goetz, he launched what would be known as the Center for Study of Public Choice in 1968 and was reunited with Buchanan. Tullock's law background provided the basis from which to build a strong foundation in the field. Public choice theory combined economics with political science.

By the 1970s Blacksburg, Virginia, had become the geographical home of the Center for the Study of Public Choice. An administrative shake-up in Blacksburg during the latter part of the 1970s caused the center to be relocated to George Mason University in 1983. The move for Tullock brought him closer to the epicenter of his universe—Washington, DC, a place where economics and politics collided.

Tullock accepted a position as the Karl Eller Professor of Economics and Political Science with the University of Arizona in 1987. Tullock brought new energy to the faculty in Tucson, a faculty that focused on experimental economics, a field of great interest to Tullock. He spent 12 years at the University of Arizona before returning to George Mason University in 1999.

Tullock served his academic communities by publishing of journals, articles, and books, and by serving the scholarly community in a variety of other capacities. Tullock was recognized as a distinguished fellow from the American Economic Association in 1998.

Gordon Tullock retired from George Mason University in 2008.

*See also:* Buchanan, James; Simons, Henry

### Selected Works by Gordon Tullock

Tullock, Gordon. *The Economics of Special Privilege and Rent Seeking*. Boston: Kluwer Academic, 1989.

Tullock, Gordon. *Public Goods, Redistribution and Rent Seeking*. Northampton, MA: Edward Elgar Publishing, 2005.

Tullock, Gordon. *The Social Dilemma: The Economics of War and Revolution*. Blacksburg, VA: University Publications, 1974.

Tullock, Gordon, and James Buchanan. *The Calculus of Consent: Logical Foundations of Constitutional Democracy*. Ann Arbor: University of Michigan Press, 1962.

Tullock, Gordon, Arthur Seldon, and Gordon L. Brady. *Government Failure: A Primer in Public Choice*. Washington, DC: Cato Institute, 2002.

### Selected Works about Gordon Tullock

George Mason University. "Gordon Tullock." http://economics.gmu.edu/people/gtullockemeritus (accessed January 2012).

Mercatus Center. "Gordon Tullock." http://mercatus.org/gordon-tullock (accessed January 2012).

Rowley, Charles K., and Daniel Houser." Life and Times of Gordon Tullock." *Public Choice*. 152, nos. 1–2 (July 2012): 3–27.

*William S. Chappell*

## TURGOT, JACQUES

Born: May 10, 1727, in Paris, France; Died: March 18, 1781, in Paris, France; French; political economy, capital theory, Physiocrat; Major Works: *Elegy to Gournay* (1759), *Reflections on the Formation and Distribution of Wealth* (1766), *Six Projects of Edicts* (1776).

Jacques Turgot, Baron de Laune, a Frenchman, was expected by his family to enter the church. Turgot instead elected for a career within the French government beginning in 1752. Although his writings related to economics were limited, he articulated the unwritten ideas of other influential theorists such as his mentor,

Jacques Claude Marie Vincent, Marquis de Gournay. Further, he introduced his own ideas and implemented these during his work as a government administrator in the region of Limoges and later as French controller-general (finance minister). Turgot died in 1781.

Anne Robert Jacques Turgot was born on May 10, 1727, in Paris, France. His initial academic training was such to prepare one for entering the church, including attendance at the Sorbonne for theology in Paris and presenting two dissertations, but he sought a role in government administration instead, ultimately rising to the role of controller-general (finance minister). Throughout his life, he studied cartography, languages (modern and ancient), religion, music, and the sciences, and made contributions to the field of economics. Brewer (1987) claims that Turgot should be considered the founder of the classical school of economics and argues that his 1767 work was foundational for the concept now known as diminishing returns. This is an impressive accomplishment for an eighteenth-century administrator who wrote comparatively little about economics during his brief career, and whose work was largely ignored or disclaimed by his contemporaries.

Through the 1750s salons of Paris, Turgot came into contact with the free-market intellectual group labeled the Physiocrats, which influenced his ideas and writings. Over time, he was affiliated with Vincent de Gournay, François Quesnay, Dupont de Nemours (later his assistant), and Voltaire, among others. His writings not only commemorated the ideas of others but were included in the notes and journals of his peers.

In the *Elegy to Gournay* (1759) following his mentor's death, Turgot articulated ideas of his mentor not recorded elsewhere. He criticized the economic statutes that were in place at the time for restricting commerce and needlessly placing economic power in the hands of few people; the free-market idea of "laissez-faire" economics is now attributed as a statement made by Gournay. Turgot also criticized restrictions on international trade; he thought they were unnecessary, as trade would be voluntary between two self-interested parties. Predating Adam Smith's later work *An Inquiry into the Nature and Causes of the Wealth of Nations* (1776), Turgot described the free market as the means by which a seller could ensure that the price of a product exceeded the cost of production and, likewise, the buyer would receive the best product for the price. Turgot thought that government regulations inherently act as a tax on the consumer.

Turgot was appointed to the position of intendant (tax collector) of Limoges in August 1761 and would serve in this role until 1774. As intendant, he attempted to create a more equitable taxation scheme within his region, reduce the contribution of his region to the French government, and spend tax revenues locally to support infrastructure rather than rely upon forced or conscripted labor. In *Reflections on the Formation and Distribution of Wealth* (1766), he reiterates Quesnay's belief that land is the only form of wealth and thus only the net product of that land should be taxed, writing previously about the problems of existing taxes while not articulating the virtues of his proposed tax only on land.

After the death of King Louis XV and the ascension of King Louis XVI in 1774, Turgot was appointed to a brief stint as minister of the navy in July 1774. In

August 1774, he was appointed as French controller-general (finance minister), which provided an opportunity to attempt the same reforms as during his experience in Limoges. He immediately provided the king with guidance to reduce spending such that there would be "No bankruptcy. No tax increases. No loans." The failure of these reforms as outlined in the *Six Edicts of March 1776* led to his ouster from the position of controller-general within two months.

The free-market reforms proposed by Turgot dealt with numerous issues: the removal of price and transportation controls on agricultural and meat products; the removal of paid petty offices; the dissolution of trade guilds that restricted opportunities for employment; and the removal of the royalty's ability to conscript farm workers for no pay in the construction of infrastructure. While unpopular with the very large working class, these initiatives were untenable due to the power of the more affluent in influencing opinion against this liberal program. Some theorists claim that the failure of these market reforms and the Flour War (*guerre des farines*) of 1775—caused by pricing differentials during periods of time when markets were nonregulated as compared to regulated—were precursors to the French Revolution in 1789.

In April 1776, he wrote of the American Revolution and the implications to the finances of France, recommending that the country not become involved in the war, projecting that the most probable outcome would be an eventual American victory over the British while positing the ramifications of each outcome.

Anne Robert Jacques Turgot died on March 18, 1781, in Paris, France.

*See also:* Malthus, Thomas; Quesnay, François ; Ricardo, David; Smith, Adam

### Selected Works by Jacques Turgot

Turgot, Jacques. "Elegy to Gournay" (1759). In *The Economics of A. R. J. Turgot*. Translated and edited by P. D. Groenewegen, 43–95. The Hague, Netherlands: Martinus Nijhoff, 1977.

Turgot, Jacques. "Reflections on the Formation and Distribution of Wealth" (1766). In *The Economics of A. R. J. Turgot*. Translated and edited by P. D. Groenewegen, 20–42. The Hague, Netherlands: Martinus Nijhoff, 1977.

Turgot, Jacques. *Six Projects of Edicts—Together with Explanatory Preambles Enacting Sundry Reforms* (1776). Translated and edited by Robert P. Shepherd. New York: Columbia University, 1903.

### Selected Works about Jacques Turgot

"Anne-Robert-Jacques Turgot." In *The Concise Encyclopedia of Economics*. Edited by David R. Henderson. The Library of Economics and Liberty. http://www.econlib.org/library/Enc/bios/Turgot.html (accessed August 2012).

Powell, Jim. "Anne Robert Jacques Turgot, Who First Put Laissez-Faire Principles into Action: Turgot Was a Man of Truth, Courage, and Compassion." *The Freeman, Ideas on Liberty* 47, no. 8 (August 1997). http://www.thefreemanonline.org/features/anne-robert-jacques-turgot-who-first-put-laissez-faire-principles-into-action/ (accessed October 2012).

Shepherd, Robert P. *Turgot and the Six Edicts*. New York: Columbia University, 1903.

*Michael B. Becraft*

# TYSON, LAURA

Born: June 28, 1947, in Bayonne, New Jersey; American; macroeconomics, industrial competitiveness, trade, public policy; Major Works: *The Yugoslav Economic System and Its Performance in the 1970s* (1980), *Trade Economic Adjustment in Eastern Europe* (1985), *Who's Bashing Whom: Conflict in High Technology Industries* (1992).

Laura Tyson is an American economist and the S. K. and Angela Chan Professor of Global Management at the Haas School of Business at the University of California, Berkeley. She is an expert in trade and international competitiveness. In addition, she is also a member of President Barack Obama's Council of Jobs and Competitiveness, of Obama's Economic Recovery Advisory Board (PERAB), and of former secretary of state Hillary Clinton's Foreign Affairs Policy Board. She was the first female chair of the Council of Economic Advisers (1993–95) and then served as part of the President's National Economic Council (1995–96) during the Clinton administration. She has published books and numerous articles on industrial competitiveness and trade.

Laura D'Andrea Tyson was born on June 28, 1947, in Bayonne, New Jersey. Her father was a World War II GI veteran who became an accountant and her

Former Clinton administration member and professor at University of California, Berkeley Laura Tyson speaks during the Clinton Global Initiative in 2011. (AP/Wide World Photos)

mother was a housewife. Tyson majored in economics at Smith College, graduating summa cum laude in 1969. She continued on to earn her PhD in economics from the Massachusetts Institute of Technology in 1974. Tyson worked as a professor of economics at Princeton University for three years before she moved to the University of California, Berkeley, in 1977. She served as the dean of the Berkeley Haas School of Business from 1998 to 2001 and as the first female dean of the London Business School from 2002 to 2006. She was the only woman to head a major U.S. business school (Berkeley) and she was the first woman to lead a top 10 international business school (London).

Tyson also founded the London Business School's Center for Women in Business. While working in London, the United Kingdom's Department of Trade and Industry appointed Tyson chair of a task force on nonexecutive directors, which authored a recommendation for the recruitment and development of nonexecutive directors. Tyson has since returned to the University of California, Berkeley, where she is the S. K. and Angela Chan Professor of Global Management at the Haas School of Business.

As part of the Obama and Clinton teams, Tyson greatly influenced the presidents' domestic and international monetary policy. As chair of the Council of Economic Advisers, she provided guidance and analysis on all economic policy concerns, the economic forecasts, and the annual *Economic Report of the President*.

Tyson has published many books and articles on trade, industrial competitiveness, and transitions of European countries to market systems. Her studies include focus on worldwide trends in gender gaps for women in education, economics, politics, and health.

In academia, her work centers on globalization, trade liberalization, the impact of high technology, and domestic economics. She regularly promotes the benefits of globalization for domestic economies, yet some fear she may favor protectionist measures due to the Berkeley campus reputation of antiglobalization. Tyson advocates concern for these ideas such as global warming and environmental impact, but promotes the ethical responsibility of the businesses involved.

In addition to her work at Berkeley where she was cited as the winner of its Distinguished Teaching Award, Tyson is also a senior adviser at the McKinsey Global Institute, Credit Suisse Research Institute, and The Rock Creek Group. She continues to write opinion columns for many sources such as the *New York Times*, *BusinessWeek*, and The *Financial Times*. Tyson is a member of the World Economic Forum's Global Agenda Council, National Academies' Board on Science, Technology and Economic Policy, and the National Academies Committee on Research Universities to name a few. She serves on the boards of directors and advisory boards of many companies such as Morgan Stanley AT&T, Newman's Own, and the Peter G. Peterson Institute of International Economics.

*See also:* Summers, Lawrence

## Selected Works by Laura Tyson

Tyson, Laura. *Economic Adjustment in Eastern Europe*. RAND Report. San Diego, CA: RAND, 1985.

Tyson, Laura. *Who's Bashing Whom: Trade Conflict in High-Technology Industries*. Washington, DC: Institute for International Economics, 1992.

Tyson, Laura. *The Yugoslav Economic System and Its Performance in the 1970s*. Berkeley: Institute of International Studies, University of California, 1980.

## Selected Works about Laura Tyson

Greenslade, Nick. "The First Lady of Business." *The Observer*, May 20, 2006. http://www.guardian.co.uk/business/2006/may/21/theobserver.observerbusiness3 (accessed August 2012).

"Laura D'Andrea Tyson (1947–)." In *Distinguished Women Economists*. Edited by James Cicarelli and Julianne Cicarelli, 202–5. Westport, CT: Praeger, 2003.

The White House. "President's Economic Recovery Advisory Board." http://www.whitehouse.gov/administration/eop/perab/members/tyson (accessed August 2012).

*Kathryn Lloyd Gustafson*

## VEBLEN, THORSTEIN

Born: July 30, 1857, in Cato, Wisconsin; Died: August 3, 1929, in Menlo Park, California; American; evolutionary and institutional economics; Major Works: *The Theory of the Leisure Class: An Economic Study of Institutions* (1899), *The Theory of Business Enterprise* (1904).

Thorstein Veblen was best known for his theories on conspicuous consumption in the area of evolutionary economics and sociology. He believed that technological advances were the driving forces behind cultural change, but refused to automatically connect change with progress. He was most known for his theories regarding conspicuous consumption. His most famous work was *The Theory of the Leisure Class* (1889). Veblen died in 1929.

Thorstein Bunde Veblen was born on July 30, 1857, in Cato, Wisconsin. He grew up in a small Norwegian community of central Wisconsin speaking very little English. Veblen began his formal higher education at Carleton College Academy, completing his undergraduate degree at Johns Hopkins University. Veblen earned his PhD from Yale University in 1884. While at Yale, Veblen was greatly influenced by Charles Darwin. During his graduate work he rejected the views of John Bates Clark, a neoclassical, and William Graham Sumner, founder of the pragmatist school of philosophy. Veblen's interest in Darwin was the springboard for his later interest and study in economics as an evolutionary science. Unable to find work after graduating from Yale, he returned to the family farm. Six years later he entered Cornell University to study economics.

Thorstein Veblen began his professional career with an appointment to the University of Chicago where he also edited the *Journal of Political Economy*. In 1906, Veblen left the University of Chicago for Stanford University. This began a series of professional moves for Veblen, moves often initiated for personal reasons or personal behavior and relationship issues with other colleagues. Veblen's credibility was often negatively influenced by a somewhat tumultuous personal life.

It is often thought that major contributors to a discipline are lifelong academics. This was not the case with Veblen. Veblen evolved from sociologist to economist. Veblen's most prominent work was *The Theory of the Leisure Class* (1899). In *Theory of the Leisure Class*, Veblen first offered two new theories both contrary to the capitalist thinking of the day. First, Veblen countered the prominent premise of private property of the period with his own idea that ownership brought excessive consumption beyond meeting basic economic wants. This excessive consumption Veblen named "pecuniary emulation." He went on to claim that pecuniary emulation would eventually spread from a personal issue to an issue for an entire economic system.

As an economist and social critic, Thorstein Veblen was one of the leading figures in the revolt against nineteenth-century social thought in the United States. Using Darwinian evolutionary theory, Veblen attacked the conservative economic doctrines of his times. He is best known for his first book, *The Theory of the Leisure Class* (1899). (Bettmann/Corbis)

From his idea of pecuniary emulation, he broadened his theory to his second major contribution to economic thought. Due to pecuniary emulation, he theorized that people sought excessive wealth beyond satisfying their basic economic wants because they liked the social prestige it gained them. One's ownership of the large estate, the fancy carriage, and the expensive suit, according to Veblen, were used as symbolic of one's wealth. It was Veblen who identified this consumption pattern as the theory of conspicuous consumption. With *The Theory of the Leisure Class*, Veblen and his ideas of "pecuniary emulation" and "conspicuous consumption" became conceptual models in historical, sociological and economic disciplines.

It was quite clear through his writings Veblen did not accept the economic theory of his day. He did not support the marginalist solutions or proposed economic cures for the capitalist economy of his day. Veblen believed the orthodox economic theories of his day were incorrect in their approaches by addressing the economy's ills directly. Through his sociological background, Veblen submitted that it was the culture and society that needed to be fixed, which in turn would solve the ills of the economy. To achieve this result, Veblen favored a complete restructuring of the capitalistic economy, not just reforming it. For Veblen, this was not enough. He promoted a total restructuring, which could be accomplished only with extensive government exploitation through a socialistic economic system.

To reference Veblen as unconventional would be a gross understatement. As sociologist Alan Wolfe writes in his Introduction, Veblen "skillfully ... wrote a book that will be read so long as the rich are different from the rest of us; which, if the future is anything like the past, they always will be."

Thorstein Veblen died on August 3, 1929, in Menlo Park, California, at the age of 72.

*See also:* Clark, John Bates; Marshall, Alfred; Marx, Karl

### Selected Works by Thorstein Veblen

Veblen, Thorstein. *Absentee Ownership: Business Enterprise in Recent Times: The Case of America*. New Brunswick, NJ: Transaction, 1923.

Veblen, Thorstein. *The Engineers and the Price System*. New York: B. W. Huebsch, 1921.

Veblen, Thorstein. *Imperial Germany and the Industrial Revolution*. New York: Macmillan, 1915.

Veblen, Thorstein. *An Inquiry into the Nature of Peace and the Terms of Its Perpetuation*. New York: Macmillan, 1917.

Veblen, Thorstein. *The Instinct of Workmanship: And the State of Industrial Arts*. New York: Macmillan, 1914.

Veblen, Thorstein. *The Theory of Business Enterprise*. New York: Charles Scribner and Sons, 1904.

Veblen, Thorstein. *The Theory of the Leisure Class: An Economic Study of Institutions*. New York: Macmillan, 1899.

### Selected Works about Thorstein Veblen

Diggins, John P. *Thorstein Veblen: Theorist of the Leisure Class*. Princeton, NJ: Princeton University Press, 1999.

Dowd, Douglas Fitzgerald. *Thorstein Veblen*. New Brunswick, NJ: Transaction, 2000.

Mills, Charles Wright, and Alan Wolfe. *The Power Elite*. New York: Oxford University Press, 1956.

Rienert, Erik, and Francesca Lidia Viano. *Thorstein Veblen: Economics for an Age of Crises*. London: Anthem Press, 2012.

*Dave Leapard*

## VICKREY, WILLIAM

Born: June 21, 1914, in Victoria, British Columbia; Died: October 11, 1996, in Harrison, New York; American; microeconomics, price theory, public finance, taxation, Nobel Prize (1996); Major Works: *Agenda for Progressive Taxation* (1947), "A Proposal for Revising New York's Subway Fare Structure" (1955).

William Vickrey was an American economist noted for his contributions in public finance including taxation, public price theory, public utility pricing, and transportation. Vickrey was considered the first to suggest congestion pricing for public transportation, raising prices during high-traffic times and in high-use areas and lower prices in less-used areas and during low-traffic times. In 1948, he was the first to suggest electronic payment of tolls on toll roads to reduce traffic congestion in toll booth areas. In the area of income tax, Vickrey asserted that the optimal income tax burden for individuals should be based on long-term earnings, not yearly earnings. He was awarded the Nobel Prize in 1996. Vickrey died in 1996.

William Spencer Vickrey was born on June 21, 1914, in Victoria, British Columbia. An American economist, he was educated in both Europe and the United States, graduating from Phillips Andover Academy in 1931. He attended Yale University and received his BS in mathematics in 1935. He studied economics while at Columbia University and received both his MA degree (1937) and his PhD (1948).

In 1945, Vickrey became a naturalized U.S. citizen. It was during the interim of his two graduate degrees when Vickrey began his work in the area of taxation. He worked for the National Resources Planning Board in Washington, DC, and the Division of Tax Research in the U.S. Treasury Department. As a Quaker, he objected vigorously to World War II. It was during this time that he designed a new inheritance tax for Puerto Rico. His doctoral dissertation, "Agenda for Progressive Taxation," completed in 1948, was later reprinted in 1972 as an economic classic. This 496-page thesis revealed that one's optimal income tax should not be based on one's year-to-year earnings but rather on a citizen's long-term economic situation.

Vickrey's teaching career began in 1946 at Columbia University as a lecturer in economics. As a New Yorker, he proposed the congestion pricing principle for its subway system. This principle, first written in 1952, was considered risky by elected officials as it recommended that subway fares be increased during peak times and in high-traffic sections and be lowered in others. This principle regarded time-of-day pricing as a way to balance the supply and demand of market forces. In 1958, he became a full professor and served as chairman of the Department of Economics from 1964 to 1967. He was later named McVickar Professor of Political Economy in 1971. He received an honorary degree from the University of Chicago in 1979. He retired as McVickar Professor Emeritus in 1982.

During his more than 60-year academic career, Vickrey researched a large range of subjects including taxation, public utilities, transportation, and urban problems. More specifically these included the efficient pricing of public utilities (electric power) in 1939 and 1940 for the Twentieth Century Fund. He was also considered to be a crusader for the efficiency of public services. In 1948, he created the idea that toll booths, which significantly slowed traffic flow, should have a means to use vehicle identifiers to be read electronically without slowing down the traffic. This electronic system is still in place today. In 1950, he and his colleague Carl Shoup helped develop a comprehensive program for revising the tax system of Japan. In 1951, he studied transit fares in New York City for the Mayor's Committee on Management Survey.

A basic economic principle is that incentives affect people's behavior. Asymmetric information is the term that refers to the fact that government officials never know as much about the people their policies affect as the people affected know about themselves. Vickrey theorized that a buyer and seller have unequal information about a transaction. Vickrey devised what is now called the Vickrey auction, where bids are sealed and the highest bid wins but the second-highest bid is the price paid.

Vickrey was interested in many interdisciplinary fields and was known for showing up at seminars around the university. His interests also included ethics and philosophy; he wrote a number of papers in both areas. He lectured widely and served as a consultant in the United States and overseas and to the United Nations. Vickrey was the founding member of Taxation, Resources, and Economic Development. A popular economist, he was a member of or associated with many professional and civic organizations. He was an active supporter of organizations promoting world peace.

In 1996, three days before his death, Vickrey shared the Nobel Prize in Economics with James Mirrlees for their fundamental contributions to the economic theory of incentives under asymmetric information. Vickrey was elected to the National Academy of Sciences and served as president of the American Economic Association in 1992. He was a fellow of the Econometric Society and received the F. E. Seidman Distinguished Award in Political Economy.

William Vickrey died on October 11, 1996, in Harrison, New York.

*See also:* Mirrlees, James

### Selected Works by William Vickrey

Vickrey, William. *Agenda for Progressive Taxation*. New York: Ronald Press, 1947.
Vickrey, William. "Auctions and Bidding Games." In *Recent Advances in Game Theory*. 15–27. Princeton University Conference, 1962.
Vickrey, William. "Averaging of Income for Income Tax Purposes." *Journal of Political Economy* 47 (1939): 379–97.
Vickrey, William. "Counterspeculation, Auctions, and Competitive Sealed Tenders." *Journal of Finance* 16 (1961): 8–37.
Vickrey, William. *Microstatics*. New York: Harcourt, Brace, and World, 1964.
Vickrey, William. "My Innovative Failures in Economics." *Atlantic Economic Journal* 21 (1993): 1–9.
Vickrey, William. "Pricing in Urban and Suburban Transport." *American Economic Review* 52, no. 2 (1963): 452–65.
Vickrey, William. "Progressive and Regressive Taxation." In *The New Palgrave: A Dictionary of Economics*. Vol. 3. Edited by John Eatwell, Murray Milgate, and Peter Newman, 1021–25. London: Macmillan, 1987.
Vickrey, William. "A Proposal for Revising New York's Subway Fare Structure." *Journal of the Operations Research Society of America* 3 (1955): 38–68.
Vickrey, William. "Some Objections to Marginal Cost Pricing." *Journal of Political Economy* 56 (1948): 218–38.
Vickrey, William. "Today's Task for Economists." *American Economic Review* 82 (1992): 1–10.
Vickrey, William. "Utility, Strategy and Social Decision Rules." *Quarterly Journal of Economics* 74 (1960): 507–35.

### Selected Works about William Vickrey

"Biography." NobelPrize.org. http://www.nobelprize.org/nobel_prizes/economics/laureates/1996/vickrey-bio.html (accessed June 2012).
National Academies Press. "William S. Vickrey by Dreze, Jacques H." http://www.nap.edu/html/biomems/wvickrey.html (accessed June 2012).
Victoria Transport Policy Institute. "Principles of Efficient Congestion Pricing, by William Vickrey, Columbia University, June 1992." http://www.vtpi.org/vickrey.htm/ (accessed June 2012).
"William S. Vickrey." In *The Concise Encyclopedia of Economics*. Edited by David R. Henderson. The Library of Economics and Liberty. http://www.econlib.org/library/Enc/bios/Vickrey.html (accessed June 2012).

*Carol Lynn Nute*

## VINER, JACOB

Born: May 3, 1892, in Montreal, Canada; Died: September 12, 1970, in Princeton, New Jersey; American; public policy, international trade, history of economic thought; Major Works: *Dumping: A Problem of International Trade* (1921), *The Customs Union Issue* (1950).

Jacob Viner was an accomplished economist of international stature, spanning the spectrum from pure theory to public policy. His major fields of research and influence were in the theory of international trade and the history of economic and social thought. Viner died in 1970.

Jacob Viner was born on May 3, 1892, in Montreal, Canada, and would later become a naturalized citizen of the United States. He graduated from McGill University in 1914, came to the United States, and received his doctorate from Harvard University in 1922, where he was a pupil of Frank W. Taussig, later becoming a close friend and colleague.

Viner was an instructor at the University of Chicago for nine years beginning in 1916 while writing his dissertation on international trade under the direction of Taussig. He subsequently held professorships at the University of Chicago from 1925 to 1946 and later at Princeton University from 1946 until 1960, when he was given emeritus status.

It was at the University of Chicago that he developed his seminal theories of international trade. Viner's first work was entitled *Dumping: A Problem in International Trade*, published in 1921. His thorough analysis of the economic significance of dumping as a method of international competition laid the groundwork for subsequent studies in international trade, including Viner's doctoral dissertation was published in 1924 as *Canada's Balance of International Indebtedness*.

Viner's lecture to commemorate the sesquicentennial of the publication of *The Wealth of Nations* titled "Adam Smith and Laissez Faire" in 1928; his *Studies in the Theory of International Trade* (1937), a history of trade theories and policies; and his "Guide to John Rae's *Life of Adam Smith*" established him, along with Joseph A. Schumpeter, as one of the leading economic historians of his time. Viner's 1940 Harris Foundation Lecture "International Economic Relations," published as *The Foundations of a More Stable World Order* in 1941, called for an international cooperation of political and economic resistance to all forms of dictatorship.

In 1950 Viner, now at Princeton University, published *The Customs Union Issue*, an important groundbreaking study analyzing the trade-creating and trade-destroying effects of customs unions throughout the nineteenth and twentieth centuries. Also in 1950, he delivered a series of lectures at the National University in Brazil entitled *International Trade and Economic Development* (1953) that applied international trade theory to present-day problems. In 1958, *The Long View and the Short: Studies in Economic Theory and Policy* was published in commemoration of Viner's 65th birthday. This compilation of previously published essays ranging from economic theory and policy, to the history of economic thought and shorter book reviews, also contained his famous 1930 essay "Cost Curves and Supply Curves," making an important microcontribution by helping to simplify the Marshallian long-run average cost or planning curve.

Viner, along with Frank Knight and Henry Simons, has been identified as a cofounder of the Chicago School of economics. Additionally, he was editor of the *Journal of Political Economy* for 18 years, served the U.S. Tariff Commission and the Shipping Board during World War I. He participated in the early planning of the Social Security program of the 1930s and was a consultant to the U.S. State Department and the board of governors of the Federal Reserve.

Jacob Viner served as president of the American Economic Association in 1939. He is a permanent member of the Institute for Advanced Study at Princeton and an honorary fellow at the London School of Economics. Jacob Viner was awarded the Frances A. Walker Medal by the American Economic Association in 1962.

Jacob Viner died on September 12, 1970, in Princeton, New Jersey.

*See also:* Knight, Frank; Schumpeter, Joseph; Simons, Henry; Smith, Adam; Taussig, Frank

### Selected Works by Jacob Viner

Viner, Jacob. *Canada's Balance of International Indebtedness, 1900–1913*. Cambridge, MA.: Harvard University Press, 1924.

Viner, Jacob. *The Customs Union Issue*. New York: Carnegie Endowment for International Peace, 1950.

Viner, Jacob. *Dumping: A Problem of International Trade*. Chicago: University of Chicago Press, 1921.

Viner, Jacob. *International Trade and Economic Development: Lectures Delivered at the National University of Brazil*. New York: Free Press, 1953.

Viner, Jacob. *The Long View and the Short: Studies in Economic Theory and Policy*. New York: Free Press, 1958.

Viner, Jacob. *Studies in the Theory of International Trade*. New York: Harper and Brothers, 1937.

### Selected Works about Jacob Viner

Ekelund, Robert B., Jr., and Hebert Robert F. "Alfred Marshall and the Neoclassical Synthesis." In *A History of Economic Theory and Method*. 5th ed., 344–80. Long Grove, IL: Waveland Press, 2007.

Roncaglia, Alessandro. "Marshallism in the United States: From John Bates Clark to Jacob Viner." In *The Wealth of Ideas: A History of Economic Thought*, 372–74. Cambridge: Cambridge University Press, 2005.

*Joseph A. Weglarz*

## VOLCKER, PAUL

Born: September 5, 1927, in Cape May, New Jersey; American; financial economist, monetarist, chairman of the Federal Reserve Board (1979–87); Major Work: *Good Intentions Corrupted: The Oil-for-Food Scandal and the Threat to the U.N.* (with Jeffrey A. Meyer and Mark G. Califano) (2006).

Paul Volcker became chairman of the Federal Reserve Board in 1979, during a period of historically high inflation rates accompanied by low economic growth rates, known as stagflation. During such periods, economic policy makers are presented with a dilemma, since policy to control inflation will often result in

Under Chairman Paul Volcker's direction, the Federal Reserve helped end a period of unprecedented inflation in the United States in the 1970s and 1980s. (AP/Wide World Photos)

depressed economic conditions, including high unemployment. Volcker, unlike previous Federal Reserve Board chairmen, implemented an unpopular monetary policy to lower inflation rates. At the time, his actions were widely criticized. Though the policy was unpopular and there were negative consequences, Volcker was successful in lowering and controlling the inflation rate.

Paul Adolph Volcker was born on September 5, 1927, in Cape May, New Jersey, and grew up in Teaneck, New Jersey. He graduated from Princeton University in 1949, obtained an MA from Harvard University in 1951, and studied at the London School of Economics after graduate school. Volcker has been awarded more than 50 honorary degrees recognizing his contributions as an economist.

Volcker's first job began in 1952 as an economist at the Federal Reserve Bank of New York before leaving government employment to become a financial economist at Chase Manhattan Bank in 1957. In 1962, he returned to government service in the Department of Treasury as the director of financial analysis and was promoted in 1963 to deputy undersecretary for monetary affairs. Volcker returned to the private sector in 1965 as vice president of Chase Manhattan Bank. Again returning to government service in 1969, he was appointed to the position of undersecretary for monetary affairs at the Treasury Department. While serving in this capacity, he was an important participant in ending the Bretton Woods agreement that had established exchange rates based on gold and removing the United States from the gold standard. In ending the Bretton Woods agreement, the dollar and the other currencies were allowed to float in determining their values. Next, Volcker became a senior fellow at the Woodrow Wilson School of Public and International Affairs at Princeton University in 1974 before becoming president of the Federal Reserve Bank of New York in 1975 until 1979.

Volcker was appointed as chairman of the Federal Reserve Board in 1979. His appointment took place in the midst of an economic period known as stagflation. During stagflation, inflation rates are abnormally high and economic growth rates are low. Inflation peaked at 13.5 percent in 1981. Immediately upon becoming chairman, Volcker implemented a monetary policy targeting money supply growth as a method to drastically lower inflation rates. In order to accomplish this, Volcker increased the federal funds rate to a high of 20 percent and the prime rate rose to 21.5 percent in 1981. This policy was widely criticized since the effect was to radically increase unemployment (9.7% and 9.8% in 1982 and 1983, respectively) and produce high interest rates (30-year fixed mortgage rates exceeded 13%), which further slowed economic activity. However, by 1983 his policy successfully lowered the inflation rate to 3.2 percent. Volcker's policy worked and inflation was brought under control. For many Americans, he went from the villain to the conqueror. Volcker left as Chairman of the Federal Reserve Board of Governors in 1987, replaced by Alan Greenspan.

After leaving the Federal Reserve, he joined the small investment banking firm of James D. Wolfensohn Inc. In 1996, Volcker became chair of the Independent Committee of Eminent Persons (became commonly known as the Volcker Commission), which investigated money held in Swiss banks by Holocaust victims. The result of Volcker's commission's investigation was to draw attention to a relationship between the Swiss banks and the Nazis. Their findings led to a $1.25 billion settlement to Holocaust survivors and their families. Volcker has served on a number of committees and foundations including: chairman of the International Accounting Standards Committee Foundation (2000–2006); head of an investigation of accounting practices of Arthur Andersen, which was responsible for auditing Enron (2002); led the UN's investigation of the UN oil-for-food program for Iraq (2004–5); and chairman of the Economy Recovery Advisory Board under President Barack Obama (2009–February 2011).

While serving on the Economy Recovery Advisory Board, he proposed in 2009 what became known as the Volcker Rule, which would have severely restricted commercial banks from capital market and trading activities—hedge funds, private equity funds, commodities trading, and derivatives—by separating commercial banks from investment banks. The rule proposed by Volcker was not enacted, but a less stringent version was passed in the Financial Reform Act of 2010.

Descriptions of Volcker include irascibly honest, an inflexible man of integrity, Mr. Incorruptible, and a fair and strong leader in troubled times. Standing at six feet seven inches tall and armed with a determined personality, Volcker was an imposing and unyielding policy maker who was successful in doing what other chairman were unable to do. He reined in inflation during a time of double-digit inflation rates, but is also criticized for putting the American economy into recession. Politically, Volcker is considered a Democrat; however, his reputation during government service has generally been that of being nonpartisan. Volcker's economic perspective is one of caution, faith in markets, and common sense.

*See also:* Burns, Arthur; Greenspan, Alan

**Selected Works by Paul Volcker**

Meyer, Jeffrey A., Mark G. Califano, and Paul Volcker. *Good Intentions Corrupted: The Oil-for-Food Scandal and the Threat to the U.N.* New York: Public Affairs, 2006.

Volcker, Paul A., and Toyoo Gyohten. *Changing Fortunes.* New York: Times Books, 1992.

**Selected Works about Paul Volcker**

Morris, Charles. *The Sages: Warren Buffett, George Soros, Paul Volcker, and the Maelstrom of Markets.* New York: Public Affairs, 2009.

Neikirk, William R. *Volcker: Portrait of the Money Man.* New York: Congdon & Weed, 1987.

Treaster, Joseph. *Paul Volcker: The Making of a Financial Legend.* Hoboken, NJ: Wiley, 2004.

*Jean Kujawa*

## WALPOLE, SIR ROBERT

Born: August 26, 1676, in Norfolk, England; Died: March 18, 1745, in London, England; English; political economy, South Sea Company, taxation, trade policies; Major Works: unpublished speeches and pamphlets on various tax policies.

Robert Walpole was a British statesman who served as Great Britain's first prime minister for 20 years from 1721 until 1742. He is recognized as the longest-serving prime minister in British history, although the title of prime minister was actually not an official title during his years of service. He believed in stimulating the domestic economy through strong finance at home and keeping Great Britain out of expensive wars. He was made Earl of Oxford in 1742 and resigned as prime minister. Walpole died in 1745.

Robert Walpole was born on August 26, 1676, in Norfolk, England. He planned to enter the clergy and studied at Eton College from 1690 to 1695; he entered Kings College in Cambridge in 1696. However, due to the death of his eldest brother in 1698, he returned home to help his father manage the family estate. His father, Colonel Robert Walpole, died in 1700, and as the eldest surviving son he inherited the family estate and the family parliamentary seat in the borough of Castle Rising. He subsequently represented the more important borough of Kings Lyon for most of the next 40 years. Following in the footsteps of his father, he was a strong Whig Party leader. He was a controversial figure in politics and was several times investigated for dishonest behavior.

Walpole's political longevity has been attributed to his strong speaking ability and careful dispensing of political patronage. Walpole believed that the best way for him to maintain the support of all constituencies and keep his political power was to maintain the wealth and prosperity in the economy. Throughout his 20 years in power, he supported economic policies to promote wealth, commerce, industry, trade, and sound government finances. He believed in low taxes and wanted to keep Great Britain out of entangling wars so that resources could be focused on building the domestic economy.

Walpole was guided by the mercantilist theory that exports should exceed imports. He repealed export duties on most English goods. He also wanted to reduce or remove most import duties, which he believed would strengthen trade. He did not publish a book or a treatise on his economic policies. However, in his speeches and pamphlets, and through actual implementation of various tax policies during his administration, it is clear he understood the impact of tax policies on economic growth and fiscal responsibility. His financial policies helped give Great Britain a strong period of economic prosperity.

In 1720, Great Britain faced a financial crisis. The South Sea Company had been granted a trade monopoly to trade with Spanish colonies in the new world. In 1719, the government allowed the company to assume responsibility for larger amounts of the national debt through the exchange of shares of government debt for shares of the company. Politicians were given bribes and in turn expressed confidence in the company's future. Eager to profit from the expected trade, speculators quickly began to buy shares and wild buying ensued as the company also continued to artificially promote the success of the company. No wealth had been created, just a lot of speculative paper profits. The crash began in September and by December the stock had retreated to its original value. Investors were left with worthless paper, having invested their savings and pension funds. The South Sea scandal is described as the first time the term "bubble" was used for excessive speculation resulting in quick and unexpected losses.

In 1721, Walpole was given the role of prime minister by appointments as first lord of the Treasury and chancellor of the Exchequer. His first challenge was to restore confidence in the government and the economy as it faced financial ruin because of the South Sea "bubble."

Throughout his career, Walpole was concerned about the national debt. He proposed a sinking fund (designed to pay down the national debt from surplus or extra revenue) to provide confidence in the government's commitment to actually fulfill national debt obligations. However, at times he decided to use these funds to pay for unexpected government expenses when extra revenue was needed rather than raise taxes. In 1737, he defeated a proposal to reduce the interest on the national debt.

Walpole had developed a warehouse system where goods would be taxed when consumed from a warehouse with an excise tax rather than paid as a customs import duty. His proposal to expand this warehouse plan on selected items to check smuggling was defeated because the general public and politicians felt this would be the beginning of a general exercise tax on all products. He did establish standard values for imports currently being taxed to prevent fraud. Walpole did favor a tax on luxuries but not on the necessities of life. He also favored a lower tax on landowners.

Walpole believed the English colonies in the new world existed not to manufacture goods but to serve as a market to buy English goods. Colonies were in return to provide the raw materials for English manufactures. He did pass restrictive rules to discourage manufacture in the colonies, but he was not concerned with enforcement. This lack of enforcement interest by the British allowed the colonies to develop and flourish economically. Also, because of the favorable trade with the colonies, he had no real interest in heavy taxation on the colonies.

Sir Robert Walpole died on March 18, 1745, in London, England.

*See also:* Cantillon, Richard; Child, Josiah; Colbert, Jean-Baptiste; Hornick, Philipp Wilhelm von; Mun, Thomas; Quesnay, François

### Selected Works by Sir Robert Walpole

Unpublished speeches and pamphlets on various tax policies.

### Selected Works about Sir Robert Walpole

Brisco, Norris A. "The Economic Policy of Robert Walpole." In *Studies in History, Economics and Public Law*. Vol. 27, no. 1. Edited by Faculty of the Political Science of Columbia University. The Columbia University Press, London: P. S. King & Son, 1907. http://www.archive.org/stream/economicpolicyof00brisrich.

Hill, Brian. *Sir Robert Walpole: Sole and Prime Minister*. London: Hamish Hamilton, 1989.

Pearce, Edward. *The Great Man: Sir Robert Walpole*. London: Pimlico, 2008.

Plumb, John Harold. *The Growth of Political Stability in England 1675–1725*. London: Macmillan, 1967.

Plumb, John Harold. *Sir Robert Walpole*. 2 vols. London: Cresset Press, 1956–60.

*Jean Kujawa*

# WALRAS, LEON

Born: December 16, 1834, in Evreux, France; Died: January 5, 1910, in Claren, Switzerland; French; equilibrium theory, quantitative economics; Major Work: *Elements of Pure Economics* (1874, 1877).

Leon Walras greatly contributed to economic thought by introducing what we call today general equilibrium theory. Walras explained how the economy fits together with many goods using mathematical modeling. His seminal work was published in 1874 and 1877: *Elements of Pure Economics*. He is also credited as one of the founders of the "marginal revolution," developing the idea of marginal utility and the Lausanne School of economics. Walras died in 1910.

Marie-Esprit-Leon Walras (pronounced Valrasse) was born on December 16, 1834, in Evreux, France. His father, Auguste Walras, was a proto-marginalist economist and schoolteacher who encouraged his son to study mathematics. Walras was heavily influenced by his father's Socialist views regarding taxation and land reform. The senior Walras particularly influenced his son regarding the application of mathematics to economics. Augustin Cournot, a friend of Walras's father, also influenced the young Walras.

As a young man Walras was enrolled in the Paris School of Mines to study engineering. Not content with engineering, Walras worked in banking and journalism. He was a published romance novelist author and a railway clerk. However, when Walras finally turned to economics he experienced professional pleasures he had never before felt from his previous endeavors. He had found his professional calling. In 1870, Leon Walras was appointed to the Academy of Lausanne in Switzerland. This was his first and only academic appointment.

The dominant economic thinking of the time was centered in Great Britain and surrounded published works in English. Walras's work *Elements of Pure Economics* (in French), published in 1874 and 1877, was largely ignored because he wrote in French and was in Switzerland at the Academy of Lausanne training lawyers. He founded the Lausanne School of economics with the help and support of Vilfredo Pareto.

In what we call today general equilibrium theory, Walras devised a mathematical model using simultaneous equations to describe an entire economy. He attempted to show how an entire economy fits together leading to equilibrium. In his model there was an equation for each unknown leading to an equilibrium price and quantity for each commodity. Through his system of equations, a unique price and quantity was hypothesized (determined) for each good in the economy. Although not successful in showing how the economy fit together, he is considered the founder of general equilibrium theory. The system of equations developed by Walras led to the idea that if all the markets of an economic system are in equilibrium, then the economic system as a whole must be in equilibrium.

A major contribution of Walras was his contribution to the concept of marginal utility. Marginal utility is the study of measuring the results of adding (or subtracting) one more unit of a good or service to the satisfaction of the consumer. Marginal analysis is also used to determine the results of adding (or subtracting) one more unit of a productive resource (land, labor, or capital) in the production process. Walras study of marginal utility came three years after William Stanley Jevons and Carl Menger. Walras had developed the idea of marginal utility in complete isolation while in Switzerland. Yet along with Jevons and Menger, today he is considered one of the pioneers of the marginal economic way of thinking.

Walras retired in 1892 at the age of 58. He was very disillusioned by the neglect of his work.

Walras's legacy to the world is the transformation of economics to a mathematical-based discipline from its literacy roots. He explained how all markets are interrelated and that relationships between variables (e.g., commodities) can be described and analyzed mathematically.

Later in Walras's life, with his health failing, he attempted to enlarge on his writings in *Elements*. In 1896, he wrote *Social Economics* and *Studies in Applied Economics*. Walras himself considered these along with *Elements* as one integrated series devoted to his general equilibrium theory models. However, the academic world of economists rejected his final two works as substandard. Some economists even regarded them as a political statement for socialism.

Joseph Schumpeter hailed Leon Walras as the one of the greatest of all economists for his equations in *Elements*. Walras has been claimed to be the third most read nineteenth-century economists behind David Ricardo and Karl Marx.

Leon Walras died on January 5, 1910, in Claren, Switzerland, having spent his last years living with loneliness and dementia.

*See also:* Jevons, William Stanley; Menger, Carl; Schumpeter, Joseph; Stigler, George; Pareto, Vilfredo

### Selected Works by Leon Walras

Walras, Leon. *Elements of Pure Economics*. Lausanne, Switzerland: L. Corbaz & Cie., 1874.
Walras, Leon. *Elements of Pure Economics*. Translated and annotated by William Jaffe. London: Allen & Unwin, 1954.

### Selected Works about Leon Walras

Blaug, Mark. *Great Economists before Keynes*. Atlantic Highlands, NJ: Humanities Press International, 1986.
Schumpeter, Joseph. *History of Economic Analysis*. Edited by Elizabeth Boody, and published posthumously in 1954.
Stigler, George J. *Production and Distribution Theories*. New York: Macmillan, 1941, 1994.

*Martha R. Rowland*

## WEBB, BEATRICE

Born: January 22, 1858, in Gloucester, England; Died: April 30, 1943, in Hampshire, England; English; economic history, cofounder of the London School of Economics and Political Science; Major Works: *The History of Trade Unionism* (with Sidney Webb) (1894), *Industrial Democracy* (with Sidney Webb) (1897), *English Local Government*, Vols. 1–10 (with Sidney Webb) (between 1906 and 1929).

Beatrice Webb was one of the cofounders of the famous London School of Economics. In 1895, she was instrumental in the cofounding of the school as a response to her convictions as a member of the Fabian Society. Webb was a major researcher and writer on the poor in London during the nineteenth century. Focusing on economic historical history, Webb along with her husband, Sydney, were considered the preeminent historical researchers when between 1906 and 1929 they published 10 volumes of *English Local Government*. Webb died in 1943.

Beatrice Martha Potter (Webb) was born on January 22, 1858, in Gloucester, England. Her father was a wealthy railway engineer and she traveled widely as a child. She received little formal education but read extensively in the areas of philosophy, mathematics, and science.

In 1883, Webb joined the Charity Organization Society (COS) and began working with the poor. In 1886, she went to work as a researcher for her cousin Charles Booth. She became involved in studying the lives of working people living in London. It was her assignment of studying and investigating the lives of dock workers and sweat labor in the tailoring trade that would later lead to the publishing of several articles published in the journal *Nineteenth Century*. She also covered other topics including Jewish immigration.

Webb's research on would lead her to believe that poverty was caused less by the individual than by the governmental systems in place, over which the poor lacked control. Later, to better understand the organizations the working class had created for itself, Webb became interested in the work achieved by the different cooperative societies currently existing in many of Britain's industrial towns. While writing *The Cooperative Movement in Great Britain*, she contacted Sidney Webb who had also researched this topic. In 1892, they married. Since Webb had a considerable income from her deceased father's estate, both began to focus on their political interests and social reform. Sidney was a leading figure in the Fabian Society, which Webb later joined. The Fabian Society was a social order that believed capitalism had created an unjust and inefficient society. Later, when the society was bequeathed a large sum of money, it was the Webbs who suggested that the funds be used to create a new university. In 1895, the London School of Economics and Political Science was founded.

During their early years, Beatrice and Sidney Webb cowrote several books including *The History of Trade Unionism* (1894) and *Industrial Democracy* (1897). Their greatest work, *English Local Government*, was a 10-volume project published over a 25-year period. It was a history of the government from the seventeenth to the twentieth century and firmly established the Webbs as first-rank historical researchers. It became the standard work on the subject of the organization and function of English local government.

Continuing to be involved in politics on all levels, the Webbs would later write the *1902 and 1903 Education Acts*, which would set the pattern for public education for years to come. In an effort to end the Poor Law system in Britain, the Webbs authored the Minority Report, which, though rejected, has long been seen as a key influence on the emergence of Britain's welfare state (i.e., the welfare of the citizen is the responsibility of the state). In 1913, Webb started the Fabian Research Department and with her husband, a new political weekly, *The New Statesman*. In 1914, the Webbs became members of the Labour Party. During World War I, Webb served on a number of government committees and continued to write for a number of Fabian Society pamphlets. In 1929, her husband became Baron Passfield; Beatrice, however, refused to be known as Lady Passfield.

In 1932, disillusioned with their lack of success in politics and the Labour prospects, the Webbs visited the Soviet Union. During this time many changes were occurring there to ensure economic and political equality for women, as well as improvements in health and educational services. Upon their return, they spent three years writing a book called *Soviet Communism: A New Civilization?* (1935). This was later followed by another book, *The Truth about Soviet Russia* (1942).

Beatrice Webb died on April 30, 1943, in Hampshire, England.

*See also:* Bauer, Otto; Engels, Friedrich; Hilferding, Rudolf; Marx, Karl

## Selected Works by Beatrice Webb

Webb, Sidney, and Beatrice Webb. *English Local Government*. Vols. 1–10. London: Longmans, Green 1906–1929.

Webb, Sidney, and Beatrice Webb. *The History of Trade Unionism*. London: Longmans, Green, 1894.

Webb, Sidney, and Beatrice Webb. *Industrial Democracy*. London: Longmans, Green, 1897.

Webb, Sidney, and Beatrice Webb. *Soviet Communism: A New Civilization?* Vols. 1–2. New York: Scribner, 1935-1938.

Webb, Sidney, and Beatrice Webb. *The Truth about Soviet Russia*. London: Longmans, Green, 1942.

## Selected Works about Beatrice Webb

Muggeridge, Kitty, and Ruth Adam. *Beatrice Webb: A Life, 1858–1943*. New York: Knopf, 1968.

Seymour-Jones, Carole. *Beatrice Webb: A Life*. Lanham, MD: I. R. Dee, 1992.
Simkin, John. *Spartacus Educational*. http://www.spartacus.schoolnet.co.uk/TUwebbB.htm (accessed October 2012).

*Carol Lynn Nute*

## WEBER, MAX

Born: April 21, 1864, in Erfurt, Prussia; Died: June 14, 1920, in Munich, Germany; German; political economy, social sciences, sociology, economic systems; Major Works: *The Protestant Ethic and the Spirit of Capitalism* (1904–05), *Economy and Society* (1921–22).

Max Weber was an influential German political economist and sociologist. His work traced the roots of capitalism from within the Protestant religion. He also examines the connections between religion, culture, and economic systems of Chinese Confucianism and Taoism, Indian Hinduism and Buddhism, and ancient Judaism. Many would consider Weber, as well as Karl Marx and Emil Durkheim, a founder of modern social science. Weber died in 1920.

Maximilian Weber was born on April 21, 1864, in Erfurt, Prussia, as the oldest of six children. His father, Max Sr., a lawyer and politician, and his mother, Helene Fallenstein, well educated with strong Calvinistic convictions, created a prosperous and intellectually engaging household. Weber's brother Alfred would eventually become a noted economist and sociologist as well. Weber studied law, economics, and history at the University of Heidelberg in 1882 and then at the University of Berlin in 1884. In 1886, he passed his "Referendar" examination (similar to the American Bar examination) and earned his doctorate in law magna cum laude in 1889. His dissertation focused on South European trading companies of the Middle Ages. Weber earned notoriety after conducting research into the conditions of rural laborers in the East Elbian provinces of Prussia recommending the breaking of large estates for the use and incentive to keep workers in the area. In 1894, he accepted a position as a professor of political economy at Freiburg University. He then moved to the University of Heidelberg in 1896.

In the summer of 1897, Weber and his father had a notable confrontation regarding Weber Sr.'s treatment of his mother. Weber's father died shortly thereafter without resolution between the two. Weber then began to suffer symptoms of a nervous breakdown and spent the summer and fall of 1900 in a sanatorium, forcing him to give up his professorship in 1903. Weber slowly returned to academia as a private scholar, writing many influential works. He later helped to shape the well-known social science journal *Archiv fur Sozialwissenschaften und Sozialpolitik* with Edgar Jaffe and Werner Sombart.

At the beginning of World War I, Weber founded and managed nine military hospitals as part of the Reserve Military Hospitals Commission. Weber's political views slowly became more public through the wake of World War I until 1917 when he campaigned for constitutional reform of postwar Germany with universal suffrage and the empowerment of Parliament. At the end of the war, Weber was asked to join the German Armistice Commission at the Treaty of Versailles as well as to help draft the Weimar Constitution. In 1919, he taught at the universities of Vienna and Munich and continued to write.

Throughout his life, Weber did not shy from either controversy or political debate. He ran unsuccessfully as a liberal Democrat for a parliamentary seat. His wife, Marianne Weber, became a leader of women's rights and Weber also publically supported universal suffrage. Their home in Heidelberg became a gathering place for intellectuals and writers.

Weber was a founder of modern sociology. Weber believed that a social scientist's work should be value free; he advocated a rigorous separation of fact and value. In his most famous work, *The Protestant Ethic and the Spirit of Capitalism*, Weber began a comparative study of world religions and economic systems. He argued that the morality of Protestantism, specifically Calvinism, was the catalyst for entrepreneurship and capitalism. The Protestant work ethic, he thought, encourages people to accumulate wealth. Protestantism also encourages thoughtful, rational stewardship, which meant that Protestants were likely to reinvest their wealth rather than spend it. Weber's analysis of Protestantism was accompanied by various explanations of why capitalism did not develop in places with different religions.

In another influential work, *Economy and Society*, Weber describes rationalization as a shift from value-oriented social organization and action to one of goal-oriented organization and action. He darkly describes this change as a "polar night of icy darkness" that ultimately traps human life in the control of bureaucratic organizations.

Weber's methodology and his systems of classification are also noteworthy. Weber introduced the distinction between social class (one's relationship to the market), status class (religion and reputation), and party class (political affiliations), as the three classes that work together to determine one's potential future.

Weber felt that the study of economics should also include economically relevant and conditioned phenomena, or as he described it, social economics. He advocated for interdisciplinary work between economics and sociologists.

Max Weber died in Munich on June 14, 1920, from pneumonia.

*See also:* Bauer, Otto; Engels, Friedrich; Hilferding, Rudolf; Marx, Karl

## Selected Works by Max Weber

Weber, Maximillian. *Economy and Society: An Outline of Interpretive Sociology*. 4th ed. Edited by Guenther Roth and Claus Wittich. Berkeley: University of California Press, 1978.

Weber, Maximilian. *The Protestant Ethic and the Spirit of Capitalism*. London: Allen & Unwin, 1930.

## Selected Works about Max Weber

Bendix, Reinhard. *Max Weber: An Intellectual Portrait*. Berkeley: University of California Press, 1978.

Rourke, Brian R. *Max Weber*. April 4, 2008. http://www.duke.edu/web/secmod/biographies/Weber.pdf (accessed August 2012).
Weber, Marianne. *Max Weber: A Biography*. New Brunswick, NJ: Transaction, 1988.

*Kathryn Lloyd Gustafson*

## WICKSELL, KNUT

Born: December 20, 1851, in Stockholm, Sweden; Died: May 3, 1926, in Stockholm, Sweden; Swedish; macroeconomics, monetary theory, inflation; Major Works: *Value, Capital and Rent* (1892), *Studies in the Theory of Public Finance* (1896), *Interest and Prices* (1898).

Knut Wicksell, a Swedish economist, is often referred to as the father of the Stockholm School of economics and of modern macroeconomics. He is known for his work fusing the Lausanne, the Austrian, and the Ricardian schools of economics. His strong Malthusian persuasion also enabled him to guide Swedish public policy with his view of a limited welfare state. Wicksell's work later influenced other notable economists such as Ludwig von Mises, Friedrich von Hayek, John Maynard Keynes, as well as fellow Swedes Bertil Ohlin, Gunnar Myrdal, and Dag Hammarskjold. Wicksell died in 1926.

Johan Gustaf Knut Wicksell was born on December 20, 1851, to a middle-class family in Stockholm, Sweden. His father, a businessman as well as real estate investor, died when Wicksell was 15. His mother had died earlier when Wicksell was seven. Fortunately, Wicksell along with his four siblings had enough financial resources for the family to finish high school. In 1869, Wicksell attended the University of Uppsala near Stockholm where he specialized in mathematics, physics, and astronomy. He graduated cum laude with a bachelor of science degree in only two years. He spent his next years as a social critic and lecturer developing his interest in social sciences. In 1885, he earned his doctorate in mathematics.

Wicksell received the Victor Loren Foundation scholarship, which allowed him to spend three years studying economics in Germany and Austria. In Vienna, he attended the lectures of Carl Menger, the founder of the Austrian School of economics. Wicksell then worked to support himself, and later his common-law wife and two sons, with small inheritances, grants, and minor income earned through public lectures and other writings.

In 1896 at the age of 45, Wicksell returned to college and earned his doctorate in economics from the University of Uppsala. He next applied for a lectureship in economics at the University of Uppsala, but was declined for his radical social views and lack of a law degree, deemed necessary for the position. He was, however, recommended for the university law school and he completed these studies in two years instead of the usual four. Wicksell was then appointed an economics lecturer at the University of Uppsala in 1899. The next year he became a professor at the University of Lund where he worked until he retired in 1916.

In his book *Value, Capital and Rent* (1893), Wicksell blended the equilibrium theory (Leon Walras), the theory of capital (Eugen von Böhm-Bawerk), and later the marginal productivity theory of income distribution (David Ricardo).

Wicksell explained that each factor of production was worth the equivalent of its marginal product generated from creating the final good. He also clarified that interest income becomes an incentive for replacing capital consumed over time.

Wicksell's *Studies in the Theory of Public Finance* (1896) illustrated the theory of marginal cost-benefit analysis with respect to government taxing and spending. Wicksell focused on those individuals who would either receive the benefits or bear the tax costs. Wicksell emphasized the importance of the rules public agents use when making decisions, stating that reform should stem from rule changes not influencing the agents themselves. Wicksell concluded that even an open economy would not equalize wealth in a society. Only those who had wealth in the first place would benefit with economic growth. Wicksell believed this was why government intervention was necessary to improve the national welfare.

In *Interest and Prices* (1898), Wicksell altered the accepted view of the quantity theory of money where a general increase in prices could not occur unless there was an increase in the quantity of money. He built upon Böhm-Bawerk's concept of the period of production and determined that the "natural rate" of interest was what market forces would establish if goods were bartered. In a complex economic system, money—used as a medium of exchange—allows the monetary authority to change the monetary supply and change the "money rate"—no longer the natural rate—used for borrowers. If this interest rate is kept below the natural rate due to monetary expansion, society would experience a "cumulative process" of increased prices. Only a return to the natural interest rate would stop the cycle. This cumulative process theory would later influence John Maynard Keynes's ideas of growth and recession and Joseph Schumpeter's creative destruction theory.

Throughout his lifetime, Wicksell was not afraid of controversy. At the university, Wicksell became interested in many social issues of his day such as drunkenness, prostitution, poverty, and overpopulation. He believed that the slowing of population growth would allow greater wealth building, but he rejected Thomas Malthus's idea of "moral restraint." On another occasion Wicksell defended the right to freedom of expression when he gave a satirical public lecture about the Immaculate Conception. He was tried, was convicted of blasphemy, and spent two months in prison.

Knut Wicksell died in Stockholm, Sweden, on May 3, 1926, from a stomach disorder complicated by pneumonia.

*See also:* Böhm-Bawerk, Eugen von; Hayek, Friedrich von; Keynes, John Maynard; Mises, Ludwig von; Myrdal, Gunnar; Ohlin, Bertil; Ricardo, David; Schumpeter, Joseph; Walras, Leon

### Selected Works by Knut Wicksell

Wicksell, Knut. *Finanztheoretische Untersuchungen: Nebst Darstellung Und Kritik Des Steuerwesens Schwedens* (German ed.) or *Theory of Public Finance*. Charleston, SC: Nabu Press, 2010.

Wicksell, Knut. *Interest and Prices*. Washington, DC: Josephs Press, 2008.

Wicksell, Knut. *Value, Capital and Rent*. Auburn, AL: Ludwig von Mises Institute, 2007.

### Selected Works about Knut Wicksell

Anderson, Richard G. "Wicksell's Natural Rate." Federal Reserve Bank of St. Louis. March 2005. http://research.stlouisfed.org/publications/mt/20050301/cover.pdf (accessed October, 2012).

Blaug, Mark. *Knut Wicksell (1851–1926)*. Northampton, MA: Edward Elgar, 1992.

Ebeling, Richard M. *Knut Wicksell: A Sesquicentennial Appreciation*. December 2001. http://www.thefreemanonline.org/features/knut-wicksell-a-sesquicentennial-appreciation/ (accessed October, 2012).

Formaini, Robert L. "Knut Wicksell: The Birth of Modern Monetary Policy." Federal Reserve Bank of Dallas. *Economic Insights* 9, no. 1 (2004).

Gardlund, Torsted. *The Life of Knut Wicksell*. Translated by Nancy Adler. Northampton, MA: Edward Elgar, 1996.

*Kathryn Lloyd Gustafson*

## WICKSTEED, PHILIP

Born: October 25, 1844, in Leeds, West Yorkshire, England; Died: March 18, 1927, in Childrey, Berkshire, England; English; Unitarian minister and lecturer, Austrian economics; Major Works: *An Essay on the Co-ordination of the Laws of Distribution* (1894), *The Common Sense of Political Economy* (1910).

Philip Wicksteed was a Unitarian minister who spent the latter part of his life as a lecturer of economics. He is best known in economics for *An Essay on the Co-ordination of the Laws of Distribution* (1894) and *The Common Sense of Political Economy* (1910). He is usually associated with Austrian economics, though he had no formal connection. His research focused on marginalism, microeconomics, and the actions of the economic individual in the marketplace. Wicksteed died in 1927.

Philip Henry Wicksteed was born on October 25, 1844, in Leeds, England, to a Unitarian minister. He received his London MA (with a gold medal for classics) in 1867 after studying at University College (1861–64) and Manchester New College (1864–67). In 1868, he became a Unitarian minister in various locations around London and Manchester until deciding to lecture full-time in 1897. While he was a minister, he developed a great interest in the ethics of the commercial society, and his study of economics led him to begin lecturing in 1884.

Wicksteed's involvement with economics began around the early 1880s as he began to study Henry George's *Progress and Poverty* (1879) and the works of William Stanley Jevons. Wicksteed was exposed to *Progress and Poverty* through his membership with the Socialist Fabian Society in the 1880s, and the books seemed to open his eyes to distribution and labor problems that lead to poverty. He expressed in a letter to George his agreement about the benefits of the expanded use of technology in agriculture and the problem of labor not being helped by increased capital. Wicksteed would also take ideas about the labor supply from Jevons and expand on them.

Despite the Socialist nature of the Fabian Society, Wicksteed was a major opponent of the views of Karl Marx. One of Wicksteed's first forays into economic writing came in 1884 in a critique of Marx's *Das Kapital*, where Wicksteed pointed out fallacies in Marx's ideas of "abstract labor" and the cost of production in the labor force. In 1888, Wicksteed published his *Alphabet of Economic Science*, which focused on utility, marginal utility, and the theory of demand. During this time, Wicksteed began what would be a more than 30-year involvement with the London Society for the Extension of University Teaching (LSEUT), during which time he would teach over 300 courses in a variety of subjects, especially economics.

In 1888, Wicksteed republished a series of articles in *Getting and Spending: Papers on the Meaning and Uses of Money*. This work focused on what our spending reveals about what we value. In 1894, he published *An Essay on the Co-ordination of the Laws of Distribution*, which dealt with expansions of ideas by Jevons and George on marginal products. In this work, he proves how the distribution of marginal factors, if paid relative to marginal product, would exhaust the total product. This relationship between marginal factors and marginal product with total product was first made by Leonhard Euler and became known as Euler's theorem.

Wicksteed's next major work was not until 1910, the two-volume *Common Sense of Political Economy*. It attempted to examine human action in a comprehensive way including morality in its analysis of economic action. This subjective approach to economics also worked against the concept of the economic man by taking economic actions as "non-tuistic." Wicksteed coined the word "non-tuistic" to describe an economic transaction where the consequences to one involved in the economic decision are not considered. He also used economics to analyze seemingly noneconomic behaviors, like spending time leisurely. Aristotle's ethical works and Jevons's marginalism were both very influential to Wicksteed's publication.

Among other insights, the *Common Sense* is known for the idea that prices will come to an equilibrium or balance point now known as the Wicksteedian state of rest (WSR). To illustrate the movement of prices, Wicksteed used the example of a fruit market, where prices are determined and changed in real time as fruit sellers observe customer behavior and factor in customer preferences. Through this process, an equilibrium price can be achieved through the actions in the market place. According to WSR, forecast errors in plain state of rest (PSR) values will lead to the ideal values of the WSR.

Wicksteed was also accomplished as a medievalist through his study of Dante Alighieri and Thomas Aquinas. Part of his work with the LSEUT included lectures on sociology, Dante, Aristotle, and other topics. He wrote *Six Sermons on Dante* (1879), *The Religion of Time and Eternity* (1899), *Dante and Aquinas* (1913), *The Reactions between Dogma and Philosophy, Illustrated from the Works of St. Thomas Aquinas* (1920), and other books and articles, as well as a translation of Dante's *Divine Comedy*. He was also a student of Old Testament criticism and Dutch liberal theology.

Philip Wicksteed died on March 18, 1927, in Childrey, England.

*See also:* George, Henry; Jevons, William Stanley; Marx, Karl; Robbins, Lionel

### Selected Works by Philip Wicksteed

Wicksteed, Philip. *The Alphabet of Economic Science*. London: Macmillan, 1888.
Wicksteed, Philip. *The Common Sense of Political Economy*. London: Macmillan, 1910.
Wicksteed, Philip. *An Essay on the Co-ordination of the Laws of Distribution* (1894). New York: Macmillan, 1932.

### Selected Works about Philip Wicksteed

Herford, C. H. *Philip Henry Wicksteed: His Life and Work*. London: J. M. Dent, 1931.
Howson, Susan. "The Origins of Lionel Robbins's Essay on the Nature and Significance of Economic Science." *History of Political Economy* 36, no. 3 (2004): 413–43.
Kirzner, Israel M. "Biography of Philip Wicksteed: The 'Austrian' Economist." Ludwig von Mises Institute. http://mises.org/page/1465/Biography-of-Philip-Wicksteed-The-Austrian-Economist (accessed April 2012).
Klein, Peter G. "The Mundane Economics of the Austrian School." *Quarterly Journal of Austrian Economics* 11 (2008): 165–87.
Newton, Bernard. "The Impact of Henry George on British Economics, I: The First Phase of Response, 1879–82; Leslie, Wicksteed and Hobson." *The American Journal of Economics and Sociology* 30, no. 2 (1971): 179–86.
Spencer, David A. "'The Labor-Less Labor Supply Model' in the Era before Philip Wicksteed." *Journal of the History of Economic Thought* 25, no. 4 (2003): 505–13.

*Joseph Lee Hauser*

## WIESER, FRIEDRICH VON

Born: July 10, 1851, in Vienna, Austria; Died: July 22, 1926, in Vienna, Austria; Austrian; Austrian School, microeconomics, cost theory, currency, taxation, social economics; Major Works: *Natural Value* (1893), *Social Economics* (1914), *Geld* [*Money*] (1928).

Friedrich von Wieser was an Austrian economist and one of the early members of the Austrian School. His views on value were important to the development of the Austrian School of economics and he is best known for developing the ideas of marginal utility and opportunity cost as aspects of his view. Wieser died in 1926.

Friedrich von Wieser was born on July 10, 1851, into a prominent family. His father was a War Ministry official in the Austro-Hungarian Empire. He entered the University of Vienna in 1868 to study law and sociology. However, while there he would read the work of Carl Menger and would switch his studies to economics. He would pursue his economic work, choosing to spend 1875–77 studying in Germany at the universities in Heidelberg, Jena, and Leipzig with his boyhood friend, Eugen Böhm-Bawerk. Böhm-Bawerk would later become his brother-in-law.

Upon completion of his studies in 1877, Wieser would enter the Austro-Hungarian civil service. He would serve there until 1883 when he would receive an offer to teach at the University of Vienna. After one year he would move to teach at the university in Prague until 1889. In 1889, Carl Menger would resign from the University of Vienna, leaving his chair open. Weiser would follow Menger as chair at the University of Vienna. He would teach there until 1922. This was interrupted when in 1917, Wieser was elected to the Upper House of the Austro-Hungarian Parliament. He was later appointed minister of commerce. Those responsibilities disappeared however with the dismantling of the empire with the conclusion of the First World War, and he would return to teaching.

While at Vienna, Wieser would leave his mark by teaching other economic notables like Ludwig von Mises, Friedrich von Hayek, and Joseph Schumpeter. He would also contribute to the field in his own right, publishing a number of influential and important works.

His first major work, *Natural Value*, explored an area described by Menger. In it, Wieser coined the term "marginal utility." He would connect the idea of cost to his description of marginal utility and would differentiate between value in use and exchange value. The former he saw as a measure of a good's usefulness and the latter a function of the income of the demander. Equally important in this work was his imputation theory to discover the value of inputs in production.

Weiser theorized that the value of an additional unit of input was ultimately based on the marginal utility of the additional units produced. Or put more simply, the value of the input was determined by the additional utility that resulted. This was different from previous explanations, which incorporated marginal revenue received by the producer.

His second major work, *Social Economics*, was published in 1914. This work, which has had great impact on economics teachers, develops the concept now known as opportunity cost. The concept illuminates the social value, in addition to the strictly economic values, coincident with economic choices. The concept helps explain why individuals make subjective choices rather than pure utility calculations.

His final work, *Geld* (*Money* in English), published in 1927, was an expansion of the quantity theory of money. Wieser would spend his closing years lecturing largely on sociology rather than economics.

Friedrich von Wieser died on July 22, 1926, in Vienna, Austria.

*See also:* Böhm-Bawerk, Eugen von; Hayek, Friedrich von; Menger, Carl; Mises, Ludwig von; Schumpeter, Joseph

### Selected Works by Friedrich von Wieser

Wieser, Friedrich von. *Natural Value*. London: MacMillan, 1893.
Wieser, Friedrich von. *Social Economics*. New York: Greenberg, 1928.

### Selected Works about Friedrich von Wieser

"Friedrich von Weiser Biography Theory." economictheories.org. http://www.economictheories.org/2008/08/friedrich-von-wieser-biography-theory.html (accessed August 2012).
Morgenstern, Oscar. "Friedrich von Wieser, 1851–1926," *American Economic Review* 17, no. 4 (December 1927): 669–74.
Obituary, Friedrich von Wieser. *The Economic Journal* 37 (June 1927).

*Timothy P. Schilling*

## WILLIAMS, WALTER

Born: March 31, 1936, in Philadelphia, Pennsylvania; American; government in economy, minimum wage, private property, libertarianism; Major Works: *The State against Blacks* (1982), *South Africa's War against Capitalism* (1990), *Do the Right Thing: The People's Economist Speaks* (1995), *Race and Economics: How Much Can Be Blamed on Discrimination?* (2011).

Walter Williams has served as the John M. Olin Distinguished Professor of Economics at George Mason University in Fairfax, Virginia, since 1980. He is the author of 10 books and over 150 publications, appearing in scholarly journals such as *Economic Inquiry* and the *American Economic Review* as well as popular publications such as *Newsweek* and *National Review*. He frequently appears on television and radio programs such as *Nightline*, *Face the Nation*, or the *Rush Limbaugh* show. He is known for his libertarian views including the limited role of government intervention with respect to minorities.

Walter Edward Williams was born on March 31, 1936, in Philadelphia, Pennsylvania. William's mother, Catherine, raised him in a single-parent home living at one point in the Richard Allen housing projects. He is second cousin to basketball player Julius Erving, otherwise known as "Dr. J." After graduating from Philadelphia public schools, Williams spent two years as a taxi driver before becoming a private in the U.S. Army. Williams began as sociology major at California State College in Los Angeles before switching to economics. Although he earned a D in his first course, he persevered and ultimately earned his bachelor's degree in economics from California State College in Los Angeles in 1965. He received his MA in 1968 and PhD in 1972, both in economics from the University of California, Los Angeles. Williams studied under Nobel laureates Armen Alchian and Milton Friedman. He also began a lasting friendship with visiting economist Thomas Sowell. Williams began to question whether government social programs like minimum wage and affirmative action were truly helping those in need. Williams then taught for eight years at Temple University in Philadelphia before joining the economics faculty at George Mason University in Fairfax, Virginia, in 1980.

Williams's work is doubtful of the effectiveness of government social programs to promote prosperity. In his 1982 book, *The State against Blacks*, Williams argues that government initiatives such as affirmative action only serve to hurt minorities and stifle their economic progress. He writes that college admission standards should be equal for all, and that minorities do not benefit from artificial measures designed to boost their enrollment numbers. Williams believes that substandard test performance by minorities is the result of substandard secondary education and family breakdown. He writes that the government has a monopoly on public education, which leads to a low quality with lack of competition. Government programs such as welfare reward childbirth out of wedlock, thus contributing to the collapse of black communities. PBS used his book *The State against Blacks* as the basis for the documentary *Good Intentions*.

In addition, Williams argues that minimum wage laws price low-skill workers out of the market and increase unemployment. In 1977, the Joint Economic

Committee of Congress asked him to write about minimum wage. Williams reported that black teenage unemployment was lower than whites' before minimum wage and higher after. His research also found that the Davis-Bacon Act of 1931 that required high worker wages for federally financed construction projects was designed to discriminate workers based on their race.

Similarly, in *South Africa's War against Capitalism* (1990), Williams argues that South African apartheid was not created for white exploitation but as a reaction to World War I, designed to encourage the hiring of higher-paid white workers. Williams again promotes his belief that capitalism without government intervention will provide the highest standard of living for all.

Williams's overall support of deregulation and laissez-faire government can be described as libertarian. Williams is one of few scholars to defend individuals' rights to sell bodily organs. He continues to write a nationally syndicated weekly column carried in approximately 140 newspapers and multiple websites. He regularly participates in national debates, conferences, and lectures, as well as provides expert testimony before congressional committees on public policy issues. He serves on the boards of Grove City College, Reason Foundation, and Chase Foundation and the advisory boards of the Cato Institute, Landmark Legal Foundation, Institute of Economic Affairs, and the Heritage Foundation. He has received numerous awards and fellowships such as the Foundation for Economic Education Adam Smith Award, Hoover Institution national fellow, and the Ford Foundation fellow to name a few. Williams is a member of the Mont Pelerin Society and the American Economic Association.

*See also:* Friedman, Milton; Hazlitt, Henry; Sowell, Thomas

### Selected Works by Walter Williams

Williams, Walter. *Do the Right Thing: The People's Economist Speaks*. Stanford, CA: Hoover Institution Press, 1995.

Williams, Walter. *Race and Economics: How Much Can Be Blamed on Discrimination?* Stanford, CA: Hoover Institution Press, 2011.

Williams, Walter. *South Africa's War against Capitalism*. Rev. ed. Cape Town, South Africa: Juta, 1990.

Williams, Walter. *The State against Blacks*. New York: McGraw-Hill, 1982.

### Selected Works about Walter Williams

Miller, John J. "Walter Williams." *Hey Miller*. March 19, 2011. http://www.heymiller.com/2011/03/walter-williams/ (accessed August 2012).

National Cable Satellite Operation. "Q&A Walter E. Williams." March 18, 2012. http://www.q-and-a.org/Program/?ProgramID=1383 (accessed August 2012).

Riley, Jason L. "The State against Blacks." *Wall Street Journal*, January 22, 2011. http://online.wsj.com/article/SB10001424052748704881304576094221050061598.html (accessed August 2012).

Williams, Walter E. *Up from the Projects: An Autobiography*. Stanford, CA: Hoover Institution Press, 2010.

*Kathryn Lloyd Gustafson*

## WILLIAMSON, OLIVER

Born: September 27, 1932, in Superior, Wisconsin; American; utility theory, governance, institutions, antitrust, Nobel Prize (2009); Major Works: *Markets and Hierarchies* (1975), *The Economic Institutions of Capitalism: Firms, Markets, Relational Contracting* (1985).

Oliver Williamson is a retired professor of economics from the University of Pennsylvania, the University of California, and Yale University. He is most well known for being awarded the 2009 Nobel Prize in Economics (with Elinor Ostrom) for his work on governance and institutions. A majority of his expansive writings have dealt with the organization of firms and how business decisions are made.

Oliver Edward Williamson was born in Superior, Wisconsin, on September 27, 1932, to Scott and Lucille Williamson, both former high school teachers. He graduated from the Massachusetts Institute of Technology (MIT) with an engineering degree in 1955. He earned his MBA from Stanford University in 1960 and a PhD in economics from Carnegie-Mellon University in 1963. His transition from engineering to business to economics was aided by taking an economics class taught by James Howell while working on his MBA and realizing that he had an interest in an economics and organization theory program offered at Carnegie-Mellon, to which he was awarded a three-year fellowship by the Ford Foundation.

Williamson won a dissertation competition through the Ford Foundation. The dissertation was the foundation for the book *The Economics of Discretionary Behavior: Managerial Objectives in a Theory of the Firm*, published in 1964. This book is considered the first effective way to base firm behavior on utility maximization instead of on profit maximization. He began teaching at the University of California, Berkeley, in 1963. He moved on to the University of Pennsylvania in 1965, where he taught until 1983. He was active in many academic pursuits including editing the *Bell Journal of Economics* in 1974 to 1977 and again from 1979 to 1981. He served the U.S. Department of Justice as a consultant from 1967 to 1969 and the Federal Trade Commission from 1978 to 1980. He served as a special economic assistant to the assistant attorney general for antitrust in 1966 and 1967.

While working as a special economic assistant, Williamson was able to contribute a great deal to the field of antitrust economics. A major focus of his work in this field was to allow economists to view horizontal integration of companies as not necessarily something that creates or necessitates a monopolistic advantage over a competitor. His viewpoint was that these integrations could simply be to improve economic efficiency for the company. Through his study of this topic, he developed the naive trade-off model, or what is now usually called the Williamson trade-off to help understand the relationship between cost savings and an increase in consumer prices. His ideas were finally incorporated into the Justice Department's Horizontal Merger Guidelines in 1997.

Williamson also provided some work that was beneficial to understanding vertical integration in a new way. In 1967, the Supreme Court ruled in *United*

*States v. Arnold, Schwinn & Co.* that companies that maintained too much control over the distribution of their product were in violation of the Sherman Antitrust Act. Williamson believed and sought to prove that some restraints placed by companies on how their product was distributed was legitimate and necessary for effective business. In subsequent court cases over the years, the Court has changed its course, finally stating in *Leegin Creative Leather Products, Inc. v. PSKS, Inc.* (2007) that certain antitrust laws should be viewed on a case-by-case basis and not with certain blanket restrictions.

After writing several articles on this topic in the early 1970s, Williamson published *Markets and Hierarchies* in 1975 and *The Economic Institutions of Capitalism* in 1985, which allowed him to demonstrate his broader view of transaction cost economics. In the latter book, he dealt with the limitations of bureaucracies to efficiently limit the size of firms in a consistent way. Due in part to his education, many of his ideas pushed the boundaries of orthodox economic thought at the time, though many of his ideas have become accepted practice by today's economists.

Williamson would leave his position in 1983 at the University of Pennsylvania to work with the School of Organization and Management, the Law School, and the Economics Department at Yale University. The nature of this work, which included being the founding editor of the *Journal of the Law, Economics, and Organization*, would be very taxing on Williamson. He left in 1988 to return to Berkeley where he taught until his retirement in 2004. He served as chair of the Academic Senate at Berkeley from 1995 to 1996, and was influential in reshaping several programs within the Haas School of Business and the Economics Department.

Williamson's crowning achievement would be the awarding of the Nobel Prize with Elinor Ostrom in 2009. He earned the award for his work in showing how firms ought to distinguish between decisions that should be made internally and decisions that should be dictated by market pressures. His body of work stresses the benefits of opportunistic decision making in firms. Williamson's ideas reflect an idea of governance opposite from Ostrom. Williams argues that governance is a problem because of human self-interest, while Ostrom says it is a solution.

Williamson continues to write and perform research through his retirement. He is active in presenting workshops and writing articles, having written hundreds of published and reprinted articles over the years. He has received 10 different honorary degrees since 1986 and several economics awards. A current workshop held at Berkeley also bears his name.

*See also:* Ostrom, Elinor

## Selected Works by Oliver Williamson

Aoiki, Masahiko, Bo Gustafsson, and Oliver E. Williamson, eds. *The Firm as a Nexus of Treaties*. London: Sage, 1989.

Phillips, Almarin, and Oliver E. Williamson, eds. *Prices: Issues in Theory, Practice, and Public Policy*. Philadelphia: University of Pennsylvania, 1968.

Williamson, Oliver E., ed. *Antitrust Law and Economics*. Houston, TX: Dame, 1980.
Williamson, Oliver. *Corporate Control and Business Behavior: An Inquiry into the Effects of Organization Form on Enterprise Behavior*. Englewood Cliffs, NJ: Prentice-Hall, 1970.
Williamson, Oliver. *The Economic Institutions of Capitalism: Firms, Markets, Relational Contracting*. New York: Free Press, 1985.
Williamson, Oliver. *The Economics of Discretionary Behavior: Managerial Objectives in a Theory of the Firm*. Englewood Cliffs, NJ: Prentice-Hall, 1964.
Williamson, Oliver. *Industrial Organization*. London: Edward Elgar, 1990.
Williamson, Oliver. *Markets and Hierarchies: Analysis and Antitrust Implications*. New York: Free Press, 1975.
Williamson, Oliver. *The Mechanisms of Governance*. Oxford: Oxford University Press, 1996.
Williamson, Oliver. *Organization Theory: From Chester Barnard to the Present and Beyond*. New York: Oxford University Press, 1990.
Williamson, Oliver E., and Scott E. Masten, eds. *The Economics of Transaction Costs*. Brookfield, VT: Edward Elgar, 1999.
Williamson, Oliver E., and Sidney Winter, eds. *The Nature of the Firm*. New York: Oxford University Press, 1991.

### Selected Works about Oliver Williamson

Earl, Peter E., And Jason Potts. "A Nobel Prize for Governance and Institutions: Oliver Williamson and Elinor Ostrom." *Review of Political Economy* 23, no. 1 (January 2011): 1–24.
Shapiro, Carl. "A Tribute to Oliver Williamson: Antitrust Economics." *California Management Review* 52, no. 2 (Winter 2010): 138–46.
Williamson, Oliver E. "Autobiography." Nobelprize.org. http://www.nobelprize.org/nobel_prizes/economics/laureates/2009/williamson.html (accessed April 2012).

*Joseph Lee Hauser*

## WOLF, MARTIN

Born: August 16, 1946, in London, England; British; economics journalism, globalization, financial crisis; Major Works: *The Resistible Appeal of Fortress Europe* (1994), *Why Globalization Works* (2004), *Fixing Global Finance* (2008).

Martin Wolf is a British economist who turned his interest to economic journalism and economic education. Beginning his career with the World Bank, he also directed the Trade Policy Research Centre as the director of studies. In 1987, he turned to economics journalism when he joined the *Financial Times* as associate editor. He later added chief economics commentator to his roles. In 2000, Wolf was awarded the coveted Commander of the British Empire (CBE) for his many contributions to financial journalism. He is the 2012 winner of Italy's highly lauded honor, the International Ischia Journalism Prize.

Martin Wolf was born on August 16, 1946, in London, England, the son of an Austrian Jewish playwright and a Dutch Jew. Though the personal journeys of his parents during the Holocaust years made him cautious about politics, it spurred his curiosity in economics. Wolf began his education at University College School, finishing an undergraduate degree at Corpus Christi College of Oxford University. While at Oxford, Wolf continued his graduate studies at Nuffield College, earning his master of philosophy in economics in 1971.

Wolf began his career as a young professional at the World Bank in 1971, becoming senior economist in 1974. He stayed on with the World Bank until 1981 when he was named the Trade Policy Research Centre's director of studies in London. Wolf joined the *Financial Times* in 1987 as chief economics leader writer. Wolf became associate editor in 1990 and chief economics commentator in 1996, both of which positions he still holds today.

A prolific thinker and candid writer on economic topics, Martin Wolf has been cast as a world authority on matters of globalization. The Leigh Bureau website labeled Wolf one of the foremost authorities on the new global economy and the financial crises. Warrant for this acclaim is found in his many contributions to the field of economics in the form of columns, editorial pieces, and major works. Many of his journalistic ventures have won wide praise among his financial peers as well as academic and political audiences.

His *Financial Times* monthly column is a staple in the world financial community. Wolf's 1994 *The Resistible Appeal of Fortress Europe* illustrates his command of economic concepts and forward thinking. In his 2004 *Why Globalization Works*, he advocates a win-win global market scenario fit for underdeveloped and wealthy nations and everyone in between. He argues that that the problems of nations rest not with their market operations but rather with the influx of government and political intervention.

An early believer in the theories of John Maynard Keynes, Wolf's position changed as he became a supporter of free-market enterprise. In his 2008 *Fixing Global Finance*, Wolf argues the finer points of how to address the financial crises afflicting world powers such as the United States. By retracing economic events and highlighting trends, Wolf's in-depth research and commentary have far-reaching implications for today's global economy. In a lessons-learned mentality, he develops a sound and respectable argument that to become economically stable across the globe, new and old economies alike must have resilient financial systems in place backed by a stable national currency. *China Business News* named *Fixing Global Finance* its "Financial Book of the Year" for 2009.

Wolf has enjoyed an illustrious career in economics, drawing the attention and admiration of institutions abroad. He served as a member of the Independent Commission on Banking since June of 2010 and also held positions at Nuffield College of Oxford University, the Oxford Institute for Economic Policy in Oxonia, and the Council on Foreign Relations. He was also a member of the board of governors of the Ben Gurion University of the Negev in Israel. Other notable positions include Forum fellow with the World Economic Forum (WEF) in Davos and member of WEF's International Media Council.

Martin Wolf has been decorated with numerous awards and distinctions. Wolf has enjoyed acclaim in his native England, receiving the highly coveted Commander of the British Empire (CBE) in 2000. He has also been honored by New Zealand, Fundacio Catalunya Oberta (Open Catalonia Foundation), Workworld Media, Editorial Intelligence, and U.S. Society of Business Writers and Editors. In 2009, he received the Ludwig Erhard Prize for outstanding contributions in economic journalism. Wolf has had several honorary doctoral degrees conferred on his behalf from Nottingham University, Warwick University, London University, and the London School of Economics.

Wolf was one of *Foreign Policy*'s Top 100 Global Thinkers in 2009, 2010, and 2011. According to the Leigh Bureau, Wolf was the first to receive *FIRST* magazine's coveted Special Advocacy Award in recognition of his well-founded commentaries on global markets. This year he claimed Italy's top-prize in journalism when he was announced as the 2012 International Ischia Journalism Prize beneficiary.

Though his positions may often be debated, his positions and views are highly respected and valued by government officials, economists, and academics. Wolf has commented on various matters involving the state of the global economy as well as nation-specific problems. His direct approach is a trademark of his commentary and perhaps a reason his honest portrayal of events has become a part of the world's financial and political landscape.

*See also:* Keynes, John Maynard; Singh, Manmohan

## Selected Works by Martin Wolf

Wolf, Martin. *Costs of Protecting Jobs in Textiles and Clothing.* London: Trade Policy Research Centre, 1984.

Wolf, Martin. *Fixing Global Finance.* Baltimore: Johns Hopkins University Press, 2008.

Wolf, Martin. *Global Implications of the European Community's Programme for Completing the Internal Market.* New York: Lehrman Institute, 1989.

Wolf, Martin. *India's Exports.* New York: Oxford University Press, for the World Bank, 1982.

Wolf, Martin. *The Resistible Appeal of Fortress Europe.* Rochester Paper 1. Washington, DC: American Enterprise Institute Press, 1994.

Wolf, Martin. *Why Globalization Works.* New Haven, CT: Yale University Press, 2004.

Wolf, Martin, and Donald B. Keesing. *Textile Quotas against Developing Countries.* London: Trade Policy Research Centre, 1980.

Wolf, Martin, Hans-Eckert Scharrer, and Christopher Johnson. *The Political Economy of EMU.* London: Royal Institute of International Affairs, 1997.

## Selected Works about Martin Wolf

Jones, Andrew. "Positive Thinking: Thomas Friedman and Martin Wolf." In *Globalization: Key Thinkers.* 130–47. Cambridge: Polity Press, 2010.

Krugman, Paul. "Martin Wolf Gets It." *New York Times*, August 30, 2011. http://krugman.blogs.nytimes.com/2011/08/31/martin-wolf-gets-it/ (accessed October 2012).

Leigh Bureau. "Martin Wolf." http://www.leighbureau.com/speaker.asp?id=272 (accessed October 2012).

Wolf, Martin. "Transcript: 'Fixing Global Finance' with Martin Wolf." SUNY Levin Institute. http://www.levininstitute.org/wolf/transcript.cfm (accessed October 2012).

*Joy Dooley-Sorrells*

## XIAOCHUAN, ZHOU

Born: January 29, 1948, in Yixing, Jiangsu province; Chinese; Chinese economist, banker (11th governor of the People's Bank of China); Major Work: "Reform the International Monetary System" (2009).

Zhou Xiaochuan is a Chinese economist and banker serving as the governor of the People's Bank of China (PBOC). He assumed his post as governor in December 2002. He is the 11th governor of China's central bank, responsible for the nation's monetary policy.

Zhou Xiaochuan was born January 29, 1948, in Yixing, Jiangsu province, China. Zhou graduated from the Beijing Institute of Chemical Technology in 1975. In 1985, he received his PhD in economic systems engineering from Tsinghua University. His career began with the Beijing Institute of Automation. In 1986, he served as assistant minister of foreign trade till 1989. During this time and to 1991, he was also a member of the National Committee of Economic Reform. Zhou also worked for the State Council on economic restructuring, serving on the Economic Policy Group of the State Council. He also held the position of deputy director of the Institute of Chinese Economic Reform Research.

He later served the State Commission for Restructuring the Economy and the Foreign Economic Relations and Trade. In 1995, he was appointed director of the State Administration of Foreign Exchange till April 1998. During this time, he also served as the vice governor of the PBOC.

In 1999, he was appointed China Construction Bank governor. During his tenure with the China Construction Bank, he was responsible for the establishment of a system to deal with the banking system's bad debts. Zhou was also responsible for overseeing China's immense quantity of foreign exchange reserves.

Prior to becoming governor of the PBOC, he held other positions at the central bank from 1996 to 1998, including deputy governor. He had previously served the Chinese government as director of the State Administration of Foreign Exchange, the governor for the China Construction Bank, and chairman of the China Securities Regulatory Commission.

Zhou became a member of the PBOC Monetary Policy Commission in March 2000. He was named governor of the PBOC in December 2002. He has since also assumed the position as chairman of PBOC's monetary policy committee. His career has been devoted to economic reform and liberalization of the financial markets.

As the country's number one banker, in 2010 Zhou came under pressure to adjust the Renminbi and revise its exchange rate-setting procedures.

Zhou Xiaochuan with Alan Greenspan in 2005. (AP/Wide World Photos)

Though Zhou has published more than 10 books and more than 100 academic articles in his homeland, Zhou has the rare distinction of being a Chinese official who has been published in the reviewed publication of the Bank of International Settlements ("Reform the International Monetary System," *BIS Review*, 2009). In his essay, Zhou advocates for the use of IMF Special Drawing Rights (SDRs), similar to Keynes's use of the "Bancor," which he proposed in the 1940s. Zhou has also made speeches where he has argued that global financial crises are made more severe by fundamental weaknesses in the international monetary system. In these speeches, he has advocated for a measured transition toward replacing the U.S. dollar as the global reserve currency, instead using IMF SDRs. He submits that the move will address the inadequacies of using a national currency as a global reserve currency, referring to the U.S. dollar.

Zhou was ranked fourth by *Foreign Policy* in the Top 100 Global Thinkers report of December 2010.

*See also:* Keynes, John Maynard

### Selected Work by Zhou Xiaochuan

Xiaochuan, Zhou. "Reform the International Monetary System." *BIS Review*, March 23, 2009. http://www.bis.org/review/r090402c.pdf (accessed October 2012).

### Selected Works about Zhou Xiaochuan

China Vitae. "Zhou Xiaochuan." http://www.chinavitae.com/biography/Zhou_Xiaochuan (accessed March 2011).
US-China Business Council. "Zhou Xiaochuan." http://www.uschina.org/public/china/govstructure/bio/zhouxiaochuan.html (accessed January 2011).

*David A. Dieterle*

# Y

## YELLEN, JANET

Born: August 13, 1946, in Brooklyn, New York; American; macroeconomics, unemployment, fiscal policy, monetary policy; Major Work: *The Fabulous Decade: Macroeconomic Lessons from the 1990s* (2001).

Janet Yellen has served the academic sector in the classroom and the public sector as an advocate for the American people. She shared her knowledge of economics at Harvard University, the London School of Economics and Political Science, and the University of California, Berkeley, and she applied that knowledge while serving on the board of governors of the Federal Reserve System. Yellen currently holds the position of vice chairperson of the board of governors of the Federal Reserve System.

Janet Louise Yellen was born on August 13, 1946, in Brooklyn, New York. She graduated summa cum laude from Brown University in 1967 with a degree in economics and earned her PhD from Yale University in 1971. Yellen taught at Harvard as an associate professor from 1971 until 1976. She also taught at the London School of Economics and Political Science from 1978 until 1980 when she accepted a position with the University of California, Berkeley. She is professor emeritus of the Haas School of Business and has served as the Eugene E. and Catherine M. Trefethen Professor of Business and Professor of Economics. She specializes in macroeconomics with an emphasis in the causes and effects of unemployment.

President Bill Clinton nominated Yellen as the chair of the Council of Economic Advisers in 1997 after she served as a member of the board of governors of the Federal Reserve, a position she was appointed to in 1994. Her efforts were primarily focused on the stabilization of foreign exchange rates and international trade. Her work during the 1990s helped lead her into numerous leadership positions during the latter part of the decade and into the twenty-first century.

Yellen was named president and chief executive officer of the Twelfth District Federal Reserve Bank at San Francisco in 2004. Her work on the current state of the U.S. economy has prompted her testimony toward guiding appropriate macroeconomic and monetary policy for the betterment of the American people. She believes that policy should improve the lives of those it governs. Her emphasis has been on promoting policy that will both reduce the breadth, depth, and frequency of economic downturns as well as focus on long-term, sustainable growth over time. These policy changes are paramount in promoting a higher standard of living for the American people. Her work emphasized understanding the disparity of wage increases over the past 30 years, exploring the implications of attaining education and the impact of technology on the workforce.

Janet Yellen, vice chairwoman of the Federal Reserve Bank, speaks at the Economic Club of New York in 2011. (AP/Wide World Photos)

Yellen was named vice chair of the board of governors of the Federal Reserve System in October of 2010. She is also concurrently serving as a member of the board of governors until 2024.

Yellen's contributions to the economic community are vast as she has worked in the Federal Reserve System and in the classroom. She has written papers, taught classes, and helped shape monetary policy in the United States. Aside from these positions, she was a member of the Council on Foreign Relations, the American Academy of Arts and Sciences, Federal Open Market Committee, the Group of 30, the executive committee of the Bay Area Council, and a research associate of the National Bureau of Economic Research. She served as president of the Western Economic Association, vice president of the American Economic Association, and fellow of the Yale Corporation, and worked with a number of other organizations.

Janet Yellen is currently vice chair of the board of governors of the Federal Reserve System.

*See also:* Bernanke, Ben; Greenspan, Alan

### Selected Works by Janet Yellen

Akerlof, George, Andrew Rose, Janet Yellen, and Helga Hessenius. "East Germany in from the Cold: The Economic Aftermath of Currency Union." *Brookings Papers on Economic Activity* 22, no. 1 (1991): 1–106.

Yellen, Janet. "The Continuing Importance of Trade Liberalization." *Business Economics*, January 1, 1998.

Yellen, Janet. *The Inequality Paradox: Growth of Income Disparity*. Washington, DC: National Policy Association, 1998.

Yellen, Janet. "Trends in Income Inequality and Policy Responses." *Looking Ahead*, October 1997.

Yellen, Janet, George Akerlof, and Michael Katz. "An Analysis of Out-of-Wedlock Childbearing in the United States." *Journal of Economics* 111, no. 2 (May 1996): 277–317.

Yellen, Janet, and Alan Binder. *The Fabulous Decade: Macroeconomic Lessons from the 1990s*. New York: Century Foundation Press, 2001.

## Selected Works about Janet Yellen

Council of Economic Advisers. "Dr. Janet L. Yellen." http://clinton4.nara.gov/WH/EOP/CEA/html/yellen.html (accessed October 2012).

Federal Reserve. "Janet L. Yellen." http://www.federalreserve.gov/aboutthefed/bios/board/yellen.htm (accessed October 2012).

Lang, Kevin. *Poverty and Discrimination.* Princeton, NJ: Princeton University Press, 2007.

*William S. Chappell*

# Z

## ZOELLICK, ROBERT

Born: July 25, 1953, in Evergreen Park, Illinois; American; diplomat for international trade, president of the World Bank (2007); Major Works: "Campaign 2000: A Republican Foreign Policy" (2000), *America and Russia: Memos to a President* (coedited with Philip Zelikow) (2000), *America and the East Asian Crisis: Memos to a President* (coedited with Philip Zelikow) (2000), *America and the Balkans: Memos to a President* (coedited with Philip Zelikow) (2001).

Robert Zoellick became the 11th chief executive of the World Bank in 2007. A career public servant, Zoellick served in the U.S. State Department and U.S. Treasury, was a U.S. trade representative, and worked in the offices of Fannie Mae and in the White House for the president. Zoellick's main focus of public service was in economic policy and diplomatic affairs. He was the lead diplomat in many U.S. trade treaties. Zoellick was an adviser to several presidents, including Ronald Reagan, George H. Bush, and George H. W. Bush. He was a personal adviser to President George H. W. Bush. Zoellick was a major player in the U.S. post–Cold War economic policy.

Robert Bruce Zoellick was born on July 25, 1953, in Evergreen Park, Illinois. In 1975, he graduated from Swarthmore College. He attended Harvard Law School, graduating with honors with his JD degree. He stayed at Harvard, receiving a master's in public policy from the Harvard Kennedy School of Government in 1981.

Following graduation from Harvard, Zoellick entered U.S. government public service. Between 1985 and 1993, Zoellick served Treasury Secretary James Baker as a deputy assistant secretary for financial institutions policy and counselor to the secretary, and as an undersecretary of state within the State Department, and spent time in the White House as a deputy chief of staff. Zoellick led the U.S. delegation for the German unification in 1989 and 1990. Zoellick assisted the president in preparing for the 1991 and 1992 Economic Summits.

In 1993, Zoellick left the White House and joined Fannie Mae as executive vice president. In 1997, he made a temporary career change when he left Fannie Mae to join the U.S. Naval Academy.

Zoellick returned to public service and economic policy diplomacy in 2001 when he returned to the administration as the nation's 13th U.S. trade representative, a cabinet position in the White House. In his new role as trade representative, Zoellick negotiated free-trade agreements with many countries. He was instrumental in developing policies for global, regional, and bilateral agreements and launching the Doha Development Agenda of the World Trade Organization (WTO). He had significant influence in many countries becoming

Robert Zoellick, U.S trade representative, arrives at a hotel for the official opening ceremony of the World Trade Organization (WTO) in Doha, Qatar, in 2001. (AP/Wide World Photos)

members of the WTO, including China, Chinese Taipei, Cambodia, Vietnam, Russia, and Saudi Arabia.

Zoellick was also very influential in the negotiations of many of the free-trade agreements for the United States. He also served as an adviser to the U.S. Congress in many trade and economic policy agreements with many developing countries. He brought free-trade agreements with many South American countries and the developing countries in Africa to completion. He had a leadership role in initiating U.S. free-trade relations with many other countries including Peru, Colombia, and Panama.

In 2005, he returned to the State Department as a deputy secretary for a year prior to entering the private sector as a vice chairman at Goldman Sachs in 2006. In 2007, President George H. W. Bush appointed Robert Zoellick to be the 11th chief executive of the World Bank.

Robert Zoellick retired from the World Bank on July 1, 2012. He joined the faculty at the Harvard Kennedy School's Belfer Center for Science and International Affairs.

*See also:* Draghi, Mario; Lagarde, Christine

### Selected Works by Robert Zoellick

Zoellick, Robert. "Campaign 2000: A Republican Foreign Policy." *Foreign Affairs* 79, no. 1 (January 2000). http://www.foreignaffairs.com/articles/55632/robert-b-zoellick/campaign-2000-a-republican-foreign-policy (accessed March 2011).

Zoellick, Robert. "The G20 Must Look beyond Bretton Woods II." *Financial Times*, November 7, 2010. http://www.ft.com/cms/s/0/5bb39488-ea99-11df-b28d-00144feab49a.html#axzz1I1Et2scK (accessed March 2011).

Zoellick, Robert B. and Philip Zelikow, eds. *America and the Balkans: Memos to a President*. New York: Norton, 2001.

Zoellick, Robert B. and Philip Zelikow, eds. *America and the East Asian Crisis: Memos to a President*. New York: Norton, 2000.

Zoellick, Robert B., and Philip Zelikow, eds. *America and Russia: Memos to a President*. New York: Norton, 2000.

## Selected Works about Robert Zoellick

National Bureau of Asian Research (U.S.) and Richard Baum. *Whither U.S.-China Relations?: A Roundtable Discussion of Deputy Secretary of State Robert Zoellick's September 2005 Remarks to the National Committee on U.S.-China Relations*. Seattle, WA: National Bureau of Asian Research, 2005.

Schneiderman, R. M. "No Return to the Gold Standard." *Newsweek*, January 23, 2011. http://www.newsweek.com/2011/01/23/no-return-to-the-gold-standard.html (accessed March 2011).

World Bank. "Office of the President—Biography, Robert Zoellick." http://web.worldbank.org/ (accessed March 2011).

*David A. Dieterle*

# Appendix: Nobel Laureates

| | | | |
|---|---|---|---|
| 2012 | Alvin Roth | Lloyd Shapley | |
| 2011 | Thomas Sargent | Christopher Sims | |
| 2010 | Peter Diamond | Dale Mortensen | Christopher Pissarides |
| 2009 | Elinor Ostrom | Oliver Williamson | |
| 2008 | Paul Krugman | | |
| 2007 | Leonid Hurwicz | Eric Maskin | Roger Myerson |
| 2006 | Edmund Phelps | | |
| 2005 | Robert Aumann | Thomas Schelling | |
| 2004 | Finn Kydland | Edward Prescott | |
| 2003 | Robert Engle | Clive Granger | |
| 2002 | Daniel Kahneman | Vernon Smith | |
| 2001 | George Akerlof | Michael Spence | Joseph Stiglitz |
| 2000 | James Heckman | Daniel McFadden | |
| 1999 | Robert Mundell | | |
| 1998 | Amartya Sen | | |
| 1997 | Robert Merton | Myron Scholes | |
| 1996 | James Mirrlees | William Vickrey | |
| 1995 | Robert E. Lucas Jr. | | |
| 1994 | John Harsanyi | John Nash | Reinhard Selten |
| 1993 | Robert Fogel | Douglass North | |
| 1992 | Gary Becker | | |
| 1991 | Ronald Coase | | |
| 1990 | Harry Markowitz | Merton Miller | William Sharpe |
| 1989 | Trygve Haavelmo | | |
| 1988 | Maurice Allais | | |
| 1987 | Robert Solow | | |
| 1986 | James Buchanan | | |
| 1985 | Franco Modigliani | | |
| 1984 | Richard Stone | | |
| 1983 | Gérard Debreu | | |
| 1982 | George Stigler | | |

| | | |
|---|---|---|
| 1981 | James Tobin | |
| 1980 | Lawrence Klein | |
| 1979 | Theodore Schultz | Arthur Lewis |
| 1978 | Herbert Simon | |
| 1977 | Bertil Ohlin | James Meade |
| 1976 | Milton Friedman | |
| 1975 | Leonid Kantorovich | Tjalling Koopmans |
| 1974 | Gunnar Myrdal | Friedrich von Hayek |
| 1973 | Wassily Leontief | |
| 1972 | John Hicks | Kenneth Arrow |
| 1971 | Simon Kuznets | |
| 1970 | Paul Samuelson | |
| 1969 | Ragnar Frisch | Jan Tinbergen |

# Glossary

**Absolute advantage** – A situation in which one party can produce more using a given quantity of resources (or the same amount using fewer resources) than another.

**Affirmative action** – Policies intended to counter discrimination in employment, education, and business by taking into account factors such as race, color, religion, gender, national origin, or sexual orientation.

***Affluent Society, The*** – The 1958 book by John Kenneth Galbraith, Harvard economist, regarding the post–World War II United States and the growth of the private sector at the expense of the public sector.

**Aggregate demand** – The sum of all expenditures (household consumption, business investment, government spending, and net exports) in a nation's economy.

**Aggregate supply** – The sum of all production in a nation's economy.

**American Academy of Arts and Sciences** – A leading center for independent policy research; election to the academy is one of the nation's highest honors; the center is headquartered in Cambridge, Massachusetts.

**American Economic Association (AEA)** – Established in 1885, AEA is the learned society in the field of economics; headquartered in Nashville, Tennessee, AEA publishes the prestigious academic journal *The American Economic Review*.

**American Enterprise Institute** – A conservative think tank founded in 1943 as an independent nonprofit organization headquartered in Washington, DC, to defend American freedom and democratic capitalism including limited government, private enterprise, and individual liberty and responsibility.

**Antidumping duty** – A tariff levied on imports usually in retaliation for selling a product below fair value.

**Antitrust** – Government legislation to prevent monopolies and deter companies from conducting business in a collusive or anticompetitive activity.

**Asymmetric information** – A situation in which two parties to a transaction have different amounts of information concerning the transaction.

**Austrian School of economics** – A school of economic thought that focuses on the actions of the individual and the study of human behavior; main tenets include the theses that economic models are unreliable and prices are determined best by the equilibrium of supply and demand when markets function freely.

**Average tax rate** – The total tax paid divided by total income.

**Balance of payments** – A system of accounts that measures the trade, financial, and foreign aid transactions between a nation's domestic economic components during a specific period of time.

**Balance of trade** – The difference between a nation's exports and imports of goods and services.

**Banking crisis** – Failure in banks that causes further failure and disintermediation to spread to other banks; a common feature when an international financial crisis occurs.

**Bank of International Settlements (BIS)** – An international organization that serves as a central bank for national central banks.

**Bankruptcy** – The condition of a person, company, or nation when its assets are less than its liabilities.

**Barriers to trade** – Transparent forms of protectionism include tariffs and quotas while nontransparent forms include specific manufacturing standards, licenses, fees, or patents.

**Bayesian games** – A game, designed by economic game theorists, in which players have incomplete information about other players and/or the payoffs for various actions.

**Behavioral economics** – A study of economics that emphasizes human behavior and the psychological aspects of decision making.

**Belovezh Accords** – The agreement signed on December 8, 1991, that declared the Soviet Union effectively dissolved and established the Commonwealth of Independent States in its place.

**Black-Scholes model** – A mathematical model of financial markets and derivative investment instruments, introduced by Fischer Black and Myron Scholes in 1973, that is widely used to price options.

**Bretton Woods conference** – A conference held in the small New Hampshire town of Bretton Woods in July 1944. The conference established the international financial and economic order after World War II. The foundations for both the World Bank and International Monetary Fund began here.

**Brookings Institution** – A liberal think tank based in Washington, DC, that conducts research and education regarding the global economy and development to provide recommendations to strengthen American democracy, improve social welfare, and support a more cooperative international system.

**Bureau of Economic Analysis (BEA)** – An agency located within the U.S. Department of Commerce that provides economic data including the U.S. gross domestic product.

**Bureau of Labor Statistics (BLS)** – An agency of the U.S. Department of Labor whose responsibility includes collecting, analyzing, and distributing important economic data regarding employment, inflation, and economic growth.

**Business cycle** – Also known as the economic cycle, the stages of an economy including contraction, peak, expansion, or trough over time.

**Capital** – A factor of production that includes tools, buildings, and other human-made intermediate goods used in producing final goods.

**Capital assets** – Producer durables and nondurable goods firms use to produce final goods.

**Capitalism** – The economic system known as the market economy where the answers to the key economic questions (what to produce, how to produce, for whom to produce) are answered in the marketplace in the interaction between buyers and sellers.

**Capital resources** – All human-made tools, machines, buildings, and technology used in the production of final goods.

**Central bank** – The national bank that serves other banks and is responsible for a nation's money supply, monetary policy, and commercial bank regulations.

**Chain-store paradox** – An apparent game-theory paradox that refutes standard game-theory reasoning.

**Chicago School** – A neoclassical school of thought that rejected Keynesianism in favor of monetary policy popularized by economists and faculty of the University of Chicago.

**Circular flow of economic activity** – A pictorial depiction of an economy identifying the key markets (product, resource, financial, foreign) and the interaction of the key participants (households, businesses, government, financial institutions, and foreign companies) within each of the markets.

**Classical economics** – Widely regarded as the first modern school of economic thought; major figures include Adam Smith, Jean-Baptiste Say, David Ricardo, Thomas Malthus, and John Stuart Mill, all of whom generally agreed that free markets will regulate themselves.

**Classical liberalism** – A political ideology that promotes restricting government involvement in the economy to providing rule of law and economic freedom.

**Cliometrics** – Originating in 1958, the systematic application of economic theory and econometrics and mathematical methods to the study of history; also known as new economic history or econometric history.

**Coase theorem** – Describes the economic efficiency that can be achieved by an economic allocation or outcome in the presence of externalities; first presented by Nobel laureate Ronald Coase.

**Cold War** – From approximately the late 1940s to the early 1990s, a continual global condition of both political and military tensions between primarily the United States and the Soviet Union.

**Command economy** – An economy where the three main questions (what to produce, how to produce, and for whom to produce) are addressed, answered, and implemented by a central authority (government).

**Commodities** – The generic term to describe the natural resources used in production of final goods such as coal, oil, and natural gas.

**Common-pool resources** – A resource such as water or fish where exclusive or defined use is hard to impossible to enforce.

**Communist League** – Established in 1847 in London, the Communist League is considered the first Marxist political party; it promoted the political and economic philosophies of Karl Marx and was disbanded in 1852.

***Communist Manifesto, The*** – An 1848 work of Karl Marx and Friedrich Engels, and the most influential book on theories of class struggle and capitalism's shortcomings; it became the foundations of the Communist Party; it was originally titled the *Manifesto of the Communist Party*.

**Comparative advantage** – A situation in which one person, company, or nation can produce a good or service with lower opportunity costs than another; useful for determining the most efficient allocation of resources; leads to trade between the two entities and increased wealth.

**Comparative economics** – The component of economics that studies different economic systems.

**Comparative economic systems** – The study of different economic organizations including market, command, and mixed economies.

**Competition** – In economics the act of several persons, businesses, or nations vying to be the most efficient, the most effective, or the most favorable for the allocation of resources.

**Congressional Budget Office** – A federal agency within the U.S. legislative branch of government, established in 1974 to provide timely, nonpartisan economic data and analysis to Congress.

**Conspicuous consumption** – The consumption of goods and services by individuals in a manner beyond basic utility such as driving a Rolls Royce instead of a Buick.

**Consumers** – Purchasers of final goods or services.

**Consumer surplus** – The difference between what consumers would be willing and able to purchase and the total amount they pay.

**Consumption** – A household consumer's spending current income on a good or service.

**Contraction, economic** – The portion of the business cycle in which a nation's economy slows down.

**Corn Laws** – Trade laws implemented to protect the cereal producers in Great Britain and Ireland against foreign imports between 1815 and 1846.

**Cost-push inflation** – Inflation caused by increases in the cost of resources (land, labor, capital), causing a decrease in aggregate supply.

**Costs** – The trade-off of using a resource for the production or consumption of a good or service.

**Council of Economic Advisers** – Established in 1946 as an agency of the Executive Office of the President of the United States, advising the president on economic policies, providing objective empirical research, and preparing the annual *Economic Report of the President*.

**Creative destruction** – Made famous by Joseph Schumpeter, an economy's inability to protect goods, services, or industries whose resource allocation has become more costly than a newer, more efficient allocation of resources.

**Currency** – Term referring to the money used as a nation's medium of exchange, store of value, or standard of value.

**Dead capital** – Any capital or land resources that do not have distinct ownership title.

**Debt** – When revenues are less than expenses over a period of time (usually several years).

**Debt to equity** – The ratio of a company's debt to the equity of a company.

**Deflation** – A constant general decrease of the average price level of an economy over a period of time.

**Deflationary spiral** – The continued decreasing of the general price level of an economy over time, resulting in significant decreases in resource and investment values.

**Demand** – A schedule reflecting a set of prices for a good or service at which consumers are willing and able to purchase the good or service, other things being equal.

**Demand curve** – A graphical picture of a demand schedule reflecting the demand for a good or service, other things being equal.

**Demand-pull inflation** – Inflation caused by increases in aggregate demand not matched by comparable increases in aggregate supply.

**Demand-side** – The Keynesian idea of focusing fiscal policies on the behavior of the consumer in the product market (i.e., demand).

**Demographics** – The population statistics reflected by data used to describe the gender, age, race, mobility, and employment characteristics of a population.

**Deregulation** – Freeing an industry from regulations imposed on it by government.

**Derived demand** – Demand for inputs dependent on the demand for the final products the inputs are used to produce.

**Development economics** – The branch of economics that studies the conditions and variables conducive for economic growth, especially for developing nations

**Diamond-Mirrlees efficiency theorem** – A thesis based on observations of market and government revenue-generating situations that suggests there should be no taxes on intermediate goods and imports.

**Diminishing marginal returns (utility)** – The principle that at some point, the returns or utility of a good or service consumed diminishes with each additional use during a given time period.

**Diseconomies of scale** – Increases in the long-run average costs as production increases.

**Disincentive** – A regulation or policy that deters a particular action by companies or individuals.

**Disinflation** – A lower rate of inflation from a previous inflation measure as opposed to the negative measure deflation.

**Disintermediation** – A failure on the part of the banking system that prevents savings from individuals being directed into business investment.

**Division of labor** – Division of labor occurs because human beings have a tendency to "truck, barter, and exchange one thing for another," that is, to trade. This causes people to become dependent on one another.

**Dynamic economic view** – A view of the economy's condition over time.

*Econometrica* – A prestigious academic journal of the Econometric Society that publishes articles highlighting the research of economic issues through econometrics.

**Econometrics** – A branch of economics that combines economics, mathematics, and statistics to develop quantitative and empirical analysis to economic theory and economic data.

**Econometric Society** – An international society to advance the study of economic theory through mathematics, statistics, and econometrics; publishes *Econometrica*.

**Economic conservatism** – An economic philosophy that promotes minimal government involvement and spending in the economy; a belief in free trade and a balanced federal budget with no national debt.

**Economic forecasting** – The process of making economic predictions regarding future unemployment, inflation, economic growth activity, and other data for a specific time period.

**Economic growth** – Increases in real per capita GDP over a given period of time.

**Economic history** – The branch of economics that studies past events and people.

**Economic index** – A statistical measure of the economy highlighting changes in a specific group of individual data derived from numerous sources; Dow Jones, GDP deflator, and Consumer Price Index are examples of economic indices.

**Economic institutions** – Nonhuman entities of an economy including businesses, governments, and unions.

**Economic liberalism** – An economic belief that the best economic decisions are those made by individuals in the marketplace and not collectively by institutions.

**Economic model** – A theoretical construct of a defined section of the economy for the purposes of studying economic behavior.

**Economic philosophy** – A normative economic ideology that defines the main structures of an economy, including its means to achieving specific ends or goals.

**Economic rent** – A payment for the use of a resource above its opportunity cost.

**Economics** – The science of the decision making behind how individuals, institutions, and nations allocate their limited resources to satisfy their unlimited wants.

**Economics of crime** – A subgroup of economics that studies the economic effects and impacts of crime on an economy.

**Economics of environment** – A subgroup of economics that studies the economic effects and impacts of environmental policies and environmental conditions on an economy.

**Economics of family** – A subgroup of economics that studies the economic effects and impacts of a family culture in an economy.

**Economics of government** – A subgroup of economics that studies the economic effects and impacts of government and government policies on an economy.

**Economics of health** – A subgroup of economics that studies the economic effects and impacts of health-related issues and policies on an economy.

**Economics of information** – A subgroup of economics that studies the economic effects and impacts of information gathering and technology on an economy.

**Economics of law** – A subgroup of economics that studies the economic effects and impacts of a nation's laws on an economy.

**Economics of war and peace** – A subgroup of economics that studies the economic effects and impacts of a nation's conditions of war and peace on an economy.

**Economic systems** – An economy's method of allocating its resources, goods and services; it is determined by who (markets, central authority, or some combination) answers the main economic questions (what to produce, how to produce, for whom to produce).

**Economies of scale** – Decreases in long-run average costs as output increases.

**Edgeworth Box** – Named for Francis Ysidro Edgeworth, the Edgeworth Box represents various combinations of resource distributions that can be achieved in an economy; often used in general equilibrium analysis.

**Elasticity** – The measure for the responsiveness of quantity demanded or quantity supplied to changes in price; if the percentage change in response (either demand or supply) is greater than the percentage change in price, the product is deemed elastic; if less, then inelastic; if equal, then unitary.

**Empirical economics** – General term used to describe econometrics, mathematical economics, or experimental economics whose means to economic solutions is quantitative.

**Enlightenment, Age of** – A cultural movement of eighteenth-century Europe and American colonies to create societal reforms through reason and science.

**Entrepreneurship** – A component of human resources; the willingness and ability of an individual to use productive resources (land, labor, capital) to raise financial capital, organize, take risks, manage, and otherwise combine resources to create a business or organization.

**Environmental economics** – A study of economics concerned with creating and promoting economic solutions to environmental issues.

**Equation of exchange** – Also known as the quantity theory of money, the equation of exchange identifies the relationship between an economy's money supply (M), price level (P), velocity of money (V), and value of its goods and services (Q) as PQ = MV. The equation states that the number of monetary units (M) times the number of times each unit is spent (V) equals the quantity of goods and services sold (Q) times the prices paid for the goods and services (P).

**Equilibrium** – The condition in which the quantity demanded and quantity supplied of a good or service is equal at a given price; equilibrium also describes the balance of an economy's aggregate demand and aggregate supply.

**Equilibrium price** – The price determined when quantity demanded equals quantity supplied.

**Euler's theorem** – A theorem in number theory named for Leonhard Euler.

**Euro** – The monetary unit of the European Union (€) first appearing in January 2002.

**European Central Bank** – The central bank responsible for the monetary policies of the Eurozone Monetary Union; located in Frankfurt, Germany.

**European Union** – Twenty-seven European nations acting together as an economic union.

**Evolutionary economics** – A subgroup of economics that focuses on interdependence, growth, competition, and economic structural changes.

**Exchange, voluntary** – Willingness of two individuals, organizations, or businesses to trade a good or service.

**Exchange rates** – The price of one nation's currency expressed in terms of another nation's currency.

**Experimental economics** – Applying experimental methods to the study of economic issues such as the functioning of markets or exchange structures.

**Exports** – The outflow of goods and services by one nation to another nation.

**Externality** – The positive or negative consequence of an economic transaction that impacts a third party.

**Fabian Society** – A British Socialist organization founded to advance democratic socialism through marginal means and not revolutionary action; the modern organization operates like a think tank.

**Federal Open Market Committee (FOMC)** – A body of the Federal Reserve System responsible for the decisions regarding interest rates and quantity of U.S. money supply through the buying and selling of U.S. securities (bills, notes, bonds).

**Federal Reserve System** – Since 1913 the central banking system of the United States, responsible for the monetary policies and money supply and regulation of the U.S. banking system.

**Feudal system** – An economic and political system of medieval Europe that emphasized the ownership of property of some and the exchange for labor by others.

**Final goods** – Goods and services produced to be sold in the product market and consumed by households; not used to produce other final goods.

**Finance economics** – The discipline of economics that studies the effects and impacts of the financial markets and financial institutions on an economy's functioning.

**Financial Reform Act of 2010 (Dodd-Frank Wall Street Reform and Consumer Protection Act)** – Signed into law in 2010 by President Obama, it called for significant changes to regulations of the financial markets resulting from the financial crisis of 2007–9.

**Fiscal policy** – The discretionary actions and policies of government through taxation and spending to achieve the economic goals of a nation's economy.

**Focal point** – In game theory, the focal point refers to the solution to a problem in which the players are not able to communicate with each other but must cooperate to reach the same point. The focal point is the point where both players believe they both are most likely to reach a common agreement or understanding.

**Foreign aid** – Payments by developed nations to developing nations for which no repayment is required.

**Foreign debt** – When a nation's repayment loan obligations to another nation exceed its ability to repay the loan over time.

**Fractional reserve banking** – A system of banking where financial institutions are required to maintain reserves that are only a percentage of total deposits.

**Free-rider problem** – A condition when the users of public goods assume others will pay the costs of the public good; one example is a user of a city park who lives in another city and does not pay taxes in the park's city for maintenance and upkeep.

**Free-trade agreements** – Agreements by countries to provide open borders for free trade and population movements creating a free-trade area; the North American Free Trade Agreement (NAFTA) is an example of a free-trade agreement.

**Game theory** – The study of interactive decision making; tries to understand the various probable outcomes when two or more individuals with limited knowledge of their situation try to calculate best outcomes.

**General Agreement on Tariffs and Trade (GATT)** – Established in 1947, an international agreement to reduce barriers of trade in world trade; was followed by the World Trade Organization (WTO).

**General equilibrium theory** – In macroeconomics the condition in which aggregate supply is equal to aggregate demand; the study of consumer and producer behaviors that result in market equilibrium as an economy of the whole.

***General Theory of Employment, Interest, and Money, The*** – The work of John Maynard Keynes that changed the way government is viewed as a participant in the economy; considered the beginnings of macroeconomics.

**Giffen good** – A Giffen good is a good that violates the law of demand; as price increases so does quantity demanded.

**Global economics** – The study of the world economy (also known as the global economy) and how national economies interact with each other in a global marketplace.

**Globalization** – The process of integrating national economies into one global economy through improved technology in telecommunications including the Internet and transportation.

**Gold standard** – A fixed exchange rate system that uses gold as its standard of value.

**Great Depression** – The worldwide depression of the twentieth century that preceded World War II; began in the 1930s and lasted through the mid-1940s and the beginning of World War II.

**Gresham's law** – Commonly known as "bad money driving out good," this occurs when a government overvalues one money and undervalues the second money so that the undervalued money disappears and the overvalued or bad money overwhelms the economy.

**Gross domestic product (GDP)** – A measure of a nation's economy by the final market value of goods and services produced by businesses, households, government, and the effects of net trade (exports minus imports) within a nation's borders over a given period of time.

**Gross national product (GNP)** – A measure of a nation's economy by the final market value of goods and services produced by the nation's businesses, households, government, and the effects of net trade (exports-imports) regardless of where geographically.

**Harrod-Domar model** – A measure of the growth rate of an economy through its savings and the productivity of its capital.

**Heckscher-Ohlin theory** – A trade theory that predicts a country's ability to export goods and services based on their abundant factors of production and import goods and services where the factors of production are relatively scarce.

**Heritage Foundation** – A conservative think tank located in Washington, DC, created to promote conservative public policies based on free enterprise, individual freedom, strong national defense, and limited government.

*Human Action: A Treatise on Economics* – The second and most popular work of Austrian economist Ludwig von Mises, which became the definitive explanation of the Austrian view; the treatise rejected positive economics in favor of viewing economic decision making through the study of human behavior; promoted a free-market economy over a government-planned economy.

**Human capital** – The productive resource of labor in the production of goods and services; human capital is based on several variables including education, experience, and the market demand for the education and experience for particular skills.

**Human resources** – Also known as human capital, the component factor of production that includes individuals in the production of goods and services.

**Immigration** – The movement of people to a country or region where they are not native.

**Imperfect competition** – A market condition where perfect competition characteristics are not fulfilled; forms of markets with imperfect competition include monopolistic competition, oligopoly, and monopoly.

**Imperialism** – Economic imperialism results when a nation's rates of consumption outpace production, forcing the country to export capital to foreign countries in order to exploit foreign markets and labor forces to supply its needs.

**Imports** – The inflow of goods and services from one nation to another nation.

**Incentives** – Positive rewards for participating in an activity.

**Income distribution** – A measurement of different income levels in an economy and the percentage of income earners in each income level.

**Index (indices)** – A statistical measure of an economy such as a stock market index or consumer price index.

**Indifference curves** – A curve composed of a set of consumption alternatives that yield the same amount of utility (satisfaction).

**Industrialization** – The transforming of an economy from an agrarian to an industry-based economy.

**Infant-industry argument** – The idea that government should impose tariffs to protect an industry that is trying to get started from import competition.

**Inflation** – A general rise in the price level of all goods and services (demand-pull) in an economy; the general rise in the costs of resources (supply-push) in an economy; when the quantity of the money supply exceeds the current price level of the quantity of goods and services produced (monetary inflation).

**Inflation-unemployment rate trade-off** – The thesis, first proposed by A. W. H. Phillips, that during times of economic growth a nation will experience either inflation with low unemployment or relative price stability with high unemployment.

**Information economics** – A branch of microeconomics that studies how information and information technology impact an economy.

**Inheritance taxes** – A tax levied on a person's accumulated wealth that remains after the person's death.

**Input-output model (analysis)** – A quantitative economic technique that studies, analyzes, and models the interdependence between the inputs (land, labor, capital) and the outputs (goods and services) of an economy or the comparison with other economies.

**Inputs** – Land, labor, capital; natural resources, human resources, capital resources.

**Institutional economics** – The study and analysis of the role of institutions in developing economic behavior.

**Institutions** – A formal or informal set of rules of behavior, limits, or constraints on an economic, social, and political society.

**Interdependence** – The reliance of two resources or economies on each other.

**Interest** – The price/cost of money expressed in nominal (stated interest rate) or real (foundation interest rate) terms.

**Intermediate goods** – Goods produced to be used entirely in the production of final goods.

**International economics** – A branch of economics that studies the interdependence of economic activity between nations and the economic development of nations including resource movements, trade, and investment.

**International finance** – A branch of economic study concerned with the money flows between nations and the international monetary systems including balance of payments, exchange rates, international trade, and foreign direct investment.

**International Monetary Fund (IMF)** – Founded during the Bretton Woods conference to administer an international foreign exchange rate system and lend to member countries having balance-of-payments problems; lender of last resort for national governments and central banks.

**International policy reform** – A future state or condition determined by government action and policy to stimulate future international trade or development.

**International trade** – The study of the flow of goods and services and productive resources between international boundaries.

**Investment** – Use of today's resources to fund future production or future consumption.

**Investment banking** – The operations of a financial institution that focus on raising capital to accommodate transactions such as mergers, acquisitions, derivatives, foreign exchange, and the issuance of securities.

**John Bates Clark Medal** – A prestigious award bestowed by the American Economic Association to an economist under 40 who has made significant contributions to economic knowledge and economic thought; considered second only to the Nobel Prize in Economics in prestige.

**Keynesianism** – The school of economic thought influenced by the writings of John Maynard Keynes.

**Knowledge-based economy/industry** – An economy or industry whose resource advantage is in the advanced application of human capital through technology and advanced production and management operations.

**Labor** – Contributions to a nation's economy by humans who work.

**Labor economics** – A branch of study in economics that focuses on the function of labor markets including the interaction of workers and employers, the supply of labor, the demand for labor, and labor patterns of an economy.

**Labor theory of value (LTV)** – Economic theory that submits that the value of a commodity or economic good or service is based on the labor needed to either produce it or acquire the commodity, good, or service.

**Laffer curve** – Based on the ideas of Arthur Laffer's supply-side economics, the Laffer curve supposes that government revenues will increase to a specific marginal tax rate, at which time the incentive to work supposedly decreases, which in turn decreases tax revenues.

**Laissez-faire** – An economic term used to describe an economy free from government intervention in economic activity including trade and market transactions; French phrase for "let us do," generally translated as "let it be" or "to leave alone."

**Land** – The natural resources available from nature including resources on the land, from the land, or located beneath the land.

**Lausanne School of economics** – Also referred to as the Mathematical School, a neoclassical school of thought known as the school that developed general equilibrium theory.

**Lender of last resort** – The role of a central bank or institution willing and able to lend to a bank with temporary liquidity problems to prevent the position spreading to a general loss of confidence in other banks or financial institutions.

**Libertarianism** – A political philosophy that emphasizes freedom, voluntary association, and liberty of the individual, which includes small government.

**London School of Economics (LSE)** – A public research university located in London, England, founded by Sidney Webb, Beatrice Webb, and George Bernard Shaw in 1895 to conduct research and teaching in the social sciences, mathematics, and statistics.

**Long-run equilibrium** – A situation in which aggregate demand and aggregate supply are equal during a time period when all resources are variable.

**Macroeconomics** – The study of a nation's economy as a whole, measuring changes in unemployment, money supply, national income, and general price level.

**Malthusian theory** – The theory named after Thomas Malthus that predicted a return to subsistence living when food production cannot keep pace with population growth.

**Marginalism** – Studying the economic impact on outputs by changing one input unit at a time.

**Marginal rate of substitution** – The rate at which a consumer is willing and able to give up one good or service for a complementary good or service without forfeiting satisfaction (utility).

**Marginal tax rate** – The change in tax payment divided by the change in income; percentage of additional dollars to be paid in taxes.

**Marginal utility** – The change in utility (satisfaction) of an activity obtained by adding one more unit to the total consumed.

**Market economy** – An economy where the key economic questions (what to produce, how to produce, for whom to produce) are addressed, answered, and implemented in the marketplace in the transactions between buyers and sellers.

**Market failures** – An economic situation or transaction in which too few or too many resources are going to a specific economic activity.

**Market price** – Also known as economic price, the price offered in the marketplace.

**Markets** – The interaction of a buyer (consumer, household) and seller (producer, business) exchanging goods or services in a variety of different settings.

**Market structure** – Structure of a competitive industry or market, based on the number of firms, product differentiation, and barriers to entry; market structures include perfect competition, monopolistic competition, oligopoly, and monopoly.

**Marxism** – A worldview for social, political, and economic change based on the division between social classes and influenced by the writings of Karl Marx.

**Mathematical economics** – The application of mathematical methods to study, analyze, and represent economic theories through empirical approaches such as statistics, econometrics, calculus, and differential equations.

**Mercantilism** – The economic system of sixteenth-century Europe that stressed the importance of exports, and not imports, for accumulating trade surpluses to boost a nation's revenues; modern mercantilism is to promote exports but stay closed to imports.

**Microeconomics** – The study of decision making by individuals, firms, and organizations.

**Minimum wage** – A legislated price floor set by a government to determine the lowest possible hourly wage rate that can be legally paid to workers.

**Mixed economy** – An economy in which the key economic questions (what to produce, how to produce, for whom to produce) are addressed, answered, and implemented through a combination of transactions between buyers and sellers and a central authority (government).

**Monetarism** – An ideology of economic thought most prominently held by Milton Friedman that views the money supply as the key variable in measuring a nation's economic output and measure of price level.

**Monetary economics** – A branch of economics that studies and analyzes the functions of money as a medium of exchange, store of value, and unit of account; studies the roles of central banks and the money in an economic system.

**Monetary policy** – Macroeconomic policies related to interest rates and money supply usually determined by the nation's central bank.

**Money** – The currency of a nation's economy used as a medium of exchange, a store of value, and a standard of value.

**Money supply** – The quantity of money circulating in an economy.

**Monopolistic competition** – A market with fairly easy entry in which a large number of firms produce comparable but not the same products.

**Monopoly** – A one-firm industry that can determine the market price of a good.

**Moral hazard** – The prospect of riskier behavior when borrowers know they may not have to be responsible for a loan; behavior that generates significant social costs.

**Moral philosophy** – Also known as ethics, the defining and defending of conduct that is considered right or wrong.

**Nash equilibrium** – Named for John Nash, a game-theory solution where each player has a chosen strategy and no player can gain by changing his or her strategies, such that none of the players change their strategies and the resulting choices and payoffs are accepted.

**National Academy of Sciences** – A U.S.-based nonprofit organization whose members are elected based on original research achievements and serve as advisers to the United States.

**National Bureau of Economic Research (NBER)** – The largest American private non-profit research organization providing unbiased research in economics for policy makers, businesses, and the academic community.

**National income accounting** – A estimate measure of an economy's national income and its components including wages, profits, rents, and interest income; one approach to measuring an economy's aggregate performance.

**National Labor Relations Board (NLRB)** – An independent agency of the U.S. government located in Washington, DC, that oversees elections of labor union representations and investigates unfair-labor-practice charges.

**Natural resources** – Those resources that originate from the environment, such as air or water; are extracted from the ground or water, such as oil; or are taken from natural habitats, such as fish.

**Natural rights, natural law** – Components of a political order based on a social contract (rather than on divine right or monarchic rule); foundational elements of government during the Age of Enlightenment.

**Negative-sum game (exchange)** – A game in which players as a group lose during the process of the game and are worse off at the game's conclusion than when the game began.

**Neoclassical** – A school of economic thought in microeconomics that posits that individuals and firms make decisions so as to maximize their utility or profits; emphasizes that people act independently based on varying amounts of information and make decisions based on rational calculation.

**Neo-Keynesians** – Economists such as Paul Samuelson who combined neoclassical economic models with new interpretations of Keynes's writings.

**Neo-Ricardian** – A modern interpretation of David Ricardo's case against marginal theory of value, offered by Piero Sraffa.

**New Deal** – Economic programs in the United States during the 1930s designed to combat the Great Depression.

**Nobel Prize in Economics (see Appendix: Nobel Laureates)** – Officially the Sveriges Riksbank Prize in Economic Sciences in Memory of Alfred Nobel, the prize was endowed in 1968 and first awarded in 1969; considered by many as the most prestigious award bestowed for outstanding contributions to the field of economics.

**Office of Budget and Management (OMB)** – The largest office within the Executive Office of the President of the United States; assists the president in the preparation, oversight, and administration of the federal budget.

**Offshoring** – The actions of individuals and businesses to conduct part of their transactions outside their domestic borders.

**Oil Producing Exporting Countries (OPEC)** – A multination organization of 12 oil-producing nations with the goal of influencing and creating a stable global market price of oil; members include Algeria, Angola, Ecuador, Iran, Iraq, Kuwait, Libya, Nigeria, Qatar, Saudi Arabia, the United Arab Emirates, and Venezuela; headquarters are located in Vienna, Austria.

**Oligopoly** – A market structure with few sellers in which each seller is aware that the other sellers will respond to any changes in prices, quantities, or qualities of products on the market.

**Opportunity cost** – The next best alternative cost (trade-off) of a decision; every decision has a cost because every decision involves forgoing an alternative good, service, or activity.

**Organisation of Economic Co-operation and Development (OECD)** – Established in 1961, an international organization of 34 developed nations committed to free trade and democracy with the goal of stimulating global trade and global economic growth; headquarters are located in Paris, France.

**Outputs** – Goods and services.

**Outsourcing** – A firm's employing resources outside the firm that could be domestic or foreign.

**Ownership** – The process of possessing the rights to defined property including the ability to defend and sell as one wishes.

**Pareto optimality** – Named after Vilfredo Pareto, an efficient economic allocation is achieved when no one can be made better off without someone else becoming worse off.

**Pareto principle** – Also known as the 80–20 rule where 80 percent of the results are created by 20 percent of the sources

**Partial equilibrium analysis** – Equilibrium analysis of just a single market within an economy.

**Pensions** – Generally, a contract between an employer and employee for a fixed sum of income or onetime payment after a defined term of service (usually in years) to be paid at one's retirement.

**Per capita income** – Measure of a nation's standard of living based on a nation's total income divided by its population.

**Perfect competition** – A market structure with many buyers and sellers in which individual decisions do not affect market price.

**Phillips curve** – Named for A. W. H. Phillips, the curve shows the trade-off or inverse relationship between unemployment and inflation.

**Physiocrats** – A group of economists originating in France during the late eighteenth century whose economic theory was based on productive work as a source of national wealth.

**Pigou effect** – Named for A. C. Pigou, the term defines the relationship between wealth, consumption, output, and employment; as wealth increases it leads to increases in consumption, which in turn stimulate output and employment.

**Political economy** – Early terminology from moral philosophy used to describe the study of buying, selling, and producing, along with the governmental laws and societal customs; used to describe the relationships between government and economy in a national context.

**Portfolio theory** – A mathematical approach to investing in which diversification (coordinated selection of diverse assets) plays a major role; has been challenged in recent years by behavioral economists.

**Positive economics** – Analysis limited to factual statements or scientific predictions; economic analysis that aims to describe "what is" rather than what "ought" to be.

**Positive-sum game (exchange)** – A game in which players as a group are better off at the end of the game then when the game began.

**Post-Keynesian** – A school of economic thought based on the work of John Maynard Keynes, specifically his seminal work *The General Theory of Employment, Interest and Money*, in an effort to reestablish Keynesianism within economic theory; post-Keynesians include Joan Robinson, Michal Kalecki, and Nicholas Kaldor.

**Poverty** – Defined in absolute terms as the inability to satisfy basic needs through income, or described in relative terms as a measure of income inequality, where an individual's or family's income is below a predetermined income level (this level differs from one society or nation to the next).

**Price controls** – Imposed by a government establishing either minimum or maximum prices to be charged for goods or services.

**Prices** – Signals the relative allocation of the distribution of productive resources to goods and services.

**Prisoner's dilemma** – Strategic game in which two prisoners have a choice between confessing and not confessing to a crime.

**Private property** – The ownership of an economy's productive resources (land, labor, capital) by the private sector of an economy.

**Private property rights** – Exclusive rights of ownership that allow the use, transfer, and exchange of property.

**Producers** – The buyers of the productive resources of land, labor, and capital (inputs) of an economy who then use those resources to create and sell the goods and services produced (outputs).

**Product differentiation** – The process through which a firm differentiates its product from that of its competitors; variables for differentiation include quality, price, or design for a specified target market.

**Production possibility curve (frontier)** – A curve representing all possible combinations of maximum outputs being produced using its full complement of inputs assuming a specific point in time, a fixed amount of productive resources, and fixed technology; also reflects the trade-offs a nation must make to change or alter a given allocation of resources for a specified output.

**Productive resources** – The land, labor, and capital of an economy used by producers to create goods and services.

**Productivity** – Measuring the economic growth of an economy through the relationships of inputs and outputs; increased outputs using the same inputs or same outputs using fewer inputs.

**Profit maximization** – A microeconomic condition where a firm determines maximum price and production levels measuring the relationship between one's marginal cost and marginal revenues.

**Propensity to consume** – The rate at which a consumer spends each additional dollar on goods and services.

**Property rights** – The ability of an owner of private property to have defined property, defend their property, and receive the benefits of the property's value including the right to transfer or exchange the property.

**Protectionism** – A nation's ability to limit imports (quotas) or tax imports in order to keep domestic industries competitive (tariffs).

**Public choice theory** – The use of economic analysis and economic tools to study the behavior of public officials and citizens as voters; public choice theory often uses tools such as game theory or decision theory.

**Public finance** – Revenue generated through taxes, fees, fines, and levies to be used by public institutions for the purpose of providing public goods.

**Public goods** – Goods and services offered by a public institution that are nonexcludable (individuals cannot be prohibited from receiving their benefit); consumption of public goods and services is shared without diminishing the benefit of the user.

**Public policy** – A government law or regulation imposed by a governmental unit on its constituency.

**Public utility pricing** – A pricing scheme in which a government subsidy is necessary to maintain production because the price is equal to marginal costs and is below the average cost.

**Purchasing power parity** – An adjustment made when converting exchange rates to account for the differences in the true cost of living between countries.

**Quantitative economics** – The use of mathematical tools to address and analyze economic problems; includes calculus, differential equations, and econometrics; also known as mathematical economics.

**Quantity demanded** – A specific price along a demand curve at which a buyer is willing and able to purchase a good or service.

**Quantity supplied** – A specific price along a supply curve at which a seller is willing and able to produce a good or service.

**Quantity theory of money** – Also known as the equation of exchange, the quantity theory of money identifies the relationship between an economy's money supply (M), price level (P), velocity of money (V), and value of its goods and services (Q) as $PQ = MV$; the number of monetary units (M) times the number of times each unit is spent (V) equals the quantity of goods and services sold (Q) times the prices paid for the goods and services (P).

**Quota** – An import restriction on the quantity of a good that one nation imposes on another country.

**Rational expectations** – A theory based on future policy changes and effects on economic variables founded on past experiences.

**Recession** – The declining economic growth portion of the business cycle measured by two consecutive quarters of negative economic growth.

**Regional trade agreements** – An agreement between groups of nations for the express purpose of granting special trade benefits and access to each domestic market such as NAFTA.

**Resolution Trust Corporation** – A U.S. government-owned management company whose purpose was to liquidate assets of financial institutions, specifically savings and loan associations, that had been declared insolvent by the Office of Thrift Supervision during the 1980s savings and loan crisis.

**Return** – A profit or rent earned by the owner of a factor of production (land, labor, capital).

**Revenue** – The amount received by a business through the sale of a good or service or a government total of taxes, fees, and fines received.

**Risk** – The potential that an economic action or lack of action will leave the person worse off than before the action was take.

*Road to Serfdom, The* – Written in the 1940s by Friedrich von Hayek, *The Road to Serfdom* expounds on the dangers of central planning as an economic system that will lead to further state control and the loss of individual freedoms; Hayek's work continues to be influential today.

**Royal Economic Society in London (UK)** – Established in 1902, it is one of the oldest professional associations promoting the study of economics; it is the publisher of *The Econometrics Journal*.

**Saving** – The amount of an individual's current income set aside for use at a later time.

**Savings-investment relationship** – An identity relationship signaling that an economy's investment is dependent on the nation's savings.

**Say's law** – Named for Jean-Baptiste Say, Say's law states that supply creates its own demand.

**Scarcity** – The basic economic problem of allocating limited resources (land, labor, capital) to satisfy the unlimited desires for goods and services.

**Securities** – Stocks and bonds.

**Shock therapy** – The use of aggressive fiscal and monetary policies to combat the excessive spending and control of government in the economy.

**Short run** – Economic time period when one input (land, labor, and capital) cannot be altered.

**Social accounting** – The process of keeping corporations accountable for their environmental impacts.

**Social choice theory** – A framework for collective decision making using individual values in the aggregate; combines the fundamentals of voting theory and welfare economics.

**Social economics** – A comprehensive term for a branch of economics that uses economic tools and analysis to study society, ethics, or philosophy.

**Social insurance** – A government program that transfers risk to an organization that provides benefits to those who represent a defined population; such programs have defined eligibility requirements and are funded through taxes or shared public-private funding.

**Socialism** – The economic system known as the command economy where a central authority answers the key economic questions (what to produce, how to produce, for whom to produce).

**Social liberalism** – The view that the government has a social foundation, and hence the proper role of government includes addressing social issues like health and education, as well as defending the rule of law.

**Social science** – The academic disciplines of economics, history, sociology, political science, geography, and the like that involve studying human behavior (both individually and collectively), society, and social groups.

**Social Security** – Old-Age, Survivors, and Disability Insurance (OADI); a federal program of the Social Security Act of 1935 to provide income to qualifying retired individuals; the single greatest expenditure in the federal budget.

**Special drawing rights (SDRs)** – A reserve asset created by the International Monetary Fund (IMF) for countries, specifically developing countries, to use in settling international payments.

**Stagflation** – Term coined to describe an economy experiencing stagnant economic growth (lower real GDP) and inflation at the same time.

**Standard of living** – A term to describe a level of material well-being including income, employment factors, poverty rate, affordable housing, gross domestic product, hours of work needed for living basics, access to health care, availability of education, infrastructure, safety, and other metrics related to a nation's quality of life.

**Static economic view** – A view of the economy's condition at a specific point in time.

**Stockholm School of economics** – A group of Scandinavian economists who influenced Swedish economic policy post–World War II, led by Knut Wicksell, Gunnar Myrdal, Olin Heckscher, and Bertil Ohlin.

**Stolper-Samuelson theorem** – A theory that states that changes in import or export prices of final goods lead to a change in the same direction of the income generated by the resources used in their production.

**Subsidy** – Government aid or payment to a domestic producer to encourage infant industries or protect domestic industries and make them more competitive with foreign competition.

**Supply** – The willingness and ability of producers to produce a good or service at a set of prices.

**Supply curve** – The graphical representation of a supplier's willingness and ability to produce a good or service at a set of prices.

**Supply-side** – A school of economic thought that contends that economic growth is best generated through low marginal income tax rates and low capital gains tax rates with reduced government regulation.

**Supply-side economics** – The proposition that incentives for producers will increase productivity, shifting the aggregate supply curve outward.

**Tariff** – A tax on imports usually levied by developed nations to protect domestic industries and by developing nations to generate revenue.

**Taxes** – One form of revenue generated by governments, used to produce public goods or redistribute income.

**Theory of the firm** – A combination of economic theories intended to identify and explain the nature of firms, companies, corporations, and their structures.

*Theory of Moral Sentiments, The* – The first of Adam Smith's two major works, the other being *Wealth of Nations*.

**Theory of public choice** – The study of how groups participate in decision making.

**Tobin's q** – Developed by James Tobin, the ratio between the market value and the replacement value of an economic good, which can be used to identify a relationship between financial markets and the markets for goods and services.

**Tobin tax** – A tax on the spot conversion of a currency to a second currency to penalize short-term currency transactions.

**Trade** – The voluntary exchange between two entities for the express purpose of improving the standard of living for both.

**Trade agreements** – Trade pacts between nations to promote free trade, or preferential trade, or to identify a tariff, quota, or other trade restriction.

**Trade-offs** – Another term for opportunity cost.

**Tragedy of the commons** – The overuse of public goods with no regard to the costs of use.

**Transaction costs** – The costs related to making, reaching, and enforcing agreements.

**Transfer payments** – Distribution of income from governments to individuals by way of money payments with no goods or services in return.

**Transitional economy** – Once developing economies whose economic measures reflect significant growth yet are still too low to be considered a developed nation; the BRIC nations of Brazil, Russia, India, and China are examples of transitional economies.

**Unemployment** – The total number of adults 16 and over who are not working but are willing and able to work and actively looking for work.

**Unemployment insurance** – A transfer payment to those who are willing and able to work but currently not working.

**Unemployment rate** – A measure of people who are not working but are willing and able to do so.

**United Nations Conference on Trade and Development (UNCTAD)** – Established in 1964 as a UN intergovernmental body; assists and serves developing nations with trade, investment, and development opportunities.

**United Nations Millennium Project (Goals)** – An initiative to implement operational means to achieve the Millennium Development Goals (MDGs) developed by the United Nations in 2000 to address poverty reduction, hunger, disease, illiteracy, discrimination against women, and environmental degradation; 2015 is the target date for achieving these goals.

**U.S. Department of Commerce** – A cabinet-level department charged with promoting economic growth and creating jobs by collecting, analyzing, and reporting economic and demographic data.

**U.S. Department of Treasury** – Established in 1789 by Congress, the cabinet-level executive department was created to manage government revenue, print paper currency, mint coins for circulation, collect federal taxes, and manage U.S. government debt instruments.

**Usury** – The charging of interest when loaning money.

**Utilitarianism** – An early theory of ethics promoted by John Stuart Mill and Jeremy Bentham; utilitarianism promotes the idea that the good is whatever has the most utility in maximizing overall happiness.

**Utility** – A representation of the satisfaction one experiences, according to one's various preferences, when consuming a good or service.

**Value, theory of** – A generic term that includes all economic theories regarding the value of prices for goods and services.

**Value added** – The price of a final good minus the value of intermediate inputs used to produce it.

**Value of the marginal product** – The value of additional revenue generated from a one-unit change in an input.

**Vector auto regression (VAR) model** – A theoretical construct designed to test cause-and-effect relationships such as the impact of increases in interest rates on the money supply or the consequences of tax cuts on growth and inflation.

**Velocity of money** – Measure of the number of times a currency revolves completely through the economy.

**Victorian era** – A period in British history named for Queen Victoria's reign from 1837 to 1901.

**Volcker Rule** – A component of the Financial Reform Act of 2010 proposed by Paul Volcker to limit a U.S. bank's ability to make certain speculative investments that do not profit their customers.

**Voluntary exchange** – Elective trade between a buyer and a seller on which both anticipate to be better off as a result of the exchange.

**Wages** – Compensation to the labor resource components in the production of a final goods and services.

***Wealth of Nations: An Inquiry into the Causes of the Wealth of Nations, The*** – Authored in 1776, the main writing of Adam Smith, which altered the study of economics and changed economic thought from mercantilism; considered the beginning of classical economics.

**Welfare economics** – The branch of economics that uses microeconomic tools, methods, and theory to assess the economic well-being of individuals and their economic activities as groups, societies, and communities.

**Welfare state** – A political unit where a government has a major role in the protection and promotion of the individual through specific government economic and social organizations; modern welfare states include Iceland, Sweden, and Norway, where significant revenue transfer from individuals to the state funds public services like education and health care.

**World Bank** – Established during the Bretton Woods conference following World War II, a multinational agency whose purpose is to make loans to developing nations to improve the development of a nation's infrastructure such as schools, hospitals, sanitation, and roads.

**World Trade Organization (WTO)** – An independent organization created during GATT talks for the express purpose of serving as the main international body to promote international trade among developed and developing nations; also serves as the refereeing body for international trade disputes.

**Zero-sum game (exchange)** – A game in which the players as a group have the same (equal) value at the conclusion of the game as they did at the beginning of the game or exchange.

# Selected Bibliography

## Austrian School

Boettke, Peter J., ed. *The Elgar Companion to Austrian Economics*. London: Edward Elgar, 1994.

Gloria-Palermo, Sandye. *Evolution of Austrian Economics: From Menger to Lachmann*. London: Routledge, 1999.

Grassl, Wolfgang, and Barry Smith. *Austrian Economics: Historical and Philosophical Background*. Beckenham, Australia: Taylor and Francis, 2010.

Koppl, Roger. *Explorations in Austrian Economics*. Bingley, UK: Emerald Group, 2008.

Schulak, Eugen Maria, and Herbert Unterkofler. *The Austrian School of Economics: A History of Its Ideas, Ambassadors, and Institutions*. Auburn, AL: Ludwig von Mises Institute, 2011.

## Bank of International Settlements

Baker, James C. *The Bank for International Settlements: Evolution and Evaluation*. Westport, CT: Praeger, 2002.

Koch, Elmar. *Challenges at the Bank for International Settlements: An Economist's (Re)view*. New York: Springer, 2007.

Schloss, Henry H. *The Bank for International Settlements*. Amsterdam: North-Holland, 1958.

## Capitalism

Fulcher, James. *Capitalism: A Very Short Introduction*. Oxford: Oxford University Press, 2004.

Schumpeter, Joseph A. *Capitalism, Socialism, and Democracy*. 3rd ed. Oxford: Routledge, 1950.

Zingales, Luigi A. *Capitalism for the People: Recapturing the Lost Genius of American Prosperity*. New York: Basic Books, 2012.

## Chicago School

Emmett, Ross B. *The Elgar Companion to the Chicago School of Economics*. Northampton, MA: Edward Elgar, 2010.

Emmett, Ross B. *Frank Knight and the Chicago School in American Economics*. Abingdon, UK: Routledge, 2009.

Samuels, Warren J. *The Chicago School of Political Economy*. Piscataway, NJ: Transaction, 1993.

Valdes, Juan Gabriel. *Pinochet's Economists: The Chicago School of Economics in Chile*. New York: Cambridge University Press, 1995.

van Overtveldt, Johan. *The Chicago School: How the University of Chicago Assembled the Thinkers Who Revolutionized Economics and Business*. Chicago: Agate, 2007.

## Classical Economics

Barber, William J. *A History of Economic Thought*. Middletown, CT: Wesleyan University Press, 2009.

Gilder, George, and Steve Forbes. *Wealth and Poverty: A New Edition for the Twenty-First Century*. Washington, DC: Regnery, 2012.

Kurz, Heinz D., and Neri Salvadori. *Interpreting Classical Economics: Studies in Long-Period Analysis*. London: Routledge, 2007.

Kurz, Heinz D., and Neri Salvadori. *Understanding "Classical" Economics: Studies in Long-Period History*. London: Routledge, 2003.

Morgan, Mary S. *The World in the Model: How Economists Work and Think*. Cambridge: Cambridge University Press, 2012.

Rickards, James. *Currency Wars: The Making of the Next Global Crisis*. New York: Portfolio Trade, 2012.

Smith, Matthew. *Thomas Tooke and the Monetary Thought of Classical Economics*. London: Routledge, 2011.

Sowell, Thomas. *Classical Economics Reconsidered*. Princeton, NJ: Princeton University Press, 1974.

Sowell, Thomas. *On Classical Economics*. New Haven, CT: Yale University Press, 2007.

Wolff, Richard D., and Stephen A. Resnick. *Contending Economic Theories: Neoclassical, Keynesian, and Marxian*. Boston: MIT Press, 2012.

## *The Communist Manifesto*

Blaisdell, Bob, ed. *The Communist Manifesto and Other Revolutionary Writings: Marx, Marat, Paine, Mao Tse-Tung, Gandhi and Others*. Mineola, NY: Dover, 2003.

Marx, Karl, and Frederick Engels. *The Communist Manifesto*. London: Arcturus, 2010.

Marx, Karl, and Frederick Engels. *The Communist Manifesto: Complete with Seven Rarely Published Prefaces*. Minneapolis, MN: Filiquarian, 2007.

## Development Economics (Economics of Developing Nations)

Acemoglu, Daron, and James Robinson. *Why Nations Fail: The Origins of Power, Prosperity, and Poverty*. New York: Crown Business, 2012.

Landes, David S. *The Wealth and Poverty of Nations: Why Some Are So Rich and Some So Poor*. New York: Norton, 1999.

Miller, Debra A. *Developing Nations*. Farmington Hills, MI: Greenhaven, 2007.

Powell, Benjamin, ed. *Making Poor Nations Rich: Entrepreneurship and the Process of Economic Development*. Palo Alto, CA: Stanford Economics and Finance, 2007.

Prashad, Vijay. *The Darker Nations: A People's History of the Third World*. A New Press People's History. New York: New Press, 2007.

## Federal Reserve System

Beckhart, Benjamin Haggott. *Federal Reserve Systems*. New York: Columbia University Press, 1972.

Greider, William. *Secrets of the Temple: How the Federal Reserve Runs the Country*. New York: Simon and Schuster, 1987.

Harris, Ethan S. *Ben Bernanke's Fed: The Federal Reserve after Greenspan*. Cambridge, MA: Harvard Business School Press, 2008.

Meltzer, Allan H. *A History of the Federal Reserve: Volume 2, Book 1, 1951–1969*. Chicago: University of Chicago Press, 2010.

Meltzer, Allan H. *A History of the Federal Reserve: Volume 2, Book 2, 1970–1986*. Chicago: University of Chicago Press, 2004.

## Friedman, Milton

Butler, Eamonn. *Milton Friedman: A Concise Guide to the Ideas and Influence of the Free-Market Economist*. Hampshire, UK: Harriman House, 2011.

Ebenstein, Lanny. *Milton Friedman: A Biography*. Basingstoke, UK: Palgrave Macmillan, 2007.

Friedman, Milton, and Rose Friedman. *Two Lucky People: Memoirs*. Chicago: University of Chicago Press, 1998.

## *General Theory on Equilibrium of Employment, Interest, and Money*

Keynes, John Maynard. *The General Theory of Employment, Interest and Money*. Ocala, FL: Atlantic, 2006.

Keynes, John Maynard. *The General Theory of Employment, Interest and Money*. Kila, MT: Kessinger, 2010.

## Great Depression

McElvaine, Robert S., ed. *Down and Out in the Great Depression: Letters from the Forgotten Man*. Chapel Hill: University of North Carolina Press, 2007.

Shlaes, Amity. *The Forgotten Man: A New History of the Great Depression*. New York: Harper Perennial, 2008.

## Hayek, Friedrich von

Caldwell, Bruce. *Hayek's Challenge: An Intellectual Biography of F. A. Hayek*. Chicago: University of Chicago Press, 2004.

Ebenstein, Alan. *Friedrich Hayek: A Biography*. New York: St. Martin's Press, 2001.

Ebenstein, Alan. *Hayek's Journey*. New York: Palgrave Macmillan, 2003.

Hayek, F. A. *Hayek on Hayek: An Autobiographical Dialogue*. Edited by Stephen Kresge and Leif Wenar. Chicago: University of Chicago Press, 1994.

Wapshott, Nicholas. *Keynes Hayek: The Clash That Defined Modern Economics*. New York: Norton, 2012.

## International Monetary Fund

Copelovitch, Mark S. *The International Monetary Fund in the Global Economy: Banks, Bonds, and Bailouts*. Cambridge: Cambridge University Press, 2010.

Danaher, Kevin, and Muhammed Yunus. *Fifty Years Is Enough: The Case against the World Bank and the International Monetary Fund*. Brooklyn, NY: South End Press, 1999.

Eichengreen, Barry J. *Globalizing Capital: A History of the International Monetary System*. Princeton, NJ: Princeton University Press, 2008.

McQuillan, Lawrence, and Peter Montgomery. *The International Monetary Fund*. Stanford, CA: Hoover Institute Press, 1999.

Vreeland, James Raymond. *The International Monetary Fund: Politics of Conditional Lending*. Global Institutions. New York: Routledge, 2013.

### Keynes, John Maynard

Keynes, John Maynard. *Essays in Persuasion*. Kila, MT: Kessinger, 2010.

Minsky, Hyman. *John Maynard Keynes*. New York: McGraw-Hill, 2008.

Skidelsky, Robert. *John Maynard Keynes: 1883–1946: Economist, Philosopher, Statesman*. New York: Macmillan, 1980.

Skidelsky, Robert Jacob Alexander. *Keynes: The Return of the Master*. London: PublicAffairs, 2009.

Skidelsky, Robert Jacob Alexander. *Keynes: A Very Short Introduction*. Oxford: Oxford University Press, 2010.

Skousen, Mark. *The Big Three in Economics: Adam Smith, Karl Marx, and John Maynard Keynes*. Armonk, NY: M.E. Sharpe, 2007.

Wapshott, Nicholas. *Keynes Hayek: The Clash That Defined Modern Economics*. New York: Norton, 2012.

### London School of Economics

Dahrendorf, Ralf. *LSE: A History of the London School of Economics and Political Science, 1895–1995*. New York: Oxford University Press, 1995.

Russell, Jesse, and Ronald Cohn, eds. *London School of Economics*. Stoughton, WI: Book on Demand, 2012.

### Marx, Karl

Marx, Karl. *The Portable Karl Marx*. Translated by Eugene Kamenka. New York: Penguin Books, 1983.

Simon, Lawrence H., and Karl Marx. *Selected Writings*. Indianapolis, IN: Hackett, 1994.

### Nobel Prize in Economics

Breit, William, and Barry T. Hirsch. *Lives of the Laureates*. 4th ed. Cambridge, MA: MIT Press, 2004.

Horn, Karen Ilse. *Roads to Wisdom, Conversations with Ten Nobel Laureates in Economics*. London: Edward Elgar, 2009.

Karier, Tom. *Intellectual Capital: Forty Years of the Nobel Prize in Economics*. Cambridge: Cambridge University Press, 2010.

Wahid, Abu N. M. *Frontiers of Economics: Nobel Laureates of the Twentieth Century*. Westport, CT: Greenwood, 2002.

### Say's Law

Kates, Steven. *Say's Law and the Keynesian Revolution: How Macroeconomic Theory Lost Its Way*. London: Edward Elgar, 2009.

Sowell, Thomas. *Say's Law: An Historical Analysis*. Princeton, NJ: Princeton University Press, 1972.

## Smith, Adam

Buchan, James, *The Authentic Adam Smith: His Life and Ideas*. New York: Norton, 2006.
Colander, David, and A. W. Coats, eds. *The Spread of Economic Ideas*. Cambridge: Cambridge University Press, 1989.
Rae, John. *Life of Adam Smith*. Charleston, SC: Nabu Press, 2010.

## Socialism

Harrington, Michael. *Socialism: Past and Future*. New York: Little, Brown, 1989.
Maass, Alan, and Howard Zinn. *The Case for Socialism*. Chicago: Haymarket Books, 2010.
Nichols, John. *The "S" Word: A Short History of an American Tradition … Socialism*. Brooklyn, NY: Verso, 2011.

## Stockholm School of Economics

Jonung, Lars, ed. *The Stockholm School of Economics Revisited*. New York: Cambridge University Press, 1991.

## *The Wealth of Nations*

Smith, Adam. *The Wealth of Nations: The Economics Classic*. With an introduction by Tom Butler-Bowdon. Mankato, MN: Capstone, 2010.

## World Bank

Danaher, Kevin, and Muhammed Yunus. *Fifty Years Is Enough: The Case against the World Bank and the International Monetary Fund*. Brooklyn, NY: South End Press, 1999.
Klees, Steven J., Joel Samoff, and Nelly P. Stromquist. *The World Bank and Education: Critiques and Alternatives*. Rotterdam, Netherlands: Sense, 2012.
Marshall, Katherine. *The World Bank: From Reconstruction to Development to Equity*. New York: Routledge, 2008.
World Bank. *A Guide to the World Bank*. Washington, DC: World Bank Publications, 2011.

## World Trade Organization

Cottier, Thomas, and Manfred Elsig, eds. *Governing the World Trade Organization: Past, Present and Beyond Doha*. Cambridge: Cambridge University Press, 2011.
Hoekman, Bernard M., and Michel M. Kostecki. *The Political Economy of the World Trading System*. New York: Oxford University Press, 2010.
Narlikar, Amrita, Martin Daunton, and Robert M. Stern. *The Oxford Handbook on the World Trade Organization*. Oxford Handbooks in Politics. New York: Oxford University Press, 2012.

# About the Editor and Contributors

**David A. Dieterle** is professor and lecturer of economics at Walsh College (Troy, Michigan) and University of Michigan, Flint. He is a national teaching fellow for the Foundation for Teaching Economics. He has served economic education centers and councils in Ohio, Nebraska, Illinois, Wisconsin, and Michigan. His previous published books include *Economic Experiences*, *Energy and Economics*, and *Entrepreneurship and Economics*. Dieterle holds a doctorate from Michigan State University.

## Contributors

**Michael B. Becraft**
Park University School of Business,
El Paso, TX

**William S. Chappell**
HCS Early College High School
Conway, SC

**Stephen H. Day**
North Carolina State University
Raleigh, NC

**Joy Dooley-Sorrells**
ENCOR Solutions
Panama City, FL

**Steven Downing**
Global Island English
Manila, Philippines

**Diane Fournier**
Tinkham Alternative High School
Westland, MI

**Aimee Register Gray**
Crescent High School
Anderson, SC

**Victoria Green**
Albany High School
Albany, GA

**Kathryn Lloyd Gustafson**
Farmington High School
Farmington, MI

**Joseph Lee Hauser**
Boiling Springs High School
Boiling Springs, SC

**Heather Isom**
Florence High School
Florence, AZ

**Rebecca Kraft**
Plymouth High School
Plymouth, MI

**Jean Kujawa**
Lourdes University
Sylvania, OH

**Cynthia Blitz Law**
White Station Middle School
Memphis, TN

## ABOUT THE EDITOR AND CONTRIBUTORS

**Dave Leapard**
Eastern Michigan University
Ypsilanti, MI

**Samantha Lohr**
HCS Early College High School
Conway, SC

**Elham Mahmoudi**
University of Michigan
Ann Arbor, MI

**Carol Lynn Nute**
River Bluff High School
Lexington, SC

**Kerry Pannell**
DePauw University
Greencastle, IN

**Andrew Probert**
Academy of the Pacific
Honolulu, HI

**Martha R. Rowland**
The University of Michigan, Dearborn
Dearborn, MI

**Timothy P. Schilling**
Davenport University
Grand Rapids, MI

**Kathleen C. Simmons**
Alamo Community College
San Antonio, TX

**Sara Standen**
Carman-Ainsworth High School
Flint, MI

**Nevena Trajkov**
Eastern Michigan University
Ypsilanti, MI

**John E. Trupiano**
Desert Mountain High School
Scottsdale, AZ

**Joseph A. Weglarz**
University of Detroit, Mercy
Detroit, MI

**Ninee Shoua Yang**
Wayne State University
Detroit, MI

# Index

*Note: Page numbers in **bold** font indicate main entries.*

Addiction, economics of, 269
*Affirmative Action around the World* (Sowell), 410–11
*Affluent Society, The* (Galbraith), 103, 105
Africa, 57, 354, 418
    HIV/AIDS in, 291, 292
African Americans, 273–74, 410
Agricultural economics, 318
    Boserup on, 32, 33–34
    European Union and, 450
    Schultz on, 367, 368
    Thunen's models for, 441–42
*Aid Watch* (blog), 74
Airline industry, deregulation of, 165, 166
Akerlof, George, **1–3**, 412
    as Nobel laureate, 1, 3, 412, 425
Alchian, Armen, **4–6**, 387
    on inflation, 4–5
    on monetary policy, 5
Allais, Maurice, **6–8**
    golden rule of accumulation and, 7
    on risk, 7
*American Capitalism* (Galbraith), 104
*American Dilemma, An: The Negro Problem and Modern Democracy* (Myrdal), 273–74
*America's Great Depression* (Rothbard), 348
Antitrust economics, 485–86
Aplia company, 341, 342
ARCH (autoregressive conditional heteroskedasticity) model, 84, 85–86
Arrow, Kenneth, **9–11**, 234, 379, 430
    as Nobel laureate, 9, 135, 137
Asset pricing. *See* Capital asset pricing
Asymmetric information, 251, 252, 425, 462, 463
Aumann, Robert, **11–12**, 385
    folk theorem of, 11
    as Nobel laureate, 11, 362, 363–64
Austrian School of economics, 79, 128, 145
    Böhm-Bawerk and, 30, 31, 47, 324, 371
    Haberler and, 117, 259
    Hayek and, 124, 259
    Machlup and, 219
    Menger and, 30, 242–43, 481
    Wieser and, 371, 481
    *See also* Mises, Ludwig von
*Austria Over All, If She Only Will* (Hornick), 147–48

Balance of payments, 162, 266
Balance of trade, 55, 152, 263, 264
Banerjee, Abhijit, 69–70
*Banking Policy and Price Level* (Robertson), 335
Bargaining model, in game theory, 270–71, 277
Bastiat, Frédéric, **13–15**
    on protectionism and tariffs, 14–15
Bauer, Otto, **16–18**
    socialism and, 16–17
Becker, Gary, **18–20**
    *Human Capital*, 18
    as Nobel laureate, 18, 19, 105
Behavioral economics, 7, 223, 438, 439
    Becker and, 18–19
    Kahneman and, 167, 168–69, 298
    organizational problem solving and, 393
    Vickrey auction, 462
    *See also* Choice behavior theory
Bellagio Group, 220, 221

Bentham, Jeremy, **20–22**
  Mill and, 21, 247, 248
  utilitarianism and, 20, 21
Bernanke, Ben
  Federal Reserve and, **22–25**, 64, 67
  on Great Depression, 23
*Best Use of Economic Resources, The* (Kantorovich), 175
*Between Two Wars* (Bauer), 16–17
Beveridge, William, **25–27**
  British welfare state and, 25, 26, 178
Bhagwati, Jagdish, **27–29**
  free trade and, 27, 28
Black-Scholes model, 245, 364, 365
Böhm-Bawerk, Eugen von, **30–32**, 254, 481
  Austrian School and, 30, 31, 47, 324, 371
  on capital and interest, 30–31, 47, 324
  Marx and, 30, 138
Boserup, Ester, **32–35**
  on Malthusian paradigm, 32, 33–34
*Bottom Billion, The* (Collier), 57
Bretton Woods system, 120, 128, 178, 335
  gold standard and, 391, 466
Buchanan, James, **35–37**
  *Democracy in Deficit*, 36
  public choice theory and, 35, 451
Buddhist economics, 369
Bull's-eye model, 30, 31
Burns, Arthur, **37–39**, 94
  Federal Reserve Board and, 38, 39
  monetary policy and, 38–39
Bush (G. H. W.) administration, 112
Bush (G. W.) administration, 22, 23, 113, 225
Business cycle, 38, 173, 313
  Haberler on, 117, 118
  Keynesian economics and, 176, 359
  Kydland and Prescott on, 196, 197, 315
  Mises on, 255
  monetary policy and, 397–98
  rational expectations and, 359
  Schumpeter on, 370, 372
*Business Cycles* (Schumpeter), 372

Cambridge School, 177, 239, 251–52, 378
  Kaldor and, 170, 171
  Pasinetti at, 300
  Sraffa and, 416
  *See also* Keynesian economics
Cantillon, Richard, **41–43**, 420
  *Essai Sur la Nature du Commerce en Général*, 41, 42
  on price as "intrinsic value," 42
  South Sea bubble and, 41–42
Capital, 125–26
  interest and, 30–31, 47
  Pasinetti's theory of, 301
  production costs and, 381
  theory of, 301
Capital asset pricing model (CAPM), 387
Capitalism, 185, 232, 305
  Böhm-Bawerk's exploitation theory and, 30
  Protestantism and, 475, 476
  Veblen on, 460
*Capitalism, Socialism and Democracy* (Schumpeter), 372
*Capital* (Marx), 232, 479–80
Capture theory, 423
Carlyle, Thomas, **43–46**
  Chartism and, 44–45
  *Sartor Resartus*, 44
Carnegie Institute of Technology, 240–41, 258, 393
Carter, Jimmy, 165, 166, 363, 423
Cassel, Gustav, **46–48**
  purchasing power parity theory, 47
Central planning board (CPB), 204–5
Chain store paradox, 376–77
*Challenge of World Poverty, The* (Myrdal), 274
*Chartism* (Carlyle), 44–45
Chicago School of economics, 93–95, 183, 216, 249, 465
  freshwater economics movement and, 358
  Simons and, 397
  *See also* Free market/trade; Friedman, Milton
Child, Josiah, **48–50**, 283
  mercantilism and, 48–49
Chinese economy, 54, 308, 331–32
  Qin Shi Huang and, 149–51

Choice behavior theory, 235, 236, 260, 269
   North and, 280, 281
   P. Romer on, 342
   *See also* Public choice theory
Circle Bastiat, 323, 348
Circular flow of economic activity, 88, 317–18, 416
   Leontief's input-output model and, 206, 207
Civil Aeronautics Board, U.S., 165, 166
Clark, John Bates, **50–52**
   marginal productivity theory and, 50, 51
Classical economics, 51, 324, 416, 454
   Friedman and, 95
   Menger's critique of, 242, 243–44
   Tullock and, 450
Climate change, 355, 417, 418–19
   "green" innovation and, 419
Clinton administration, 112, 430, 455
   Reich in, 321, 322
   Stiglitz in, 424, 425
Cliometrics, 91, 280
*Coal Question, The* (Jevons), 160
Coase, Ronald, **52–54**
   on externalities, 53, 310
   "Nature of the Firm, The," 53
   as Nobel laureate, 54
Coase theorem, 53–54
Cognitive psychology, 236
Cointegration, 109
Colbert, Jean-Baptiste, **54–56**
   mercantilism and, 55, 56, 318
   Versailles and, 56
Collective action, 289–90
Collier, Paul, **57–58**
   on global poverty, 57
   *Plundered Planet, The*, 57–58
Commission on Growth and Development, 412, 413
Common-pool resources, 294
*Common Sense of Political Economy* (Wicksteed), 480
*Communist Manifesto* (Marx & Engels), 83, 231–33
Comparative advantage, 118, 326–27

Competition, 51, 158
   imperfect, 337
*Conditions of Agricultural Growth* (Boserup), 33–34
Congressional Budget Office, 328, 329
Conspicuous consumption, 459–60
Consumer behavior, 94, 95, 356
   advertising and, 105
   consumer demand models, 182, 428–29
   indifference curve and, 76
   Veblen on, 459–60
   *See also* Behavioral economics
Consumer surplus, 71, 72, 230
"Contribution to the Theory of Economic Growth, A" (Solow), 407, 408
Corn Law debates, 283, 327, 421
   Malthus and, 222, 223
Corporate finance, 250, 258
Cost-benefit analysis, 35, 51, 478
Cost-push inflation, 357
"Costs and Outputs" (Alchian), 5
Council of Economic Advisers, 1, 112, 225, 339
   Bernanke on, 23
   Burns on, 38
   Heller on, 133, 134
   Okun on, 287
   Solow on, 408
   Stiglitz on, 424, 425
   Tobin on, 447
   Tyson on, 456
Cowles Foundation, 59–60, 186, 227, 447
   Shiller and, 388, 390
Creative destruction, 111, 370, 372, 478
Credit Lyonnais Affair, 449

Debreu, Gérard, 7, **59–61**, 314
   mathematical economics and, 59, 60–61
   as Nobel laureate, 60, 61
Debt-deflation theory, 89
Demand, elasticity of, 264
Demand curve, 71, 210, 230
   *See also* Supply and demand
*Democracy: The God That Failed* (Hoppe), 146

*Democracy in Deficit* (Buchanan), 36
Demographics, 222, 381, 428
De Soto, Hernando, **62–64**
    Institute for Liberty and Democracy and, 62
    on property rights, 62, 63
Developing countries, 171, 187, 209, 498
    appropriate technology and, 369
    global economy and, 51
    IMF and, 203
    microeconomics in, 69–70
    Myrdal on, 274
    policy reform in, 189, 190
    Sachs on, 353, 355
    Schultz on, 367, 368
    sex-selective abortion in, 292
    Stiglitz on, 426
    Stolper-Samuelson theorem and, 356
*Development as Freedom* (Sen), 379
Development economics, 87, 209
    Collier on, 57
    Duflo and, 68–70
    Easterly on, 73–74
    Kregel and, 187–88
    Lewis on, 209, 210
    Romer on, 341
    Sen and, 379
    *See also* Developing countries
Diamond, Peter, **64–66**, 236, 262, 311
    Diamond-Mirrlees efficiency theorem, 64, 251, 252
    Social Security system and, 64, 65
*Discourses upon Trade* (North), 282, 283
Discrimination, economics of, 18
    *See also* Affirmative action
*Distribution of Wealth, The* (Clark), 51
Division of labor, 109, 180, 403–4
Domar, E. D., 119, 120
Draghi, Mario, **66–68**
    European Central Bank and, 66, 67
Duflo, Esther, **68–70**
    Banerjee and, 69–70
    development economics and, 68–70
    microfinance and, 70
*Dumping: A Problem in International Trade* (Viner), 464

Dupuit, Jules, **71–72**, 78
    relative utility and, 71–72
Dynamic economics, 197

Easterly, William, **73–75**
    on aid to poor countries, 74
East India Company, 48, 248, 263–64, 421
*Econometrica* (journal), 169
Econometrics, 85, 115, 182, 216
    Frisch and, 97, 98, 444
    Granger causality test, 109
    Heckman and, 129, 130
    McFadden and, 235–36
    Prescott and, 313, 315
    Tinbergen and, 444, 445
    Tobin model, 448
    vector auto regression and, 399
    *See also* Mathematical economics
*Economic Approach to Human Behavior, The* (Becker), 19
*Economic Consequences of the Peace, The* (Keynes), 178
Economic growth, 447
    as creative destruction, 370, 372
    government and, 290
    Harrod-Domar model of, 119, 120
    human capital and, 18, 152
    in India, 402
    mathematical models, 429
    microeconomics and, 69–70
    national income accounting and, 193, 194–95
    Okun's law and, 287–88
    Quesnay on, 317–19
    Solow on, 407, 408
    Spence on, 412, 413–14
    technological change and, 341, 342
Economic growth of developing countries. *See* Developing countries; Development economics
Economic history, 348, 373, 374, 464
    Ekelund and, 78
    Fogel and, 90–93
    Heilbroner and, 131, 132
    Hollander and, 143–45

North and, 279–81
Robbins and, 333
C. Romer and, 339–40
Sargent and, 359
Economic policy, 314, 399, 422, 465
mercantilism and, 49
Russian reform of, 101, 102
Economic Recovery Advisory Board, 467
Economic rent, 141, 142, 223, 326, 381, 451
Economic Report of 1962 (Council of Economic Advisers), 447
*Economics: An Introductory Analysis* (Samuelson), 356
*Economics in One Lesson* (Hazlitt), 128–29
*Economics of Being Poor, The* (Schultz), 368
*Economics of Imperfect Competition* (Robinson), 336, 337
*Economics of Regulation* (Kahn), 165
"Economics of Superstars, The" (Rosen), 343–44
*Economic Sophisms* (Bastiat), 14
*Economics Survey 1919–1939* (Lewis), 210
Economies of scale, 192, 294
*Economy and Society* (Weber), 476
Edgeworth, Francis, **75–77**, 298
Edgeworth Box, 76–77
*Mathematical Psychics*, 76
Education, 269, 322, 381
early childhood, 130, 411
earnings and, 344
opportunity cost of, 367, 368
as positive externality, 309, 310
Spence on, 413
student incentives and, 346
"Education and Self-Selection" (Rosen & Willis), 344
Ehrlich, Paul, 395
Eisenhower administration, 38
Ekelund, Robert B., Jr., **77–79**
Dupuit and, 78
*History of Economic Theory and Method, A*, 78
Elasticity, 230, 264
*Elegy to Gournay* (Turgot), 453
*Element of Pure Economics* (Walras), 471
*Elusive Quest for Growth, The* (Easterly), 73

Ely, Richard, **80–82**
Socialism and, 81
Wisconsin Idea and, 80
Employment. *See* Labor and labor market; Unemployment
"Endogenous Technological Change" (Romer), 341, 342
Energy depletion theory, 160
Energy efficiency, 418
Engels, Friedrich, **82–84**
*Communist Manifesto*, 83, 231–33
Marx and, 82, 83, 232
Engerman, Stanley, 92
*England's Treasure by Foreign Trade* (Mun), 148, 264
Engle, Robert, **84–86**
ARCH model and, 84, 85–86
as Nobel laureate, 84, 109
*English Local Government* (Webb & Webb), 474
Entrepreneurship, 42, 120, 184, 368
Calvinism and, 476
Schumpeter on, 370, 371, 372
transaction costs and, 53
Environment, 105, 324, 395
climate change and, 355, 418
*Equality and Efficiency* (Okun), 288
Equation of exchange, 89
Equilibrium, 7, 60, 406, 480
Edgeworth Box and, 75, 76–77
exchange rates and, 47
flexprice/fixprice taxonomy and, 136–37
game theory and, 270–71, 278, 376
general theory of, 47, 136, 188, 471, 472
global economy and, 51
input-output analysis of, 206, 207
Kaldor and, 170, 171
Sharpe's CAP model and, 387
*Essai Sur la Nature du Commerce en Général* (Cantillon), 41, 42
*Essay on the Nature and Significance of Economic Science* (Robbins), 333
*Essay on the Principle of Population, An* (Malthus), 222
*Essentials of Economic Theory* (Clark), 51
*Ethics of Competition, The* (Knight), 184

Euro (monetary unit), 265, 266, 267
European Central Bank (ECB), 66, 67, 449, 450
Exchange markets, Tobin tax and, 448
Exchange rates, 118, 267, 448
  purchasing power parity theory, 47
*Experimental Economics: Induced Value Theory* (Smith), 405, 406
Exploitation theory, capitalism and, 30
Externality, 53, 309–10

Fabian Society, 26, 473, 474, 479
Family, economics of, 19
Federal Open Market Committee, 23, 112, 339
Federal Reserve System, 374–75, 400, 409
  Bernanke as chairman of, **22–25**, 64, 67
  Burns as chairman of, 38, 39
  Great Depression and, 23, 117, 241, 348, 374
  Greenspan as chairman of, 23, 111, 112–13
  interest rates and, 112, 113, 359
  Meltzer's history of, 241–42
  Volcker as chairman of, 38, 465–67
  Yellen on board of governors, 493, 494
Finance economics, 188, 466
  Black-Scholes model, 245, 364, 365
  Colbert and, 55
  deregulation and, 430
  Johnson and, 162
  Long-Term Capital Management and, 245–46, 364, 365–66
  Markowitz and, 226, 227
  Miller-Modigliani theorem and, 249, 250, 256, 258
  Scholes and, 364–65
  Sharpe and, 386–88
  Tobin's portfolio theory, 447
Financial markets, 365–66, 386–87, 388
  portfolio theory, 447
Fiscal policy, 197
  Mundell and, 267
Fischer, Ernst, 17
Fischer, Stanley, **87–88**

Fisher, Irving, **88–90**, 398
  debt-deflation theory of, 89
Focal point, in game theory, 363
Fogel, Robert, **90–93**
  on American slavery, 92
  cliometrics and, 91
  *Railroads and American Economic Growth*, 91
"Folk theorem" (Aumann), 11
Food production, population and, 222–23, 367
*Frederick the Great* (Carlyle), 45
Free market/trade, 93, 249, 255, 403
  Bastiat and, 13, 14–15
  Bhagwati on, 28
  Buchanan on, 35
  George and, 107
  government role in, 397
  Hume's defense of, 152
  interest rates and, 49
  Irwin's defense of, 157, 158
  Knight and, 184
  List and, 211, 212
  Meade on, 238
  Mill's defense of, 248
  Mun's defense of, 264
  North on, 282, 283
  offshoring and, 27
  Reisman on, 324, 325
  Rothbard on, 348
  shock therapy and, 102
  Smith and, 140, 212, 404
  Turgot and, 453–54
  Zoellick and, 498
Free-rider problem, 289, 290, 419
*Free to Choose* (Friedman & Friedman), 96
French economics
  Colbert and, 54–56
  Lagarde and, 202–3
  Napoleonic government of, 361
  Say and, 360–62
  Turgot and, 452–54
Friedman, Milton, 7, 18, 23, **93–96**, 135
  free markets and, 93
  Lucas and, 216, 217
  *Monetary History of the United States, A*, 95, 374
  monetary reform and, 397, 398

at NBER, 94, 95
  Rosen and, 343
  Samuelson and, 356–57
  Schwartz and, 95, 162, 374
  shock therapy and, 353
  Stigler and, 423
  *Theory of the Consumption Function, A,* 94, 95
Friedman, Rose, 93–94, 96
Frisch, Ragnar, **97–98**
  econometrics and, 97, 98
  as Nobel laureate, 98, 444

Gaidar, Yegor, **101–3**
  shock therapy and, 101, 102
Galbraith, John Kenneth, **103–6**, 131, 200
  *Affluent Society, The*, 103, 105
  Keynesian view and, 104, 105
Gale-Shapley algorithm, 385
Game theory, 9
  Aumann and, 11
  bargaining model, 270–71, 277
  chain store paradox, 376–77
  equilibrium point and, 270–71, 278, 376
  focal point in, 363
  Gresham's law and, 271
  Harsanyi and, 122, 123
  mechanism design and, 153, 154, 233–34, 270, 272
  Morgenstern and, 259, 260
  Nash and, 11, 122, 277, 278–79, 375, 376
  organ transplant market and, 345, 346
  Schelling and, 362–63, 364
  Selten and, 375, 376
  Shapley and, 384–85
GDP. *See* Gross domestic product
General equilibrium theory, 136, 471, 472
  Cassel and, 47
  Edgeworth Box and, 75, 76–77
  Kaldor and, 170, 171
  Kregel and, 188
  *See also* Equilibrium
*General Theory of Employment, Interest, and Money, The* (Keynes), 131, 178, 273, 310, 337

Robertson and, 335
  Sraffa and, 416
  Tobin and, 446
George, Henry, **106–8**
  land use and, 107
  *Progress and Poverty*, 107, 479
  protectionism and, 107
  on tax reform, 106
  Wicksteed and, 479, 480
German Historical economics, 80
Giffen good, 344
Globalization, 28, 402, 413, 443
  protectionism and, 456
  Wolf and, 488
Global poverty, 74, 354–55
  Collier on, 57, 58
  Duflo and, 69–70
  Myrdal on, 274
  *See also* Poverty and the poor
Global warming, 418–19
Glut Controversy, 360, 361–62
GNP. *See* Gross national product
"Golden Rule of Accumulation" (Phelps), 7, 304
Gold standard, 264, 326
  Bretton Woods system and, 391, 466
  Harrod on, 120
  Machlup on, 219, 220
  Mundell on, 265, 266
  Nixon administration and, 391–92
  Sennholz and, 383, 384
Government, Locke on, 213, 214
Government intervention, 36, 117, 140, 414, 423
  externalities and, 309–10
  famine and, 379
  individual rights and, 324
  Kalecki on, 172
  Keynes on, 178
  Olson on, 290
  Reich on, 321–22
  Stiglitz on, 425
  Wicksell on, 478
Granger, Sir Clive, **109–10**
  econometrics and, 109, 110
  as Nobel laureate, 109
Great Depression, 128, 333, 339, 405

Allais and, 6–7
Bernanke on, 23, 24
debt-deflation theory of, 89
economic data in, 195
Ely and, 81
Federal Reserve and, 23, 117, 241, 348, 374
Lewis on, 210
Simons and, 396, 397
*Great Depression, The* (Robbins), 333
Great Recession (2008–9), 332, 350, 389
"Green" industrial revolution, 419
Greenspan, Alan, **111–13**
on Federal Reserve Board, 23, 111, 112–13
Gross domestic income (GDI), 195
Gross domestic product (GDP), 195, 288, 341, 379
Gross national product (GNP), 287, 339, 379
*Growth and Fluctuations* (Lewis), 210
Growth theory, 1, 171
See also Economic growth

Haavelmo, Trygve, **115–17**, 186
econometrics and, 115
as Nobel laureate, 115
Haberler, Gottfried von, **117–19**, 259
on business cycle, 118
*Theory of International Trade*, 117–18
Harrod, Sir Roy F., **119–20**, 408
economic growth model of, 119, 120
on entrepreneurs, 120
on international monetary relations, 120
Harrod-Domar model, 119, 120
Harsanyi, John, **122–24**, 377
game theory and, 122, 123
as Nobel laureate, 122, 123, 277, 279
Harvard University, 9, 131, 329, 363, 430, 432
Hawkins-Simon theorem, 393
Hayek, Friedrich von, **124–27**, 170, 210, 254, 259
at London School of Economics, 125, 333
as Nobel laureate, 124, 126, 272, 274
*Road to Serfdom, The*, 126

Hazlitt, Henry, **127–29**
*Economics in One Lesson*, 127–28
Mises and, 128
*Head to Head: The Coming Battle among Japan, Europe, and America* (Thurow), 443
Health economics, 269, 291–92
Hébert, Robert, 78
Heckman, James, **129–31**, 236
on early childhood education, 130
econometrics and, 129, 130
at NBER, 129–30
Heckscher, Eli, 162, 285, 286
Heckscher-Ohlin theory, 162, 285–86
"Hedonic Prices and Implicit Markets" (Rosen), 343
Heilbroner, Robert, **131–33**
*Worldly Philosophers, The*, 131, 132
Heller, Walter, **133–35**
on Council of Economic Advisers, 133, 134
on taxation, 134
"Hepatitis B and the Case of the Missing Women" (Oster), 291, 292
Hicks, Sir John, 6, **135–37**
on compensation criteria, 136
flexprice/fixprice taxonomy and, 136–37
Kaldor-Hicks efficiency theory, 171
as Nobel laureate, 9, 135, 137
Hilferding, Rudolf, **137–39**
as Austro-Marxist, 137, 138
Historians. See Economic history
*History of Economic Theory and Method, A* (Ekelund & Hébert), 78
*History of the Federal Reserve, A* (Meltzer), 241–42
Hobbes, Thomas, **139–41**
*Leviathan*, 140
Hobson, John, **141–43**
critique of imperialism by, 141, 142–43
Hollander, Samuel, **143–45**
*Studies in Classical Political Economy*, 143, 144
Hoppe, Hans-Hermann, **145–47**
on government officials, 145–46
on monopoly, 146

Hornick, Philipp Wilhelm von, **147–49**
   mercantilism and, 147–48
Housing market, 389
Huang, Qin Shi, **149–51**
   Li Si Huang and, 149, 150
   standardization under, 149, 150
*Human Action: A Treatise on Economics* (Mises), 255
Human capital, 18, 152, 322
   Phelps on, 305
   Romer on, 341, 342
   Schultz on, 367–68
   *See also* Labor and labor market
Hume, David, **151–53**
   on free trade, 152
   *Treatise on Human Nature*, 151
   utilitarianism and, 151–52
Hurwicz, Leonid, 9, **153–55**, 235
   on mechanism design theory, 153, 154, 234
   on social choice, 153–54

IMF. *See* International Monetary Fund
Imperfect competition, 337
*Imperialism* (Hobson), 142
Impossibility theorem, 9
Income distribution, 94, 298, 300–301
   *See also* Wages
India, 177, 251–52, 378, 401–2
   economic reforms in, 27, 401, 402
   *See also* East India Company
Indifference curve, 76, 77
Induced value theory, 406
Induction, probability and, 160
Industrial organization, 209–10
Industrial policy, Reich on, 321–22
Inflation, 8, 38, 121, 152
   Alchian's theories of, 4–5
   Burns's policies to combat, 38–39
   Cantillon on, 41, 42
   central banks and, 359
   cost-push, 357
   debt-deflation theory, 89
   interest rates and, 89, 197, 359, 467
   Kahn and, 166
   Mundell-Tobin effect, 266
   price freeze and, 392
   stagflation, 95, 118, 465–66

Inflation-unemployment trade-off, 217, 305, 306, 307, 466
Information economics, 219, 220, 400, 423
   asymmetric information, 251, 252, 425, 462, 463
Input-output analysis, 206, 207, 393, 408, 428
*In Quest of an Economic Discipline* (Allais), 7
*Inquiry into the Principles of Political Oeconomy* (Steuart), 420
Institute for Liberty and Democracy (ILD), 62
Institutional economics, 280, 281, 485
Institutional sclerosis, 290
*Interest and Prices* (Wicksell), 478
Interest rates, 215, 283
   bull's-eye model and, 30, 31
   Cassel on, 46–47
   Federal Reserve and, 112, 113, 359
   free trade and, 49
   golden rule of accumulation and, 7
   inflation and, 89, 197, 359
   Keynes on, 47, 178
   Kydland on, 197
International Monetary Fund (IMF), 266, 350, 426
   Krueger at, 189, 190
   Lagarde's leadership of, 202–3
International trade, 237, 238, 282, 438
   balance of, 55, 152, 263, 264
   Haberler on, 117–18
   Heckscher-Ohlin model of, 162, 285–86
   human capital and, 342
   Krueger and, 189, 190
   Krugman on, 191, 192
   Leontief paradox, 207
   mercantilism and, 48–49
   national economic systems and, 211, 212
   Stolper-Samuelson theorem, 356
   Viner on, 464
   *See also* Globalization; Protectionism
*Interregional and International Trade* (Ohlin), 285–86
Intrinsic value, price as, 42
Intuitive prediction, 168

"Investment under Uncertainty" (Prescott & Lucas), 314
*Irrational Exuberance* (Shiller), 389–90
Irwin, Douglas, **157–58**
   critique of protectionism, 157–58

Jevons, William Stanley, 46, **159–61**, 333, 472
   Cantillon's *Essai* and, 41, 42
   Jevons paradox, 160
   marginal utility theory and, 159–60, 230
   Wicksteed and, 479, 480
"Job Creation and Job Destruction in the Theory of Unemployment" (Pissarides), 311–12
Johnson, Harry, **161–63**
   possibility theorem of, 161, 162

Kahn, Alfred, **165–67**
   airline deregulation and, 165, 166
Kahneman, Daniel, **167–70**, 236
   behavioral economics of, 167, 168–69, 298
   as Nobel laureate, 167, 169
Kaldor, Nicholas, **170–72**
   Keynesian economics and, 170, 171
   Pasinetti and, 300, 301
   on taxation, 171
Kaldor-Hicks efficiency theory, 171
Kalecki, Michal, **172–74**
   on business cycle, 173
   Keynesian theory and, 172, 173
Kantorovich, Leonid, **174–76**, 185
   on linear programming, 174, 175
   as Nobel laureate, 175, 185, 186
   on resource allocation, 175–76
Kennedy, John F., 105, 134, 287, 447
Keynes, John Maynard, 162, **176–79**, 200
   business cycle and, 176, 359
   *Economic Consequences of the Peace, The*, 178
   Friedman and, 96
   Galbraith and, 104
   Haberler's critique of, 118
   Harrod and, 119, 120
   Hayek and, 124, 126
   on interest rates, 47, 178
   Khaldun and, 180
   Leontief's critique of, 206, 207–8
   Lucas and, 216
   Marshall and, 177, 229
   on measure of growth, 195
   Ohlin and, 286
   Pigou and, 177, 309, 310
   Robertson and, 334, 335
   Robinson and, 336, 337, 338
   Say's law and, 362
   Schumacher and, 369
   Sraffa and, 415, 416
   Wicksell and, 478
   Wolf and, 488
   *See also General Theory of Employment, Interest, and Money, The* (Keynes)
Keynesian economics, 1, 131, 176, 182, 425
   aggregate demand in, 38
   Buchanan on, 36
   Kaldor and, 170, 171, 300
   Kalecki and, 172, 173
   Kregel's critique of, 188
   Mankiw and, 224, 225–26
   Meade and, 237, 238, 239
   Okun's law and, 287
   Pasinetti and, 300
   Robbins and, 332, 333
   Samuelson and, 356, 357
   Tobin and, 446
   *See also* Keynes, John Maynard
Khaldun, Ibn, **179–81**, 200
   history theories of, 180
Klein, Lawrence, **181–83**
   Keynesian ideas and, 182
   mathematical economics and, 181, 182
   as Nobel laureate, 181, 182, 313
Knight, Frank, **183–85**
   *Risk, Uncertainty, and Profit*, 183, 184
Koopmans, Tjalling, 64, **185–87**
   Cowles Foundation and, 186
   as Nobel laureate, 175, 185, 186
Kregel, Jan, **187–89**
   critique of Keynes, 188
   United Nations and, 187–88
Krueger, Anne, **189–91**
   IMF and, 189, 190

Krugman, Paul, 28, **191–93**, 200
  on economies of scale, 192
  on international trade, 191, 192
Kuznets, Simon, **193–96**, 339
  Friedman and, 94, 95
  on national income accounting, 194–95
  as Nobel laureate, 193
Kydland, Finn, **196–98**
  on business cycle, 196, 197, 315
  dynamic economics of, 197
  Prescott and, 197, 313, 314, 315

Labor and labor market, 76, 261–62, 311, 479
  division of, 109, 180, 403–4
  education and, 344
  elasticity supply of, 210
  human capital, 18, 152, 322, 367–68
  offshoring and, 27
  Reich and, 321, 322
  signaling productivity in, 412–13
  value of, 223
  wage inequality in, 268
  *See also* Human capital; Unemployment
Labor theory of value, 303, 327, 403, 404, 421
Labor unions, free-rider problem and, 290
Laffer, Arthur B., **199–201**
  supply-side economics and, 199, 200–201
Laffer curve, 200
Lagarde, Christine, **202–3**
  IMF and, 202–3
Laissez-faire, 49, 67, 396, 397
  Reisman on, 323, 324
Land taxes, 453
Land use, 107, 303, 441–42
Lange, Oskar, **204–5**
  market socialism and, 204–5
Lausanne School of economics, 297
Law, John, 41
*Law, The* (Bastiat), 15
*Lectures on the Theory of Production, The* (Pasinetti), 301
Leontief, Wassily, **206–8**
  critique of Keynes by, 206, 207–8
  input-output model of, 206, 207, 408, 428

Leontief paradox, 207
  as Nobel laureate, 207, 208
*Leviathan* (Hobbes), 140
Lewis, Sir Arthur, **209–11**
  on development economics, 201, 210
  *Economics Survey 1919–1939*, 210
  as Nobel laureate, 209, 367, 368
Libertarianism, 348–49
Life cycle hypothesis, 257
Linear programming, 174, 175
List, Friedrich, **211–13**
  on national economies, 211, 212–13
  *Outline of American Political Economy*, 211–12
Location theory, of Thunen, 441–42
Locke, John, 152, **213–15**, 283
  on natural rights, 214
  on self-interest, 214–15
*Logic of Collective Action, The* (Olson), 289–90
London School of Economics (LSE), 2, 23, 136, 162, 171, 418
  Hayek at, 125, 333
  Meade at, 238, 239
  Pissarides at, 311
  Webb and, 473, 474
Louis XIV, King of France, 55, 56, 318
LSE. *See* London School of Economics
LTCM. *See* Long-Term Capital Management
Lucas, Robert, Jr., **216–18**
  critique of Keynes, 216
  Friedman and, 216, 217
  as Nobel laureate, 197, 216, 217, 314
  rational expectations theory of, 216, 217

Machlup, Fritz, **219–21**
  Bellagio Group and, 220, 221
  on gold standard, 219, 220
  on information economy, 219, 220
Macroeconomics, 4, 5, 120, 446
  Burns and, 38
  Kalecki and, 172, 173–74
  Keynes and, 176
  Okun's law and, 288
  Sims and Sargent and, 358, 359, 399

Smith and, 404
Wicksell and, 477
Yellen and, 493
Malthus, Thomas, **222–24**, 326, 361
   Corn Law debates and, 222, 223
   demographic economics and, 222
   *Principles of Political Economy*, 223–24
   rent theory and, 223, 326
Malthusian paradigm, 32, 33, 381, 477
*Man, Economy, and State* (Rothbard), 348
*Manifesto of the Communist Party* (Marx & Engels), 83, 231–33
Mankiw, Gregory, **224–26**
   new Keynesian theory and, 224, 225–26
Marginal cost, 210, 344
Marginal rate of substitution, 76
Marginal utility theory, 71, 482
   Jevons and, 159–60, 230
   marginal productivity, 50, 51, 442, 480
   Menger and, 159, 244, 472
   Walras and, 160, 471, 472
Market design, 345–46
   *See also* Free market/trade
*Market Signaling* (Spence), 412–13
Market socialism, 204–5
Markowitz, Harry, **226–28**
   as Nobel laureate, 226, 227–28, 387, 388
   *Portfolio Selection: Efficient Diversification for Investments*, 227
Marschak, Jacob, 227, 257
Marshall, Alfred, **228–31**, 309, 332, 461
   consumer surplus and, 71, 72, 136
   Keynes and, 177, 229
   Sraffa's challenge to, 415–16
   on supply-and-demand curves, 228, 229–30
   Taussig and, 437
Marx, Karl, 30, 298, 404, 410
   *Capital*, 232, 479–80
   Engels and, 82, 83, 232
   *Manifesto of the Communist Party*, 83, **231–33**
   Robinson and, 336, 337
Marxism, 173
   Bauer and, 16–17

Hilferding's defense of, 137, 138
Sweezy on, 433, 434, 435
Maskin, Eric, **233–35**
   mechanism design theory and, 233–34, 270, 272
Massachusetts Institute of Technology. *See* MIT
Mathematical economics, 88, 181, 182, 472
   Debreu and, 59–60, 61
   Frisch and, 97
   linear programming, 174, 175
   Mirrlees and, 252
   Samuelson and, 356
   Sargent and, 359
   Shapley and, 385
   *See also* Econometrics
*Mathematical Psychics* (Edgeworth), 76
McFadden, Daniel, **235–37**
   choice behavior theory of, 235, 236
Meade, James, **237–39**, 427, 428
   Keynesian economics and, 237, 238, 239
   as Nobel laureate, 237, 238, 286
Mechanism design theory, 153, 154, 270, 272
   implementation theory and, 233–34
   *See also* Game theory
Meltzer, Allan, **240–42**
   at Carnegie Institute of Technology, 240–41
   on Federal Reserve, 241–42
Menger, Carl, 31, 159, **242–44**
   Austrian School and, 30, 242–43, 481
   marginal utility and, 159, 244, 472
   paradox of value and, 243–44
   *Principles of Economics*, 30, 242, 243, 254
Mercantilism, 48–49, 56, 147–48
   balance-of-trade theory and, 55, 152, 263, 264
   Hume's critique of, 152
   imperialism and, 143
   Quesnay's critique of, 318, 319
   Smith's critique of, 404
   Steuart and, 420
   Walpole and, 469
Merton, Robert, **245–47**, 364
   Long-Term Capital Management and, 245–46
   as Nobel laureate, 245, 365

Microeconomics, 4, 228, 298, 406
  consumer theory and, 76
  Duflo and, 69–70
  Ekelund and Hébert on, 78
  marginal utility and, 71
  Phelps and, 305
Microfinance, 70
Mill, John Stuart, 160, **247–49**
  Bentham and, 21, 247, 248
  *Principles of Political Economy*, 43, 247, 248
Miller, Merton H., **249–51**
  Modigliani-Miller theorems, 249, 250, 256, 258
  as Nobel laureate, 227, 249, 250, 388
*Mind and Society* (Pareto), 298
Mirrlees, James, **251–53**
  Diamond and, 64, 251, 252
  on moral hazard, 252
  as Nobel laureate, 64, 251, 463
Mises, Ludwig von, 117, 124, **253–55**
  critique of socialism, 254
  Hazlitt and, 128
  Machlup and, 219, 220
  Rothbard and, 255, 347–48
  *Theory of Money and Credit, The*, 254
MIT (Massachusetts Institute of Technology), 27, 64, 85, 236
  Fischer at, 87
  J-PAL at, 69
  Maskin at, 234
  Samuelson at, 356, 407, 408
  Solow at, 407, 408
  Stiglitz at, 425
  Thurow at, 442, 443
Modigliani, Franco, 245, **256–58**, 301
  Duesenberry-Modigliani hypothesis, 256, 257
  life cycle hypothesis, 257
  Modigliani-Miller theorems, 249, 250, 256, 258
  as Nobel laureate, 249, 250, 256
Monetarism
  Bernanke and, 24
  Draghi and, 67–68
  Fisher and, 89
  *See also* Friedman, Milton

*Monetary History of the United States, A* (Friedman & Schwartz), 95, 374
Monetary policy, 5, 197, 339, 445
  Bernanke and, 23
  Burns and, 38–39
  Chinese, 491
  employment and, 21
  exchange rates, 47, 267
  Federal Reserve and, 242, 466, 493
  Friedman on, 95, 353, 397, 398
  H. Simons on, 397–98
  Keynes and, 178
  shock therapy, 101, 102, 353, 354
  Tobin and, 447
  Volcker and, 466, 467
Monetary system, 265, 283
  balance of payments and, 162, 266
  Indian, 177
  Keynes on, 178
  Machlup and, 220
  Menger on origins of, 244
  new Keynesian theory and, 225
  "quantitative easing" and, 24
  *See also* Gold standard
*Money* (Harrod), 120
Money supply, 95, 120
  cumulative process theory and, 478
  Fisher's equation of exchange and, 89
  inflation and, 8, 326
  interest rates and, 215
  prices and, 42, 89
MONIAC (Monetary National Income Analog Computer), 306, 307
"Monograph, The" (Debreu), 60
Monopoly, 146, 210, 397, 434
  antitrust economics, 485–86
  possibility theorem and, 161, 162
  state-owned, 7
  Stigler's capture theory and, 423
*Monopoly Capital* (Sweezy), 434
*Monthly Review*, 433, 434
Mont Pèlerin Society, 126, 423
Moral hazard, 252, 425, 426
Moral philosophy, 151, 185, 403
Morgan Stanley (financial firm), 330, 331
Morgenstern, Oskar, **259–61**
  Austrian School and, 259
  game theory and, 259, 260

*On the Accuracy of Economic Observations*, 260
Mortensen, Dale, **261–63**
   on labor market, 261–62
   as Nobel laureate, 64, 65, 261, 262, 311
Mummery, Albert, 142
Mun, Thomas, **263–65**
   balance-of-trade theory and, 263, 264
   *England's Treasure by Foreign Trade*, 148, 264
Mundell, Robert, **265–68**
   euro and, 265, 266, 267
   on gold standard, 265, 266
   as Nobel laureate, 265, 267
Murphy, Kevin, **268–70**
   health care research of, 269
   on wage inequality, 268
Muth, John, 359
Myerson, Roger B., **270–72**
   on mechanism design theory, 234, 270, 272
   as Nobel laureate, 270, 272
   on political economy, 271–72
Myrdal, Gunnar, **272–75**
   *American Dilemma, An*, 273–74
   on global poverty, 274
   as Nobel laureate, 272, 274
*Mystery of Capital, The* (De Soto), 63

Nash, John F., 197, 271, **277–79**
   game theory and, 11, 122, 277, 278–79, 375, 376
   paranoid schizophrenia of, 277, 279
   Selten and, 122, 123, 277, 375, 376, 377
National Bureau of Economic Research (NBER), 206, 280, 339, 388
   Becker at, 18, 19
   Bhagwati at, 28
   Burns at, 38
   Friedman at, 94, 95
   Heckman at, 129–30
   Kuznets at, 194
   Schwartz at, 373, 374, 375
National debt, 470
National economic system, 212–13, 427, 428
National income accounting, 193, 194–95, 427–28
Natural rights, 214, 403
*Natural Value* (Wieser), 482
*Nature and Necessity of Interest, The* (Cassel), 46
"Nature of the Firm, The" (Coase), 53
Neoclassical school, 46, 226, 310, 450
   Marshall and, 230
   Sargent and, 358
Neo-Keynesian economics, 171, 425
   *See also* Keynesian economics
Neo-Ricardian economics, 171, 300
   *See also* Ricardo, David
Neumann, John von, 259, 260
*Next American Frontier, The* (Reich), 322
*Next Asia, The: Opportunities and Challenges for a New Globalization* (Roach), 331–32
Nixon administration, 39, 95, 112, 391–92
North, Douglass, **279–82**
   cliometrics and, 280
   on institutional economics, 280, 281
North, Sir Dudley, **282–84**
   *Discourses on Trade*, 282, 283
   on interest rates, 283

Obama administration, 430, 455, 456, 467
Objectivist Movement, 112, 323, 324
Office of Information and Regulatory Affairs, 431–32
Office of Management and Budget, 199, 328, 330, 391
Offshoring, 27
Ohlin, Bertil, **285–87**
   Heckscher-Ohlin model, 162, 285–86
   as Nobel laureate, 237, 238, 286
Okun, Arthur, **287–89**
   *Equality and Efficiency*, 288
   on unemployment, 287–88
*Olbie* (Say), 361
Olson, Mancur, **289–91**
   on free-rider problem, 289, 290
   *Logic of Collective Action, The*, 289–90
*On the Accuracy of Economic Observations* (Morgenstern), 260

"On the Mechanics of Economic
    Development" (Lucas), 217
Open-market policies, in India, 402
    *See also* Free market/trade
Oppenheimer, Frank, 129
Opportunity costs, 482
Optimality, Pareto, 60, 297–98
Option-pricing model, 245, 364, 365
Options contract, 365
Organ transplant market, 345–46
*Origins of Modern Microeconomics* (Ekelund
    & Hébert), 78
Oster, Emily, **291–93**
    health economics and, 291, 292
Ostrom, Elinor, **293–95**, 486
    on common-pool resources, 294
    as Nobel laureate, 293, 295, 486
*Outlines of the American Political Economy*
    (List), 211–12

Pareto, Vilfredo, **297–99**, 471
    on income distribution, 298
    on power elites, 299
Pareto optimality, 60, 297–98
Pasinetti, Luigi, **299–302**
    on capital theory, 301
    on income distribution, 300–301
    on Ricardian system, 300
Pecuniary emulation, 459–60
People's Bank of China, 491
Petty, Sir William, **302–4**
    Royal Society of London and, 302, 303
    on taxation, 302, 303
Phelps, Edmund (Ned), 6, **304–6**, 313
    "Golden Rule of Accumulation," 7, 304
    on Phillips curve, 305
Phillips, A. W. H., 217, **306–8**
    MONIAC and, 306, 307
    on stabilization policy, 307
Phillips curve, 305, 306, 307
*Philosophy of Wealth, The* (Clark), 51
Physiocrats, 140
    Cantillon and, 41, 42
    Quesnay and, 317, 319
    Turgot and, 453
Pigou, A. C., 184, **309–11**, 334
    on externalities, 53, 309–10
    Keynes and, 177, 309, 310, 359

Pigou effect, 118
Pissarides, Christopher, **311–13**
    as Nobel laureate, 64, 65, 262, 311
    on unemployment, 262,
        311–12
*Plundered Planet, The* (Collier), 57–58
Political economy, 159, 173,
        189, 309, 353
    Cantillon and, 42
    Edgeworth and, 75
    George and, 107–8
    Hobbes and, 139
    institutional sclerosis and, 290
    Knight and, 184
    Laffer and, 199, 201
    List and, 211–12
    Malthus and, 223–24
    Menger and, 242
    Mirrlees and, 252
    Myerson and, 271–72
    North's *Discourses on Trade* and, 282
    Petty and, 302, 303
    Reich and, 321
    Reisman and, 325
    Say on, 361
    Senior on, 380–81
    Stern and, 417
    Steuart and, 420
    Walpole and, 469
    Weber and, 475
*Poor Economics: A Radical Rethinking of the
    Way to Fight Global Poverty* (Duflo &
    Banerjee), 69
Poor Laws (Britain), 381
Population growth, 381, 395
    agrarian development and, 32, 33–34
    food production and, 222–23, 367
*Portfolio Selection: Efficient Diversification
    for Investments* (Markowitz), 227
*Positive Program for Laissez Faire, A*
    (Simon), 397
Possibility theorem, 161, 162
"Potato Paradoxes" (Rosen), 344
*Poverty and Famines* (Sen), 379
Poverty and the poor, 69, 252,
        379, 381, 479
    global warming and, 419
    *See also* Global poverty

*Preferential Policies: An International Perspective* (Sowell), 410–11
Prescott, Edward C., **313–16**
   Kydland and, 196, 197, 313, 314, 315
   as Nobel laureate, 196, 217, 313
Price and price theory, 7, 46, 187, 422
   competition and, 120
   congestion pricing, 461, 462
   elasticity of demand and, 229–30
   flexprice/fixprice taxonomy and, 136–37
   freeze on wages and, 392
   hedonic, 343
   Kregel on, 188
   labor theory of value and, 404
   marginal cost and, 210
   money supply and, 42, 89, 326
   option-pricing model, 245, 364, 365
   paradox of value and, 243–44
   Wicksteedian state of rest and, 480
*Principles of Economics* (Marshall), 229
*Principles of Economics* (Menger), 30, 242, 243, 254
*Principles of Political Economy* (Malthus), 223–24
*Principles of Political Economy* (Mill), 43, 247, 248
*Principles of Science, The* (Jevons), 160
Private property. *See* Property rights
"Problem of Social Cost, The" (Coase), 53
Production costs, 5, 381
Production theory, 301
Productivity, 50, 51, 442, 480
   division of labor and, 180
   signaling, 412–13
   Solow paradox and, 408
   wages and, 381
Profit maximization, 120, 301, 421, 441
*Progress and Poverty* (George), 107, 479
Property rights, 5, 36, 294, 319
   Coase theorem of, 53–54
   de Soto on, 62, 63
   Hume's defense of, 151–52
   self-interest and, 214–15
Protectionism, 55, 117, 162, 413
   Bastiat and, 14–15
   George and, 107
   globalization and, 456
   Irwin's critique of, 157–58
   *See also* Tariffs
*Protestant Ethic and the Spirit of Capitalism* (Weber), 475, 476
Psychological hedonism, 21
*Public Choice* (journal), 450, 451
Public choice theory, 35, 423, 451
   impossibility theorem and, 9
   McFadden's discreet choice, 235
Public debt, 36
Public price theory, 461, 462
Public works, Dupuit and, 71, 72
Purchasing power parity, 47

Quesnay, François, 207, **317–19**, 453
   Physiocrats and, 317, 319
   *Tableau économique*, 317–18

*Race and Economics* (Sowell), 410
*Railroads and American Economic Growth* (Fogel), 91
Rand, Ayn, 112, 323, 348
RAND Corporation, 9, 227, 385, 387
Rational expectations, 216, 217, 358–59
Rationality, bounded, 377
Rational rights concept, 323–24
Reagan, Ronald, 112, 135, 392, 410, 429
   Friedman and, 93, 95
Reaganomics, 199–200, 329, 383–84
   *See also* Supply-side economics
Recession, 112, 134, 210, 467
   (2008–9), 332, 350, 389
*Reforming the World's Money* (Harrod), 120
Regulation, capture theory and, 423
Reich, Robert, **321–23**
   on human capital, 322
   on industrial policy, 321–22
Reisman, George, **323–25**
   on "green" energy resources, 324
   objectivism and, 323, 324
   rational concept of rights, 323–24
Relative utility, 71–72
Rent theory, 141, 142
   Ricardo and, 223, 326, 381
   Tullock and, 451
Resource allocation, 174–75, 186, 395
   common-pool, 294
   efficiency in, 154, 176

*Resourceful Earth, The: A Response to Global 2000* (Simon), 395
*Reviving the American Dream* (Rivlin), 329
Ricardo, David, 300, **325–27**, 362, 404
  comparative advantage concept of, 326–27
  Corn Law debates and, 222, 223, 327
  Mill and, 247, 248
  rent theory and, 223, 326, 381
  Senior and, 380, 381
  Sraffa and, 415, 416
*Rise and Fall of a Nation, The* (Olson), 290
Risk, 184, 226
  Allais paradox and, 7
  capital asset pricing and, 387
  moral hazard and, 252
  options market and, 365
*Risk, Uncertainty, and Profit* (Knight), 183, 184
Rivlin, Alice, **328–30**
  *Reviving the American Dream*, 329
  *Systemic Thinking for Social Change*, 329
Roach, Stephen, **330–32**
  Chinese economy and, 331–32
  at Morgan Stanley, 330, 331
*Road to Serfdom, The* (Hayek), 126
*Road to Socialism, The* (Bauer), 16
Robbins, Lionel, **332–34**
  *Essay on the Nature and Significance of Economic Science*, 333
  on Great Depression, 333
Robertson, Sir Dennis, **334–36**
  *Banking Policy and Price Level*, 335
  Keynes and, 334, 335
Robinson, Joan, **336–38**
  *Economics of Imperfect Competition*, 336, 337
  Keynes and, 336, 337, 338
  Socialism and, 337–38
Romer, Christina, **338–41**
  on Great Depression, 339
  on tax changes, 340
Romer, David H., 338, 339
Romer, Paul, 2, **341–43**
  "Endogenous Technological Change," 341, 342
  on human capital, 341, 342

Roosevelt administration, 104, 195
  *See also* Great Depression
Rosen, Sherwin, **343–45**
  "Economics of Superstars, The," 343–44
  "Potato Paradoxes," 344
Roth, Alvin, **345–47**
  as Nobel laureate, 345, 385
  on organ transplant market, 345–46
Rothbard, Murray N., 323, **347–49**
  Hoppe and, 145, 146
  libertarian views of, 348–49
  Mises and, 255, 347–48
Roubini, Nouriel, **349–51**
  Great Recession and, 350
Royal Society of London, 302, 303
"Rules Rather than Discretion" (Prescott & Kydland), 314

Sachs, Jeffrey, **353–55**
  Earth Institute and, 355
  Millennium Project and, 354
  shock therapy and, 353, 354
Samuelson, Paul, 6, 217, 245, **355–57**, 430
  cost-push inflation and, 357
  Keynesian approach of, 356, 357
  as Nobel laureate, 355
  Samuelson-Modigliani model, 301
  Solow and, 307, 408
Sargent, Thomas, 217, **358–60**
  as Nobel laureate, 358, 359, 399
  rational expectations theory and, 358–59
*Sartor Resartus* (Carlyle), 44
Savings behavior, 31, 257, 324
Say, Jean-Baptiste, 13, 142, **360–62**
  Glut Controversy and, 360, 361–62
  Napoleonic government and, 361
Say's law, 224, 326, 360, 361–62
Schelling, Thomas C., **362–64**
  game theory and, 362–63, 364
  as Nobel laureate, 11, 362, 363–64
Scholes, Myron, 246, **364–66**
  Black-Scholes model and, 364, 365
  Long-Term Capital Management and, 364–65
  as Nobel laureate, 245, 364

Schultz, Theodore W., 18, **366–68**
   on human capital, 367–68
   as Nobel laureate, 209, 367, 368
Schumacher, Ernst, **369–70**
   Buddhist economics and, 369
   *Small Is Beautiful*, 369–70
Schumpeter, Joseph, 132, **370–73**, 434
   on business cycles, 370, 372
   on creative destruction, 370, 372, 478
   on entrepreneurship, 370, 371, 372
Schwartz, Anna, **373–75**
   Friedman and, 95, 162, 374
   at NBER, 373, 374, 375
Self-interest, 36, 140, 309, 381, 404
   collective action and, 289
   Locke on, 214–15
   mechanism design model and, 154, 234
Selten, Reinhard, **375–77**
   chain store paradox, 376–77
   as Nobel laureate, 122, 123, 277, 279, 375–76, 377
Sen, Amartya, 292, **378–80**
   as Nobel laureate, 378, 380
   *Poverty and Famines*, 379
   social choice theory and, 379
Senior, Nassau, **380–82**
   Malthusian paradigm and, 381–82
   Ricardo and, 380, 381
Sennholz, Hans, **382–84**
   gold standard and, 382, 383
   Reaganomics and, 383–84
Shapley, Lloyd, **384–86**
   game theory and, 384–85
   as Nobel laureate, 346, 384, 385
Sharpe, William F., **386–88**
   capital-asset pricing model and, 387
   as Nobel laureate, 228, 387, 388
Shiller, Robert, 2, **389–91**
   *Irrational Exuberance*, 389–90
   *Subprime Solution*, 390
Shock therapy, 101, 102, 353, 354
Shultz, George, 199, **391–93**
   Laffer and, 199
   in Nixon administration, 391–92
   Reagan and, 392
Simon, Herbert, **393–94**
   Hawkins-Simon theorem and, 393
   as Nobel laureate, 393, 394
Simon, Julian, **394–96**
   *Resourceful Earth, The*, 395
Simons, Henry, **396–98**
   on monetary policy, 397–98
Sims, Christopher, **399–401**
   on information theory, 400
   as Nobel laureate, 358, 359, 399
SIMSCRIPT (programming language), 227
Singh, Manmohan, **401–3**
Sismondi, Simonde, 361
*Small Is Beautiful* (Schumacher), 369–70
Smith, Adam, 140, 247, 264, **403–5**
   Bentham and, 21
   Cantillon and, 41, 42
   Hume and, 152
   "invisible hand" concept of, 60–61, 132, 404
   Khaldun and, 180
   labor theory of value and, 403, 404
   List and, 211, 212
   Locke and, 215
   Ricardo and, 325–26
   Say and, 360, 361
   self-interest and, 309, 404
   Sen and, 379
   Senior and, 381
   *See also Wealth of Nations* (Smith)
Smith, Vernon, **405–7**
   experimental economics and, 405, 406
   as Nobel laureate, 405, 406
*Social Choice and Individual Values* (Arrow), 9
Social choice theory, 153–54, 379
Social contract theory, 140
*Social Economics* (Wieser), 482
Socialism, 13, 26, 126, 138
   Bauer and, 16–17
   Ely and, 80–81
   Fabian Society and, 479
   Kalecki and, 173
   labor theory of value and, 403, 404
   Lange and, 204–5
   Mises on, 254
   *Monthly Review* and, 434
   Robinson and, 337–38
   Schumpeter on, 372

Social issues
    economic decisions and, 50, 51, 268–69
    *See also specific issues*
Social Security system, U.S., 65
Social value, opportunity costs and, 482
Solow, Robert, 7, 307, **407–9**
    on economic growth, 407, 408
    as Nobel laureate, 407, 408
    Solow paradox, 408
"Some Unpleasant Monetarist Arithmetic" (Sargent), 359
South Sea bubble, 41–42, 470
Sowell, Thomas, **410–12**
    affirmative action and, 410–11
    on education, 411
Spence, Michael, **412–14**
    on economic growth, 412, 413–14
    on job market signaling, 412–13
    as Nobel laureate, 1, 3, 412
Sraffa, Piero, 300, **415–17**
    Marshallian economics and, 415–16
    Ricardo's papers and, 415, 416
Stabilization policy, 307
Stagflation, 95, 118, 465–66
Stanford University, 190
    Arrow at, 9, 10
*State against Blacks, The* (Williams), 483
"Statistical Estimation of Simultaneous Economic Relations" (Koopmans), 186
Statistical model, 116, 194
Stern, Nicholas, **417–19**
    climate change and, 417, 418–19
    Commission for Africa, 417, 418
Steuart, James, **420–22**
    *Inquiry into the Principles of Political Oeconomy*, 420
Stigler, George, 19, **422–24**
    capture theory of, 423
    *Theory of Competitive Price, The*, 422
Stiglitz, Joseph, **424–27**
    Clinton administration and, 424, 425
    as Nobel laureate, 1, 3, 105, 412, 425
Stockholm School, 46, 273, 285, 477
Stock market crash (1987), 112
Stolper-Samuelson theorem, 356
Stone, Sir Richard, 238, **427–29**
    consumer demand models and, 428–29
    as Nobel laureate, 427
    systems of national accounts and, 427–28
*Strategy of Conflict, The* (Schelling), 363
*Studies in Classical Political Economy* (Hollander), 143, 144
*Study in Industrial Fluctuation, A* (Robertson), 335
*Subprime Solution: How Today's Global Financial Crisis Happened, and What to Do about It* (Shiller), 390
Summers, Lawrence, **429–31**
    in Clinton administration, 430
    Waterman Award and, 429
Sunstein, Cass, **431–33**, 439
    at Harvard Law School, 432
    Office of Information and Regulatory Affairs and, 431–32
Supply and demand, 7, 42, 243, 344, 421
    curves, 228, 229–30
    Giffen good and, 344
    Say's law and, 360, 361–62
Supply-side economics, 135, 199, 216, 384
    tax cuts and, 200–201, 216
    *See also* Reaganomics
Supreme Court, U.S., 485–86
Sustainability, 160
Sweezy, Paul, **433–35**
    on Marxist economics, 433, 434, 435
    *Monopoly Capital*, 434
    *Monthly Review* and, 433, 434
*Systemic Thinking for Social Change* (Rivlin), 329
Systems of national accounts (Stone), 427–28

*Tableau économique* (Quesnay), 317–18
Tariffs, 14, 107, 421, 437–38
    mercantilism and, 49, 55
    possibility theorem and, 161, 162
    trade agreements and, 157
Taussig, Frank, **437–38**
    on tariffs, 437, 438
Taxation, 55, 134, 171, 252, 315
    Diamond-Mirrlees theorem, 64, 251, 252
    Georgist reforms, 106, 107

on land, 453
Meade on, 239
on negative externalities, 309–10
Okun on, 288
Petty on, 302, 303
Rivlin on, 329
Romer on, 340
Sennholz on, 383
Simons on, 398
supply-side economics and, 200–201, 216
Tobin tax, 448
Turgot and, 453
Vickrey on, 461, 462
Walpole on, 470
*See also* Tariffs
Thaler, Richard, 169, **438–41**
on behavioral economics, 439
*Theory of Capitalist Development, The* (Sweezy), 433, 434
*Theory of Competitive Price, The* (Stigler), 422
*Theory of Economic Development* (Schumpeter), 371
*Theory of Economic Growth* (Lewis), 210
*Theory of International Economic Policy, The* (Meade), 238
*Theory of International Trade* (Haberler), 117–18
*Theory of Money and Credit, The* (Mises), 254
*Theory of Moral Sentiments* (Smith), 403
*Theory of Social Economy, The* (Cassel), 47
*Theory of the Consumption Function, A* (Friedman), 94, 95
*Theory of the Leisure Class, The* (Veblen), 131, 459, 460
*Theory of the Political Economy* (Jevons), 159
Third World countries, 62, 73–74
*See also* Developing nations
Thornton, Mark, 78
Thunen, Johann von, **441–42**
*Isolated State, The*, 441
profit and location theory of, 441–42
Thurow, Lester, **442–44**
on global economy, 443
*Zero-Sum Society*, 443

*Time on the Cross: The Economics of American Negro Slavery* (Fogel), 92
Tinbergen, Jan, **444–46**
econometrics and, 444, 445
as Nobel laureate, 98, 444
Tobin, James, **446–48**
Cowles Foundation and, 227, 447
as Nobel laureate, 446, 448
Tobin's q, 447
Tobin tax, 448
Tollison, Robert D., 78
*Towards a Dynamic Economy* (Harrod), 120
Trade. *See* Free market/trade; International trade
*Trade and Welfare* (Meade), 238–39
Transaction costs, 53
*Trattato di sociologia generale* (Pareto), 298
*Treatise of Taxes and Contributions* (Petty), 302, 303
*Treatise on Human Nature* (Hume), 151
Trichet, Jean-Claude, **449–50**
European Central Bank and, 449, 450
Tullock, Gordon, **450–52**
*Public Choice* and, 450, 451
Turgot, Jacques, **452–54**
*Elegy to Gournay*, 453
free-market reform and, 453–54
Tversky, Amos, 167, 168–69, 236
Tyson, Laura, **455–57**
globalization and, 456
at University of California, Berkeley, 455, 456

*Ultimate Resource, The* (Simons), 396
Underconsumption, theory of, 125, 142
Unemployment, 2, 197, 350, 408
Beveridge on, 25, 26
inflation and, 217, 305, 306, 307, 466
monetary policy and, 38, 39
Okun's law of, 287–88
Phillips curve and, 305, 307
Pissarides on, 311–12
stagflation and, 95, 467
Yellen on, 493
Unions, free-rider problem in, 290

United Nations (UN), 187–88, 209, 379
  Committee for Development
    Planning, 445
  Millennium Project, 354
University of California, Berkeley,
    60, 236, 280
  Tyson at, 455, 456
University of Cambridge, 252
  See also Cambridge School
University of Chicago, 130, 162, 185, 216
  Friedman at, 93–94, 96
  Markowitz at, 226–27
  Murphy at, 268
  Rosen at, 343
  Shultz at, 391
  Simon at, 393
  Tullock at, 451
  See also Chicago School of
    economics
University of Vienna, 481–82
  See also Austrian School of
    economics
Utilitarianism, 20, 21, 123, 247
  Hume and, 151–52
Utility
  choice and, 260
  marginal, 71, 159–60, 244, 472
  relative, 71–72

Value, 223
  intrinsic, 42
  labor theory of, 303, 327, 403,
    404, 421
*Value, Capital and Rent* (Wicksell),
    477–78
Veblen, Thorstein, 104, **459–61**
  pecuniary emulation concept,
    459–60
  *Theory of the Leisure Class, The*, 131,
    459, 460
Vector auto regression (VAR)
  model, 399, 400
Vickrey, William, 252, **461–63**
  as Nobel laureate, 251, 461, 463
  public price theory of, 461, 462
  on taxation, 461, 462
Viner, Jacob, **464–65**
  on international trade, 464
Volcker, Paul, **465–68**

  as chairman of Federal Reserve, 38,
    465–67
  stagflation and, 465, 467
Volcker Commission, 467

*Wage Dispersion* (Mortensen), 261
Wage lag inflation, 4
Wages, 51, 408, 442, 493
  inequality in, 268
  of performers, 343–44
  and price freeze, 392
  productivity and, 381
  wage ratio principle, 445
Wallis, W. Allen, 94
Walpole, Sir Robert, **469–71**
  as prime minister, 469, 470
  South Sea bubble and, 470
Walras, Leon, 207, 297, **471–73**
  Cassel and, 46, 47
  marginal utility and, 160, 471, 472
*Wealth and Welfare* (Pigou), 309
*Wealth of Nations, The* (Smith), 42, 215,
    309, 421
  division of labor in, 180, 403–4
  free-trade principles in, 158, 404
  Khaldun and, 180
  Turgot and, 453
Wealth transfer, 288, 297
Webb, Beatrice, **473–75**
  at London School of Economics, 473, 474
Webb, Sidney, 473–74
Weber, Max, **475–77**
  *Protestant Ethic and the Spirit of
    Capitalism*, 475, 476
Welfare economics, 25, 136,
    309, 379
*White Man's Burden, The* (Easterly), 74
"Why Money?" (Alchian), 5
Wicksell, Knut, 335, **477–79**
  *Interest and Prices*, 478
  *Value, Capital and Rent*, 477–78
Wicksteed, Philip, **479–81**
  Wicksteedian state of rest, 480
Wieser, Friedrich von, 371, **481–82**
  marginal utility and, 482
Williams, Walter, **483–84**
  libertarian views of, 483, 484
  *State against Blacks, The*, 483

Williamson, Oliver, **485–87**
    antitrust and, 485–86
    naive trade-off model and, 485
    as Nobel laureate, 293, 486
Willis, Robert, 344
Wisconsin Idea, 80–81
Wolf, Martin, **487–89**
*Women's Role in Economic Development* (Boserup), 34
*Work of Nations, The* (Reich), 322
World Bank, 426, 497, 498
*Worldly Philosophers, The* (Heilbroner), 131, 132
World Trade Organization, 28, 497–98

Xiaochuan, Zhou, **491–92**
    People's Bank of China and, 491

Yellen, Janet, **493–95**
    Akerlof and, 2, 3
    on Federal Reserve board, 493, 494

*Zero-Sum Society, The* (Thurow), 443
Zoellick, Robert, **497–99**
    as U.S. trade representative, 497–98